3.50

LILLIAN HELLMAN
Her Legend and Her Legacy

LILLIAN HELLMAN

HER LEGEND AND HER LEGACY

Carl Rollyson

ST. MARTIN'S PRESS
NEW YORK

Grateful acknowledgment is made for permission to reprint from the following: *Dashiell Hammett: A Life* by Diane Johnson. Copyright © 1983 by Diane Johnson. Reprinted by permission of Random House, Inc. *The Thin Man* by Dashiell Hammett. Copyright © 1933, 1934 by Alfred A. Knopf, Inc. and renewed 1961, 1962 by Dashiell Hammett. Reprinted by permission of Alfred A. Knopf, Inc. *Memoirs* by Raisa Orlova. Translation Copyright © 1983 by Samuel Cioran. Reprinted by permission of Random House, Inc. *Pentimento: A Book of Portraits* by Lillian Hellman. Copyright © 1973 by Lillian Hellman. Reprinted by permission of Little, Brown and Company. *An Unfinished Woman: A Memoir* by Lillian Hellman. Copyright © 1969 by Lillian Hellman. Reprinted by permission of Little, Brown and Company. Permission was granted from the following libraries to examine material that proved indispensable in the writing of this biography: Academy of Motion Picture Arts and Sciences, Margaret Herrick Library, Beverly Hills, CA; Lewis Milestone Collection, Merle Oberon Collection, Motion Picture Association of American Production Code, administration files, Hal Wallis Collection, Fred Zinneman Collection: Alabama Department of Archives and History, Montgomery; Tallulah Bankhead papers: Boston Public Library; Edwin O'Connor papers: Boston University, Mugar Memorial Library; Bette Davis Archive, Anne Revere Collection, Edmund Fuller Collection, Marjorie Osterman Collection: University of California at Berkeley, Bancroft Library; Sidney Coe Howard papers: Indiana University, Lilly Library, Bloomington, Indiana; Laves papers: Library of Congress, Recorded Sound and Manuscript Divisions; Recordings of Lillian Hellman, Archibald Macleish papers, Janet Flanner-Solito Solano papers, Lillian Hellman playscripts for "The Dear Queen" and *The Autumn Garden*: University of Michigan, Harlan Hatcher Graduate Library; Roy Cowden papers: The New York Public Library, Special Collections; Correspondence between Lillian Hellman and Herbert Mitgang, and from Lillian Hellman to Alfred Kazin: The New York Public Library, Bill Rose Theatre Collection; Correspondence from John Golden to Lillian Hellman, Correspondence from Lillian Hellman to George Freedley: University of North Carolina at Chapel Hill, Southern Historical Collection; Eugenia Rawls and Donald Seawell Theater Collection: University of Pennsylvania, Van Pelt Library; Van Wyck Brooks Collection: Rutgers University Libraries, Special Collections and Archives; Unpublished Hellman essay, "Richard Harding Davis": University of Southern California, Doheny Library; Edward Small Collection, Warner Brothers Collection: University of Texas, Humanities Research Center; Dashiell Hammett Collection: University of Washington Libraries; Theodore Roethke papers: University of Wisconsin, State Historical Society; Arthur Kober papers, Kermit Bloomgarden papers, Herman Shumlin papers, Moss Hart papers: Yale University Library; Henry E. Sigerist Papers.

LILLIAN HELLMAN: HER LEGEND AND HER LEGACY

Library of Congress Cataloging-in-Publication Data
Rollyson, Carl E. (Carl Edmund)
    Lillian Hellman: her legend and her legacy / by Carl Rollyson.
    p.   cm.
    ISBN 0-312-00049-9
    1. Hellman, Lillian, 1906–1984—Biography. 2. Dramatists,
American—20th century—Biography. I. Title.
PS3515.E343Z87   1988
812'.52—dc19   87-28398
                                                                    CIP

First Edition

10 9 8 7 6 5 4 3 2 1

To Lisa

My At-Home Editor

God helps those who invent what they need.

—Lillian Hellman, *The Little Foxes*

CONTENTS

ACKNOWLEDGMENTS

A great many people have contributed to this biography by sharing with me their memories of Lillian Hellman in personal interviews and in correspondence. I want to thank them for their generous help. Many of them reviewed their remarks for accuracy and suggested other corrections that have saved me from making many errors: John Abbott, William Alfred, Rupert Allan, L. Scott Bailey, Margaret Bailey, Carlos Baker, Walter Jackson Bate, Howard Bay, Peter Benchley, Stephen Birmingham, Heywood Hale Broun, Zoe Caldwell, Robert H. Chapman, Virginia Bloomgarden Chilewich, Ruth Conte, Malcolm Cowley, Richard de Combray, Philip Dunne, Leon Edel, Florence Eldridge, Frances FitzGerald, Louis Fraad, Robert Fryer, J. C. Furnas, Martha Gellhorn, Lee Gershwin, Stephen Gillers, Herbert Gold, Stephen Greene, Albert Hackett, Julie Harris, Diane Johnson, Alfred Kazin, Michael Kinsley, Catherine Kober, Maya Koreneva, Emmy Kronenberger, Ring Lardner, Jr., Max Lerner, Harry and Elena Levin, Ephraim London, William Luce, Jo Marshall, Jay Martin, Sam Marx, Walter Matthau, Thomas McBride, Peter J. McCrohan, John Melby, Howard Meyer, Hilary Mills, Raisa Orlova, Ralph Penner, Martin Peretz, Daniel Pollitt, Marilyn Raab, Tally Richards, Mary Robinson, Joseph Rauh, Robert Silvers, William M. Sloane, Isabel Stein, Ken Stuart, Alex Szogyi, Telford Taylor, Diana Trilling, Decherd Turner, Jose Vega, Bobbie Weinstein, Richard Wilbur, Arthur Wilde, Meta Carpenter Wilde, Emlyn Williams, Thomas H. Wolf, Jane Wyatt, Talli Wyler, Louis Zetzel, and Maurice Zolotow.

The interviews and correspondence were initiated in the spring of 1986 and completed by the fall of 1987.

Some of my interviewees did more than respond to my questions. Ken Stuart provided his class papers and his remarkable journal of Hellman's 1961 Harvard class; Virginia Bloomgarden Chilewich, Martin Peretz, Heywood Hale Broun, and Herbert Gold went out of their way to identify and recommend sources of information; Scott and Peg Bailey invited me to stay the night at their lovely Princeton home so that I could see for myself the environment in which part of *Days to Come* was imagined; Stephen Greene turned over letters and photographs; Jo Marshall shared with me her Hellman correspondence; Emlyn Williams sent me a long, thoughtful statement on *Montserrat* and on his dealings with Hellman; Maya Koreneva sent a fifteen-page handwritten letter of her impressions of Hellman in the Soviet Union; Catherine Kober provided photographs and much insight into painful memories; Hilary Mills supplied her files on her own extensive investigation into Hellman's life and career, thus saving me many hours of research time; Tally Richards wrote at length about Arthur Cowan and sent me many photographs; Louis Zetzel discussed his medical examinations of Hellman and their friendship and gave me two lovely photographs of her.

I owe a very special debt to Robert Newman and John Melby. Mr. Newman generously allowed me to make extensive use of his forthcoming book *Cold War Romance: Lillian Hellman and John Melby* (University of North Carolina Press, 1988), responded many times to my requests for information, and provided significant information from Hellman's passport file and from Joseph Rauh's papers. His critique of my manuscript saved me from making several errors. John Melby most graciously responded to my questions and comments and followed up with correspondence that helped clarify my views on many aspects of Hellman's life.

Several friends and colleagues suggested profitable lines of research, helped arrange interviews, brought their expertise to bear on my biographical problems, and in many other ways made my task easier: Rupert Allan, Nancy Allen, Shaye Areheart, Barbara Barnett, George Barnett, John Bassett, Kay Bassett, Vincent Blasi, Jeanne Hauben, Paul Hauben, Mary Hrabik-Samal, M. Thomas Inge, Tonette Inge, Michael Millgate, Paul Orlov, Seymour Riklin, Virginia Rock, Beulah Rollyson, Norman Rosten, David Saunders, Roslyn Schindler, Andy Silber, Arthur Wilde, Meta Wilde, Rea Wilmshurst, Saul Wineman, and Maurice Zolotow. Professor Vincent Blasi of Columbia University Law School provided important information on the law of libel.

Frances Saunders, a distinguished biographer, was a constant source of support, advice, and information. My understanding of Hellman's brief but important period in Princeton would be much diminished without her expert help.

In the early stages of my research, several scholars provided invaluable information and advice: Jackson R. Bryer, Bernard F. Dick, Richard Layman, Richard Moody, and Theresa Mooney.

Carol Binkert and Joseph Spilmann, Jr., were prompt and efficient researchers who helped me get off to a quick start in writing this biography.

A number of people kindly gave permission to examine correspondence in various libraries and archives: Christopher Davis, Frances FitzGerald, Blair Fuller, Stephen Greene, Catherine Kober, Marjorie Osterman, and Diana Trilling.

In researching the background of Hellman's family, I had the assistance of several historical societies, libraries, and individuals. I wish to thank Mrs. James C. Armistead, responding for the Marengo County (Alabama) Historical Society; Carolyn A. Bercier of Gallier House (New Orleans); Mary Ann Brown of the Miami Purchase Association; Jonathan Dembo of the Cincinnati Historical Society; Wayne Everard of the New Orleans Public Library; Edward F. Haas of the Louisiana State Museum; and Mabel Simmons, Books Editor of the New Orleans *Times Picayune/States Item*.

Many librarians and historians responded helpfully to my queries. I will begin at home by thanking Professor Melvin Small, Department of History, Wayne State University, for quickly putting into my hands material on the Freedom of Information Act. Professor Philip Mason and Warner Pflug of the Reuther Archives provided information on the labor-history-informing *Days to Come*. Irving Bluestone, Director of the Master of Arts in Industrial Relations degree program at Wayne State, sent me material on Hellman's friend Elizabeth Hawes. Nancy Allen put me in touch with film librarians in California. Roy Nuffer at Purdy Library searched several indexes for me and facilitated my research through the use of interlibrary loans.

In Ann Arbor, A. L. Bader directed my attention to the Hopwood Room at the University of Michigan, where Andrea R. Beauchamp, a Hopwood Program Associate, alerted the faculty to my interest in Hellman's contacts with University of Michigan faculty members and the Hopwood Program. Kathryn Brown kindly made available the Hellman correspondence on the Hopwood awards.

I am grateful to the many libraries and archives that responded to my requests for information, providing material as well as suggesting other profitable avenues of research. In New York: Mary

Corliss of the Film Stills Archive, Museum of Modern Art; Ron Magliozzi of the Film Study Center, Museum of Modern Art; Louis A. Rachow of the Hampden-Booth Theatre Library, Karen St. Pierre of the Museum of Broadcasting; Bernard A. Crystal of the Rare Book and Manuscript Library, Butler Library, Columbia University; Nancy Johnson of the American Academy and Institute of Arts and Letters; James B. Poteat of the Television Information Office; Lola L. Szladits, Special Collections, the New York Public Library; Dorothy L. Swerdlove of the Billy Rose Theatre Collection, Lincoln Center Library for the Performing Arts, the New York Public Library; Adrienne Fischier of the Harvard Library in New York.

In New Haven: Marcia Bickoff, Ferenc Gyorgyey, Mary C. La-Fogg, Christa Sammons, Patricia Bodak Stark, and Lynn J. Stewart of Yale University Library. In New Brunswick: Edward Skipworth of Rutgers University Library. In Philadelphia: Daniel Traister and Georgianna Ziegler of the Van Pelt Library, University of Pennsylvania; Geraldine Duclow of the Theatre Collection, the Free Library of Philadelphia. In Boston: Margaret R. Goostray and Howard B. Gottlieb of Mugar Memorial Library, Boston University; and Roberta Zonghi of the Boston Public Library. In Cambridge: Elizabeth Shenton of the Arthur and Elizabeth Schlesinger Library on the History of Women in America, Radcliffe College. In Washington, D.C.: Rick Bickel, Samuel Brylawski, James H. Hutson, Katharine Loughney, Edwin M. Matthias, and Donna Thacker of the Library of Congress; and Garnett McCoy of the Archives of American Art.

In North Carolina: Richard A. Shrader of the Wilson Library, the University of North Carolina at Chapel Hill. In Georgia: Frances Van Horn, Director of Alumnae Affairs, Wesleyan College, Macon. In Texas: Cathy Henderson, Sally Leach, and Decherd Turner of the Henry Ransom Humanities Research Center, University of Texas at Austin.

In Wisconsin: Maxine Fleckner Ducey, Director of the Film Achive, University of Wisconsin–Madison; Joanne Hohler, and Harold Miller, State Historical Society of Wisconsin, Madison. In Minnesota: Steven Eric Nielsen of the Minnesota Historical Society, St. Paul. In Indiana: Joel Silver and Saundra Taylor of the Lilly Library, Indiana University, Bloomington. In Illinois: R. Russell Maylone of Northwestern University Library; Sheila Ryan of Morris Library, Southern Illinois University at Carbondale; and Carolyn

A. Sheehy of the Newberry Library. In Washington: Janet Ness, University of Washington Library, Seattle.

In California: Diana R. Brown of Turner Entertainment Company; Ned Comstock of the University of Southern California Library, Los Angeles; Sharon E. Farb of the Theater Arts Library, University of California, Los Angeles; Leona Schonfeld and Jon Stefansson of the Huntingdon Library, San Marino; Ann G. Schlosser of the Louis B. Mayer Library, American Film Institute, Los Angeles; Samuel Gill of the Margaret Herrick Library, Academy of Motion Picture Arts and Sciences, Beverly Hills; Lilace Hatayama of the University Research Library; University of California, Los Angeles; Bonnie Rothbart, Picture Research Library, MGM Entertainment Company, Culver City; Bob Petrucco, Burbank Public Library; and Mary-Ellen Jones, the Bancroft Library, University of California, Berkeley.

I owe a special debt of gratitude to Samuel Gill of the Margaret Herrick Library, Academy of Motion Picture Arts and Sciences and to Ned Comstock of the University of Southern California library, both of whom responded patiently and enthusiastically to so many of my queries. In Mr. Gill's case, I received extraordinarily detailed, written descriptions of the Academy's holdings. Mr. Comstock identified an unproduced screenplay by Lillian Hellman that seems to have eluded other researchers.

Several people should be acknowledged for responding to my requests for information: Daniel Aaron, William Abrahams, Leon A. Berman, Robert Brustein, McGeorge Bundy, Blair Clark, Edward T. Cone, Paul Cowan, David Richard De Combray, William Doering, David DuVivier, K. R. Eissler, Isidore Englander, Jo-Ann C. Ewing (for Patricia Neal), Hamilton Fish III, Gerard Fountain, Fred Gardner, Ruth Goetz, Constance Goodman (for George Kennan), Alexander Grinstein, John Hersey, Charles C. Hoerske, Fay Holloschutz, Roy Hoopes, Janet Howard (for Averell Harriman), Irving Howe, Thelma B. Ingersoll, Garson Kanin, Penn Kimball, Arthur F. Kinney, Valentia G. Kozintseva, Harry J. Kraut (for Leonard Bernstein), Christopher Lehmann-Haupt, Anthony Lewis, Norman Mailer, Mary McCarthy, Judith McNally, Arthur Miller, Sophia Mumford (for Lewis Mumford), A. Obrasztsova, Donald Pizer, Norman Podhoretz, Richard Poirier, Stephen Rivers (for Jane Fonda), Ray Roberts, Kenneth Rowe, Daniel E. Schneider, Maureen Stapleton, Francis Steegmuller, William Styron, Roger

Wall (for Elizabeth Taylor), Jerome Wiesner, and Margaret Zilboorg.

Under the Freedom of Information Act, I requested information from the following federal agencies: the FBI, the CIA, the National Security Council, and the National Security Agency. After long delays and with the assistance of my congressman, George Crockett, I was able to obtain Hellman's FBI file. The CIA supplied a file of Hellman correspondence the agency had intercepted in the 1960s. Robert Newman sent me the valuable correspondence between Hellman and Elizabeth Shipley of the Passport Office, Department of State. The Organization of American Historians has a helpful pamphlet on how to apply for material under the Freedom of Information Act.

A generous grant from the American Philosophical Society allowed me to do some of the essential traveling to libraries and archives. Dean Garrett T. Herberlein and Associate Dean Thomas V. Getchell of the Graduate School, Wayne State University, encouraged my research and allowed me to maintain a flexible schedule during the writing of this biography. My wonderful agent, Elizabeth Knappman, of New England Publishing Associates, has been the source of much shrewd and cheerful advice. Without her, my initial conception of the biography would have been much poorer. Toni Lopopolo, my editor at St. Martin's Press, had faith in this book from the very beginning and has been its champion ever since. I do not believe there is a page of this book that I have not talked over with my wife, Dr. Lisa Paddock, or a page she has not read with critical advice and discernment. Much more than an at-home editor, she has often been the inspiration for this book.

CAST OF CHARACTERS

The Principal Players
(In alphabetical order)

Alfred, William: American playwright, Harvard professor, and close friend of Hellman's.

Aunt Lily: As a child, Hellman was much taken with her aunt's apparent elegance, although quickly enough she turned "another way" against her aunt. Aspects of Lily can be observed in the character of Albertine Prine in *Toys in the Attic*.

Bankhead, Tallulah: Star of *The Little Foxes* and Hellman's nemesis.

Bay, Howard: Set designer for most of Hellman's plays, beginning with *The Little Foxes* in 1939. Bay was a very close personal friend who viewed her with a critical eye.

Bernstein, Leonard: Hellman's collaborator on *Candide*. He stayed her friend while often feeling oppressed by her bossiness. He called her "Uncle Lillian."

Bethe: A relative from whom Hellman learned, early in life, about the powers of sexuality and womanhood.

Bloomgarden, Kermit: Hellman's producer, beginning with *Another Part of the Forest*; before that, he was Herman Shumlin's business manager.

Broun, Heywood Hale: Cast member of *My Mother, My Father and Me*.

Chilewich, Virginia Bloomgarden: Wife of Hellman's producer, Kermit Bloomgarden.

Cowan, Arthur: Eccentric Philadelphia attorney who promised Hellman money from a will that was never found.

de Combray, Richard: Hellman's close friend, one of those young men she enjoyed having around her in the last ten years of her life.

Ducky, Caroline: A black retainer in Aunt Lily's household, confidant of Uncle Willy and of Hellman. Caroline used the word "shit" more than any other person Hellman knew as a child.

Dunne, Philip: In the 1930s served with Hellman on the negotiating team for the Screen Writers Guild, a liberal who disagreed with her Stalinist positions. Saw Hellman socially throughout her life.

Eldridge, Florence (Mrs. Fredric March): This renowned actress played two roles in Hellman plays and observed firsthand the playwright's discomfort in the theater and her rather dictatorial style.

Field III, Marshall: The principal backer of *PM* and Hellman's staunch friend.

Fonda, Jane: Starred in the movie *Julia*, which enhanced the legend and the legacy of Lillian Hellman.

Gershwin, Lee: The wife of Ira Gershwin, one of Lillian's best friends throughout the late twenties and the thirties.

Gillers, Stephen. Worked as Executive Director for the Committee for Public Justice.

Goldwyn, Sam: Hellman's movie boss who admired her enormously and took her word for almost everything. She invented some of his famous Goldwynisms.

Greene, Stephen: An American painter who met Hellman in Rome in 1953 and remained a close friend.

Hackett, Albert and Frances: Screenwriters who became fast friends with Hellman and Hammett after the Hacketts successfully adapted *The Thin Man* for the screen. They also adapted the *Diary of Anne Frank* for the stage.

Hammett, Dashiell: The aloof novelist who helped guide Hellman's career; her lover; a Marxist; a man she could never quite grasp in their thirty-year, on-and-off relationship.

Harriman, Averell: Ambassador to the Soviet Union during Hellman's trip to Moscow in 1944.

Harris, Julie: Actress who starred in *The Lark* and had a small part in *Montserrat*.

Helen: Hellman's black servant about whom Hellman writes in *An Unfinished Woman*.

Hellman, Jenny and Hannah: Lillian's aunts. Part of her childhood years were spent in their boarding house, where she got to observe a wonderfully rich variety of people. Jenny and Hannah, and their love for their brother Max, became the inspiration for *Toys in the Attic*.

Hellman, Julia Newhouse: Lillian's delicate, pretty, and somewhat "goofy" mother; the model for Birdie in *The Little Foxes* and Lavinia in *Another Part of the Forest*.

Hellman, Max: Lillian's father. She adored him and idealized him as a strong, handsome, and witty man.

Hemingway, Ernest: Hellman said she liked him, that she was "one of his girls," but her memoirs demean him and are contradicted by most other accounts.

Hunter, Kim: Actress who played Karen in the 1952 revival of *The Children's Hour*.

Ingersoll, Ralph: A brilliant journalist and founder of *PM*. His love affair with Hellman was intense, and her example influenced his own politics.

Johnson, Diane: Dashiell Hammett's biographer, who had to put up with Hellman's interference in the writing of her biography.

Julia: In *Pentimento*, the beautifully imagined companion of Hellman's childhood, standing for all the attractive physical, mental, and political qualities Lillian coveted for herself. Vanessa Redgrave (Julia) and Jane Fonda (Lillian) made the film *Julia* an international hit.

Kazin, Alfred: This notable literary critic came to despise Hellman's snobbery and self-important accounts of her career.

Kober, Arthur: Hellman's first and only husband. A charming, gentle man who remained an important part of her life after their marriage broke up.

Kober, Catherine: Arthur's daughter.

Kober, Maggie: Arthur's second wife.

Koreneva, Maya: Hellman's translator on her 1967 trip to Russia.

Kronenberger, Emmy: Wife of Louis Kronenberger; an outspoken Hellman critic and one of those younger women who had married a man with whom Hellman had been intimate. Hellman often had trouble accepting the presence of such women in her men's lives.

Kronenberger, Louis: Engaged to Hellman at age eighteen, he wrote a play with her and remained a lifelong friend. He was a very close friend but often was critical of her more outrageous behavior.

Lardner, Jr., Ring: Screenwriter and Hellman friend.

Levin, Harry and Elena: Hellman's friends at Harvard.

Luce, William: Author of *Lillian*, a play personally approved by Hellman and based on her memoirs.

MacLeish, Archibald: American poet, public servant, and close Hellman friend.

Mailer, Norman: The source of much conflicting feelings on Hellman's part. She admired his work but also criticized it. She told Diana Trilling that Mailer once tried to rape her.

Marshall, Jo: Dashiell Hammett's daughter.

Marx, Sam: He first met Hellman in the 1920s. He hired her as a script reader at MGM but had no idea she wanted to become a writer. They disagreed about almost everything yet remained friends.

Mason, Sophronia: Hellman's black nursemaid; a firm but loving woman who became a model for many of the honest, tough-talking servants in her plays.

Matthau, Walter: Cast member of *My Mother, My Father and Me.*

Melby, John: Foreign Service officer who fell in love with Hellman during her 1944–45 trip to Moscow.

Meyer, Howard: Business manager of the *Columbia Spectator*, who met Hellman in 1923, became her lover for a few months in 1925, and renewed their friendship many years later, during the production of *Candide.*

Miller, Arthur: Author whom Hellman attacked for exposing his personal life with Marilyn Monroe in *After the Fall*. She also did not think much of his House Un-American Activities Committee (HUAC) testimony, even though his stand was really more courageous than hers.

Newhouse, Jake: Sophie's brother and even more formidable than Sophie. His conniving and comical character informs Hellman's creation of Ben Hubbard in *The Little Foxes.*

Newhouse, Sophie Marx: Hellman's grandmother, who presided over her family and enjoyed business speculation. Some of her characteristics appeared in Regina in *The Little Foxes.*

Parker, Dorothy: Worked closely with Hellman in organizing the Screen Writer's Guild. The two women were warm friends and were the grande dames of radical politics.

Penner, Ralph: A student of Hellman's at Yale.

Perelman, Laura: Wife of S. J. Perelman, sister of Nathanael West, and the model for the character of Cora in *Days to Come.*

Perelman, S. J.: Screenwriter, humorist, and brother-in-law of Nathanael West; friend of Hellman and Hammett.

Peretz, Martin: Publisher of *The New Republic*, member of the Committee for Public Justice, and close friend of Hellman's until he attended a fund-raising party at Roy Cohn's house.

Pollitt, Daniel: Assisted Joseph Rauh in representing Hellman before HUAC.

Rauh, Joseph: Hellman's attorney before the HUAC, and one of those Americans for Democratic Action (ADA) liberals she attacked for being soft on McCarthyism. They remained fond friends in spite of disagreements over communism.

Redgrave, Vanessa: Starred as Julia in the film based on Hellman's memoirs and stoutly defended Hellman when doubts were raised about the authenticity of Julia.

Shumlin, Herman: He first employed Hellman as a play reader, then served as director and producer of her plays. During *The Little Foxes* he was her lover.

Silvers, Robert: Editor of *The New York Review of Books*; active with Hellman in the Committee for Public Justice.

Smith, Randall "Pete": Seaman, activist in Henry Wallace's presidential campaign, and Hellman's casual lover.

Stuart, Ken: One of Hellman's students at Harvard.

Szogyi, Alex: Hunter College professor and Hellman friend.

Taylor, Telford: Prominent attorney who first met Hellman in the early 1950s and later was invited by her to participate in the activities of the Committee for Public Justice.

Trilling, Diana: Social and literary critic, wife of Lionel Trilling, and a former friend of Hellman's; she defended her late husband against Hellman's anti–anti-Communist remarks.

Trilling, Lionel: Distinguished American literary critic who became the target of a Hellman attack because he considered Whittaker Chambers an honorable man.

Uncle Willy: Hellman was in love with him for a time because of his bluff, hardy opposition to the Newhouse clan.

Vega, Jose: Assistant Stage Manager for *Another Part of the Forest* and *The Children's Hour* (1952).

Wallace, Henry: Presidential candidate on the Progressive Party ticket in 1948. Hellman campaigned for him, even though she had doubts about him and knew that Communists were infiltrating his organization.

Weinstein, Bobbie: One of Hellman's close female friends.

West, Nathanael: Celebrated author of *Miss Lonelyhearts* and *Day of the Locust* and manager of the Sutton Hotel, where Hellman and

Hammett lived for a time. Hellman's fling with West broke up his engagement to another woman.

Wilbur, Richard: One of America's finest poets. He collaborated with Hellman on the musical version of *Candide* and was a close friend for many years.

Wyler, Talli: Wife of William Wyler. She got to know Hellman in the late 1930s, took several trips with Hellman, and agreed to have the playwright in her home during what turned out to be Hellman's last winter months.

Wyler, William: Director of several Hellman films who became her close friend and loyal supporter.

Zetzel, Louis: Hellman's doctor in Cambridge.

Zilboorg, Gregory: Psychiatrist for Hellman, George Gershwin, and Ralph Ingersoll; involved in the controversy over *PM*.

1

A LEGEND IN
HER OWN TIME

I cannot and will not cut my conscience to fit this year's
fashions.

—Lillian Hellman, letter to John S. Wood

Lillian Hellman will be best remembered for a line that comes
not from one of her plays, but from the drama of her life. On
May 21, 1952, she appeared before a subcommittee of the House
Un-American Activities Committee (HUAC). In a letter to the
subcommittee's chairman, John S. Wood, she offered to be frank
about herself and her activities. But, she wrote, she would not
"bring bad trouble to people who, in my past association with
them, were completely innocent of any talk or any action that was
disloyal or subversive." She pointed out that she was "raised in an
old-fashioned American tradition and there were certain homely
things that were taught to me: to try to tell the truth, not to bear
false witness, not to harm my neighbor, to be loyal to my country,
and so on." When Hellman invoked the cause of her conscience,
then, she was speaking not only for her convictions, but for an
American way of life.

The subcommittee must have sensed that they had been had.
Unlike previous witnesses, Hellman was neither submissive nor
combative. She could not be damaged by admissions of guilt or by
self-righteous declarations of her beliefs. She took her stand on
what every true-blue American believed. Everyone remembered

her phrase. Years later, in interviews about Hellman, friends might get it slightly wrong—"tailor my conscience" or "fit my beliefs to." But Hellman's way of hitting exactly the right tone was uncanny. "I cannot and will not"—the sturdy individual who is constitutionally incapable of changing first principles; "this year's fashions"— here was one person who would not be intimidated just because others had tattled on their friends. The reference to her upbringing, the innocence and awkwardness of a phrase like "bad trouble," made Hellman all the more blameless. Questioning her proved fruitless. Even forcing her to take the fifth amendment did not embarrass her because she had maneuvered the subcommittee into a position where their rules were made to seem like a form of coercion against an honest American.

Like so much of Hellman's writing, the letter to the subcommittee seems perfectly straightforward, the kind of document that would be produced by a right-thinking person with a clear conscience. In fact, the letter went through several drafts and was the product of much calculation. In one rejected draft—which surely would have changed Hellman's public image—she admitted her membership in the Communist Party from 1938 to 1940. Most of it was written by her attorney, Joseph Rauh, although he freely concedes that the telling phrases in it are hers. Without Rauh's counsel, however, she might have given way to her first inclination, which was to tell the subcommittee "to hell with all of you." As in the productions of her plays, Hellman profited enormously from having a good director. On her own she probably would have done herself great harm.

The key to Lillian Hellman's character, to what made her a legend in her own time, was her sense of herself as a grande dame. There was something very grand about putting herself above this year's fashions, above the hoi polloi who do not have the nerve or the style to be independent. At the same time, Lady Hellman professed the politics of the oppressed and was for all sorts of radical and liberal causes. She was for the Spanish Loyalists, labor unions, environmentalism, and civil liberties; and against Franco, big corporations, the FBI, and Richard Nixon. She loved making lots of money and was proud of her Hollywood salaries and the profits from her plays, yet she often cried poverty to her friends. Like all legends, she was a peculiar blend of opposites; and like most figures who become legends in their own time, she worked very hard at it.

After Hellman posed in November 1976 in a fur for a Blackglama advertisement with the caption, "What becomes a legend most?" an old friend from the thirties, Philip Dunne, kidded, "I thought you were an environmentalist, Lillian." "I know," she said, "but there was money in it." John Melby, one of her many lovers, has a different interpretation of the advertisement: "Like a lot of people I was a little startled by it, thought she had gone a little too far, but fancy explanations are a lot of nonsense: She knew exactly what she was doing: in exchange for the use of her picture she was conning the capitalist system out of a very expensive fur coat, Period! And laughing about it."

Above all, Hellman "loved attention—any way she could get," recalls Richard de Combray, a young writer and photographer who got to know her well during the last ten years of her life. She would talk loudly in restaurants if she was not getting "quite enough attention. She was an exhibitionist, deeply an exhibitionist . . . She thought of herself as an actress, always. In fact, she said that to me once." Negative attention seemed to her the same as positive attention. "I wouldn't be surprised if it wasn't more interesting to her to get negative attention. I remember her making a chilling scene in a store in Martha's Vineyard when a child mistakenly trod on her foot." Hellman would scream and didn't care how unpleasant her behavior became. Indeed, she seemed to thrive on it. "There's a kind of character who will take it where they can get it, no matter what," de Combray concludes.

On the beach Hellman would wear revealing bathing suits. She knew she was no beauty, but "she always thought she was sexually attractive, and probably always was," de Combray suggests. As this biography reveals, she longed for a beauty she could not have and would compensate for it by sleeping around and by getting even with more attractive women. She was the classic case of the funny looking girl with the great personality, grabbing the guys away from the gorgeous girls. Hellman never let up, she never stopped.

Hellman loved money and celebrity. She was on a "notoriety kick," said Howard Bay, who knew her for more than forty years. As a result, everything about her life became grander in the rewriting of it. When parts of the past were lost to her, she filled in the gaps to make her stories complete. Talli Wyler, with whom Hellman lived just months before she died, remarked that Lillian was so good at "overstepping herself," at inventing details, that it was probably impossible for her to separate fiction from fact.

Jo Marshall, Dashiell Hammett's daughter, also suspected Hellman of lying. She was intrigued by the way Hellman jumped around so much in telling the story of her life. It was a good way to cover her tracks, to move from point to point swiftly, so that no one was quick enough to question her veracity. When Marshall spoke with Hellman, she found that it was often difficult to determine when certain events happened—or whether this event occurred before or after other events that were alluded to. Marshall was not alone in suspecting that these leaps from topic to topic were an elaborate form of lying. In her own experience, she knew Hellman was perfectly capable of making up stories Marshall was sure had not occurred. There was a line from *The Little Foxes* that in Marshall's view summed up Lillian Hellman's storymaking: "God forgives those who invent what they need."

Whether it was catching fish or writing prose, Lillian Hellman was a very competitive person, and her lying can be regarded as a form of competition with herself and with others. She wanted to land the most fish and the biggest fish, to create the best and the biggest stories. If Hemingway had Spain, the bullfights, other sports, and other wars, Hellman had "Julia," the comrade she aided by traveling into the heart of Nazi Germany.

Lee Gershwin, who first met Hellman in the late twenties, suggests how lighthearted the young Hellman was about telling the truth:

> Sam Marx and I are the only two people that know she's the biggest liar in the world. Anybody else tell you about that little throb in her throat? She had this crazy little throb right here [at the base of her throat]. It would start before she began speaking and accelerate. Sam Marx—who gave her her first job in Hollywood—and I were the only people who knew it. It was amusing. She would lie about anything—a man, a woman, it could be anything—for what we used to call "a pretty good story." We didn't care, as long as we had fun.

It was all so plausible, so pleasing to a writer who thrived on good stories. When you *know* certain things are true, you sometimes forget whether you learned them firsthand or secondhand, or whether the details are just right. When one claims—as Hellman did to Talli Wyler and Philip Dunne—to have a photographic memory, then surely there are enormous opportunities for mischief, for turning the past into one's completely personal reserve. For example, Lilly and Dash—as they called each other—were very close; her writing about Dashiell Hammett, however, turned into a romantic myth. "Dash would have laughed at it," Howard Bay said, "the legend in her own time crap. Her best friends kept her in line somewhat, *somewhat*, but she was sick for years. And if Bill Blass would take her somewhere, it was important—getting over a sill of a door or off of a curb was a major undertaking." Fame was a kind of restorative, in Bay's view.

Hellman always wanted to appear "with it" and to be surrounded by young men, especially in her last years. She wanted to be admired and desired. The glamour of it all—of Hollywood, the theater, radical politics, worldwide travel, entertaining and playing the perfect hostess—was her craving, even though she would complain about all of it some of the time. To be in a Blackglama ad was to be *seen*, to have proof positive of success. Even negative reviews of her life and work were better than no reviews at all; she thrived on all of the attention. Her funeral was reported in *Vanity Fair* as "suffused with all the significance of a major social event." It was a funeral "full of intrigue, glamour, and big important names from New York, Washington, and Hollywood." Norman Mailer, Katharine Graham, Warren Beatty, Scotty Reston, Mike Wallace, and Mike Nichols all came "flying and ferrying" to Abel's Hill Cemetery in Chilmark, Massachusetts, not far from Vineyard Haven, where Hellman had spent much of her last years. The guest list was full of intriguing intimations as to who was in and who was out. The range of invitees was indeed impressive, from Jerome Wiesner, former president of MIT, to Carly Simon, to the rightist Reverend Paul Moore, Jr., the "freeze-nik bishop of the Episcopal Diocese of New York"—as Bob Colacello wrote in *Vanity Fair*.

Hellman had, after all, the face of a national monument and had built herself into a *monstre sacre*, as Talli Wyler puts it. Another of Lillian's good friends, Louis Kronenberger, joked about her George Washington nose. In later years, her craggy face resembled one of the facades etched in stone on Mount Rushmore. Lillian Hellman was an institution. "Lillian Hellman presents" could have been used as the introductory phrase for all of the activities with which she was associated in the last two decades of her life. She founded organizations such as the Committee for Public Justice, meant to protect citizens from the government's encroachment on civil liberties. Yet she befriended people in power—like Averell Harriman, various figures in the Roosevelt administration, and the Kennedys.

Hellman was brilliant at assembling a huge circle of friends, and she loved to be showered with gifts. During World War II she sent a message to friends stating that a gift for Lillian Hellman was a "blow against fascism." Talli Wyler remembers how Lillian used to say, "I have a T.L. for you." The expression dates back to perhaps the twenties and is used in Act Two, Scene 2, of *The Children's Hour*. T.L. meant "trade last": somebody had said something nice about you, but you wouldn't get to hear it unless you could trade back something nice to the person who had the T.L. for you. For decades Lillian would approach her friends with T.L.'s, "and that meant you had to rack your brains and come up with some fine compliment for Lillian. Oh, Lord," an amused Wyler recalled.

Hellman's public following was based on her portrayal of herself as the genuine article, the uncompromising heroine of American culture. She was Big Lillian, the feisty, untactful truth teller, and admirers meeting her for the first time were often surprised to see how small of stature she was. She so identified with her own heroic image that it is doubtful she could see the contradictions in her character and the lies she spread about her past. In her own mind, she was larger than life and not bound by conventional standards. This is the dark side of a woman who could not imagine that her conscience just might lead her astray.

No one was ever as pure as Lillian Hellman, so her behavior was sacrosanct even when she violated her own principles. Sam Marx, who first met Hellman in the twenties, recalls that in 1937, while he was working with her at the Goldwyn Studios, there was a strike by the scenic artists. Hellman called Goldwyn to say she would not cross a picket line. Goldwyn told her to work at home. Hellman, whose sympathies were naturally with the strikers, continued to work at home and sent her material to the studio by messenger. But one day she showed up and had lunch at the studio. She was questioned as to why she had gone to work when there were pickets outside. "They're dopes," she told Sam Marx.

"I came up to this picket line and asked if I could go through and they said sure."

Although Hellman dramatized herself as a great democrat, she had an authoritarian personality. She believed in controlling access to information about herself and about her friends. She tried to block a biography of Dorothy Parker and made things very difficult for Diane Johnson, the authorized biographer of Dashiell Hammett. When it became known that William Wright had the audacity to begin a work on her life, she sent letters and telegrams and called friends, forbidding them to speak with this interloper. Just months before she died, Hellman appointed her own authorized biographer, her editor William Abraham, who she no doubt felt could be trusted to keep her legend intact. Her life was anything but an open book. The myth of Lillian Hellman depended on censorship.

In an interview on National Public Radio with Susan Stamberg, Zoe Caldwell admitted that it was a trial to recreate Lillian Hellman's life on stage. The actress was starring in *Lillian*, William Luce's dramatization of Hellman's memoirs. Caldwell called Hellman "a strong-willed woman" who was "difficult and intriguing." She was "very, very bright, but she did have a wild sense of anger . . . quite an uncontrollable sense of anger." That intelligence and anger is so apparent in her plays that one critic said she could blow a stage to bits. Off stage she often did the same—for instance, demolishing an ice-cream parlor in Dashiell Hammett's home when she discovered he was with another woman. Hellman, often to Hammett's amusement, waged war on everything that affronted her. Her dramas both gain and lose power because she could never let up on people. In 1964 she published a merciless satire on Arthur Miller's play *After the Fall*, because she believed he had broken the rules: he had shamelessly exploited his life with Marilyn Monroe for profit. Of course, Hellman saw no parallel between Miller's play and what she had done to Hammett—even though she had finagled to get the copyright to his literary work which should have gone to his daughters.

Hellman tried to account for her keen sense of truth and justice in her memoirs, but the reasons for her presumed rectitude were not probed very deeply by her or by others. Indeed, her memoirs hide a great deal. Although she shows some of her less flattering sides, Hellman cleverly follows the style that won her fame as a dramatist. She pares away her life until it resembles a fable. The gaps in her written life are truly astonishing, and the contradictions in her testimony suggest not only lapses in memory but a rigidity of character that rarely questions itself. Yet the title of her first autobiography, *An Unfinished Woman*, implies an incomplete story.

"Dear Lillian," said John Hersey at her funeral, "you are a finished woman, now." This would not have coincided with Hellman's own view of her impending death, to which she could never reconcile herself. Right to the end she remained combative; nothing about her life seemed settled—not even her feelings about Hammett. Diane Johnson reports in *Vanity Fair* that Hellman could not let go of Hammett and wanted to be featured in Johnson's biography much nearer the beginning, even though the playwright entered her lover's life relatively late. She wanted to repossess him and to redeem their relationship by proving that he had always loved her and that she had taken first place in his affairs, in spite of all the instances of his unfaithfulness.

Always, something was missing for Hellman. She made literary capital of the gaps she could not fill by creating an elliptical style that tantalizes readers, who can only suspect that there was more to her experience than she put into words. Although most of her plays were very successful, she did not feel at home in the theater and it did not fulfill her highest ambitions. Many of the actors in her plays hated her. One of them refused to be interviewed for this book because he said he could not think of a single good thing to say about her. A fellow playwright and friend of Hellman's vehemently declined to be questioned about her for similar reasons: "She was a *viper*."

Zoe Caldwell was astonished by the deep hatred of Hellman expressed by people who knew her and who would come backstage to say things like, "She was such a goddamn liar." At Hellman's funeral, an unidentified friend suggested that even Hellman's most supportive intimates had strongly divided feelings about her:

> It's not so much that they worshiped her—that's not the precise word. It's more of the feeling that people have for a mother, which has to include a lot of ambivalence. All the people who loved Lillian the most knew that she had deep, deep faults and flaws, and they were very, very critical of them—and rebellious

about her. I can't tell you how many times I've heard people who've known her much longer than I have talk about how this was the year they weren't going to accept her dinner invitations or were not going to subject themselves to Lillian's mean tongue, and yet, year after year, they did and they loved it and they loved her. It was *real love*—a very personal love.

Richard de Combray speaks for many of her friends who admired her, miss her now, and yet feel ambivalent about her legacy: "She must have known she was dying, and she must have had terribly lonely moments. Anyone else would have let go. She wanted to pull all the scenery down with her."

How can one convey the hold Hellman had on people? She cared about so many things. It could be a nightmare having to deal with Lillian about so many details, but it could also be wonderful because her interests were so wide-ranging. Stephen Gillers, an Executive Director of the Committee for Public Justice, and now a law professor at New York University first met her in early 1971 in a Greenwich Village restaurant, The Cookery. "Lillian tried a little bit of everyone's plate, which endeared her to me. She had to see what everything tasted like." Visiting her Park Avenue apartment was a delight for him. There were pictures everywhere—of her beloved Sophronia, of Dashiell Hammett—and books everywhere. He felt comfortable among her "old, slightly worn, but good furnishings." Lillian "would sit there and smoke incessantly." She had a highly stylized way of holding her cigarette in an elevated position out from her body. Even in her last days "her voice was very strong, her mind was very strong—and her sentence structure never changed. Lillian had this wonderful sentence structure and a capacity for pauses. Her silences were as articulate as her sentences. She would suddenly stop and take a deep drag on a cigarette, and then she would continue." She always found a way of heightening the drama of her words. "I often felt she was watching herself as a character, and I liked that." Everything she did had a style, an identity. She was "Miss Hellman," never Ms.— "she hated that term," Gillers remembers. And her first name had to be pronounced with two syllables (Lil-yan), not three (Lil-i-an). She would often preface a statement by saying, "I have something important to tell you," or "I met a man on the plane who told me an exceptional story, and I want to know your view of it." She got your attention. "The other thing she did is repeat adverbial phrases: 'His behavior was very bad, very bad,' or 'How could she say that, how could she say that?' She italicized it in your mind."

As in her plays, she was able to cut to the quick of things, to really listen to people and advise them with extraordinary insight: "If she liked you, she immediately knew all there was to know about you. She knew your children's names, how many times you'd been married, whatever. And she never forgot."

Catherine Kober, the daughter of Arthur Kober, Hellman's husband, had an uneasy relationship with Hellman that finally ruptured. Yet to this day Catherine Kober honors Hellman for having pointed out to her a path in life that has proven successful. Catherine had had a very difficult time of it. As a child she watched her mother die of a slow, wasting, degenerative disease. None of the people close to her seemed to know what to do. Catherine was so unfocused. In her mid-thirties, Catherine was floundering. Teaching did not work out for her. At a party, she and Hellman talked things over. "You really ought to go to social work school," was her advice. "It would give you the broad base you need." Catherine had a fit. She figured she would have to study statistics and would never pass the course. "It's *not* statistics," Hellman assured her. "It's a research project, and if you want to, you'll get through it." Catherine dismissed the suggestion. But eventually, in 1982, she did enroll in a social work school. "If I had followed her advice then, I would have saved myself a tremendous amount of trouble. When I got into the research course—which was *not* statistics—I remembered her with great affection. She was right on the mark. This is another thing she could do. She could see things that were hidden in people. Everybody else said, do this, do that, or 'oh, poor Catherine, what will she do with her life?' " Hellman defined Catherine's direction in just a few sentences. Their whole conversation at the party could not have lasted more than five minutes. Hellman picked right through Catherine's scattered thoughts. "In one stroke of empathetic genius," said Catherine, "Lillian could see that with the social work degree I would have the basis to do any [job] I chose." Hellman had a way of authoring people's lives, of instilling a confidence in the noble purposes of life, that was truly astonishing.

Yet there was a significance to Hellman's experience and to the lives she wrote about that somehow eluded her. *The Little Foxes* and *Another Part of the Forest* were meant to be part of a trilogy—

based in large part on her family history—which she never completed. Her final book, *Maybe,* is also heavily autobiographical and inconclusive, although in some ways it may be her most honest work. In *Maybe,* she turned the growing blindness in the last years of her life into a metaphor for her memory of events that had become shadowy—like a light that was "masked with an unknown fabric."

There was an injustice in the very scheme of things, and Hellman felt thwarted. In *Scoundrel Time,* she gave way to fierce attacks on liberals for not vigorously defending blacklisted writers during the McCarthy era. She singled out Lionel Trilling, for instance, because of his insistence that Whittaker Chambers was a man of integrity who was genuinely concerned about Alger Hiss and other fellow travelers who abetted Communist efforts to subvert American policies and programs. In place of wavering progressives like Henry Wallace, she held up Hammett's staunch commitment to Marxism, even though she had significant disagreements with aspects of his political philosophy. She suspected most American intellectuals of not being loyal to their own beliefs or to their friends when careers were on the line and when writers were called to testify before Congress about their political associations. What most appalled her, in other words, was a defect in human character. That friends could publicly disown one another—whatever their differences—astonished and enraged her. Hellman never forgave certain liberals like Clifford Odets for appeasing Congress by recanting a radical past. One *lived* with one's mistakes, as Karen puts it in *The Children's Hour,* and no amount of expiation could cancel one's past transgressions.

"She quarreled with everyone, often over the most trivial issue—she broke with Bill Styron for an entire summer in a dispute over the proper way to cook a ham," Robert Brustein recalls. He believes these fights kept her vital and defiant of death. She could be generous with old friends, like Joseph Alsop, whose opinions differed markedly from her own, because of her compulsive need to be hospitable and to nourish her friends. But challenging her on any matter would provoke in Hellman an extreme effort to vindicate herself, as if in all things that touched her most closely—like her cooking and her politics—she had to be not only right but victorious.

Lillian Hellman's place in American theater is not clear, even though her plays are revived frequently in New York and all over the world, and her work has endured better than that of other dramatists in her generation. Unlike many celebrated playwrights she did little to promote or explain her work. Even her immensely popular memoirs do not concentrate on her theater career, so that some readers, acquainted only with *An Unfinished Woman, Pentimento*, and *Scoundrel Time*, have assumed that playwriting held only an episodic value in her life, and that life itself was her finest achievement. As a dramatist, Hellman wrote no manifestos for the theater. In contrast to Arthur Miller, for example, she did not campaign for tragedy and the common man or experiment with expressionism and other theatrical styles. She remained, for the most part, a practitioner of realism and showed little interest in questions of form and creativity, telling her *Paris Review* interviewers that "one form is as good as another. . . . there are a thousand ways to write. . . . If you break into a new pattern along the way, and it opens things up, and allows you more freedom, that's something. But not everything, maybe even not much." She avoided symbolism, except in her play titles, and no single character of hers can rival Willy Loman or Blanche Dubois in mythic suggestiveness. Hellman's writing does not deal in pathos; she has to be the most unsentimental major playwright America has produced.

Whether one is speaking of Hellman's political or esthetic position, she is America's finest radical playwright. Her radicalism is characterized by a depth of belief and integrity of principle that is uncommon in American drama. She required a realistic and unambiguous form in order to attack the appeasement of iniquity. Several of her plays explore the weaknesses of liberalism, of its tendency to be too lenient with evil, even while professing allegiance to the highest humanistic ideals. There is a penitent tone and a let-us-be-reasonable manner in some of her liberal characters that result in an obfuscation of evil that is deadly real. Hellman's view of Miller's *After the Fall* and of his appearance before Congress during the McCarthy "witch-hunting" period sums up her critique of liberalism:

> I never much liked his House Un-American Committee testimony: a little breast-beating and a little apology. . . . I suppose, in the play, he was being tolerant: those who betrayed their friends had a point, those who

didn't also had a point. Two sides to every question and all that rot.

Hellman had no name for what she believed, but in order to evade the Communist label she told Margaret Case Harriman, who was writing a profile of the playwright in 1944 for the *New Yorker*, "she would like to be a liberal if she could tell, these days, exactly what the hell a liberal is."

While many of Hellman's political and historical arguments in her memoirs carry the conviction of personal example and the examples of others whom she is able to revivify, her decision in *Scoundrel Time* to "stick to what I know, what happened to me" is disabling. It may seem sensible and modest, but actually it is a form of blindness that bars her from perceiving crucial dimensions of the events in which she played a part. Her account of the *Hiss-Chambers* case, for instance, is seriously in error and significantly compromises her personal Cold War history.

This is a critical biography of an American writer about whom controversy will continue for as long as she is read. Views of Hellman in the literary community are sharply divided. The novelist John Hersey, one of her very closest friends, has referred to her in print as a kind of moral touchstone. Richard Poirier, a distinguished critic and one of Hellman's literary executors, has written an admiring preface to her collection of memoirs, *Three*, and on several occasions has vigorously defended the quality of her plays. Robert Brustein, eminent theater critic and director, has mixed feelings about her life and career.

Alfred Kazin, who corresponded with Hellman a few times, grudgingly acknowledges her significance:

> I can see that Hellman, though really not a very interesting writer, was dramatic enough in her life and political opinions to provoke a whole literature about her! . . . Hellman and I were hardly friends, and as you can see from my review of *Scoundrel Time*, near the end of her life I came to detest her—not so much for her political views, though they were detestable, as for her combination of "radicalism" and snobbery and a general inclination to take herself too seriously.

Hellman's plays and, indeed, nearly all of her prose, are polemical. To read Hellman, even to read about her, is to start an argument. She did not believe in balance; having convictions means taking sides. Principles are not arrived at through compromising one's feelings for the sake of social amity. As a result, one is never done with Hellman, and she holds on to her readers until they are either persuaded or put off by her positions. The chapters of her life in this biography reflect the melodramatic rhythm of her existence as she plays, by turns, the villain and the heroine.

A fine cook, she rarely savored her own meals; a highly sexed woman, she never forgave Hammett for refusing her his bed. Even in *The Autumn Garden*, her most mature play, there is little sense of the wisdom, or at least the resignation, that sometimes accompanies age. Lillian Hellman's life, in short, was not as she would have had it. Near death, she spoke of being blocked. This biography shows what got in her way.

2

AN ONLY CHILD
New Orleans/New York
Paris/Hollywood
(1905–1930)

MB: You wanted someone to limit you in some way. You
were a spoiled only child.
LH: Yes, that's right. I did seek limits. That's right, I did. I
did. I wanted somebody to say, "Nix, knock it off."

—Lillian Hellman and Marilyn Berger
in *Conversations with Lillian Hellman*, ed. Jackson R. Bryer

Lillian Florence Hellman, the only child of Max Hellman and
Julia Newhouse Hellman, was born on June 20, 1905, in New
Orleans. Max Hellman's family had come to the city from Germany
sometime between 1845 and 1848. His father, Bernard, and his
mother, Babette Koshland Hellman, are both buried in Ahavas
Sholem on Frenchman Street in New Orleans. Max, born in January 1880, lived with his mother until his early twenties. Then, like
his father who died in 1895, Max began work as a bookkeeper
before becoming a salesman and then president of the Hellman
Shoe Company in 1905.

Julia Newhouse's family had moved to New Orleans from Demopolis, Alabama, and Cincinnati, Ohio, many years before she
was born. In Demopolis, her mother, Sophie Marx, married Leonard Newhouse, a wholesale liquor dealer who died eight years

before his granddaughter Lillian was born. It was Sophie's side of the family—the Marxes—that were uppermost in the author's mind when she described the Newhouses as rich, powerful, and avaricious, a "banking and storekeeping" clan contemptuous of Max Hellman's poor prospects. The Marxes and the Newhouses emigrated from Germany in the 1840s, establishing themselves in Mobile, Alabama, before the Civil War. During Reconstruction, both families moved up the Tombigbee River to Demopolis, a vigorous center of commerce with good connections to Mobile and the Gulf of Mexico. As another of Hellman's biographers puts it, "Demopolis in the nineteenth century, prided itself on being more worldly, more tolerant and more spirited than other smaller southern towns." Sophie's brother Jake, a successful banker in Demopolis and New York, solidified the family's presence in two very different worlds that were to play such a strong role in Lillian's education and in her dramas. *The Little Foxes* and *Another Part of the Forest*, in particular, are infused with ironical treatments of the southern setting that owe much to Sophie's and Jake's hardheaded speculations. It took considerable nerve, therefore, for Julia Newhouse to marry Max Hellman, a man whose impending failure in business made her especially vulnerable to her family's crass competitiveness. Max apparently received no help at all from the Newhouses, although he and Julia may have lived with them for a while after their marriage.

Hellman's memories of her first five years in New Orleans were extremely vague. When she was four, she was taken to see the musical *The Pink Lady*, and was impressed by the pretty costumes. She had a mammy, the first of a series of black women who nurtured Hellman and who received, in return, her devotion. When she was about six years old, her father's shoe company failed, and he took the family to New York City, where he eventually established himself as a successful traveling salesman for a clothing business. Hellman thought of herself as a "transplanted Southerner," since until she was about sixteen, her family spent half of each year with her father's sisters in New Orleans. In *An Unfinished Woman*, she remembered how hard these transitions were on her growing mind:

> This constant need for adjustment in two very differ-
> ent worlds made formal education into a kind of frantic
> tennis game, sometimes played with children whose

strokes had force and brilliance, sometimes with those who could barely hold the racket.

In New Orleans, Hellman was a self-taught loner; in New York she had trouble keeping up with her classmates. She never did very well in school, for her life lacked the evenness and balance that encourage consistent performance. Her education, in every sense of the word, was erratic.

New Orleans was a segregated city, with separate accommodations, theaters, night clubs, restaurants, and recreational facilities for blacks. As Hellman matured, she became increasingly aggravated to see how black people, who meant so much to her, were relegated to inferior positions. At a very early age, she became angry at the injustice of it all and struck out on her own. After proudly watching her father stand up to white ruffians molesting a black woman, Hellman resolved on her own course of righting the world's wrongs. With Sophronia Mason, her devoted black guardian and the "first and most certain love" of her life, she had always sat in the back of the streetcar, in the "Negro section." Not this time. Positioning herself directly behind the driver, she pulled the black woman next to her. After a brief scuffle, in which Hellman was opposed by both the conductor and Sophronia, she found herself in a panic on the street, crying and wishing to run away. Sophronia, "past the runnin' age," chided Hellman for giving in with reckless abandon to her feelings. Hellman wanted to feel good about having expressed the proper sentiments, but Sophronia was not impressed. To her, the incident must have seemed like one of those liberal gestures that could not begin to change the fundamental structure of things. Later, in her plays, Hellman would be very hard indeed on well-intentioned liberals. The curious thing about Hellman is that she reacted to inequality so personally—as if racism, for example, thwarted her own efforts to develop into an independent person. Society, in toto, conspired against her. As an only child with several sets of parental figures, she almost immediately put herself at the center of things.

Some of Hellman's earliest memories were of visits to the Newhouse apartment in New York City. Because of her father's financial difficulties, she keenly sensed she was at a disadvantage in the company of her mother's family. The Newhouse gatherings were like corporation meetings, presided over by Lillian's grandmother, "the silent, powerful, severe woman, Sophie Newhouse," and by

Sophie's brother Jake, "a man of great force, given, as she was given, to breaking the spirit of people for the pleasure of the exercise."

Lillian feared her mother's cruel family, and it was not until much later, in her mid-thirties, that she was able to see their machinations as comic and deserving of the sneaking admiration she accords them in *The Little Foxes*. As a child, she was much fonder of her father and his two sisters, Hannah and Jenny Hellman. In her memoirs, she portrays Max as handsome and charming and funny, although some of her friends in later years remember him as rather fat and ordinary and without much resemblance to the romantic figure of her writing. He prided himself on his business acumen—that is clear from Arthur Kober's diary, which is filled with references to Max's conversations about the stock market and about the money he had invested for Lillian's ex-husband. Kober was obviously fond of Max, although he fretted over Max's garrulity. But in Lillian's eyes, there was something heroic about Max, for her mother had defied her family to marry him. Even when Lillian rebelled against him, she saw her orneriness as similar to his own.

Hannah and Jenny were Max's loving servants. "Funny" and "generous" are the words Hellman uses in her memoirs to describe her aunts, who owned and managed a New Orleans boarding house. She reveled in the intense domesticity of her aunts' work. It was her job "to clean the crayfish for the wonderful bisque." She was taught "how to make turtle soup, and how to kill a chicken without ladylike complaints about the horror of dealing death, and how to pluck and cook the wild ducks that were hawked on our street every Sunday morning." Life at the boarding house seemed "remarkably rich" to Hellman, and she spent considerable time trying to figure out its inhabitants. "I was crazy about other people's lives. . . . I guess I was the only one who ever listened to the guests, and they talked to me for hours." There was Mr. Stillman, "a large, loose, good-looking man" who flirted with her mother, Collie (a favorite among the female boarders) "a too thin, unhappy looking, no-age man, [who] worked in his uncle's bank and was drunk every night," and "two faded, sexy, giggly sisters called Fizzy and Sarah, who pretended to love children and all trees." Another boarder, Gaston Crespie, owned a notions shop just three blocks from the house. Thus, Hellman was exposed to different kinds of people. She had

great fondness and respect for colored people. . . .
They were very nice to a little girl and much more fun
than anyone else. The ladies in the boarding house
always had a headache and were resting. You weren't
considered a lady unless you had a headache and were
resting.

Her aunts fed the poor and advised the young without fuss or
fanfare. New Orleans, as Hellman remembered it, in *An Unfinished
Woman*, "was a city of many poor people," and her grandfather
had set down a family law, never disobeyed by his children, to
feed the unfortunates (as many as eight or ten, black and white)
who came to the boarding house kitchen. "Jenny, the prettier and
more complex, had frequent outbursts of interesting temper,"
Hellman remembers. So brim-full of anger herself, Hellman saw
this as a virtue—especially in comparison to her mother's placid,
sweet innocence. Julia was treated by Hannah and Jenny "as if she
were a precious Chinese clay piece from a world they didn't
know."

As a child, Hellman had contempt for what she regarded as her
mother's delicacy and weakness and was irritated by her eccentricities and her simple, religious nature. As an adult, she regarded
her mother affectionately and found a lot of the things she said
"wonderfully goofy." For Richard Wilbur, Hellman once recalled a
time when she and her mother drove past a house that her mother
had considered buying. Her mother looked at it and said, "What
an ugly house. I wouldn't buy that for a song." That twisting of a
usual expression made "perfect sense" to Hellman—just as many
of Sam Goldwyn's mind-twisters did. "I don't think she made fun
of her mother so much as she enjoyed a kind of hazy malapropism
in her," Wilbur concludes.

It was not until after Julia Newhouse's death in 1935 that Hellman realized her mother's strengths. Max had seemed a far more
powerful and intriguing figure: "kind of bright and funny—gay,
full of life and interested in everything," Hellman told an interviewer. Julia, on the other hand, was "a gentle, very pleasant
woman, nice-mannered—an innocent woman." Max's infidelity
only increased Lillian's sense of her mother's unworthiness. Julia
was not a passive person in her daughter's life, however. She
wielded an influence Lillian never quite acknowledged. Julia had a
very strong sense of right and wrong; she was a moral person who

would not countenance injustice. When she gave Lillian a hard time about living with Hammett, she may have seemed small-minded and moralistic. She made Lillian feel less than an adult. But Julia's bedrock belief in good and evil was later reflected in *Another Part of the Forest*, where Lavinia's purity of religious principle helps destroy her corrupt husband, Marcus Hubbard.

Although Lillian Hellman became a far more complex person than her mother, in many ways her morality was her mother's. How else to explain her fundamental inability to see moral ambiguity, except to say that Hellman never outgrew her childhood wish for absolute standards of conduct? When she discovered, at the age of eight or nine, that her father was seeing another woman, she wanted to "kill them for it." Instead, full of fears and rage, she threw herself to the ground from her cherished fig tree and broke her nose. "The fig tree was heavy, solid, comfortable," her "first and most beloved home." In it she had "learned to read" and sweated "in the attempt to understand the world of adults I fled from in real life but desperately wanted to join in books." To fling herself from its security meant that her whole vision of things had been shattered. In "hideous pain" she went to Sophronia, who enjoined her never to say a word about her father and Fizzy: "Don't go through life making trouble for people."

More than any other incident in Hellman's life, the fall from the fig tree and its aftermath has invited comment and conjecture. Bill Moyers asked Hellman whether she had been searching her whole life for another fig tree. Zoe Caldwell based her stage characterization of Hellman on the fall, calling the broken nose a "badge of courage" and Sophronia's advice a guiding principle to which Hellman held throughout her life. The child's promise never to inform on her father echoes in Hellman's letter to the HUAC, in which she spoke of her moral upbringing and willingness to talk about herself but not others.

The obvious symbolism of Hellman's fall from innocence should not obscure the fact that, in important ways, she never grew up—that she was, indeed, an unfinished woman spoiled into regarding her own sense of right and wrong as sacrosanct. If it were *wrong* for her to be an informer, she could not imagine that, under certain circumstances, it might be *right* for someone else. Once learned, the lessons of morality never changed for her, and she would be outraged by points of view that differed from her own.

Hellman was nine or ten when she first met her Aunt Lily and her husband Willy at their St. Charles Avenue house. Like Max, Willy was a good-looking, robust man who had married into the Newhouse family, had made a fortune with borrowed Newhouse money and lost it, and had become successful again. He was unfaithful to his wife and was a romantic figure for Hellman well into her adult years. Hellman also enjoyed the confidence of Caroline Ducky, a black woman more irascible than Sophronia and apparently more willing to indulge the child's immense love of intrigue. Hellman desperately wanted to understand the intimate affairs of adults. It was in Ducky's presence that Hellman learned when Willy needed money—when he was close to ruin but gamely facing down Lily and the other Newhouses. Aunt Lily, a coarse and corrupted version of Julia, at first bewitched Hellman and then repelled her:

> Her jewelry, the dresses from Mr. Worth in Paris, her hand-sewn underwear with the Alençon lace, her Dubonnet with a few drops of spirits of ammonia, were all fine stuff to me. But most of all, I was impressed with her silences and the fineness of her bones.

The things in Aunt Lily's house that once appeared "beautiful and foreign" to a child of ten seemed to a sixteen-year-old "ornate copies of French and Italian miseries, cluttering all the tables and running along the staircase walls and newel posts on up to the attic quarters of Caroline Ducky."

In New York, the Hellmans lived in a "quite pleasant, comfortable apartment" on West Ninety-fifth Street between Riverside Drive and West End Avenue. The advent of World War I provoked Hellman and a friend, Helen Schiff, to follow suspicious-looking persons who they thought might be German spies. Evidently the two girls actually chased two "long-haired fellows"—one carrying a brief case and the other a violin case—and reported them to a police sergeant, who "discovered them to be a professor of Greek from Hunter College and a second violinist from the Palace Theatre." Hellman told Margaret Harriman that she and Helen had a "stooge" paid to "eavesdrop on conversations of suspects and report them to the two head spy-catchers." But the stooge's reports were dull and her arm had to be twisted before she invented a story that satisfied Hellman's request for something "more *interest-*

ing." Hellman uses a version of this incident in *The Children's Hour,* where Mary Tilford twists the arm of her playmate to enforce her more provocative and more damning version of the intimacy between her teachers, Karen Wright and Martha Dobie.

As a spoiled, only child, Hellman had little patience, was self-centered, and was quick to find fault in others. That her meanness of character has not put off readers of her popular memoirs is attributable, in large part, to making her reminiscences of child-hood so crucial to her adult experience. One simply cannot blame a child; a child is not responsible for his or her actions; a child is easily frustrated by the contradictory and hypocritical actions of adults. When Hellman has one of her fits, it is presented as a kind of constitutional defect she cannot change. No American writer has ever made a greater virtue of her ignorance, of a willful blindness that again is not blameworthy because it is so cunningly a part of her childhood self, a purer self that would not traffic with adult corruption: "I never thought one should establish communi-cation with one's parents. I didn't come across that idea until years later in my reading. Adults were my enemies—good to stay away from."

Hellman hardly sentimentalized childhood, her own or anyone else's. "I must have been a prize nuisance child," she told an interviewer, "I formed everything in the form of a question. And I would pull at everybody's coats or dresses to tell me what I wanted to know along a street." To another questioner she confided that "I don't think I like the picture of myself as a child. I don't know why. I was no worse than anyone else." At about ten or twelve she began to write stories and poems. She remembered that at thirteen or fourteen she wrote her first story "outside of school." It was "half-cribbed . . . from somebody," and her family laughed when she told them she did not understand it herself, although she took her incomprehension as a sign of advancement. She was, in her own words, "an aimless child" who lacked ambition and wandered about. One observer was surprised that Hellman should still apply the word "aimless" to her adult self, yet this pretense of not having a purpose, a direction, in life served Hellman well, for she could thus appear to be without guile or an agenda.

Looking back at her childhood in *Pentimento,* Hellman realized how dreams and fantasies entered her life and "how the dream, the need of dream, led to distortion of what happened. And so I knew early that the rampage angers of an only child were distorted nightmares of reality." These words introduce Hellman's memories of her dearest childhood friend, Julia, memories she trusted "absolutely": a New Year's Eve at Julia's grandparents' "great Fifth Avenue house" when both girls were twelve, weekends in New York City together, a trip to the Adirondacks with Julia's parents, camping trips on or near Lake Champlain. This was the life of the "very rich," with late dinners consisting of "courses of fish and meats and sherbets in between to change the tastes" in a house with "endless chic-shabby rooms, their walls covered with pictures, their tables crowded with objects whose value I didn't know." Each New Year's Eve, Hellman recalled that night at Julia's grandparents when Julia recited poetry—Dante in Italian and Heine in German. Hellman knew no foreign languages but read Mother Goose to her friend, her alter ego, her better half. Julia seemed to convey a sense of what lay ahead, of what could be "fine and fulfilling," if only Hellman could find her way.

"It was in our nineteenth year that she went away to Oxford," Hellman writes in preparation for a story about a close companion she was never to know as intimately again. Although she visited Julia in her second year at Oxford, the two women met only briefly and corresponded sporadically until Julia's death in 1937. Like so many of Hellman's relationships in her memoirs, the one with Julia is parabolic. She is a facet of Hellman's own self, a closeted part of her personality, a "memory" in the sense that Julia is retrieved from an only child's mind as a fitting comrade. "All my life I've divided myself into two and sometimes three parts. And they talk. They put me in my place or they have little dialogues," Hellman told journalist Marilyn Berger in describing "Nursie" and "Madam," two characters she had invented for herself.

Hellman's feelings about Julia were "too strong and complicated to be defined as only the sexual yearnings of one girl for another." Julia had the beauty, the culture, the resolute and radical devotion to a career and way of life that Hellman had always wanted for herself. Julia's rejection of luxury, her Robinson Crusoe-like independence (even hunting and skinning a rabbit for a delicious meal Hellman never forgot), her discussions of Freud and Marx as well as of "romantic love" made her an only child's perfect dream figure.

Julia was as much a rebel against her family as Hellman was against hers. As Hellman shows in *Pentimento,* she was drawn to relatives defiant of convention like Uncle Willy and Bethe Bruno

Koshland. By the age of thirteen, Hellman was interested in knowing "what attracted men and what didn't." It bothered her that both Bethe and Aunt Lily made mention of her unattractiveness, of her straight, muddy-blonde hair. Bethe not only had had her share of men, she had spurned both the Hellmans and the Bowmans—the two families responsible for the welfare of this immigrant woman, sent to them by European relatives who had arranged her marriage to Styrie Bowman. "No longer am I German. No longer the Bowmans. Now I am woman and woman does not need help," Bethe told Hellman after taking up with an Italian lover. On the sly, Hellman saw Bethe eight or nine times, until at age sixteen she stopped spending half of each year in New Orleans. When Bethe met her lover, the child sensed a sexuality she could not yet articulate:

> He was sitting alone at a table, staring at a wall, as if to keep his face from us. I asked Bethe for a glass of water and found her staring at the man, her lips compressed as if to hold the mouth from doing something else, her shoulder rigid against the chair. The man turned from the wall, the eyes dropped to the table, and then the head went up suddenly and stared at Bethe until the lips took on the look of her lips and the shoulder went back against the chair with the same sharp intake of muscles.

All in one, the movement of the lovers toward each other is registered by the keenly observant only child who recalls in adulthood how "all that I saw related to me." It was a new experience, and it pained her: "as if I were alone in the world and always would be." She ran away as Bethe returned to their table.

Fourteen was perhaps Hellman's most difficult growing-up year. She was beginning to feel "sexual stirrings." She was turning into a "handful," and one of her aunts' boarders complained that she was "just plain disgusting mean." She clobbered one of her companions, James Denery III, over the head with a porcelain coffee pot in retaliation for his hitting her hard during a tug-of-war. She had also refused to go back to dancing class. Her one tribute came in the form of a lock of hair given to her by a boy who then shoved her into the gutter. She treasured his gift by putting it into the back of her new watch, a birthday gift from her father. When the watch stopped the next day, her father insisted on taking it back to the "unreliable" jeweler. When the hair was discovered and his daughter refused to explain, he became very angry. Hellman became even more upset and physically sickened by a rage she could not control. She was "astonished" by the pain in her head and by her clumsiness, turning an ankle when she tried to stand and falling a few steps when she tried to climb the stairs to her room.

In *An Unfinished Woman* Hellman explains that she decided to leave home. She walked a long way down St. Charles Avenue, spent part of the night in a doll house on the grounds of a mansion, tried to clean herself up in the railroad station, moved through the French Quarter, past St. Louis Cathedral in Jackson Square, and found herself at the whorehouse section of Bourbon Street. She was having menstrual cramps; she was coming of age and felt she "had gotten older." Eventually, she found refuge in a "nigger" rooming house, where she claimed she belonged because she was "part nigger," a relative of her nurse, Sophronia Mason. When her father came for her, there was a standoff between child and adult, with neither conceding a point to the other. Max Hellman noticed how his daughter talked to herself. It looked like praying, as if she were preparing to be "the first Jewish nun on Prytania Street." Lillian laughed and the quarrel between them was dropped. She confided to him her "secret"—that she was bleeding and going through a change of life. Hellman realized she was putting her parents through a test of wills, a power game in which she could "take the punishment" and survive the battle. Her final comment in *An Unfinished Woman* on this episode suggests how important it was for her to win, no matter how insignificant the contest: "That the issue may be trivial, the battle ugly, is another point."

At fourteen, Hellman swung wildly between her conflicting moods. In one of her "many religious periods," she yelled across a dinner table at a great-aunt, "You have a spatulate face made to dig in the mud for money. May God forgive you." On some days, her "heart was with the poor," on others "it was with those who ground them under." What to do with a personality that identified with both the meek and the powerful? "I remember that period as a hell of self-dislike," Hellman remarks in *Pentimento*. It would take her many years to realize that she "lived under an economic system of increasing impurity and injustice for which I, and all those like me, pay with ridiculous wounds to the spirit." Not until the writing of *Days to Come* and *The Little Foxes* would she begin to understand how the psychology of individuals is bound up with the way they choose, or fail to choose, to make a living.

This is why Uncle Willy was so fascinating to Hellman at fourteen. He was powerful, he made money, but he did not act with the meanness of the Newhouses. Newhouses exploited blacks; Willy was at ease with all races and took Caroline Ducky into his confidence. Newhouses intimidated children; Willy talked to Hellman as though she were an equal. Willy was spontaneous while the Newhouses were calculating, never making a move unless it was absolutely in their best interest. Hellman "was not ever to fall in love very often," but with Willy it was "certainly . . . the first time." Leaving the stuffy climate of "the most immaculate of houses, the imitated eighteenth-century elegance of Aunt Lily's house," Willy took Hellman on a wonderful fishing trip into bayou country. He did not seem to care—or perhaps he did not even notice—that she was there to see him go off for the evening with his Cajun mistress. As with her father, Willy's infidelity enraged her. She considered avenging herself with Willy's murder but instead "revenged myself on myself" by recklessly leaving the fishing camp and taking off on her own into the swamps. A few years later she shocked her mother by calling Willy a murderer because of his involvement in his company's violent suppression of its Central American workers. Yet her love for him was only temporarily diminished, and it revived quickly on one of her later visits to New Orleans. Only Hammett's stern reminder that Willy—for all his seemingly eccentric independence—was really a company man, kept her from going off with him on an expedition to Central America.

At fourteen, however, Hellman was hardly in a position to understand that one might have to live with deeply divided feelings. Like many adolescents, she demanded but rebelled against the discipline of authority figures. Brooding over her father's order to be home at eleven, she went out with a nineteen-year-old Columbia student and did not return home until well past midnight. Angered by her father's disapproval, she called on the Columbia sophomore, announcing that she had left home and that he should look after her. Instead, he escorted her home. She responded to her mother's tears of grief very much like Mary in *The Children's Hour*: "Mother, I have heart trouble."

There was not much in Hellman's New York school life that attracted her. Wadleigh High School "was a large, smelly, unpleasant dump" where she was taught "nothing." Said Hellman, "In those days I spent a good deal of my spare time looking up the naughty words in the dictionary." Her report cards for 1921 and 1922 indicate that she took drawing, English, French, intermediate algebra, history, physical training, grammar, trigonometry, journalism, hygiene, Latin, and geometry. Her best subjects were English (with a score of 89), history (88), grammar (95), Latin (80), and hygiene (80). She never scored above 70 in her mathematics courses. Of more interest to her was her participation in dramatics. She was assigned the villain's part in a school play. Although she had few lines, she capitalized on an unfortunate occurrence during the play's performance: when she could not make a final exit because of a stuck door, she pleased herself by remaining on stage, arranging herself on the sofa of the drawing-room set and creating "a dazzling scene, which fattened up her own part by a number of showy remarks." It took about five minutes for the horrified drama coach to get the door unstuck and to wave the villain offstage. "It Seems to Me, Jr.," a column Hellman wrote for the school newspaper, was another opportunity to show off. It was "a light, chatty, socially insignificant" contribution she wanted to forget—although she could not resist mentioning it to at least two interviewers.

Hellman's report cards for 1921 and 1922 show twenty-three absences. According to her school chum, Helen Schiff, the two girls would cut classes because of freezing weather. Walking along the frozen Hudson River they would often come home late. Hellman had already taken up smoking and would "airily" toss her cigarette out of a high-story window when Helen's mother appeared. Hellman was considered such an unruly child that at one point Helen's mother was warned by the school principal that Hellman was a "bad influence on her daughter."

In the summer of 1921, on a trip to Cincinnati, sixteen-year-old Hellman met Louis Kronenberger, who was to become a lifelong friend. A friend of his, Stan Simon, had shown him one of Hellman's letters, and Louis was profoundly impressed. He had never seen such a funny and marvelous letter. Her literary talent was already apparent, and he was intrigued by her "high-flying" temperament. A few years later, in New York City, they were engaged—although Kronenberger's mother disapproved of this nonconformist young woman. The engagement was short-lived, for Kronenberger was penniless and had to return to Cincinnati while Hellman, equally at a loss for income, remained in school in New York.

In Hellman's view, there was not much to say about her college years. By seventeen, she was a "wild and headstrong girl . . . overproud, oversensitive, overdaring because I was shy and frightened." She was supposed to go away to school—Smith was her choice; her parents picked Goucher—but her mother's illness made it obvious to Hellman that she was to stay at home. Going to New York University was probably something of a relief to a young woman who was not ready to venture out on her own. The Washington Square branch of the university had an excellent small faculty that Hellman felt, at least in retrospect, was the right environment for an insecure rebel who probably would have been lost elsewhere. "All I got out of it was a notebook. I still have it. I wrote in it that I thought Greek art was all right," she told a reporter in 1935. Dante was also "okay," according to the same notebook, in which she recorded her reactions to courses taken in the summer sessions of 1922 and 1923 at Columbia University. Dostoyevsky and Melville made a significant impression. She briefly considered writing biographies of Dante and Lewis Carroll. She was irritated by Alexander Woollcott's NYU class and would walk out in the middle of his "gibe-wit" lectures. One of Hellman's classmates remembers her as a "very homely and very unhappy" young woman who complained about NYU. Ann Haber, another fellow student, remembers gossiping with Hellman, who impressed her as reserved yet lively and perceptive. During an exam, Hellman copied Haber's paper and justified the cheating by saying, "I know what *I* think about the plays, but for the test I have to know what the *instructor* thinks about them." Only one professor excited her interest by introducing her to Kant and Hegel and to "a little, very little, of Karl Marx and Engels." Her favorite memories, however, were of Lee Chumley's, a Greenwich Village restaurant, where she would curl up with a book or argue with "a brilliant girl called Marie-Louise and her extraordinary, foppish brother, up very often from Princeton, carrying a Paris copy of *Ulysses* when he wasn't carrying Verlaine."

It was during the Columbia summer session of 1922 that Howard

Meyer first met eighteen-year-old Lillian Hellman. He was the business manager of the *Columbia Spectator*. His office in East Hall, in a central location on campus, was the place from which all Columbia publications were issued. He had a little office with a window that looked out on a path coming from the philosophy building and on to the main courtyard. She came by with a girlfriend, perhaps even younger than herself. "We kidded around for maybe fifteen or twenty minutes," Meyer remembers, and then she said, "how about walking me home?" So he did. Hellman lived in a walk-up in an old, not very distinguished building on Ninety-fifth Street. Hellman had been carrying a tennis racket, covered by a case that was turned inside out. When Meyer left her, he looked at the name that was written on the tennis racket case: Barbara Warren. So all attempts to contact her after that were completely frustrated. In a few years, however, they would meet again when Hellman was working at Liveright, although Meyer cannot remember how he happened to see her again. Their first encounter impressed him enormously. He was quite taken with her directness and sexiness, which seemed uncommon for the time.

By her junior year, Hellman had lost all interest in college and set off with her mother on a long tour of the Midwest and the South. In her memoirs she calls the trip her mother's reward for quitting school; to a reporter she claimed to have talked her mother into taking her to New Orleans. Mother and daughter returned to New York in June 1924 for Hellman's nineteenth birthday. At that point she began, as she puts it, what "was then called an 'affair.' " It was probably her first sexual involvement. The man in question may have been Gerald Sykes, who at that time was rooming in New York City with Louis Kronenberger. In *Maybe*, Hellman mentions Alex, "a tall thin young man of twenty-three when I was nineteen, gentle, just out of college and on his way to a Ph.D. . . . He had been the first man I had ever slept with." In retrospect, Hellman characterized the affair as neither pleasant nor passionate, but she was inclined to discount the damage inflicted by the "tinkering malice" of a young man bent on paining his friend rather than on pleasing her. Richard Moody, speculating on the anguish this liaison may have caused Hellman, notes that romantic scenes in her writing "have frequently been tinged with a touch of cynicism. When men and women in her plays are drawn to each other, their magnetic fields are often charged with perversities, eccentricities, and selfish calculations." It is a fact that she was never able to write a purely romantic love scene or to imagine one for herself.

In the autumn of 1924, feeling pleasantly "aimless" yet searching for some kind of meaningful employment, Hellman met Julian Messner, vice-president of Horace Liveright's publishing firm, and talked her way into a job. In spite of this rather bold entry into one of the most exciting American publishing houses of the 1920s, she did little to distinguish herself and was not regarded with much interest. Edmund Wilson met her during this period and took her for "a shy girl who spoke very little." The truth of it was, the job bored her. In the midst of Liveright's high-class talent—and the parties where that talent was often paraded—her own contribution was minimal. In *An Unfinished Woman* she describes her job as "a little advertising work, a little publicity, and a lot of manuscript reading." And Hellman did not get the exciting material—Hemingway, Anderson, Dreiser, or O'Neill. Instead she got "the stuff that no one else wanted to read."

But Hellman was stimulated by the robust, spontaneous, and inspiring periods in the office when Liveright or one of his colleagues discovered a new talent. She also found exciting the attention of the men in the firm who would make a grab for her as she would sprint up and down the staircases. As Howard Meyer remembers it:

> She was never a beauty, but she had a beautiful figure. One of her tales, when she was working for Liveright, concerned an editor who wanted her to read a manuscript, and she was just an office girl who probably had made her brightness apparent. A second editor asked, "Why in hell do you want Lillian to read it?" "Because she has a beautiful figure," the first editor replied.

But she also mystified her employers and troubled herself. She was of a generation that was supposed to be sexually experienced and in revolt against sentimentality. After Versailles and a world that had not been made safe for democracy, she shared the rather common feeling among urban, middle-class youth that traditional

American values were to be questioned. She was "skeptical of democracy, of romance, of Socialism, of humanitarianism in general, and of puritanism in particular." One is hard put to gauge Hellman's feelings at nineteen because she refused to commit herself to a point of view. Words of love did not impress her; indeed they were almost distasteful. She and her friends were "pretend cool" about romance, yet their seemingly clear-eyed view of men cut them off from genuine emotions. Too young to have been a part of the feminist movement, Hellman could not appreciate how the agitation for women's rights had made it possible for her to behave as a man's equal. As a result, she had no sense of what she was about or of how she should behave. She was quiet because she was at a loss.

In June 1925, Hellman expected to be fired. She had misplaced an important manuscript, did not know how to file, was an erratic typist, and her manuscript reports were "severe." That she was also pregnant, however, provoked the sympathetic interest of every member in the firm. Suddenly she was a "showcase," the object of advice and curiosity. The men expected her to break down, name the child's father, and enact the role of helpless female. Instead, she withdrew from them in anger, refusing to talk or to be sent home—even after an abortion. Hellman was naturally angry about their snoopy solicitousness, but she appears to have hidden her own feelings from herself. One reads about this episode in *An Unfinished Woman* and wonders how she felt about Arthur Kober, the father of the child who married Hellman six months later.

Although Kober paid for it, he was out of town on vacation the day of the abortion, and Hellman made a date that evening with Howard Meyer. He was closest to her during this period, and because he and Hellman were quite intimate he thought she needed him to have a shoulder to cry on after the abortion. But she did not seem too upset and in fact seemed to take it all in stride.

Her mother wanted her to marry Meyer, not Kober, and Hellman seemed to favor him as well. Meyer came from a comfortable German-Jewish family, whereas Kober came from less desirable, poorer Eastern European Jewish stock. But Meyer was not in a position to consider marriage. He was a college student with no source of income and was just beginning what was to become a distinguished career as an architect. Says Meyer, "Lillian would come up to the drafting room, and we would set off by taxi to wherever she wanted to go. It was pretty hot and heavy for a couple of months." They would do "crazy things," Meyer remembers fondly, "like walking from her Ninety-fifth Street apartment to the Biltmore Hotel to the Cascades, where Lillian loved to dance. That's quite a walk." She was "crazy in a nice way . . . and it was her sexiness that kept us going." In Meyer's memory, Hellman was unique, with a mind of her own and "a very capable tongue. She didn't pull any punches." He had no idea that she would become a writer. She had a fine intellect, but her interests had not yet jelled, so far as he could tell. Their German-Jewish backgrounds were similar, although Meyer does not remember anything particularly Jewish about Hellman—just that most of her friends who Meyer knew were Jewish. When she married Kober, Meyer saw her once more at a party the couple hosted, and then he disappeared from her life for more than thirty years.

The most Hellman can say in *An Unfinished Woman* about her feelings immediately after the abortion is that she was "increasingly muddled by the Puritan conscience that made me pay for the adventures" her very young self decided were worth having. Evidently, she was out to impress herself and others that she could handle anything that came her way. The problem with that approach, as she learned years later, was that it left her unable to discriminate between values—between what made one kind of experience truly worthwhile and another not.

Her marriage to Kober on December 21, 1925, was an example of Hellman's inability to define her own real needs. She let Arthur do it for her. He was charming and good-looking and full of promise. This snappy and energetic man could carry her along on his good spirits without overwhelming her, for he was also shy and sensitive—always a "sweet man," according to many of his friends. Kober had had it rough. Born August 25, 1900, in Austria-Hungary, his family came to New York City when he was four years old and lived on East Sixtieth Street. The Italians and Irish beat up the Jewish kids living in two tenements on the same block. Life in that neighborhood was "hell," as Kober described it in "Having Terrible Time," his unfinished, self-mocking memoir. But he came out of it a high school graduate who had been a stock boy in the glove department of Gimble Brothers and later worked as a bookkeeper for a real estate company, a stenographer and typist, a reviewer of vaudeville shows, and a cub press agent for the

Shuberts from 1922 to 1925. Most of all, like Hellman, Kober wanted to write. He adored the theater and was determined to be a successful playwright.

The first four months of 1926 they spent in Paris. Hellman worked on short stories, publishing a few in the *Paris Comet*, a magazine Kober edited, but set aside her writing when she realized it was "lady writer" stuff: "the kind of stories where the man puts his fork down and the woman knows it's all over." Once again, she was "aimless," playing bridge, reading, and rediscovering how much she liked New Orleans cooking. Just before leaving Paris, Hellman met Lee Gershwin (the wife of Ira Gershwin) in the American Express office. They were introduced by a mutual friend, Henrietta Malkiel. Hellman said, "I'm so sorry that we just met. I have to leave this afternoon for America. But I'll see you in a few days." It was agreed that Lee would call her in New York. The two women soon struck up a friendship that Gershwin fondly remembers for its fun. They loved going shopping together and buying fabric for dresses. Hellman was always thinking up things for them to do—even if it was only a trip to look at a dress Hellman liked. "Wouldn't you like to see it?" she would ask in a way that made Gershwin feel she was Hellman's special girlfriend. At big parties in New York, they would go into the ladies' room and change into each other's evening clothes. To them it was a big joke. As Gershwin got to know Hellman better, however, she realized her friend preferred the company of men. Often men would join them for lunch, and Gershwin would have the feeling she ought to leave, although the attention Hellman paid her was not lessened by the presence of a male. As far as Gershwin was concerned, Hellman did not discriminate among her men. She went after them all. As Gershwin puts it, Hellman spent "a great deal of time on herself." To make herself attractive for men was very important. (Years later, Diana Trilling would be amazed at the enormous display of makeup bottles and perfumes in Hellman's bathroom.) In the mid-thirties, Gershwin had a chance to observe her friend picking up men at Goldwyn Studios. She worked very fast and would suddenly disappear with her conquests. Gershwin thought that several of Hellman's seven abortions were the result of these fleeting liaisons.

Back in the States, Hellman turned to press agentry for a musical revue, *The Bunk of 1926*, but it failed to attract an audience, in spite of the district attorney's well-publicized efforts to close the "smutty" show. On September 26, 1926, her book reviews began appearing in the *New York Herald Tribune*. She was a judicious and generous critic; even with books she did not like she found something to praise, although she could not help having some fun with silly books like *Summer Bachelors*:

> There is no sham about the writing—plain sensational bunk of the more powerful sort. And from that you should be able to guess that the heroine's name is Desideria (with its ancient connotations), and that dear Desideria is suffering from the problems of sex and its many pangs and hard knocks. She is a constant visitor at night clubs, is worshiped by every man who meets her, and stays up until too late discussing whose body belongs to whom, why and what you are supposed to do about it.

Each review was a conscientious job, for which she was paid $4.70 a column. And when she had a chance to review a serious novel, William Faulkner's *Mosquitoes*, she was extremely careful to convey the complexity of characters and themes as well as his wit and irony. While recognizing that parts of *Mosquitoes* were "overwritten," too consciously "Joycean," and "overloaded with description," she favored his "lusty writing" and "healthy, fresh pen." Searching for a valid style herself, she was most impressed with Faulkner's versatility.

Between writing reviews, Hellman read play scripts for Leo Bulgakov, Harry Moses, Anne Nichols, and Herman Shumlin. Hellman's one notable discovery was *Grand Hotel*, the big hit of the 1930–31 season (with 257 performances) which was produced and directed by Herman Shumlin. Much of Hellman's theater work came about as a result of Kober's connections. He had moved on from the Shuberts in 1925 to Edgar Selwyn and Jed Harris. Compared to Kober and his vitality, Hellman seemed idle. Although she had proven herself capable of finding her own jobs, it was so much nicer to let Kober look after her. One night, after playing cards with his friends at the Hoyle Club, Kober bemoaned his losing night: "The little woman won't like it. . . . No money to bring home for our breakfast of caviar and champagne. Helpless little girl, she depends on me." While he may have been exaggerating Hellman's helplessness, she characterized this period in the late 1920s as a "jumble of passivity and wild impatience." Howard Benedict, who in 1925 was a press agent for the Shuberts (who used to shoot dice with Hellman, her father, and Kober), recalls that Hellman played one or two games at the Hoyle Club. "She always fancied herself as a great poker player but she never knew the value of the chips, who the dealer was, or how many cards [she should have]. She was a very bad poker player."

Kober had, in the words of Sam Marx, "a sly sense of humor and a droll personality." The two men first met during Kober's days at the Shubert press department. Kober told Marx that his marriage to Hellman had been the result of his frustrating efforts to produce a play entitled *Me*. If Kober would marry Hellman, her father promised, he would back the show. To Marx, Kober claimed that "he intended to void the pact and buy his way out with the play's profits." But *Me* was an almost instant failure and "Lillian Hellman became Mrs. Arthur Kober, not in name but in actuality." Marx himself doubts the story because it was so obvious that Kober was in love with Hellman. Yet it seemed to be Kober's inclination to cast Hellman in the role of dependent. "It was like a joke—putting down the woman I am married to," Marx concludes. Howard Benedict remembers her as being "mellower and in an inferior position. Later she became much more dominant and the acid in her was evident." Leo Friedman, also in the Shubert press office in the 1920s, thought of Hellman as "one of those astute and smart Jewish girls who were always trying to get ahead because that was her goal—to be ahead." Making it in the literary world was her goal. "I honestly think she married Arthur because she thought he had a promising future as a playwright," said Friedman. "She always said he had a great future, and I think that meant a great deal to her—to be associated with someone who had a future."

By the spring of 1929, Hellman knew she had to do something on her own. She went to Rochester, New York, for four months to work as a publicist for Cukor-Kondolph, a theater stock company. She loved to gamble every night with Rochester society, to win money for a trip to Europe that summer. She also had a good time reading, drinking, and listening to a gangster tell about Rochester's underworld. It was typical of her to swing this way between high and low; she was—even later in life—the type of person who liked to dress elegantly for dinner and then complain about the "rat-fuck" food she was eating.

She made it to Germany that summer and decided to stay for a year in Bonn, studying at the university. Hellman enjoyed the camaraderie of the university boarding house and imagined she was hearing from the healthy, blonde students a brand of socialism she liked. Actually, she had become involved with a Nazi youth group that apparently accepted the Germanness of her last name. Upon learning this, she left Bonn the next day and came back to New York. Many years later, she transformed this brief brush with anti-Semitism and with the naiveté Americans often reveal in their contacts with other cultures into two superb plays: *Watch on the Rhine*, and *The Searching Wind*.

These months spent away from Kober apparently did not signal that there was something missing in the marriage, although Richard Moody records that Hellman had "hasty flirtations" that troubled her "Puritan conscience." In some sense, she was declaring her independence. Sam Marx remembers that "rumors of romances and even extramarital affairs circulated among Kober's associates almost before the ink on their wedding certificate was dry. In *Maybe*, Hellman admits to a brief affair with an Englishman during a visit to Lake Maggiore in 1926. Yet Hellman and Kober were not so different from other young couples of their generation. As Dorothy Herrman points out in her discussion of the Sid and Laura Perelman marriage:

> It was considered important to preserve one's privacy and sense of independence. Extramarital affairs were tolerated as long as they were casual and discreetly conducted. Sexual freedom proclaimed one's emancipation and need for diversion, while monogamous love was regarded as sentimental, confining and hypocritical.

Marx recalls that Hellman "had her own coterie, a notch higher intellectually than her husband's lower-browed group." Bright men were attracted to her; they loved being around her. She had a charisma and a kind of laugh that were very appealing. Marx cannot remember having seen Hellman and Kober very much as a couple. They rarely appeared at the same parties or gatherings, and they had different interests. She would never be found, for example, mixing with Kober's cronies in the Shubert press office. When Marx first met Hellman, he thought "she was a rather nice, homely girl . . . a thin, bony slip of a girl then, with rust-colored hair and an unpretty face. She was in a state of perennial indignation about the human condition; to her, every cause was a good one. She felt there were no bad causes, just the fact that it was a cause made it good and she supported it." She and Marx seemed to disagree about everything, and in the midst of their heated debates, "mild-mannered Kober held his tongue." Marx was "never sure what side he [Kober] was on," though years later it was clear to him that Kober had relished Hellman's anger; it seemed to energize him.

Marx, of course, was not in a position to see other sides of Hellman. Mildred Kober Mendelson, Arthur's sister, remembers how good Hellman was to Kober's mother. Mildred could also see that Hellman cared deeply for Kober, a feeling Hellman also communicated to Howard Benedict, Arthur's friend. She was generous with her husband's family and deeply concerned about his career. She was wholly supportive of his decision to give up press agentry in favor of playwriting. But when the stock market crashed, in his words, it "crushed all my plans and wiped out everything Lillian and I had saved." He was forced to take up his career again as Broadway press agent for Marc Connelly's *The Green Pastures*. Just before the opening of the play in February 1930, Paramount offered him a seven-year contract as a screenwriter at $450 a week. Initially "elated at the prospect of a long period of work, especially when our country was undergoing a Depression," his spirits fell when he realized that "seven years would be the term if *all* the options were renewed. What the studio was actually guaranteeing me was three months of steady employment," Kober concludes in his unpublished autobiography.

Kober and Hellman decided they should keep their New York apartment and that he should go alone to Hollywood to serve his probationary period; if he was not a success, he would hurry back to New York. Although Kober had a modest reputation in New York as a *New Yorker* short story writer and a newspaper columnist, in Hollywood he found himself to be a "distinguished nonentity." He was bothered by how little there was to do besides write for the movies. But his option was renewed and Hellman, after much dilatory behavior, joined him in the fall of 1930 in a one-room apartment with a Murphy-bed on Sunset Boulevard. She did not relish the role of Hollywood wife, and may have been reluctant to leave New York, where she had apparently become involved in a passionate affair with David Cort, "a bright, egotistical young would-be writer . . . who would later become the foreign editor for the yet unformed *Life* magazine."

Hellman found Hollywood even less to her liking than had Kober. As he became more certain of his position, they moved first to the Garden of Allah, "a Hollywood hotel popular with screenwriters and resembling a Moroccan villa with stucco bungalows and palm trees," and then to what she remembered as a "dark house in Hollywoodland, the hilly section above the already junky Hollywood Boulevard." Even years later, in *An Unfinished Woman*, Hellman could not see any value in that time or place. She was morose about it. All she did was read and learn to "drink hard." She had turned twenty-five that June and felt completely alone.

Evidently, the strain was too much for the couple. In "Having Terrible Time," Kober remarks, "It would be an easy thing to say that the dullness of the town and its intense pre-occupation with one subject—movies—affected our marriage, and so I shall say it." He persuaded Marx, then MGM's story editor, to give Hellman a job. Hellman was restless and hated Hollywood, and, Kober confided to Marx, their marriage might not otherwise survive. It looked like she was going to leave him. Film historian Bernard F. Dick reports that "in its heyday, the reading department at MGM handled 20,000 pieces of literature a year, ranging from magazine articles to novels in galley." Marx was very impressed with Hellman's test; she admirably met the requisite of writing clear and accurate summaries of material that might make good motion pictures. She was paid fifty dollars a week, a good salary for a reader. At that point, he had no idea that Hellman had ambitions to write; Kober had asked him to provide a job, not a junior writing assignment.

In an interview with Dick, Marx took exception to Hellman's characterization of her work as writing "the kind of idiot-simple report that Louis B. Mayer's professional lady storyteller could make even more simple when she told it to Mr. Mayer." Marx had marvelous, carefully selected readers. By and large, they were content with the standard fifty-dollars-a-week salary and happy to be doing something they enjoyed. Most readers wanted to be writers. And to some of them, the reading department was a refuge from poverty. They were marking time until they could write. Hellman's gloomy memories and her anxiety over the fact that she was unable to do any of her own writing obscured from

her the fact that she was learning script writing in a disciplined
fashion. She began at an elementary stage most established authors would not deign to essay. She found it demeaning to work
in a rickety building that shook from the smallest tremor, sit in a
room with more than a dozen writers, read "junk," and pound
out on "half-broken typewriters," two or three summaries a day.
It was slave labor, as far as she was concerned, and she tried to
organize the writers. Hellman wanted more money, different
hours, and different work. The readers were beginning to look at
Pratt as their worst enemy. The reading department's head, Dorothy Pratt, was so enraged by Hellman's stirring up the readers that
she threatened to quit. Marx had no choice. Hellman was just
another reader, and he had to let her go. She did not seem to
mind; in fact she said she was dying to get back to New York. In
spite of his troubles with Hellman, Marx remembers that in her
year at MGM she was a thoroughly reliable employee who delivered beautiful synopses.

Hellman was never one to pay attention to why the studio
system functioned the way it did. A different kind of observer—
Garson Kanin, for example—would realize that the reason Sam
Goldwyn often had several writers tell him the plot of a film over
and over again was not because he was stupid but because he
would eventually have a better grasp of the story than would any
individual writer. Hellman, whether she cared to know it or not,
was learning the most effective way to tell stories on film. The
process of learning may have been boring—even humiliating—but
she was teaching herself the fundamentals of movie plot construction. This training eventually allowed her to write whole screenplays with virtually no collaboration—a feat that Faulkner and
Fitzgerald never managed. She was rarely used just to doctor
dialogue or to invent one or two scenes, for she had a professional
command of the total film product that very few novelists or
playwrights could match.

Hellman's employment at MGM must have seemed even shab-
bier than it was because of the class system. In *An Unfinished
Woman* she recalls how she hated going to the studio commissary,
where she would have to "pass a large table for famous directors
and writers, some of whom knew my husband and thus had to
make the kind of half rise-bow" that told her she was "above the
ordinary but not enough above it" to be accepted into that distinguished circle. She remembered a woman at a party telling her it

took "too damn long to tell" whether her clothes were "good" or not. Such comments said it all: Hellman was good, but not good enough. She was also confused about what she had a right to expect from people and what they could rightfully demand from her.

Hellman, in other words, had an incipient style, but not enough of it showed yet. Her marriage had had its good moments—even in Hollywood—but it, too, was not good enough. There was no dramatic, definite break with Kober. Indeed, for almost another four years he hoped to regain her affection. They separated, as she said in *An Unfinished Woman,* "without ill feeling," and she went back to New York. Her letters to him reflected a loyalty to their love she would never abandon. But Kober could not lay down the law to her; he was all for giving her as much latitude as she seemed to want. She would always chafe at any sort of restraint, yet in retrospect she admitted her need of "a teacher, a cool teacher, who would not be impressed or disturbed by a strange and difficult girl." Kober's inclination, to the end of his life, was to be impressed by Hellman, to lean on her, and to measure his actions by her advice and example. While she found this aspect of Kober attractive, it also meant there was too much give in his character. That was fine in a friend, but flaccid in a lover. Hellman, the child and the adult, reveled in the test of wills. Personality, the Newhouses had shown her, was born out of conflict and developed in the bruising of egos. With Kober she could be comfortable but she could not mature. And it was time. She was past due for growth, for deliverance.

3

SHE-HAMMETT
Hollywood/New York
(1930–1934)

Like other writers, he knew the odd way life catches up
with things that you write, after you have written them.

—Diane Johnson, *Dashiell Hammett: A Life*

I would say I wanted to get everything straight for the days
after his death when I would write his biography and he
would say that I was not to bother writing his biography
because it would turn out to be the history of Lillian
Hellman with an occasional reference to a friend called
Hammett.

—Lillian Hellman, *An Unfinished Woman*

Lillian Hellman was twenty-five years old when she met Dashiell Hammett in the fall of 1930. He was thirty-six, the author
of several successful novels, and an elegant, if often dissolute,
presence in the society of writers, which deeply attracted Hellman.
Although she had been planning since childhood to be a writer,
all she had to show for her efforts were a few short stories, book
reviews, and diaries. She had been around—New York, Paris,
Hollywood—and knew some things about literary life, but her
career, like her marriage to Arthur Kober, lacked definition.

In her memoirs, Hellman remembers being introduced to Hammett at a Hollywood restaurant. They spoke of their interest in

T. S. Eliot and they ended up in his car talking about books "until daylight." Biographers have taken her word about this meeting, although she confesses to some doubt about her recollection of a first encounter with Hammett. Lee Gershwin witnessed it: "I was there the night she met him. The stories aren't quite right." The Gershwins were "big stuff" when they came to California in 1930. Producer Darryl Zanuck had taken them, Hellman, and Kober to a movie premiere, and then suggested they accompany him to Bing Crosby's opening at the Roosevelt Hotel, which was directly across the street from the theater. After insisting they could not walk but must take a limousine to the hotel, Zanuck ushered them to a table directly in front of Crosby. The lights started to dim and then come up on Crosby as Hammett was making his way to the men's room. "Lil said to me, 'Who's that man?' " Gershwin could not identify the distinguished, gray-haired, handsome man. She turned to Zanuck and asked him if he knew who it was. Zanuck, in turn, checked with one of his companions, who recognized Hammett. When Gershwin turned to tell Hellman, somebody else had already told her and she was up and out of her seat. She grabbed Hammett and started walking with him on the way to the men's room. "That's how fast she was," says Gershwin. It is curious that Hellman should forget this meeting, since Gershwin teased her about it more than once. Hammett, Hellman, Kober, and the Gershwins all became good friends.

In *An Unfinished Woman*, Hellman suggests there was no mistaking Hammett's sharp-edged character. He was a "line of a man" with a "knife for a nose" that, on a later occasion, took the wind out of her sail as she became caught up in him, "the handsomest sight" she had ever seen.

Hammett had his pick of women, and Hellman could not, in any sense, have been considered the loveliest. There was that mannish face with the bold nose—broken by a fall from a fig tree. The fall itself was prophetic of her later character, for she had taken the angry jump after observing her unfaithful father out on the town with his girlfriend. With his many women, Hammett had to have reminded her of her father, who was waited on by his adoring sisters and who was the focus of his daughter's romantic feelings. Dash, as she liked to call him, rekindled her deeply divided feelings about the love between men and women.

Hammett had left a wife and family with whom he could not share his writing life. On what terms would he accept Hellman?

He acknowledged that she had talent, and he had always been generous with young authors. She had strong convictions and dressed with style, a style that perhaps could be put in words. He sensed that she needed the proper form to harness her energies; otherwise, her vigor would be spent on shooting at too many targets. By her own estimation, she was still an amateur when she wrote her second play, *Days to Come*, which failed because she felt compelled to write about everything she knew.

In his person and in his books, Hammett stood for economy of purpose and for professionalism. He wrote about detectives because he had been a Pinkerton detective, and he enjoyed pointing out the improbable aspects of mystery fiction written by hacks who were unfamiliar with criminal behavior and police work. When he met Hellman, his writing career was almost over; he had exhausted the material over which he could be an undisputed authority. While he continued his efforts to complete another novel, he always stopped himself short. He was uncertain what he was trying to accomplish by writing another book, and he did not want to repeat himself. Instead, he passed on his story ideas to Hellman, who he could goad into action. Hammett's endpoint—a recognition of corruption—was the fuse that set off Hellman's creativity. By the time he met her he was beyond the stage of being shocked by evil. Until the day she died, Hellman could never reconcile herself to the fact of injustice. These two individuals were not so much opposites as complements of each other. The man could be as gentle as the woman could be tough. She was almost his equal as a hard drinker, but she knew long before he did when it was time to call a halt to their alcoholic binges. One helped supply what the other lacked.

In retrospect, it is clear that Hammett's writing life was winding down when Hellman first met him. "The five-day drunk had left the wonderful face looking rumpled, and the very tall thin figure was tired and sagged," she later recalled in *An Unfinished Woman*. They met again a few weeks later and then lived together, off and on, for the next thirty years until his death in 1961. In 1930, he was a celebrated writer presumed to be at the top of his form. In April of 1931, his fourth novel, *The Glass Key*, was published, and he was looking forward to completing his last full-length work of detective fiction, *The Thin Man*. A fragment of that last novel was making the rounds in Hollywood as a kind of teaser for a screenplay that would provide Hammett with the income to sustain his expensive habits. Yet he was already tired of the detective fiction formula he had worked so hard to develop into an art form, and was anxious to get on with other kinds of writing. Other types of fiction—perhaps even plays—interested him.

Hammett enjoyed his success and took advantage of his status as best-selling author of *Red Harvest* (1929), *The Dain Curse* (1929), and *The Maltese Falcon* (1930). He was free with his money and an avid partygoer, yet it was in his nature to remain aloof and enigmatic. Perhaps he had been attracted to detective work because it was usually a solitary job. An "operative," as Pinkerton agents called themselves, could be out all day on his own following a suspect, interviewing people, and setting his own plans for apprehending criminals. After a number of drinks, Hammett could open up and begin to tell stories about his Pinkerton past. In his cups, the ex-detective confessed that he had often had to lie to get his man; deception, in fact, was at the heart of the job. Hellman could see how sensitive the writer/detective was about the morality of his work. He was a committed person who made her own desire to write all that more urgent—if only she could be as ruthlessly honest with herself as he evidently was.

She was a restless person, and it bothered Hammett that she did not want to stay put. Although Hellman had a job reading scripts for Metro-Goldwyn-Mayer, by March 1931, after they had been together four months, she took a leave of absence and was off to New York. She wanted to visit her parents and to think over her growing involvement with Hammett and her neglect of her husband.

Because Hellman's memoirs make so much of Hammett and so little of Kober, it has been assumed that she was not affected very profoundly by her only marriage. In the 1950s, Kober began an autobiography that was still unfinished at the time of his death in 1975. Fred Gardner, one of Hellman's former students who was planning a book about her, wrote to Kober asking to see the autobiography. Kober replied on February 7, 1967, that he was suffering from one of his "perennial workblocks. . . . You'll be through with your book, I'm sure, long before I write about Lillian. I'm half way through my book and we haven't met. I wonder if we ever will." To many friends, the Kober-Hellman marriage had been "all laughs"—to use Albert Hackett's phrase. They put a breezy and whimsical face on a relationship that remained for all of their lives deeply serious and troubled but often greatly satisfying and comforting to both partners. Kober would joke about his "work-blocks" and say that for "two pins (jeweled and expensive, of course), I'd give it [the autobiography] up." But he signed himself to Gardner "in despair," for, as his diaries reveal, he never quite caught up with Hellman, either personally or professionally.

It was not at all unusual for Hellman to show up at parties given by George and Ira Gershwin with both Kober and Hammett. Ruth Conte remembers one party in which the women went upstairs to a Victorian sitting room while the men remained below. Hellman sat in a Victorian barber's chair, pulled out a cigar, and proceeded to tell the other women stories about her sexual exploits. When the women rejoined the men, one of Hellman's confidants said, "Arthur, we were upstairs and Lillian was smoking a cigar and telling us racy stories. What did you do?" He said, "Oh, we were exchanging recipes."

Kober was a charming and amusing man. But when Lee Gershwin asked her friend why her marriage was not working, Hellman replied that she was sick of always taking his head out of the stove when he got drunk. Hellman did not believe in and was bored with her husband's suicidal feelings. She thought he was just trying to impress her. "Oh Lillian, be kind to him. He's such a sweet man," Gershwin said. "I don't want a sweet man," Hellman shot back. Although not as heavy a drinker as Hammett, Kober would drink enough to get loaded. Then he would go dancing, then he would start to cry. This was invariably his pattern at the Gershwins. One night Kober actually put his head in the Gershwins' oven, and Lee Gershwin saw what Hellman had meant. Thereafter, Gershwin would devise things to keep Kober occupied—including putting him in charge of the barbecues. Catherine Kober remembers that her father had a morose sense of humor and also wonders about the extent to which his suicidal gestures were serious. Clearly, he was disturbed, but announcing his intention to do away with himself at a party was surely the best way of preventing suicide.

Kober could see how crazy Hellman was about Hammett. He knew that Hellman and Hammett were having a fling, and he assured Hammett's wife, Josephine, that the affair should not be taken seriously. He had good reason for not giving up hope that she would return to him. In the early spring of 1931, Hellman was writing Kober letters from the St. Moritz in New York City that suggest how closely she felt bound to him. To his complaint that she was not supplying him with enough information about her activities, she noted she had sent him twice as many letters as he had sent. They had been trying to have a child, and she was writing him to say she had got her period. She was very upset and thought her plight was unfair. She was being punished. She was going to see a doctor. She told him, pleading with Kober not to take it hard. They could always "try again."

She was not certain of his reaction. Did he still want a divorce? She wanted to be consoled and was ashamed to discover she was not the "super-creator of babies" she imagined herself to be.

Kober had written a play and Hellman was trying to get it produced. She wanted Kober to feel she was intimately involved in his work and urged him to send her more letters. She wanted him to love her. She missed him but coped with her loneliness by talking about him constantly. Kober was a far more powerful figure than she was and would have had many more connections in the theatrical world. It is hard not to suppose that Hellman was rationalizing the time spent away from her husband.

Another letter to Kober followed almost immediately as Hellman went into great detail about her social life—dinners, visits with friends, attendance at plays, and so on. Was it a slip of the pen or a deliberate ploy for his attention when she wrote about Russell Crouse's intention to take her to *As I Desire You*, a play that was actually titled *As You Desire Me*? She was still feeling "lousy about getting the curse. I'm an old weakling." At the same time, she bragged about her attractiveness and reassured her husband that although she was "a very popular young woman," she remained devoted to him. In spite of all her dates, she would return to Kober soon—right away, if he said so. She really loved him and hoped their marriage would last. She had already written him three letters that week.

Hammett's letters to Hellman during this same period were warm and chatty. He spoke openly of his love for her, but it was usually in the guise of some joke about himself and her friends: "The emptiness I thought was hunger for chow mein turned out to be for you. . . . I ran into Arthur [Kober], Sid [Perelman], and Laura [Perelman] in the Brown Doiby [sic]. I tried to pump Laura about your conduct in New York. . . . Suspected you of the loosest sort of conduct. . . . Just a she-Hammett." He wanted to know when she was coming home and seemed restive without her. Screenwriting commitments kept him pinned down in Hollywood.

His friendly references to Kober (they had been to the fights together) reflected none of the strain and despair Kober would confess in his diary. The Perelmans, already fast friends with Hellman, now had taken happily to Hammett as well.

On the way back to California, Hellman visited her aunts in New Orleans. The whole family, she knew, would be disturbed and perplexed about her divorce from a husband everyone, including Hellman herself, liked. Although she consistently portrays herself in her memoirs as a rebel defiant of convention, having an intimate relationship with a man outside of marriage troubled her. Many years later, she confessed to Jay Martin, Nathanael West's biographer, that "in those days, in the late 20s and 30s, we all thought we *should* be sexually liberated and acted as if we *were*, but we had a deep uneasiness about sex too."

Hellman felt her aunts would disapprove, but rather than explain herself she went on the offensive—as she almost always did in cases where her own position was vulnerable. Instead of talking about Hammett and Kober, she engaged her aunts in discussions of the past. Opening a closet, she noticed a canvas valise they had once given her and taken back, and she remembered the valise once contained a letter from Bethe, the distant relative who had embarrassed the family by living with an Italian man. The aunts had given Bethe up because, Hellman told them, "she loved a way you didn't like." Obviously, Hammett was on her mind.

In fact, Hellman learned, both aunts quietly supported Bethe. They even took Hellman on a visit to see this woman who had gotten in trouble by associating with criminals, this woman whose lush hair and figure represented to Hellman "the beautiful side of my father's family." Much of Bethe's story, recounted in *Pentimento*, is fragmentary, with some of it evidently kept from Hellman in that valise which her aunts never did return to her. Bethe seemed to be a lost person and an example of what could happen to a woman—in this case a warm-hearted German immigrant— who did not live conventionally.

Hellman always wanted to be sure that friends and family would be loyal to her, that she would be backed by them no matter what mistakes she made. Hammett was a serious concern, for he was, by his own admission, only more or less faithful to her. Soon she would rage against his infidelity, but now it must have seemed too early for her to make exclusive claims on him. One drunken night a few months later in New York she tried to tell him about Bethe and became angry when he said he did not understand what she meant. What did Bethe have to do with them? Hellman knew but could not say, and became so angry that she drove away to Montauk (Long Island) on a snowy day "and came back two days later with the grippe." These words conclude the "Bethe" episode in *Pentimento* and underscore how often Hellman had to see her life again in writing in order to make any sense of events that petered out in illness, drunkenness, and confusion.

When Hellman returned to Hollywood from New Orleans in the fall of 1931, she found her lover depressed and suicidal. He had not been able to write or to stop drinking. The success of *The Glass Key* did not assuage his anxieties; indeed, as with many writers, he may have been feeling the letdown that often comes after the accomplishment of a great work. Hellman, on the other hand, was brimming with energy and not particularly concerned about his condition. She was curious, but not disturbed by his despair. It did not make any sense, she told him, dismissing his self-destructiveness in a way that made him feel ashamed. He told her, "I'm a clown"—his way of concluding this most recent round of self-disparagement. Faced with her puzzled reaction to his talk of suicide, he just quit it, even though he could not resist his own intimations of doom and drinking bouts that debilitated his already fragile, tubercular constitution.

Hammett's dour moods and Hellman's bright future were reflected in his fiction. In "On The Way," published in the March 1932 issue of *Harper's Bazaar*, a taciturn and apparently disenchanted screenwriter called "Kipper" is an unmistakable self-portrait of the author. Kipper is "a long, raw-boned man," who dresses, like Hammett, in "brown silk pajamas under a striped silk robe." His girlfriend, Gladys, has just landed a movie contract, and is set to begin work on "Laughing Masks" (the title of a short story Hammett wrote in 1923). The opening dialogue of "On The Way" is a version of what Hellman would say to Hammett just a few years later, after the success of *The Children's Hour*:

> "You're as much a part of it as I am. You gave me
> something that—"
>   His eyes did not avoid hers, though they seemed
> about to. He patted her shoulder with his empty hand
> and said awkwardly, "Nonsense. You always had

things—just a little trouble knowing what to do with
them."

Kipper is scrupulous about his words and about what Gladys does
not owe him. Regarding his own deep feelings he is silent, preferring, like Hammett, to ignore questions or to give the shortest
possible answers. And, like Hellman, Gladys has to strain to get a
sense of what her lover and mentor is thinking.

"On the Way" is as enigmatic as is its author. Is Kipper a failure?
He is out of work, but then his attitude toward Hollywood is "wry"
and he is "wearily contemptuous" of his milieu, so that he projects
an aloof superiority amidst brash, garrulous characters. His personality has no give to it at all: "Kipper's lean face was stony."
Meanwhile, Gladys works hard to show her gratitude and, in the
story's last scene, even proposes they marry. Their last terse
exchanges, like the next thirty years of Hellman and Hammett's
relationship, are ambiguous:

> He cleared his throat harshly. "I'll do anything you
> say." He took a deep breath. "I'll stay if you say so."
> She began to tremble and tears came out. She whis-
> pered desperately, "I want you to do what you want
> to do."
> His lower lip twitched. He pinched it between his
> teeth and stared through the window at street lights
> they passed. He said slowly, "I want to go."
> She put a hand up on his cheek and held it there.
> She said, "I know, darling, I know."

Kipper holds on to his emotions, controlling a twitch by biting his
lip. Hammett and Hellman behaved similarly. Moved by deep
feelings, they nevertheless chose not, in most instances, to be
explicit. It was always an open question with them: who was to
go, who was to stay? Neither wanted to be kept, yet it was always
Hellman who forced the issue, who kept them from drifting
irrevocably apart. Hammett came to count on her strength, even
though, as in this story, it was never clear that the couple would
be able to remain together.

What attracted Hellman to Hammett was his penchant for extremes. She once told him he was a "Dostoyevsky sinner-saint."
Provoked by the sight of this slender white man sailing on the

water in the sun—with his white hair, white pants, and white shirt—she remembered his womanizing and carousing that gave way in later years to an austere, almost ascetic—and virtually silent—existence in which he took care never to be a burden to anyone. He did not like to make trouble for others, an attitude Hellman liked to think she shared with him.

By late fall, 1931, Hammett was in New York trying to get his writing life back on track. A few stories, a preface to a book parodying detective stories, some lectures—this is what he had planned. But his attention was easily diverted by his drinking companion, William Faulkner, whose friend, Ben Wasson, had become Hammett's agent. Hellman again heard about things through her lover's letters. Faulkner was familiar to her, for she had favorably reviewed his second novel, *Mosquitoes.* And, like Hammett, she would be drawn to Faulkner's Southernness and to his intense commitment to writing.

Later in the year, Hellman joined Hammett in New York, and soon she was a part of those vibrant discussions of books Hammett and Faulkner championed. Faulkner liked to call her "Miss Lillian." This fellow Southerner had a deep respect for her talent, which in Hollywood he conveyed to his beloved, Meta Carpenter. Years later, he would fondly remember how Hellman would "sit curled upon on a sofa" as the argument raged about literary values, about Faulkner's supposedly having written *Sanctuary* for money, and about Hammett's dismissal of *The Magic Mountain* as "long-winded," a charge both Faulkner and Hellman rejected. She had a knack for getting along with male writers—it showed in the taciturn Faulkner's willingness, even two decades after those New York days, to confide in her about what he was currently working on.

Arthur Kober enjoyed Hammett's company. He always wanted to be close to those who meant the most to Hellman, and he seemed fascinated with Hammett's tough-guy reputation. There was an Italian restaurant in New York called Tony's that Kober and other theater people like Albert Hackett frequented. During Prohibition it turned into a gin mill; the clientele also changed, so to Hackett it seemed that there were a lot of strangers there. Kober told Hackett that he joined Hellman and Hammett for drinks one night at Tony's. A couple of men made some sort of nasty remark and Kober said, in a quiet but serious voice, "If you'd like to settle this thing, come outside." So the two guys got up and, just as quietly, said, "Okay, let's go." Kober turned to Hammett with a significant nod. The tough guy did not talk. Kober thought Hammett had a big blade in his cane, but, "once outside—bang! Down goes Dash. And then—bang! Kober was hit and . . . so startled. Dash hadn't even put his hands up. So he helped Dash get up, and all Dash said was, 'where we going now.' Kober was so disappointed," Hackett remembers.

After the divorce from Kober in early 1932, Louis Kronenberger engaged Hellman's attention as they began working on a play, *The Dear Queen*. At first their collaborative efforts seemed more like the *jeu d'esprit* of friends than a serious commitment to the stage. The play is about an eighteenth-century monarch, Sophia, suffering from the ennui of court life and determined to start over as a commoner. Her family is hopeless. Her son, King Charles, is obsessed with bridge, with his stamp collection, and with the speech he gives each year on Ascession Day. Her grandson is devoted to picking out tunes on his accordion. Her granddaughter, Elizabeth, is attached to her spinning wheel, and her other son regularly importunes her to provide money for the illegitimate children he thinks he has begotten. Sophia prefers to live simply, in a house with her name in the telephone book. The farcical plot continues with Sophia marrying a commoner, a rope manufacturer, in a fake ceremony arranged by her court ministers. It takes just one evening with him and his friends for her to see that the middle class is no more genuine than royalty. Indeed, her husband's friends are "snooping, mean, dirty-minded fatheads." So she drops her disguise and returns to court. While Sophia has been away, King Charles and Elizabeth have also tried to escape the court routine, but he returns because he has to use the royal bathroom and Elizabeth has not been able to pick up a sailor. Elizabeth is captivated, however, by a new delusion: "It's not the bourgeoisie who are free and fine. It is the peasantry. The house of thatch, the tilled field. It is toward that I stretch out my arms and toward that I will be journeying tomorrow." Sophia dismisses all of these silly notions, and the whole family returns to its usual foolery.

The eighteenth century was Kronenberger's specialty, but the pre-Marxist setting of the play may have suited both authors equally. Sentimentalizing any segment of society would immediately invite Hellman's ironic counterattack. She had little patience with proletarian literature, in spite of her obvious sympathies with the Left. Because she found it impossible to commit herself to a strict dialectical view of society, in which one class has the right—indeed the historical mission—to rule over another, she found such simplistic works unappealing. Her feelings about her own family, the rich and the poor, were too subtle and too mixed to permit her to condone the faults of either side.

The Dear Queen, according to Emmy Kronenberger, heralded the wacky comedies of the thirties even as it summed up the kind of playful behavior characteristic of her husband and Hellman's relationship in the twenties, in which nothing was taken very seriously. Kronenberger and Hellman were sincere enough about *The Dear Queen* to have it copyrighted at the end of 1932, and plans were announced in the *New York Herald Tribune* for its production, which never materialized. At some point, George Kaufman had a look at the play, and Kronenberger always felt Kaufman had stolen some of the spirit of *The Dear Queen* for his play *You Can't Take It With You*. As late as the summer of 1934, the authors were attempting to revise the play. In January and February 1936, after the success of *The Children's Hour*, Hellman wrote to John Golden seeking a producer for *The Dear Queen*. He was uncertain: "Yes, I've 'thought more'—and more about 'Dear Queen' but I haven't thought who's to do it—have you?" Three weeks later, he sent her a note in which he confessed, "Personally, I don't know whether I am being urged by a desire to do one with you, or whether I really do like some of the great material that's in the script." The play never found backers, and Hellman and Kronenberger later disowned it. *The Dear Queen*, nevertheless, provides an interesting first glimpse of Hellman as social critic and satirist. The rather wild comedy, the attack on several targets at once, is curiously like her last play, *My Mother, My Father and Me*, which also concentrates its black humor on the contradictions of middle-class life.

By May 1932, Hellman and Hammett were living at the Biltmore Hotel in New York City. Her divorce from Kober was nearly settled, but again she was leaving Hammett to visit her family in New Orleans. He could not find the money to pay his hotel bills, support his estranged wife, or pay the damages awarded to an actress who said he had roughed her up when she refused his advances. Yet he had been rewriting old material and preparing himself for a final attempt to complete *The Thin Man*. His conversations with Faulkner were, in reality, a way of revving himself up for the total concentration it would take to write a novel.

After several changes of hotel (he had to sneak out of one because he could not afford the bill), Hammett finally found a haven in late September at the Sutton Place, a hotel run by Nathanael ("Pep") West, S. J. Perelman's brother-in-law, now a Hammett confidant. Hellman also felt herself at home there. West had already written *The Dream Life of Balso Snell* (an experimental novel). Later he became famous as the author of *The Day of the Locust* and *Miss Lonelyhearts*. He intrigued Hellman. She may even have been in love with him for a time. He was bemused by the conceit that "his ancestors were of gentle birth," as Jay Martin puts it. Hellman described West as "certainly not delicate and not quite aristocratic, but . . . both distinguished and casual." The phrasing could have fit herself, Hammett, and many of their friends. Heywood Hale Broun, a confidant of S. J. Perelman and a casual friend of Hellman's, points out that,

> Nat West was one who prided himself on his skill at shooting birds in the English gentleman tradition, and he and Sid [Perelman] both wore clothes from London. Despite the defiant broken beak, Hellman was always a very smart dresser and was also one who wanted you to know that she knew the difference between breast of pheasant sous cloche and breast of pheasant au poivre. They all aspired to a kind of novelesque elegance. I guess that's why [Hammett's] Ned Beaumont said "never silk socks with tweeds."

Sometimes people who would become a part of Hammett's and Hellman's circle would overdo it. For instance, on first meeting the couple at a party in 1931 hosted by William Rose Benet, Dorothy Parker, who could cut anyone down to size with her tongue, embarrassed Hammett when she dropped to her knees and kissed his hand, as if in obeisance to the detective novelist's superior talent. Hellman, already uncomfortable in the company of people much older than herself, realized that Parker, a sincere admirer of Hammett's writing, had failed to carry off a scene that was "meant to be both funny and serious."

As an aspiring writer, Hellman was fascinated and deeply influenced by the behavior of established writers and by the environments they chose to build around themselves. Pep West's Sutton Place was rather seedy, but it was conducive to the writing regimen Hammett put himself through. S. J. Perelman described the hotel as "an impersonal sixteen-story barracks with a myriad of rooms so tiny that their walls almost impinged on each other, a honeycomb full of workers and drones in the minimum cubic footage required to avert strangulation." Nevertheless, West thought of it as a "Paris of the imagination," for it was a place where he was free to let loose his fantasies, and to provide sanctuary for indigent writers who came to live there for months at a time. West would often socialize with his guests over coffee in the evening as a way of feeding his voracious imagination. Hellman eventually became his accomplice in steaming open his guests' letters so that he could follow the intimate details of their lives.

Hellman was never candid about this period at the Sutton. Jay Martin, who spoke with her several times about his biography of West, found her "somewhat remote emotionally." Before beginning work on West, he had met her on numerous occasions when she was a visiting professor at Yale. "She was, of course, friendly, sophisticated, and polite, as befits her professional relation with me in that context," Martin recalls. But she repeatedly drew back from telling the biographer what West meant to her. During Hellman's stay at the Sutton, West was engaged to Alice Shepard, "a real beauty" of a woman, according to Edmund Wilson. She had been introduced to West by his sister, Laura Perelman, in the fall of 1930. She was the chief outstanding model of the costume designer, Elizabeth Hawes, and for West—deeply attracted to the world of fashion and wealth—she became a "romantic ideal." Yet he was uneasy and hesitant about deep emotional attachments and was wary of any involvement that might threaten his dedication to writing, that might tie him down to family life. He had only to look as far as Hellman and Hammett to observe quite a different way of having one's lovers and writing too.

One evening after a party, West drove Hellman and Shepard uptown, dropping Shepard off at Grand Central Station to catch a train for New Rochelle, and accepted Hellman's invitation to sleep with her. Shepard spent the night calling West's room. The next morning, when he finally answered, he told her about Hellman. "Why?" she asked Pep. "Because she asked me to," he said sheepishly. Shepard broke things off; she simply could not forgive him for his misguided chivalry. For West, the one night stand was an effective, if crass, way of severing himself from Shepard.

This was what Hellman would not tell Martin: why it was necessary to go after West. It was one way of proving her independence from Hammett, but it was also childishly cruel behavior—calculated to hurt another woman, a lovely woman Hellman could not damage in any other way. Hellman's lack of good looks bothered her. Louis Kronenberger used to say she had George Washington's nose, and Sid Perelman "often made derogatory though witty remarks about Lillian's looks." As a little girl she dreamed of "being a beauty." Alice Shepard *was* a beauty—her pictures appeared in the magazine. So Hellman beat out a real beauty. It was important that men took notice of her. Hellman wanted Hammett to write poems to her; he wrote none. Emmy Kronenberger remembers Hellman talking admiringly about an attractive blonde, "candy-box pretty" woman. Then Hellman would suddenly appear in very feminine, frilly dresses, even though she looked her best, Kronenberger thought, in fairly conservative, dark clothes. "I was always jealous of great beauties," Hellman admitted in interviews, but she would not own up to the unpleasant consequences of this envy. Albert Hackett, who met her after writing the screen version of *The Thin Man* with his wife Frances Hackett, recalls that "Lilly never made any point of being kind to other women. There was a whole group who were ready to cut her head off." Frances Hackett saw "Lilly get rough with other women and said 'if she ever let out on me like that, it would be the end.' But Frances was very admiring of Lilly and very vocal about it. I think Lilly knew there was a temper there too."

In September 1933 and January 1934, Hellman published in the *American Spectator* "I Call Her Mama Now" and "Perberty in Los Angeles," two comic short stories that satirized contemporary attitudes toward sex. Both stories are told in the first person by Eden, a young girl fed up with her family's efforts to initiate her into "the new sex freedom." She does not want to hear about her mother's lovers, to see her Uncle Wallace naked, or to read Stekel, a then-popular "authority" on sexuality. Eden says she is an old-fashioned girl. She reads Oswald Spengler on the decline of the West, even though "in the Marxist sense" he does not have "the proper historical balance." Eden wants none of the so-called "modern, intelligent life." She may marry a waiter who is ashamed of sex. She is a self-admitted throw-back who escapes her family because she does not want to hear her Aunt Minnie's lectures about "perberty" as being a "beautiful awakening" for a woman. Eden is something of a Puritan who admires "the beautiful, severe prose of Xenophon" and scandalizes her mother's generation "which went through the war with high disillusionment," as her Aunt Minnie puts it.

Behind these two amusing trifles was Hellman's continuing uncertainty about sexual experimentation. It was ridiculous to bring up a child without a strong sense of right and wrong or a respect for authority. "I Call Her Mama Now" is about the child's desire to have a "mama," not a parent who thinks she and her daughter should be on a first-name basis. Somebody had to set limits or all kinds of promiscuity would proliferate. An absolutist at heart, Hellman was bothered by the relativity of "free love" even as she tried to practice it. Why else would she get so angry over Hammett's straying with other women? What claim could she have on him in an era of "anything goes"? Hellman's nature, in other words, sought an anchor in Hammett—even if, from time to time, one would be set adrift from the other by some momentary affair.

In her memoirs, Hellman's eye is exclusively on Hammett. At the Sutton, she was struck with the way he locked himself in. There were to be no diversions—no drinking, no parties, not even a walk, "for fear something would be lost," she recalled in *An Unfinished Woman*. Like West, Hammett was drawing on material close to hand. *The Thin Man* tells as much about Hammett and his "she" as he was ever to reveal.

In *The Thin Man*, Nick Charles is forty-one and his wife Nora is twenty-six. He has retired from detective work, but Nora, the police, former clients, and friends keep turning to him to solve crimes. In this case, he is called in to investigate three murders. The prime suspect is Clyde Wynant (the thin man), an aloof, eccentric inventor and the employer of one of the victims, Julia Wolf. Wynant is an elusive figure throughout most of the novel and communicates with Nick and others only through written notes. Herbert Macaulay, Wynant's attorney, is the only one who claims actually to have seen him. Wynant, Nick eventually deduces, has been Macaulay's murder victim. Macaulay collaborated with Julia Wolf in defrauding Wynant and then killed her because he could not trust her. He then has to murder a criminal who is trying to blackmail him.

Nick's impressiveness, like his author's, derives not from what he currently does but from his past accomplishments. Nick is reluctant to take on any new assignments. He is, rather, a charming alcoholic who is weary of a profession that others still find romantic and exciting. He is content with managing his wife's inheritance and prefers not to say any more than is absolutely necessary. His attitudes are the result of years of manipulating people in order to solve crimes, and he is now wary of anyone who wants answers from him.

Like Nick, Hammett was intractable, unwilling to affirm Hellman's own perceptions, to commit himself entirely to her or to anyone else. Like Nora, Hellman was charmed by this independence and cultivated it in herself when she spoke in *Scoundrel Time* about being "nobody's girl." Nearly all of the dialogue with Hammett in her autobiographical writings is inconclusive, understated, enigmatic. Like Nick, Hammett was retired and he withdrew further and further into himself. He was quite willing to husband Hellman's talent—to manage her fortune, so to speak, just as Nick looks after Nora's investments—but in league with his fictional counterpart, Hammett was never less than his own man. As Hellman later put it, he was a person with "reserves so deep that we know we cannot touch them with charms or jokes or favors."

Women are attracted to Nick, but he is loyal to Nora. She takes his attractiveness in good-humored stride. Seeing him with a young woman, Nora remarks:

> "She's pretty."
> "If you like them like that."
> She grinned at me. "You got types?"
> "Only you, darling—lanky brunettes with wicked jaws."
> "And how about the red-head you wandered off with at the Quinns' last night?"
> "That's silly," I said. "She just wanted to show me some French etchings."

This is the elegant, sophisticated love affair as Hellman would have liked it, with the woman keeping the man in line without in any way compromising his independence. Yet Hammett has his say—the last word, in fact—in these witty dialogues between husband and wife. Although Nora is described by another character as a "woman with hair on her chest" because of her intrepid participation in Nick's adventures with criminals, she is, for the most part, a fine example of the docile woman Hammett wryly joked about preferring to the difficult Hellman. Nora has almost none of Hellman's fabled anger and very little need to assert herself, until the end of the novel when she tries to get Nick to wrap up the case neatly. Nora's tidiness and thoroughness—her craving for a final, authoritative summing up—is all Hellman, and is firmly resisted by Nick/Hammett.

Mimi, the villainess in *The Thin Man*, is given the bad temper, the tendency to be profane that marked Hellman in her arguments with Hammett. Hellman felt good about being the model for Nora, but never could be sure if Hammett was joking when he said she was also the inspiration for Mimi, a pathological liar. Mimi goes into uncontrollable violent fits when she cannot have her way. In her memoirs, Hellman speaks often of her own "rampage-anger" and of a high temper that stops just shy of Mimi's abusive behavior.

Lying is an important theme in *The Thin Man* and is tied to Nick's malaise. "What's worrying you now, son?" Nora asks Nick, and he replies "riddles, lies, and I'm too old and too tired for them to be any fun." Of Mimi, an exhausted Nick complains, "She keeps trying and you've got to be careful or you'll find yourself believing her, not because she seems to be telling the truth, but simply because you're tired of disbelieving her." Hammett's weary tone in Hellman's writing recalls Nick's fatigued reluctance to credit Nora's speculations about Nick's cases, her tendency to create stories and plots about the crimes she tries to solve.

Nora is fresh and direct and eager, as was Hellman, to know all about her lover's detective work. Nora is also frankly sexual in ways inspired by Hellman:

> "Tell me something, Nick. Tell me the truth: when you were wrestling with Mimi, didn't you get excited?" [Hammett originally wrote, "didn't you get an erection?"]
> "Oh, a little."

She laughed and got up from the floor. "If you aren't a disgusting old lecher," she said.

Although Hellman was right to say in *An Unfinished Woman* that Nick and Nora's marriage is one of the few "in modern literature where the man and woman like each other and have a fine time together," the distinction between Nick's laconic "a little" and Nora's moralistic "lecher" should not be ignored. Throughout the novel, Nora wants to categorize things and to organize Nick's case: "Listen, why don't we make a list of all the suspects and all the motives and clues, and check them off against . . ." He interrupts her and dismisses the whole idea: "You do it. I'm going to bed." She wants not only the criminal but some kind of clear apportionment of justice in the scheme of things—just as Hellman so often did.

To a very large extent, the novel is about Nick's education of Nora and about her unwillingness to accept completely his notion that knowledge is built on surmise, that a detective's statements fill in but do not eradicate gaps in the evidence that lead to the arrest of the murderer, whose means of disposing of one of his victims is still in doubt. Contrary to what Nora supposed, Nick knew almost nothing from the beginning. Instead, he has guessed and reconstructed a murder from the pattern of details he has slowly accumulated. "I don't want to go against your idea of what's right and wrong, but when I say he probably dissected the body so he could carry it into town in bags I'm only saying what seems most probable," he instructs Nora. There ought to be, in her view, certain a priori methods and principles (a right and a wrong), and not just what the detective learns from experience.

Nothing is very exact in Nick's world, and this comes as a shock to Nora: "I always thought detectives waited until they had every little detail fixed in . . ." To wait for such perfection in detection is to make virtually certain that the criminal will escape, he tells her. The case is closed, but Nora is upset by the uncertainty of the methods used to solve the crime. The last words of the novel are hers: "it's all pretty unsatisfactory." The world Hammett describes is dangerously unstable, for lies have no clear opposite. Nick is not telling "the truth" at the end; he is only explaining what seems probable.

The Thin Man is a book addressed to Hellman, a fiction that explores the ramifications of her own personality in relation to

Hammett's. She had a tendency to rearrange the order of things in an attempt to prove a certain view of the world. Whereas Hammett believed his writing followed the ambiguity of events to a certain, only partial, resolution, Hellman wavered between exposing the inconclusiveness of events and giving them a sharper contour, a final "act" that would provide a satisfactory "curtain."

Hammett must have wondered how she would handle her own case, a crime that would test her rigid sense of right and wrong. On a fishing trip in the Florida Keys in the spring of 1933 (made possible on the strength of *The Thin Man*'s magazine sale), he suggested to Hellman that William Roughead's book, *Bad Companions*, contained a chapter that could serve as the starting point for a play. The chapter, "Closed Doors; Or the Great Drumsheugh Case," is an account of an actual lawsuit and trial in nineteenth-century Edinburgh. Two female teachers, friends since their college days, were accused of lesbianism by one of their pupils. Although the women were ultimately vindicated ten years after the accusation, they lost their teaching positions and their careers were ruined.

By the fall of 1933, after a spring and summer in Florida spent fishing and reading with Hammett, Hellman returned to New York to struggle with the first draft of her play. To Herman Shumlin, a producer and director with whom she had worked several years earlier during her stint as a play script reader, she confided the story line of her drama. He suggested that she quit writing plays, and she surprised herself by accepting his job offer as a play reader for fifteen dollars a week.

Hellman was a painstaking writer who worked from a strong factual base. She relied on Roughead for many of her characters and for some of her plot. She borrowed from him in the same sense that Shakespeare took the stuff of his plays from Plutarch. In more than a year of intense work, she produced at least six drafts of the play.

In the notes for *The Children's Hour*, Hellman displayed considerable indecision about how to treat the relationship of Karen Wright and Martha Dobie, the two school teachers accused of being lovers. To what extent would either woman recognize that they shared more than feelings of friendship? To what degree would one of the women, Martha, acknowledge her latent lesbianism? Even in its final form, the play does not resolve this nexus of friendship, love, and sexuality.

Almost thirty years later, in *Pentimento*, Hellman was still trying to understand why the Karen-Martha relationships gave her so much trouble. She connected *The Children's Hour* to her concern with her friendship with Julia. While Hellman was writing her play, Julia was in Europe fighting fascism.

In *Pentimento*, Julia is a figure in the autobiographer's imagining of the past, a fantasy functioning more like an alter ego or dramatic complement to the playwright's personality than a historically verifiable presence in her life. It is essential to the writer's purpose that we do not know more about Julia, for "Julia" is meant to be about the way Hellman conceived of her life: she had to have both a male lover and a female confidant—just as Karen Wright does in *The Children's Hour*. It would definitely not be in Hellman's interest to make it possible for others to check the facts of Julia's life. Julia, like Hammett, had to be all Hellman's.

Exactly what did Julia mean to Hellman? What kind of commitment was Hellman expecting from her friend? It is a question that also might be asked of Martha Dobie in *The Children's Hour*. What does she want from Karen? Martha's, rebelliousness, outspokenness, and irritability all seem modeled on the playwright's own traits. As Doris Falk puts it, "Hellman's complicated, half-understood feelings must have given her some insight into Martha Dobie—one of the few Hellman characters whose fate could be called tragic."

By early 1934, Hammett was wearing Hellman down with his drinking and with the constant guests at their house on Long Island. He was in an irritable mood, but he generously gave her money "to get away from all of it." In *Pentimento*, Hellman states that her ostensible purpose was to stay away a long time to finish her *The Children's Hour*, but after a month in Paris, feeling "lonely and tired of work," she called Julia, with whom she had been in phone contact several times, to arrange a visit to Vienna. Julia advised against it and would not talk for long on a phone she was sure was tapped, but said she would relay a message to Hellman when it was safe to arrange a meeting. Eventually, Hellman received a call from a John Von Zimmer in Vienna, informing her that Julia was in the hospital. She had been hurt during a violent clash (February 12–15) involving Austrian troops, Nazis, and Socialist workers.

After an initial visit to the hospital, at which she found her friend unable to communicate because of bandages covering most of her head and face, Hellman was not allowed to see Julia for the next two days. There had been an operation and the recovering patient still could not talk; instead, "she raised her right arm and touched my hand," Hellman recalls in *Pentimento*. The moment of intimacy was over as Julia withdrew her hand, as if she knew that Hellman had always considered it "too large even for this tall girl, too blunt, too heavy, ugly."

The recognition of incongruity at such a time, and Hellman's immediate reference to the fact that she could not understand Julia's gesture—a raised hand pointing to the window with a pushing motion—suggests a division between these women that was the result of more than physical separation from each other over many years. Cast like a spell over so much of Hellman's writing about her life is the sensation of a meaning that has been missed, a significance she found hard to put in words or shape into dramatic form. Julia's absence from Hellman's life is like a void in the author's own character.

According to *Pentimento*, Hellman returned to Paris quickly, as soon as she received Julia's urgent command to leave Vienna and await word in Paris. A month passed with no communication, and by then Hellman found it impossible to ascertain Julia's whereabouts or to contact her associate, Von Zimmer, who had arranged Hellman's brief stay in Vienna. Julia vanishes, like so many characters in Hellman's memoirs, as if she never existed at all. The autobiographer seems to paint over her canvas of life whenever it suits her imaginative purpose.

Hellman returned home to New York, and with Hammett's help, finished *The Children's Hour* there. Although the surviving manuscripts of the play show no sign of his holograph, Hammett evidently corrected several drafts and kept after her until she had it right. He relished this sort of mentoring, of bringing a fictional idea to fulfillment.

By May 1934, Hellman had shown her script to Herman Shumlin. Lee Gershwin remembers her husband Ira phoning Shumlin about the play and insisting he read it. On a rainy day, Shumlin, Gershwin, and Hellman met to go over the play. Lee remembers Hellman getting up several times and walking to the window, and Ira would tell her to sit down. Shumlin would then get up, and Ira would tell him to sit down. The whole play was read. Ira kept pushing Herman to commit himself: "Are you going to do it or not?" Finally Shumlin agreed to produce it. "I don't think Lil ever appreciated that," says Lee. She continued to make revisions until late October or early November. She also tried to revise *The Dear Queen*. In a letter to Kober about the hot summer in New York that made her sick to her stomach, she complained about her collaborator, Kronenberger, who kept their playwriting sessions "carefully sandwiched between his engagements." It did not go well: "two headaches, a lot of screaming, apologies, and no results."

Hellman's attitude toward Kober was maternal. He had a throat infection and she pleaded with him not to go into the swimming pool: "Pay attention to mama, and take care of yourself," she urged in one letter. She wrote to keep him abreast of her life—her father had had a fall and refused to see a doctor; her mother was acting as if Hellman's having gone away with the Shumlin's for a few days without leaving an address had caused the accident. What if someone died while Hellman was away, her mother wanted to know. Hellman was chagrined that at twenty-nine she had to report her itinerary to her mother. One day her mother would discover she was not a virgin, and that would destroy their "beautiful friendship."

Hellman had several dreams about Kober—that he had four children and was leading them by the hand down Fifth Avenue. She was not sure how they should treat each other, or if they should do anything. She thought about him too much. He had sent her a new typewriter, and she let him know it had arrived. He was such a lovely, generous man and she loved him very much:

X X X X X - from me
X X X X X - from the typewriter and me

Hellman wrote to console Kober about his feeling that Hollywood was no good, saying he would just have to make it until November, when his contract would end and he could decide what to do. Again, she complained about her mother's monitoring of her activities, especially with a "visiting unmarried gentleman." She would spend a few days each week at Dash's house in Huntington, Long Island. She was having trouble with one of her friends, a fanatical Communist, and had spent an evening arguing with him. He had a sharp intellect, but he also got "confused and dogmatic." They had "screamed at each other for several hours." She had also been up until four A.M. with Kronenberger the previous evening, still trying to get *The Dear Queen* right without much progress. She doubted they did the play much justice. Kronenberger seemed as frustrated with *The Dear Queen* as she was. She was exhausted "and sick from heat and cigarettes and lack of sleep," and she had become a ".work dog." The most positive note was that she had just about completed final revisions of *The Children's Hour* after having worked on it until two or three in the morning for a couple of nights.

Unlike some writers who rely extensively on cut-and-paste methods, Hellman retyped each new draft of *The Children's Hour*. Her first typescript included outlines for the action of each act, so that subsequent drafts represented revisions in scenic structure, fine tuning of dialogue, and various changes of location—but not in the author's vision of the whole. Changes in wording often resolved inconsistencies or vagueness in characterization. Slowly and carefully, Hellman settled on a vocabulary for her characters that made them stand out as individuals. She pruned certain speeches and divided others that were too long. She overcame the prosaic quality of her initial work and gave the play pace and crispness. Even slight modifications, like the following exchange between Mary Tilford and her grandmother, emphasize the author's growing ability to individualize her characters and to dramatize the gap between the genteel adult and the manipulative child. First draft:

> MARY. I missed you. (*Looks up at Tilford and smiles.*) I
>   was homesick
> TILFORD. I'm glad that's all it was. I was frightened
>   when Agatha said you were sick. . . .

Final draft:

> MARY: I missed you so. [*Smiling up at Mrs. Tilford.*] I
>   was awful homesick.
> MRS. TILFORD: I'm glad that's all it was. I was frightened
>   when Agatha said you were not well.

Mary's use of exaggeration and her grandmother's resort to euphemisms are quickly established. The refined Mrs. Tilford will not be able to see through the child's shocking lie about her teachers' lesbianism—a word so revolting that Mrs. Tilford cannot bring herself to say it aloud.

The first full draft of the play continues to reflect the author's uncertainty about how to dramatize the relationship between Karen and Martha. Martha, for example, is an "Unconscious Lesbian," and at thirty-two is five years older than Karen. In later drafts, Hellman drops the discrepancy in ages and makes Martha's sexuality far less explicit. As a result, the dramatic impact of Martha's fury over Mary's lie is all the greater, since it is only through her vehemence and her belated recognition of her lesbianism in the last act that the unconscious is revealed. Similarly, Hellman removes the implication that Karen and Joe Cardin have been lovers, thus strengthening Joe's doubts about Karen's sexuality. Their tragedy, in Edmund Fuller's words, is also heightened by separating Karen and Joe "before any fulfillment of their relationship has been attained."

In the simplest, most basic terms, the play is about a child who makes trouble for adults. Mary Tilford is a headstrong thirteen-year-old with a "half-grown mind"—Hellman's definition (in the earliest surviving notes on the play) of a young girl who is surely the dark side of Hellman herself, a girl who had to be warned by her nursemaid, Sophronia, not to "go through life making trouble for people."

In Roughead's book, Mary's original was Miss Jane Cumming, the bastard offspring of an aristocrat's liaison with a black woman in India. Roughead links Cumming's malevolence to her race and sense of illegitimacy; she is a "half-caste" determined to have revenge on the female disciplinarians who have punished her for breaking the rules. Hellman did not pursue this aspect of her source and was probably put off by Roughead's racism, yet throughout her life she tended to identify with wayward adolescents and to side with minorities—even transforming herself into a kind of "half-caste" when she ran away from home at age fourteen.

In the introduction to *Six Plays*, Hellman confessed that some of Mary Tilford's behavior was her own. As a child, Hellman did disturb adults, fake a heart attack, and experience Mary's half-awakened sense of sexuality derived from reading books. She was also capable of telling lies that came "from [the] unconscious pushing against nothing," as Hellman describes it in her notes about Mary. (In fact, one of the achievements of *An Unfinished*

Woman is Hellman's ability to convey the frustration of a child-woman who does not know her own mind, who is "pushing against nothing" because adult experience is lacking.)

Mary pretends to see her teachers, Karen Wright and Martha Dobie, making love. She is confused about what she might accomplish by this lie, but she senses how effective it will be in her campaign to remain at home with her grandmother rather than return to the punishment that awaits her at school. Hellman's notes for the play reveal considerable sympathy for Mary and a closeness to her way of thinking, for Mary is "against the completely accepting minds of the rest [of her classmates]." Readers and viewers of the play, on the other hand, have tended to see Mary as diabolic, not as a rebel gone wrong.

As Hellman as a child learned from her two aunts, Mary picks up and responds to tensions that exist between two women living together. Karen Wright is the voice of reason, "straight, clear, dull but educated, balanced, unemotionally awakened," as Hellman put it in her preliminary notes. Martha Dobie, on the other hand, has some of Mary's fire, for Martha is nervous and high-strung. She is "half one thing, half another." "A forced neurotic calm" covers up her reaction to "a tough childhood."

Martha is bedeviled by her aunt, Lily Mortar, who has been permitted—against the better judgment of both teachers—to instruct the students in literature. Mortar herself is a liar, an ex-actress who exaggerates her theatrical past. Entirely lacking in candor or in the sympathetic but firm manner that is needed with the adolescent girls she harangues, Mortar responds to her niece's disapproval of her teaching by picking on Martha's jealous possessiveness and on her dislike of Karen's fiancé, Dr. Joseph Cardin. Two of the girls hear Mortar accusing Martha of "unnatural" feelings for Karen, and Mary eventually devises the dramatic stratagem of whispering Mortar's words to her shocked aunt, Mrs. Amelia Tilford.

There is a melodramatic perfection in the play's structure and in its characters that deeply satisfied Hellman's own need for clarity of purpose. The play is like a piece of music—an opera, perhaps. In Hellman's preliminary notes for the first act, in which the characters of the two teachers are slowly revealed, she emphasizes that "nothing has been hit hard, nothing awakened." Act one, she writes, is "an overture, and distinctly the overture, to the end." Act two is "the action of the charge. What has been indefinite becomes definite now." Mary will come out with her lie and overturn the conventional order of things. In act three, "the theme has been dropped, the case has been stated." At the beginning of the play's last movement, it is clear that Karen's and Martha's lives have been ruined. They have lost their court case against Mrs. Tilford (who spread Mary's lie about the teachers' lesbianism), and they have lost faith in their ability to go on. There is no longer much hope for Karen to have a normal life with Cardin. The bleakness of act three's opening lines beautifully realizes the playwright's intention that "no one must talk with the same words or rhythms as they have before."

> MARTHA: It's cold in here.
> KAREN: Yes.
> MARTHA: What time is it?
> KAREN: I don't know. What's the difference?
> MARTHA: None. I was hoping it was time for my bath.

The absence of rhythm, the coldness of the lines, demonstrate that life no longer has meaning for these characters.

Martha commits suicide when she realizes there may have been some truth in Mary's lie. In her notes to the play, Hellman puts the issue of the relationship between Martha and Karen in the form of a question: "Could the kid have been right. Could she, because of her own and different abnormality, have seen what they couldn't see themselves, have sensed it and unconsciously known about it." Hellman's own complicated and unresolved feelings about her sexuality, about her relationship with Hammett, and about her love for Julia surface in her characterization of Martha. Martha fumes at the injustice of her accusers, but her sense of outrage also masks internal conflicts. Leaving for Europe—the option Karen and Cardin invite Martha to consider—is one that Hellman often took when she could not straighten out her own life.

Hellman had considerable trouble ending *The Children's Hour* and was never quite satisfied with its conclusion. The play, like the memoir of Julia, is incomplete. Rather than coming to terms with her feelings about Julia, Hellman shifts attention to Julia's unfeeling family and the cruel world that did her in. Similarly, in *The Children's Hour*, Mrs. Tilford's third-act apology to Karen

throws the burden on society and its representatives who have
wronged Karen and ruined Martha's life. In an early version of the
play, there is even a reconciliation scene between Karen and Mrs.
Tilford, in which Tilford declares not only her sympathy but her
"love" for Karen.

> KAREN: *(Smiles)* You love me?
> MRS. TILFORD: It's odd, Karen; you're all I have left.
> KAREN: It's over for me now, but it will never end for
> you. She's harmed us both, but she's harmed you
> more, I guess. *(Sits down beside Tilford and kisses her.)*
> I'm sorry. I'll do whatever I can.
> TILFORD: *(Clings to her, kisses her)* Then you'll try for
> yourself.

In an early draft of the play, another character, Judge Potter, was
introduced in act two to heap still more blame on Mrs. Tilford.
When she takes it upon herself to telephone the parents of the
schoolchildren about Mary's charge of lesbianism, Potter makes
several attempts to point out that the child may be merely hysterical. He decries Tilford's "swift punishment" of the schoolteachers
and suggests that she is "after blood." "Are you society, Amelia?"
he asks, in order to demonstrate how much Tilford has taken upon
herself. In rejecting his advice, she bluntly tells him, "I don't give
a damn what you'd do." The dramatization of Tilford's outrage is
so extreme that Hellman took Hammett's advice and cut Potter
from the play. She also toned down the nastiness of Tilford's
anger, which was out of keeping with her genteel personality.

In Roughead's book, Dame Helen Cumming Gordon, the model
for Mrs. Tilford, is portrayed as an obdurate, nasty opponent of
the two teachers, who does not for a moment entertain the possibility that the women are innocent. As subsequent drafts of the
play shifted the focus in act three from outrage over the unjust
accusation to a probing of how the two women felt about each
other, a subtler dramatization of Tilford's character was also called
for. She could be as impulsive as her factual counterpart, but she
also had to be shown as having doubts about Mary's story, which
Mary shrewdly resolves by constantly enlarging the implications
of her lie.

In spite of Hellman's increasing concern with her characters'
psychologies, the feelings Karen and Martha have for each other

are never adequately probed; rather, they are deflected by turning Mary into an incarnate evil, so that the injustice of her accusation rather than the reasons why she chose that particular lie is dramatized. There is, for example, an undeveloped link between Martha and Mary. Like Mary, Martha had been a jealous, possessive child. And it is Martha who first recognizes that there is something "wrong" with Mary. Later, Martha uses the same words for herself: "There's always been something wrong."

In the final scene, after Mary's lie has been revealed, Karen tells Mrs. Tilford that Mary is her "own," an evil she will have to live with for the rest of her life. Karen's line is itself an ironic echo of Tilford's disgust with Karen's and Martha's alleged lesbianism: "This—this thing is your own." This need to complete the circle of accusation, to put the final details in place—as Nora in *The Thin Man* also wanted to do—is characteristic of Hellman's fastidious knitting together of loose ends. The tightness of this moral universe is also reflected in the value-laden vocabulary of the characters. The word *bad* is used repeatedly. Mary is "bad for the other girls," Martha remarks. "You know, it's really bad having you around children," Martha says to her aunt. Running away from school is "a very bad thing to do," Mrs. Tilford tells Mary. Cardin refers to Mary's "bad temper," and Karen tries to convince Mrs. Tilford that Mary is a "bad girl." Near the end of the play, Martha concludes, "There'll never be any place for us to go. We're bad people." Her endpoint has been prepared by the relentlessness and consistency with which words like "bad" are applied to the actions of the characters.

Only Cardin consistently speaks in a language that might free the characters from moral absolutes. Like Karen, his first inclination is to reason with Mary. Indeed, by juxtaposing Cardin's and Karen's talks with Mary, one can fit together a rational world view that her lying defeats.

> KAREN: Let's try to understand each other. If you feel that you *have* to take a walk, or that you just *can't* come to class, or that you'd like to go into the village by yourself, come and tell me—I'll try to understand. *(Smiles)* I don't say that I'll always agree that you should do exactly what you want to do, but I've had feelings like that too—everybody has—and I

won't be unreasonable about yours. But this way,
this kind of lying you do, makes everything wrong.
CARDIN. *(walking about in front of Mary)* Look: everybody
lies all the time. Sometimes they have to, sometimes
they don't. I've lied for a lot of different reasons, but
there was seldom a time when, if I'd been given a
second chance, I wouldn't have taken back the lie
and told the truth. You're lucky if you ever get that
chance. I'm telling you this because I'm about to ask
you a question. Before you answer the question, I
want to tell you that if you've l—, if you made a
mistake, you must take this chance and say so. You
won't be punished for it.

But Mary is obdurate, as Hellman often was with her elders, and
will not admit error. The only point that registers with her is that
she has been cornered, and in the face of an inquisition she is
uncannily like the adult Hellman in shifting attention to her
persecutors and away from her own behavior. She starts to cry and
laments the fact that "everybody is yelling at me. I don't know
what I'm saying with everybody mixing me all up."

Lying and character assassination turn a whole society upside-
down and mix everyone up. Liberals—like Cardin and Karen, who
would reason with Mary—are helpless. Indeed, lies are so corrupting that Cardin, near the end of the play, confesses to doubting
Karen and Martha. Because he cannot take the radical view—that
a lie is just that, a false insupportable assertion—he is doomed to
half-believing in the lie he would try to persuade Mary to reject.
Hellman's plays imply that the liberal mentality goes only half-way
toward opposing evil. Liberalism is too flexible for her own rigid
nature. Concede nothing, get a firm grip on the recalcitrant child,
seemed to be her philosophy. As Sophronia did with Hellman as
a child, so Hellman did later in life and in art: the weak, the
childish must be firmly *controlled*. Otherwise, everyone pays for
the trouble.

The casting for the original Broadway production of *The Children's Hour* proved difficult because several actresses turned down
the parts of Karen and Martha, sensing the controversy they would
stir up. As late as October 19, 1934, Herman Shumlin was telegraphing Arthur Kober to see if he could help in getting an actress

to accept Martha's part. Finally, Katherine Emery was cast as Karen and Anne Revere as Martha. Twenty-five years later she would play in the starring role of Anna Berniers in *Toys in the Attic*. Robert Keith was chosen for the role of Joe Cardin. Katherine Emmet (Mrs. Amelia Tilford) was the only cast member to repeat her role in the 1952 revival of *The Children's Hour*. Eugenia Rawls, one of the young actresses cast as a schoolgirl, five years later toured the country playing Alexandra to Tallulah Bankhead's Regina in *The Little Foxes*.

This was a combative play that took on society. Other dramas on Broadway, notably *The Captive* (1925), had addressed lesbianism, but *The Children's Hour* struck hard at the pieties and conventions of contemporary life. "This play . . . could land us all in jail," Hellman remembers the owner of the theater, Lee Shubert, saying when he watched the rehearsal for "the confession scene, the recognition of the love of one woman for another."

Hellman had just had an altercation in the theater with Shubert, who had ordered her to get her "dirty shoes off my chair." She claims he did not know who she was, that Shumlin had to tell him, "That girl, as you call her, is the author of the play." Hellman's part in the rude exchange with Shubert is characteristic of the obstinate, tough child-woman who wrote the play:

> I said, "My shoes aren't touching the chair, Mr. Shubert," but, after a pause, he pushed my right leg to the floor.
> I said, "I don't like strange men fooling around with my right leg so don't do it again."

Worries about censorship and the banning of the play in some cities, however, were balanced by the excitement generated by Hellman's boldness. The expectation was that audiences would be attracted by a drama that radicalized their emotions. In the words of the press agent who promoted several of Hellman's plays, she had "power and punch." In spite of Shubert's misgivings, Shumlin proceeded to direct the play as Hellman had written it. She had only him to rely on, since Hammett was in Hollywood, writing her how much he missed her and rejoicing in her report that rehearsals were going well. He was still carousing with Kober, for whose family Hellman considerately set aside opening night tickets.

According to *Pentimento*, on opening night, Hellman was drunk.

Years later, she remembered very little, except holding on to a rail at the back of the theater and hearing the enthusiastic audience yelling for a curtain call. Even before the first reviews, the excited responses of the audience and of the critics in attendance indicated that her first produced play would be a big hit. She seemed numbed by it all and unable to accept the signs of her success. Her parents were proud of her but unable to show it. They were frightened for her in "a world they didn't know," and they proceeded to argue nonsensically about Julia Hellman's claim that her daughter was "the sweetest smelling baby in New Orleans," an honor Max Hellman reserved for himself.

Hellman appreciated this comical diversion, since she could not come to terms with either the theater or her adult life. She found herself in an alcoholic haze in the company of people she did not know or like. She telephoned Hammett in Hollywood, but a woman identifying herself as his secretary answered, saying it was a strange hour to be calling. Dizzy from beer, it took Hellman two days to realize that she had called him at "three A.M. California time and that he had no secretary." Drinking heavily again, she flew the same day to California, went immediately to the house Hammett had rented from Harold Lloyd, smashed the soda fountain there to pieces, and took the night flight back to New York. Hammett was proud of the play and happy that all the hard work had "paid off," but Hellman could not put up with his disloyalty, with the good times that excluded her, with the life he insisted on having without her.

Kober, still out on the West Coast, was having a very hard time finishing a play of his own. "Perhaps it is Lil's success which makes me feel that I can hardly hope for a similar reception," he confided to his diary on November 27. He hated to admit it, but he missed her. She was constantly on his mind, and he felt "all alone." A woman he was with wept and told him "how empty I am of emotion." On November 30 he received a long letter from Hellman and a copy of *The Children's Hour*. She told him about her "success with all the acclaim & excitement of a hit." The next week she was writing him about the fabulous offers she was receiving. Three days later, on December 11, Kober finally acknowledged in his diary that, in spite of the divorce, he had never given up hope of getting Hellman back:

This day received a long, honest letter from Lil stating the case & her gratitude toward Dash & how I'm completely & entirely out of the scheme—which is as well, but why I was allowed to dangle, why I wasn't sawed off, why I tortured & wracked myself these many months is unexplained.

This was the only complaint he allowed himself. By December 20 he had become reconciled to Hellman's telling him about the strong ties between her and Hammett:

> I see now how silly it is for me to make an obsession of her. Time would have parted us completely but for correspondence & sentimental jags I indulge in.

December 31, 1934, marked the anniversary and the real end of Kober's first marriage—although in many ways it was the beginning of an enduring relationship:

> This day nine years ago I married Lil with whom I had lunch & very nice it was, for no one bores me less, no one I can be more at ease with than her. And no one disturbs or upsets me more.

Having put it all in perspective, he was able to work most of the day. In many ways, as Kober was later to realize, Hellman would be in a position vis-à-vis Hammett that resembled his own place in her life. If Hellman grieved Kober over the men she had, Dash pained her over the women he pursued. In his diary, Kober had ended the year 1934 with a summing up that was prophetic of the feelings of a lifetime.

4

THREESOMES
New York/Hollywood/New York
(1934–1937)

Sometimes he asked Lillian to make a threesome. It interested him to see how far she would go.

—Diane Johnson, *Dashiell Hammett: A Life*

Looking to the Academy [of Motion Picture Arts and
Sciences] for representation was like trying to get laid in
your mother's house. Somebody was always in the parlor,
watching.

—attributed to Dorothy Parker in
Nancy Lynn Schwartz, *The Hollywood Writers' Wars*

At nite Howard & I call for Lil & Morris & we to Brown
Derby for dinner & pleasant, too, with talk being loose &
the dinner good & lots of wine & bill over $20 which we
match & Howard stuck. I see the feminine in action, how,
for Lil with all her money is still a girl & exempt from
matching. I recall how annoyed I was in the courtship days
to find myself constantly on paying end—remember?

Arthur Kober's diary, May 16, 1935

The reviews of *The Children's Hour* in early December 1934
praised the play for its dramatic force and originality. Reviewers were also impressed with Hellman's ironic and tragic sensibil-

ity. The character Mary Tilford, they believed, was the dominant figure, and the third act—which lacked her evil genius—lost the tension that kept the audience riveted to the play. While sympathizing with Hellman's need to show the consequences of Mary's lie, critics still objected to the moral accounting that coerced Mrs. Tilford back into the play's conclusion with an apology to Karen and an offer to do whatever is necessary to rectify the injury to her reputation.

Years later, Hellman admitted she had "overburdened" her play with that last "summing-up" scene, but insisted that the fault resided in the scene, not in the attempt to resolve what the play was really about. Joseph Wood Krutch, one of Hellman's most perceptive critics, identified the playwright's dilemma:

> Whatever the original intention of the author may have been, it is plain enough that the play as it stands is a play about a Machiavellian child, not a play about two women falsely accused of a Lesbian attachment. But the mistake was made, partly at least, because the author could not imagine a satisfactory end to the real story and so gave us instead the end of a different one.

Krutch could not have known that Hellman's preliminary notes revealed an acute understanding of Mary Tilford's character but were quite vague in imagining how the relationship between the two women would be developed. From the beginning, Hellman knew what the consequences of Mary's lie would be, but she had trouble calculating how Karen and Martha would respond to the lie and to each other. Mary was close to the author's heart, a character through whom Hellman could gain perspective on her own "naughty" childhood. Karen and Martha were not as individualized as Mary, and their lives lacked a background, a history, against which their behavior could be perceived. In the main, they reacted to Mary and did not demonstrate how their affection for each other had been formed. In the coming year, Hellman would write *These Three*, the first movie version of *The Children's Hour*, remedying this lacuna in her characters' lives.

In spite of the reviewers' reservations about the play, they recognized it as a daring and original work. It was extremely popular in New York City and ran for 691 performances—a record of box office success not equaled by any other Hellman play. *The*

Children's Hour stayed in the public's mind throughout 1935 and 1936 as newspapers reported on its road tour and on the controversy surrounding its impending production in other cities. In London, it was banned by the Lord Chamberlain, Earl Cromer, censor of the English stage: "Plays on this theme are automatically forbidden irrespective of merit," *The New York Times* reported on March 12, 1935. In late 1935, a number of articles in the *Times* covered the banning of the play in Boston and marked the one-year anniversary of its Broadway debut. On December 16, Hellman was quoted as saying that she and Herman Shumlin would take "every step legally possible to fight the executive order of Mayor Mansfield [of Boston]. . . . If it is possible to do so, I should like to make a test case out of this arbitrary ruling."

Hellman's reputation for being frank and provocative was already attracting much notice. She was pursued by Hollywood producers hoping to sign her to a contract. Hammett had been working for MGM since late October 1934, and Hellman was eager to join him. In Hollywood, she was flattered by all of the attention from the studios and was intent on enjoying her success. She was young enough to be pleased by the hard-drinking crowd of friends, new and old, that seemed so interested in her.

Hellman saw Kober at least once a week, often in the company of Hammett (who lavished expensive furs and other gifts on her) and of the Perelmans for dinner and dancing, although on many occasions she and Kober ate and drank alone. They were enormously fond of each other and for a night or two resumed intimate relations, although Kober, keeping his distance, noted in his diary little sexual satisfaction with Lillian. He wondered whether he would have sought consolation elsewhere were he still married to her.

On December 27, 1934, Hellman delivered a screenplay to Edward Small Productions, an independent company. How she had time to write this complete script while being so heavily engaged with *The Children's Hour* and other activities is a mystery—one she does not clear up in her memoirs, which make no mention of this work, an adaptation of *The Melody Lingers On*, a silly romantic novel by Lowell Brentano. Perhaps she did not acknowledge writing for which she received no screen credit. When *The Melody Lingers On* was released in 1935, Philip Dunne and Ralph Block were listed as the authors of "screenplay and dialogue." Dunne cannot remember ever seeing the Lillian Hellman script.

Although Hellman retains many of Brentano's characters and much of his plot, the first part of her screenplay concerns a love triangle not found in the novel. Ann Prescott falls in love with Carlo Salvini, a great Italian tenor, but their life together is destroyed when Catherine, his former mistress, murders him. The second part of the screenplay concentrates on Ann, whose proximity to Carlo excites the police's suspicion. She is arrested and tried for Carlo's murder, but Catherine's suicide helps to clear Ann, and the next part of the story centers on Ann's efforts to recover her son by Carlo. Since Ann and Carlo have lived in sin, she has been declared an unfit mother. Her life becomes dedicated to her son and his singing career which she hopes will compensate for her lover's death. It is a trite story but an interesting episode in Hellman's biography, for the scenarist makes Ann into an adult figure—much more mature than Brentano's naive victim. Hellman's Ann knows from the beginning that Carlo will never marry her, but through the force of her devotion and will she is able to break Carlo of his lady's-man lifestyle. It would be misleading to push too many parallels between Hellman's life and this screenplay, but the young woman falling in love with a great artist, a very handsome lady's man, in a knowing, determined fashion is the story of Hellman and Hammett that many of her friends still tell. Ann's subsequent devotion to the legend of Carlo Salvini is a sentimentalized version of what Hellman would later do with Hammett. If the screenplay did not fully satisfy Edward Small—even after Hellman submitted revisions on January 12, 16, and 17, 1935—it is probably because the extremely sentimental plot of the novel still dominated Hellman's writing. Dunne and Block took Hellman a step further by making Ann a feisty, flirtatious, and slightly cynical character—although reviewers still complained about the highly sentimental plot.

By the end of January 1935, Hellman had accepted Sam Goldwyn's handsome offer of $2,500 a week, making her one of the highest paid screenwriters in Hollywood. In *Pentimento*, she writes of this powerful, independent producer with much affection. "Lily and people who worked over there for Goldwyn had more fun just making jokes," Albert Hackett remembers. Goldwyn's staff would sit around and think up "Goldwynisms," those peculiar inversions of speech ("include me out") that so delighted writers. Once somebody repeated one of these Goldwynisms, and Hellman put her claim in: "that was my joke on Goldwyn. I made that up." But above all, Goldwyn wanted to make good pictures and he wanted to make money. He had risen from a rough background and from poverty, and he aspired to a place in an affluent, cultured world. He wanted to treat writers well, and had even reserved a table for them in his studio commissary which served excellent food prepared by a fine chef.

Lillian Hellman baffled Sam Goldwyn. He was not used to writers who were not impressed by his wealth. She was to earn more than $125 thousand from *The Children's Hour* and spend it quickly, but the profits from the play must certainly have strengthened her self-assurance. She liked Goldwyn's offers of big money, but she could walk away from a project that did not suit her, especially when it involved a director like Sidney Franklin, who consulted with his card-playing buddies about revisions of her script. When she left Hollywood in disgust after several weeks of inconclusive story conferences, Goldwyn offered her a new contract, stipulating that she would have considerable independence in deciding which movie properties to work on. Hellman usually got along well with Goldwyn, but sometimes they argued and she would tell him to "fuck himself." In *Pentimento* she suggests she was valuable to him "for reasons he did not understand." That she seemed unattainable made it all the more desirable to have her on his payroll. Goldwyn did not like "aggressive females," but he was fascinated by this lady who could talk tough and deliver good scripts on schedule. Philip Dunne tells the story of the time Hellman, Dottie Parker, and her husband Alan Campbell were all working for Goldwyn, who was in an expansive mood at lunch. "You know I'm delighted with the work that's being done. From now on I'm going to hire nothing but women writers," Goldwyn vowed. Then he noticed Alan and said, "But if one wants to bring her husband along, that's okay too!"

Sam Marx goes so far as to say Hellman dominated Goldwyn. When she complained about screenwriter Virginia Kellogg ("her fucking typewriter distracts me. . . . She never stops to *think!*"), Goldwyn got rid of Kellogg, and the script she was working on "was abandoned without a trace of explanation or compassion," according to Marx. He remembers her as the only woman in an all-male group—laughing, joking, drinking, and gambling with them.

Hellman always called the producer "Mr. Goldwyn," as if to maintain her distance and her independence. Goldwyn was just one of several paternalistic Hollywood moguls who viewed making movies as a family enterprise. He was suspicious of unions, of any organization representing employees who should have been personally loyal to him. The heads of Hollywood studios had established the Academy of Motion Picture Arts and Sciences on May 11, 1927, as a way of retaining their absolute power. It was a company union designed to forestall the formation of collective bargaining agreements that would have given writers, directors, actors, and technicians some say over their working conditions. Right from the beginning of her Hollywood career, Hellman took up with Dorothy Parker, Frances and Albert Hackett, and other screenwriters who found in unionization a "sense of commitment and common destiny they had never before shared."

In reflecting upon these early Hollywood years, Hellman noted that "Roosevelt gave you a feeling that you had something to do with your government, something to do with better conditions for yourself and other people." There is no doubt that she was in a militant mood. "Lil talks revolution," Kober remarked in his diary on May 6, 1935. Hellman even frightened her fellow writers because she was so aggressive, "so powerful in her speech—saying nuts" to the movie producers, as Albert Hackett remembers so well. "She was somebody wonderful to have on your side, but then you were afraid she'd go too far," he concludes. Hellman campaigned for the passage of the Wagner Act, which affirmed the right of employees to engage in collective bargaining and prohibited employers from discriminating against union members. It was voted into law by Congress on July 5, 1935. However, Goldwyn and the other producers would not obey the Wagner Act until its constitutionality had been reviewed by the Supreme Court.

By the summer of 1936, Hellman was deeply involved in an organizing drive for the Screen Writers Guild (SWG). Maurice Rapf, a junior writer at MGM, later recalled how impressed he was with Hellman, this "famous lady writer," coming into his cramped little office "wearing one of her extraordinary hats, and chain smoking," and personally asking him to become an SWG member. A rival organization, Screen Playwrights (SP), was formed with the aid of the producers, and the SWG then had to contend with separate deals offered to struggling screenwriters if they would abandon their loyalties to the militant union. Even when the SWG had apparently failed, underground organizing efforts continued, with Hellman, Hammett, Parker, and other writers providing their homes as meeting places. By April 12, 1937, when the Supreme

Court declared the Wagner Act constitutional, Hellman and many others had been able to sustain the political will of their cause while the SP failed to negotiate a contract with the producers.

Never one to relish talking about her own work for the stage and screen, Hellman leaves the impression in her memoirs that this work did not mean much to her. Certainly she talked about movies with her fellow screenwriters. One might say "nice job" or "you've done it again!" But in general the writers did not become too specific about another writer's work, Philip Dunne recalls. Indeed, in *Pentimento* Hellman dwells on her amusing side adventures in Hollywood—like rolling condoms to fit into small matchboxes as a practical joke on director Henry C. Potter, a "prep-school handsome, respectable, grandson of a bishop." Hellman meant to stay only a month in Hollywood but remained for six. Goldwyn listened to her ideas, and she became caught up in the process of making movies.

In *Pentimento*, Hellman calls *The Dark Angel*, her first project for Goldwyn, "an old silly." It had been a stage play and then a silent film about a World War I British romance. In the play, Captain Hilary Trent and his beloved Kitty Fahnestock are unable to marry in time of war but pledge to be faithful to each other. Kitty, however, has a premonition, an allegorical dream that tells her Hilary will meet the angel of death. When he does not return from the war, she makes plans to marry Gerald Shannon. Hilary, in fact, has been blinded and retires to a cottage, where Kitty discovers him. He relieves her of her divided feelings by encouraging her to marry Gerald. In the silent film, Kitty stays with Hilary when she realizes her love for him has never diminished.

Hellman imposed her own vision on this tearjerker by elaborating on the central elements of *The Children's Hour*: the love triangle and familial relationships. In an opening scene that occurs ten years before the war, Gerald Shannon (Herbert Marshall), Alan Trent (Fredric March), and Kitty Vane (Merle Oberon) are shown as childhood friends. Gerald lives next door to Kitty, and Alan and Gerald are cousins. Through a silly misunderstanding, Gerald comes to believe a report that Alan has been unfaithful to his fiancée, Kitty, and when Alan refuses to explain himself to Gerald, hard feelings develop between the two men. At the front, Gerald, now Alan's commanding officer, will not permit him a leave because he suspects Alan will visit "the other woman." Blinded in action, Alan is visited after the war by Gerald, who has been informed of his cousin's whereabouts by a doctor who knows of Alan's love for Kitty. In realizing the mistake he has made about his cousin's character, Gerald gives up Kitty and leads her back to Alan.

Kitty's plight and predilections for two men may have exercised some appeal for Hellman, who liked having both Kober and Hammett at her side. Although Kitty must choose between Gerald Shannon and Alan Trent, she would prefer to have both of them remain close to her. Near the beginning of the film, with Alan at her side, she announces her engagement to Gerald. Then, looking at Gerald, and knowing how deeply hurt he has been by her favoring of Alan, she affirms, "We shall all be together—always—now."

In Hellman's version of *The Dark Angel*, the personalities of the characters become paramount; she concentrates an ironic eye on people who are closely related to each other and yet clearly mistaken about each other's motivations. In *The Children's Hour*, trouble is caused by a busybody aunt and a child who overhears that aunt. In the play, words weigh heavily in convicting the two teachers. In *The Dark Angel*, Gerald takes on faith eyewitness testimony that Alan has been *seen* deceiving Kitty with another woman. In other words, in terms of both plot and technique, Hellman had no apparent trouble in making the transition to screenwriting—perhaps as a result of Goldwyn's fine ensemble of experienced professionals: screenwriter Mordaunt Shairp, director Sidney Franklin, and cinematographer Gregg Toland.

Reviews of *The Dark Angel*, which was released in September 1935, were enthusiastic, and Hellman must have realized that even an "old silly" could be shaped into serious themes and that her career, in both Hollywood and New York, could have some continuity. Of course, the film is sentimental and trite, but it is also understated. Sparely written scenes depend on tactful cinematography and acting. Hellman's own tendency to say too much, to moralize, is kept in check by the need to overlap sounds and images. Dissolves and cuts keep the story moving and show simultaneously the feelings of characters in different settings and times—at home and at the front, in childhood and in adulthood.

This filmic play with time and space and with persons and locations—in which chronology counts for very little and facts are rarely separate, discrete entities—is exactly what readers relish in

Hellman's prose. Her memoirs are constantly fusing disparate moments—is there any chapter of her life in which she is not several ages at once? One episode recalls another before or after it because of an image or sound she decides to follow with the camera of her mind. Film taught her to be artful about her work and her life at the same time, and it became a principle of her memoirs not to revive her career, like a stage play, but to remake it, like a film.

In June 1935, on her way to New York from Hollywood, a dust storm forced Hellman's plane to land in Albuquerque, New Mexico. She had just completed her work on *The Dark Angel* and she was looking forward to *These Three*, her screen adaptation of *The Children's Hour*, which was still running on Broadway. Ralph Ingersoll was also returning to New York after finishing a successful assignment for *Fortune* magazine, and he had just accepted a promotion as general manager of *Fortune*. In a euphoric mood and with his senses heightened by the champagne he had drunk to celebrate his success, Ingersoll stepped out onto the tarmac and saw illuminated by the green-and-white beacon lights a blonde woman whose face interested him. She was not pretty and her name, Lillian Hellman, meant nothing to him. She was frankly irritated by his ignorance but impressed with his career as managing editor of the *New Yorker* and then of *Fortune*.

At a restaurant hotel provided by the airline, Hellman and Ingersoll talked about their lives. She told him about her plans for *These Three* and about *Days to Come*, her next play, and he spoke of his efforts to write a novel and his rise in Henry Luce's publishing empire. As Ingersoll remembered it, their physical attraction was immediate and intense; they took it "for granted" and went up to Hellman's room as soon as it was ready—even forgetting to close the door until one of them noticed an astonished face observing their lovemaking. Their passionate, angry, and often comical affair continued throughout the next year with frequent interruptions because of Hellman's devotion to Hammett and Ingersoll's concern for his tubercular wife, with whom he "could not have normal sexual relations." Very early on when Ingersoll first met her, Hellman was very put out with Hammett. He had gone bust and she had given him five thousand dollars "to stay alive." He had come back a week later broke again, and she was furious. When she roared at him, demanding to know what he had done with the money, he said, "I went to a whorehouse, found a pretty girl and gave it to her." Hellman called him a "son of a bitch" and beat him. Ingersoll and Hellman were "abrasive, ambitious, and egocentric," to use the words Roy Hoopes applies to Ingersoll alone. It is not surprising that their love, and later their friendship, would be stormy.

On Tuesday, July 9, 1935, Kober heard from Sid Perelman about "the shocking story of Dash & Laura." Dash had hired a call girl to appear naked in Sid's hotel bathroom, and Laura, Sid's wife, had discovered her husband and the woman "flagrante delicto" and had run off with Dash. Kober was sympathetic to Sid's decision to leave his job and Laura. To Kober, Hammett was "absolutely cheap and despicable & probably proud of it too." After helping Sid move from his hotel to an apartment, Kober observed Hellman that night at "21." Not feeling well, she walked out. Was it because of Hammett? Kober wondered. Sid had told him that Hellman and Hammett were planning to get married— "so nice for Lil," the diarist wryly concluded. By Friday, Laura had gone back to her husband. "How like my own marriage & how Lil now experiences the heartaches I felt—and I'm sorry for her, too," mused Kober. The Dash-Laura liaison lasted less than a week, but it was a subject Sid and Hellman never touched. In fact, she was so angry at Sid for telling her about Dash and Laura that she refused to speak to him for an entire year. She had never thought much of the Perelman marriage. Soon she would use its failings as material for a play.

Kober saw a good deal of Hellman in New York that summer, and together they enjoyed long talks, dinners, socializing with the Shumlins, and a party at the Maxine Elliott Theatre celebrating three hundred performances of *The Children's Hour*. However, he did tire of the heavy drinking, of "this game which seems to have taken possession of the place." He was annoyed at Hellman for getting into a petty quarrel, but he succeeded in comforting her and himself, giving a wink, in his diary, to what was apparently a sexual liaison, repeated the next evening after a party at the Gershwins. In his end-of-year diary summation, he would refer to these brief erotic interludes as "hits on the wing." The next day, July 23, she had to leave, and she did so in a fashion that showed him she could not be his—"the Hammett influence heavily seen in the careless, sweeping way in which her money is thrown around." Later, in September, he would get a good look at her New York apartment and conclude she had "successfully washed every last trace of years with me away."

Back in Hollywood, Hellman wrote to Kober congratulating him on the publication of *Thunder Over the Bronx*, a collection of his *New Yorker* stories. Hammett was "very excited" and "impressed" with it. She was lonely and she missed Kober. As so often in her letters to him, she was bolstering his ego and encouraging him to get on with his play. She referred to several good reviews and promising sales of *Thunder Over the Bronx* and suggested he should have more confidence in his own abilities. She brought Kober up-to-date on their friends and mentioned having gone to the Trocadero, a favorite night spot, with the Wylers. William Wyler was about to direct *These Three*. Work on the script was going slowly, in part because she was acting as "a kind of producer on it." She was angry about having spent three hours at a meeting talking Miriam Hopkins into playing the part of Martha. Goldwyn and Hopkins kept interrupting each other, to Hellman's great irritation. She was puzzled by the solicitude Goldwyn showed toward her. She was certain he had discovered she was "his illegitimate child by Hilda Wilinchowski in Minsk," she told Kober. He promised her next assignment would depend on her liking the picture. She thought it was "all very screwy."

Hellman could not hope to preserve her play's concern with lesbianism for a movie audience, but she knew that Goldwyn, with a reputation for accomplishing "the impossible," wanted to find a way to bring such a notorious stage success to the screen. His purchase of the rights to *The Children's Hour* for fifty thousand dollars had amused and puzzled Hollywood, for he had agreed to the following restrictions set down by Joseph Breen of the Hays Office, Hollywood's self-imposed censorship board: To not use the title of the play or make any reference, "directly or indirectly, in advertising or exploitation of the picture, to the stage play; and to remove from the finished production "all possible suggestions of lesbianism and any other matter which is likely to prove objectionable." It has often been said that Hellman sanitized her play and tacked on a happy ending for the movies; but in fact, she sold Goldwyn and Wyler on a script that preserved the principal theme of *The Children's Hour*—the power of a big lie—and the story of the love triangle was resolved better in the movie than in the play.

Both Goldwyn and Wyler were impressed with the integrity of Hellman's screenplay. She made no apology for changing *The Children's Hour*; on the contrary, she was enthused about transforming it into a film. There was a tough-minded quality in her approach that implied there was nothing sacrosanct about the play. *These Three* would have a life of its own; the movie would be made on its own terms. Years later, in a *Paris Review* interview, Hellman affirmed the artistic value of film scripts. She never apologized for her Hollywood work—as did many New York artists who clung to their reverence for the legitimate stage or novelists who refused to regard screenplays as literary achievements.

Hellman's first decision in altering *The Children's Hour* had to do with putting the focus immediately on Karen and Martha. In a thirteen-page treatment received by Breen's office on July 24, 1935, the initial setting was shifted to a small English village. Martha becomes a distant cousin of Karen's family and their ward when her father unexpectedly dies, leaving her only one hundred pounds a year. The two girls were like sisters as they grew up together, sharing the same governess, the same schools, the same friends and pleasures. But then Karen's father dies, "a wreck from the [First World] war," and his death so disturbs Karen's mother that she dies shortly after her husband. Mrs. Mortar is their flighty chaperon, the black sheep of the family because of her theater career, which has dwindled "for lack of talent." Not equipped for business or professional life, the two girls decide to start a school in America, where they have friends and where their English background will give them a certain cachet. From that point, the treatment follows the outlines of *The Children's Hour*.

Whether Hellman really intended to start the film this way or was writing a treatment to obtain Breen's approval is not clear. She may have realized that in her haste to establish Karen's and Martha's relationship, her story went too far into the past. In the completed screenplay, the action moves much more quickly and is a model of efficient, cinematic exposition. Instead of a schoolroom scene with adolescent girls, Hellman begins with the two women graduating from college. Amidst the seniors congratulating one another and greeting their families, Karen (Merle Oberon) and Martha (Miriam Hopkins) walk alone, virtually unacknowledged. They are obviously more important to each other than to their classmates, and they are disturbed by the sudden appearance of Martha's aunt, Lily Mortar. Karen starts to walk away from the disagreeable relative, but Martha discreetly holds on to her friend's sleeve so that they can suffer the boorish Mortar together.

This shrewdly directed scene establishes the bond between Karen and Martha, their isolation from others, and the disturbing entrance of a third party; the scene foreshadows their tragic fate. Mortar's overbearing attitude toward Martha is irritating and somehow troubling, even though she is presented as an apparently trivial, humorous figure. In their dormitory room following graduation, the two women muse over an uncertain future. Martha will teach somewhere. Karen has no family left—just a bit of land and a farmhouse. Casting about for likely plans of action, Karen suddenly importunes her friend to help her turn the old property into a school: "Martha, take a chance with me and come." It is a kind of proposal—a romantic one, in the sense that Martha realizes how much hard work will be involved in making Karen's vision a reality. Although there is no hint of a sexual attraction between the women, Karen has, in a manner of speaking, pressed a suit upon Martha. They become wedded to the idea of making a success of the school and of themselves as a couple.

That we are to think of Karen and Martha as a couple—as women deeply committed to each other—is emphasized in their arrival at the dilapidated farmhouse. Discouraged by its sad state of disrepair, they are about to abandon their plans for the school when the sound of shingles being tossed off the roof draws their attention to a bizarre figure crawling out of a window wearing, they later learn, bee-keeper's gear. It is Dr. Joe Cardin (Joel McCrea), a genial man who identifies himself as their neighbor. Although he is very friendly, the women are wary and even a bit rude to him. Not at all like Lily Mortar, he is still a disturbing third party. They act as if he were an alien but eventually warm up to him, reluctantly accepting his offer of sandwiches and eventually trusting him to help with the restoration of the farmhouse.

A quick succession of shots framing Karen in a window she is cleaning and Martha pulling off old wallpaper mimic the speed with which these industrious women happily take hold of their new career. The first disturbing sign of a division between them comes when Martha takes off her glasses and straightens herself up as she sees Joe on his way to help with the house. She makes a point of meeting him first and of telling him, "we missed you yesterday." Then she waxes poetic about the old newspaper on the walls she has just uncovered describing the opening of the

Brooklyn Bridge, "two great cities united." Joe is his usual friendly self, but he momentarily looks away from Martha as if he is not entirely enthralled with her flowery speech. Almost immediately, Karen calls him for help and he abruptly leaves Martha. The camera lingers a moment on Martha: she is disconcerted and a little disappointed—perhaps because she has tried too hard with Joe. Miriam Hopkins plays Martha subtly, making her character first thoughtful, then less animated, and finally very still. Martha has just experienced the premonition of a great pain: she will not have Joe for herself.

From the very beginning of the film, Karen has been the more understated of the two women. She does not express her dislike of Lily Mortar; she simply walks away. Although she likes Joe, she will not tell him so. Unlike Martha, Karen seems entirely independent. As a result, Joe enjoys pursuing her and feels he must declare his heart, for she is a women he must win. Indeed, at one point he gets quite angry and frustrated because she will not passively await his proposal. But as soon as he manages to express his love, she accepts him without any fuss or florid speeches.

It seems that nearly half of the film is taken up with establishing this love triangle. As an exploration of men and women in love, *These Three* is far superior to *The Children's Hour*. In the play, the emotions of childhood are meant to predominate and the mature complexity of Karen's, Martha's, and Joe's feelings is never clearly dramatized. In the film, the tensions in the triangle shift subtly from moment to moment without any one of the threesome predominating. If Martha is frustrated with Joe, then Joe is frustrated with Karen. Karen, in turn, is torn between her affection for Martha and Joe.

Lily Mortar arrives to upset the delicate equilibrium of the triangle. Instead of accusing her niece of an "unnatural" attachment to Karen, as in the play, she implies that Martha and Joe are having an affair. At this point, *These Three*, with some reassignment of dialogue, follows the direction of *The Children's Hour*. The young student Mary's (Bonita Granville) malevolence is aroused by school gossip concerning a night Joe spent in Martha's room. She exaggerates that incident into an enormous lie that provokes her grandmother, Amelia Tilford (Alma Kruger), to make certain that all of the children are removed from the school. Mary's character is no less vicious in the film than in the play, but she has been introduced so much later in *These Three* that she is not allowed to dominate the action.

In place of the bleak lines that open act three of the play, the film, in a long shot, frames Martha and Karen in a window looking out at a world to which they now have no connection. As Martha, sitting in an easy chair, distantly gazes toward the window, the camera pulls back and away from this isolated couple—far more isolated now than they were at the beginning of the film. As if to recall their innocent beginning, Martha catches hold of Karen's hand in sympathy with Karen's admission that she did indeed wonder if Martha and Joe had had an affair. Once it is proven that Mary has lied, Martha leaves town, sending a message to Karen encouraging her to follow Joe—whose career was ruined in the court case against Mrs. Tilford—to Vienna where he has resumed his hospital work. The price for staying with Karen, Martha knows, is ostracism by the community.

These Three was released in March of 1936, and reviews of the film were positive and enthusiastic. A few critics lamented the absence of the lesbianism charge, but others favored the film over the play—a highly unusual judgment, especially since *The Children's Hour* was still playing on Broadway. Most films suffered when compared to their stage originals, but *These Three* was received as a work in its own right. If it was sentimental and if it lacked the strident energy of the play, the film was, in some ways, more stirring, mature, and lifelike—in Graham Greene's view: "I have seldom been so moved by a fiction film as by *These Three*."

1935 was a Hollywood year for Hellman. On September 25, she gave a lecture at New York University on "The Difference Between Writing a Screen and a Stage Play." She was home in New York for Thanksgiving. Her mother had been ill. Kober had visited Mrs. Hellman on November 21 and thought she was better, but on November 30, Julia Hellman died. It was a deep shock to her husband, who cried every time he spoke of her. Kober was there to help him get through a bad night and make the necessary calls. Kober was profoundly moved by Julia Hellman's remembering him in her will, leaving him ten thousand dollars in trust. Lillian and her father were worn out with making the funeral arrangements, and the next day had a "mild set-to" over Max's concern that they get to the chapel very early "out of respect." At the funeral, a rabbi delivered a short prayer that nevertheless seemed interminable. At the cemetery, everyone watched Julia's casket being lowered into the grave as Kober tossed a lily on it.

As Hellman remarked in her memoirs, she did not realize how much she loved her mother until after she had died. Because Julia Hellman had put up with her husband Max's philandering for years, there was more than a little contempt in the way Lillian brushed aside her mother's concern over her love life. It was Kober, at the moment, who felt intensely Julia's kindness and sweetness. And he wanted to comfort Hellman over the loss she had yet to truly acknowledge. Although he could not spend New Year's Eve with her, Hellman, en route by train to Los Angeles, sent him a telegram from Chicago, commemorating the tenth anniversary of their marriage and expressing her "love and affection" for him.

Hellman spent a few months in Hollywood working on a new play, but in the early spring she decided to spend three or four weeks in Ohio, traveling between Cincinnati and Cleveland. It was an "atmosphere tour" of small communities that "served as a sort of sop to her professional conscience." She was going to set her next play in a small Ohio town beset by labor troubles, and she wanted to "see what the people looked like and how they spoke." She had been thinking about this play for perhaps five or six years, long before writing *The Children's Hour*, but it may have been her union-organizing activity in Hollywood that finally spurred her to finish the work within a period of eight months.

On May 30, Kober recorded in his diary that Hellman was leaving for Cuba on June 4 in order "to get away from it all." To him, it seemed "a strange place to go this time of year." She fretted over Hammett's sickness, and confided to Kober her fear over the "warts"—presumably a reference to one of Hammett's frequent bouts with venereal disease. After securing an apartment at 14 East Seventy-fifth Street in New York, Hellman sailed for Havana. The trip must have worked like a tonic, for Kober reported receiving a wonderful letter from her on June 24. He marveled at the "naturalness" of her writing and the "quick humor of her cracks." She labored on the play before returning on the Grace Liner *Santa Elena* on June 30, 1936. A photograph and caption announcing her arrival in the city mentions that after completing the play, she will resume her screenwriting career. In the photograph she looks elegant. A fur piece sweeps around her upper body and part way down her back, and a large hat is tilted at a stylish angle, contributing to her smart appearance. She seems rested and comfortable after her cruise. A confident and serene writer—arms folded, smiling, and gazing forthrightly ahead—she is completely at ease in front of the camera.

In fact, Hellman, as usual, was struggling with her stage work and her triangulated love life. Even Kober, who at this point did not figure as a lover, felt the force of her seductive powers.

> Note from Lil this morning wondering why I don't write & she does this trick quite often putting guiltless one on the defensive. I find I miss her letters & that I can't quite stop thinking of her. She no longer is the actual person she was, but a character in my mind & this picture helped by her letters so that when I fail to receive them I'm disturbed.

As Ralph Ingersoll put it, she could not let go of anyone who had been close to her.

The summer was to be spent in a cottage on Tavern Island, off the coast of Norwalk, Connecticut, where along with Hammett she would rest and revise the play. Ralph Ingersoll was still seeing Hellman, although their affair had cooled. He thought of Hammett as a rival for Hellman's love, but Hammett was so detached he would not compete. Ingersoll never got to know him well and called him "the most silent man I ever knew." One weekend, with Herman Shumlin and Kober also present, Ingersoll went through an emotional crisis. He was intimidated by these articulate people and unable to sleep with Hellman, unable to find at least some reassurance to mend his bruised ego. Like Hellman, he was given to strong opinions, and he had been arguing with her for days about fascism, communism, capitalism, and the Spanish Civil War, which had begun with Franco's revolt against the Republican government in July. Their words were like blows, with Hellman "screaming virtually one whole night that he was 'an anti-Semitic son of a bitch.' " In her usual uncompromising fashion, she listed the faults of capitalism and socialism and claimed that one must make a choice between the two. "God damn it, no!" replied Ingersoll, who wanted "to take the best of capitalism and communism, while avoiding their faults." She completely unnerved him, and that weekend, the affair ended for good. They swore never to see each other again, then broke their vows and continued to quarrel. Ingersoll was grateful to her for challenging his values, and he attributed his resolution to establish his own radical publication, *PM*, to the days of raging debates with Hellman that "shook [him] out of a monolithic complacency." He even invested five thousand dollars in *Days to Come*.

Acquiescence to the status quo infuriated Lillian Hellman. The argument with Ingersoll was similar to what Kober had observed a year earlier in a discussion of communism:

> Sid [Perelman] swinging from side to side with simian agility & Lil who has just found the cause speaks like expert & like all those eloquent dogmatists will not allow anyone else to think or listen to what is being said.

Hellman wanted to write about a community unable to come to terms with the very issues of labor and capital that she had fought over with Ralph Ingersoll. On Tavern Island, she read Kober part of her new work. He was "amazed at her dramatic skill" and looked forward to "an exciting and interesting play. She has another act to do & I feel that these first two build up beautifully toward it." Three weeks later, on September 20, she completed a draft of the third act.

Hellman's spring trip to Ohio had been part of her attempt to convince herself of the authenticity of what she was writing. In her extensive notes for the play, she recorded her observations of a brush factory. Wages, working conditions, and personal impressions of the people she had seen were all thoroughly described. She made lists of characters, considered their stage movements, and set down details about minor figures. She entertained changing the names of characters and of the town, and critiqued each act of the play.

Hellman's early drafts concentrated on the strike in the Rodman factory, not on the troubled marriage of the factory owner. Several of her proposed titles for the play—all of them drawn from *Isaiah* and *Ecclesiastes*—reflected her concern to anchor her drama to the biblical question: "What profit hath he that worketh in that wherein he laboreth?" In *Ecclesiastes*, the accumulation of capital, the solidarity of friends and family, and the acquisition of all of the things that mean wealth to the laborer are destroyed by "vanity and vexation of spirit." No man can "rejoice in his own works . . . for who shall bring him to see what shall be after him." The title of the play Hellman finally settled on, *Days to Come*, follows *Ecclesiastes* in predicting the inescapable discontent of an acquisitive society: "All the labor of man is for his mouth, and yet the appetite is not filled." An evil time can fall suddenly upon the richest man, *Ecclesiastes* warns: "time and chance happeneth to them all."

Although Callom, Ohio, the town in Hellman's play, and Hollywood, California, did not seem to have much in common, they were both provincial communities torn by labor disputes. On March 8, 1933, just two years before Lillian Hellman arrived in Hollywood to work for Sam Goldwyn, the movie industry faced a crisis. Except for MGM, the studios could not meet their payrolls. Wage cuts of between 25 percent and 50 percent—depending on the level of the employee's salary—were put into effect for an eight-week period while studios attempted to remedy their cash-flow problems. The one organized group of workers, the International Alliance of Theatrical Stage Employees (IATSE), threatened a strike, never did accept the pay cut, and forced the producers into negotiations that resulted in reductions in salary only for the highest-paid employees. As Nancy Lynn Schwartz concludes in her book *The Hollywood Writers' Wars*, the wage cuts taught motion picture employees "that producers didn't think contracts were sacred. And they saw the protection that had rendered IATSE unions immune to any tampering with salaries. It was time to unionize." After 1933, Hollywood was no longer the province of a paternalistic, family-owned movie industry where a studio executive like Carl Laemmle would be called "Uncle" by his employees. A significant number of studio employees still thought in terms of personal loyalty to their bosses or resisted the idea of collective bargaining, but it was abundantly clear that Hollywood had become just another part of corporate America that was beholden to bankers and Wall Street firms that had lent the money for the studios to stay in business.

In *Days to Come*, Andrew Rodman, the third-generation owner of a brush factory, faces the same dilemma as the studio executives: loss of control over his business and his community. On the one hand, he is pressured by bankers to whom he owes money; on the other hand, he has to contend with Leo Whalen, the union organizer brought into town to direct the striking workers. Irving Thalberg, head of production at MGM, told a group of screenwriters what a "great deal" they had and how the producers would not tolerate unionization, which he said was tantamount to turning their industry over to "outside interests." Similarly, Rodman imagines Callom, Ohio, as a self-contained community with interests identical to his own. From the high point of Tucker's Road he likes to look down on the town: "It always looks so scrubbed and clean and I thought the way I used to, when I was a kid: that I could stop in any house and have a good breakfast and they'd be glad to see me." This naive view of capital and labor is related to the way a Thalberg or an L. B. Mayer sentimentalized Hollywood. Like many of the screenwriters who admired Thalberg and expected him to resolve the labor dispute, Andrew Rodman's workers, led by Thomas Firth, expect their employer to settle the strike. Leo Whalen is the character who comes closest to embodying Hellman's own hardheaded views. He is not given to long speeches, but his radical position is clear: the factory will have to make fewer kinds of brushes and standardize its products, and the workers will bargain for jobs that require less skill. Whalen refuses to emotionalize the workers' plight or to commiserate with the difficult choices Rodman must make to save his company, but Whalen cannot prevent the strike from turning violent once the strikebreakers are deputized and provoke the strikers into defending not just their jobs but their very place in the community.

In many ways, *Days to Come* is a brilliant reflection on Hellman's organizing experience in Hollywood and on the crisis of labor-management relations during the Depression. Under the Roosevelt administration the labor movement had been invigorated, with union membership doubling within the first five years of the New Deal—in spite of violent attacks on unions and various union-busting tactics. In 1934, there were more strikes in Ohio than in any year since 1920, and in New York City, several plays dealing with the question of labor were running. Hellman did not overburden *Days to Come* with labor history, but her characters' references to wage rates, to concerns about immigrant workers, and to how strikes are broken by management demonstrate her careful research.

One quotation from *Isaiah* seems to have guided Hellman in creating Callom, Ohio: "How is the *faithful city* become a harlot! It was full of judgement; righteousness lodged in it; but now murderers." In *Days to Come*, Andrew Rodman reluctantly agrees to import strikebreakers who are to work in his factory. Among these men are two criminals, one of whom murders the other. The murdered man is then dumped upon the doorstep of Leo Whalen, to implicate him in the crime and to provide the excuse for attacking the union. More important, Rodman's decision to rely on strikebreakers corrupts the atmosphere of the community; it becomes no more than a company town—like "Poisonville" in Hammett's novel *Red Harvest*.

There is no question that Hellman was writing from Hammett's experience as well as from her own. He had taken part in breaking the IWW Anaconda strike in 1920–21. Years later, he regretted his actions and criticized Hellman for her admiration of her Uncle Willy, a man who worked for a company that exploited and murdered its workers. Comparing himself to Willy, Hammett noted, "I was in that racket for a lot of years and I don't like it." Although a great deal has been made of Hammett's glorifying in his Pinkerton past and of Hellman's relishing his stories about detective work, there can be little doubt that he was deeply ashamed of having been a company man.

Days to Come has a Marxist orientation insofar as the conflict between labor and capital is inevitable. Nineteenth-century paternalism and capitalism have become outmoded; the old economy is breaking down and cannot be repaired by resurrecting feelings of fellowship. There is no such thing any longer as a community of interests. Workers will have to organize and to struggle for their rights. But this Marxism is tempered by a tragic, biblical vision of history. It is not at all clear in the play that the working class will triumph; the working class is not idealized or seen as somehow in the vanguard of history. Indeed, no working-class mentality emerges in the play, and years later, Hellman would remark on how *Days to Come* prophesied the latter-day conservatism of the labor movement.

In *Days to Come*, it is a moral argument, not a political one, that Hellman makes. Andrew Rodman has let down not only his workers but his wife Julie and his whole family. He is personally and politically impotent. In sexual frustration, Julie turns first to her husband's attorney, Henry Ellicott, and then to the more powerful Leo Whalen, but in each case she has only the vaguest idea of what she wants. Andrew's sister Cora is immature and terrified of sex, and her hysterical prudishness, her playing with neatly arranged glass figurines, is meant to symbolize how far removed the entire Rodman household is from the realities of love, work, and the fight for decent moral and economic standards of living.

Cora is a puzzle in the play. She appears sporadically and is always complaining. She is tormented, however, by the same issues that confuse Andrew and the other characters. What does the strike mean, and on what terms will capital and labor be able to coexist? She does not know how to begin to live her own life. She exemplifies critic Joseph Wood Krutch's observation that Hellman is "a specialist in hate and frustration, a student of helpless rage. . . ." In her introduction to *Six Plays*, Hellman admits "I knew a woman like Cora and I hated her." Cora's futility seems to have been borrowed from Laura Perelman. Like Cora, Perelman loved "fragile miniature objects." According to Dorothy Herrman, Perelman's home in Bucks County, Pennsylvania, "was filled with over a hundred tiny china dogs and cats." Absolutely obsessed with her brother Nathanael West, just as Cora is with her brother Andrew, Perelman could not seem to define any purpose for her own life. In her diary, Perelman deplored the lethargy that seemed characteristic of both her brother and herself; both of them depended on Sid Perelman for social contacts. As in *Days to Come*, brother and sister had no verve or stamina, and Perelman, like Cora, felt stultified by her life as a housewife. She felt trapped. In her boredom, Perelman—like her stage self—lashed out.

Pervading the whole atmosphere of the play is Andrew Rodman's weary acceptance of defeat; he sounds almost like the voice of *Ecclesiastes*, except that Andrew's words have none of the vigor of that biblical text. He fails to judge people: he is all too tolerant of his wife's unfaithfulness, his sister's paranoia, and his own incompetence. *Days to Come* might have worked as a novel exploring the psychological complexity of its characters. As a play, it is static and diffuse. Andrew, in particular, is paralyzed. Near the end of the play, he confesses, "I don't know where I stand anymore."

The final draft of *Days to Come* was written at 90 Cleveland Lane in Princeton, New Jersey, where Hammett had rented a Colonial-style, five-bay, three-floor, seventeen-room house in the fall of 1936. Isolated near the end of a street that contained only a few homes, it seemed the ideal place for Hammett to get away from New York City and Hollywood, sober up, work on a new novel, and be near Hellman as she readied *Days to Come* for its Broadway opening in mid-December. The house (circa 1830) had been moved in 1925 from busy Nassau Street and was now situated in the country. It was built for quiet, genteel people accustomed to servants, who could be easily and unobtrusively accommodated on the third floor. Years later, Hellman remembered that the house was unusually furnished with "lovely Empire and regency pieces." The collection of furnishings—a high-boy with Napoleonic insignia, portraits of Napoleon, doorways from a Jerome Bonaparte house, and other reproductions of the Empire style—had been acquired by a Princeton professor, William Milligan Sloane, author of a famous biography of Napoleon, and added to by his son, the owner of 90 Cleveland Lane who rented the house to Hammett while the Sloane family was spending the academic year in New York.

In *Pentimento*, Hellman makes a point of mentioning this brief playwriting period in Princeton without divulging how the house and *Days to Come* are connected. When 90 Cleveland Lane's current owner, L. Scott Bailey, wrote to her in 1969 about her memories of the house, she was quite vague, but in a subsequent phone call to her he learned that she regarded her Princeton days as unhappy and unproductive. It was the site, she said, of her "only failure."

Things got out of hand quickly in Princeton, and much of the sense of thwarted purpose, sexual frustration, and infidelity tormenting the characters in *Days to Come* paralleled the Hellman-Hammett relationship. They were lovers with separate bedrooms and separate lives, with Hellman often away in New York and Hammett free to indulge his appetites.

Shortly after the school year started, Frank Severance, a member of the English Club at Princeton, asked his friend, Thomas H. Wolf, to accompany him one evening out to Hammett's house to see if the writer would be willing to speak on campus. They arrived at 90 Cleveland Lane at dusk. The house was set back from the street, and Wolf remembers "a threesome coming down the path: Hammett, Hellman, and a large brown poodle. Hers, I'm quite sure." Although the students did not want to intrude—they had not called ahead—Hammett was insistent that they come in, which they did. They started talking and drinking, and the next thing Wolf knew it was morning and he had a "Godawful hangover."

In the months that followed, Severance took a number of classmates to the "Hammett *ménage*." The evenings were all of a piece: drinking, dinner, Hammett talking in sentences that always began

"So . . . ," and more drinking. Wolf sensed that "Dash used to bring women down when he was mad at Lillian."

> I remember one particularly whose first name was Prudence—known to him as "Pru." One evening when I arrived, Hammett had a black eye. I asked about it and he replied: "Oh, Pru. So she always wants attention. So she always wants to screw. So, is she sexy? No. She just thinks you can't fuck her without paying attention to her. So I took a paper to bed and did a crossword over her shoulder while I screwed her. So she hit me."

Hammett's behavior seems to have been a trial for everyone in Princeton, and the legend of his stormy stay has grown with the years. In 1936, "town and gown were very much more interlocked than they are now," recalls William M. Sloane, the son of the owner of 90 Cleveland Lane at the time Hammett rented it. Everyone knew everyone else, and stories of Hammett's outrageous behavior spread quickly. He was not the normal kind of neighbor, especially in days when it was still the custom to visit newcomers with a calling card. A lady who lived two houses down from Hammett came over, perhaps a little before noon, and rang his bell. He finally came down, bleary-eyed in his bathrobe, yelling, "What the hell do you want?" She withdrew nervously, explaining she had meant to welcome him, and scooted away. Evidently, Hammett regretted his rudeness and decided to favor his neighbor with a visit. He knocked on her door, and after much waiting she appeared in her nightgown. She accepted his apology graciously but could not resist pointing out to him that it was 1:30 in the morning. "Well, goddam it, those are my calling hours," he said as he stomped back to his house. The incident is indicative of his inability to sustain either his poise or purpose in this period in Princeton.

William M. Sloane was away at school, but he remembers the period of Hammett's residence in the house as a difficult one for his family. Considerable damage was done to the house as a result of Hammett's entertaining. There were cigarette burns in the hardwood floor and a large hole in the living room rug, where a fire had started after some party guests tried to remove embers from a smoky fireplace that would not draw properly. The Sloane family went to considerable trouble in getting Hammett to make restitution for the damage done to the house and furnishings.

The Princeton episode is evocative of dissolute years for both writers that weakened their work. Hellman seemed to associate the incongruities of living in the handsome house with those disheveled days of her relationship with Hammett. They aimed for style, grandeur, but their lives lacked structure, and she came to develop a peculiar guilt over the failure of *Days to Come* that was never quite resolved. She accused herself of not thinking hard enough about the play. She had not done "what the writer must do: kick and fight his way through until the whole is good."

The fall of 1936 was a trial for Hellman in many ways. She was having big fights with her father, who was now living in her apartment. For some unexplained reason, he held a grudge against her. Dash's drinking was getting worse, and Kober reports that she was "very blue & discouraged." He could see how much she leaned on Hammett for help with her writing. Sometimes Shumlin, Hammett, and Kober would get together to discuss the play and to argue over the characters. Yet she coped remarkably well, and there were evenings with Max and Lillian that surpassed in pleasure anything Kober had experienced during their marriage. She was taking preparations for the play calmly. In her place, Kober imagined he would be "mad and fouled by indigestion," and he admired her "dignity and perspective."

On December 4, Kober attended a rehearsal. He began to see structural problems. The first act seemed fine in outline and in presentation of character, but there were bad moments in the second act, and the third seemed uneven and too long. Shumlin seemed very solemn, so it was difficult to talk about the play. Kober supposed that once the actors knew their lines and the action picked up, their performances would not seem so troubled and shallow. Two days later, Kober ran into Hammett, and was drunk, at "21." With the help of Marc Connelly, he took Hammett to his apartment, where Hammett proceeded to read aloud the final act of *Days to Come*. He disapproved of the final curtain, which, he said, would "have to be fixed."

Florence Eldridge,* who played Julie Rodman, remembers that "there was an enormous respect and admiration between Herman

---

*Eldridge would later play Lavinia opposite her husband, Frederic March (Marcus) in the film version of *Another Part of the Forest* (1948).

Shumlin, the director, and Miss Hellman, so that he considered every word of the play sacrosanct, and she considered her director perfect in every respect." It was intimidating for actors to work with Hellman. "It was not a group project in any sense and the actors were not expected to ask questions or make any suggestions about a scene involving them," Eldridge notes. There was a line that she was sure would "get a very bad laugh in a very wrong place." With no preparation, Julie has to tell Leo Whalen, the union organizer, that she loves him. It was ridiculous, and Eldridge could never find a way to say "I love you" with which she felt comfortable. Shumlin told her, "Now Lillian knows what she is writing. Just go ahead." And Hellman said, "Herman will see that you don't get a laugh. And of course opening night the line got a laugh." In spite of her problems with the part, however, Eldridge had no forewarning that the play would be a failure, and the cast rehearsed with the hope of producing a hit.

Shortly before the curtain went up on opening night Hellman came to Eldridge's dressing room to wish her well. As Eldridge looked into the long mirror she noticed, to her horror, that a bit of lace on her petticoat was protruding under her skirt;

> There was no time to change, so I grabbed my scissors and cut off the lace border on the skirt—a great sacrifice as we wore real lace in those days! The curtain rose and as the play progressed it was obvious that it was not going well. One knows it—one feels it in one's bones. Suddenly from the basement under the stage we heard a small rumble which increased in volume as the author and director tried to escape blame by putting it onto his or her colleague. Her writing! His direction!

Kober had gone backstage and found Hellman in an alley "weeping hysterically on Herman's shoulder." Hammett and Kober took her to a cellar office to comfort her. She was wildly proclaiming she had written a flop and there was nothing ahead for her.

The play made the first night audience uneasy. By nine o'clock, Richard Maney remembers, people were restless. Hellman recalls that the light cues were mistimed and the props were misplaced and mishandled. She surprised herself by vomiting in a side aisle of the theater. In the middle of the second act, William Randolph

Hearst made a loud departure with six of his guests. The final curtain was greeted with only meager applause. After the play, Hellman's friends waited for her at Ralph Ingersoll's new apartment on Fifth Avenue. It was like a "dirge," Eldridge recalls. Everyone was embarrassed and uncomfortable. Two hours later, the playwright entered, "stormed past them all and down the hall and into [Ingersoll's] deserted bedroom, slamming, and locking, the door behind her." Ingersoll regarded her behavior as a "graceful gesture. Who knew what to say to her in her agony." But she hardly seemed in control of herself when she appeared an hour later, "tight," to quarrel with the early negative reviews. She called on Hammett for help: "Dash, didn't you tell me last week that *Days to Come* was the best script you'd ever read?" He took his time responding. "You son of a bitch, you said it was good!" she taunted him. Hammett stood erect, broke off his conversation with James T. Farrell, took up his cape, whirled it around his shoulder, and confessed, "Okay, I did. I've changed my mind." Without another word, he abandoned the group.

Days to Come closed after only six performances. In an introduction to *Six Plays* and in her memoirs, Hellman admits the weaknesses of her work, although she felt the director and the actors were confused and did not do the play justice. One Hellman comment, in particular, remains vivid in Eldridge's memory: that the leading lady was so careless that she entered the stage on opening night with her petticoat showing. "Alas, my poor alençon had been sacrificed in vain," Eldridge concludes.

One opening night reviewer remarked that "the performance is directed to move at the pace of a snail's funeral party. . . . It highlights every chink in the script, gives the generally good texture of Miss Hellman's writing no sheen, no excitement at all." Critics also noted that, as in *The Children's Hour*, where the playwright switched attention from Mary in the first two acts to Karen and Martha in the third, in *Days to Come*, she shifted from an intense concern with the strike to the domestic problems of the Rodmans. Hellman had not yet learned how to meld internal and external conflicts into a single dramatic center for her plays.

Hellman brooded over the play and avoided the public, reminding Kober of Martha and Karen's behavior in the last act of *The Children's Hour*. On the whole, however, he thought she had taken the failure gracefully. He had had such high hopes for the play and had invested in it. In his customary end-of-the-year summation, he could not help remarking how surprised he had been by Hellman's weakness.

In early January, 1937, Hellman was briefly hospitalized. Kober visited a "wan and pale" Hellman but was heartened to see Herman Shumlin there, "hale & hearty," and Ralph Ingersoll, who seemed "very fond of Lil & she of him for there is tenderness in her face." Two days later, Kober was at her apartment acknowledging her "steadying influence" on him, but he was saddened to see "how much the failure of the play [still] affected her." She was talking about not going back to Hollywood, about taking a year off. She was like "one returning from a dream world." But he found it hard to judge her, to measure "the extent of her fragile nerves" or "the height & desires of her ambitions." Yet, less than a week later, she was in the theater helping Kober with his play. She went at it with her usual intensity and was all for Kober taking a firmer hand with his director, Marc Connelly. The mild-mannered Kober was happy enough if the direction approximated what he wanted and dismissed Hellman's "nonsense of tantrums & following a temperamental pattern." She only succeeded at upsetting Connelly.

The next month, Hellman was back in Hollywood writing the screenplay for *Dead End*, Sidney Kingsley's sensational Broadway drama about slum children living along the East River in New York City. The play depicts human character as the product of one's environment. Gimpty, a crippled, unemployed architect, has grown out of the gang mentality of the ghetto, but he is still a child of the streets. He capitulates to poverty and idolizes a rich young woman, Kay, who has fallen in love with him. He ignores his loyal childhood girlfriend, Drina, until the end of the play, and never feels equal to Kay, even though she favors her upper-crust boyfriend largely because she fears destitution. Gimpty almost gives up on himself, until he realizes he must fight for his neighborhood by reneging on his childhood fealty to the gang leader, Baby Face Martin, who has become a vicious criminal. In the end, Gimpty must inform on Martin to the FBI, even though he realizes the gangster is a victim of society. Gimpty's adult decision to betray Martin is contrasted with the adolescent Spit's venal decision to inform on Tommy, the leader of his gang, who has stabbed a rich man in a desperate attempt to avoid punishment for brutalizing the man's prissy son. *Dead End*, as a play, is aptly named; the East

River is a constant presence and a state of mind that cannot be permanently transcended. Only the vulgar energy of its kids—their rough humor and sport with one another—relieves the grim message of this Depression-era drama.

Hellman had to have known that Sam Goldwyn would not stand for a naturalistic treatment of ghetto life. William Wyler wanted to shoot the film in New York, but Goldwyn insisted on building an elaborate set that everyone—except Wyler—admired for its authenticity. The director called it a phony. He was both right and wrong. To shoot the film as Kingsley had constructed the play certainly required a trip to New York. But Goldwyn and Hellman put the emphasis on character, not on environment. Gimpty, in Hellman's hands, becomes the stalwart hero, Dave, played by Joel McCrea, who was considered an all-American ideal young man. The whole plot of the film organizes itself around his efforts to defend his community from the purely evil menace of Baby Face Martin. As Bernard F. Dick puts it, "Martin is an enemy of society, not a victim of his environment, and hardly a tragic figure." As in so much of Hellman's work, good and evil in *Dead End* reside in the conflict between opposite kinds of characters and not in a conflict within individuals.

Goldwyn gave Wyler a hard time throughout the making of *Dead End*. The producer worried about the dirtiness of the set. It is easy to laugh over his idea that his expensive slum should look better than an "ordinary slum." But Hellman knew what he meant. Movie audiences wanted a hero, not a cripple. The indication of a slum was sufficient for both Goldwyn and Hellman, since Dave had to transcend his surroundings, not be hindered by them. Quite a different value system imposed itself on the original material. There was a powerful identification between Hellman and Goldwyn; in his and her own way, each wanted to transform reality by denying it, by sublimating it into the character of the hero. In other words, the conventions of Hollywood film fit perfectly Hellman's frame of mind.

The censorship of the time would have made it difficult for Hellman to write otherwise. On April 25, Joseph Breen had specified his key objections to *Dead End*. The scene showing people stepping on cockroaches had to be omitted. And, said Breen, "we would like to recommend, in passing, that you be less emphatic, throughout, in the photographing of this script in showing the contrast between conditions of the poor in tenements and those of the rich in apartment houses." The filmmakers should not show "the presence of filth, or smelling garbage cans, or garbage floating in the river, into which the boys jump for a swim," although all of these details were in the original play. Breen suspected that such scenes would "give offense." In addition, Francey, Baby Face Martin's girlfriend, could not be shown to be suffering from venereal disease, as in the play, and the movie should *affirmatively* establish the disease from which she was suffering.

Although it is discussed in the film, the actuality of slum life is hardly an issue for Hellman. Even when characters speak the lines of Kingsley's play, the force of personality, not of setting, is what gets expressed. Drina, for example, shows almost none of the weary, almost apathetic air of the downtrodden that is apparent in the play. In the film, she is first seen ironing, but even that kind of labor becomes a vigorous expression of her desire to make a better world for herself and her brother Tommy. She is a striker who defies the status quo. She pursues Dave rather than just waiting for him—in contrast to the Drina in the play, who frets over Gimpty's mooning for the glamorous Kay.

As Bernard F. Dick observes, "there were several reasons why Hellman built up Drina's role at the expense of Kay's." Sylvia Sidney was cast as Drina, and she was a much bigger star than Wendy Barrie, who played Kay. Hellman wanted Drina to stand for the tough, resilient personalities she admired in the labor movement. Once again, a Hollywood film allowed Hellman to pinpoint personalities and themes she had not satisfactorily portrayed in a previous play. *Dead End* captures a historical moment in the thirties far better than *Days to Come* insofar as Dave and Drina surmount the forces of repression—represented in the movie by the police and the inhabitants of the luxurious apartment house that borders the slum. "The year 1937, when *Dead End* was released, was a year of strikes, 4,720 in all, eighty-two percent of which were settled in favor of the unions," Dick points out.

Part of the problem with *Days to Come* is that it does not weld together the personal and political troubles of its characters. In the film of *Dead End*, on the other hand, Drina and Dave are as one; their passions and their politics are the same. Dave tells Baby Face Martin (played with maniacal neuroticism by Humphrey Bogart) to get out of the neighborhood before he corrupts the kids who may follow his advice to use dirty tactics in fighting a rival gang. Similarly, Drina tells off a policeman who is trying to arrest her brother Tommy. She defiantly shows him her bruised forehead—the result of a battering she has taken from another cop trying to stop a strike. Kingsley's characters also have some feistiness, but Gimpty is full of self-pity and is all too understanding when Kay confesses she cannot live in poverty with him. In the movie, Dave merely acknowledges Kay's feelings about being poor and later rejects them when he sees her running out of his tenement, scared and revolted by its seaminess. That Hollywood should have stars impersonate working people, that Joel McCrea—the male focus of *These Three*—should play Dave in *Dead End* was exactly to Hellman's purpose: she wanted clean-cut definitions of character and a leading man sufficiently attractive but not dynamic enough to overshadow the two women.

With McCrea, Hellman could keep a romantic focus on the triangle without blurring the moral and political implications of her story. As in *These Three*, he is a linking figure attracted to two women. Drina tends to be levelheaded and down-to-earth. Kay leans toward a flighty, insubstantial romanticism. Drina ultimately wins Dave because she demands more from him and commands not simply his love but also his social conscience. Just when it looks like she will lose him, Hellman gives her lines that bring him back to her. She tells Dave he wants only to please Kay and no longer wants to build a better world.

While *Dead End* is a far more successful work than *Days to Come*, it is also less ambitious and the product of the Hollywood screenwriter's inclination to simplify characters and themes. In Kingsley's play, Gimpty turns informer, pointing out Baby Face Martin in the street to federal agents, who kill him in a shootout. The neighborhood is rid of a corrupting influence, but Gimpty is partly motivated by the reward money and by anger over Martin's contemptuous treatment of him. In Hellman's version, Dave does not inform on Martin. On the contrary, Dave foils Martin's plot to kidnap a rich kid, engages in a gun duel with the gangster, and scorns the reward money.

The political implications of Hellman's deviations from Kingsley's play are prophetic of the stand she would take in *Scoundrel Time*. Right from the beginning of the film, informing is condemned, when a boy from a rival gang is singled out by the scar on his face that shows he has been a "squealer." Dick is right, of course, that "in the movies the romantic lead is not an informer." But this is just another instance of how Hellman bent Hollywood values to her advantage. Nothing should be seen to compromise Dave. It would never be right to inform in any circumstances—this is the logic of Hellman's absolutist code. There must be a decisive split between right and wrong; evil must be external to the hero, not a part of him, and he must be viewed as accomplishing his victory on his own.

The hero's self-sufficiency is matched by the community's independence in Hellman's version of *Dead End*; that is, when the police arrive after Dave's fight with Martin, they are treated as disrupters of an organized neighborhood's way of life. "I live on this block and I work on this block and I got a right to see what's going on," a rugged-looking, middle-aged woman tells a policeman who is trying to disperse the crowd that has formed to discuss the shooting. Another, younger woman, tells the same officer, "Don't push me," when he prods her to go on home.

In many ways, *Dead End* demonstrates that Hellman was at war with the institutions of society. In Kingsley's play, the authorities must be called on to restore order. In Hellman's film, one of the slum kids reads an exaggerated account of the killing in a newspaper and comments, "but that ain't the way it happened." Baby Face Martin's mother is described in the article as "a plump pink-cheeked woman who lives in a cottage near Sunny Side, Long Island," when in fact, the film has shown her to be a tenement dweller, an exhausted old woman ashamed of her son's evil notoriety.

As in *These Three,* in which Hellman sometimes reassigned the lines of *The Children's Hour* or gave the lines—slightly altered—to different characters, in *Dead End* she has Kay plead with Dave for his love, saying they "could have a year of happiness." In the play, Kay rejects Gimpty, saying she could have "only a year of happiness" with him. Even at the very end of the film, Hellman holds the romantic and political elements in perfect balance. It is certain that Dave and Drina will marry, but all Dave can manage is a remark that he no longer thinks of her as a "little girl." Politically and personally, the couple comes to an understanding, but there is no lovemaking. Drina seals their bond by giving her hand to Dave. There is no kiss, no sentimentalizing of their union. Indeed, the scene plays more like an agreement between them, a simple acknowledgment of solidarity.

Very few reviewers were in a position to study the extent to which Hellman made *Dead End* (released on August 24, 1937) express her vision of people and politics. Most reviews were laudatory and praised Hellman for producing a taut script without sacrificing too much to Hollywood's sanitization of the play's language. John McManus in *The New York Times* noticed how she had simplified characters, and a few negative reviews stressed that the film was not faithful to its gritty original. In general, though, the film enhanced Hellman's screenwriting reputation.

The day after *Dead End* opened in New York, Hellman sailed for Europe on the *Normandie* with Dorothy Parker and her husband Alan Campbell. She had an invitation to attend a theater festival in Moscow. By October, she would be in Spain. Eight months earlier, Hellman, Dorothy Parker, and Archibald MacLeish had founded an organization called Contemporary Historians, to support film director Joris Ivens's project to make a documentary on the Spanish Civil War. She had collaborated with MacLeish on the story for *The Spanish Earth*, although illness prevented her from seeing the film through to completion. Perhaps it was her aborted effort on the film that kindled the desire to see Spain firsthand. By her own account, she was deeply disturbed by George Gershwin's "terrible death" that summer of 1937 and wanted to get out of Hollywood. (Kober had kidded Gershwin about his poor piano playing, not knowing that a brain tumor had caused his lapses at the keyboard.) Hellman had also been having trouble with Hammett, and told Kober about her lover's "change of feelings." On July 28, Kober joined the couple at the Brown Derby and observed how "they behaved very much like [a] quarreling married couple." Hammett said Hellman could not resist the summons to visit other places. He could picture other locations through his books and had no desire to leave home. Hellman, on the other hand, always had to be off. For her, the present never sufficed; she was always on the point of departure.

5

DAY IN SPAIN
Hollywood/Paris/Berlin/Moscow/
Valencia/Madrid
(1937)

And so I was living on an island off the shore of Connecticut when the Spanish Civil War began in 1936. Never before and never since in my lifetime were liberals, radicals, intellectuals and the educated middle class to come together in single, forceful alliance.

—Lillian Hellman, *An Unfinished Woman*

It is the easiest thing in the world nowadays to become so socially conscious, so Spanish war stricken, that all sense of balance and values goes out of a person. Not long ago in Paris Lillian Hellman told me that she would give up writing if she could ameliorate the condition of the world, or of only a few people in it. . . . It is a form of egotism, a supreme form.

—James Thurber to E. B. White

The Republican *causa* in Spain did indeed unite a generation. Lillian Hellman, Ernest Hemingway, Martha Gellhorn, and many other writers were persuaded that the fight for the Spanish republic was the preliminary battle of World War II. Winning against Franco and his Fascist forces might prevent world cataclysm—or, at the very least, buy time for the democracies to gird themselves against Hitler and Mussolini. In "Day of Spain," an article written after her trip to Spain, Hellman concentrated on what she had been able to see for herself: men in the international brigades from America, Canada, Germany, Czechoslovakia, England, and many other countries were fighting for democracy. She prayed, "for the first time in many years, that they would get what they wanted." She thought that "these foreigners from everywhere were noble people." Noble was a word she had "never used . . . and it came hard, even to say it to myself."

"Day in Spain" defines the change not only in Hellman but in a whole generation of writers. In the twenties, she had been looking for a cause (any cause would do, an unsympathetic Sam Marx suggests). But in fact, she was troubled by the discrepancy between her anger and the fairly trifling causes to which she could attach herself. At that point, she had no clout as a writer and could bring no pressure to bear on her world. After the failure of Versailles and the League of Nations, politics seemed like a futile, hypocritical occupation. Writers should write and perhaps go into exile, as Hemingway and the "lost generation" had done. Of course, there were writers committed to changing society, and the legend of John Reed, the epitome of the writer/activist, remained a compelling, romantic idea. Yet it was embarrassing to use words like noble without sounding like a fake. And how could an untested writer like Hellman possibly make a declaration of faith in democracy when her betters had disowned political rhetoric altogether?

The truth is that writers were starved emotionally and politically by Hemingway's austere, understated style. The holding back of emotion and the cynicism implied by such a style had a withering effect on writers and increased their sense of alienation. If writing contributed to no cause, if the writer was completely on his or her own hook, then what to do if one had no experience, if one had not seen war as Hemingway had? If a writer growing up after Hemingway had never had faith in, say, democracy, then how could he or she go around lamenting loss of belief? It was kind of a sham for Hellman. What had she done, for good or evil, that compared with Hammett's strike-breaking, Pinkerton past?

The Depression, however, made it difficult for writers to live "a deliberately private existence." Except for the most successful writers, it became impossible to make a living writing. A writer's destiny was tied to the fate of the economy. No one could stay outside of politics—this is the message Hellman brought to screen-writers in her organizing efforts. Her politics coincided with a reversal in Communist party policy that now made it desirable to recruit writers. Before the mid-thirties, writers had been used by the party, but they were considered unpredictable and were rarely trusted. The Popular Front period (1935–39) was characterized by the party's far greater tolerance of idiosyncracy. Indeed, as Nancy Lynn Schwartz puts it, "In Hollywood in the thirties, the Commu-nist party was barely distinguishable in policy and activities from the noncommunist Left." One could be for Roosevelt and for the party. The party lent "a structure and context to political efforts in Hollywood" and "suffused everything with meaning."

In Hollywood, on July 10, 1937, less than two months before her trip to Europe, Hellman attended a showing of *The Spanish Earth* in the home of Fredric and Florence Eldridge March, at which Hem-ingway spoke for the Loyalist cause in the hopes of raising dona-tions for ambulances. Various accounts of the party differ signifi-cantly from hers, especially in describing Hemingway's behavior, which comes off very badly in *An Unfinished Woman*. Florence Eldridge March remembers he had written what he wanted to say on Hollywood Hotel stationery. After the picture had been shown, Hemingway just sat there like an old bear, and Florence finally said to him: "If you want to talk to people, you better begin pretty fast because they're going to start to move away." So he said, "Well, yes, I guess I should say something. But first . . . I gotta take a leak." Fredric saw Florence's startled look and came over to her to ask what Hemingway had said to her. She looked as though Hemingway had hit her. In fact, the novelist felt considerable anxiety about speaking in public and may have been in genuine distress when he spoke to Florence. When he returned, he read a very moving speech, describing the filmmakers' efforts to capture the conditions of wartime Spain, the indiscriminate bombing of the civilian population, and the deaths of his friends. A contribu-tion of one thousand dollars would get an ambulance to Spain. There was virtual silence after the speech, then people began to come forward with donations and to say a few words to the writer. Dashiell Hammett was the first to pledge one thousand dollars. As Hemingway biographer Carlos Baker points out, the combination of "Ernest's fame, his obvious sincerity, and the effect of the film itself immediately brought in enough money to buy and equip twenty ambulances." A very pale and withdrawn F. Scott Fitzgerald, whose presence at the party almost went unremarked by the Marches because he had changed so much in appearance, was full of admiration. The next day he wired Hemingway that "THE PICTURE WAS BEYOND PRAISE AND SO WAS YOUR ATTITUDE." Fitzgerald later confided to Max Perkins that Hemingway's "nervous tensity" had "something almost religious about it." The importance of this event lay, in part, in Hemingway's public demonstration of himself as a writer committed to social and political action. This was a striking change in the persona of a novelist whose works up to this point seemed to have created a deliberate estrangement between the writer and society.

In *An Unfinished Woman*, Hellman places the March party in 1938, after her trip to Spain. She presents Fitzgerald as absolutely terrified of Hemingway. As she and Fitzgerald arrive at Dorothy Parker's house for a nightcap, they are "stopped dead at the sound of smashing glass"—Hemingway had just thrown his highball glass into the fireplace. (Others at the party do not remember this incident or the pugnacious image of him that Hellman fashions.) A year or so later, at the Stork Club, Hemingway's behavior was even more abominable. He hectored Hammett and challenged him to bend a spoon between the muscles of his upper and lower arm. Hammett quietly admitted he probably could not equal Hemingway's feat of crumpling the spoon. "But when I did things like that I did them for Pinkerton money. Why don't you go roll a hoop in the park?" Hammett suggested to Hemingway as he left the table. The lines seem pure Hellman, not Hammett. In fact, they are remarkably similar to Mrs. Ellis's advice to Nick Denery, the fretful bully in *The Autumn Garden*: "Try to make a paper hat out of the newspaper or get yourself a nice long piece of string."

Hemingway's involvement in Spain is made to seem irrelevant to the cause; he got involved because of his gigantic ego. That there may be truth in Hellman's view does not in the slightest mitigate the fact that she felt compelled not just to criticize him, but also to cut him down to size. And it is only after she has belittled him in *An Unfinished Woman* that she returns to proper chronological sequence, to her visit to Paris in the autumn of 1937.

Hellman was quite taken with the charming but somehow superannuated Murphys, Gerald and Sara, who founded on the Riviera the "center of a brilliant world of writers and artists attracted by the originality of their style as people. The rules that the Murphys had overturned seemed to anybody of my generation interesting but not important. . . ." They came "from another world and time" and were not to the taste of Hellman's "duller and certainly less talented" Depression generation that favored loyalty, "or the rhetoric of it," to Dorothy Parker and Ernest Hemingway's clever sniping at each other, kept in control only by Gerald Murphy's "often overcivilized hand." Hellman, as a politically active writer coming of age in the thirties implies that Parker, Hemingway, and the Murphys were all part of the twenties emphasis on *personal* style which, to her, seemed petty—although she is careful not to use that word.

The point of Hellman's long prologue in *An Unfinished Woman* to her Spanish diary—the party at the Marches, the Stork Club confrontation, the Parisian idyll, and her brief stay in Moscow—is to make her appear fresher, more open to experience, and less compromised by the prejudices of a preceding generation of writers. Similarly, she says she quickly lost interest in the rather stodgy theater festival in Moscow (the ostensible purpose of her visit), and was put off by American diplomats. "Most of them . . . were frivolous men who might have functioned well in the Vienna of Franz Joseph." She discounted most of what they said, for it was hard to tell fact from invention; so much of it was "mixed with blind bitterness about a place and a people." As a result, she wrote, "I did not know I was there in the middle of the ugliest purge period." Some of this anti-Soviet bias turned out to be well-founded, she concedes in *An Unfinished Woman*, but the fact is that she was never to make more than a grudging admission of how profoundly wrong she was about Stalin. Nor does she allow her readers to learn that she behaved like a partisan by signing an advertisement in *The New Masses* defending the trials. She thought she knew enough to approve of Stalin's measures to protect the Soviet Union from what the advertisement described as a Fascist disinformation plot aided by Trotskyist "enemies of progress." The defendants in the trials were "spies and wreckers" of Soviet democracy.

In *An Unfinished Woman,* Hellman maintains that in Paris, Otto Simon, a Communist, journalist, and early anti-Fascist, persuaded her to overcome her "fear of the danger of war" and to act on her "strong convictions" about the war by visiting Spain. Yet the diary entries covering Hellman's month in Spain are presented so as to disclaim bias:

A great many people have told me a great many things—atrocities on one side and the other; nuns and priests torn by the limbs in Republican villages; peasants and intellectuals burned alive on Franco's side; why what government fell when; the fights among the Anarchists and Communists and Socialists; who is on what side today who wasn't yesterday—but this is not the way I learn things and so I have only half listened, although my head will soon come off from the polite up-and-downs it has been making, and the fixed smile might grow into a tic. If I have anything to do here, anything to say or write, I am better off by myself.

The passage reads like an authentic example of the confusion experienced by a newcomer to what was, in fact, a most complex conflict. As Jeffrey Hart observes in a review of books on the war, in addition to the fight against Franco and his Fascist sponsors, Hitler and Mussolini, there were the internal battles between "monarchists and republicans, anti-clericals and the Church, landowners and labor unions, Basque and Catalonia separatists and Madrid centralizers, Communists, anarchists, and the Fascist Falange." Moreover, Spain was an ideological battleground, the forerunner of the "internationalized postwar conflicts in Greece, Korea, Vietnam, and now Nicaragua." It is no wonder that at the time, Hellman could not see all of this clearly, but it is less excusable for her in her memoirs not to confront the fact that the Spanish Civil War was no simple fight for democratic rights. Her only criticism of the Soviet Union, for example, is that it failed to give adequate support to the republican Loyalists. Yet "what the Russians brought to the Republic was unmitigated repression and terror—a civil war against the Spanish Left," concludes Ronald Radosh in a recent article that details the massive weight of evidence against the Stalinists that George Orwell and others began to accumulate before the war was over. Some liberals, like Philip Dunne, were very much aware that the Communists were sabotaging the republic, and "this is the main reason we were trying to get Roosevelt to send support, so that all supplies did not come in from the Soviet Union," he notes. Of course, the Soviet strategy to subvert the republican government and to turn it into a Stalinist satellite is much clearer in the light of subsequent history—such as the Soviet Union's failure to return the Spanish gold reserves entrusted to its safekeeping. What is undeniable is that Hellman, Hemingway, and many other writers willfully blinded themselves to the atrocities committed by the Communists. When John Dos Passos inquired after his missing friend, Professor Jose Robles Pazos, who had accepted a War Ministry post in the republican government, he was deliberately deceived by Josephine Herbst and others who had reason to know or to strongly suspect that Robles had been murdered by the Communists. Dos Passos could not believe that his friend had committed treason, and he could not support a cause that demanded such horrible and arbitrary sacrifices. Hemingway, on the other hand, shrugged off Dos Passos's humanitarian concerns and argued, "after all . . . this is war."

Spain somehow inspired disillusioned Communists, who should have known better, to put their faith once again in Stalin. Gustav Regler, a German Communist who befriended Hellman during her short stay in Spain, had barely escaped Moscow with his life. He had observed Stalin "consolidating his dictatorial powers [by] purging Old Bolsheviks. Important people vanished." Yet he was overjoyed to obtain an exit visa to Madrid, stating that "Spain was the place for a Communist to make a stand for an idealized vision of the cause."

By October 1937, the beginning of Hellman's month in Spain, the republic held hardly more than one-third of the country, and Franco's forces were threatening to cut the republic in two. In less than a month, Dorothy Parker would be writing about the siege of Madrid and about a republic that, in spite of the war, was building "more schools in a year than ever were in all the years of the kings." Similarly, Hellman recorded in her diary evidence of the solidarity and generosity of the Loyalists, who offered her food when they had so little for themselves. Above all, her diary (quoted in *An Unfinished Woman*) records the intense struggle to stay alive that makes every moment meaningful. The most honest passages in the diary are devoted to Hellman's passionate wish to remain with these dedicated people and her simultaneous aching, gnawing need to leave the terror, the hunger, and the devastation of war. Hemingway might make a show of his commitment, but she was prepared to admit her guilt over leaving what she felt was her fight, and to reveal how far she was from the reality of Spain: "Last night I packed a jewelry case—what a ridiculous thing to have brought to Spain. . . ."

If the war in Spain was "little"—a "minute of history," Hellman called it—then her time there was barely a second. She stayed long enough to admire the bravery of the Republicans, to visit a hospital where she was urged to petition Roosevelt for help, to experience hunger and dizziness, the fear of bombing raids, and the insensitive behavior of other Americans. Hemingway comes off rather badly, an egomaniac reveling in the beauty of the shelling of Madrid, and Dos Passos "hadn't brought in any food but had eaten everybody else's." Most of all, however, Hellman came to witness a people dying for their beliefs. It was as if she had had a vision of what she had "missed in the world." One had to make hard choices in Spain, Hellman learned as she spoke to a Czech woman about her visit to Prague. The woman condemned her two brothers, owners of a newspaper: "Liberal pigs. Pigs. They will kill all the rest of us with their nothing-to-be-done-about-it stuff. They will save themselves when the time comes, the dirty pigs." This scene, like so many of the scenes in Hellman's plays, reveals great contempt for liberals.

In spite of such opinionated passages, Hellman's Spanish Civil War diaries are inconclusive. "My pieces here about Spain do not say all or even much of what I wanted to say," she admits in *Three*, the 1979 edition of her memoirs. For one thing, the disjointedness of the diaries in *An Unfinished Woman* prevents her from taking center stage, even though all of the experiences she describes were her own. Somehow, her own life, her own ego, was not really at stake in *An Unfinished Woman*. In *Pentimento*, she divulges the reason why: it seems that she had omitted the story of her 1937 trip through Berlin to Moscow because she did not feel she could write about Julia. From Paris, Hellman had originally planned to travel to Vienna to see her friend. Over the phone, Julia advised Hellman to stay in Paris for a few days, until "a friend" came to see her. A Mr. Johann arrived to ask Hellman to carry fifty thousand dollars by train from Paris to Berlin for the anti-Fascist underground. She wavered. Although she was told that the risk seemed minimal, the enormity of the responsibility weighed heavily upon her. At the station, she was given a hatbox and a box of candy. The train trip was nerve-wracking, although Hellman's instructions were quite simple: at the border she was to "leave the candy box on the seat," open the hat box, and wear the hat, which had the money in its lining. Throughout the trip she was full of hesitations—as one might expect of someone in her position—and a variety of helping figures (Mr. Johann, "the big girl," and "the little girl" on the train) guided her foray into active antifascism. At her destination, a restaurant in Berlin, a calm and collected Julia congratulated Hellman for doing "something important."

The story of Julia in *Pentimento* overshadows the passages in *An Unfinished Woman* on Russia and on Spain, but these are retroactively validated by *Pentimento*. Notified on May 23, 1938, of Julia's death, Hellman tried to retrace the pattern of events, to determine how her friend met her fate and discover where Julia's child had been hidden.

The Julia story gives Hellman's political convictions personal authority. Julia was a friend Hellman had to create in order to justify her politics and her personality. To put it another way, Hellman had to feel personally injured or threatened by the forces she opposed politically. She made this quirk apparent, late in life, in an exchange with Dan Rather. In considering his point that she had been able to see "what was wrong" with McCarthy but not with Stalin, she responded, "I was injured by McCarthy, for one thing. I was not—I was personally not injured by Stalin, which is—is not—a very high-class reason, but it's a very—it's—it's a good practical reason." There is an astonishing lack of proportion in Hellman's reply to Rather; after all, what had Hitler done to her *personally* to justify her antifascism? Through Julia, or the Julia figure, however, all of Hellman's emotional resources were brought to bear in the cause of antifascism. There were simply no feelings left over for second thoughts about Stalin.

What has been said of Dorothy Parker proves to be equally true of Lillian Hellman:

> Parker could never look critically at the Communist Party, once she had decided that the Party really wanted to help suffering humanity. . . . She was a very, very *grande dame,* and contrariness was the wellspring of her Communism. She was anti. She was anti the Establishment.

Hammett often took to dubbing Hellman "Madame" in his letters about her because of the loftiness with which she would state a position. As John Keats points out, radicals of the thirties often expressed their anti-capitalist views with a fervor and an intolerance that made it impossible for them to rethink the ideology to which they had converted:

> They believed together with Marx that the new world could be reached only after a class struggle. They were also convinced that anyone who did not agree with them was potentially, if not overtly, an enemy.

For Parker and Hellman, however, ideology was embedded in a temperament that was already high-toned and contemptuous of other points of view. Thus, when Hellman became outraged at William Carney, a *New York Times* correspondent whose reports from Spain were, to her, obviously pro-Fascist, she wrote not just to refute his articles but to destroy his reputation. From the safety of a resort, Hellman claimed, Carney filed "paper stories based on what the Fascist propaganda agency has just told him." Carney's dispatches not only got front-page attention, they were also the subjects of *Times* editorials. Was he related to the boss? Hellman wanted to know. Carney, she remembered, was the journalist who newspapermen were telling "strange stories" about several years earlier. She does not say what the stories were; it is enough that she has impugned his integrity. Her attack was never published, and parts of it are crossed out, as though Hellman had second thoughts about her anger. Did she realize that she was reporting gossip that would call into question her fairness and her facts?

Hellman's stay in Spain was a turning point for her. It let loose all restraints on her radicalism. Back in the United States in November, she would work feverishly for the Loyalists and begin her involvement in numerous Communist and fellow-traveling organizations. The idea of *The Little Foxes* also came from her trip to Spain. At the time, she thought her intense involvement with the play was a way of relieving the terrible sense of responsibility she felt toward the fighters for the *causa*. Yet *The Little Foxes* is—if not a Marxist play—certainly a devastating revelation of the corrupting power of the capitalistic mentality. The Hubbards are anything but collectivists, and their brand of economic individualism is the ruination of society.

Hellman was ready to write a play fired by personal and political convictions. She would draw on her family background—a new tack for her made possible by virtue of her trip to Spain. As she confessed in *An Unfinished Woman*, her time there constituted a confrontation with herself, her fears, and her ability to withstand hardship. It seems that she had been looking to grapple with this historic event in order to get a perspective from which to write. Traveling—as Kober suggested in his diary on January 28, 1937—held out hope of insight:

> The most important function of travelling is not to escape or beat reality but on the contrary to realize or try to understand the many aspects it assumes at the various ends of the earth. For that three things are necessary, to see a place just in the terms and from the vantage point of its inhabitants (after all these people *live* here)—to see it in terms of one's own personal experience (that native girl is just my age) and to contrast it with one's necessarily limited knowledge of its significance with respect to the rest of the world.

At its best, Hellman's writing about Spain fulfills Kober's requirements, for she is able to see the natives clearly, to identify with them, and to place them against her "necessarily limited knowledge of the world." In June of 1942, she presented parts of her Spanish diary as "The Little War" in *This Is My Best*, a collection of writings edited by Whit Burnett. Hellman beheld herself in the lives of others, on a street in Valencia on October 13, hearing the approach of bombers:

> I went through a square, towards my hotel, and when I first heard the noise of the motors I didn't want to turn to see where they were. I thought: in that hotel room is a toothbrush, a clean nightgown, a cake of soap, an old coat and a box of lousy candy. Yet I am hurrying to it, it is where I am trying to go, it is the place where I have what belongs to me, it is home. And I knew, then, why even the poorest women in Valencia wanted to stay with what was theirs. It hasn't got anything to do with how much you have.

In *An Unfinished Woman*, the bombers approach on October 14 and Hellman's descriptions are a little more concrete, a little more dramatic. A policeman shouts at her and shoves her under a bench, and later she dashes across the square. Several phrases from "The Little War" are amended—usually to enhance the pictorial quality of the narrative. Was Hellman remembering more of her experience in Spain, polishing her diaries, or both? It is impossible to say for a writer compulsively bent on rewriting her life.

6

THE LITTLE FOXES
New York/Hollywood/New York
(1937-1939)

Take us the foxes, the little foxes, that spoil the vines, for
our vines have tender grapes.

—Song of Sol. 2:15

Put all your eggs in one basket and then watch the basket.

—Andrew Carnegie's business motto,
recorded in Hellman's notes for *The Little Foxes*.

B y November 17, 1937, Hellman was back in New York and
looking fit. Arthur Kober took her to "21" for dinner, and
they were joined by Ralph Ingersoll. Throughout the next few
months, she saw a great deal of Kober, the Gershwins, and the
Campbells. Spain was much on her mind. To Kober, she seemed
bitter about Hemingway and even described herself as "one of his
girls." Exactly what she meant by the remark is not clear from
Kober's diary. In *An Unfinished Woman*, there is no suggestion of
an affair. According to Hellman, Hemingway made a point of not
sleeping with her, but perhaps she was alluding to the charismatic
spell he often cast over men and women. Certainly, her memoirs
imply that she was bitter about his behavior. Kober's diary suggests she was suffering from feelings of rejection.

On November 21, during a long walk in the country, Hellman
told Kober about her ideas for plays, in particular, one (probably

Watch on the Rhine) that seemed inspired by Henry James's tales. On December 7, she and Kober visited Albert Maltz's class on playwriting at New York University and were questioned by a group of "earnest, serious students." Hellman and Kober had a brief romantic revival, and it seemed to him like "old times"—as if the years had not passed at all. On November 30, after seeing Ina Claire in a performance of Barchester Towers Hellman did not like, Kober stayed the night with her. Her unsigned review of the play appeared in Time magazine on December 13. She complained that the stage adaptation of Anthony Trollope's novel had weakened his superb storytelling ability by removing the bite and the realistic characterization. "Even Miss Claire's fashionable audience gave up giggling during the second act and sat back to chat in peace. Broadway connoisseurs were waiting for the big actress scene that would explain why she had chosen the play. The scene never came." Hellman was more amused with a new poodle and with serving hearty breakfasts for Kober. At one dinner with Kober and her father, she quizzed them on whether they "were pretty or not as children."

By the end of the year, Hellman was helping Kober look for a new apartment, and he spent Christmas with her and New Year's Day as well, when they were joined by Dorothy Parker and Alan Campbell. With the new year, the cozy Kober-Hellman friendship continued: "we have a very good time telling each other how fond we are of each other, which is true," Kober confided to his diary on January 3. And Hellman looked out for Kober: "Mrs. Bush, the renting agent tries to pull a fast one & Lil thwarts her." Both were deeply concerned about the quarreling Campbells; Dorothy was tearing Alan "to pieces." The next day, Hellman addressed a tea party on the war in Spain. January and February were filled with such activity. At one such speaking engagement, Kober thought it strange that the Soviet Union was being upheld as the "ideal democratic state," but at another meeting he was impressed with Hellman's "well spoken, direct, and honest" talk about Spain.

Throughout this period, Hellman was writing. She had not yet begun a draft of The Little Foxes, but instead showed Kober a short story. It was not very good. To him, it seemed "childish as far as style, manner, construction is concerned." She was trying to get Walter Winchell, a syndicated newspaper columnist for the Hearst chain, to deliver on his promise to put her piece on Spain in his column. Winchell was clearly having trouble and was, in Kober's words, "unusually reserved." William Randolph Hearst refused to allow her piece to be published. Less than six months later, in April 1938, "Day in Spain" appeared in *The New Republic*.

The clearest sign that Hellman had not settled down to write a play was her willingness to consider an assignment from Sam Goldwyn. Dealing with Goldwyn was always a challenge. Ralph Ingersoll remembered how she would "fight like hell" over the phone for half an hour. She would get a lot of money that way and would fight until she got it. She wanted a reluctant Kober to accompany her to New Orleans to visit her father before going on to California. By February 17, after a few days of socializing with Kober and Louis Kronenberger, she was excited to be off, wiring Hammett in California that she would be coming after a short stopover in New Orleans. He had written her a Christmas letter counseling her not to spend her time on insignificant writing assignments. During a long period of sobriety, he was working on a movie, *Another Thin Man*, a "new fable of how Nick loved Nora and Nora loved Nick. . . . nobody ever invented a more insufferably smug pair of characters."

The tone of self-disgust was obvious, especially since Hammett mentioned he was being paid forty thousand dollars for the script. In a few months, he would suffer a complete collapse. Although he was never one to admit how shaky his grip was on things, he was anxious to have Hellman with him and sent another wire to her in New Orleans: "It is raining here but only on the streets where they don't know you are coming. Dotty expects you for dinner and I love you."

Hellman had agreed to work at Goldwyn Studios on an adaptation of *Graustark*, a novel by George Barr McCutcheon, published in 1901, about a "love behind the throne." The novel had been dramatized in 1926 by Grace Hayward. It was Hellman's task to update the property for the screen. Her writing did not go well, and later she admitted she did not do a good job on the script, which was never produced. Yet she liked Sam Goldwyn and described herself as his "oldest living employee. He's been very decent to me; he really charms me. He calls me Lillian, but I always call him Mr. Goldwyn. I don't think he notices it." Hellman's April 4 inter-office communication addressed to Sidney Howard suggests that she was having a good time in spite of her script troubles. Her memo concerns a fellow writer, the "mystery man," Howard Estabrook. Goldwyn, or "Sam the Good," as she dubbed him, announced the imminent arrival of Estabrook. A sign had appeared on a door with Estabrook's name printed on it, yet a month later the writer still had not appeared. In her frequent trips around the building, drinking at the water fountain, visiting her fellow writers Sidney Howard and S. Raphaelson, and pacing the corridor, she had not seen "anyone who could be Howard Estabrook."

Hellman questioned a "smirking" Reeves Espy, a Goldwyn executive whom she referred to as "a disappointed former conman from Seattle," about Estabrook. Occasionally, in darkened projection rooms, Espy identified an entering newcomer as Estabrook. "Obviously a lie. Obviously chicanery. . . . A gigantic plot has been put over on Sam the Good," she concluded. Her surmise: Estabrook "has been dead for several months." Espy, she had discovered, was the "illegitimate child of Estabrook's grandmother." Espy knew of the death and had hired a man from Central Casting who "looked like a writer, God should forbid." Sam the Good was fooled by Espy, who had coached the actor to say nothing. "This was fine, since that is the way a writer should act," Hellman added in a parenthetical aside. Then she begged for action. She called for a "committee meeting" at which she would reveal evidence that proved Espy was cashing "the unfortunate" Estabrook's salary checks while doling out only a tenth of the income to Estabrook's family. She closed her memo with the exhortation: "Save Goldwyn. Save Austria. This is a pure example of Fascist terror and deception. Save United Artists!"

Espy retaliated on the same day with his own "confidential" memo to Howard. He pointed out that Hellman was crazy:

> Lillian is not violent. It is merely essential that we humor her. There is no indication of monomania, megalomania, paranoia, amentia, lycanthropy, or of any specific type. I would describe her condition as allergy of the brain.

Espy concluded that Hellman might be suffering from "something elementary such as sex frustration." He was going to have her studied by a psychopathist, who "diagnoses with the naked eye; by stealthy observation." In a postscript, he noted that "Lillian says she is a writer. Encourage her." To Hellman, however, Espy wrote "there is something in what you state." If she promised to discontinue her communications on the matter and to give her word of honor in writing, he would give her "the facts on Estabrook."

Writers should say nothing—they might not even exist and still get on the payroll. This was Hellman having fun, but she was also getting in her digs. In March, she was named, along with Hammett, to the new SWG board of directors and met with Nate Witt, executive secretary of the National Labor Relations Board (NLRB), who visited California in March 1938 to investigate news of labor unrest. Witt remembered several years later that Hellman was "immersed" in politics but "not really on top of it." Hammett seemed the most "politically astute" of the writers he met. Philip Dunne, who served with Hellman on the SWG negotiating team during this period, has similar recollections. She was not a strident radical. Her sentiments were undoubtedly on the left, but she was quiet about them during actual negotiations. Charles Brackett, a conservative writer and a Republican, was much more vocal. With his mustache bristling, he would drive home his team's points as aggressively as possible. He was outraged to find that his outspokenness was equated with radicalism. Alfred Wright, the attorney for 20th Century-Fox, sized up the writers seated across from him at the bargaining table and told Dunne that he liked Hellman very much: "She's fine, but you ought to get rid of that damn Communist Brackett!"

By early spring, Hellman was back in New York and ready to begin serious work on her new play. *The Little Foxes* was to be set in the South at the turn of the century. Everything about the setting and the time had to be authentic. As one of her interviewers put it, "night after night she prowled through various libraries, unearthed faded magazines, tattered theatre programs, yellowed newspapers—anything, in short, to bring her closer to the way of life in 1900." She had done similar research for *Days to Come*, in which she had tried to blend facts with feelings about people she knew, but *The Little Foxes* was to draw directly on her family background, and she wanted her sense of the period to be grounded in history.

Aided by a researcher and a secretary, Hellman compiled a notebook of 115 typewritten pages divided into several sections covering American life from 1880–1900. She made separate studies of "the Negro," the cotton economy, the industrial South, and the agricultural South. A "Historical Background" section concerned the United States and Europe from 1890 to 1905. Political events like the assassination of President McKinley and the 1904 Russo-Japanese War were noted, and a bibliography was assembled to organize her extensive research. Various observers of this material have suggested it constitutes much more information than could possibly be put into a single play. Hellman's purpose, however, was not so much to extract dramatic substance from her archive as it was to provide a guide. She showed it to Howard Bay, her stage designer, who was astonished by the detail: "It had little ground plans for truck gardens . . . and the Reconstruction banking laws." Although very little of this material was specifically mentioned in the play, Bay notes that "it was amazing how much she got in in an unobtrusive fashion. It was in the atmosphere, in the warp and woof." He found it helpful to have such a rich body of information from which to select telling details for the set. The research book, in other words, served as the framework for the whole play.

In fact, Hellman had gone to considerable trouble to reconstruct what Glen Whitesides in his Ph.D. dissertation describes as the "plan of a representative upper middle-class house and garden of the period." All of the details a designer would need were there: "rambling roses growing just outside the parlor, hollyhocks by the kitchen, and honeysuckle and lilacs by the stables." Every kind of furnishing for a living room was described; one would even know how to set the table from Hellman's notes.

Hellman was most interested in national trends in which the South had taken part. She was less concerned with the agrarian tradition that emphasized the distinctiveness of the region than in the industrial policies of the "New South" fostered by Henry Grady and others. She favored statistical and empirical studies. She relied, for example, on the work of Howard Odum, .who argued the importance of the South as a region that contributed significantly to the country's economy. Because of her New Deal politics and her family background, she gravitated toward an ironic rather than a romantic view of the South. While she would sympathetically present characters who expressed a rootedness and sense of community—virtues the agrarians prized—her dynamic characters would be the materialists, the ones bent on making the country grow. The past, in and of itself, would not be lauded, and Southernness, per se, would not be her focus. It had never been her family's special concern. Her Uncle Jake, after all, had been a successful banker in both Demopolis, Alabama, and New York City.

Alabama, the setting of the play, received special attention. Hellman knew how long the school year lasted, how much education the average Alabaman had, and the approximate cost of commodities like eggs. She knew the songs people were singing, the books they were reading, and other new amusements like the player piano, the telephone, and the automobile. Typical Southern names filled a page of research. As she began to imagine her characters, she could set them into a completely realized world.

The very heart of *The Little Foxes* is, of course, Regina Hubbard. In a separate notebook filled with character sketches and plot outlines, the playwright essayed her first impressions of Regina:

> Good looking but not attractive. Has headaches and uses them whenever necessary; she is an insane housekeeper; wipes her fingers on walls, floors, etc., to see if they are clean. If she loves anybody, it is her son, but she is strict with him too. She is not interested in the daughter. Has always been angry that her husband isn't richer than her brothers; but he is rich enough for her not to be put aside by them. Ben or Oscar has a carriage she likes and wants. Perhaps all through play wants to move to bigger town.

Regina's son, but not the daughter, Alexandra, would be cut from the play—as would a number of other ancillary characters—but the sense of rivalry with her brothers, her high-strung perfectionism, and her desire to have a prominent place in a world far larger than the one she inhabits are abiding qualities in the final version of the play.

Regina was a most unsympathetic character in the first draft of the play and seems to have been modeled after Thomas Beer's description of the "Titaness" in *The Mauve Decade*. She was a type of woman that became increasingly dominant in a rising leisure class after the Civil War and during a time of rapid industrialization. She is Beer's kind of cunning and manipulative woman, using her sexuality to get her way. At this point, Hellman may have been too influenced by Beer and her other period sources, for she had Regina savagely bullying her husband Horace into a deal with her brothers Ben and Oscar, who have become partners with a Chicago businessman, William Marshall, in a cotton processing plant. When Horace refuses Regina, she exiles him first to an unbearably hot third-floor sewing room and then to the Hubbards' former slave quarters. Later drafts would tone down her villainy and much more subtly situate Regina within the competitive climate of her family.

The sketch for Horace is remarkably faithful to the finished version of the character who would appear in the ninth and final draft:

> Sick, tired by the time we see him. Hates Regina because he has come to see through her and because he has come to hate the life he has gotten into. Maybe smokes expensive tobacco that she has always objected to. When supply is used up she won't let him have more, although doctor said it didn't matter anyway. Alexandra tries to get it for him and has fight with her mother. He has been successful, but could have been more successful if he had been more ruthless. When first comes home, makes one last effort to touch her, be friendly with her; when this is refused, he grows increasingly bitter toward her.

In the first draft of the play, Horace is explicitly against not only Regina's business deal but also rapid industrialization, and he expresses his dislike of factories and "the boys who owned them" in Birmingham, Alabama. Horace is Old South, and in the final draft takes his moral stand against the Hubbards, whom, he knows, "will pound the bones of this town to make dividends" for Regina to spend.

Ben Hubbard was conceived, right from the beginning, as a wily and humorous figure, a much-needed counter to his sister Regina's stridency and his brother Oscar's stolidity:

> Probably big, calmer, although more talkative than the rest. He and Regina are smarter than the others and always have been. His is the final word. He makes jokes, and knows all about very rich families of the time. He plays the piano; nobody knows why. He has a large store and is also a cotton trader. It has been his idea to start the factory. Likes horses. He is rather jolly

and far less solemn than the others, and far more dangerous. Keeps saying he is no good at figures.

Although the final draft of *The Little Foxes* does not show Ben playing the piano or reveal things like his taste in horses, the text is true to the original conception of a character who is likeable. Ben's comic spirit and his evil are inseparable; he commands attention because of his ironic vision, his powers of observation.

Oscar, on the other hand, is portrayed in Hellman's notes and in the finished drama as a conspicuous waste of human character, a man who hoards everything and who cannot see beyond self-interest:

> Mean, without the eccentricities of his brother. He puts into words what he knows Ben wants done. Has great pleasure out of shooting, and shoots everything he sees. The house is always supplied with much more than it can use. When he gets too much, just lets it rot, and won't give any away. Has contempt for his wife. Has indigestion always.

It is fascinating to see on stage how well Ben and Oscar mesh, how Ben can imply what Oscar has to say in so many words. Ben becomes a capitalist by choice; Oscar seems blindly driven to it, and Regina is pressured into economic speculation just to hold her own with her scheming brothers. Oscar has to have absolutely everything he sees—hence his indigestion and his eternal disappointment. He cannot consume everything, and it is doubly ironic and funny when he becomes the one whose share in the cotton mill is reduced by Regina's subtle maneuvering.

Oscar's wife, Birdie, is, as her name suggests, flighty. Hellman must have had her mother in mind in penning this initial portrait:

> Is soft and fading—pretty. She tries to talk, tries to pretend that she has some place, but nobody pays any attention to her. Drinks sherry in increasing amounts. Is usually gardening. Likes something in living room and has always wanted it for her own room. Has insomnia.

Julia Hellman, as Lillian remembers her in *An Unfinished Woman*, was a kind of gentle flower, out of place among the crude Newhouses. She was treated all too delicately by Hannah and Jenny, Max's sisters, and she was often left out of Hellman conversations that were in German. Julia was pitied by the Newhouses for picking a husband not nearly as financially successful as themselves. As in life, where Julia had an almost other-world quality about her, in the play, Birdie's love of music suggests an idealization of human nature which the Hubbards scorn.

With such detailed and clearly conceptualized notes, the first draft of the play was in remarkably good shape. Leo, at this point, was another brother, although in the next draft he became Oscar's son. Many fine speeches, theater scholar Richard Moody reports, were sacrificed in subsequent drafts so that the dramatic structure could be tightened. In general, many allusions to the period were dropped by the time Hellman brought her play into production. Such revisions were her way of weaning herself away from her reading and of sharply individualizing her characters. From some of the earliest notes for the play, it is clear that the black servant Addie—probably created with Sophronia in mind—was to serve as a moral guide. In the first draft, she opposes Ben's plan to set whites against blacks by hiring both for the same low wage. At strategic intervals Addie is on stage—not saying much, but making pointed, sharp comments that reveal how Ben has transgressed against the moral code of his community.

In the first draft of the play, Addie tells Alexandra the story of Joe Keyes, who borrowed money from old man Hubbard, the unscrupulous father of Ben, Oscar, and Regina. Instead of acknowledging Keyes's ten-dollar overpayment, old Hubbard amused himself by predicting that the extra currency would lead to millions. In the first four drafts of the play, Addie's attention is on Alexandra, as Sophronia's was on Hellman. Addie fears that Alexandra will turn into another Birdie, Oscar's genteel wife, who remains helpless as the Hubbards take over her family's plantation and dominate the economy of a whole community. In draft four, Addie speaks of Birdie and Alexandra "standing round all your lives watching. Watching them [the Hubbards] eat the earth and its people. Standing there, growing old, sweet as the day you were born." But in the last four drafts, Alexandra's character is strengthened, and Addie's criticism is directed exclusively at the little foxes. At the conclusion of the play, Addie's line becomes Regina's tribute to her daughter: "Well, you have spirit after all. I used to think you were all sugar water." These lines were first addressed to Hellman by her Uncle Jake, as the playwright would point out years later in her memoirs. The assignment of the lines to Regina made the acknowledgment of Alexandra's independence especially powerful; like Hellman, the young woman of *The Little Foxes* learns to hold her own with her formidable family. In the manuscript first used when the play went into rehearsal, Hellman followed Kober's suggestion to alter the play's ending, which had Addie praising Alexandra's spirit: "That's my girl." Kober felt the final words should be between mother and daughter, and Hammett, almost always an astute critic of Hellman's work, had been complaining about all the servant talk. With Alexandra now able to act on her own, the moralistic tone of Addie's speeches could be severely cut, even though Herman Shumlin, according to Moody, "liked the original 'coda' and hated to see it go."

Unquestionably, *The Little Foxes* was a profound improvement over Hellman's previous two plays, for she had learned how to handle the interplay between highly individualized characters and their environment. As Hellman scholar Katherine Lederer points out, "Oscar's speech is jerky in rhythm, whiney in tone. Ben's is more expansive, more public in tone, as befitting a man who is always 'on' for someone. Birdie, the lost alcoholic Southern lady, is more lyric and repetitive than the others." At the same time, the Hubbards, as a family and as a business, are inseparable. There is a congruity in their relationships that gives their scenes together enormous dramatic power. Both Birdie and Regina are excited by the appearance of the Chicago businessman William Marshall and want to please him—Birdie, because he represents culture, manners, education, and all of the privileges of wealth her aristocratic family once enjoyed; and Regina, because Chicago represents "crowds of people, and theaters, and lovely women," and all of the honor and attention she craves. In spite of their differences, Birdie and Regina both reflect "a certain naive or innocent quality" that Hellman associated with the South in this period. Similarly, the men, particularly Oscar's son Leo, are out to impress this sophisticated Northerner and respond in this fashion to Marshall's comment on the beauty of the Hubbard ladies:

> BEN: Our Southern women are well favored.
> LEO: *(laughs)*. But one must go to Mobile for the ladies,
>   sir. Very elegant worldly ladies, too.
> BEN: *(looks at him)*. Worldly, eh? *Worldly*, did you say?

OSCAR: *(hastily,* to Leo). Your Uncle Ben means that worldliness is not a mark of beauty in any woman.

In this way, the Hubbards speak and shape each other's words and cannily take up each other's meanings while remaining irrepressibly themselves. Oscar interprets Ben for Leo; Ben interprets Regina for Oscar; and Regina interprets both of her brothers for everyone's benefit. When Ben and Oscar prefer to get the final third of the capital needed for the new cotton mill from Regina and Horace, it is Regina who unmasks their motivation: they do not want to include another business partner outside of the family. Even Horace, who opposes the Hubbards, relishes their machinations and smiles at the comprehensiveness and coherence of their plans. As a member of the family who has done business with Ben and Oscar before, Horace knows, "Everybody will get theirs."

The Hubbards drive hard bargains with themselves, just as they have with others, and are not surprised for long when Regina demands more than one third of the profits from the mill. Ben is being ironic when he assures Marshall that the Hubbards are "very close," since they are hardly a loving family. But, in another sense, they are "very close" in the way they try to outfox one another while making sure that the family, as an economic enterprise, prospers. In other words, the Hubbards attempt to contain within the family the fierce competitiveness of capitalism.

All three Hubbards try to capitalize, literally, on what they have learned from one another. Regina, for example, explains:

> It would seem that if you put up a third you should only get a third. But then again, there's no law about it, is there? I should think that if you knew your money was very badly needed, well, you might say, I want more. I want a bigger share. You boys have done that. I've heard you say so.

This speech indicates in wonderfully concrete terms that the Hubbard greed is boundless, that every family relationship is transactional and open to negotiation—including the possibility that Regina might "manage" to have Oscar's son Leo marry her daughter Alexandra, so that Oscar and son can share in the fortune of Regina's ailing husband.

Ben knows that the South is readying itself for industry and capitalistic competition. He predicts that his family's rapacity will be replicated many times over in the course of the nation's economic growth: "There are hundreds of Hubbards sitting in rooms throughout the country . . . and they will own this country someday." Ben knows that the Hubbards, unlike the southern aristocrats he despises, will be quick to change, to adapt to whatever complex of economic forces they encounter. Yet for all their confidence, the Hubbards live under enormous tension, which is most often visible in the nervous smiles and laughter that punctuate much of their conversation. This is a world in which the "balance of power," as Hellman scholar Lorena Holmin puts it, is constantly shifting from one brother to the other or from the brothers and Horace to the sister—a dynamic the playwright dramatizes by the use of a staircase, at the top of which the audience can usually find the family member who currently has the upper hand. At the end of the play, Regina has triumphed over her brothers, but the family strain remains, since Ben and Alexandra suspect that she has achieved her supremacy by somehow hastening Horace's fatal heart attack.

Although politics plays no explicit part in *The Little Foxes*, Hellman clearly means the Hubbards to be broadly representative of a modern evil which Alexandra rejects at the end of the play when she characterizes her family as among those people who Addie said "ate the earth." Alexandra declares herself a fighter. Such a statement, in retrospect, at least, sounds like the prelude to Hellman's anti-Fascist plays, in which the weak-minded and usually liberal characters struggle to face up to an insatiable menace.

The research and writing of *The Little Foxes* took less than a year, an extraordinary feat, considering how painstakingly Hellman revised and rewrote eight complete versions of the play at a time when she was under considerable stress. In late May 1938, just as she was beginning to write the play, Hammett was having a breakdown in California. He had lost twenty-five pounds and looked gaunt and white. He was holed up in the Beverly Wilshire Hotel, supposedly working on a novel, but friends were worried about his increasing absences. He stayed in bed all day. After fourteen months without a drink, he had called Hellman, then written her, then broken through the seeming even temper and gay spirits of his letters to her and gone on a binge, starting with several bottles of liquor from the hotel pharmacy. Frances Hackett discovered Hammett in his room, unable to get up from his bed. She called her husband Albert; there were consultations with Philip Dunne about what to do. Hammett had just been elected president of the Motion Picture Democratic Committee, and Dunne was one of three vice-presidents who would have to assume Hammett's duties. The thing about the incident that Dunne would never forget was Hammett's feeble blue eyelids which looked like those of a bird. The hotel would not let the writer leave until he paid an eight-thousand-dollar bill, but the Hacketts eventually managed to sneak Hammett out of his elegant suite, now in considerable disarray, and "airmail" him to a "terrified Lillian," who met him in New York with an ambulance.

The next few weeks were a trial for Hellman. Kober phoned her from California on June 3 and she sounded tired. The "Dash business" had her down, and she was gently affectionate with Kober. Yet by July 18, he received a letter from her announcing that she had completed the first act of *The Little Foxes* and was planning to go into production by November. "Whew!" was Kober's only comment. In her memoirs, Hellman does not even mention the grief Hammett caused her. Perhaps this is because by June 25 he had righted himself. In a letter to an MGM executive, Hammett reported, "I've gained twenty pounds since leaving Beverly Hills and am beginning to feel like something human again." He was at work on a book called "My Brother Felix." Hellman was grateful for how helpful Hammett was in the writing of her play. She respected "the toughness of his criticism, the coldness of his praise" that "came from the most carefully guarded honesty I have ever known, as if one lie would muck up his world." He was persistent and patient, and never intimidated by her saying that if a draft was not any good she would kill herself. "If I never wrote again, he said, what difference did it make? If I wasn't going to be any good, I should stop writing anyway. Go back now and try again." Hammett exhibited "the care and sacrifice of a scholarly and warm-hearted man who knows about writing, who wants it to be good, who is generous enough to give help." His "sense and balance" were invaluable in the shaping of *The Little Foxes.*

As Hellman reveals in her memoirs, the casting of Regina proved difficult. Stage stars Ina Claire and Judith Anderson both turned down the part because it was "unsympathetic, a popular fear for actresses before that concept became outmoded." Shumlin had it in mind to try Tallulah Bankhead. Hellman does not say what her first reaction to his proposal was, although she is reported to have had her doubts. Years later Shumlin told Gary Blake, a Ph.D. student, that he admired Bankhead's "presence on stage." She was a daring actress, but Lillian was nervous about what Shumlin called Tallulah's "scarlet" reputation. At thirty-six, Bankhead might have been considered a little young for the forty-year-old Regina. But the director sent the actress a script, and she "wired back immediately that she loved it." Shumlin's account to Hellman was that the flamboyant actress was "wild" about the play, and he thought she would "do fine" if her propensity for staging outrageous scenes could be held in check. According to Hellman's account in *Pentimento*, Bankhead insisted on seeing Shumlin while in bed with her husband, John Emery, and at the end of their meeting "threw aside the sheets, pointed down at the naked, miserable Emery, and said, 'Just tell me, darling, if you've ever seen a prick that big.' "

It would be up to Shumlin to keep Bankhead in line. The director was in complete charge of the production. Hellman had almost no technical sense of the theater and no insight into the casting of plays. Although she would certainly have her strong say on anything that bothered her, she was content to have Shumlin hire whoever pleased him. He had been the business manager for the legendary theatrical genius Jed Harris—a brutal boss who never gave his boyhood friend Shumlin a fair share of the profits from their extraordinarily successful productions. Having been bullied by Harris since they were teenagers, it took Shumlin years to launch his own career. Now in his prime, he was a formidable, quick-tempered, and authoritarian director. In her autobiography, Bankhead calls him a "taut and unhappy man" who approached his dual roles as producer and director with "uncommon industry and ability." He could also be extremely sensitive in his handling of actors, but he would tolerate no opposition to his instructions.

Howard Bay was twenty-seven years old when Shumlin hired him to design the set for *The Little Foxes*. Hellman had taken a dislike to Aline Bernstein, who had done the sets for *The Children's Hour* and *Days to Come*, although Bernstein remained as the costume designer for *The Little Foxes*. Bay thought it was Bernstein's drinking that bothered Hellman. Kober noted in his diary that Hellman derided Bernstein's book, which had just gotten a good review in *The New York Times*. When Shumlin decided he wanted

Bay to do the show, he introduced the young man to Hellman in his office. Bay had been actively involved in the Federal Theater from 1935 to 1939 and was, in his words, "sort of a star," having designed the sets for two important productions of the "living newspapers" and for several experimental productions.

According to Bay, "things were rough sometimes" during the rehearsals of *The Little Foxes*. Shumlin could be tough and arbitrary. "Part of it was his perfectionism," Bay recalled. "He knew all the actors there were in this world, and if he did not get the one he wanted, he would not do a show." He never compromised on what he felt was the proper casting. "And we had the perfect cast on *The Little Foxes*. But Tallulah had never been directed before, and that took a bit of acclimation," Bay concludes. Publicly, the actress praised the director for his shrewd understanding of the actor's psychology. He understood the actor's sensitiveness, and he was tactful. After *The Little Foxes* had become a hit in February 1939, Shumlin extolled Bankhead's power, style, and authority. Her personal qualities were admirable, and he singled out her "honesty, lack of selfishness and a straight mind that goes to the heart of a job." He acknowledged that she had had fears of being not "quite good enough." But he liked her lack of complacency about her talent. She had told him that she was shy and self-conscious during rehearsals and that he should not expect much from her in the first two weeks, when she was feeling her way into the part and getting used to the others in the company. Shumlin's approach was just the opposite. Two days would be spent reading and discussing the play, then rehearsals would begin at full pitch. "Right or wrong," he wanted her to "do it with conviction from the start."

When Shumlin criticized Bankhead's interpretation of a line, she angrily left the stage. He ran after her, and in her dressing room he explained that more than her "instinct and nerve" were needed for the role. She could get by with that much, but he wanted her to know *why* she did the part well, so that she could "be sensational on opening night and every other night." Given time to think about it, she wearily agreed with her director. She was having trouble breaking a lifetime pattern in the theater: "I've lived on my nerve. From the second night on, every part I have ever done has been torture to me." Bankhead "ended up fitting into the ensemble," Bay recalled. She accepted Shumlin's direction and "it all worked out." But before opening night in New York, there had been a lot of shouting going on out of town: "Herman and Tallulah, Lillian and Herman, Lillian and Tallulah and a little bit all way around."

One anecdote that survived the rehearsal period of the play and made its way into theatrical lore concerns a flare up between Hellman and Bankhead. As a good old radical, Hellman was inveighing against Heywood Broun, who had just joined the Catholic Church: "How dare he betray the radical movement by joining up with the Scarlet Woman of Rome!" Apparently, in the middle of this tirade, Bankhead spoke up and declared, "If Heywood Broun became a fire worshipper, I should continue to respect him. Can we get on with it?"

Shumlin was careful never to go too far with the principals. Instead, he would take out his frustrations on stage managers and designers. He hated technical matters. On out-of-town tryouts of plays, Shumlin would send ahead his business manager, Kermit Bloomgarden, to set up. When Shumlin came to town, he would walk around the block three times before he could bring himself to enter the theater. Finally, he would come in, walk down the aisle, and slump into the first seat in the first row, shake his head, and say, "No, Howard." Then he would clump up onto the stage and test the props or scenery. If there was a staircase, he would take the railing and shake it like crazy; or if there was a door, he would go to it and shake it. Then he would go back to his seat and say again, "No, Howard." He had a fetish about measurements and would have a tape measure in his briefcase, along with a script and a thermometer (to take the temperature of the theater). For some reason, the director was of the opinion that the sofa in *The Little Foxes* had to be raised an inch and a half, and the whole thing was taken apart to comply with his persnickety request. He never liked sets much—except perhaps after a successful production when someone would compliment him on the set.

A production with two such temperamental people as Hellman and Shumlin could never be easy. Complicating matters was the fact that they were also "boyfriend and girlfriend at the time," in Bay's words. Shumlin was married, and Kober felt Hellman had a "lot to do with wooing" Shumlin away from his wife, "tho they would inevitably have parted." Evidently, Kober was angrier about the affair than he realized. After a rally against Nazism at Madison Square Garden on the night of November 21, Kober, Dorothy Parker, Alan Campbell, Hellman and Hammett met columnist

Leonard Lyons. Kober noted in his diary that he had said "something cheap about Lil" to Lyons, and he rued his words all night. On December 3, with Hellman at Aline Bernstein's "new quarters," he observed "poor Rose [Shumlin]" playing "the lady with broken heart, glass in hand." Until the production of *The Searching Wind*, Hellman had great confidence in Shumlin's theater knowledge—his casting and direction—but after their professional relationship and lovemaking ended, she took up with Jed Harris for a brief period. "After Shumlin," she told Howard Bay, "I might as well go back to the gen-u-ine original."

During the rehearsal period of *The Little Foxes*, Hellman also leaned heavily on Louis Kronenberger for advice about her play. There were sumptuous dinners with Kober, Shumlin, and Kronenberger—all lovers of Hellman's at one time or another and all still deeply involved in her professional and personal life. Sometimes Max Hellman would be there as well. William Wyler's wife, Talli, who had just met Hellman in Hollywood, remembers that the word she had been given about Hellman was that she had to have at least two men around her. If one was good, two were better, especially if they had had affairs with her. Once Hellman had you, you were hers *forever*.

However possessive Hellman might have been about her friends—who were mostly men—she had a tremendous gift for friendship. She was enormously helpful to Kober in the writing of his plays. She made concrete suggestions about how to improve them and in general was a very important source of moral support for a man who easily doubted himself, who suffered from terrible writer's blocks, and who desperately needed others to believe in him. She nursed him when he was sick and visited his family. She was almost always affectionate with Kober and usually had no trouble entertaining and satisfying her various men.

> Sunday, December 11: Lil visits me this morning & crawls in bed beside me & this bundling so much like the old days when we used to play so crazily together. Dash comes & takes Lil to meeting. . . .

However, Ralph Ingersoll observed occasions when Hellman was "terrible to Arthur." She could be high-handed and extraordinarily oblivious of other people's sensitivities. Emmy Kronenberger remembers many occasions when Hellman would call early in the morning and begin screaming at Louis. She demanded absolute loyalty and undeviating attention from her friends. In return, she was prepared to go to enormous lengths to help their careers and to make them feel they were extraordinary human beings.

The women Hellman liked had either an endearing frailty about them or were fellow professionals—for example, Frances Hackett and, especially, Dorothy Parker. Similarly, Elizabeth Hawes, a fashion designer, educational director for the United Auto Workers, and columnist for Ralph Ingersoll's newspaper, *PM*, and Eleanor Merrill, an antiques dealer who helped Hellman decorate many of her homes, seemed to suit a woman who was very sensitive about the presence of other women in her circle. Hellman prided herself on her femininity and good taste. She tended to be spiteful of women younger and more attractive than herself— women like Talli Wyler and Virginia Bloomgarden, who had married men who were Hellman's professional peers. In the years to come, these women would be wounded by the playwright's acid tongue. Only Emmy Kronenberger would have the nerve to speak up and contradict Hellman at Hardscrabble Farm, the very court of Hellman admirers.

Kober's diary reveals that personalities, politics, and the theater were all pretty well mixed together in Hellman's get-togethers. Discussion might center on Kronenberger's work at *Time*, where he was working on a profile of Clifford Odets in November 1938, or on André Malraux: was he still a revolutionary or was he a counter-revolutionary? Kober conferred with Hellman about re-marrying. Wait, Hellman advised him, until he was over this low period in his life; the marriage should come at a "high moment," not when he was feeling lost. Hellman's politics were moving sharply to the left. The word *communism* never appears in Kober's diary, but he seems to have it in mind in his references to Hellman telling him about the "movement" and suggesting lists of books to buy. There also seems to be a cryptic reference in the diary to Hellman's connections with Communist party members. She was actively involved for a brief period in a "small Marxist study group of intellectuals," according to John Melby, who became her lover in 1944.

In her memoirs, Hellman is silent about this crucial period in her personal and political development. The war was ending badly for the Loyalists in Spain; Stalin was about to sign his non-aggression pact with Hitler and to invade Finland and Poland; the world was edging toward a much larger and devastating conflict; and Hellman was rehearsing a play that certainly dealt with the dark and violent side of human nature—if not specifically with the politics she was espousing. There is much that is left unexplained about her convictions and about her playwriting. In her memoirs, she deflects hard questions about both her life and her work by taking refuge in admissions of confusion and in delineating the colorful personalities engaged in the production of *The Little Foxes*.

In 1967, during a revival of *The Little Foxes*, Hellman confessed that in 1939 she was not sure whether she "understood what good actors and what good work Herman Shumlin was putting on the stage." She remembered doing a lot of complaining and fussing. She drank as much as Bankhead. A mint julep for Bankhead "made her temper flashing and often attractive." The same drink for Hellman often fixed her "in a kind of gloom whose quiet was broken by sudden swings of anger more unpleasant, I guess, because they were preceded by soft politeness." But, Hellman explained, on that production "almost everybody fought with somebody." It was fashionable to believe in the "civil rights of something called temperament," although Hellman now thought such argumentativeness a "comic waste." Bankhead immediately challenged the playwright's memories, emphatically stating "with all honesty that no one fought with anyone. It was the most pleasant experience I ever had in the theater—thanks to the kindness and understanding of the producer and director, Mr. Herman Shumlin, and the other members of the cast and crew."

In January 1939, *The Little Foxes* must have seemed like a make-or-break enterprise. Hellman had failed very badly with *Days to Come* and Bankhead's recent Broadway plays had been near misses or flops. There were also some problems with the ending of the play. Hellman needed to rewrite the last four minutes, although Bankhead thought fifteen minutes should be cut from the last act. En route to Baltimore for the out-of-town opening night, Bankhead came down with a bad cold, aggravated by worry over the quality of her performance. She was very nervous. Her mouth was so dry that petroleum jelly was used to keep her lips from sticking to her teeth. Patricia Collinge, who played Birdie, wanted the theater warm. Bankhead objected that the steam heat suffocated her. The opening-night performance stumbled along, and Bankhead, in particular, fared badly in the reviews, with one critic suggesting, "She encourages the suspicion that she is confusing Regina and

Shakespeare's Lady Macbeth." Another review may have scared Hellman: "The character does not hold up generally." After an opening-night party—about which Bankhead's and Hellman's memories are again at odds—Hellman seems to have suffered a failure of nerve. For several days, during which her assistance was required to rectify problems in the play, she was nowhere to be found.

Only a month later, the play was a raging success on Broadway. The entire cast was superb: Abbie Mitchell (Addie), Patricia Collinge (Birdie), Carl Benton Reid (Oscar), Dan Duryea (Leo), Charles Dingle (Benjamin), Florence Williams (Alexandra), and Frank Conroy (Horace). Not much had changed in the written text, but Bankhead's opening-night performance in New York was a triumph. The reviews read:

> Miss Hellman has given Miss Bankhead something substantial to work on, and this is a lot. Miss Bankhead, using few of the old tricks and relying instead upon insight, does a very fine job with the abashing Regina; makes her hard and vicious and rather frightening, as the author intended, and always authentic in the grain (*New York Sun*). February 16, 1939

> Miss Tallulah Bankhead offers the finest performance of her career, a portrayal that is honest, merciless, and completely understanding (*The New York Times*). February 26, 1939

> She radiates ruthlessness; she is seductive and dangerous. When, in the last act, she sits motionless and menacing while her husband dies in front of her eyes, you are convinced that the woman Miss Bankhead has built up would have done just that (*Theatre Arts*). April, 1939

> In its extraordinary variety, its combination of charm, common-sense, courage, avarice, and utter unscrupulousness, her Regina is a figure who might have stepped out of the pages of Balzac (*Commonweal*). March 3, 1939

There were a few unfavorable reviews and a fair number of mixed responses to the play, but *The Little Foxes* was a resounding triumph. It would run for 410 performances on Broadway and tour the country for two years. Hellman was more annoyed and troubled by the reviews than she was pleased by them. Certainly, she wanted a success, although she feared she would not know how to handle it. As in the case of *The Children's Hour*, she seemed to shy away from her prominent place in the theater. She stayed away from New York. She had some sense of the mistakes and virtues of *The Little Foxes*, but in *Pentimento* she suggests she was looking for "an interesting critical mind" that could go beyond her own analysis. She could not agree with the criticism that the play was melodramatic and explained why in an article for *The New York Times* (February 26, 1939) and then in her preface to *Six Plays*. The term itself had become corrupted, she argued. It was a good word when used to define the difference she saw between two fundamentally different views:

> If you believe, as the Greeks did, that man is at the mercy of the gods he might offend and who will punish him for the offense, then you write tragedy. The end is inevitable from the beginning. But if you believe that man can solve his own problems and is at nobody's mercy, then you will probably write melodrama.

The playwright believed in the humanity of her characters—in their ability to make choices and their responsibility for their own actions. Critics made too much of her "bad" and "good" characters; she did not assign them such values, and she was surprised when reviewers did. In conversation many years later with Richard Wilbur, she was still exercised about the subject. The character Ben, for example, is not presented simply as a dreadful, predatory animal. He may be interested in getting money by whatever means, but he is a good gambler and a good loser. There are moments when he laughs, and one thinks, well, he's a good sport. In *Pentimento*, Hellman implicitly makes the same point by following her discussion of *The Little Foxes* with descriptions of her Uncle Jake and her mother's other greedy and unscrupulous relatives. They were "comic as well as evil," and by the time she was sixteen, she began to enjoy "the family dinner with the talk of who did what to whom." Was this really so unusual? "I had meant the audience to recognize some part of themselves in the money-dominated Hubbards; I had not meant people to think of them as villains to whom they had no connection." What she liked about her own family was that they were "high-spirited." She had no use for weak-minded characters like Birdie and was outraged when audiences sympathized with her.

Tallulah Bankhead interpreted Regina as a "completely unsympathetic character." She did not want people to sympathize with Regina, "a woman with whom everything is seething under the surface." It would be easy "to let go, emotionally," but Bankhead was determined to "hold back, repress especially in the early part of the play." Her memoirs suggest that she saw Regina as having no redeeming or enviable qualities, and this surely is not so. Her rugged determination to best her brothers, her unwillingness to give up her ambitions, and her realization at the end of the play that her plans have cost her her daughter's affection clearly mark her as a complex and vulnerable personality. The truth is that Hellman saw the world as a tough place that called for a hardness of character which often was not pretty to behold. This is why her first notes on Regina mentioned that she was "good looking" but not attractive. It is tempting for actors to play Hellman as melodrama—the elements are there—but a more sophisticated and more realistic approach is required, which demands that the actor look for other aspects of the character. The villainous side will play itself, as Fredric March remarked to his wife Florence when he was preparing to play Marcus Hubbard in the movie version of *Another Part of the Forest*.

Somehow, Hellman was never able to articulate why she could not sanction the success of *The Little Foxes*. It had to do with the fact that her play was accepted on the wrong terms. By not admitting the evil inherent in everyone, reviewers were able to dismiss her characters as melodramatic fiction. Yet "1939 was the holocaust year of our century," as she puts it in her 1967 *New York Times* article, and after having been to Spain and seen the Loyalists' failure to stop Hitler and Mussolini, she "felt shame and sorrow at all liberal impotence in the face of the hurricane" which she was sure was just off her country's coast. Death was "around the corner." After the play's opening, she spent a brief time in an isolated village in Cuba, thinking about how to change her life, and decided to buy a farm in Westchester County, on the outskirts of New York City. Although she would constantly leave her country home for the city, there is the suggestion in her writing that she felt betrayed and that her decision to own and operate a farm was a kind of exile from liberal New York.

7

THE PACT
New York/Hardscrabble
(1939–1940)

On September 17, 1939, German and Soviet troops entered Poland. . . . If we were for Hitler, then what were we supposed to do about the antifascists? . . . I had absolutely no understanding that in 1939 the country of Poland had been wiped off the map of the world. And we had been co-participants in that act. . . .

In November 1939 our troops attacked Finland. . . . The thought that Finns were dying there as they protected their soil did not penetrate in the least. . . . [A] war of expansion was turned into something different. After all, we had been taught since school that *White* Finns had fought against us in the Civil War.

—Raisa Orlova, *Memoirs*

I recall how fiercely, almost half a century ago, [Hellman] scolded a group of us for failing to raise funds with which to help poor, powerless Russia defend itself against the murderous onslaught of a vast army of Finns.

—Brendan Gill, in *New Yorker*, January 27, 1986

On June 7, 1939, *The New York Times* announced the purchase of a country home:

Lillian Hellman, well-known playwright, has purchased from Richard M. Lederer his 130-acre estate in the town of Mount Pleasant, Westchester, midway between Pleasantville, Chappaqua and Briarcliff. The property lies between the Saw Mill River and Bronx River Parkways and faces on Hardscrabble Road.

The land is divided about equally between woodlands and fields and there is an eight-acre artificially created spring-fed lake with three islands. Besides the large main residence, which is surrounded by a screen porch, there are a six-room caretaker's cottage, two guest houses, game house, barns, stables and poultry houses.

The approach to the main house is a driveway about 1,000 feet long. The grounds are planted in rock gardens, orchards, vegetable gardens, grape arbors, and there are a network of bridle paths and a riding ring.

Hellman did not like the term "estate." She preferred to think of her place as a farm where she raised and sold poodles, pigs, and young lambs, and planted asparagus, giant tomatoes, and crossbred ducks. She made and lost money on her farming ventures. She got to know a lot about "trees, birds, wildflowers, vegetables, and some animals; about how to make butter and cheese and sausages; how to get the muddy taste out of large-mouth bass." Sometimes, however, her experiments failed: "The elegant Gerald and Sara Murphy grew very ill on skunk cabbage I had disguised according to an eighteenth-century recipe." The point for Hellman was to work herself to weariness, to feel "good-tired from writing, or spring planting, or cleaning chicken houses, or autumn hunting." Anyone who visited the farm—and there were many visitors—came away marveling at her command of her little kingdom. She was the perfect hostess and a fine cook.

Hammett spent the better part of his time at Hardscrabble, according to Hellman. Their days together were certainly the closest she ever came to having him entirely to herself. She would rag him about her reading, which was her way of trying to learn. He was so erudite and had made up his mind about things Hellman still puzzled over. He was a committed Marxist. "No one is as certain about his beliefs as my father appeared to be," his daughter, Jo Marshall, suggests. "But somehow, very early on, he had perfected a facade of utter confidence that was uncrackable and could be very intimidating. Part of it was that he really seemed indifferent to what other people thought, just shrugged off any arguments and never tried to convert anyone to his side. "I was trying, without knowing it, to crack his faith, sensed I couldn't do it, and was, all at one time, respectful, envious, and angry," suggests Hellman in *Pentimento*.

Hammett was the one man who forever eluded Hellman's grasp, the one man she most wanted to control and could not. "Turtle," a story in *Pentimento*, encapsulates their ambivalent affairs during the first spring of their residence at Hardscrabble. The story makes plain that Hellman looked to Hammett for certitude about herself and about their place in the universe—although she would not put the episode in such portentous terms. Their frustrating efforts to capture and kill a turtle, which had crippled Hammett's favorite dog, recurred to her after an incident at Martha's Vineyard, when she had almost drowned. Just when she was sure she was about to go under and was hoping she "had sense enough to go quietly and not make myself miserable with struggle," she bumped her head against the pilings of the West Chop Pier and was able to save herself. It occurred to her then that the turtle and Hammett had understood each other. They were survivors. Was she a survivor? she wanted to know from Hammett. As usual, he refused her a definitive answer.

The turtle that would not die, even after its head was chopped off—the turtle, an example of "the oldest living species that had remained unchanged"—obviously reminded Hellman of Hammett. The doggedness of the turtle, its withstanding all attempts to kill it, provoked Hellman to ask the fundamental question: "What is *life*?" Hammett had no patience with such questions; it was as if he was beyond them. Like the turtle, he could not be moved. He regarded her question as puerile because by thirty-four, her character, as far as he was concerned, was formed. It was too late to question the nature of existence itself. The couple actually quarreled over this turtle, with Hammett retiring to his own room and refusing to help her bury it. Even his concession to her feelings carried with it a rebuke to her self-indulgence: "My first turtle is buried here. Miss Religious L.H." read his neatly painted, small, wooden tombstone.

"Turtle" reveals that Hellman's mind was in turmoil, but the story also diverts attention from her precise feelings at the time. Indeed, she is expert at evading responsibility for the politics she espoused by describing herself in *Scoundrel Time* as "a woman who was never to be committed . . . facing a man who already was." Up to this point, she had been known as a fierce anti-Fascist. In the *New York World-Telegram* on December 11, 1935, she had been quoted as saying:

> California is the home of Fascism. There is considerable nationalism prevalent, and in Los Angeles there is an anti-Semitic organization. While I was there a proclamation against the Jews was inserted in the *Los Angeles Times*.

By 1940, she had joined a number of anti-Fascist organizations, many of which contained considerable Communist representation. The party and the Soviet Union were in the forefront of the opposition to Hitler and Mussolini. Her FBI file alleges that she attended the National Communist Convention in 1938. At the third National Congress of the League of American Writers in New York City, June 2, 3, and 4, 1939, Hellman signed the Call of the Congress for "Cooperation of this country with other nations and people opposed to Fascism, including the Soviet Union, which has been the most constant defender of the people."

That Hellman had a radical resume, that she was an enthusiastic fellow traveler, seems obvious—although the FBI had a hard time distinguishing between radicals and liberals who joined many of the same organizations in the Popular Front period.

Where the FBI and Hellman could have been most helpful— what were her reactions to the Hitler-Stalin pact of August 1939?— there is virtual silence. This period of nearly two years, which ended when German armies invaded the Soviet Union in June 1941, is the most telling episode in her political life. Her handling of the pact would mark out a position from which she never really deviated for the rest of her life. If she had been associated with liberals in the Popular Front period and even called herself a liberal from time to time, her unwavering support of the Soviet Union during the pact and afterward leaves little doubt as to her radicalism—even if she could never feel as secure about it as Hammett evidently did. For a brief period (1938–1940), she considered herself a Communist party member.

With her friends, Hellman was candid about her support of the Hitler-Stalin alliance. Philip Dunne, a liberal all of his life, was an associate of Hellman's during the SWG's organizing efforts in the thirties. He distinctly remembers that they parted company on the subject of the pact. From 1940 until her death, they remained friends, saw each other socially many times, but never discussed politics. The wounds from the pact period were so deep that they never healed. Like many liberals, Dunne was shocked that Hellman could suppress her fervent antifascism for almost two years, until the Soviet Union was invaded by German armies. Before August 1939, liberals and radicals had joined in a united cause under the doctrine of "collective security for all anti-Fascist nations."

At the time, Dunne was still serving on the Motion Picture Democratic Committee, and he vividly remembers that group's reaction to the pact. Hammett had been elected president, although he had never really taken up his post, and Dunne assumed duties as acting president.

> DUNNE: When the pact was first announced, everybody was against it, then all of a sudden—pssh!—the word came down. The first thing Melvyn Douglas and I did was to call a board meeting and obtain a unanimous vote of condemnation. A week later, they called a meeting (which any board member was entitled to do under our constitution) and rescinded the vote. Apparently the word had come down.
>
> ROLLYSON: When you say "they," you mean Communists?
>
> DUNNE: The people who followed the Communist line in this period.

Dunne's distinction is important. He did not *know* that either Hellman or Hammett were Communists. The use of "they" to refer to Communist sympathizers or fellow travelers was common at the time, especially among liberals who did not want to be viewed as redbaiters and name-callers. In his diaries, Kober uses precisely the same terminology, referring to Hellman's radical activities as "the movement" or to her Communist friends as "they."

Ring Lardner, Jr., recalls that Hellman had no doubts about the pact. Some party members considered Stalin's agreement with Hitler a purely tactical maneuver taken for his own defense, but they were disturbed by the carving up of Poland by Hitler and

Stalin. Lardner does not think Hellman had such reservations. He suggests that she was like a number of fellow travelers in the American League Against War and Fascism, which changed its name to the American League for Peace and Democracy. This organization was of the belief that the war in Europe was "phony" and would be turned against Russia. The fear was that Chamberlain and Daladier would unite with Hitler against Stalin.

Hellman's attitudes were similar to those of Ralph Ingersoll, who joined a Communist study group for a short period and was sympathetic to the party's support of "racial equality, fair dealing with labor, medicine practiced for patients not profits," and other "humanistic values." Laura Z. Hobson, in love with Ingersoll then, remembers that they quarreled over his sympathetic view of Stalin. They would spend weekends in Pleasantville, and she would feel "a great gulf" between herself and Ingersoll, who would take fellow traveling sides with Hellman and Hammett in talking about "the imperialist war." She knew they all hated Hitler and fascism as much as she did, yet it infuriated her to see how they trusted Stalin.

A short time later, Ingersoll became leery of Hellman because of the undeviating line she espoused:

> I never talked politics with her. I suspected she was very close to the Communist party. An actual break with her occurred at the Stork Club. She said I was a son of a bitch. I said, "Who told you that?" she said, "They told me." I said, "Who are they?" And she said, "None of your business." I said, "If you don't want to tell me, I don't want to know." I presumed it was the "they" of the Communist party.

Code words in regard to the party were common, and secrecy, an air of mystery, was often cultivated wherever Communists were active—in Hollywood, in New York, and in Washington, D.C.

In such an atmosphere, there was a great deal of confusion about who was actually a party member, but it was not difficult at all to tell who was following the party line, since support of the pact dictated such a volte-face on the subject of fascism. Unlike Hammett, whose public support of the pact can be easily documented, Hellman was unusually circumspect. FBI informants (whose names are blacked out in her file) reported that she belonged to organizations promulgating the party's opposition to the "imperialist war" in Europe, yet the FBI produces no records of her membership in such organizations.

Far more revealing of Hellman's true color is her attitude toward the Soviet invasion of Finland on November 30, 1939. Her account in *Pentimento* is one of her more disingenuous efforts. She never identifies where she stood. Instead, she introduces the subject of the invasion by noting that she had been in Helsinki for two weeks in 1937, where she observed "giant posters of Hitler pasted to the side wall" of her hotel and attended a "large rally of Hitler sympathizers." Although Hellman is careful not to state that the Finnish government was pro-Nazi, the implication is that the Finns deserved no sympathy. How that justifies a Soviet invasion she does not say; nor does she find it relevant to remember the pro-Nazi rallies in her own country.

Instead, Hellman belittles Tallulah Bankhead's support of the Finns by making her seem a dupe, attacks the actress's highhandedness, and suggests that Shumlin and Hellman were the victims of anti-Communist hysteria:

> Finland's ambassador to Washington was a handsome and charming man who met Tallulah at a dinner party. The day following Tallulah's meeting with the ambassador she announced that *The Little Foxes* would give a benefit for the Finnish refugees. The day following that Shumlin and I announced that *The Little Foxes* would not give a benefit. I can't remember now whether we explained that we had been refused a benefit for Spain, but I do remember that suddenly what had been no more than a theatre fight turned into a political attack: it was made to seem that we agreed with the invasion of Finland, refused aid to true democrats, were, ourselves, dangerous Communists. It was my first experience of such goings-on and I didn't have sense enough to know that Tallulah's press statements, so much better than ours, or more in tune with the times, were being guided by the expert ambassador.

This is an outrageous piece of nonsense. Bankhead hardly needed the help of the Finnish ambassador. As Maurice Zolotow has pointed out in *No People Like Show People*, she was an active member of the Committee to Defend America by Aiding the Allies. Throughout the thirties, she was an outspoken anti-Communist. Her support of Finland was no momentary enthusiasm inspired by a good-looking man, and it is typical of Hellman's contempt for most actors that she should cast Bankhead in such a demeaning position. In her own defense, the actress remarked that she thought the Russian invasion of Finland "the brutal act of a bully"—her words here anticipate what Hellman herself would say about Russia when she expressed admiration for Tito's feisty independence in 1948. Furthermore, neither Shumlin nor Hellman had ever asked the cast of *The Little Foxes* to give a benefit performance for the Spanish Loyalists. In fact, Bankhead recalled rehearsing the play on the day Barcelona fell and in her dressing room giving Hellman a shot of brandy "to ease her anguish." Bankhead had adopted two Spanish children, "hungry and homeless because of Franco's fury." During the controversy over Finland, Hellman never brought up the subject of a benefit for Spain. This is why she cannot "remember" having done so.

Bankhead's press statements were indeed more "in tune with the times" than were Hellman's. "The first week in February was designated Finland Week in the Legitimate Theatre," Bankhead biographer Lee Israel reports. With the exception of Shumlin's productions of *The Male Animal, Life with Father*, and *The Little Foxes*, every show on Broadway held benefit performances for Finland. On January 19, 1940, *The New York Times* reported that there were over half a million refugees as a result of the invasion. Herbert Hoover, national chairman of the Finnish Relief Fund in the United States, had already succeeded in sending more than six hundred thousand dollars to Finland, declaring that the very fate of civilization was at stake.

Over thirty years later, Shumlin told Gary Blake, a student of his career, that Mannerheim, head of the Finnish government, "had gained the reputation of being reactionary when he quelled a particular strike. I felt that the Nazis would overrun Russia, and that we couldn't allow that to happen." In 1939, Shumlin stated that the relief effort for Finland was an example of an "unneutral attitude" and that charity should begin at home for unemployed stage workers and other needy Americans.

This was in fact, the party line Hammett followed: America should avoid involvement in events that might lead to war and "concentrate on pressing for socialist reforms here at home." This was patently ridiculous and made a mockery of his and Hellman's earlier efforts on behalf of the Spanish Loyalists. In rebuttal, Helen Hayes noted, "When you get in the habit of helping your fellow-man, you don't stop to ask where he lives." Bankhead openly took the risk of being labeled a redbaiter when she suggested that the real reason for Hellman and Shumlin's refusal to aid the Finns had to do with their pro-Soviet bias. In the January 20, 1940, issue of *The New York Times*, she pointed out how active the playwright and producer had been on behalf of Spanish and German refugees, so "why should Mr. Shumlin and Miss Hellman suddenly become so insular?"

The very next day, Hellman was quoted in *The New York Times* as saying, "Theatrical benefits for Finnish relief would give a danger-ous impetus to war spirit in this country." This was a strange statement for a militant anti-Fascist to make. In both *Watch on the Rhine* and *The Searching Wind*, she would excoriate liberals for not having stood up to Hitler and Mussolini, yet in 1940, she was following the party line as dictated by the pact. Had she suddenly become a pacifist in 1939 and 1940? A few days after the announce-ment of the pact, Philip Dunne asked Herbert Biberman, a party-liner, what had become of "collective security," the doctrine that bound all anti-Fascist nations together. "Collective security for peace, not for war," was the baffling reply. At this time, Dunne in Hollywood and Zolotow in New York heard absurd and vicious attacks on President Roosevelt; Communists claimed that the pres-ident might "lead the nation into war *on Hitler's side.*" There is no evidence that Hellman went this far. Instead, she held her tongue and apparently bided her time. Her anti-Fascist play, *Watch on the Rhine*, first produced on April 1, 1941, was clearly, if momentarily, out of sync with the party line. She must have known the Hitler-Stalin alliance would not hold.

To understand how Hellman could write an anti-Fascist play that would be attacked by the party before the Soviet Union was invaded and then praised by the party as soon as the pact was dissolved, her rather old-fashioned code of friendship has to be examined. She was deeply loyal to her friends—most of all to Hammett, who faithfully followed the party line even when he knew it was nonsense. Hammett supported the party because it tried, however fruitlessly, to implement the principles of Marxism. He would vote for the Republican party, he told his daughter Jo

Marshall, if it adopted a Marxist platform. He knew that many of the Communist party officials were foolish. Marshall remembers a time when he was almost in tears because the party would not permit a friend of his to implement a program Hammett knew was the right thing to do. Party discipline was harsh. Hammett had been ordered to tell his friend the bad news precisely because he thought it was a good plan. "So it was an example of how the party expected demonstrations of obedience and submission—a situation particularly hard on one as brain-proud as my father," Jo concludes. He was also old-fashioned about certain things. His relationship to the Party seemed to his daughter like a marriage, and no matter how sour the marriage might become, her father would not betray the vows he had taken. In this, he was like a devout Catholic. The party was his church. Many ex-Catholics like Hammett were, in fact, attracted to the authoritarianism of the party, as Ralph Ingersoll would note after his experience with a Marxist study group and with Communists on the staff of his newspaper, *PM*. Philip Dunne relies on a religious term to describe Communists who never forsook the party or its allegiance to Moscow. The term applies to Hammett. He was an ultramontanist, with Moscow as his Vatican. Hammett would stifle his dissent, and so would Hellman—although she could never quite maintain his degree of loyalty. Friendship with Hammett and with other Communists and fellow travelers meant that Hellman could never attack them. The positive side of her position was that she refused to be a snitch, to name names when she was later called before Congress; the negative side was that she perpetuated the myth of the party's authority, of its right to speak for the radical movement and to exculpate Stalin from the hideous tyranny of his rule in Russia. She was not Dunne's kind of "wheel-horse Communist [with] a digestive system like a goat's [that] apparently can swallow anything," but she was never able to have anything more than a lover's quarrel with the Soviet Union.

Hellman certainly felt, as did most radicals and many liberals, that the West had pretty much ganged up against the Soviet Union. Woodrow Wilson had sent in troops to fight the Bolsheviks, and the Communists felt beleaguered right from the beginning because of hostile American administrations. The Soviet government was not officially recognized until the Roosevelt administration. For many years, Winston Churchill maintained that the Communists were worse than the Fascists. Hellman's fear about the "war spirit" in America perhaps carried with it the hint that anti-Soviet feelings over Finland might turn into a war against Russia. Undoubtedly, she could see why Stalin had made the pact with Hitler. The Soviet leader had not been able to form an alliance with the West, and the West seemed incapable of stopping Fascist advances. As Dunne points out, Stalin was making a purely nationalistic maneuver, but to cloak his deal in idealistic terms—as many American Communists did—was unpardonable. If they did not become pro-Nazi, they did stop their criticism of fascism. Even the Soviet invasion of Poland was rationalized; at least half of the country would be "saved," was the incredible justification Zolotow and others were offered.

This was a particularly tense time for Hellman and her friends. On January 14, just before the fight with Bankhead was aired in the press, everyone seemed on edge. Kober reported going to the opening of a Shumlin production, *The Male Animal*. Waiting around, he became "jittery with Dash's high spirits, Lil's profanity, Louis's preoccupation." On January 18, he took note of how sad he was to see "Lil unhappy of late . . . always on point of tears—Herman too difficult & irrational, Dash too weak & too tortured." Lee Gershwin, probably Hellman's closest woman friend since 1928, was astonished to see Hellman stand up at a party and announce that she was not Communist and never had been. It had never occurred to Gershwin that Hellman was a party member; their friendship had never involved politics and she was disturbed to see Hellman raise the issue. The Gershwins were patriotic and apolitical. Lee Gershwin did not understand any of this talk about communism, although she came from a very liberal family. She had heard rumors about Hellman running a kind of Communist cell (such terms were used very loosely at the time) at the Beverly Wilshire but she never said anything to her friend about it. Kober, Shumlin, and Hammett were all living together—at least that was the implication of the reports Gershwin heard.

Hardscrabble Farm became a refuge for all of them. Hellman would take walks with Kober to the lake and back to the house. She helped him with a play he was writing. Shumlin, Kober, and Hellman went ice skating on the lake. Shumlin was good at it, and Hellman was just learning to "stand on her feet with skates attached." They were at Hardscrabble on the weekend of January 20 and 21 when, in Kober's words, Bankhead started "cutting up about giving [a] benefit for Finland & pointing to Lil & Herman as horrors for not aiding the brave little nation." They were all very angry, with Kober giving vent to his feelings a few days later in his diary: "I feel enraged at this drunken foul-mouthed degenerate bitch & I think of letters to write & things to say denouncing her."

In January, February, and March, the newspapers remained filled with the controversy over Finland. *Time* magazine printed a nasty story about Shumlin. The best of times were still to be had at Hardscrabble, even though Kober found it terribly chilly in his guest cottage. He played Ping-Pong with Hammett and almost always lost. Hammett, Shumlin, and Hellman all contributed useful comments on his play, although Hammett's comments, as usual, were the most candid and devastating. On February 22, at Hellman's apartment in the city, Kober attended some kind of study group headed by Hammett. "Find subject so abstruse I follow little of it," he remarked in his diary. He was cold-sober but doubted whether a single thing Hammett said had made an impression on him. There were also Drama Guild meetings— usually boring for Kober except when Hellman attended and spoke her piece.

By the spring of 1940, *The Little Foxes* was on a road tour, and Tallulah Bankhead continued her efforts on behalf of the Finns. She made everyone in the cast contribute blankets for Finland, ushers in the theater wore Finnish costumes, and Bankhead sent a check—the equivalent of a week's salary—to the Finnish ambassador. Clearly, the actress was as stubborn as the playwright. Eugenia Rawls, who played Alexandra, remembers that the star was "not to be crossed, and not to be stopped from doing what she wanted to do." Rawls had been one of the schoolgirls in the original production of *The Children's Hour*. Her attitude toward Shumlin was reverential, and the confrontation between Bankhead and the director shocked her:

> In Boston, Mr. Shumlin called a rehearsal on stage at the Colonial Theatre. Tallulah said she would not rehearse with him. To me, conditioned by two years of "The Children's Hour" to treating him with awe, this seemed impossible. She stayed in her dressing room. In the work light backstage, I saw his face, lined and set. He and Miss Hellman had decided that if Tallulah did not rehearse, they would not continue the tour. Something had to give.

That afternoon, after the company was dismissed, Tallulah came out on stage, Shumlin sat in the back of the theatre, and she walked through the part. They never exchanged a word.

Rawls, who became a dear friend of Bankhead's, recalled that as a child in Alabama, Bankhead, determined to have her way, would have temper tantrums. She would "hold her breath until she turned blue and her grandmother would slosh a bucket of water over her." If Shumlin had delivered the water treatment to Bankhead, perhaps "she might have gasped and laughed and they could have talked things through," Rawls suggests. As it was, "she was angry and he was hurt," and they never reconciled their differences. Richard Maney, press agent for the play, remembered rather facetiously that "relations between star and author became so strained that they communicated only through semaphores. When visibility was poor, I served as liaison officer, carrying water on both shoulders." More was at stake than personalities, however. As Rawls notes, "I always associate 'The Little Foxes' with grey, snowy skies, and the tension of a country not yet at war but aware that we were close to being involved. Everything we did was colored by this awareness."

Soon Hellman would begin the writing of her first war play, *Watch on the Rhine*, which had been on her mind even before her work on *The Little Foxes*. With the dissolution of the Popular Front, the play would be trickier to write now. It would have to attack liberals, yet call on them and all anti-Fascists to band together for their "collective security." It would not be an anti-Communist drama, even though its activist message contradicted the party's current avowal of neutrality toward the European war. Similarly, Hellman's screen version of *The Little Foxes* would feature a bolder Alexandra, a more worthy opponent of Regina and a heroine fit for wartime.

8

THE SPLENDOR OF
PLEASANTVILLE
(1939–1940)

We are a group which believes in the existence of Right and
Wrong and we believe the Right lies to the Left. But how
far?

—Ralph Ingersoll, *A Proposition to Create a New Newspaper*

I remember I walked into Zilboorg's office once after Lillian
was leaving and his back was turned and he said, "But she
really *thinks* she's a princess."

—Ralph Ingersoll, interview with Hilary Mills

Again to Liss [a psychiatrist] & this time melancholy seizes
me . . . and again I'm deep in its grip. He forces speech
from me & translates it as envy & jealousy of Lillian & her
success, which I vehemently deny.

—Arthur Kober's diary, August 26, 1940

The success of *The Little Foxes* settled nothing in Lillian Hellman's character, even though it solidified her standing in the
theater. In May and June 1939, for example, she was one of five
judges at the finals of the Works Progress Administration (WPA)
Community Drama's annual Spring tournament and chaired a
three-hour discussion of the problems of contemporary drama at
the New School for Social Research. As in the case of *The Children's*

Hour, celebrity made her uncomfortable and she feared she would not know how to handle it. Setting herself up as a landowner promised the stability she desperately needed. She would have a return on her investment and avoid the conspicuous waste of resources that had spoiled her first theater triumph.

Heavy drinking accompanied Hellman's first stage success, and a similar period of drunkenness followed *The Little Foxes*. It frightened Hellman, and she had sense enough to know she was headed for a breakdown. She took a desperate step, one she would not have countenanced even a few years earlier—she consulted a psychiatrist. Ralph Ingersoll remembered that she had always been against psychoanalysis. But she was convinced that it made a change for the better in his case. In fact, she went to Ingersoll's analyst, Gregory Zilboorg.

Zilboorg had also analyzed George Gershwin, and Hellman may have seen the affectionate drawing Gershwin made of his burly therapist. The drawing bears out Virginia Bloomgarden Chilewich's memory of a heavily mustached, walrus-looking personage. Ingersoll described Zilboorg as a "small man with a large head, ornamented with a scraggly, over-sized and drooping mustache and great overhanging eyebrows. His almost bald pate was circled by equally scraggly, overlong black hair. But his eyes were what dominated the whole wild effect. They were dark, and at once warm and intense, and extraordinarily expressive." Later, Hellman would become good friends with Marshall Field III, another Zilboorg patient. Field, Ingersoll, Hellman, Hammett, and Zilboorg would soon become enmeshed in the production of *PM*, Ingersoll's independent, liberal newspaper. Indeed, an article in *Life* would exaggerate the psychiatrist's influence as the foreign guru of the radical rich and left-wing writers.

For Hellman, Zilboorg had many attractions. He was deeply interested in politics and had served as secretary to the minister of labor in the Kerensky government. He was steeped in the ways of Communists and freely advised his patients, including Ingersoll, on their involvement with radicals. Zilboorg was enormously cultured and was proud of his theater translations. He wrote several books interpreting Freud's ideas for the public; in one of them, he included a discussion of *Watch on the Rhine*. There is plenty of evidence to show that neither Ingersoll nor Hellman slavishly followed Zilboorg's advice, but he was a formidable figure whose opinions they could not easily dismiss. Although Hellman had come to him about her drinking, she was reluctant to think of herself as an alcoholic. "Do you ever have a drink before you go out to a party?" he asked. "Oh yes, I always do," she replied. "Then you are an alcoholic," he concluded. Hellman told Chilewich that, like any good analyst, Zilboorg had allowed her to discover the true nature of her alcoholism.

Within the profession, questions were raised about Zilboorg's ethics. Some analysts felt he became much too involved in his patient's lives. Certainly, he was Hellman's guest several times at Hardscrabble. Then there was his ego—it was enormous, one analyst remembers. Chilewich remembers him as very amusing and "holding forth like a egomaniac." But another analyst recently said, "They were all like that in those days. The early analysts did not always have the scruples that one in the profession would observe today." There is no question that Hellman felt she had benefited as a person and as an artist from her years of analysis with Zilboorg. For one thing, he helped her become much more aware of the kind of personality she had. She was the only patient he had ever had who talked about herself as if she were another person. "He meant no compliment. He meant that I had too cold a view of myself," Hellman told an interviewer. She was able to appreciate her analysis when it became possible for her to apply what she had learned the second before something happened—rather than the second after. It is doubtful, however, that she really knew what her analysis was about until near the end of it, when she wrote *Another Part of the Forest,* the play she dedicated to Zilboorg.

Practically every Hellman intimate in this period had either undergone analysis or was about to do so. Kober would be in therapy for years. In his diary for April 20, 1940, Kober notes that Herman Shumlin was in "good spirits" and confessed he had been seeing a psychiatrist for months. Hammett would also seek out a psychoanalyst, although he claimed to have learned more about himself from Zilboorg's treatment of Hellman than Hellman had learned about herself. She did not readily go into details about her sessions with Zilboorg, but friends noticed the difference in her behavior. Some of them envied the rapport she had with Zilboorg; others might ask her advice about therapy but shy away from her analyst, who could be overpowering.

It was Zilboorg who advised Ralph Ingersoll not to follow through with his plans for a radically different kind of newspaper.

The psychoanalyst detected a self-defeating quality in the journalist's endeavor. Ingersoll wanted to prove he was a greater publisher than his mentor Henry Luce, the inventor of the Time-Life empire. Ingersoll would have to depend on the backing of several wealthy investors, and, thought Zilboorg, in the end, they would fail him. The journalist had also carried on a dangerous flirtation with the Communist party, and although he was in the process of extricating himself from a Marxist study group, his fellow traveling friends, especially Hammett and Hellman, were deeply involved in creating the dummy issue of the newspaper, which Hellman had dubbed *"PM."* In the prospectus, Ingersoll had announced that *PM* would be against "people who push people around." Hellman may have supplied him with that pugnacious line.

Throughout the first half of 1940, Ingersoll visited and consulted with Hellman. Kober heard them compare notes on Henry Luce and Sam Goldwyn, two authority figures they must have enjoyed measuring themselves against. Like Hellman, Ingersoll had "an unerring belief in the rightness of any cause" he adopted. *PM* was such a cause. Hellman sent letters to her fellow writers, including Richard Wright, who she hoped would be interested in a job at *PM*. "All of us have great hopes for its importance and its influence," she assured him, as if speaking for the multitudes. But that is the way Ingersoll himself thought: the paper would be revolutionary, would accept no advertisements, and therefore would be beholden to no one. As he recruited his staff, the eager publisher was treating his brainchild like a success even before the appearance of its first issue. Hodding Carter, who became a distinguished journalist and publisher, was somewhat doubtful about Ingersoll's idealism, but signed up to work on what he called "this newspaper of tomorrow." According to Carter, *PM* would throw out the traditional who-what-when-where formula for writing news stories. All "stereotypes, all hackneyed phrases, all that spelled impersonal dullness and useless convention and superficial treatment" would be abandoned. The newspaper would expose issues and delve in the "why" of its stories. "It would tell the shopper what was what, where the bargains were, and what were bargains. *PM* would be a beautiful newspaper. More like a daily magazine in appearance, its high-grade paper would be printed partly in color . . . [and] would tell as much of the story in pictures as possible." No wonder *PM* seemed a place where serious writers and artists were welcome. And no wonder Lillian Hellman would be disappointed when Ingersoll failed to abide by his own exacting standard.

It was never Ingersoll's intention to offer Hellman a job on the paper. She would work on the dummy issue and write one article, but she was no journalist. As *PM* neared its publication date in June 1940, she was beginning to doubt that it would survive, for in addition to hiring several experienced journalists, Ingersoll had risked his enterprise on many writers with no experience in meeting the deadlines of a daily newspaper. The publisher himself had made his mark in weekly magazines. Marshall Field III, who was to become the principle backer of *PM* after the other investors dropped out, first encountered Hellman at a meeting of *PM* stockholders. She had a very small share in the paper and bluntly complained that the prepublication dummies of *PM* were "a mess—badly written, no stance, cute and unprofessional." Field was much impressed with her incisive intelligence and intolerance of hypocrisy. Louis Kronenberger, also on the staff of *PM*, noted Field's "great elegance as well as good looks." As a "reformed princeling playboy with a sense of social obligation and a real wish to be of use," Field would have a special appeal for Hellman, who was always so well turned out herself and so good at being a high-society radical.

Advising Ingersoll on *PM*, however, was hardly Hellman's principal activity. She was putting a new wing onto her home at Hardscrabble. It was almost finished when Kober arrived on Sunday, March 17, to have lunch with Hellman and Hammett on the back porch. The next Sunday, at a snow-covered Hardscrabble, Kober enjoyed an Easter roast beef dinner with the couple. As usual, Hammett bested him in Ping-Pong. Kober thought it was a beautiful day—"nice and sharp"— and Hellman was already at work on the screenplay for *The Little Foxes*. She was finding it a struggle. Kober thought the first part of the screenplay too talky, a common enough problem for a playwright trying to put her drama into cinematic terms. On Sundays in April at Hardscrabble Kober found himself in the company of the Kronenbergers. There were more hearty lunches, picnics by the lake, and a roast beef dinner that made Kober and Hellman sigh about the weight they were adding. Emmy Kronenberger was never one to let Hellman get away with anything, and Kober sensed that this was a woman who would stand up to his formidable ex-wife. Always one to fall under Hellman's charm and her outspoken convictions, Kober regarded "little Emmy Kronenberger" (actually, she was no smaller than Hellman) as an "ear chewer and quite fixed in her opinions, too. . . . We are both victims of Emmy's officiousness. This is further evidenced when Lil criticizes an idea Louis has for play & instead of being quiet and listening to an expert Emmy interrupts, gives her opinions and seems dogmatic about it, too." Hellman's letters are full of snide asides on Emmy Kronenberger.

With Kober for lunch at "21" on May 10, Hellman said she had a script for *The Little Foxes* that William Wyler, all set to direct it, seemed to like. Sundays in May at Hardscrabble included visits from Hellman's father, Ralph Ingersoll, and Herman Shumlin. On Saturday, May 17, the distinguished historian of medicine and science, Henry Sigerist, visited Hellman for dinner at her country home. Sigerist had befriended Ingersoll, who had invited him to write articles on health care for *PM*. Zilboorg and Sigerist had similar interests in medicine, and after Sigerist's death, Zilboorg served on a committee to complete the publication of Sigerist's manuscripts. An expert on Soviet medicine, a successful scholar and teacher at Johns Hopkins, and a virulent anti-Fascist, Sigerist was a revered figure for Hellman—as many of her letters to him reveal. He found her fascinating as well: "[Hellman was] dressed all in white, a flowing robe, bare legs, sandals. She looked Greek, and yet she is a very modern woman. I have a great admiration for her. She has an extraordinary psychological flair and yet is very modest, almost timid. Very refined dinner with excellent wines and conversation like fireworks. Sometimes life is very good." Except for finding Hellman "timid," which may have been her way of showing her enormous respect for him, Sigerist's impressions faithfully render the effect Hellman could have on her guests.

By Sunday, May 12, the magnolia's were in full bloom on the estate, and Hellman, Hammett, and Kober inspected "the garden & other blooms." Kober was with Margaret Frohnknecht, soon to become his wife. He had brought her earlier for Hellman's approval—Hellman having rejected several other women in his life. But Frohnknecht was lovely and quickly adapted to life at Hardscrabble. Hammett was to become very fond of her, and Hellman would become a significant source of support and guidance for the couple. It was all so serene and lovely at the lake that Kober almost forgot his thoughts of "war abroad of Holland being raided & soon by the Nazis, of Belgium being invaded, of the low countries being rendered lower."

On Sunday, June 2, Kober found Shumlin and Hellman in the garden picking vegetables. Then they all went off to the lake and built a fire for a picnic lunch of hamburgers. Hellman, Kober, and Frohnknecht went canoeing. It was warm enough for Kober to take his first "bare-assed" swim of the season. The next Saturday, the new wing was ready to be decorated. It was a "riot of color the wallpaper & the rugs brilliant & flowery. The chair a rich red, the bed a green & the vallences a peppermint green. It [was] audacious & aggressive & so like Lil," Kober noted in his diary. He helped her shelve books. With Shumlin and Jim Benet, he walked through the woods, and they all ended up swimming nude in the lake. Kober's bucolic rest, however, was disturbed on this night, as it would be on others: "again to bungalow for needed sleep & what the roosters don't do for noise the dogs more than make up." Kober never did take to country living like Hammett did. He was not good at frogging by the lake and was often tormented by bugs and flies. "The insect world" was getting him down, he observed in one of his diary entries. But throughout the summer of 1940 he records his delight in the fish, steak, and chicken dinners and the "al fresco lunches" of hot dogs and hamburgers that Hellman provided with considerable panache.

The beginning of Hellman's summer idyll was interrupted by a brief trip to Philadelphia to cover the Republican convention as a "distinguished guest writer" for PM. Like so much of her journalism, her report is a disappointing piece—two paragraphs on cynical, wheeling-and-dealing Republicans and seven on the city that is afraid to speak its mind. A taxi driver says he has been "instructed not to talk about politics, the war, or the state of the nation." In the South Street slum section there are "a lot of colored people in the street, not all of them looking healthy or very happy." At a corner store, the boss says, "We don't think around here much. It's too hot to think. Makes your dogs hurt." People like the boss keep looking away from Hellman, avoiding her direct questions, and she lets them know she is not fooled: "I said mine always hurt even when I didn't think." Everyone seems scared. A shoeshine boy says he has no ideas, that "sometimes it wasn't smart to have ideas." Hellman knows they want her to go away, and by now she is ready to leave, concluding that Lincoln "might not like" his deal-making party or a climate in which people are "too suspicious and too tired and too frightened to exercise their primary right of free and easy speech"—as if nineteenth-century Republicans did not make deals, as if Lincoln was not a politician! What she found was undoubtedly cause for some concern; worries over the fate of democracy in a world at war were understandable, and fascism certainly had its sympathizers in the United States. But Hellman's tone is so knowing and captious. Did she take the time to learn about these people, to establish some rapport? Or did she behave like the smug, out-of-town intruder? While in a Philadelphia hotel lobby, she ran into Thomas E. Dewey, an acquaintance. She asked him if he was planning to stay the entire week. As Dewey "wanly passed on," a Hellman friend present at this occasion said to her, "Look, dear. The poor guy just hopes to get nominated. Remember?"

The peaceful splendor of Pleasantville was shattered in late July, when Shumlin arrived with a memo Ingersoll had sent to *PM* investors. In Kober's words, it was about "his 'commy friends.' " Ingersoll wrote about Hellman and Hammett in "outrageous terms." Kober was appalled at the publisher's betrayal of his friends and shocked that he had not consulted them. Hellman was very upset and was unable to reach Ingersoll by phone. The next evening, Kober listened to Hellman's discussion of the charges against her and Hammett, and he was "terribly distressed at [the] picture of a frightened guy striking at friends to hide his terror." It also came as a surprise to Kober to learn that Hellman had not been as close and friendly with Ingersoll of late as he had supposed.

What had precipitated Ingersoll's panic? Right from the beginning, *PM*'s involvement in contentious subjects invited attacks. In Brooklyn, Reverend Edward Curran, in league with the pro-Fascist Detroit priest, Father Charles Coughlin, called *PM*'s first issue licentious because it carried four pictures of Gypsy Rose Lee. The photographs were not particularly revealing, but they were enough to set off a campaign in Brooklyn pulpits and in Coughlin's weekly magazine, *Social Justice*, that charged the newspaper with being atheistic and pro-British. Next came the charges of militant anti-Communists, circulated in an unsigned handbill that was distributed to New York newspapers: "Although card holding party members are in the minority at *PM*, they control some vital desks and otherwise are in positions to doctor the copy to suit." There followed a list of twenty-four Communist party members or sympathizers. Ingersoll was outraged at this scurrilous attack, and without consulting anyone but Hammett, planned to publish the photographs of the twenty-four staff members, a copy of the handbill, and a signed editorial condemning the charges and welcoming an FBI investigation. Hammett opposed Ingersoll's response and convinced the publisher he was dignifying an anonymous attack that could bring trouble to the people listed on the handbill. Ingersoll then reversed his decision, calling Hammett and telling him he would go to press with his original plan. The final blow for Hammett that ended his work for *PM* was Ingersoll's complete failure of nerve: "Incidentally, Dash, things are pretty hot down here right now on this Red issue. Maybe you'd better stay away from the shop for a month or so until it cools off." It was naive of Ingersoll to think he could settle things this way. Hodding Carter, certainly no radical, seems to have it right when he suggests that the failure of *PM* had a lot to do with Ingersoll's personality:

> He was given to emotional decisions, we thought, and was easily swayed first by one partisan group and then another; he listened too readily to the associates to his left, and not enough to those in the middle. . . . He commanded considerable loyalty but not much confidence among the rank and file. He was a good prima donna, but he made the mistake of hiring too many other prima donnas.

The controversy over *PM* did not hinder Hellman's research and writing of *Watch on the Rhine*, the first draft of which is dated August 15, 1940. There is no telling whether her fight with Ingersoll influenced the writing of the play, but it must have rankled her to be regarded as a tool of the Communist conspiracy, and she may have taken particular care to prove her independence. It took her only one draft to sever the connection between communism and anti-fascism in order to unburden her hero, Kurt Muller, of the weight of radical politics and of long-winded passages containing his affirmations of socialism. Here are the lines Hellman gave Kurt in the first draft before developing him into a more universal and less politicized figure:

I think a working Anti-Fascist is, what you call a radical. One who wishes to adjust society. One who works at that adjustment.

No. I am not a Communist. But I work with many of them.

In the finished play, Kurt would become the model of the good man, the freedom fighter without any specified political affiliation. Not until the creation of Julia, the Socialist (a model for Kurt, the author claims in *Pentimento*), was Hellman able to restore the link between radical politics and antifascism.

As with *The Little Foxes*, *Watch on the Rhine* was the product of much research, including interviews with people who knew about the underground movement against Hitler in Germany. Her trip to Spain had also prepared her to understand Kurt's anti-Fascist mentality and the details of his political work. Even so, she would ask herself pointed questions about her characters' backgrounds, especially Kurt's: "What was he doing in Germany? Scientist? Trade Union Movement? Maybe China? What was going on 1920–1932? Maybe they have only been here about 6 months? What was he doing here?" Shortly after the play opened in New York City, Hellman told Robert Van Gelder that she had made digests of twenty-five books before she began writing. She covered everything—"political argument, memoirs, recent German history." Her notebooks contained more than one hundred thousand words, even though this material figured directly in only two speeches. Somehow she needed it all to feel sure of her ground and to keep her "mind on the job." Hellman always felt that her writing had to spring from a completely realized world, the kind a novelist presents. She tried out various German names for Kurt's family. There were notes on the entrances of characters, plot outlines for each act, notes on the characters and on the structure of each act, and synopses of several scenes. In all, Hellman wrote eleven rough versions of the play and four complete drafts.

As Kober's diary demonstrates, Hellman had an intense social life during the writing of *Watch on the Rhine*. She could have been easily distracted from her work. Indeed, in his diary entry for September 15, 1940—one of her very social Sundays—Kober notes his admiration of Hellman "for her strength in withdrawing to her room & working on her play." This is how she remembered her schedule:

My friends come to stay and amuse themselves any way they want to—most of them read. We meet at meals. When I write I still leave myself plenty of time around the meal hours; work three hours or so in the morning, two or three hours in the afternoon, and start again at 10 and work until 1 or 2 in the morning.

It was not always so easy coping with guests, however. Sometimes she would have to move from room to room in Pleasantville in search of a quiet place to write. On one occasion, she posted a notice on the door of her workroom:

This room is used for work
Do not enter without knocking
After you knock, wait for an answer
If you get no answer, go away and don't come back
This means everybody
This means you
This means night or day
        By order of the Hellman-Military-Commission-for-
        Playwrights.
Court-martialling will take place in the barn, and your
        trial will not be a fair one.

At Christmas in 1940, several guests were "court-martialled," including "Herman Shumlin, former *regisseur*; Mr. Samuel Dashiell Hammett, former eccentric; Mr. Arthur Kober, former itenerant [sic] sweet-singer; Mr. Louis Kronenberger, born in Cincinnati, lynched by me." Emmy Kronenberger "perished" with her husband, and Max Hellman, a "most constant offender," was spared because of his age. The playwright warned that "this sentimentality may not continue."

As usual, Hellman did a lot of rewriting, and her play went through several drafts. At strategic points—usually the completion of an act—she would read the material to Kober and Hammett. On September 24, Kober heard a draft of the first act and was tremendously impressed. On September 27, Hammett told Kober how much he liked *Watch on the Rhine*. Hellman seemed to thrive on the attention and was rarely discouraged by criticism. She importuned Kober to come for weekends and to stay for many meals. In some ways, he was more reliable than Hammett, who Kober thought was looking very poorly during this period. Hammett seemed to be convinced that if he restricted himself to beer, he could handle his drinking problem, but this did not seem to be working. On October 26, Kober saw some faults in the play, but considered it wonderful material if Hellman used it properly. Right through to the end of the year, Kober saw Hellman and her numerous friends thirty-nine times—sometimes in the city, usually at Hardscrabble—and he reveled in the way she treated him to lively discussions of her work, his work, politics, food, and personalities. It was so "pleasant in Pleasantville," he remarked—picking fruit, eating breakfast, and gossiping about the slumbering guests, enjoying the beauty of the lake, walking the country paths and woods in the fall, and watching the "colored leaves departing from the trees." Applying lotion to his poison ivy blisters was less pleasant.

On the eve of his marriage to Margaret Frohnknecht, during this time of intense friendship with Hellman and while he was having the most grave misgivings about his own ability to write, Kober was undergoing an analysis that made him confront directly his and Hellman's personalities. Except with Lee Gershwin, Hellman had always shied away from explaining her divorce from Kober. Sam Marx called him the "great forgotten figure" of Hellman's memoirs, and Kober himself once joked that he had been married to Hellman for seven years, and she had given him only one sentence in her memoirs. In a note to him dated January 4, 1940, she kidded him about an old letter of his she found in a world atlas. She had many more in her files, but she thought he would like to have this one. She told him that her attorney had advised her that since Kober was getting married, he might find it prudent to purchase certain letters dating back to 1925. She imagined that fifty thousand dollars would be satisfactory, though she might "take more." This is how Hellman always wanted her friends to see her life with Kober—all laughs—and this is how her friends would faithfully report the Hellman-Kober liaison, except for those who were too puzzled to know what to think. He seemed too tame for Hellman; "she could have had him for breakfast" is how Talli Wyler puts it.

Kober talked over his marriage plans with his psychiatrist. They analyzed his dreams. One of them was about candles—which Kober associated with the old-fashioned and puritanical Jewish life of his mother's home and with the "gay, live world of the theater."

Both worlds used artifice, Kober noted in his cryptic diary entry for October 18, 1940:

> Make-up to simulate another character—stage—relig-
> ion the wig & the raiments. The conflict between the
> old & the new. Of artifice in both cases to conceal
> truth. On assimilation—on the influence of Ma & Lil
> (Ma again) & throwing off apron strings to make one's
> own decisions (Maggie).

Hellman was everywhere in Kober's past and present:

> Monday, October 21: Tell Liss of marriage & of plans,
> of what Lil said about if she can't be maid of honor
> then she'll be maitre d'hotel.

Kober's psychiatrist kept probing:

> Monday, October 28: To Liss & on argumentative side
> I telling him Lil's Dr. doesn't ask her for dreams,
> doesn't rush her thru.

Kober was becoming increasingly put out with himself:

> Friday, November 1: Disturbed at self for kind of
> dreams I have & for flaunting my weakness on my bed
> clothes. Tell Liss about dream & he tries to make
> connection between Lil's phone call to tell me how
> happy she is over marriage, how she's giving us some
> of her land as wedding present & Liss tries to make
> the connection with dream, Lil being mother, stuff of
> dream, the repression of sex activity toward mother.
> That bird talk or bird crap! What it may be is that Mag
> is to be my wife & I'm dreaming [?] for whoring
> pleasures. On Mag being a child & my desire for
> women.

In another session with the psychiatrist on November 8, Kober conceded that Hellman appeared in the mother role in another dream, "taking care of us and feeding us." On November 22, Liss pulled the wires together—to use Kober's phrase—in pointing out that both Frohnknecht and Hellman were acting as mothers, nurturing him and providing him with music and cultural (Frohnknecht and her family) and literary and social (Hellman) activity. If Hellman had carried him through one breakdown was Frohnknecht destined to do the same now? "I feel insecure as I did then," Kober remarked on November 26.

Max Lerner, who had been Frohnknecht's teacher at Sarah Lawrence College, got to know Kober well during this period. Lerner mentions the fondness everyone had for Kober and the feeling that "Arthur somewhere had lost the mainspring of what moved him in writing. . . . It was a sad thing. He was one of those writers who flashed through the heavens . . . and then was no longer able to sustain that." Kober would often talk to friends about his difficulties and his therapy. Frohnknecht's German-American family was very cultured, very European, permissive and tolerant and very supportive of the couple. This meant a great deal to the floundering short-story writer and playwright who had tied himself up so deeply with Hellman. Yet "all the way through one had a sense of Lillian as the presiding spirit over Maggie and Arthur," Lerner recalls. To Lerner, Kober seemed to have the best of both worlds: still married, in a sense, to Hellman but married in fact to the very beautiful Frohnknecht.

For all his personal and professional anxieties, Kober thought he was a happier person than Hellman. Whether or not this was true, by December, he was beginning to put their years together in perspective and to put some emotional distance between himself and Hellman. To his psychiatrist he brought up the subject of marriage, fidelity, and the failure of his last marriage—"what a role infidelity played, how we quarreled, etc." The decidedly retrospective tone of his comments reflected the fact that he was completing his formal analysis. It had been "a bad year and a good year." He was very happy about his marriage proposal and felt "a deep personal sense of development in my own home, my own wife & the family I will have. Fifteen years ago the time it was with Lillian, but that was doomed by her restlessness, her personal satisfactions." Hellman accepted Frohnknecht "so warmly and wholeheartedly," and so many people were "pleased & confirm my judgment." On the last page of his diary for 1940, he wanted to record a wish for Hellman's happiness. He hoped that she could straighten out her affair with Herman Shumlin, who occasionally appears in Kober's diaries for 1940 as disgruntled and headachy.

Kober wished her all the best for her new play. The writing had gone smoothly in just a little over six months, and *Watch on the Rhine* was ready for rehearsal. There were also high hopes for a book Hammett was working on. Kober spoke as if he were closing a chapter of his life. In many ways, he was. Although he would remain close to Hellman throughout his life, their marriage had finally ended.

WATCH ON THE RHINE
(1941)

Miss Hellman has skirted the question of war without eliminating it as a possibility; she has avoided mention of the working class as the leaders in the struggle for the better world, and nowhere does she indicate that a land of socialism has already established the permanent new life of peace and freedom, morality and comradeship and is the greatest guarantee that the ultimate struggle will be won. . . . The war is on everyone's lips; our nation seethes for and against the Roosevelt pro-British policy. And the Soviet Union and Communism are equally the center of a vast propaganda campaign of lies and distortion. Now, if ever, is the time to tear away the veil. And it is this veil, a fabric of omissions, which hangs between "Watch on the Rhine" and its audience. Kurt Mueller [sic] either is or is not a member of a Communist group fighting for German freedom. But in the play he dodges the question: "Are you a radical?" And we never really know.

—Ralph Warner, in *The Daily Worker*, April 4, 1941

D id Lillian Hellman ever fully realize that *Watch on the Rhine* was an effort to rewrite *Days to Come*? While working on *The Little Foxes*, she had the idea for a play to be set in a "small Midwestern American town, average or perhaps a little more isolated than average," disturbed by a titled European couple "pausing on their way to the West Coast." But somehow, she could not dramatize this idea. Then it occurred to her to write a play concentrating on the reaction of poor Europeans in a wealthy American home. Still she was stuck, and a new play had to evolve out of these two ideas and separate sets of characters. As a screenwriter, she had been exposed to the emigration of Europeans from Hitler's Germany. These visitors were usually warmly welcomed by naive Americans who did not realize that some of their guests were actually Nazi sympathizers, while others had seamy backgrounds that made their presence in the United States highly suspect. Hellman had also been reading Henry James on the subject of complacent, well-meaning, and all too tolerant Americans who did not recognize how much their comfortable, self-indulgent existence removed them from the recognition of evil. There was, for example, the head of an American household in *The Europeans*: "Mr. Wentworth was liberal, and he knew he was liberal. It gave him pleasure to know, to feel it, to see it recorded." The same could have been said of Andrew Rodman in *Days to Come* or Fanny Farrelly in *Watch on the Rhine*.

Days to Come, however, has no center, and Andrew Rodman's anguish over his ineffective liberalism proves to be wearing. Leo Whalen, the tough union organizer, is a dynamic character, but his story gets confused with the Rodman marriage, and no single plot line ever takes control of the play. *Watch on the Rhine*, on the other hand, is dominated by the character Kurt Muller. Even when he does not speak, most of the action has to do with him. He is as strong as Leo Whalen but also as vulnerable as Andrew Rodman. Kurt is European, but he is married to an American and returns with his wife Sara to her home in Washington for a brief respite from his anti-Fascist activities. Sara's mother, Fanny Farrelly, is a *grande dame*, a staunch liberal who only has to be shown the way out of her ignorance in order to act vigorously on Kurt's behalf. Hellman lent many of her own gruff but charming qualities to Fanny. Fanny's son, David, a much weaker version of his deceased father, a distinguished diplomat, nevertheless shows some backbone in his support of Kurt when he is blackmailed by the Romanian nobleman, Teck. David has fallen in love with Marthe, Teck's American wife and friend of the Farrelly family, whose choice of husbands has proven to be just the opposite of Sara's. That all of these characters should find themselves in Fanny's Washington home is precisely Hellman's point about liberals: on the one hand, they are warm-spirited and generous and apt to accommodate people of many different political persuasions; on the other hand, through their ignorance, liberals fail to make crucial distinctions and thus help to perpetuate evil.

In *Days to Come*, Hellman forces the action because of what she has to say; in *Watch on the Rhine*, the action has grown naturally from world events, and the characters, not the message, come first. Americans were hosting precisely the kinds of characters Hellman writes about. In fact, the playwright herself had been taken in a poker game arranged for the amusement of some Europeans in London. She obviously took her revenge on one of her fellow card sharpers, Romanian Prince Bibesco, by making him the model for Teck.

Although there is a great deal of criticism of liberals in *Watch on the Rhine*, it is a crowd-pleaser because it suggests that ultimately liberals will do the right thing. Early drafts of the play were harsher. Kurt implies, for example, that he has to come to the United States illegally because "working anti-Fascists" are not wanted; they are called "radicals" in America. Here Kurt expresses Hellman's feelings, which were published on December 10, 1940, in *The New Masses*. Along with Lion Feuchtwanger, a German-Jewish historical novelist, she was appealing for aid to the anti-Fascists who had fought for democracy in Spain but who now found themselves interned in French concentration camps. Thinking of men like Kurt Muller, Hellman noted that "there were days, not so long ago, when a political refugee was honored and welcomed by the liberals of every country in the world. But the places where he can be welcomed have each month grown fewer." The implication of Kurt's remarks and Sara's in the early drafts of the play is that American liberals *say* they are against fascism because it is the fashion to do so. They do not really want to support the anti-Hitler revolution in Germany. In the final draft, Fanny is given the pointed remarks and Kurt is circumspect:

> FANNY: Are you a radical?
> KURT: You would have to tell me what that word means to you, Madame.
> FANNY: *(after a slight pause):* That is just. We all have private definitions. We are all Anti-Fascists, for example—
> SARA: Yes. But Kurt works at it.

This is cunning revision. Everything Kurt says is measured and precisely spoken. It is up to Sara to deliver the rebuke to her mother (with a line originally given to Kurt). When Fanny forces Kurt to detail his political activity, he responds not with political opinions—sure to offend some members of the audience—but with an anecdote about Kirchweih, a gay holiday that gradually turns somber as the German economy deteriorates and the Nazis take control of the country. In this speech, Hellman manages to incorporate some of her extensive reading on post–World War I history and at the same time to make Kurt's antifascism spring entirely from his personal experience.

Watch on the Rhine has one of Hellman's most carefully defined sets. It is an early-nineteenth-century house with furniture of many different periods carelessly provided by four or five generations of aristocrats. Every item in itself has been contributed by "people of taste," but the overall effect is crowded and lacking in definition. In this setting, Kurt Muller's formal English bespeaks a man who has carefully shaped his convictions by fighting for them, by not taking them for granted. For example, he denies that he was careless in leaving twenty-three thousand dollars lying around to be seen by Teck, who then demands ten thousand dollars from Kurt in exchange for not telling the German embassy Kurt's whereabouts. "It was careless of you to have in your house a man who opens baggage and blackmails," Kurt informs Fanny.

Kurt must murder Teck. The lives of Kurt's fellow anti-Fascists cannot be risked by allowing Teck to leave Fanny's home with information that could be used against them. Kurt knows that murder is immoral. Nevertheless, he feels it is necessary to combat the violently sick world of the Nazis, even if taking Teck's life might be a sign of Kurt's own sickness. Fanny and David become accomplices to this murder so that Kurt will have the precious time to escape and return to Germany with the money he has collected for the anti-Fascist cause.

Several critics have commented favorably on Hellman's handling of characters in this play. Kurt, in particular, is a well-rounded, complex being. With his broken hands he is remarkably fragile and shows his fear, self-doubt, and great weariness. In many ways he is a ruined man, a vulnerable hero—as his wife Sara senses when she encourages him at the end of act two, "Don't be scared, darling. Don't worry, you'll get home. Yes, you will." His children bear much of the burden of stating his ideas, and as a result, he is allowed to speak and act with virtually no sentimentality. His conversations with Teck are extraordinary, for he talks familiarly with a fellow European accustomed to dealing with evil, never resorting to the blustering self-righteousness of Fanny and David. While Fanny prides herself on the principles she has absorbed from her husband Joshua, Kurt doubts that civilization itself has come very far: "Thousands of years and we cannot yet make a world." This is radicalism in its truest sense, a radicalism that confronts the fundamental problem of humanity.

More than any other Hellman play, the writing of *Watch on the Rhine* came out in one piece. Extensive revisions mostly had to do with paring away excess dialogue, tightening the dramatic structure, and relating the characters more closely to one another. In rehearsal, Hellman and Shumlin had their usual arguments, but the hard-working cast of Paul Lukas (Kurt), Mady Christians (Sara), Lucille Watson (Fanny), John Lodge (David), Helen Trenholme (Marthe), and George Coulouris (Teck) may have been the best ensemble of actors the director ever put together, and in her memoirs the playwright terms the production "a pleasant experience." That is about as enthusiastic as she ever became about most actors in her plays. In *Pentimento*, Hellman cannot resist pointing out that Hungarian-born Paul Lukas, cast as Kurt, was lazy, indulged in comic "capers," and betrayed Bela Kun (the Hungarian Communist leader) and joined Kun's enemies. Lukas, in Hellman's words, "saw nothing contradictory in now playing a self-sacrificing anti-Fascist." Lukas cheated at tennis and was so hated by Eric Roberts, who played his twelve-year-old son, that some nights Roberts "rubbed his hair with foul-smelling whale oil" before climbing into Paul's lap, according to Hellman.

When Kober read the finished script on February 4, 1941, he was terribly excited and felt it was better than anything else Hellman had ever written. In late February, he attended a rehearsal and was particularly struck by Paul Lukas's moving portrayal of Kurt and by Herman Shumlin's direction. Several reviewers would echo Kober's opinion. In April, the play opened to glowing notices and won the Drama Critics' Circle Award for the best American play. Such an award was long overdue Hellman. *The Children's Hour* had been scandalously denied a Pulitzer Prize because its subject matter shocked at least one of the judges. *The Little Foxes* had received more votes than any other play in 1939 but not enough to gain a majority. Although the whole cast was praised, Paul Lukas was singled out in many reviews. In the June 1941 issue of *Theatre Arts*, Rosamond Gilder sums up many of the actor's fine points:

His manner is quiet, restrained; he plays with his fellow actors, not against or over them; he is a keenly attentive listener, a gentle, kindly presence, yet he succeeds in conveying throughout a sense of Kurt's anguish and preoccupation, the fear that haunts him, his desolation at the necessity of going back into a way of life against which his whole soul cries out. Miss Hellman's Kurt Mueller [sic] in Paul Lukas' hands becomes the prototype of all those who like Hamlet, revolt against the "cursed spite" that calls upon them to set right by violence a world gone out of joint.

The reference to Hamlet is appropriate, for in Muller—as many critics noticed—Hellman had created a modern hero, one of the very few figures of the contemporary stage who deserved such an appellation.

There were a few negative reviews, and even highly admiring appraisals identified flaws in dramatic structure and characterization. In *The New Republic* (April 14, 1941) Stark Young spoke for several critics when he suggested that "some of the first act appears to lose time or wander too amiably—for one instance, perhaps with the scene of the children in which so many lines are given to Bodo, the comical, pedantic little boy." The last act also seemed slow; after the murder of Teck, too much time was taken up with Kurt's farewells to his family. Most reviewers praised Shumlin's direction, although a few thought his handling of the play too "reverential," which perhaps accounts for some of the slowness other reviewers complained of.

Except for Communist reviewers, almost no one found fault with the play's political message. The critic in *Commonweal* (April 25, 1941) wanted to know why Hellman used the word *Fascist* throughout the play instead of the more precise *Nazi*: "Perhaps the clue may be found in some remarks interjected by the youngest member of the cast, the anti-nazi's ten-year-old son. These are decidedly of a Communist tinge, and it may be that Miss Hellman wanted to write such a play but didn't dare." While it is true that the playwright censored her Communist sentiments, it seems unfair to deny her the term *Fascist*. After all, Kurt Muller fought in Spain and traveled throughout Europe for the anti-Fascist cause.

In *The New Masses* (April 15, 1941), Alvah Bessie handed down the party line on *Watch on the Rhine*. He admired Hellman's sincere and effective effort to get her audience's emotional consent to Kurt Muller's antifascism. But what was the basis of Kurt's politics? The play did not say. And what would be the "cure for this pestilence of our time"? Only a "world-wide organization by the working people against their separate home-grown brands of fascism." As a popular Broadway playwright, Hellman must have known that Bessie's line would prove to be much too controversial. She even deleted from an early draft Kurt's statement about an anti-Nazi organization's "attempt to teach the working mass of the German people." *Watch on the Rhine*, Bessie contended, "can be and has already been misused by those who would like to whip us or cajole us into imperialist war under the banner of fighting fascism in Germany." There it was: the implied rationale for supporting the pact. Because of Stalin's agreement with Hitler, the current war must be imperialist. After the Soviet Union was invaded, however, the war was no longer imperialist. Russia was now America's ally, and *Watch on the Rhine* was rehabilitated by American Communists.

Hellman's statements in the press during the production of *Watch on the Rhine* clearly show how much care she took to exclude many of her own political opinions from the play. As a dramatist, she came nowhere near her feelings about the persecution of the Jews or about home-grown fascism. At an authors' luncheon on January 9, 1941, sponsored by the American Booksellers Association and the *New York Herald Tribune*, she identified herself as a writer and a Jew. She wanted to be "quite sure" that she would be able to "say that greed is bad or persecution is worse . . . without being branded by the malice of people who make a living by that malice." She wanted to go on saying she was a Jew "without being afraid that I will be called names or end in a prison camp or be forbidden to walk down the street at night." Having been in Europe, she had returned "to see many of the same principles of propaganda and censorship apparently existing here," and she was particularly upset by the "private definitions" of terms like *Americanism* which she deemed especially "impertinent." She was already reacting to the campaign against so-called Communist subversives that would go into full swing after World War II.

In February 1941, as Hellman was going into rehearsals for *Watch on the Rhine*, she made arrangements with Goldwyn to hire Kober, Dorothy Parker, and Parker's husband Alan Campbell to work on the revision of her screenplay of *The Little Foxes*. Except for a slow beginning, Kober thought Hellman had done a fine job on the script. He regarded his own contribution as very minor and in July asked to have his name removed from the screen credits. But Hellman insisted that his work should be acknowledged, especially since Goldwyn had told her that Campbell was "cutting up about it." Goldwyn hoped to get out of the quarrel by telling Hellman what a wonderful man Kober was for claiming no credit, but she pointed out that she had submitted a complete list of credit cards a month earlier. She was so fond of Parker that she wanted no quarrels with Campbell. Hellman thought Goldwyn had lied when he said he could not give each of her three script collaborators a separate credit card. It would be too expensive, he claimed. She believed it would cost no more than two hundred and not the three thousand dollars he quoted her. After prolonged argument with her boss, she finally offered to put all of their names on her credit card. The important point, she reiterated, was that she had always thought it important that Kober be given credit. If it meant including Campbell, then they might as well admit he had them "by the balls and give up." She gave Kober instructions to consult William Wyler on the cost of a separate card and have him argue her case with Goldwyn, and to call Goldwyn himself, if necessary. To Kober, Hellman expressed her exasperation. Campbell had "maneuvered" her into the middle, realizing she would not accept a solution that deprived Kober of his credit. To not have her own card, she pointed out, meant compromising on her contract, and she had always made a point of not doing that with Goldwyn.

Parker and Campbell have been credited with introducing a new character, David Hewitt, but William Wyler's letter of February 10, 1941, to Hellman indicates clearly that she had already written David into the script, for the director suggested cutting a page or so of redundant dialogue concerning Horace's feelings about David. Wyler also thought Hellman had cut too many lines from Regina's part and that there was too much dialogue in other parts. He made detailed suggestions about the placement of other characters so that the stage play would move more quickly and realistically in cinematic terms:

> Couldn't we, in the picture, have Horace go straight to
> bed for a rest and play the scenes as they are now,
> partly up in his room. I feel that after the strenuous

trip, Zan should insist on Horace lying down in his room if not go to bed.

Wyler was also very concerned about the ending of the screenplay. Alexandra's speech to her mother was too long. Somehow they had to "find a way of dramatizing . . . the fact that Regina has won all that she fought for, but lost in the sense that she's now a lonely woman, who, however, faces the future with the same courage and ambition she has shown throughout." Shumlin had told Wyler that this view of Regina had never been executed by Tallulah Bankhead, and Wyler was concerned to "find a way to pictorially dramatize this idea at the end of the story."

Bette Davis's revised shooting script for *The Little Foxes*, dated May 2, 1941, reveals how Wyler finally resolved his dilemma. He seemed to lean toward a vanquished Regina in contrast to a triumphant Alexandra. Alexandra goes off in a carriage with David Hewitt, who has, all along, counseled her to stand up to her mother.

219
CLOSE SHOT: REGINA: NIGHT: RAIN
She determines that even this will not conquer her. We see her steeling herself against any emotion. She looks away and then looks again. Only her eyes betray her this time.
220
LONG SHOT: STREET: NIGHT: RAIN
The carriage drives off.
221
CLOSE SHOT: REGINA: NIGHT: RAIN
She looks after it for a moment, then starts to turn as if toward Horace, then turns back and looks after the carriage, her face getting closer and closer to the pane. The rain has been increasing in fury. It beats against the glass in gusts and streams down it. Perhaps it is only the reflection of its shadows on Regina's face, but as we leave her, she looks like an old, tired, defeated woman.

It is not clear that Bette Davis's expression in this last scene is exactly what the script suggests, but certainly the rain and Alexandra's departure strongly convey Regina's loneliness and her hollow victory over Horace and her brothers.

When Hellman saw the completed film, shortly before its release, she wrote to the Kobers that it was a "fine picture as pictures go, but it should have been better and I think Willy did a bad job." She had sent him a "vague telegram" and would follow up with a more honest letter. She predicted that the reviews would be good—judging by the enthusiasm generated at the screening for the press. For her, the picture pulled back too much, did not "hit hard enough," was "choppy in the beginning," and jumped around too much. In her view, Wyler was scared of being called melodramatic. Her comments are apposite in light of the battle Bette Davis had had with her director. She felt the only way to play Regina was as the villainess Tallulah Bankhead had patented on Broadway. Wyler wanted to see more humanity in Regina, less melodrama: "I wanted her to play it much lighter. This woman was supposed not just to be evil, but to have great charm, humor, and sex. She had some terribly funny lines. That was what our arguments were about." For all her criticism, Hellman had to admit in her letter to the Kobers that Wyler's direction was far superior to anything she had seen in "a long, long time."

Hellman was right; the reviews were very good indeed, and were due, in part, to the excellent cast. Patricia Collinge (Birdie), Charles Dingle (Ben), Carl Benton Reid (Oscar), and Dan Duryea (Leo) repeated their stage roles. Veteran screen actor Herbert Marshall gave a moving performance as Horace. The reviewer in *Newsweek* (August 25, 1941) noted that Alexandra's (Teresa Wright's) role had been amplified and that her romance with David Hewitt (Richard Carlson), the young newspaper editor, brought a "welcome leaven of warmth and humanity." As with *Watch on the Rhine*, it seems as though Hellman was introducing a degree of heroism and an appealing good nature in her characters. In a meticulous study of *The Little Foxes*, Bernard F. Dick has also noticed how Hellman builds up Addie's role as "part of her attempt to humanize the blacks in the film so that they would be more than domestics entrusted with the exposition," as had been the case in the stage play. Hellman paid a price for this new mellowness. In the *New York World-Telegram* (September 13), John Mason Brown pointed out that the film lacks "the horrendous concentration of Miss Hellman's melodramatics." The "screen technique has diffused the dramatic ferocity of the story," observed Don Herold in *Scribner's Commentator* (November 11). It would be in the nature of a Hollywood film, though, to make sure that there were strong counters to evil characters, so that David and Alexandra would have the "life-force to carry on after the Hubbards have burned each other out"—as Philip T. Hartung put it in *Commonweal* (September 5). Hellman admitted in an interview with Eileen Creelman in *The New York Sun* (June 19, 1941), that since Alexandra's part had been built up, "we needed someone for her to talk to. . . . Besides that, the movies always want a boy."

What is most striking about the "boy" is his sense of humor. David kids Alexandra all the time because she is so high and mighty and yet so quick to do everyone's bidding. In *Pentimento*, Hellman admits that in Alexandra she aimed to "half-mock my own youthful high-class innocence." Hellman often took herself too seriously, but she was capable of laughing at herself and of making her characters, including the Hubbards, point out the ludicrous aspects of their own personalities. There is a comic buoyancy in her depiction of human nature that is rarely acknowledged by critics, who get caught up in moralizing about the Hubbards. The fact is, their shenanigans are just plain fun to watch, just as the Newhouses' dealings were for Hellman. For instance, Kober would note in his diary for February 17, 1942, her telling him "a gem of a tale about Gilbert Newhouse & his screwing a chauffeur out of dough."

In her memoirs and plays, Lillian Hellman demonstrates tremendous affection for domestic life. Family matters—the very idea of family—concerned her deeply. In spite of her upset with Tallulah Bankhead—which continued when Hellman got wind of the actress's hamming it up on the road tour of *The Little Foxes*—Hellman acknowledged the death of Bankhead's father in September 1940. She wrote the actress to say she did not know or believe there was a proper "word" for "consolations." But she wanted to tell Bankhead "how sorry" she was to hear about her loss and to know that Hellman sent her "all good wishes."

Even as the Hubbards vie against each other for shares in a fortune, they remain a family, a coherent unit for which there can be no substitute. This is why, when it came to writing a political, anti-Fascist drama, Hellman would have to set it within the context of a family. Although she never remarried, she behaved with Kober and his wife, and with other very close friends, as if they were all a single family—of which she, of course, was the head. She presented them with lavish gifts and expected the same in return. In a letter to Kober in late July 1941 she mentions a gift of shirts for his birthday. She was pleased that he wanted them; he could have as many as he liked. She had divined that Kober's wife was "making like a baby for Kobe's birthday present." She was full of instructions: "For God's sake be careful: make it right. No fooling around, now, just plain, simple baby making. No comedy, no drama, just do it plain." They were expected to write and tell Mama Hellman all about Arthur's "birthday-wirthday." She missed them very much, promised to leave all her money to their baby, and closed with this injunction: "Hide the weenie, now, and don't fool around." The letter was signed "Lilly, the advise girl."

Hellman would find an apartment for the Kobers when they decided to move, and she wrote them several detailed letters about the rental and moving arrangements. She would have made an excellent real estate agent. She negotiated with Broadway playwright Moss Hart for the rental of his apartment and wrote the Kobers about the furnishings, including the beautiful rugs and draperies: "They are very much like the ones in my new wing." She had eaten out twice with Moss on their behalf. "I point this out because my birthday is June Two-Oh," she reminded them. Her letters were always very affectionate, with just a little chiding if she felt she was not receiving enough attention.

Her letters also reveal Hellman's enormous energy, good humor, and endless socializing. She may have already begun an affair with St. Clair McKelway, a *New Yorker* editor, who visited her at Hardscrabble along with the Kronenbergers during the summer of 1941. Zilboorg would not be around; he had gone away for six weeks and she did not feel good about it. In her correspondence, she would sometimes tick off the various items of her private and public agenda: 1.) She missed them very much. Did they get the note about Moss's house? 2.) She announced the prize for *Watch on the Rhine* and the contradictory reactions to the play, which made her "howl." 3.) She was sorry Arthur did not finish work on a picture. 4.) She had to break a luncheon engagement with Maggie Kober's mother to do interviews. 5.) She would take good care of the Kobers' apartment during her temporary stay, "except the nights I have parties for hundreds and we lay about with cocaine and flood the hall for water-polo." 6.) On the day her prize for *Watch on the Rhine* was announced, she had difficulty convincing United Press that it was Kober, not Shumlin, she had been married to. "I almost had to write you for the papers."

Hellman had it in mind to write a play about Versailles, about the events after World War I that were surely leading to a second international catastrophe. But she could not yet put her mind to the task of writing and was, as usual, heavily involved in politics. After several years of leftist activity, she had come to the attention of the FBI. A memo dated June 16, 1941, detailed her sponsorship of numerous events, organizations, and petitions under the governance or the influence of the Soviet Union, of the American Communist party, or of party sympathizers. There was, however, no evidence of a direct connection between Hellman and the party. An unidentified FBI source in San Francisco said as much, "but gave it as her belief that Miss Hellman is sympathetic with the Communist Party." Much was made of the *Daily Worker* review of *Watch on the Rhine*, as though the party had wholeheartedly endorsed the play, when, in fact, the reviewer had serious reservations about Hellman's politics. In many instances, the quality of the FBI reports is so poor as to be ludicrous: "On April 11, 1940 a reliable source advised that Lillian Hellman of Hollywood had been assigned by the Communist Party to devote her activities to 'smearing the FBI' in connection with her work on the newspaper *PM*." "Unverified" information in her file had it that in June 1941 she and some other unidentified party "were financing the American Peace Mobilization picket of the White House." In the FBI's view, these were Communist war protesters. Efforts to prove Hellman's support of the pickets were futile, even though the FBI went to the trouble of checking her bank accounts.

What made Hellman especially suspect was that she was clearly not a liberal dupe of the party. The FBI summarized a *New York Times* article (May 4, 1941) in which Hellman was quoted as expressing " 'shock' at the cowardice of some Liberals. . . . You cannot be a Liberal to a Republic and not to a Communist." As Hellman would demonstrate many years later in *Scoundrel Time,* she found it hard to imagine that anyone with integrity could be a liberal and an anti-Communist at the same time. Most damning of all to the FBI was her participation in the Fourth National Congress of the League of American Writers on June 6, 7, and 8, 1941. The pamphlet announcing the meeting urged that America should stay out of the European war. The congress opened with a public antiwar rally held at Manhattan Center in New York City. Both Hammett and Hellman signed the call of the Fourth Congress. Two weeks later, the Soviet Union was invaded by German armies. Less than a month after that, the FBI noted, Hellman signed a League of American Writers call to "All Creative Workers" in the United States "to demand full support to Great Britain and the Soviet Union in their struggle for the 'demolition of Fascism.' " Thus she had flip-flopped "in close sympathy with the line of the Communist Party in the United States," the FBI concluded.

In the late summer of 1941, Hellman attended a dinner for Averell Harriman and the American Mission to Moscow. She had been invited by both sides—the Russians and the Americans. At the dinner, a senator from Texas had asked a Russian dignitary whether he was not fearful that Stalin would "cut his head off" if he returned home. The Russian official took this kind of talk without objecting; indeed, he found the senator "charming." About this episode Hellman wrote Arthur and Maggie Kober: "You can understand why the Russians are doing well. The world of the great and the rich, rich, is all in Washington. I think we hear a good deal about the liberal new dealers, but they are heavily mixed with the New York upper set." But then, so was she. The newspapers were already beginning to refer to her as a "Red," yet she moved easily among Washington and New York politicians and diplomats, and seemed at home on both the Soviet and American sides.

In the fall of 1941, Hellman got into trouble over her sponsorship of the "Dinner Forum on Europe Today," a fund-raising affair for the anti-Fascists still imprisoned in French concentration camps. Originally, Governor Lehman of New York and other prominent liberals supported the forum, but they withdrew when it was alleged that several Communist front groups were involved. Hellman was outraged when a *New York World-Telegram* article suggested that the event would be used as a way for the Communists to "crawl back into favor." She branded the article "hysterical" and "malicious." She did not "give a damn" about the "politics or the religions or the colors of those who sponsor the Dinner or who will attend it." Her objective was to save fifty anti-Fascists. She was certain the publicity would do the dinner harm, yet she noted that reservations continued "to pour in, and our speakers, evidently being men of sense and courage, are undisturbed." She would provide a strict accounting of the financial results of the dinner, which she did on October 17, 1941 in a letter to Horace Kallen, one of the sponsors.

All of Hellman's political activities were a matter of public record. There was absolutely nothing clandestine or the least bit fraudulent about her leftism. She was a staunch supporter of the Soviet Union but never saw herself as disloyal to the United States. According to another unidentified FBI informant, "Lillian Hellman is one of the few Communists or Communist sympathizers who will discuss Communism openly and honestly." The FBI, on the other hand, was charged with keeping its investigation secret. No one was to know, least of all Hellman, that an extensive dossier was being compiled.

As with most FBI files, there is considerable material on Hellman that is blacked out on the grounds that the confidentiality of sources must be protected, the inner workings of the FBI must not be exposed, or the national security put in jeopardy. So it is possible that this inaccessible part of the file holds conclusive evidence of Hellman's subversiveness. But this is most unlikely. The file is full of hearsay and summaries (sometimes inaccurate) of newspaper articles and reviews of Hellman's plays. There is virtually no effort made to determine which of the reports is important, or which items within the reports have particular value. Instead, a repetitious collage is constructed, and each successive summary of the "evidence" appears to be taken at face value. Absolutely no effort appears to have been made to read Hellman's plays or her personality. No coherent picture of her emerges from the file.

Margaret Case Harriman's lively *New Yorker* profile of Lillian Hellman appeared on November 8, 1941; parts of it went into the FBI's *"Reader's Digest"* file on her radicalism. Harriman seemed charmed by "Miss Lily of New Orleans." The playwright was "genuinely feminine to a degree that borders engagingly on the wacky." She had little sense of direction—she had gotten lost on her own farm—and puzzled over such scientific insights as the fact that heat rises: "If that's true," she remarked to Herman Shumlin, "why doesn't your hand get burned worse if you hold it a foot above a radiator than it does if you put it right on top?" Of Hellman's appearance, Harriman remarked that she was "five feet three inches tall, and slim with reddish hair, a fine, aquiline nose, and a level, humorous mouth." The FBI's New York field office made Hellman a "key figure" that year, and that seemed to require several recapitulations of her vital statistics: sex, race, age, height, weight, build, color of hair and eyes, shape of nose, religion, and occupation. Unfortunately, Harriman's observation of this "key figure's" resemblance to an American revolutionary was not included: "When she is in repose or talking business, her nose and mouth give her a fleeting and curious resemblance to the familiar Gilbert Stuart portrait of George Washington."

After a reprise of Hellman's biography and career to date, Harriman pointed out that the playwright "has been called a Communist." Harriman found her "coy" on the subject of her allegiances. The reporter only got a vague reply that Hellman "would like to be a liberal if she could tell these days, exactly what the hell a liberal is." Rather than be pinned down—which surely would have meant getting into the issue of the pact—Hellman switched attention to her antifascism. Yet Harriman sensed Hellman's discomfort over having to waffle:

> Once, in her presence, a friend of hers set out to prove to a heckler that Lillian was not even sympathetic to the Communists, and gave a number of convincing reasons. "Isn't that true, Lillian?" the friend said, turning to her rather breathlessly. "Well . . ." said Miss Hellman.

Soon the issue of Hellman's "allegiances" would not matter. On Saturday, December 6, 1941, the Kobers, Shumlin, Hammett, and Hellman were at Hardscrabble. Hellman had been in bed for a few days with a cold. With the leaves off the trees, the countryside seemed shabby and bleak to Kober, now that nothing was concealed by summer's beauty. Hammett was playing the host. There were walks in the woods with Salud, Hellman's dog. Returning toward the farmhouse, Kober saw more chickens than he had ever seen. The tool house had been converted into a place for the ducks. Kober marveled at it all and sighed, too, to think about how much this country retreat must have cost "poor rich Lillian." The next day he heard his wife and Hammett up in Hellman's bedroom fiddling with the radio. Suddenly, Kober's wife said, "Have you heard the news?" He rushed up to the bedroom to hear the announcement that Japan had bombed Pearl Harbor, and that many ships were bombed and sunk. "Japan declares war on us when our leaders are negotiating with their representatives," Kober noted in his diary. All day they listened to the radio reports from Manila. The damage seemed to be considerable, and he realized, "This will do more to unite the nation than any act of Congress trying to get us into war. We were at peace when this happened. Remember Pearl Harbor is echoed over the air."

10

HOLLYWOOD GOES TO WAR
Hardscrabble/New York/Hollywood
(1942–1943)

. . . pure Bolshevist propaganda . . . as bad as Warner Bros.
Mission to Moscow only more insidious, it could not be
more flagrant if it were paid for by Stalin.

—Comment on *The North Star*, in *New York Journal-American*
November 5, 1943

. . . binds two great peoples even closer together in their
united struggles against fascism . . . The presence of
Marshal Stalin and the philosophy of his party in the life of
the villagers . . . might have provided a more complete
picture of Soviet life.

—Review of *The North Star*, in *Daily Worker* November 5, 1943

The year 1942 started with plans for the film version of *Watch on the Rhine*. Hammett would write the screenplay and a worried Shumlin (never having done a movie) would direct. In Pleasantville, the lake was still frozen, and one Sunday in January Kober and Hellman went skating, after which they feasted on a heavy lunch of spaghetti and meat balls. Hammett was talking about doing a one-hour mystery story for Shumlin, to be presented twice a night on national radio, but Kober doubted that anything would come of it. Hellman seemed disturbed by two visits from Morris Ernst, a prominent attorney, and told Kober shocking stories about the meetings. At the moment, she seemed enraptured with St. Clair McKelway, and Kober teased her about the way she cooed to her lover over the phone.

Kober could see that Hellman was very excited about the January 25 "command performance" of *Watch on the Rhine* for President Roosevelt. The play had been selected by the entertainment committee for the Washington celebration of the president's birthday. In her memoirs, Hellman points out that this was to be "the first public appearance of President Roosevelt since war had been declared." Her fondness for him is apparent in her description of his entrance into the theater: "The bold, handsome head had so much intelligence and confidence that the wheelchair in which he sat seemed not a handicap but an interesting way to move about." A few days afterward, she regaled Kober with tales about dinner with Roosevelt and the Russian ambassador Maxim Litvinov. There were stories about Mrs. Litvinov's fascination with Muriel Draper's "Freudian hat," the shortage of tea cups, and gossip about other Washington notables.

In *Pentimento*, Hellman recounts Roosevelt's repeated questions about when she had written *Watch on the Rhine.* He was surprised when she explained that she had begun the play a year and a half before the war, for Morris Ernst had told him that Hellman was "so opposed to the war" that she had financed the "Communist" war protestors who had picketed the White House before the German invasion of Russia. She could not tell Roosevelt why Ernst had promulgated this "nonsense story." The president laughed when she observed: "Ernst's family had been in business with my Alabama family long ago and that wasn't a good mark on any man." Ernst's story was red-baiting, as far as Hellman was concerned. It was like her, though, to put him in his place without making clear that she had indeed opposed the war before Germany's attack on Russia.

Hellman was especially tender toward Maggie Kober, who was suffering through a troublesome pregnancy. There were many visits to the expectant mother to cheer her up, and Arthur remarked on how "good and generous" a woman Hellman was and "how different from the thoughtless, restless, idle one I married." Although she was at the peak of her powers—a collection of her work, *Four Plays*, had just been published—she seemed very unhappy. On February 26, Kober jotted down in his diary the suspicion that McKelway had "wandered from home." Hellman confirmed Kober's hunch the next day, admitting she felt rejected. Her solution was a brief trip to Nassau in early March.

On March 16, Catherine Kober was born. A week later, Hellman and Dotty Parker accompanied Kober to see his wife in the hospital and to do some "window-shopping," as he put it, peering at Catherine through the hospital window. For perhaps the only time in his life, Kober felt a kind of serenity—maybe even a smug satisfaction—that these two women would never achieve: "I see Dotty watching baby with tears in eyes & Lil so envious. I really believe she'd give everything she has to be happily married & have child." If Hellman was envious, she was very good about telling Arthur how much she liked the baby. She also lavished gifts on Maggie and devoted herself to Arthur's well-being. They talked about so many things together, and he had to admit that "she was one of the most interesting gals to be around with." The trip to Nassau must have helped. By April 30, as she was about to depart for Hollywood, she looked as if she were blossoming. As usual, Kober found her in the garden picking strawberries, the "country lovely & green & luxuriant." They played gin rummy on the porch. She was apparently a poor player, since Kober made a point of saying so more than once. In June, he would win fifty dollars from her which he was "loathe to take" and she was "loathe to give me." Shumlin was already in Hollywood and from a call he placed to her at Hardscrabble, Kober suspected she had changed "a lot of stuff Dash put in [the] movie version of play." The next day, she had Kober moving furniture.

Evidently, there were some problems with *Watch on the Rhine*. At Hardscrabble, Hammett was slowly writing the script in installments and getting letters and telegrams from the film's producer, Hal Wallis encouraging and importuning him to finish it. Hellman was discouraged about the poor treatment a studio executive was giving her script, according to Kober. It was not her script, strictly speaking, but she would have a hand in rewriting and editing it. On April 4, Shumlin wrote to Wallis explaining that Hellman was "very anxious about the casting." She had not been informed about who was being considered for the leading parts which were still open. She was not looking forward to her trip with Hammett in early May to Hollywood, where they would go over their work with Wallis. But the cast proved to be excellent and certainly contributed significantly to the splendid reviews the film received. Out of respect for his magnificent portrayal of Kurt, Bette Davis

(Sara) gave Paul Lukas top billing. George Coulouris (Teck) and Lucille Watson (Fanny Farrelly) also successfully adapted their stage performances for the film. Geraldine Fitzgerald (Marthe) and Donald Woods (David) ably executed their supporting roles.

Hammett's early drafts of *Watch on the Rhine* were turgid. Kurt was given long, philosophical speeches about the rise of Hitler and nazism and about human evolution. Joshua Farrelly, Fanny's husband and David's father, was made into a Supreme Court Justice, "the greatest liberal lawyer of his age," and a political philosopher. Hammett even included a shot with a quotation from a book by Farrelly: "There is in our social organizations an institutional inertia, and in our social philosophies a tradition of rigidity. Unless there is a speeding up of social invention, grave maladjustments are certain to result." A man with a prodigious intellect, remarkably well read, Hammett tried to cram his reflections into the screenplay. For once, the roles were reversed; Hellman took the blue pencil to Hammett's disquisitions.

Even though several of Hammett's scenes were bloated with excess dialogue, he had hit on a cinematic structure for the play that survived subsequent revisions. The movie opens in Mexico, a country particularly hospitable to refugees from the Spanish Civil War. The Mullers gradually become acclimated to the United States by their train trip to Washington, and at the same time, the Farrelly household is having breakfast on the terrace. As Bernard F. Dick points out, "the Mexican opening allows two actions to develop simultaneously," so that by the time the Mullers arrive in Washington, viewers know a good deal both about Kurt's background and about the Farrelly family. For example, on the way downstairs to breakfast, Teck observes to Marthe, "It's unfortunate that early American liberals were such a hardy people. Breakfast promptly at nine. Outdoors. Dinner promptly at eight." At about the same time, Kurt is having a discussion on the train with an Italian-American about his anti-Fascist activities in the Spanish Civil War.

Hellman admired the way Hammett could articulate human character and politics in movie scenes that were not in her play: "He's put in one scene that I'd have given anything to have written," she remarked to Eileen Creelman. "Do you remember the villain talking about a poker party in the German Embassy? Well, he's written in that poker party. And it's marvelous." In the play, Marthe points out to Teck that he has played on so many sides in Europe's political wars that she does not understand why they have not come out better. In the movie, we see Teck playing cards, and he is easily identified as a man who has something to sell, a man whose motivations are transparent to the Nazi intelligence officer who deals the cards. Seated at the table are a German baron who serves but despises the Nazis and their vulgar, "paper hanger" leader, a diplomat who never gives away his game, and a businessman who will deal with anyone for the right price. The round of poker aptly sums up the ideological, cynical, and collaborationist forces aligned against Kurt. Hellman's own contribution to the movie, a coda that takes place six months after the point where the play ended, was not well received. Some reviewers thought it was superfluous to show Sara discussing the future with her son Joshua, who traces on a map his father's route back to Europe as a way of preparing himself to take Kurt's place.

Although Hellman was only in Hollywood for a month, she managed to write a short screenplay entitled *The Negro Soldier* for director Stuart Heisler. As the FBI knew, she had been active for some time on behalf of civil rights for blacks. On April 8, 1942, for example, she had joined Paul Robeson and others as speakers at the Council on African Affairs at Manhattan Center. A resolution was adopted at that meeting advocating the end of all racial discrimination in the armed forces and government services. Robeson and Hellman would be associated with various fund-raising events for anti-Fascist refugees and for campaigns against racial discrimination. On September 25, 1943, at Hunter College, she led a group discussion of Jim Crow in the armed forces, sponsored by the Citizens Emergency Conference for Inter-Racial Unity.

In February 1944, *The Negro Soldier*, a forty-minute semi-documentary film, was released, but Hellman was given no credit. Given the way the film was produced and reviewed, it is not surprising that Heisler found Hellman's work unacceptable. Evidently, he wanted an upbeat film that concentrated on the achievements of blacks and on their participation in every war the United States had fought. All controversial topics, like racial discrimination, are avoided; Paul Robeson is not even mentioned.

Hellman had in mind something quite different. Her movie is set on an evening in which Joe Louis defends his world heavyweight title. A dialogue takes place between Chris, a thirteen-year-old newspaper boy, and John, a soldier. Both are black. Chris is upset because "Private Joe Louis" is turning over his part of the gate receipts to the families of the armed forces. John, on the other hand, admires the fighter's ability to rise above bitterness. He imagines that Louis, like himself, is not fighting for "what's bad [but] for what's good now, and what'll maybe get better." This attitude angers Chris, who points to the headlines of his newspaper: "RIOTS OVER NEW NEGRO HOUSING PROJECT. WHITE NEIGHBORS REFUSE OCCUPANCY TO NEGRO TENANTS IN BUILDING GOVERNMENT ERECTED FOR THEM."

John does not deny the evils of racial discrimination, but he counsels Chris not to become a "bitter and useless man." He suggests that "if you're going to make the lot of the black man better, you got to fight for the white man, too." The movie illustrates his point by flashing back to an episode in which a much younger John witnessed the aftermath of a lynching. A white man had boldly stood up to Klansmen and thereafter made it impossible for the Klan to ever lynch blacks in that part of Alabama again. In this heavily didactic script, Chris cannot help but get the point—which is rousingly orchestrated at the end by Paul Robeson and the Fisk Jubilee singers. Hellman's work is well-meaning but terribly talky, contrived, and static. Yet her script did attract attention. At one point she announced in a letter that Goldwyn was going to make "the negro picture with some money put up by me and Herm." Hellman wanted to see it done quickly, and if the film would not cost too much, that was the way the deal would be made, with William Wyler as director. Evidently, the arrangement with Goldwyn fell through, because on June 22, 1942, she wrote to Hal Wallis, who produced *Watch on the Rhine* at Warner Brothers, that she was "delighted about the negro short." As late as October 8, 1942, Jack Warner was urging a subordinate to "lose no time on rewriting Lillian Hellman Negro short." The very next day, Warner was told in a memo that Vincent Sherman was enthusiastic about directing the Hellman script and wanted to rewrite it himself with a collaborator. A script was produced bearing virtually no resemblance either to Hellman's draft or to the film that was eventually released.

By May 26, Hellman and Hammett had returned from Hollywood—Hellman with her usual quota of wild stories and with Goldwyn's plan to send her to the Soviet Union to do a documentary. She told Kober she was less than enthusiastic about traveling to a war zone, although if anything happened to her, Goldwyn would probably feel it was "good publicity." On June 14, a Sunday at Hardscrabble, Kober met Wyler, who was curious as to why Hellman did not want to go to Russia with him to work on the film.

That summer, Hammett's daughters, Mary and Jo, came from California to visit their father. The best part of the visit was at Hardscrabble. Hammett loved nature and enjoyed teaching his daughters how to fish. Mary, however, was unmanageable; she would drink and fight with her father, and Hellman thought her a "brat straight from hell." Sixteen-year-old Jo was much more pleasant than her older sister. A docile girl, in Hellman's view, Jo was three or four when she first met Hellman at the Beverly Wilshire Hotel. To Jo, Hellman always seemed pleasant, if a little scary because of the tough persona of a New York Jewish woman. But it was interesting to observe the Southern belle side. There would be moments when Hellman would defer in an almost girlish, flirtatious way to others. "What do you think, *really?*" she might ask. Jo thought that her father, raised as a Maryland Catholic, found Hellman intriguing and perhaps a bit exotic, a bit of forbidden fruit. Hammett asked Jo what she thought of Hellman. Jo did not know what to say. He explained that he had been with Hellman so long he did not know how to think of her anymore. Occasionally, Hammett and Hellman would joke about sex, and at first Jo was shocked, having been brought up by her mother as a strict Catholic. Evidently, Hellman restrained her cursing around Jo. On one occasion Jo did hear a "goddam," and Hellman said, "Oh, excuse me, Josephine." Jo did not take this as a sincere apology; it seemed a little showy. "Josephine, you're very religious, aren't you?" Hellman once asked her. In retrospect, Jo sees this as a rather rude way to put such a question to a child. At seven years old it made her uncomfortable. Hammett came to the rescue. He said, "Well, Jo feels that there is nothing wrong with being religious. If it turns out that there is a God, then she's that much further ahead of the game." Not particularly interested in children, Hellman nevertheless could be very funny and generous with them. Jo received from her a lovely locket in an antique frame, a Hellman family treasure.

It was a relief to see the children go home. "Things were becoming strained anyway between Hammett and her, with his drinking, the cold way he seemed sometimes, his moody silences," reports Diane Johnson. Hammett indulged himself with other women, especially in Harlem whorehouses, and continued to plaster himself with liquor. Hellman, her nerves raw from her analysis with Zilboorg, felt she had come to the end of something in her relationship with Hammett. While driving him into town one night, he began to paw her. He fixed her with a drunken leer and suggested they make love. She had never refused him, but this time it was no. Her denial upset him. A man given to extremes, he determined never to make love to her again. He kept his vow. He never spoke of it, and Hellman could not have known what the consequences of her first refusal would cost her. No one can say for sure why Hammett made such an absolute decision, but it must have occurred to him that if she had declined to have sex once, she might do so again. In all likelihood, a man as self-contained as Hammett, who prided himself on needing no one, who could not stand the idea of being manipulated by the desires of others, could not accept Hellman's independence on this issue, no matter how just her reason for refusing him.

Throughout this summer, Hellman got reports from Hollywood about the progress of the *Watch on the Rhine* production. As Shumlin feared, he was having a difficult time directing the movie. He kept getting memos from the studio about using too much film. He was shooting full takes of too many scenes. As in the theater, he would rehearse his cast before going in front of the cameras. Set-ups for camera angles were a problem and he fell behind schedule. Gradually, however, the film took shape, largely under the guidance of veteran cameraman Hal Mohr and Hal Wallis, who supervised all aspects of the production.

Of even more serious concern to Hellman were censorship problems. On June 22, she wrote Wallis, indicating she wanted to send a letter to Breen's office. She considered the objections to *Watch on the Rhine* "not only as unintelligent as they were in the old days, but . . . growing downright immoral." On July 9, Wallis wrote to her suggesting she reply to Breen. Her letter of July 13 is scathing. She found "deeply shocking" Breen's stipulation that Kurt would have to be assassinated in recompense for having killed Teck—a scandalous suggestion in a country at war with the Nazis. What about American soldiers who killed Nazis? Should they also pay with their own lives? Nobody in her picture promoted anything immoral. She dismissed another Breen suggestion that a love affair between Marthe, a married woman, and David was promoted by the other characters. After all, she was married to "a Nazi and a villain," Hellman pointed out. This was not quite accurate, but Hellman was in no mood to concede even the smallest point to a censor. Other Breen objections seemed equally ridiculous to her—like the suggestion that the display of liquor bottles in Fanny's home promoted drinking. "It is not 'drinking' to have a drink," was Hellman's terse reply. She concluded by saying there was "no justice in these objections to the script and I cannot believe you agree with them." She was sure he believed in what the picture had to say, and she asked his help. On July 13, Hellman also wrote to Hal Wallis warning that "if they continue with the insistence that Kurt be punished, I would like to gather some more material and do a piece about the Hays office censorship." The result of her adamant stand was that she won on every point.

The summer splendor of Pleasantville was also disturbed by Hammett's enlistment, at forty-eight years old, in the army. Hellman was shocked and was sure he would not be able to bear up under strenuous military discipline. After he left Pleasantville in the fall, she felt "lonely and useless." It was difficult watching others go off to a war she wanted to be a part of. The plan to go to Russia for Goldwyn was wrecked when he insisted, according to Hellman, that she and Wyler do the picture for free, out of their love (as radicals) for Russia and their patriotic duty to America. Hellman knew Goldwyn was not serious about not paying them; he merely wanted to reduce their price. But by the time they were reconciled, Wyler had taken a commission in the Air Force and Hellman was not willing to go to Russia with another director. Goldwyn still wanted his Russian picture, and evidently so did Washington, since presidential advisor Harry Hopkins seemed to have had a hand in encouraging the production of *The North Star*.

Here was Hellman's opportunity to have her say about what was going on in Russia. As she puts it in *An Unfinished Woman*, "America was moved and bewildered by the courage of a people who had been presented to two generations of Americans as passive slaves." She had begun a new play, but finishing that was put aside to research and to write her only produced original movie script. In late September, she wrote to Kober saying what a "tough, tough job" it was working on *The North Star*. "I'm just no good at writing about people and places I don't know about." Yet she felt bolstered by the "thick research book" she and a Goldwyn researcher had spent seven weeks compiling. Hellman also spent six months rereading Russian novels and having issues of *Pravda* translated. Two scenes in the script were based on news stories, she told an interviewer. Germans had actually taken blood transfusions from undernourished children, who had subsequently died for lack of medical attention in Poland and Russia. And Russian pilots really had "dived their planes straight into lines of enemy tanks." *The North Star* was set in a farming commune, and Hellman felt her trip in 1937 to a collective farm near Moscow had helped her in forming a "mental picture of that for use now. The little things kept coming back to me—the way a dining room table was laid, the faces of village people as they walked along the road or shopped in the village store, and snatches of their conversations." She claimed that Soviet filmmakers were very pleased with the authentic script.

In a letter to Kober, Hellman confessed that there had been plenty of "Goldwyn trouble" and that she had had to do "some workmanlike screaming and lot of declaration of principles of my art [before] everything quieted down." Goldwyn had now divided his week between a "childlike period" (the script was great and the money had not been wasted) and a "graveyard period" (there was no way to get his money's worth out of the picture except to "bluster, telephone, flatter, bully and phone back"). Hellman was out of sorts, she admitted, "half in bed and half working, which only fucked up the work and my health." She was down with the grippe. Everyone seemed to be deserting her. Herman Shumlin was to get his military commission in December. Dash was writing her cheery letters from Fort Monmouth, N.J.: one of them under the heading "Private Hammett reports" listed sixteen military accomplishments, including: "1. That he passed prick inspection last night with flying colors. 2. That he was accompanied by Private Gottlieb, one of your people," on a jaunt to town. His only complaint was his desk job. "He seems to want to be in the African landing force," Hellman wrote Kober. *The North Star* was all the tougher to get through because of her loneliness, which was apparent at the end of her letter to Kober. She had "seven little pigs" and he could eat one if he ever came home. She had "five cows, three pregnant: everything here is pregnant, except me, and I wish I was. Please write me." She sent her love and wanted him to know how much she missed him. On November 27, she wrote to say she hoped to finish the script by December, when she could join the Kobers in California for a visit.

Although she does not specify the causes, Hellman's personal anguish during this period had much to do with Shumlin, according to a letter she wrote Kober. She would do one more play with Shumlin, but the signs of a break between them were becoming apparent to Hellman. Her psychoanalysis was much better, but it seemed to have come too late to repair a breach with Shumlin. They had "come to the end." She could not manage the relationship any longer. The "fights and confusions and the foolishness" had settled nothing—indeed they seemed "a step backwards . . . so far backwards" that she did not want to risk further involvement. She was not laying blame on anyone, but it felt better just to confront her feelings. The best she could hope for was some kind of "friendly arrangement" with him.

Hammett seemed unaffected by Hellman's affairs with other men. He was never jealous. When the Hellman-Shumlin liaison was at its most passionate, when the two would tear into each other during the rehearsals of *The Little Foxes*, Hammett would just roll his eyes at his buddy, Howard Bay, and seem entirely aloof from the fracas. His letters to her from Fort Monmouth and later from Seattle were amusing and very supportive, but he cared nothing about her romantic entanglements, and he teased her about his own sexual adventures. In one letter, he gave her instructions for the turtle traps at Hardscrabble and then reported he was going to town for a ball game and "to see if any old friends have daughters, and that darling is how we are winning this war."

Filming of *Watch on the Rhine* was completed by November 1942, and Shumlin wrote Wallis to say, "Lillian really liked the picture very much, but was angry at herself for putting certain repetitious speeches back in the script." Complimentary letters were also exchanged between Hellman and Jack Warner, and she expressed her hope she could work for his studio again "and often."

By mid-December 1942, Hellman was in Hollywood for six weeks of script conferences with Goldwyn and director Lewis Milestone. All seemed to go well, although she always found spending an extended period with Goldwyn a trial. In January, she wrote to Kober saying she had incorporated some of his suggestions into what was probably an early draft of *The Searching Wind*, a play that departed from her usual single-set, chronologically structured dramas by employing flashbacks to tell the twenty-year history of European and American reactions to fascism. She had "transposed some scenes," so that the whole thing was "less jerky and the end is fuller and more moving. Me, I like it and am sick of it and never want to hear about it again." The same month, she had an approving letter from Hammett about the new play; he suggested cutting some of the early parts, but praised her for achieving the "desired documentary effect."

The North Star continued to trouble Hellman. In a letter to Kober, she confessed to increasing irritability. She and Goldwyn had been "love-birds" until she had lost her temper "over very little" and could not regain her equanimity. Goldwyn was going crazy, throwing money in all directions—a sure sign of "indecisiveness."

Back home at Hardscrabble in March, Hellman received another letter from Hammett, who sensed what a hard time she was having writing her play without him. To his "dearest Lily" he confided that she was breaking his heart about her new play. "I think we're going to have to make a rule that you're not to tackle any work when I'm not around to spur, quiet, goad, pacify and tease you, according to what's needed at the moment. It is obvious that you're not capable of handling yourself." Hellman was also fretting over the release date of *Watch on the Rhine*. On March 9, she wrote Jack Warner to express her dissatisfaction that *Watch on the Rhine* was "once again postponed" in favor of *Mission to Moscow*, a movie based on Ambassador Joseph E. Davies's trip to the Soviet Union in 1937–38. She pointed out that she had interrupted writing a new play to come to Hollywood for four weeks of work on the movie, and that she and Shumlin had closed the road tour of *Watch on the Rhine* early to accommodate Warner Brothers. Warner replied that a release date in the fall of 1943, when movie attendance was at its greatest, would garner great attention and publicity for the film. When the movie of *Watch on the Rhine* appeared in September 1943, some critics rated it the best film of the year, and Paul Lukas won an Academy Award as best actor. Hammett was commended for faithfully adapting the play for the screen.

In March 1943, Lewis Milestone, the director of *The North Star*, wrote an article about the making of the movie that noted *The North Star* would not "glorify war. There will be no phony heroics. The script by Lillian Hellman is realistic, an objective job of reporting and in adapting it to the screen I intend to follow the same line." Had he stuck to his word, perhaps her intentions for the script would have been fulfilled. With his decision to have all of the actors playing Russians retain their American idioms, he destroyed Hellman's effort to achieve a "semi-documentary" quality. Milestone's point was to drive home to Americans the idea that "but for the grace of God this might be an American village instead of a Russian" one invaded by Nazis. Unfortunately, with Hollywood production values, this approach meant virtually obliterating anything distinctively Russian about the village and its people. William Cameron Menzies, one of the premier art directors (an Oscar winner for *Gone with the Wind)* constructed an elaborate Russian village that took up the entire back lot of the studio. Everything that was supposed to be in a Russian village—thatched-roof cottages, hospital, school, radio station, railroad station, farm administration building, livestock, and hundreds of trees—was supplied, at a cost of $260,000. In this case, the expensive quest for an authentic setting overwhelmed whatever truth the script told. Hellman had wanted a simple film concentrating on characters in a Russian village; what she got was an extravaganza with a musical score by Aaron Copland, lyrics by Ira Gershwin, and an all-star Hollywood cast: Anne Baxter (Marina), Dana Andrews (Kolya), Walter Huston (Dr. Kurin), Walter Brennan (Karp), Ann Harding (Sophia), Jane Withers (Claudia), Farley Granger (Damian), Erich von Stroheim (Van Harden).

Before the film's release in November 1943, the scenarist publicly aired her complaints to Theodore Strauss in *The New York Times* (August 29, 1943). While affirming that "the film is a valuable and good picture which tells a good deal of the truth about fascism," she was most censorious about Milestone's trifling with her script—about "whole pages of dialogue written by him in a sort of Gregory Ratoff patois, which I was asked to touch up as best I could." In May 1942, Hellman returned to Hollywood to see a rough cut of the film, an "extended opera bouffe peopled not by peasants, real and alive, but by musical comedy characters without a thought or care in the world." Scenes that were absolutely essential to reveal the characters had been "shortened or cut entirely to make room for the extension of other scenes out of all proportion to their dramatic importance." What Hellman did not say for print was that she was so angry with Goldwyn for siding with Milestone that she bought back her contract for thirty thousand dollars and never worked for the producer again. What most upset her was that the possibility of producing an honest picture had been sabotaged. She criticized the film "on the basis of what she believe[d] it might have been," she told Strauss.

A close inspection of Hellman's published screenplay, Milestone's shooting script, and the film itself shows that Hellman was right. For example, Hellman's peasant, Karp, is a rather melancholy, wistful peasant; Milestone's Karp (played by Walter Brennan) is a merry old Hollywood coot. Hellman's Karp sighs over memories of romantic love and gives an unsentimental tweak to the young Russian lovers, Damian and Marina; Milestone's Karp simply laughs and is truly a one-dimensional figure. In general, where Hellman's peasants are self-reflective or critical, Milestone's are jolly and complacent. Where Hellman puts in a laugh, Milestone adds two or three more.

Rather than exploring the characters, Milestone often interrupts conversations with ludicrous musical scenes, with peasants collectively singing:

> Let the locomotive labor
> While we dance and join our neighbor
> > In a jingle,
> > In a jingle.

Milestone cuts out the good-natured bickering between the peasants, which gives at least some reality to the village life Hellman portrays in this scene from the published screenplay:

THE ROAD—KARP'S WAGON
Karp looks off and sees a tractor on the side of a hill.
He pulls up his horse, speaks to the tractor.
KARP: You ought to get a horse.
Boris, a nice-looking man about forty, sticks his head
    out from under the tractor.
BORIS: Jokes don't get better with age.

Nothing survives from this scene except Karp and Boris exchanging innocuous conversation. Absent also is Karp's wry comment on romantic love in this scene from Hellman's published screenplay:

DAMIAN: Ever been to Kiev, Karp?
KARP: Of course. There was a pretty girl there who lost
    her head over me. Years ago. It was a sad case.
BORIS: It must have been.
KARP: *(sighs):* Love is sad. *To Damian:* You disagree?
DAMIAN: *(smiles):* Yes, I disagree.

KARP: She was a charming girl. Of course, love is sad.
It should be. But I don't remember her name. The
one in Kiev who loved me so much.

The rhythms of village life, the deep sense of familiarity these
people have with each other, are largely destroyed—especially in
the ridiculous first half of Milestone's film—because the director
whisks his characters from one fabulous setting to another with a
kind of hollow vibrancy.

Milestone did leave Hellman's story more or less intact, which
helped him a great deal in the second half of the film, when he
allowed her taut drama to unfold. The plot is simple. On June 22,
1941, Germany invades the Soviet Union. Members of a Soviet
collective farm, North Star, are hiking to Kiev. Much of the movie
is taken up with their efforts to get back to the village once they
encounter the invasion forces. The village's effort to protect itself
and to adopt a policy of resistance to the German occupiers is a
moving and well-told story. The love interest is between Damian
(Farley Granger) and Marina (Anne Baxter). Toward the end of the
film, there is an exciting confrontation between a Nazi doctor, Von
Harden (Erich von Stroheim), and the Russian doctor, Kurin (Walter Huston). Von Harden is not so much a dedicated Nazi as he is
a collaborator, a believer in might makes right. He authorizes the
blood transfusions that threaten the lives of the village children.
Kurin, a humane, peaceful man, a scientist who has retired to
village life, is forced to kill Von Harden in a compelling encounter
in the hospital. The conflict between the two doctors is reminiscent
of the Teck de Brancovis–Kurt Muller confrontation in *Watch on the
Rhine*.

The North Star turned out to be a successful film, and reviewers
were quick to condemn it or praise it for political, historical, and
esthetic reasons. It was inevitable that critics would complain that
the "humble peasantry are too clean, too noble, too handsome."
In *Commonweal*, it was also noted that there are absolutely no
references to religion. Surely, the Soviet government had not been
able to wipe out centuries of Christianity in one generation. Yet
the people in the film "live very happily without churches, and
they die very heroically without any thought of God. I cannot
believe this is a true picture of the Russian people," concluded
Philip T. Hartung. Bosley Crowther in *The New York Times* singled
out Dr. Kurin's speech to Von Harden as lifting the film to a

"thrilling peak": "You are the real filth—men who do the work of Fascists and pretend to themselves they are better than those for whom they work, men who do murder while they laugh at those for whom they do it." He was bothered, though, by the film's prettiness and "theatrical ornamentation."

The harshest criticism of *The North Star* came from Mary McCarthy. She objected to the portrayal of the Soviet Union as an "idyllic hamlet, with farmhouses and furniture that might be labeled Russian Provincial and put in a window by Sloane." Harping on the German invasion "might be all very well if no one remembered the Pact and Stalin's long armament program and the terror which held the country in domestic siege long before the first German company moved across the frontier." Here was the essential point: the Soviet Union had never been innocent and this is where liberals like McCarthy parted company with Hellman. Russia was no peace-loving country, as the film suggested. Echoing a phrase she would use many years later about Hellman herself, McCarthy observed, "The picture is a tissue of falsehoods woven of every variety of untruth." She cited three instances. First, the collective seemed to be autonomous. Where was the central authority, the directives that were "coming down from above"? The characters were like "feudal Serbian mountaineers, or Norwegian fisherman, acting naively on their own initiative." Second, the country is presented as so "unsuspecting" of an invasion that a pilot goes off with peasants on a hike "when the bombs from the air tell him that it is time to be off with his squadron." And finally, on the first day of the invasion, with no Russian planes in the air yet, German planes "are shown wasting their war material by dive-bombing a couple of peasant carts on a country road."

The North Star is a tendentious film. Lillian Hellman knew she was writing propaganda. But she was right to insist that there was a reality in her sentiments that never got filmed. Usually, no matter how rough the going was in Hollywood, she could put it behind her. On May 18, 1943, when she returned to Hardscrabble from a week's worth of battling with Goldwyn and Milestone, she was, in her own words, "tired and nervous." The studio head had never before sided with a director against her. She had always thought the writer came first. The episode had "done me in," she wrote Kober.

There was always a sure cure for fatigue: Hardscrabble itself. She wanted Kober to know that it was a "particularly lush year," and that she was just in time to catch "the dogwood and the lilacs and the wood violets before they were gone. If all this doesn't sound like a bad English poet I'll hang myself on Goldwyn's grave." Hammett had come for a brief visit, toothless—his cure for chronic dental problems. He looked horrible to Hellman and she had screamed on first seeing him. She did not think it troubled him at all. "He goes straight along in an incredible fashion." She was wrong, though. When the handsome Hammett had first seen his sunken face in the mirror, he was shocked. Then, too, Dash liked to play The Stoic to Lillian the Fretful.

11

THE SEARCHING WIND
New York/Hardscrabble
(1943–1944)

I got the title for "The Searching Wind" from a colored
maid who used to work for me. Some mornings when she
came she'd say, "It's a searching wind today." She meant
one of those winds that go right through to your backbone.
I suppose in my title I was thinking of the wind that's
blowing through the world.

—Lillian Hellman, interview with Helen Ormsbee,
in *New York Herald Tribune, April 9, 1944*

Commitments to screen work on *Watch on the Rhine* and *The
North Star* delayed completion of the play *The Searching Wind*
until just before rehearsals in early 1944. According to Richard
Moody, Shumlin saw a draft in August 1943, but Hellman told her
press agent, Richard Maney, that she did not commence the actual
writing of the play until that month. She found that her elaborate
research for *Watch on the Rhine* served her well for the new play,
which was to be about a romantic triangle: two women, Cassie and
Emily, who vie for the love of Alexander Hazen, a career diplomat.
Alex and Emily's son, Sam, is home from the war with a serious
leg wound. As his elders argue over their responsibility for not
having opposed fascism strongly enough, Sam realizes that his
father's weak liberalism has been, in part, responsible for the rise
of fascism. The earliest version of the play concentrated on the

personal affairs of these characters, and the two women were given parts that were cut considerably in the final stage production. The play Hellman finally wrote makes private lives and public affairs of equal and parallel importance. Each scene has a historical dimension: Washington (spring 1944) after Sam has returned wounded from the war, Rome (October 1922) during Mussolini's takeover of the Italian government, Berlin (autumn 1923) just after Hitler first tries to come to power, and Paris (September 1938) on the eve of the Munich conference. Thus the personalities of the characters are seen to arise from their times. Cassie is the clear-eyed, politically involved anti-Fascist; Emily is the apolitical, society-oriented abettor of fascism; Alex is the appeaser.

The Searching Wind explores twentieth-century diplomacy, and, like *Watch on the Rhine*, it dramatizes the lives of men and women who have not been able, in Kurt Muller's words, to "make a world." The play's cast is especially noteworthy: Dudley Diggs (Moses Taney), Montgomery Clift (Sam Hazen), Dennis King (Alex Hazen), Cornelia Otis Skinner (Emily Hazen), Barbara O'Neil (Cassie Bowman). Although *The Searching Wind* was a success when it opened in the last year of World War II (318 performances), subsequent critics have not rated it highly, probably because it lacks Hellman's usual tautness of structure. Coming after the acclaimed *Watch on the Rhine*, in which she shows a new subtlety of characterization, *The Searching Wind* can seem especially disappointing because it sacrifices character development for argument and seeks to demonstrate how foreign policy and domestic life dovetail. Both the times and peoples' lives are out of joint in this play, which contains the dramatist's nastiest attack on liberalism. *The Searching Wind*'s unusual form—it features Hellman's only use of flashbacks and scenes directly tied to historic turning points— would have been more manageable in a novel or a motion picture.

In act one, Sam's grandfather, Moses Taney, suggests that the Hazens have engaged in "diplomatic doubletalk." Alex never squarely faces the evil implications of Mussolini's march on Rome, just as he never confronted his true reasons for marrying Emily while continuing to see Cassie. In politics, as in love, Alex has never been willing to commit himself wholeheartedly to one side. The culmination of his indecisiveness is a memo he dictates on the eve of Munich downplaying Hitler's aggressive plans for war. Alex should know better. He has witnessed an anti-Semitic note in

Berlin, and experienced firsthand the menace of fascism. Cassie has tried to stir his conscience and his courage, but Alex persists in believing Moses and Cassie have made too much of the peril posed by Mussolini and Hitler. In truth, Alex has been afraid to commit himself and his son's generation to a war that the play demonstrates is inevitable.

Sam's speech at the end of the play assigns his parents a heavy burden of blame for not battling the evil that led to war, the evil that will now take his leg from him. He may seem hysterical and illiberal in holding them so personally responsible for the war, but his attitudes are a precise result of his parents' sense of culpability. In act one, scene 3, Emily supports Sam's effort to "learn how to put things together, see them when they come." She tells him: "Don't let us discourage you. Our generation made quite a mess." The play reflects Hellman's restless quest to chart history, to put it on a human scale, to make it amenable to judgment, to *personalize* it, as Cassie does when she twits Alex for his constitutional inability to believe in supreme evil: "Dear Alex. You haven't changed. Nobody's that bad, even when the proof is outside the door."

It is curious that for all of the controversy surrounding Hellman's politics, almost no one has troubled to quarrel much with the political vision of *The Searching Wind*. At most, critics have said the personal and political themes do not converge and that the play, therefore, is disjointed. Can one equate the personal failings of individuals with the failings of the world at large? Eugene Earl, a cast member of *The Searching Wind*, puts forward Hellman's argument succinctly:

> Individuals "messy" in their private lives, when multiplied by the millions, make a "messy" world—a world so weakened by moral slack, so undermined by blind selfishness and careless disregard for consequences, that it is easy prey to the Hitlers, Mussolinis, and Tojos. To Miss Hellman there is a fundamental bond between the moral verities which hold between individuals in their personal lives and those which govern the relations between nations.

Most critics have been uneasy with this equation of the private and the public but have not rejected it outright—perhaps because it is difficult to prove or disprove the playwright's contention. It is a workable dramatic premise, and that is all that is needed as long as the characters and the plot hold up.

Only one reviewer of *The Searching Wind* noted that one key event in the history of appeasing Hitler was not dramatized. Flashbacks to Mussolini's march on Rome (1922) to the rise of fascism in Berlin (1923) led inevitably to the third, Munich (1938) and Neville Chamberlain's sellout to Hitler. There should have been a fourth flashback commemorating the Soviet-German pact, argued Margaret Marshall in *The Nation* (April 22, 1944).

> But it is clear from the context that Miss Hellman is one of those people who assume that there is a moral difference, though they never explain why, between Chamberlain's attempt to turn Hitler east and Stalin's attempt to turn him west.

Hellman's context is the failure of the liberal world. From her play nothing can be learned about the Soviet Union's efforts to stop Hitler in the early thirties or of its about-face in August 1939. Several reviewers of *The Searching Wind* did complain that Hellman offered no solution to her liberal characters' dilemma. If fascism was a menace, then how should they have combated it—other than speaking out against it, as Cassie does? Hellman could have provided an answer. The Communists were fighting the Fascists in post–World War I Germany and elsewhere. Samuel Sillen in *The New Masses* (May 2, 1944) charged that the play ignored the fact that there was a "great popular movement against fascism which embraced millions" after World War I. To raise this point, however, would have put Lillian Hellman—popular and distinguished Broadway playwright—smack into controversy again. How could she justify the pact? Everyone supposes she was never one to duck a fight—and this was usually true of her public pronouncements— yet when it came to writing successful theater, she was never so extreme and never so daring as to risk damaging box office receipts. Instead, she told part of the truth: liberals had crumbled, had not been radical enough in opposing evil.

In an article written shortly after the production of *The Searching Wind*, Earl provides fascinating insights into Shumlin's direction and, indirectly, into why *The Searching Wind* became the occasion for the split between Shumlin and Hellman. The cast in *The Searching Wind* was particularly slow to understand the point of the play. They seemed at a loss as to how to approach their own parts. It took weeks of rehearsal to realize the subtlety of the playwright's characters, and often it was only in performance that an actor suddenly discovered the riches of his or her role. It came as a shock to Earl to see the director violate a cardinal rule of the theater: Shumlin actually read the lines to his star actors on the theory that they must *hear* what was "*in* and back of the words." Speech after speech was read to the cast, for this was the director's way of getting to the heart of the play. It is no wonder that up to this point Hellman adored her director—no matter that they had terrible fights. He put a premium on getting the sense of the play right. Actors, as creative collaborators, seemed not to concern him at all. The cast was never taken into the director's or the playwright's confidence; they were mere interpreters of Hellman's words—a notion of acting that would later get her into deep trouble with every production she directed. "It seemed almost as if playwright and director had entered into a tacit conspiracy to prevent us from seeing too far beyond our individual scenes, or inquiring too intently into what they meant in relation to the play as a whole," Earl observes.

Shumlin's approach was authoritarian. Earl remembers that he was almost "always somber and in dead earnest," rarely smiling or relaxing, with an inexorable, painstaking, and demanding technique. A perfectionist, he was indefatigable and dogged about the slightest detail. Julie Harris, directed by Shumlin many years later, recalls that he seemed very old-fashioned. "He would say things like 'raise your hand a little higher when you say that.'" It just was not possible for an actor to be thinking about such minor matters in moments of intense emotion. Actors often felt backed into a corner by such mechanical concentration on minute details.

That Shumlin was often successful with his approach had a lot to do with the fact that actors saw him as a kind man. They tolerated his dictation of lines even if it was not their way of learning a part. Harris remembered him as a "sweet man," and Earl makes a point in his article of singling out Shumlin's considerateness and gentleness. He never raised his voice and always seemed extraordinarily calm. He might be brusque, but he never lost his temper, never gave in to "the temperamental outbursts that are legend in the theatre." Instead, he brooded, and nothing escaped his eagle eye.

Hellman had always approved of Shumlin's directorial style. This time, however, it was at odds with the kind of play she had written, and she questioned him more than usual. In many ways, *The Searching Wind* was her most ambitious work. It covered more than twenty years of history; it used dramatic scenes that had to have different period flavors; and it carried on a historical debate that was inseparable from the emotional lives of its characters. Earl puts it best when he refers to the characters' "blind absorption in themselves, preoccupied in their individual 'isolationism.' " The epoch, not only these characters, was isolationist, and thus the actors were called on to interpret an intellectual theme that was never properly explored in rehearsals. As a result, the actors were puzzled and never did grasp *The Searching Wind* in its entirety. Audiences left the play wondering exactly what it meant. With the exception of *Days to Come*, every other Hellman play had such raw emotional power that Shumlin's calm, rationalistic approach to acting may not have mattered—in fact, his emphasis on careful reading of speeches may have kept Hellman's fiery melodramas in check, so that her meaning was more easily taken by the audience. In *The Searching Wind*, Hellman was more aloof from her characters; "they were no better, nor worse, than the rest of us," Earl notes. There was an aimless quality in the Hazens, for example. They had none of the drive that characterizes the Hubbards in *The Little Foxes*. Shumlin's quest for "a solid, clear, objective narrative" helped the audience to see the broad historical outlines of *The Searching Wind*, but he was not able to balance that objectivity against his actors' need to get inside their roles. Earl observed that the actors' "interpretations at times lacked the simple, direct, spontaneous, personal force of inner reality. They did not seem to live enough with their characters; often there was the vigor of rhetorical recitation rather than the subjective nuances of imagined experience." To some extent, he believed this was Hellman's fault. She had written too many words in explanation of the issues over which the characters contended. Her didacticism congested her drama.

At the heart of the quarrel that developed between Shumlin and Hellman was the casting of Cornelia Otis Skinner and Barbara O'Neil in the female roles. For the first time, Hellman doubted that Shumlin had chosen wisely. It did not ever seem to have occurred to the playwright that her severe cutting of Cassie's and Emily's roles made it virtually impossible to get their emotions in proper focus. Shumlin never edited Hellman, never suggested changes in the play as written, especially since she was so good about removing any excess wordage from her scripts. But this time he openly suggested that the script had weaknesses. Kermit Bloomgarden, then Shumlin's business manager and soon to become the producer of Hellman's subsequent plays, sometimes had to plead with the playwright not to cut her material so drastically. It was inevitable that she would find fault with the production, and actors were always fair game for Hellman. She seemed to treat them like dumb animals. Exactly what disturbed her about Shumlin probably did not matter at this point. They had almost broken up over *Watch on the Rhine*, and it was only through Bloomgarden's intercession that Hellman did not go through with her threat to fire Shumlin.

Bloomgarden's new twenty-one-year-old actress wife, Virginia Bloomgarden Chilewich, attended some of the rehearsals and remembers Shumlin's migraine headaches and the way he would hold his head to the side. To her, both director and playwright seemed like tough, formidable people not willing to concede much to others. Shumlin was a "nightmare" to her and, like Hellman, seemed to resent her presence. At the time of *The Searching Wind*, Shumlin may have seemed worse than Hellman. According to Richard Maney, the director would get "grim and taut" with foreboding as opening night approached, whereas Hellman was "more elastic, more likely to dismiss a qualm with a quip." Soon Virginia was in therapy and would say to her psychiatrist on one occasion, "you can send that bill to Lillian Hellman." Shumlin and Hellman seemed to have no compassion at all for young people who might be struggling and who could not bring the background to the theater that was acquired through years of strenuous work. During one of the rehearsals of *The Searching Wind*, Virginia remembers telling her husband how much Shumlin troubled her because he was so distant and cool. Bloomgarden asked if she felt the same way about Hellman. "I don't know, but I'm sure going to find out," she replied. A week later, she told her husband no, that with Hellman it was different. Virginia could "kind of communicate with her" because Hellman respected the causes Virginia had become involved in. Although she was young, she had had some experience and a "point of view." She had been head of the hostess committee at the Stage Door Canteen for U.S. servicemen during

World War II, and she had successfully fought to desegregate it at a time when the armed forces were still segregated. The confrontations with Shumlin and Hellman would come later, and the fights would be devastating, resulting in a "loss of self" for a time. The director was kind when the spirit moved him, but he could get vicious and violent with Bloomgarden. The "benevolent paternalist," Virginia used to call Shumlin, though "not to his face—I didn't dare." At the tryout of *The Searching Wind* in Baltimore, Herman threw his hip out trying to kick Howard Bay when he came into the theater late. With such powerful personalities as Hellman and Shumlin, who gave every impression of existing on an echelon far higher than cast and crew, it is no wonder the actors never felt in command of their roles. They were temporary help; they never owned their parts. Even Bay and Bloomgarden were rarely thanked for their services. Work well done was rarely recognized. After a silent dinner with Shumlin, Virginia remarked to her husband, "It's so quiet I can hear the soup going down my throat. Don't you ever talk to each other?" "Not if I can help it," Bloomgarden replied. With his work, Shumlin was all business; social friends, on the other hand, fondly remember him as warm, charming, generous, and erudite.

In the "Theatre" section of *Pentimento*, over and over Hellman claims that she cannot remember much from the productions of her plays. How could she when the casts and crews were held in such low esteem? Most of them she hardly got to know. Occasionally she expresses a tender word for someone—in the case of *The Searching Wind*, it was the veteran actor Dudley Diggs and the newcomer Montgomery Clift, who would spend much time together going through scenes from Shakespeare, Ibsen, and Chekhov. Several times a week she enjoyed watching from the wings "the delicate relationship between the dedicated old and the dedicated young."

Shumlin remembered Clift's "amazing amount of intensity" in the closing speech of the play, characterizing the actor's handling of the speech as "instinctive." Instinct was never enough for Shumlin, however. It was typical of the director to make Clift perform the whole speech at every rehearsal, even when they were "just running through lines in the Green Room." As with Tallulah Bankhead, Shumlin refused to let Clift walk through a scene.

> I wanted him to capture the essence of it technically as well as emotionally. At times he seemed infuriated

that he was being forced to play in such high gear. "I can do it, Herman, I can do it," he'd mutter, and then I'd shout, "Then do it, Goddam it!" The end was dazzling.

From the actor's point of view, the director must have seemed brutal.

Nearly all of the reviews of *The Searching Wind* were respectful. In *PM* (April 3, 1944), Louis Kronenberger spoke for many critics:

> The play offers the kind of hard-hitting, genuinely adult writing that only Miss Hellman brings nowadays to the American theater. *The Searching Wind* is in no sense Shavian, but it does resemble Shaw in its incisive dialogue, its provocative ideas, its political awareness and its force of personality. On these grounds it greatly deserves success, and will have it.

Kronenberger nevertheless detected flaws in the writing and in the production that would be echoed in even the most positive reviews. The characters Cassie and Emily troubled him. They were "granted no elbow room, no chance for a real development and play of personality: they must meet in hurried rather high-pitched conversations, they seem to live only in crises." Cornelia Otis Skinner and Barbara O'Neil played these scenes "all too stagily." Another admirer of the play, Arthur Pollack of the *Brooklyn Daily Eagle*, had to admit, "there is something in the feverish manner of the actors and the play that Miss Hellman and Mr. Shumlin . . . are aware of and feel the need of hiding. The battle of the women does not stand up alone as drama. It leans on the author's ideas, as they are intended to lean on it for elucidation." In the *Commonweal* (April 28), Kappo Phelan confirmed Hellman's worst suspicions of Shumlin:

> I am not sure Mr. Shumlin's direction has been of the greatest assistance. To begin with, I am uncertain of the worth of casting Miss O'Neill and Cornelis Otis Skinner in the leading feminine roles . . . [T]hese two are rather more alike than various, their quality, pace, even physical attributes being matched.

Phelan, Stark Young (*The New Republic*, May 1), and other reviewers had strong reservations about the staging and acting. Although *The Searching Wind* ran for more than three hundred performances, and Hellman was acclaimed as one of the foremost playwrights—perhaps the greatest American dramatist of her time—the reviews were devastating to the Hellman-Shumlin relationship. Several of the reviews began by noting that Shumlin had produced all of her plays and that this theater team had made remarkable contributions to the New York stage. It was that much harder to take, then, when, for the first time, questions were raised about the handling of the production. Even with that dismal failure, *Days to Come*, he had been chided for nothing more than a too "reverential" approach to Hellman's work.

As lovers and fellow professionals, Hellman and Shumlin had a falling out that would not be repaired for nearly ten years, and even then he would have nothing to do with her plays. He had been part of a succession of lovers, an anchor she seemed to need to balance herself against Hammett. As in *The Searching Wind*, it was always a three-cornered world for her—even if Hammett would not acknowledge it. Bobbie Weinstein, who first met Hellman around the time of *The Little Foxes* and became a close friend, notes that Hammett's affairs upset Hellman very much: "She controlled it and didn't talk about it, but it was very upsetting to her because she was jealous of him and he was never jealous of her." Hellman and Shumlin thought alike politically. He was always for the underdog, as she was, and she found him physically attractive—although no man would ever measure up to Hammett.

The Searching Wind was about trying to balance one's choices in love and in politics. There was more than a little of Hellman in the opinionated, radicalized Cassie and in the conniving, high-living Emily. When Hellman wrote the screenplay for *The Searching Wind*, she made Cassie a reporter uncomfortable with the society of politicians and diplomats who made history; she was on the outs. Hellman, when she acted as a journalist, had her pieces published in *The New Masses*, *The New Republic*, and *PM*—all anti-establishment papers. Yet she could cozy up to the Harrimans and other high society and government officials and, in just a few months, would make herself a part of the American Embassy group in Moscow. She would be, in some ways, living out what she had imagined in *The Searching Wind*.

12

RUSSIA

Hardscrabble/New York/Hollywood/ Seattle/Fairbanks Moscow/Leningrad/Kiev/Lublin/The Front (1944–1945)

What is party spirit *(partiinost)*? Party spirit means acting at all times, in all places, and in all things as a party, as a group, a mass, a very great mass now. But how can one know how a mass thinks? In other words, party spirit means acting the way the Central Committee deems necessary. That is what party discipline is all about.

—Raisa Orlova, *Memoirs*

In truth, I was nobody's girl.
—Lillian Hellman, *An Unfinished Woman*

Summer 1944. After a cold spring, July was blazing. Early summer receipts from *The Searching Wind* had "slipped rather sharply," according to Herman Shumlin in a letter to Arthur Kober on July 20. But the good weather and general business conditions found the play "bouncing back with almost equal sharpness." Hellman wrote Arthur and Maggie Kober that she was feeling lazy and was in a "bad, bad humor." With attorneys, she was considering contracts from Hal Wallis about a movie version of *The Searching Wind*, and that made her "sick and ill tempered." Hellman was finding it impossible to write. "I hate like hell to write anything, and as the years go by that gets worse." She was sleeping most of the time and hating herself for not doing more. She had guests only once at Hardscrabble. There had also been a weekend on Shumlin's boat. They were both working on the Independent Voters Committee of Artists, Writers and Scientists for the Reelection of Roosevelt. On August 1, Shumlin would write to Kober, who was working in Hollywood, asking for a five-hundred-dollar contribution. He and Hellman were trying to raise five thousand dollars and were two thousand dollars short of their goal.

In late July, the following cablegram arrived at 63 East Eighty-second Street, the playwright's new New York City residence:

ON BEHALF OF THEATRE ET CINEMA SECTIONS OF VOKS UNITING LEADING WORKERS SOVIET CINEMA ET THEATRE INVITE YOU TO VISIT SO-VIET UNION AND BE GUEST OF VOKS ANXIOUS WAITING YOUR REPLY—(SIGNED) KEMENOV MOSCVIN PUDOVKIN

Hellman took the cablegram to Consul General Kisselev, who suggested writing to Ruth B. Shipley at the Passport Division of the State Department and quoting the contents of the cablegram. She did so, requesting a passport and information about arranging transportation to the Soviet Union. She also notified Shipley that the British Ministry of Information had asked her to do a film in London—a commitment she would like to fulfill on her way back from Russia.

Twice before, Shipley had rejected Hellman's applications for passports. On April 28, 1943, the reason for refusal was stated as "reported to be an active Communist." On May 12, 1944, she was denied a passport for travel to England in order to write a screenplay of *War and Peace* for the British company of Metro-Goldwyn-Mayer "because of the present military situation." This time Shipley was reacting to an April 22 FBI report detailing Hellman's status as "one of the key figures in the Communist Party in the New York area." Hellman was not given this information.

Hellman had been dealing with Shipley at the passport office since March 1939 on a variety of matters. On January 17, 1942, Hellman wrote requesting a meeting with Shipley to talk about her plans for a trip to London to direct a production of *Watch on the Rhine*. The playwright was not clear about "how our entrance into the war would affect your allowing me to have a visa or a passport, or how it would affect my being able to get transportation." When the trip was canceled in February, Hellman sent a letter to Shipley explaining that the English producers were "impatient," and she felt she should not hold them up "on the chance that transportation would come through." She hoped that when the play came to Washington, Shipley would accept tickets from her. On March 30, 1942, she wrote Shipley requesting the return of an expired passport taken from her by an immigrant inspector after her trip to Nassau. Although it had not been renewed, Hellman wanted it for her "identification papers." Then there was correspondence in June 1942 about the proposed trip to Russia with William Wyler. A passport for Hellman would not be considered until the Department of State received "some detailed word from Major William Wyler as to his plans," came the reply from Shipley on August 1. On August 11, Hellman wrote Shipley in the hope that her passport would be held, pending the possibility that Wyler could get "a leave in order to make the Russian picture."

On August 18, 1944, the FBI sent Assistant Secretary of State Adolf A. Berle, Jr., a two-page memo listing Hellman's membership in organizations following the Communist line, among which were:

American Council on Soviet Relations
Jewish Council for Russian War Relief
United States Soviet Friendship Congress
Committee for Medical Aid to Russia
American Russian Institute
American Societies for Cultural Relations with Russia

In addition, the memo claimed, Hellman's lectures indicated a "pro-Soviet and pro-Communist point of view and have consistently followed the Communist Party Line." Nevertheless, Hellman did get her passport and began to make plans immediately for her winter trip to the Soviet Union. In the company of Ring Lardner, Jr., she went shopping for long underwear.

Lardner, a Communist, represented one wing, so to speak, of Hellman's social and political life. A much closer friend, Archibald MacLeish, a liberal on most matters, represented nearly the opposite wing. He was a poet and government servant—Librarian of Congress, head of the Office of Facts and Figures, and associate director of the Office of War Information. He sought Hellman's advice on a wide range of subjects and obviously respected her sensible and shrewd comments. She wrote him in early September about a documentary he was planning on the post–World War I period. She was aware, she said, of the "political pitfalls." The Wilson legacy was dangerous ground. It would be best to pick a theme, like isolationism, and stick with it. She then outlined five parts to the program: (1) "a short, simple background history of Europe beginning in about 1910 and going up to 1914"; (2) the quick return to isolationism after World War I—Senator Lodge's opposition to President Wilson's plans for peace; (3) what lay behind Lodge's speech—"the causes—political, economic, etc."; (4) how European politicians took advantage of a bickering U.S. Senate; and (5) "the need to make a peace before war weary people are sick and cynical." These points were bolstered by her analysis of their timeliness. MacLeish was in a position, she implied, to show the world how it had another opportunity to deal with postwar expectations. Her letter showed off not only historical knowledge but how that knowledge might be put to use via the medium of film.

On September 17, Hellman sent a wire to Hal Wallis explaining that in about ten days she would be leaving for the West Coast en route to Seattle, Fairbanks, and her plane to Russia. She was making notes for the screen version of The Searching Wind. On September 28, she wired him to say her departure depended on weather conditions. The very next day, she sent telegrams to Wallis and to the Kobers announcing her arrival in Los Angeles Thursday, October 5, on the train the Super Chief. The Wallis office was to get a hotel room for her father, who had accompanied her on the trip.

On October 7, the FBI reported her stay at the Kobers on Stone Canyon Road in Beverly Hills. A notice in Variety on October 11 mentioned that while she was in Russia she would contemplate a new play using the characters from The Little Foxes. By October 12, she was in Seattle, a guest of the Washington Athletic Club at the request of Jay C. Allen, Jr., a "reporter and lecturer, who was in Spain during the Civil War and was allegedly sympathetic to the Loyalist regime," it was noted in her FBI file. She was also spotted in the company of Dwight L. Spracher, a sales representative for

Paramount Pictures. An FBI search of her luggage on October 14 turned up nothing more subversive than a contract to do articles for *Collier's* magazine. She was followed to the Frederick and Nelson Department Store and was observed making several telephone calls. At the book department she purchased several mystery stories, "including 'Kent's Last Case' " and a twenty-five-cent pocket bible. At the Seattle airport, an FBI agent prevailed upon a customs official to have a look at Hellman's "two small gray and blue canvas duffel bags . . . and one large gray fiberboard suitcase." Thus it was learned that she had ninety two dollars in cash, a cablegram inviting her to visit Russia, several identification cards, passport, visa, and other personal items. She left behind two packages the FBI was most interested in examining. The contents of the first package:

> A book, "How to Say it in Russian"
> Two small French dictionaries
> One Kroll Map of Alaska
> A New York Drivers license issued to subject
> One Captain of Port identification
> A number of small blank notebooks

The contents of the second package:

> The 10/7/44 issue of "Colliers" magazine. It is noted that this issue contained the article by WENDELL WILKIE, "Citizens of Negro Blood."
> One copy "The Little Oxford Dictionary" by GEORGE OSTLER
> One copy "The Kings English" by FOWLER.
> A power of attorney issued to HERMAN SHUMLIN dated Sept. 1944.

Another *Collier's* contract, a letter from the British Information Service about her work on a film, and an envelope containing blank typing paper was the sum total of material turned up in FBI sleuthing.

Evidently, the Bureau did not intercept the amusing and touching letter Hellman wrote the Kobers from the Seattle Athletic Club. She was to leave for Fairbanks at 7:00 A.M. She was scared about her flight, but "no bomber trip could be much worse" than her train trip from Los Angeles to Seattle. She had shared her compartment with "an interesting roach." What little food was available was "beyond belief," and the filth was comparable to "The Peasant Express from Bucharest."

In Seattle, her hair had been "washed & waved by a girl who is crazy about Frances Parkinson Keyes as a writer." Hellman now resembled "a piece of ten cent store amber on which somebody has vomited." She was repacking and sowing after the previous night's "hour" with "the city's intellectual Republicans." They had made her appreciate her "own company." She was enormously grateful to the Kobers for making her feel "happy & comfortable & lovingly treated." Their affection meant a "great deal" just then, and she loved them both "very much." She promised to write from Fairbanks.

She might complain about Republicans, yet what radical would even associate with such pillars of the establishment? As Robert Newman observes, she counted among her close friends and admirers Loy Henderson, "conservative chief of the State Department Division of Eastern European Affairs . . . Christian Herter, later Secretary of State under Eisenhower (succeeding Dulles) and Mrs. Herter . . . Adele Lovett, wife of Robert Lovett, Assistant Secretary of War in 1944 and later Secretary of Defense."

Never one to stint on comfort when she could have it, Hellman knew her journey to Moscow in wartime would be rough and perhaps risky as well. She would be flying from Fairbanks across Siberia. Later, she would learn from Robert Lovett that had he known about her route, he "would have forbidden it." It was that dangerous. From Fairbanks, she managed to get a message off to Shumlin, who relayed it to Maggie Kober on October 24. Hellman was in "good shape." She had fortunately made her stay in a home of a Paramount friend. There had been a "couch to sleep on and a tub to bathe in, two articles which are obviously very scarce in Alaska."

U.S. State Department cables sent to the Embassy in Moscow made it clear that Hellman was not on official government business, even though she herself felt she was an unofficial good-will and cultural ambassador who owed her mission to behind-the-scenes maneuvering by Harry Hopkins, one of President Roosevelt's closest advisors. Later, the FBI would dutifully note an anonymous informant's claim that the "pro-Russian and pro-

Communist" Hopkins had had an affair with Hellman. At the moment, however, the FBI was busy bugging conversations between Russian military personnel at Ladd Field in Alaska and at the Russian Embassy in Washington, D.C. Neither Colonel Kisilev in Alaska nor General Rudenko in Washington knew anything about Lillian Hellman.

The fourteen-day flight to Moscow was a harrowing experience that was not without elements of black humor. On a C–47 airplane, capable of a maximum speed of 240 miles an hour, Hellman endured what she calls in *An Unfinished Woman* "physically, the hardest time of my life." The plane had no heat after the second day and could only fly in good weather. On the ground, she holed up in cabins on Siberian airfields. Because of a ludicrous misunderstanding, she drank the salts that were meant for soaking her ankle. She then came down with pneumonia and was subject to crying jags. Perhaps what saved her was the cheerful Kolya, her Russian escort, who brought her through the ordeal like a son.

It is a puzzlement as to why Hellman states in *An Unfinished Woman* that she spent five months in the Soviet Union, when at most it was three. She arrived on November 5 and was gone before the end of January 1945. The diaries she quotes from in *An Unfinished Woman*, which must be the same diaries she read in 1967 to Raya Orlova, her Russian translator in 1944, should have verified the dates of her stay. News reports at the time of her arrival in the United States in February 1945 from England also had it wrong, putting her stay in the U.S.S.R. at four months.

In Moscow, she divided her time between her rooms in the National Hotel and her accommodations at Spaso House, Ambassador Averell Harriman's residence, where she became friends with his daughter Kathleen. It was characteristic of Hellman to have two places, one of which (the hotel) could be reserved for work. She was also of two minds about the Americans and the Russians. The conversation at Spaso was, in her word, "glum." She heard nothing but complaints from the Americans. They felt hemmed in by Soviet secrecy and forced to entertain one another. Even diplomats who were sympathetic to the Soviets soon felt isolated and frustrated and treated more as enemies than allies. In retaliation, most of what Americans had to tell Hellman about the Russians was negative.

"It was great fun having Lillian there," Kathleen Harriman Mortimer remembers. The playwright was a good guest and enthusiastic about Russia. She was so lively and so well done-up, an attractive figure to have around. When the Americans got too much for her, she could always go over to the Metropole and look for interesting foreigners to talk to. She did that almost every day, in order to hear the colorful stories about the night before, a few of which she recounts in *An Unfinished Woman*.

If Hellman admired the Russians, she also shrewdly sized them up. She sensed tremendous ambivalence among intellectuals. The purge period of 1937–38 had left them at first baffled, then doubtful as to the innocence of the accused, and finally half-convinced that Stalin was right: the revolution had been betrayed by the men on trial in Moscow. Sergei Eisenstein was perhaps the only intellectual she got to know very well. Although they spent much time alone together, they did not speak much of themselves. He was a great admirer of William Wyler and spoke of the director's fine work on *The Little Foxes*. Eisenstein apparently symbolized for her the ambiguous status of the Soviet intellectual. On the one hand, he seemed to have his government's respect as a great artist and was left free to work on his film *Ivan the Terrible*. Although he was not careful about the foreigners he met and the places he visited, she could see he was not entirely his own man. Hellman found Russians "romantic and dawn-fogged about sex." Their talk about "love and fidelity [was] too highminded for my history and taste," she admits in *An Unfinished Woman*.

Hellman's divided reactions to Russia, and to the Americans' role in Russia, came quickly into focus once she made friends with her Russian translator, Raya Orlova, and fell in love with an American foreign service officer, John Melby. At the beginning, it was difficult for Orlova. Having learned Oxford English, American accents threw her. Yet Hellman was very nice about it and patient, even though patience, Orlova was to learn, was not one of the playwright's virtues. Nor was political consistency. She was never an unthinking Stalinist. In fact, Stalin seemed to have very little to do with her warm feelings about Russia. As Orlova puts it in her *Memoirs*:

> I even found confirmation of the fact that she was not "one of us." She once said: "I'll start listening to the victories of socialism after you've built the kind of toilets that don't make you want to retch at all the airports from Vladivostok to Moscow." I gave her a

very sharp and dumb reply about our people who had
been killed, about the blood that had been spilled, and
about the fact that we were protecting them, the Americans. And besides, was it possible to evaluate socialism by such lowly criteria!

Whether on a poorly equipped train from Los Angeles to Seattle
or in wartime Russia, Lillian Hellman was the same person—the
grande dame concerned with her own comfort and blunt enough to
admit that such "lowly criteria" counted.

It "annoyed me that Raya was always late—all Russians are,"
Hellman notes in a preface to *To Be Preserved Forever*, a book by
Orlova's husband, Lev Kopelev. Orlova wanted to know all about
American novels and Hellman wanted to discuss the war. It
disturbed Hellman that Orlova rejected Freud: "That feeling was
of her time and place, and I didn't like what the Russians thought
about the great man." Sometimes it was a trial to listen to her
translator's enthusiastic encomiums to communism. Perhaps that
is what provoked Hellman's commentary on Russian toilets. In
spite of hunger and bitter cold, Orlova found it difficult to admit
her suffering and to accept anything from Hellman. It would
always be so—even in 1966, when Orlova and her husband were
in jeopardy because of their criticism of the Soviet government.
She reluctantly asked Herbert Gold, a Hellman friend visiting
Russia, to convey her acceptance of Hellman's offer of help.

In 1944, two of Hellman's plays were being staged in Moscow,
and Orlova began to read her work. She was profoundly affected
by the plays and would sometimes translate the questions the
director and the actors had for Hellman. Although the plays were
examples of realistic drama, in retrospect, Orlova remembers their
having a kind of black humor to them of the kind explored by
Beckett. In later years, Hellman would cite him as the theatrical
genius of her time. Orlova remembers that Hellman was extremely
popular in Russia. Her plays made an especially deep impression
because so little American literature had been translated. She was
recognized as a friend and ally, although her dramas were not
considered ideological.

Hellman was thirty-nine and Orlova was twenty-four when they
met. The translator had not been briefed about the arrival of this
distinguished writer. To Orlova, Hellman seemed an old woman.
When Hellman mentioned something about a broken love affair,

Orlova was startled, because thirty-nine seemed too old for romance. Instead, it was an age when one started to think of dying. Hellman was not a beautiful woman, but within a few minutes Orlova forgot about the playwright's appearance—her long nose, for example—and was completely taken in by her talking, laughing, and joking. Hellman had enormous power and charm; she emanated charisma.

Although it was hardly love at first sight, John Melby, a career foreign service officer, also fell under Lillian Hellman's spell. He was a New Deal Democrat, a Ph.D., and already a veteran of various posts in Mexico and Venezuela. He had welcomed the so-called "hardship duty" in Moscow. In charge of the embassy mess, Melby fed forty people a day and supervised a laundry operation. As he wrote his parents: "Very broadening business is the foreign service." Melby admired Ambassador Harriman, a descendant of a railroad tycoon who could "dish it out" but also "take it—which makes it all ok." Harriman's daughter Kathleen also got high marks for being the only woman Melby ever knew who could also "slug it out." He would soon find another.

Melby had a wife and two sons in El Paso, Texas. He missed his boys and was frustrated by his wife's letters, which never seemed very clear about the home situation. His letters home reveal a man dedicated to his job and intensely interested in how Americans perceived Russians and how they were received in Russia. He had seen *The North Star*: "It stinks but the Russians for some weird reason love it." He felt the Russians had been excluded in a high-handed fashion from some of Roosevelt's and Churchill's important decisions. At the same time, he noted that the Russians had "relentlessly and cynically pushed us by all means at their disposal in to military ventures which would help them, but be unduly costly to us." The Russians resented the fact that Americans would not suffer nearly the number of casualties that had been inflicted on the Soviet Union. Like the character Alex Hazen in *The Searching Wind*, Melby had a powerful intellect capable of analyzing diplomatic complexities. Unlike Hazen, he was no waffler. He had firm convictions that could be acted on, and he was getting promoted more rapidly than were most of his colleagues.

Lillian Hellman did not notice John Melby the first night they met at dinner. Perhaps she regarded him as just another anti-Russian embassy official. He would not have gone out of his way to speak with her, since he was only vaguely aware of who she was. Apparently, neither of them was looking for romance. Hellman had been cut off from Hammett for some time, but he sent her a steady stream of letters—first from his various stateside locations and then from the Aleutian Islands. She got to know all about life in the military, the beauty of Alaska, his reading (Marx and *Wuthering Heights*, among other things), his running a newspaper, and the intricacies of urinating with or against the wind. He bemoaned his lack of a sex life, then told her about visiting the fleshpots of Alaska. He missed her and thought much about Hardscrabble and their life together.

After bouts of the flu, both Hellman and Melby attended a big Thanksgiving Day party at Spaso. They danced in the ballroom, and the attraction seemed almost immediate. There were drinks at the bar, and the couple discovered similar interests in the arts and world affairs. Before their acquaintance could deepen, however, they were interrupted by Annelise Kennan asking Melby for a dance. By the time he returned, Hellman had retired. The next morning at breakfast marked the beginning of their intimacy.

In *An Unfinished Woman*, Hellman names Melby only once—although she alludes to him in another passage having to do with the ruin of his career during the McCarthy period. She was very fond of the passage in which she describes their experience in a state-owned antique store. She coveted a photograph of the "real faces of Garbo and the director Rouben Mamoulian, with crudely faked bodies arranged in one of the poses of love." Melby had drawn her attention to it by touching her arm and pointing to a high shelf, then he had pulled her to the door when she had put out her hand to take the picture. Out on the street, he held her arm and would not allow her to return to the store. "Some joker had put it there, but as foreigners we would never be forgiven for buying it," Melby explained. The picture was no more than an amusement, but the love between Melby and Hellman is intimated in the different ways he touches her in this scene.

On November 28, Hellman sent Hal Wallis a wire announcing that she was going off on an important trip. She wanted to know how much "extra time" she could have to finish her movie script of *The Searching Wind*. She thought he would like what she had done so far. From November 30 to December 8, she was away from Melby visiting Leningrad after the siege. Although it was still something of a privilege for a foreigner to visit the city, she was not impressed with the invitation and did not write about this trip in her memoirs. Although she was besieged by Russian officials trying to please her with an interesting itinerary, she professed almost no curiosity about the places or people they mentioned, including Stalin. Evidently she did make comments about Leningrad in her diary, because she read them to Orlova in 1967. Orlova remembers one Hellman diary entry that suggests that Hellman took her Russian hosts at their word: "Raya says that everyone is starving equally." The translator shuddered, for she knew there was a hierarchy in the Soviet Union—that certain officials had "special rations" and even "special tennis courts." Years later, William Alfred, a dear friend of Hellman's, was shocked to hear her say Isaac Babel had died of a heart attack. "Oh, for heaven's sake, Lillian, how could you say that?" Alfred asked. "Oh, I know a very charming man in the Russian foreign service who told me that he died of a heart attack." And then Alfred just changed the subject. She was completely convinced that her Russian source was right and that everybody else was wrong, that Babel's reported death in a concentration camp was probably propaganda.

By December 9, Hellman was back in Moscow. The very next day, she had dinner with Melby. There were drinks around the Franklin stove in Kathleen Harriman's room, then he walked her back to the National Hotel, where they spent their first night together. It was to be commemorated in telegrams to each other for several years afterward. The lovers had a wonderful, high-spirited time in Moscow, although they were also careful to observe the proprieties. Robert Meiklejohn, Harriman's aide-de-camp, noted in his diary that meals had been "enlivened since Kathleen and Melby found they could make toast on the electric floor heater." For some time, the toast was daintily handed around the table, "but yesterday Miss Hellman let herself go and started tossing it about like feeding the fish."

It was Christmas time. Hellman and Melby would spend the afternoon at her hotel, "warm and easy and comfortable and very Christmasy," as he put it in a letter to her a year later. He remembered Hellman getting drunk and eating the foul embassy sandwiches, while Melby got sore because a colleague was making passes at her. It was a rowdy, brawling time. Early on Christmas morning at Spaso, Hellman "came padding down the hall in . . . oversize pajamas and made a dive into the bed." Melby wanted her like this every morning. The telegrams, the bundling in bed— it was reminiscent of her feelings for Kober.

Two days later, Melby was helping her pack for a trip to the front. He did not like the idea of being without her and was jealous that he could not go with her. They had quite a time getting her things together—the coat, books, and cigarettes. But she "looked very fetching bundled up and wearing valenki." In *An Unfinished Woman*, Hellman recalls she did not want to report on the war, said she was not a journalist, and was frightened at the prospect of a visit to the front. Orlova remembers Hellman's reactions somewhat differently. After arriving in Moscow, Hellman expressed an interest in seeing the front but made no formal, written application to do so and was not eager to go when Orlova informed her that they had been granted permission to do so. To Orlova, Hellman's reactions were normal. She knew Hellman had been to Spain, had seen fighting, and would have had at least a passing urge to see the front. The invitation was such a rare privilege, and Hellman was so envied by journalists and diplomats that she seemed to have no choice but to go.

Hellman's article in the March 31, 1945, issue of *Collier's* gives an account of her travel to the Warsaw-Vistula front. By train they took a long, five-day detour through the Ukraine and Kiev and then back north and west again to Lublin, Poland. There was almost no water on the train; it hurt to wash her hands in snow; and it did almost no good to clean her teeth with cold tea. She was "tired of canned sardines and elderly sausage." In spite of the hardships, she was treated grandly by her Russian hosts, and her article is a tribute to their courtesy and courage.

It was a very dangerous trip. Orlova and Hellman got very close to the front lines. The playwright felt she was there just to absorb the environment, and the Russians were surprised she did not ask more questions. That was not the way she learned, was her reply. She saw no value in coming up with "smart-sounding questions." Rather, she listened to what people felt they had to say. Given Hellman's very proper notions of what it meant to be a guest—to accept hospitality—it is likely that she would have regarded hard, journalistic questioning as rude. In retrospect, Orlova suggests that Hellman's "pro-left and pro-Russian politics" and her work on *The North Star* probably meant that officials at the highest echelon knew she would do nothing to offend.

The gaiety and friendliness of the soldiers pleased Hellman:

> Dinner tonight with the eight generals . . . I think they liked having a guest who was a woman. The

Russians know they are men simply without thinking about it and, like all such men, they like women and act well with them.

In her *Collier's* article, Hellman suggested there was something gallant and touching about an evening of amateur entertainment in a "freezing, shabby room filled with men trying hard to have a good time with the props, costumes and musical instruments they made themselves." She allowed herself very few autobiographical flourishes; the focus was to be on the Russians, except insofar as they had definite reactions to her:

> As we were going out to the cars, I caught a look at myself in a mirror. I stopped to stare and laugh. I had on ski pants, two sweaters and a blouse, long woolen underwear, which bulged in strange places, woolen stockings, socks, shoes, boots, an American Army sheep-lined coat with hood, and a large shawl to keep the hood in place.
>
> I said to Major Zeidner, "I want you to know that all American women don't look like this."
>
> Ria [Raya] said, "You look like the widow of a soldier who has inherited only his coat and is on her way to a government office to claim her pension!"

The Russians impressed her with their sincerity, "their ability to speak about war, death, love and hate without self-consciousness and without fake toughness; they speak simply, like healthy people who have never, fortunately, learned to be ashamed of emotion," Hellman concludes in her *Collier's* article.

William Wright has cast a suspicious eye on Hellman's memories of this trip because she includes much more dramatic material in *An Unfinished Woman*. After noting similarities between the memoir and the *Collier's* article, Wright notes that only in *An Unfinished Woman* is Hellman's sleep disturbed by fleeing German soldiers on her first night in Lublin, does she visit the Maidanek concentration camp, is she actually shot at because a reflection from her binoculars attracts enemy fire, and is she present at the interrogation of a Polish soldier fighting for the Nazis. Orlova, who describes herself as being inseparable from Hellman for the two-week trip to the front, confirms many of the incidents Wright questions. There had been shooting in Lublin, and Hellman's sleep was disturbed by the Moscow major assigned to her, who asked why she was still in bed. At Maidenek the ashes were still warm, Orlova recalls, and Hellman was appalled at what she saw. At the interrogation of the Polish soldier, Orlova remembers Hellman asking questions about the man. Who was he? What kind of family did he come from? How had he become involved with the Germans?

Wright misses the point about the person and the writer, although his own words can be used to explain most of the discrepancies between the accounts in *Collier's* and in *An Unfinished Woman*: "the variations in the two stories are not in the way Russia is depicted, but in the way Hellman depicts herself." Precisely so. For *Collier's*, she was not writing a memoir, and the reactions she seems to have had to Maidenek would have been inappropriate for that magazine:

> I was down in the blackness of deep water, pushed up to consciousness by monsters I could smell but not see, into a wildness of lions waiting to scrape my skin with their tongues, shoved down again, and up and down, covered with slime, pieces of me floating near my hands.

This is a rather overdone effort to describe her horror. The author uses a kind of language that came to her in retrospect, and it would have been entirely out of place in her journalistic report on the front line Russians.

Of more importance in gauging Hellman's reactions to her front-line trip is the glimpse Orlova provides of what Hellman chose not to write about at all. In *An Unfinished Woman*, she makes several references to the Moscow major assigned to her and Orlova. His job is to make certain that no improper questions are asked. He is a dull, politically timid functionary who is greeted contemptuously by a Russian general: "I dare say somebody will bring you a message when and if you are ever needed." In her *Memoirs*, Orlova remembers Hellman making up a perceptive story about the major:

> Look, Raya, like all military types, he was at the front at the beginning of the war. Let's say that he was in a platoon. There they immediately saw what kind of bird he was. But how to get rid of him? So they decided

to advance him, to "promote" him to a regiment. Then to a division. Then to the Political Department at the front. And, finally, to the Chief Political Department. What to do with him, what kind of job to give him so that he would cause the least amount of harm? They decided to send him off to the front with this eccentric American woman.

In April 1967, Hellman wrote Orlova: "Do you remember the name of the man we called 'the idiot major' who took us from Moscow to the front?" Orlova thought she had much more in common with the shrewd Hellman than with her stupid compatriot. At Lublin they attended the first session of the State People's Council, with the Polish leaders Bierut and Gomulka at the head of the table, installed there by the Russians. Walking away from the meeting, Hellman turned to Orlova and remarked, "There was no Lenin among those people, am I right?"

In the *Collier's* article, Hellman would not have thought it proper to include such irreverent remarks. They were for private, to be shared among friends—like her comment on Russian toilets. She was probably not dishonest when for *Collier's* she remarked on instances where Russians were courteous to Poles, even though forty years later, in *Commentary*, (October, 1984) she was fair game for Herbert Loebel, who castigated her for her pro-Sovietism. Having escaped from a "sub-camp of Auschwitz," Loebel had taken refuge with a "farmer's wife, her daughter, and one young Polish farm worker, awaiting the 'liberators.' " The Russians had come, raped the women, and wrecked the farmhouse. "The first experience with the 'Great Red Army' was followed by many others I had over a period of one year, none of them supporting Hellman's glowing description of the Red Army," Loebel wrote in a letter of protest. But Orlova points out that he referred to events that took place the spring after Hellman's visit.

Back at the embassy, Hellman told Melby all about her trip, especially the visit to Maidanek. She was baited for her pro-Soviet views. Melby noted that "it tended to become Miss Hellman vs. the field." She was personally and deeply offended, and probably made her sympathies for the Soviets more pronounced. At the same time, Melby saw how she "passionately defended the United States and everything American." He observed her in many arguments with Russian intellectuals. This often meant she attacked "something Russian I had previously heard her defend to us." In assessing Hellman's politics, her temperament and the situation she found herself in were crucial factors. Averell Harriman, for example, never was able to engage her in a serious discussion about Russian-American relations. Kathleen Harriman suspects that her pragmatic father would not have been receptive to Hellman's theoretical and philosophical views. Since Hellman was hardly a deep thinker on the subject of Marxism or on the future of Russia, this explanation seems unlikely. More to the point is Melby's conjecture that Hellman "did not have enough respect for Harriman's views to risk abusing his hospitality with arguments she knew would grow heated." This would be just like Hellman— to hold her tongue when she was in the position of guest.

It was clear to Hellman that staying too long in Moscow would sour her spirit. Everyone at the embassy was bitter. On December 8, she had sent a wire to Wallis indicating she "would like until the middle of February when I will have part of script." Another wire sent on December 24 stated she hoped to finish the script in May. Depending on the flying weather, she would leave for London in about ten days. In any event, it proved to be January 18 before she could leave. She had become very fond of Melby, and it was clear that they would see each other after Moscow. At this point, his feelings seemed to be stronger than hers, but there was no question that she was smitten. On the eve of her departure they had a confused night, too much of it spent on hurried travel preparations. Toward morning Hellman had said, "I was bad tired; now I am good tired." She seemed to be telling him about both her exhaustion and her fulfillment. At the airport, he kissed her goodbye and watched her plane "disappear into snow flurries."

13

ANOTHER PART OF THE FOREST
London/New York/East Hampton/
Hardscrabble
(1945–1946)

Perhaps I am beginning to wear that Lillian Hellman look
on my face. I hope you won't object too strenuously.

—John Melby, letter to Lillian Hellman, March 1945

. . . things move along rather dispiritedly and with too
much compromise. Very badly the moral genius and
personality of Roosevelt are missed.

—John Melby, letter to Lillian Hellman, spring 1945

T he trip to London via Teheran and Cairo was grueling, with
rough flights, open sewers, and corruption in Iran especially
hard to take. En route, Hellman sent a cable and a letter to Melby.
Arriving at the comfortable Savoy Hotel in London on January 31
was a great relief, and she immediately dispatched another cable
to Melby. She was also relieved to learn that she was not pregnant.
Although she was in love with him, she was not ready to commit
her life to him—as her second telegram suggested: "I miss you too
much." Yet she wanted to treasure their time together and asked
him for a photograph and "a calendar of significant events" of
their life together in Moscow. Already deeply devoted to Hellman,

Melby complied with her requests and suggested that missing him too much was an impossibility.

On February 2, 1945, the *Daily Worker* carried a United Press report claiming that the day before, Hellman had "branded as 'red-baiters' those who claim the Soviet Union is laying the foundation for a third world conflict." Hellman was quoted as saying the charge was irresponsible and "risked involving the world in another war." According to the report, Hellman said all the Soviets wanted was peace; soldiers wanted to return home to repair their country.

> "Anything you have read about the devastation of Russia is only a half truth," she said. "Nobody else knows what devastation means. Nobody else knows what work or privation mean until you see the Russian sacrifices."

Russian soldiers knew much more about Americans than Americans knew about them, she declared. Soviet soldiers knew about the GI bill of rights, for example, and were eager to see how it compared with their own benefits. Even in remote Siberian villages there was some familiarity with American culture, she pointed out, and "they knew more about our relations with Argentina than I did."

With the war almost at an end, there seemed little need to write the documentary that had been the original reason for Hellman's stopover in London. Instead, she took nearly a month to recuperate from her arduous travels, and returned to the United States on February 27. The FBI was anxious to question her but had difficulty locating her point of entry into the country. Not until May 16, 1945, did Fred Hallford, Special Agent in Charge, report to J. Edgar Hoover that she had arrived at Baltimore. When questioned about her time abroad, she responded with "some indignation that a person of her prominence should be subjected to any questioning upon entrance in the United States." There was no search of her person or her baggage.

Melby wrote Hellman constantly. His letters during this period run to eighty-five single-spaced pages and are filled with declarations of his love, his wish to marry Hellman, and to have children with her. He found an antique frame for her photograph: "the first thing that strikes your eye when you come into my room. So there

you sit for all the world to see, a regal picture in a regal setting."
She had not encouraged such an ardent commitment—at least not
in so many words, Melby admitted, but he was bound to break
down her skepticism that they could share a life together. He spent
many frustrating and comical hours trying to cut through the
stolid Soviet bureaucracy that hindered the shipment of all of the
fine items she had purchased in Moscow. Politically, the couple
seemed close to agreement, and Melby carried on her quarrels
with intellectuals, particularly with Ilya Ehrenburg. Melby startled
his foreign service colleagues by admitting it might take a generation to eradicate fascism in America. To even suggest that fascism
existed in his country "put the brand" on him in certain diplomatic
quarters. He believed the Russians understood the threat of fascism everywhere—not just in Germany—better than did Americans. Melby was thinking like a Marxist when he noted that the
"primary objective" of fascism was the "sanctity of property or the
glorification of the physical State (which is after all just another
form of property). Property, rather than labor or human life, is the
criterion used." In contrast to Hellman, he would later modify his
views considerably when he saw how determined Stalin was not
only to glorify the state but to enlarge it at the expense of defense-
less nations. But right now he was more preoccupied with weakness in the American system: "the vested interest in property,
whether it be great wealth or merely a supposed security in a
clerical job." Industrialization and materialism threatened American values. The "corruption of things" led to fascism, and the
problem to ponder, "could an individual once corrupted by things
be made honest again?" Evidently, Melby saw no irony in his
passionate efforts to get Hellman's property out of Moscow—
perhaps because she never bothered to square her proletarianism
with her love of luxury and of fine things.

Even at their closest, Melby could see that Hellman was much
more "disposed to give the Russians the benefit of the doubt." A
man of great integrity, Melby never divulged the details of his
work, and she never inquired about his job, but from the political
opinions expressed in letters to her she could not have failed to
see the Cold War taking shape. Indeed, her public statements
would soon reflect her dismay that the wartime alliance with Russia
was being abandoned so quickly.

Watch on the Rhine, in rehearsal in Moscow for more than six
months, finally premiered on February 24, 1945, and Melby wrote

Hellman about it. From his letter, it is easy to see why she had no great hopes for the production. "Your work on Sara was a success in that she only once had to resist a temptation to do a spread-eagle act on the table and gave a quiet dignified performance." Hellman hated the extravagance of Russian actors. The actress playing Fanny Farrelly clowned her way through the play, but "the Russians loved it." How eccentric Americans were! seemed to be the Russian reaction. The playwright could not have been pleased to hear that the actors had taken some liberties with her lines. She had thought her plays would be produced in the great tradition of Stanislavsky's Moscow Art Theater, and instead she found Russians struggling with the unfamiliar culture and idiom of her work.

On March 2, Hellman held a press conference in New York. She reported conversations with Red Army officers, who were very concerned about fascism in South America: " 'What will the United States do about Argentina?' " Miss Hellman countered, " 'What will Russia do about Franco?' " She found Russians in general to be " 'polite, Puritan, romantic, terrific,' people about whom too little is known, too much misunderstood." She suggested that they were grateful for American help and proudly displayed American-made goods obtained through lend-lease. She was wrong when she supposed the Red Army was "too well disciplined" for "individual reprisals against Germany," and less than candid when she avowed, "Artists are treated like kings in Russia in the respect and remuneration accorded them." She seemed to have a low opinion of Soviet literature, but rated Soviet music better than American. Although the FBI clipped the record of this press conference for its files, it made no comment on her most intriguing statement: "I wouldn't want to see Communism here. . . . We're never going to have it. It is no problem with us. I see no signs of it here." After Hellman's *Collier's* piece on the front-line Russians appeared on March 31, Westbrook Pegler published a column noting that her trip had been paid for by the Russian government. He stated that she was a "cozy friend of the Communists," infamous for her support of the invasion of Finland, and was listed forty-two times in the cumulative index of the HUAC for her support of Communist front groups.

Also in March, at a dinner in her honor that was part of a $750,000 fund-raising campaign for refugees from the Spanish Civil War, Hellman spoke of her Soviet trip, including a young man later identified in *An Unfinished Woman* as Kolya, who toasted his love for "Stalin, Roosevelt, Churchill, Betty Grable and Dotty Lamour." She attacked William L. White's anti-Soviet book. It was up to Americans not to approve or disapprove of communism but to acknowledge that the Russian people had fought for it remarkably well. The Spanish refugees, she said, were a "moral symbol of those we abandoned."

More news come from Melby in early April about the opening of *The Little Foxes* in Moscow. He was impressed with the Southern atmosphere and the competence of the cast, although there was still that regrettable "tendency to overact." The staging and costuming were splendid. The whole production seemed heavily influenced by the movie version of the play. He thought it was particularly effective to have a sign over the stage in huge block letters reading HUBBARDS. "I suppose it was intended to fix in the Russian audience's mind the identity between family and business."

Melby was making plans to return to America for the meeting of the United Nations in San Francisco. Roosevelt had said at Yalta that world leaders had failed the men who fought World War I—the war to end all wars. "We failed them then. We cannot fail them again, and expect the world to survive, again." These words would be used as a prologue to the movie version of *The Searching Wind*. The cause of world peace seemed achievable in the waning days of World War II, even as diplomats like Melby sensed the United States and the Soviet Union jockeying for strategic advantages. There still seemed time to reform international relations, to prevent a third world conflict. On April 12, Roosevelt died. The Russians were devastated by his death and were distrustful of Truman, a man they did not know. Ambassador Harriman convinced the distressed Vyacheslav Mikhailovich Molotov, Stalin's foreign minister, who was at a loss as to what to do, that sending a high-level delegation to the United Nations in San Francisco would be the appropriate response. Russian doubts about Truman were echoed in some liberal quarters in America, for much of the New Deal energy had already dissipated and Roosevelt's postwar foreign policy had not yet jelled. Soon, certain liberals would look to Henry Wallace as Roosevelt's heir and attack Truman for hardening his approach to the Russians. On this very issue, Melby and Hellman—like other liberals of their generation—would soon split, with Hellman joining the Wallace Progressives in the cause of world peace, a cause they supposed could be accomplished in league with the Soviet Union.

April 15, 1945. Hellman and Melby were nervous about meeting again. When he arrived at LaGuardia Airport, he called. No answer. Several more calls, a few drinks, and a connection was made. They met under a street light. She ran into his arms. It seemed, he wrote her later, "the most natural thing in the world." They stayed the night at her Eighty-second Street house. The next day he accompanied her on the train to Washington for a performance of *The Searching Wind*. Melby met several of Hellman's friends, including Ruth Gordon and Garson Kanin. By April 21 he was on a plane to San Francisco. Hellman had cabled ahead for him, asking Kober if he might be able to put up Melby for a few days, since hotel rooms were scarce. Shortly after he arrived, Melby sent a letter telling Hellman she was a "lusty wench" and that his love for her was such that he would take it "on any terms." She got a ringside view of how the United Nations was hammered into shape, with fights over the Russian-installed Lublin government in Poland and over Russian efforts to exclude Peron's Argentina from the world organization. In all, Melby wrote fifty-nine pages about the two-month conference in which he acted as a liaison officer or, as he put it, "a combination of nursemaid, office boy, and messenger." There were comical incidents—like the one with "the Arabian with no knowledge of English who tried to make [seduce] an elevator girl in the elevator by whispering 'pussy, pussy, pussy.' "

Long-distance calls were not enough to make up for the lovers' separation. In his letters, Melby would reminisce about Hellman's exuberance, for she was the spring of his affection. She would make "strange noises and gurgles in springtime. . . . There are times when your inarticulate sounds are quite as wonderful and meaningful as the articulate ones—no cracks, please—sometimes more so, and always exciting." There was that wonderful set of contradictions in Hellman—at once fresh and girlish, sardonic and cynical.

Melby's hopes were still high for Russian-American cooperation, but he could not blink away the strong anti-Soviet attitude he detected, and, feeling dispirited, he wanted to return to Hellman. There were charges on both American and Russian sides of not having lived up to the Yalta agreement. "Sweetheart, where does all this come out? I remember that we sat in your lovely living room and you wondered whether there actually could be any basis for a genuine understanding." Hellman did not like being without Melby. She was pleased, however, that her shipment of china had arrived from Moscow.

Hellman must have sensed that Melby would not give up his foreign service career. His letters everywhere reveal his passionate commitment to international relations, and by May 8 it was becoming apparent that he would be posted as a political advisor in Chungking. It was an "important job" the State Department wanted him to take on. The conflict between Chiang Kai-shek's Kuomintang and Mao Tse-tung's Communists was coming to a head. American interests had to be protected, especially since there was great worry about Soviet influence in China. The United States needed a "new and constructive foreign policy," in Melby's view. It was a risky assignment, but Melby was game for it, and he asked Hellman, "Won't you come along, darling?" If, as Robert Newman notes, she took this in stride, it may have been because she could not imagine Melby making any other sort of decision.

Melby thought he would be in China for six months. He was waiting to hear about a possible assignment that would take him back to Europe. South America, his area of expertise, was another possibility. In any case, he did not foresee a long separation. Hellman seemed disposed to wait for him. She put her claim on him, and he saw flashes of the Hellman temper when she could not reach him by phone in San Francisco for most of an evening. He had to smooth things over in a letter and to account for his whereabouts. He had never lied to her, he said, and she ought to know by now that he loved her. Her anger suggested to him that she cared more about him than she had "so far been willing to admit, or perhaps even want." This was shrewd, for Hellman must have considered how hard it would be to have this man for herself if he was determined to travel the world. Whatever her misgivings, by the end of May she acknowledged in a phone call to Melby that their love had deepened and that it would bind them together for the rest of their lives.

July, 1945. A summer with Hellman. At Hardscrabble, Melby met many of her friends: Gregory and Margaret Zilboorg, Louis and Emmy Kronenberger, Arthur and Maggie Kober and their daughter Catherine, Herman Shumlin, Gerald and Sara Murphy, Archibald MacLeish, Paul Robeson, and Dorothy Parker. He learned more about his lover's past. "In my affair with Herman I thought that sex was enough, that it would keep people together, and I was wrong about that. It isn't enough," she confided to Melby. Melby found it interesting that he and Hellman could be frank about things. "Nobody was going to get mad about it." On one occasion as Louis Kronenberger was leaving the house, he looked up at Melby and Hellman on the second floor landing and remarked, "You two look as though you belong together." At a lunch with Melby's friend, Ed Flynn, there was talk of arranging a special mission having to do with a plan for a Vatican-Kremlin detente. Hellman seemed uneasy at the way foreign service officers could be "summarily uprooted and sent halfway around the world," as Robert Newman puts it.

After a brief, painful trip to visit his family in El Paso, Melby returned to New York. During a dinner of roast duck, Hellman got a bone stuck in her throat. She had been having terrible problems with her teeth, and a new set of dentures may have contributed to the accident. A throat incision had to be made, and the incident evidently caused her some embarrassment.

The couple decided to rent a vacation house in East Hampton. But Hellman detected a certain reserve in the listing agency's response to her call and soon realized there was a restrictive covenant against Jews. With her indignation at full strength, she mobilized her friends and, perhaps out of the fear of publicity, the agency found her a place. Long walks on the beach, fishing, picnics—sometimes with Hellman's friends but more often alone—were the order of their days in East Hampton.

By August, Hammett was out of the army and aware that there was someone new in Hellman's life. If not jealous, he was feeling neglected. Back in February, for example, he had written a short letter to Hellman's secretary, Nancy Bragdon, noting that as a "good soldier," he had "picked up the frayed ends" of his correspondence with Hellman. He was going to write letters until her desktop was covered. She had been "gone so long," he was not certain she would "ever come back." He also wanted Bragdon to "warn" Hellman that she would have to find some good excuse for not having sent him any letters from London.

Hammett had his own apartment in New York and would divide his time between the city and Hardscrabble. He and Hellman had always had separate residences and other lovers. But in the past, Hammett had usually been a big topic of conversation between Hellman and her lovers. Not this time. Melby remembers meeting Hammett without knowing how big a role he had played in

Hellman's life. In her memoirs, she indicates that the postwar years (1945–48) were rough ones with Hammett and that they saw less of each other. It may also be that her failing to speak much of Hammett was an indication of how deeply she felt about Melby. Hammett's only comment about that summer was that she was leading a very social life. She would come home from town each week with new guests—all manner of "grotesques," he called them, and he "ignored them or mingled as he pleased," according to Diane Johnson.

On October 18, Melby was on his way to China. He would keep up a steady correspondence with Hellman, declaring his love and providing her with fascinating insights into diplomacy and politics. He would be there three years and send her 390 pages of cablegrams and letters. At some point, Hellman must have written him about Hammett, because Melby acknowledged her feelings on December 2: "I think I can understand what Dash means when he says you two no longer have points of contact." She was also openly discussing a permanent relationship with Melby and frankly telling him not only about Hammett but about Kober and Shumlin. For some reason, she decided to omit any mention of Ingersoll from her list of lovers. Melby thought he and Hellman had to "clean a lot of debris out of our backyards" so that they could "live together at peace with each other and with the past." Hellman threw a fit when she met a colleague of Melby's who suggested Melby did not really want to divorce his wife. Melby wrote in anger about Luis Quintanilla, who certainly knew how serious Melby was about Hellman, and by the end of the year the lover's quarrel was entirely forgotten, although she was melancholy and expressed considerable anxiety about his return. Hellman was writing again, finishing up the screenplay for *The Searching Wind* and beginning work on *Another Part of the Forest*, the second play in her projected trilogy on the Hubbards. Melby was most encouraging.

As in *These Three*, Hellman's film adaptation of *The Children's Hour*, her first inclination was to get to the point more quickly in the screen version of *The Searching Wind* than was possible in the play. *The Children's Hour* had begun in a schoolroom in which the personalities of the characters were allowed to emerge through dialogue. In *These Three*, such a scene would have been static, so the screenwriter opted for a quick-paced scene *showing* the intimacy between Martha and Karen and their plans for establishing the school. In the original movie script for *The Searching Wind*, Hellman abandoned the play's opening drawing-room scene and the expository dialogue in favor of a dramatic war scene, in which Sam Hazen is confronted by his friend Leck's words about Sam's family, words that are only repeated by Sam in the play. Leck has read in the papers about the Hazen parties, "those 'brilliant gatherings'—half of them are full of Nazis and people who are good and work along with them. Just so their own hides are safe. . . . It's people like your mother and father who got us in the spot we're in now, and if you know what's good for you, you'll get away from them." Sam heatedly defends his parents, then there is an attack—presumably it is the battle in which Sam is grievously wounded in the leg.

This opening was not used, but Hellman's concern to get the picture moving more quickly than the play was honored. In the drawing-room scene, the opening dialogue is contentious. Dudley Diggs repeats his stage role as Moses Taney, Sam's grandfather and the retired owner of a liberal newspaper. Moses has always been critical of Alex's diplomatic waffling about the events that led to the Second World War. In this opening scene, Moses berates Alex (Robert Young) for errors in political judgment that Alex refuses to acknowledge. Their fight about Alex's weak response to Fascism is interrupted by Sam's (Douglas Dick) awakening from a nightmare about his war experiences. His fears about losing his leg and the political differences between liberals about the appeasement of Hitler that led to war are immediately linked. Had men like Alex acted decisively, perhaps Sam would not have gone to war. As in the screen version of *The Little Foxes*, where the focus is immediately on Alexandra, making her into a heroine, in *The Searching Wind*, Sam's story becomes the frame within which the debates and the romances between his elders take place. The other notable addition in the film, which otherwise follows the play faithfully, is a flashback to the Spanish Civil War. As Bernard F. Dick notes, Cassie is given much stronger language in the movie, in which she condemns Alex for not reporting that German planes are bombing Madrid. "You have nothing to do with death because you have nothing to do with people. . . . You're a diplomat." Dick observes that Cassie (Sylvia Sidney) speaks for Hellman here—or rather, it might be more accurate to say, for a part of her. Hellman, after all, was in love with a diplomat, and Alex Hazen, for all of his faults, is sympathetically treated in both the play and the film.

In fact, he is somewhat more forceful in the film, and Cassie is less sorry for him and more angry that he has not lived up to his potential. It is tempting to imagine Hellman's feelings for Melby creeping into her movie work. In some ways, such as the use of montage and the juxtaposition of newspaper headlines to convey the passage of time, the film is a better vehicle than the play for Hellman's flashback technique. The film received mixed reviews and was a modest success.

According to an interview with Lewis Funke, Hellman actually started writing the first act of *Another Part of the Forest* in early March 1946. Ward Morehouse was given a December 1945 date and told the play was not finished until just before the beginning of rehearsals in October. It had been on her mind for much longer than that—probably from the beginning of her analysis with Zilboorg in 1940. She would not need to do additional research for the new play, set in 1880, since she had done so much work for the background of *The Little Foxes,* set in 1900. The very title of the new work suggested that it was a continuation of the earlier drama, but *Another Part of the Forest* was also about origins and stood by itself. How the Hubbards had formed their personalities was her concern now, just as how she had become Lillian Hellman was the topic of her sessions with Zilboorg.

Wambly Bald reported in the *New York Post* (November 12, 1946) that while writing, Hellman would drink twenty cups of strong coffee a day and smoke three packs of cigarettes. She rewrote the whole play four times, working in "fits and starts, sometimes going without sleep for two whole days," pacing the floor in "loose-fitting nightgowns and bathrobes to make her more comfortable." It was like a pregnancy, she suggested, although she did not develop a taste for pickles—just a lot of heavy eating at breakfast, particularly lamb chops. This was not the first time she had exhausted herself with a play: "When I finished 'Watch on the Rhine' I was so groggy I fell to the floor and bumped my head," she told the *Post* reporter.

It was no accident that *Another Part of the Forest* was written right after the end of World War II, for Hellman was intent on exploring how a world had developed out of war. "The war's over, the old times are finished," is what Regina says to her lover's Confederate family, the Bagtrys. In 1945, the balance of power in the world was changing. In 1880, in *Another Part of the Forest,* the balance of power was shifting from the Southern aristocrats to the self-made businessman who, like Marcus Hubbard, had profited from the Civil War. Marcus, however, is soon to be displaced by his son Ben, who is all business, whereas his father still cultivates the gentlemanly pastimes of writing music and reading Aristotle. Ben would have Regina "marry money," while Marcus dotes on his daughter and calls on his son to "put aside your plans for your sister's future. Spend with profit your time today going over the store books. *(Amused)* You'll find we are short of cash. Call in some cotton loans or mortgages. *(Giggles)* Then go to church." Marcus can be satirical about business and religion because he regards both of them as means to an end: self-aggrandizement. He has been spending money at a great rate because money itself is not his object. Making it has been one of his amusements and so is spending it. Ben, on the other hand, measures everything in terms of profit and loss and, in reference to Regina's and Oscar's affairs, says he is "sick of love."

Throughout act one, Marcus is in total control of his family, so that their efforts to become independent appear futile. But he has contempt for everyone, and his life is so lacking in balance that it comes as no surprise that Ben finds a way of assuming command by blackmailing his father. The stage setting foreshadows Marcus's limitations, for *"there is something too austere, too pretended Greek about the portico, as if it followed one man's eccentric taste and was not designed to be comfortable for anyone else."* Indeed, at the end of the play, Ben will announce his plans for building a new house and point out that his father has not quite made it into the modern age. Ironically, it is just when Ben seems to have failed and when he uncharacteristically reveals himself that he succeeds. He tells his father, "I spent twenty years lying and cheating to help make you rich. I was trying to outwait you, Papa, but I guess I couldn't do it." Ben's mother, Lavinia, takes her son's confession as an admission of sin, which is hers as well because she has also tried to "outwait" Marcus, to excuse his venality. "Benjamin," she calls after her son, the "firstborn" of her sin, to whom she will reveal how Marcus had been able to buy a pass which he had used to "prove" he had not led Yankee soldiers to an encampment where twenty-seven Confederates were killed.

It is curious that Hellman makes Lavinia the agent of change. She has written in her bible an eyewitness account of how Marcus went about constructing his false alibi. She resembles the delicate,

other-worldly Birdie in *The Little Foxes*, yet Lavinia has a strength
that the earlier version of Hellman's mother is never able to
summon. Lavinia has some of Julia Hellman's religiosity but also a
shrewdness which is missing in Birdie. Lavinia will not part with
her bible, for she knows it is her trump card. In both artistic and
autobiographical terms, *Another Part of the Forest* is an advance. As
Hellman scholar Doris Falk observes:

> [Lavinia] is neither a crazy woman nor a saintly one,
> although she has a touch of each, and her presence in
> the play means that some good blood has been
> brought into the Hubbard clan. . . . It was Hellman's
> way of setting things to rights with the ghost of her
> own eccentric, misunderstood mother, who had been
> a source of irritation and embarrassment at times to
> her daughter.

Although critics have preferred *The Little Foxes* to *Another Part of
the Forest* and have treated the latter almost as an afterthought, the
firm control of the speech rhythms and contrasting voices certainly
equals the achievement of the first Hubbard play:

> MARCUS *(softly):* You don't have to marry a man, Re-
> gina, just because—We can go away, you and I—
> OSCAR *(goes toward kitchen door):* I certainly don't know
> what's happened here. I certainly don't. I'm hun-
> gry. *(Calls in)* Where's breakfast, you all?
> REGINA *(sharply):* Order breakfast for me, too, selfish.
> BEN *(laughs):* That's my good girl. *(Picks up the newspa-
> per)* Nothing for anybody to be so unhappy about.
> You both going to do all right. I got ideas.

Oscar, essentially a character of brutal appetites, has never understood his father's successes or failures and cannot keep his mind
on either. Regina has always felt that she has been served last in
her brothers' scramble for wealth and now has to contend with
Ben's plan to have her marry Horace Giddens. Ben relaxes in his
father's role and is almost tender with her, now that she cannot go
to Marcus to have her own way. The modulation of sound from
soft to loud and from sharp to mellow tones captures the family in
its entirety. Moreover, the play's very last stage movement brings

Another Part of the Forest full circle back to *The Little Foxes,* to the jockeying for power that will now prevail as a consequence of Marcus's defeat:

> MARCUS *(softly):* Pour me a cup of coffee, darling. *(Regina looks at him, gets up, crosses to table, pours coffee, brings it to him. Marcus pulls forward the chair next to him. Regina ignores the movement, crosses to chair near Ben, sits down.)*

Regina's treatment of her father at the end of the play sums up much of what Hellman felt about human psychology and about the power of money. Regina and Marcus have catered to each other and tried to manipulate each other. Their closeness is the result of complex feelings, both selfish and loving. There is the strong implication that Marcus's attachment to Regina is incestuous, and Ben predicts (before he has bested Marcus) that the father will never let the daughter marry, never allow her to leave home. How Regina reacts to her defeated father, then, is the crux of the drama, as it seems to have been for Hellman vis-à-vis her father during her analysis with Zilboorg.

From Hellman's memoirs, it is clear that as a child she became terribly angry about her father's infidelities, but she never admits in so many words that she was jealous of other women for taking him away from her or that she was never able to forgive him for neglecting her. She wanted all of his attention but could never get it. She scorned her mother for being the weak link in the family triangle, for putting up with her father's philandering—just as Lavinia in *Another Part of the Forest* pathetically puts up with Marcus's ruthless dismissal of her feelings. Yet the play also makes clear that Regina is ready to leave her father—to go to Chicago and start a life of her own—at about the same age as Hellman was prepared to lead an independent life. The Freudian analysis with Zilboorg must have delved into controlling patterns from childhood, into Hellman's deep attachment to her father but also into her resentment over his influence. Melby suspected as much when he wrote to Hellman on May 10, 1945, about a Zilboorg book she had just sent him. Reading the psychiatrist's book emboldened Melby to

> . . . stick my neck into a bucket of water: I have been interested in and thinking about what you wrote me

about getting your pa to get married again. You once suggested that the root of your neurosis you thought would turn out to be the relationship between you and him. I have also noticed that you have from time to time spoken of wishing that he would marry. It would be nice for a lonely old man; but is there something of the other in it too? It may be coincidence, and probably is caused by something else, but all your letters since you told me of the contract [her father's marriage contract] have a different tone to them, somehow a feeling of an inner peace that is not usually there. Or am I just being clever-ignorant?

It is not hard to imagine Hellman wrestling with her feelings for her father while at the same time struggling to express Regina's reactions to her father, for the ending of the play went through several changes:

Version I: Regina pours a cup of coffee for Marcus, ignores his gesture for her to sit beside him, and quite deliberately stays away from him.
Version 2: Regina ignores Marcus when he tries to sit next to her, then moves over to create a place for him beside her.
Version 3: "Marcus is now slightly outside the circle formed by the other three [Oscar, Ben, and Regina]".
Version 4: Regina rejects Marcus by taking a seat next to Ben.
Version 5: Marcus is left to sit alone, with no place for him at the family's dining table.

In all of these versions and in other slight variations, the playwright considers how Regina can acknowledge and yet separate herself from her father. Psychologically, the ending Hellman finally uses restores a modicum of dignity to Marcus and of humanity to Regina without weakening the brutal outcome of the drama. She not only pours a cup of coffee for her father; she brings it to him. Rather than gesturing for her to sit down, he merely makes available a chair next to him. The movement to Ben, however, completes her development in the play: the balance of power has indeed shifted.

Even more than *The Little Foxes, Another Part of the Forest,* is about being in control of one's destiny. Not only Regina, but also Ben and Oscar, long for some kind of independence. John Bagtry, Regina's Confederate lover, leaves for South America in pursuit of his destiny. Lavinia finally turns against him because he will not allow her any sort of autonomy. Marcus's regime, like that of Hellman's formidable grandmother, Sophie Newhouse, and her brother Jake, is ruthless. It is time for the next generation to assume control over its own affairs.

This spirit of independence led Hellman to cast and to direct *Another Part of the Forest* by herself. A very young and beautiful Patricia Neal played Regina Hubbard. Bartlett Robinson was chosen as John Bagtry, Regina's Confederate lover. Stage veterans Mildred Dunnock as Lavinia Hubbard and Percy Waram as Marcus Hubbard gave splendid performances as the mother and father. Leo Genn, the accomplished English actor, took the role of Benjamin Hubbard and Scott McKay played the other brother, Oscar. Jean Hagen had the wonderful comic part of Laurette Sincee, the girl who was no better than she should be and who Oscar is "deeply and sincerely" in love with.

Although Hellman continued to see Shumlin after *The Searching Wind*, she never seems to have considered him for the new play, and they parted company sometime in 1946 in a dispute over taxes she thought he should have paid. Evidently, she took him to court and lost. For the newspapers, she steadfastly refused to criticize him. In *Pentimento*, she simply says, "I had a good time directing the play, not because I wanted to, but because I was tired of arguments and knew no director I thought was right for me." In an interview with Ward Morehouse in the *New York Sun* (November 15, 1946), she suggested that she had "wanted to direct for a long time—it's a natural outgrowth for a writer—and that's pretty much the only reason Herman didn't produce this new play. It all came about with no ill feeling." This simply was not true. There may have been no big scene between Hellman and Shumlin, but the resentment was there.

Hellman's new producer was Kermit Bloomgarden, "a nice and decent guy," she told Morehouse. She admitted that in her usual absentmindedness she had "embarrassed Kermit for many months" by not telling him what she took for granted—that he would produce her play. Bloomgarden had worked as Shumlin's business manager since 1935 and was fairly new at producing plays. He would go on to have a distinguished career in the theater, but he never directed and often found himself unable to control Hellman as playwright or as director.

Bloomgarden's wife, Virginia, remembers the routine involved with producing a Hellman play:

> We used to sit at breakfast at 8:30 or 9:00 at home and the phone would ring. It would be Lillian. This was day after day after day after day. I remember saying to him once "Can't you tell her we're having breakfast? Who is she?"

The demands were inexorable, and it obviously troubled Virginia that no one stood up to Hellman except Hammett, who seemed to be the only person she would listen to. Jose Vega, the assistant stage manager for *Another Part of the Forest*, remembers that Bloomgarden was there just "to service" Hellman. "You couldn't stand up to her, or she would get someone else." Bloomgarden was a very bright man who "couldn't reach her."

About her experience as director of *Another Part of the Forest*, Hellman noted in *Pentimento* that it was "so good I fooled myself into thinking I was a director, a mistake I was to discover a few years later." Had Hellman forgotten how much of an ordeal the cast and crew, with the exception of Patricia Neal, found it to work with her? Or even worse, had Hellman not noticed that theater professionals, who respected her talent enormously, nevertheless found her a terror? At the time, she admitted to Ward Morehouse that she had "fumbled around for a week" and that she did not "know the technical words of direction"—they never interested her. Wambly Bald got the story that she had been nervous the first few days, "set the motion too fast," but then settled down.

Jose Vega vividly remembers Hellman's direction:

> It was very strange. For a woman as talented as she was, she had *absolutely* no idea of how to translate what she wrote to the stage. She did not know how to work with actors. For example, she had Bartlett Robinson [John Bagtry] and Patricia Neal [Regina Hubbard] play a love scene from opposite sides of the stage. These were all very good actors and made what she made them do as good as possible.

Vega remembers there was no questioning Hellman's direction: "If you came up and said very nicely, 'Look, maybe we ought to try so and so,' she wouldn't even hear you. But if you came up very aggressively and said 'UNLESS YOU DO SO AND SO,' then she'd listen." As long as you were sure of your own professionalism, you could get along with Hellman. But if you were afraid of her, "forget it." Vega liked her very much for her brightness and her talent. She could talk about practically anything brilliantly. But her intelligence seemed to have very little to do with success in the theater. Somehow she had gotten the idea that she could do anything, yet "she was not a director at all," Vega concludes.

Hellman did not even block out the play. Actors would be behind furniture or in corners or talking upstage. None of that bothered the playwright; she was just listening to her words. The actors simply stumbled around until they found something. "There was a revolt on *Another Part of the Forest*," Vega remembers. The actors were frustrated and uncomfortable because she was giving them things that were impossible to do well. She did not even bother to explain the meaning of the play. To her, it must have seemed obvious.

The only actor in the cast who was close to Hellman was Patricia Neal, then very young, beautiful, and in her first major stage role. "With people Hellman liked she was extraordinarily nice. People she just worked with she didn't even see. She would walk in, and there would be people all around her saying hello, and she didn't even hear them," Vega recalls. Her behavior did not seem calculated to him. She was just "two different people. She would do *anything* for Patricia Neal." If Neal coughed during a rehearsal or looked a little tired, Hellman would stop and say, "Let's take a break." Someone else could have been walking around with a broken leg, and if she didn't happen to like him, she would say, "Come on!" How someone could be so insightful and so insensitive was more than Vega could understand.

Hellman always came across as fully in command of herself. There was a tough, masculine quality about her. But Vega remembers a time when Hammett was seated in the theater during a rehearsal. He had come to pick Hellman up, and there was a complete change in her. It was as if a mask had dropped away and suddenly she became vulnerable. A feminine self flowered. Around Patricia Neal, especially in the dressing room, Hellman again seemed slightly vulnerable, but utterly comfortable. "It gives me pleasure that I found an unknown girl, Patricia Neal, and watched her develop into a good actress and woman," Hellman remarks in *Pentimento.*

"Lillian behaved extremely well the opening night of *Another Part of the Forest,*" Virginia Bloomgarden Chilewich recalls. There was a party at Hellman's house at East Eighty-second Street with many of her dear friends. Reviews were coming in, and Virginia remembers being called upstairs, where the tension was terrible. After a negative review had been quoted, Virginia's eyes welled up. Hellman said, "Stop it, Ginny. I told you once nobody asked me to write for them. And nobody asked Kermit to produce it. So take your lumps." This was the kind of speech Virginia would hear again after *The Autumn Garden*—the kind of speech that as the years went on Virginia began to distrust. Hellman tended to make such incredible statements. Were they for the effect? It was as if the playwright had this Lillian Hellman role to play. Certain kinds of grand statements were expected from her.

In the critical literature, *Another Part of the Forest* has suffered under the shadow of *The Little Foxes.* The second Hubbard play has been called even more melodramatic and mechanical than the first. Curiously, the opening night reviews seem sounder than the considered analyses of academics. Several reviewers rated *Another Part of the Forest* higher than *The Little Foxes,* or at least its equal. For Louis Kronenberger (in *PM,* November 22), the new play was "less effective but more interesting, less controlled but more complex." Perhaps he was getting at the simplicity and economy of the power struggle in *The Little Foxes*; it is a contest of wills without the overlay of psychology Hellman brought to *Another Part of the Forest.* Richard Watts spoke for several reviewers who were taken with Marcus, with his "sententious but earnest striving for culture and his scorn for the romantic pretensions of the Confederate South which makes one understand a great deal about him." He was not simply a scoundrel but a human being, Watts observed in the *New York Post* (November 21). He was entranced with the Hubbards, who were "plagued by their own sins, and the relationship of the mother and father." There is no question that Hellman's first night audience responded well to her probing of the psychological roots of human character.

Yet *Another Part of the Forest* had only a modest success; it lasted less than two hundred performances, and the road tour had to be canceled after just getting started in Chicago. This lack of popular-

ity had little to do with the quality of the play but a great deal to
do with its savage tone. Hellman was ruthless in this play, especially in the long, third-act encounter between father and son. It
was unpleasant to watch. There was an Elizabethan coarseness in
the familial quarrel that must have shocked middle-class audiences. In *The Nation* (December 7), Joseph Wood Krutch contended
that there also were political overtones to the play's reading of
history:

> I am not unaware of the fact that all this is supposed
> to have, for the initiated, a meaning. It is, that is to
> say, a Marxian study of the decline of the Southern
> feudal aristocracy and the rise of the capitalist ex-
> ploiter. There are no admirable characters because, by
> antecedent premise, there cannot be any. Dying aris-
> tocrats must be dim-witted and rising capitalists must
> be villainous because otherwise the dialectic process
> could not have taken place as it did. Even the fact that
> the scoundrels seem somewhat more likable than their
> victims is precisely according to formula, since capital-
> ism, though evil in itself, advances the dialectic pro-
> cess one stage beyond feudalism and is to that extent
> more admirable. But none of this is pointed out explic-
> itly in the play itself, and I suspect that most of even
> the initiated will disregard it in order to join with the
> innocent in getting what fun they can out of a play in
> which dog bites dog, and bitch snarls at bitch for two
> hours and a half during which no spectator need ever
> remember that any of the virtues exist except in the
> futile imagination of the insane or the half-witted.

Hellman had wavered between cutting and adding explicitly political speeches in early drafts, where Ben, in particular, dissected
the southern economy and discussed the coming of northern
money to his region. By failing to adapt to new economic conditions, Marcus had gone Southern—according to Ben, in draft
four—and ruined himself. Much of this specifically southern material (including a long story about "Old Lena," a boat from the
seige of Mobile) was pruned from the play; it has less of a documentary effect than *The Little Foxes*, Richard Moody notes. Hellman
decided in the final draft, as Theresa Mooney shows, to rely on

"the characterization of Bagtry, Lavinia, and Marcus to convey her message more subtly." Marcus, in particular, became much less coldly selfish in later drafts.

Having been taken to task for having written a nasty, brutish play, Hellman took an unusual step. She replied to Brooks Atkinson in *The New York Times* (December 18, 1946). She did not really answer his charges about the melodramatic and harsh quality of her work. "Answering critics is a sucker game," she contended. "Writing is not a gentleman's game and is not properly played with gentleman's material," she explained. In other words, she had no excuses for writing plays that have "action on the stage," "evil people," and violence. The critic's taste, she implied, was tepid. There was no way of arguing him out of his viewpoint or of changing her mind; critic and playwright were natural enemies. She would never accept his terms, or he hers.

It was a hard-boiled view of things, but surely no more savage than Shakespeare's. The postwar world did not seem ready for such a play or such a tough writer. She had more energy than could be accommodated on the stage. In *Pentimento,* she seemed to enjoy quoting a critic's line against herself: "I blow a stage to pieces without knowing it." Even Henry Sigerist, a historian of science and an extravagant admirer of the woman and her works, had to admit she wore him out:

> After having seen Lillian Hellman's *Another Part of the Forest*, and having reread her *Little Foxes*, both brilliant plays about wicked and morbid people, it is a great relief to read a simple and beautiful book such as Rumer Godden's *Thus Far and No Further*, the diary of half a year that she spent during the war with her two children and three dogs on a tea plantation near Darjeeling. The day by day observations and thoughts of a sensitive woman.

"All I wanted was a docile woman," Hammett used to say, "and look what I got."

14

COLD WAR
New York/Martha's Vineyard/
Hardscrabble/Europe
(1946–1949)

We are out to expose those elements that are insidiously
trying to spread subversive propaganda, poison the minds
of your children, distort the history of our country, and
discredit Christianity.

—Congressman John Rankin

The hysterical anti-Communism of the 1940s and 1950s was
. . . virulent, overstepping the bounds of politics and
nationalistic feeling and entering the realm of religiosity.

—Philip Dunne, *Take Two: A Life in Movies and Politics*

O n February 12, 1946, Albert Maltz published an article called
"What Shall We Ask of Writers?" in *The New Masses*. As a
dedicated Communist and screenwriter, he was concerned about
creative works that were judged on the basis of whether or not
they conformed to the party line. Maltz thought it was wrong to
criticize literature on purely ideological grounds. Rather, the esthetic quality of the work of art—its contribution to an understanding of human character and society—should be the primary criterion. To support his argument, Maltz focused on the reception of
Watch on the Rhine. The play had been attacked in *The New Masses*

when the party line advocated support of the pact; the movie version of the play was praised in *The New Masses* when the party line once again was anti-Fascist.

Perhaps it was bourgeois of Maltz to think that a work of art could be evaluated purely on its own terms, but the fury of the Communist attack on his article surely had more to do with his frank discussion of the party line. He had embarrassed the party. The next issue of *The New Masses* carried several denunciations of his apostasy, and the pressure against him became so intense that he finally recanted and admitted his views were reactionary. Neither Hellman nor Hammett responded in public to this controversy, even though their own work was at issue and they had known Maltz for several years. So outspoken on so many public issues, neither writer had a word to say when it concerned a critique of radicalism. Maltz's article deserved more than diatribes, but his brief period of independence ended when radicals like Hellman and Hammett decided not to lend their dignity and prestige to the debate. Hellman has been branded a Stalinist; her silence at such crucial moments in the history of American radicalism is part of the reason why. Her opponents have shown she was not at all reluctant to criticize her own country and to take vehement issue with anti-Communist liberals.

It was possible for Communists to beat each other back into line, but liberals already appeared to be irrevocably divided. On the one hand, the Progressive Citizens of America (PCA) called on the Left—including Communists—to resist the anti-Communist hysteria that threatened to ruin the important reforms instituted by the New Deal. On the other hand, the Americans for Democratic Action (ADA) aimed at perpetuating New Deal policies while scrupulously excluding Communists. Cold War scholar Richard Walton and journalist Garry Wills have charged that this anti-Communist slant contributed to the extremism of the times, no matter how strenuously ADA members might have deplored red-baiting. Philip Dunne, a participant in the political wars of that era, takes vigorous exception to Wills's introduction to *Scoundrel Time* by pointing out that many ADA members, including Hellman's attorney Joseph Rauh, fought for everyone's civil liberties. If organizations like the ADA did not want Communist members, it was because liberals had found them, in Dunne's words, to be "dogmatists" and no respecters of free speech. Communists had persecuted their presumed allies—the socialists, anarchists, and

Trotskyists—in the Spanish Civil War; dissent had been brutally repressed in the Soviet Union; and in America, the party relentlessly attacked Trotskyists and other deviant Marxists and supported court judgments against them. For these kinds of reasons, liberals no longer wanted an alliance with Communists. "To say that we carried out our 'own purge of Communists' because we barred them from membership is the exact equivalent of saying that a woman who locks her jewels in her safe is guilty of persecuting burglars," Dunne concludes.

Lillian Hellman saw things quite differently. Domestic opinion was swinging wildly against Communists and fellow travelers. Anyone associating himself or herself with far-left causes was asking for trouble. Liberals, especially those involved with Communist front groups in the thirties, hastened to declare their differences with Communists. Hellman witnessed the betrayal of friendships; she came to have contempt for liberals who would not defend their radical friends. That many of these liberals felt their own sense of betrayal never concerned her. On the day the pact had been announced, liberals saw many of their radical friends slavishly accept Stalin's deal with Hitler. What did a liberal owe to a radical after that?

Roosevelt's death had left an immense void in American political life, and Truman had to shoulder the enormous burden of working out a postwar accommodation with the Soviets. Some liberals were dismayed at how quickly the wartime alliance was abandoned and were sure it would have been otherwise under Roosevelt. On January 31, 1946, for example, Democratic Senator Claude Pepper of Florida, perhaps the most prominent critic of Truman's foreign policy, declared that "sinister and reactionary forces" were thwarting Roosevelt's plans for postwar peace. The press, Pepper pointed out, carried almost daily attacks on the Soviet Union.

On February 9, Stalin gave a Cold War speech that confirmed the worst suspicions of anti-Communists. He observed that since the causes of World War II, capitalism and imperialism, had not been eradicated, there was no possibility of achieving world peace. No expense would be spared in making certain Russia had a superior national defense, even if this meant a shortage of consumer goods. On March 5, in Fulton, Missouri, Winston Churchill answered in kind. With Truman sitting on the speaker's platform, Churchill called the Communists "a growing challenge and peril to Christian civilization." Only a "fraternal association of the

English-speaking peoples" could combat a Soviet regime that had divided Europe with its iron-curtain policy.

Henry Wallace, the secretary of commerce in the Truman administration, noted in his diary for February 12:

> I thought [Stalin's speech] was accounted for in some measure by the fact that it was obvious to Stalin that our military was getting ready for war with Russia; that they were setting up bases all the way from Greenland, Iceland, northern Canada, and Alaska to Okinawa, with Russia in mind. . . . Stalin obviously knew what these bases meant and also knew the attitude of many of our people through the press. We were challenging him and his speech was taking up the challenge.

"In some measure"—that is the crucial phrase in Wallace's response. To what extent was Russia responding to American aggressiveness, and to what extent was Stalin pursuing his own goals which were independent of American actions? Wallace anticipated a much later generation of American revisionist historians who believe that Truman moved too quickly and too harshly against the Soviets and actually promoted the Cold War. Hellman would always remain in this camp, believing that the cause of world peace had been destroyed by the unseemly vigor with which Truman and other politicians proceeded to harp on the Communist issue. Until the fall of 1947, Hellman was getting expert letters from Melby in China that suggested he thought it was still possible to make peace with the Communists.

The FBI continued to follow Hellman's political activities. Her name had appeared on the reception list of the National Council of American-Soviet Friendship, and she had been a sponsor of the World Freedom Rally—USA–USSR Allies for Peace—on October 26, 1945. At the Russian consulate on March 7, 1946, she had spoken at a tea commemorating International Women's Day. The *Daily Worker*—the FBI's favorite source—reported on March 17 that she had taken part in "a week of protest against Churchill's war speech," delivering her own public statement: "The stage is being set for future wars. Let us not be asked to arrange crusades against socialist Britain, Communist Russia or radical France." In October, she was involved in a union campaign to get higher wages for department-store employees in New York City, and she was still very active on behalf of refugees from the Spanish Civil War. By the end of the year, she became vice-chairman of the PCA.

Wallace's break with Truman came a week after Wallace's September 12, 1946, speech urging an improvement in Soviet-American relations. Truman had read and approved his cabinet member's statement, but that did not stop him from firing Wallace a week later. Melby was outraged and wrote Hellman a letter on September 21 claiming, "it just about adds up to having the last redeeming feature of the Truman administration fade out." In the early stages of Wallace's movement away from the Democrats, Hellman and Melby seemed to be in complete agreement that Truman was not giving the Soviets nearly enough room to negotiate.

Most of Hellman's time in the fall of 1946 was taken up with the production of *Another Part of the Forest*, but she found Melby's absence a strain. She wrote to him accusing him of wanting to stay in China. He was deeply disturbed by her accusations and explained that his plans had been delayed but he had not changed his mind about coming back to her. After eleven months in China, he was fearful that a prolonged separation could do their love "no good," but he was hopeful that she could see there was a reason for it. The Department of State had been postponing transfers, and the political situation in China remained extremely sensitive. By March 10, 1947, Melby received a letter from Hellman reporting she had seen one of his State Department colleagues who had left her with the impression that Melby was inclined to stay in China. She demanded "answers in full" from him.

At the same time, the political understanding between John Melby and Lillian Hellman unraveled. On March 12, 1947, President Truman spoke in favor of aid to Greece and Turkey in order to resist Communist aggression. Melby was not yet aware of this development when he wrote Hellman his "answers in full" and, in Robert Newman's words, his "intellectual justification of precisely the theme Truman had sounded." Communists, Melby argued, had no respect for democracy. Hellman should have been sympathetic to her lover's view, since she was supposed to be against "people who push people around." But she had a higher priority: a pact of peace with the Soviet Union. Therefore, she was not able to accept Melby's diagnosis of world affairs, especially when the Truman administration established a loyalty-security program for government employees. She was already acutely aware that government was being given the power to accuse its own employees of disloyalty without establishing guidelines for their protection. Employees would not be given the opportunity to know the precise charges against them or the names of their accusers.

In March 1947, however, protests centered on the Truman Doctrine, which justified aid to Greece and Turkey. Addressing nineteen thousand people at Madison Square Garden, Henry Wallace attacked Truman's support of "unconditional aid" to anti-Soviet governments, claiming that this would "unite the world against America and divide America against itself," for the governments of Greece and Turkey were undemocratic and "every fascist dictator will know that he has credit in our bank." Melby wrote Hellman that he thought protests over aid to Greece and Turkey were hysterical and that he shared the view of the political establishment—including Averell Harriman and other Hellman friends well-placed in Washington—that Wallace's anti-Truman speaking tour abroad was unseemly. "If he disagrees, let him do it at home," Melby wrote Hellman on April 20. According to Newman, the tone of Melby's letters to Hellman turned cool. She wrote to him about her participation in the PCA, soon to be transformed into a third political party supporting Wallace. It was just possible that a third party might "serve to break a kind of deadlock," was Melby's reply, though he could not agree with her defense of Wallace's speeches in England.

In the summer of 1947, Hellman decided to accept the invitation of Julian Huxley, head of the United Nations Educational, Scientific, and Cultural Organization (UNESCO), to participate in the organization of the International Theatre Institute in Paris. She would return in three weeks for rehearsals of *Another Part of the Forest*, which was about to begin a road tour with some new cast members. It was a hectic and worrisome time for her. Max Hellman's health was rapidly failing. During the opening-night performance of *Another Part of the Forest*, he had been talking to himself and to the audience and crisply counting his money. Zilboorg had warned Hellman that her father was showing signs of senility, but she was unprepared for the breakdown that occurred six months later. Now her two aunts were insisting on a visit, and "no amount of telephone calls and letters can stop them," she wrote Kober. If they wanted to stay in Pleasantville, she would have no trouble accommodating them, but if they wanted to be in New York City with Max, then she hoped that Kober would let her borrow his apartment for two or three weeks—she would have it thoroughly cleaned after they left.

Hellman was also mindful of the bad time Kober was having. His wife Maggie had gone through an operation for a chronic neurological disease, which would take her life five years later. Hellman and Hammett (who was in California visiting his daughters) were immensely fond of Maggie, and Hellman said no more in her letters than was true: Maggie was "truly a noble lady." On June 25, five days after her birthday, Hellman sent a telegram to Kober explaining she would be leaving for Europe on July 19, but she would return in time to remember his birthday, which was "more than" he had done for her. She was not bitter, but it would be wise for him to send her a "congratulatory telegram immediately." She supposed she sent him "much love."

An undated letter was sent to Kober not long after this telegram. Hellman was in Washington—in part, to hear a Henry Wallace speech. She was anxious to learn about Maggie's operation. Max had been given treatments and was a little better, but his condition was uncertain. "What is certain is that my aunts are arriving, God help me. And thank you for the apartment. With true Hellman stubbornness they are insistent about staying at the Windsor Hotel." She was doubtful about whether she should attend the UNESCO conference, but then it might be good "to get away." She had found the last six months "tough going." Perhaps she would visit Kober in California in the fall. He was "one of the few people" she really missed.

Plans for the European trip did not go well. On July 9, Solomon V. Arnaldo, UNESCO's acting resident observer at the United Nations, wrote Maurice Kurtz of the theater sub-section of UNESCO in Paris that "Miss Hellman, whose problems we thought had been solved, burned the telephone wires yesterday." Hellman was upset because her travel expenses had not been refunded and she was not kept up-to-date on her itinerary. In fact, she was disgusted with just about every aspect of the proposed trip. Hellman threatened to withdraw and was not mollified by Arnaldo's assurance he would process a refund immediately. "This was not the point, she said. She could afford to wait, but how about others who may not be similarly situated?" He took her point, but noted that there were ways of accommodating such people as long as UNESCO was "duly advised."

It is unlikely that Hellman really considered canceling the trip, although she wrote to literary historian Van Wyck Brooks expressing doubts about the value of the UNESCO mission. No matter what difficulties she encountered, voyages overseas almost always worked as a tonic. She would stay at Claridge's in London for a few days before going on to Paris.

What the playwright did not know was that about a week before her departure for Europe, Charles A. Thomson of the Department of State had sent a letter marked "confidential" to Walter H. C. Laves, the deputy director-general of UNESCO in Paris, noting congressional concern over "Americans who are Communists or near-Communists" invited to consult with UNESCO. The presence of such un-Americans, the letter said, might lead to Congress "withdrawing its authorization for the United States to participate in UNESCO."

On August 6, Hellman's secretary, Edith Kean, wrote to Arthur Kober noting that "Milady seems to have had a good time in London. . . . Paris, she writes, is hot and lacks the flavor of the old days." Throughout this trip, Hellman wrote Melby, but she did not follow up on his remarks that "the Russians for their own ends are prepared to precipitate chaos all over Europe. I think it is damned disgraceful. It will be more than interesting to hear what you pick up in Europe on this score." On August 20, she sailed for America on the *Queen Mary*.

As usual, Hellman returned from Europe with gifts—among them, a white nightgown for Maggie Kober and a little early-nineteenth-century chair for Catherine. From Pleasantville, Hellman wrote Maggie about her pleasant memory of "very happy weeks in Antibes" with the Wylers. "You were quite right about Tally, she is an extraordinary girl and I became very fond of her." Most of the news, however, was grim. The road tour of *Another Part of the Forest* was doing "very bad business," and Hellman's "Pa" was still in the hospital. To her father, she was now "the villain." To make things worse, his sisters had sided with him. This hurt Hellman because she was "fond of them," which in itself was a rare feeling "in a family that hated one another." Hospital visits to her father were an ordeal, since she could not get accustomed to the "unbalanced dislike" of her he seemed to show.

In many such letters, Hellman would end by saying how much comfort she found in Maggie Kober. Above all, she wished she could visit again, for she missed her so much. Maggie had left a vacancy in Hellman's life, and she hoped Maggie would "come back some day soon and fill it again." She knew it would be a "bother" for the ailing Maggie to write, "but ask your stinky, mean, nasty, pig-like husband with the cute face to spend six dollars occasionally to telephone me and tell me the news. I can't go on courting him after twenty two years: it is beginning to be prideless and unfeminine."

More letters arrived from Melby. They revealed a widening gap in the couple's perceptions of the world. Melby put it baldly to her: "I do, in fact, think you are wrong about events and about a lot of people." There was a Cold War, a "situation which is not of the choosing of the United States, even if we have at times unwittingly compounded it." If the Russians were "honestly motivated by fear of external aggression," or if their actions were "the logical outcome of their rigid and narrow ideological blinders," then there was no gain saying that America was confronted by "an expanding Slavic power which is completely without scruples of any kind."

Melby did not see how one could dispute the fact that "the regimes in the Soviet satellite states in Europe are ruthless dictatorships which would be turned out over night if the majority had any freedom of choice." There was no evil design in the Marshall plan, "yet Molotov at Paris shamelessly and cynically junked the whole thing . . . for what can only be interpreted as the objective of prolonging and deepening the economic misery and collapse of Europe in order to install communist regimes in power all over." To Melby's way of thinking, "political liberties and civil rights . . . are the most important things in life." Yet the Communists in China allowed no one to express opposition "more than once." So it was "academic whether there is any direct line to Moscow, the fact is everything they put out and every view they express might just as well have been written in Pravda. In Manchuria the Russians did a job from which the area will not recover for decades." The Russians had slaughtered the Mongols. How did Hellman "interpret all this," Melby wanted to know. He conceded that politicians at home "are taking advantage of the times to do ugly things," but on the scale of wrongs he obviously ranked what was to become known as McCarthyism as of far less importance than Communist tyranny.

Hellman did not answer Melby's long letter for two months. She made it clear that they had a difference of opinion, but she did not engage in lengthy explanations. Melby having served in both Russia and China as a foreign service officer who was genuinely curious and open-minded about communism, his condemnation of Marxism-Leninism must have shaken Hellman. She had too much respect for his honesty and professionalism to question his motives. Although she destroyed her letters to him, Melby is confident in his memory that she never mounted an argument in her correspondence to him against his Cold War brief. Had they been living together, he has no doubt that they would have quarreled over his views. They certainly disagreed when they again enjoyed each other's company upon Melby's return to the States, but even then Hellman could not find it in her to assault his assumptions—as she does with her opponents in *Scoundrel Time*. Out of her days with Melby in Moscow and in East Hampton, she came to have a deep respect for him and his opinions, and she was not about to challenge him on very much of anything, even when her views became diametrically opposed to his.

It is a wonder, however, that Melby's eloquent letters did not make Hellman pause in her PCA activism. Melby has spent years thinking about how it was they came to such different conclusions after having begun, more or less, with the same views:

> I came out of that Depression generation, as she did, and we had been sold a bill of goods on the happy land of the workers and peasants and so on. . . . We bought it when I was in college. So I wanted to go and have a look for myself. I pulled all sorts of strings to get there. It didn't take me very long being there before I realized that I couldn't live there. I couldn't live that way. I'm too much of a radical myself. Nobody can tell me what to do. I'm not a very good organization man. If I believe in the organization, fine, but if I don't, I'm going to say so. And that is, of course, what Lillian saw—that I couldn't take it, couldn't take the foreign service at a certain point. . . . When we were in Moscow Archibald MacLeish, then Assistant Secretary for Cultural Affairs, was very anxious that Lillian go back to Moscow as cultural attaché. Averell was interested in having her come back. And she just said

flatly no! What she said to me was "I know I could never live there. I'd become just like the rest of you here—anti-Soviet and just as petty as everybody else in the Embassy. I just couldn't take it."

Hellman was a person who knew herself well, Melby thought. In retrospect, he also realizes that she was right on every judgment she would make about his life in the years to come—perhaps because they were so alike in their independence and in their passion for peace and justice. Yet she feared the destruction of her dreams, of that noble land of workers and peasants one can still observe in *The North Star*. Averell Harriman kidded her about her illusions and called her a "fellow-wanderer." George Kennan and other embassy diplomats had ridiculed her, and Melby remembers that she bore it well. She could have made a diplomat's wife, a cultural attaché, if she had wanted to, Melby insists. But she knew what it would cost her.

Not only was this a man who had given Hellman his heart, this was a man who profoundly respected her intelligence and integrity. He felt he had learned more fundamental things about life from her. Although he was thirty-one, married, and the father of two boys when he met her, he had not really grown up. "What she did for me really was to make a man out of me," he says unabashedly. "And for that . . . nothing else really matters." This was a woman known for her outspokenness and yet who at the same time was very feminine. "She knew how to make a man feel like a man. No quarrels about it." There was a personal, intimate, and absolutely sincere quality about her. "You were respected, looked up to, you were given the deference that one person owes to another. It was just as simple as that." Meeting her at that time of his life crystalized his convictions, made him take responsibility for what he thought. Through knowing her, he took himself seriously in a way he had never done before.

Perhaps the global perspective of a seasoned diplomat was more than Hellman, mired in domestic politics, could absorb. She had her own battles to fight. In the fall of 1947, HUAC decided to investigate communism in Hollywood. As Philip Dunne points out, these were not

ordinary Congressional hearings at all, but de facto trials—extra-legal trials in which the accused were denied normal constitutional safeguards, in which the prosecutor's witnesses could not be cross-examined, and in which the committee itself acted as prosecutor, judge, and jury. Legally barred from sentencing those they "convicted," they passed this function on to the private sector—to the American Legion, *Red Channels*, the Hearst newspapers, the other volunteer agencies and individuals who stood ready and eager to enforce the sentence openly encouraged by the Congressional inquisitors: the blacklist, the ruin of reputation and deprivation of livelihood.

While Communist subversion was never proved in these hearings, it was easy to make the equation between Communists and traitors because the party had always hewed to Moscow's line. The loyalty of American Communists seemed to have been given to a foreign power. It was in this year, as Hellman recounts in *Scoundrel Time*, that she had to turn down the movie contract of her dreams. It was worth nearly a million dollars over an eight-year period; she could write and produce without interference any story she liked with control over the final cut. All she had to do was to sign a clause swearing that none of her political activities "would be different from what the studio would allow." She balked and thereafter was blacklisted.

HUAC heard a succession of "friendly" and "unfriendly" witnesses. The so-called "Hollywood Ten"—one producer, two directors, and seven writers—defied HUAC by refusing to play by its rules. They went to prison. There was an atmosphere in which "almost everyone in Hollywood who ever had been remotely connected with any radical or liberal cause was publicly accused of subversive activity," Dunne points out. In "The Judas Goats" (*Screenwriter*, December 3, 1947), Hellman crafted some of her most vitriolic prose to discredit not only HUAC but its "friendly" witnesses. "Craven men" lied and tattled, "pushing each other in their efforts to lick the boots of their vilifiers, publicly trying to wreck the lives, not of strangers, mind you, but of men with whom they have worked and eaten and played, and made millions." She had in mind witnesses like Adolph Menjou, who reported to the committee a director's comment that capitalism was doomed. This was presumably both communistic and un-American, in Menjou's expert opinion—even though, as Dunne remarks, he had heard in

Depression-era America similar statements made by bank presidents and corporation executives. It was all so ridiculous and outrageous to Hellman:

> There has never been a single line or word of Communism in any American picture at any time. There has never or seldom been ideas of any kind. Naturally men scared to make pictures about the American Negro, men who have only in the last year allowed the word Jew to be spoken in a picture, men who took more than ten years to make an anti-Fascist picture, those are frightened men and you pick frightened men to frighten first. Judas goats; they'll lead the others, maybe, to the slaughter for you.

She was defiant. She believed there were people who would fight to preserve their civil and political rights; there were people who would not "frighten so easy. It's still not un-American to fight the enemies of one's country. Let's fight," she concluded.

Did Hellman know that HUAC did not need proof of the presence of Marxist-Leninist ideas? In her own FBI file, it would be noted that the film of her play *Another Part of the Forest* "showed the Communist technique to play up the weak spots of American life. According to the informant, this film tended to revive the hatred of the North and South in a villainous form." What is curious is that the FBI did not see the film for itself to draw its own conclusions. As with HUAC, the testimony of informants or witnesses sounded, somehow, more impressive—as though some kind of investigation had actually taken place, when in fact, no thinking at all about the terms *un-American*, *Communist*, or even *liberal* was ever entertained. No wonder Hellman was apoplectic about such asinine behavior.

By the end of 1947, Henry Wallace had declared his candidacy for the presidency, and Lillian Hellman enlisted in his campaign. On February 10, 1948, she gave a speech at a "Women for Wallace" lunch. "These have been two black years since Mr. Roosevelt's death and the end of the war." The New Deal agenda had been sidetracked. HUAC had turned into a "dangerous circus." Fascism was alive and daily life was "a great struggle of high food prices, inadequate housing, shoddy clothes enormously overpriced." Atomic energy was not being used to "relieve man's great labor burden," but to prepare for war. Biologists were not working on "life-saving drugs, but with their own form of warfare, supposedly more deadly than the bomb." Death, in fact, seemed to be the country's preoccupation. There were honest men with "reasonable and intelligent doubts about" Wallace's Progressive party, "but many of them are simply middle-aged liberals who, in [Heywood] Broun's definition, always get out of the room when a fight begins."

What would Hellman have said to Melby? By this time, he was firmly opposed to Wallace, and Melby was not the sort of weak liberal Hellman was found of castigating. Already he could see that Communists were infiltrating the Wallace movement—a fact Hellman denied in her February 10 speech but later admitted in *Scoundrel Time*. Wallace was a "fool" if he did not realize that Communists would use him "for their own ends and that those ends are bad," Melby wrote on February 3. The next two months saw the overthrow of the Czech government, the mysterious death of its leader Jan Masaryk, and the Soviet blockade of Berlin. Communists claimed Masaryk's death was a suicide, while anti-Communists were sure he had been thrown from a window. Wallace suggested that the Communists were just protecting their interests in response to the American "get tough policy." Melby wrote Hellman at the end of February that Wallace was completely "off base," and in March, Melby gave a speech to the National Catholic Educational Conference in Nanking pointing out there were great similarities between nazism and communism—the latter being the equivalent of an "iron helmet over the minds of men."

At this point, Melby and Hellman were on opposite sides. His letters to her still reflected his affection, but he had begun seeing another woman, and soon Hellman would take up with a new male companion. Surely Melby would have been shocked to read the following FBI report of a Lillian Hellman speech on June 17—if he trusted the bureau's ability to get their facts straight. She was quoted as saying that the Truman Loyalty Order legalized "spying on the American people," and that "this cold war is in many ways worse than a hot war. They are using this cold war hysteria to destroy, in the name of Americanism, our way of life in a more ruthless manner than the fascists of Germany ever dared." If she actually said that, it is no wonder that her politics lacked a sense of proportion, that she could not see that Stalinism was a far greater menace than the challenge to civil liberties at home. Think how angry Melby's letter in August must have made her when he disposed of Wallace and the Progressive party with this analogy: "I am afraid there is altogether too much of the whole rabble-rousing business which is strangely and uncomfortably reminiscent of the early days of the Nazi party."

Throughout the spring and summer of 1948, Hellman campaigned vigorously for Henry Wallace, taking time out to teach for a week at Indiana University and give a cocktail party for the Wiltwyck School. She wrote Maggie Kober about this very "remarkable institution" which welcomed both black and white children from the ages of eight to twelve with criminal records and gave a kind of psychiatric treatment that was lacking in most such schools at the time.

Hellman was enjoying the warmer weather at Hardscrabble, where she was "putting the farm to rights" after a storm in early April, and at Vineyard Haven, where a new man entered her life. Randall "Pete" Smith had been one of several elected officials in the National Maritime Union (NMU), a very progressive organization, who had been purged because of Communist or far-left sentiments. For a while, he worked in an election campaign for a liberal New York congressman and kept in touch with the Wallace Progressives. At NMU, Smith got to know the educational director, Columbia professor Leo Huberman, who for a time had been associated with *PM* and with Hellman in various political activities. Huberman knew that Smith was floundering and had no income and invited him to Martha's Vineyard to clear poison ivy off his property. One weekend in April, Huberman announced, "Hellman's here!" The name did not mean much to Smith, although he knew she had authored *The Children's Hour*. "She's coming over for dinner," Huberman told him, "Now you clean up and behave yourself."

At dinner, Smith was not terribly impressed. She was nearly ten years older than he was. She said she wanted to go fishing. Huberman said, "well, Pete here will take you fishing." And Smith said, "yea, sure, if you rent the boat." The next day, the two got acquainted on the boat. "She used me more for that than for sex," Smith recalls. Fishing was an important hobby to Hellman, and a man was useful in getting together tackle. "She'd tell you where to go and what bait to put on the hook. Hammett had made her into a good fisherwoman. And then she exulted in the cooking of jambalaya, chowders, bouillabaisse." It was fun—an amiable, easy-going relationship that "didn't strain your I.Q. a bit," according to Smith. He liked her saltiness, and she liked the fact he was a genuine member of the working class—"although I wasn't really," Smith notes. He had been a seaman and a veteran of the Spanish Civil War. They got to talking about Spain, he remembers. A bond was quickly established, and they went home to dinner.

Smith was hardly a roughneck, and his courage and political activism impressed Hellman. Until the Depression, both his parents were moderately affluent practicing physicians in Warren, Ohio. At school, his ratings on achievement tests went high off the charts, and he was recognized for his leadership qualities. Smith's sister, Isabel Stein, points out that rather than just theorizing about communism and the better world it promised, he actually crossed the Pyrenees into Spain to fight for what he believed in. Many years later, Stein met, by accident, a former longshoreman who had never forgotten her brother's union leadership. Tears came to the longshoreman's eyes as he exclaimed, "My God, we *worshipped* that guy!"

Hellman was living in a beautiful big house up on a hill. Smith began to "hang out with her." He was very impressed with her big Cadillac which she allowed him to drive. She had plenty of money, so they could have dinner wherever they wanted. She dressed extremely well, although he noticed clothes did not hang well on her, with her broad shoulders, large breasts, narrow hips, and no bottom "that amounted to anything." But she was always elegantly neat. He moved from Huberman's shed to a nice bedroom at her house. There was plenty of good Scotch available. The two felt no great passion for each other, but there was a kind of drunken intimacy between them; "it was more absent-minded than erotic. She was a little lonely, and I was a little lonely." Smith was breaking up his marriage to a "commissar," a very intense Marxist-Leninist woman who was challenging him for his "petty bourgeoisisms." The Bloomgardens visited and Smith met others of Hellman's friend. Then Hellman invited him to Pleasantville.

Smith was nonplussed at her magnificent farm layout. But she would not let him get involved in farming, even though he wanted to impress her with his knowledge of livestock and farm life. This was her show. One day she announced, "Norman is coming up"— she always seemed to be dropping names that meant nothing to Smith. This time she was referring to Norman Mailer. Smith was not impressed. He knew about *The Naked and the Dead* but had not read the book. Anyway, Smith was a veteran of World War II and the Spanish Civil War, whereas Mailer had been in only one war. He was rather patronizing to the young author as they sat by the lake and "shot the breeze." Mailer seemed like a little twerp with no great experience or depth, and Smith did not pay much attention to him. Hellman was at work on a play adaptation of *The Naked and the Dead*. On August 4, she wrote to "Arthur Baby Darling" Kober that the adaptation had her "worried and depressed." Maybe she should not have started it, although her misgivings were probably "the usual birth pains." Nevertheless, she had "done almost nothing."

Hellman nagged Smith about visiting Hammett. She cared about Hammett deeply, although in their presence Smith does not remember having seen any signs of affection. Hammett seemed lonely, and the more lonely he got, the more he drank. Hellman was afraid he would hurt himself and thought that perhaps Smith could help her look after him. "You and Dash would get along fine. Dash would like you. You would like Dash," Hellman assured Smith. Again, about all "Dash" meant to Smith was a title: *The Thin Man*. Eventually, the two did get together at Hammett's place in Greenwich Village. Smith imagines that Hammett's first unspoken reaction to him must have been, "Oh shit, here's another one from Lillian recruited to look out for me. But he's okay." They talked about their fondness for San Francisco, when Hammett felt like talking, but very little about his politics came out. Smith would get to the Village about eleven in the morning. Hammett would just be getting up from the last night's drunk, and they would drink breakfast and idle away the day. They did become good friends. Smith would accompany Hammett to the Stork Club and make sure his host got home all right. As at Hellman's, whiskey, cigarettes, and lunch, were always available. "I was really a bum—hustling in the sense that I was totally lost. I didn't know what the hell I was going to do," says Smith. The labor movement had been his purpose in life, and the labor movement had "gone to hell. The left-wing had gone to hell. It is not a period I am particularly proud of. But I can understand the mess I was in at that time."

Hellman and Hammett were always courteous and friendly when Smith showed up, even though he feels he did not have much to offer them. He did not talk theater, he did not talk books, and he barely talked politics. He had been a Communist and knew what was going on in the world, but he did not have an independent point of view. Although Hellman followed the party line on many things, Smith was very impressed with her support of Tito. He knew about her affair with Melby in Moscow and realized that she spoke her own mind. This really shook him up, because he was coming from a situation on the waterfront where nobody prized integrity as much as pragmatic effectiveness in the labor movement. She had guts. "If it was true, she said it. If it wasn't true, she opposed it," he recalls. Hellman was one of the very few persons in his life who had taught him something. He envied her capacity to "pluck the thorn. She didn't look around. She didn't count to ten before she answered. She was spontaneous." And she never patronized Smith for what he did not know. When she mentioned the death of Zelda Fitzgerald, for example, Smith needed a fifteen-minute talk to get a sense of why her death disturbed Hellman. Hellman knew that Smith's education had been "lopsided." Spain and the waterfront were his education. He knew about labor leaders and politicians, but "that was about it."

Smith remembers that one of Hellman's assignments was to take care of Henry Wallace's wife, Ilo, a "dummy" who kept stumbling into reporters who would pump her for information about her husband, and she would say "stupid things." So the idea was for Hellman to invite Ilo and her daughter up to the Vineyard for a few weeks, and Smith was involved in helping keep the candidate's wife away from New York City. The Wallaces also visited Pleasantville. In these circumstances, Virginia Bloomgarden saw other facets of Hellman that were not apparent during the production of her plays—her femininity, her extraordinary ability to run a house, her marvelous, crazy, New Orleans sense of humor, and her graciousness as a hostess. At the Vineyard, Ilo seemed confused about her husband's ethnic background. "He's Scotch-Irish," Bloomgarden remembers an exasperated Hellman saying. "If Henry were dead, he'd turn over in his grave." Then there was a terrific argument having to do with Oliver Cromwell. Hammett was called in California to settle the question because everyone knew he would have the answer—which he did, correcting both Hellman and the Wallaces. The house they were staying in was beastly hot. After turning into bed, Bloomgarden heard some horrendous snoring. Tiptoeing downstairs, she took a chaise lounge out on the lawn, and then heard someone else coming down the stairs. It was Hellman. "The two of us got sheets and Lillian joked about what you could tell the press about the wives of presidential candidates," Bloomgarden recalls. "We decided that night that since the Wallaces were staying on, Lillian was going to have to say she was leaving. We took a room in Edgartown, and I remember being driven crazy because Lillian smoked all night." Hellman was an insomniac, although Bloomgarden is sure that nobody could have slept through Ilo Wallace's thundering snores.

Hellman thought Henry Wallace was a jerk, according to Randall Smith. "Yet he looked okay and had good credentials, as credentials went in those days, and he took a fairly good position when compared to Truman. The issue was war or no war," as far as Hellman and Smith were concerned. But like Hellman, he was troubled by Communist domination of the Progressive party and of the campaign. When Wallace asked her if the charges of Communist infiltration were true, she told him straight out that they were. John Melby remembers a letter in which Hellman took an even stronger position: " 'Look, Henry, you've got to admit the Communists are running your organization. I don't care whether they are or not, but I do care that you admit it. And if you won't admit it, then I'm through with you.' When he wouldn't admit it, she went off to Yugoslavia."

The picture of Wallace in *Scoundrel Time* is of an enigma—the word Penn Kimball, then on the staff of *The New Republic*, uses to describe Wallace's baffling behavior. Other than his sincere opposition to war, Kimball and the staff at the magazine had trouble fathoming what their editor stood for. Hellman seems to have it just right when she suggests, "Roosevelt had held tight rein over the conflicts in Wallace's nature and the strange digressions of his mind." There was really no excuse for his subsequent attack on Communists when Hellman clearly had given him the lowdown. Sometimes he seemed not very well connected to reality. "When he smoked, he would spill ashes over his vest as he became enraptured with his own thoughts," Kimball remembers. He was apparently an aloof figure for everyone, including his family. "One day he left a letter from his own son open on the hall table. It began: 'Dear Mr. Wallace,' " Kimball remembers.

By the fall of 1948, Lillian Hellman had had it with Henry Wallace. On September 23, she wrote to Mrs. Shipley at the passport office announcing she had been invited by the ambassador of Yugoslavia to attend two premieres of *The Little Foxes* in

Belgrade on October fifth and tenth. It was the playwright's hope that her trip would contribute in some small way to "good cultural relations between our two countries." Hellman wanted to know if her traveling papers were in order, and she apologized for the short notice. Her request was quickly granted.

One of Hellman's great concerns in leaving the country was Hammett. He would go on binges for days and disappear. Hellman would not hear from him; nobody knew his whereabouts. Then he would show up again. She knew that Virginia Bloomgarden enjoyed Hammett's company immensely and that she felt grateful to learn from this wise man. One day at Pleasantville, Hellman asked Bloomgarden to come upstairs with her. She had a favor to ask. "You're going to be staying here. Dash is very fond of you. I worry about him." There were tears in Hellman's eyes. "Would you have dinner with him, would you look after him? Play ping pong with him?" Of course, Bloomgarden said she would. To her, it was no hardship. Indeed, she found it enthralling to sit up nights with Hammett as he recounted his colorful Pinkerton past. Hellman's emotion, which rarely showed, made an indelible impression on Bloomgarden, for it was also the year that Hammett stopped drinking.

In a series of articles for the *New York Star*, (November 4–5, 7–10, 1948) Hellman charted her trip across Europe to see Tito, who had agreed to be interviewed right in the midst of his break with Stalin. The Cominform—the association of Communist parties of Bulgaria, Czechoslovakia, France, Hungary, Italy, Poland, Rumania, and the Soviet Union—had expelled Yugoslavia for challenging Soviet supremacy. As her articles revealed, Hellman was far less interested in the politics of the split than she was in Tito's expression of independence, which she admired enormously. He was a man of courage. Later, Hellman told Virginia Bloomgarden that it was really quite remarkable to her that Tito did not think of himself as a big hero. She was thinking not only of his recent trouble but of his guerrilla campaign during the war. "I don't know how I would behave under those circumstances." It was as if in considering Tito's behavior, she was trying to take her own measure. In just a few years, she would be confronting her own moment of trial, and the trip to Yugoslavia served her in good stead.

The articles in the *Star* reveal that Hellman had a great deal of trouble thinking in postwar terms. She was strongly prejudiced against a plane load of German-Americans returning to Germany to see their families. She disliked these people who called Germany, never America, home. They were soft and sentimental with one another, but they were a cold, hard lot with others. In Amsterdam, she wondered what it had been like for a German-occupied city during the war, and this led her to memories of Kiev, another occupied city, and to her prejudice in favor of Russians. She remembered asking a Russian official if he was not disturbed by wondering which of his people collaborated with the Germans. He replied that he did not like not knowing who had helped the Nazis, "but Russians never hate for long, and have a hard time remembering other people's sins. People who have had trouble don't judge others too sharply in the end." This is manifestly not true, but Hellman agreed that Russians were "a kind people. That's very easy to see." Even the Russian official would not go that far. He thought his attitude was just a fact of Russian life.

In Prague, Hellman had a discussion with two Yugoslavs from the embassy, who claimed to be baffled by the Cominform attack. They were saddened by the unfriendliness of the Czechs, and they were certain of their close ties to the Russians. Hellman concluded her first article with the observation that she did not know

> who is right and who is wrong, or even what is right or wrong in such situations, but the Yugoslavs are not lying when they say they think they are right. They act very like a proud son who has been taken to task by a strong father. The son is hurt by the treatment of the father, but he is sure what he had done is honorable, and Papa will some day understand, and once more love.

This is a remarkably sentimental way to look at politics. It might also be charged that Hellman is dodging the issue by claiming to be an agnostic. Yet everything about her character suggests she was telling the truth. She had no mind for politics and did not think of herself as a political person—although her outrage at injustice inevitably led her to become involved in politics. John Melby never heard her sustain a level of argument comparable to his own. She admired Tito, but that is not the same thing as saying she understood or felt competent to judge his political convictions. Rather, she regarded him as having taken part in a family quarrel. It was the personal value she could inject into politics that sustained her interest—witness the way she intertwined personalities and diplomacy somewhat dubiously in *The Searching Wind*. She recognized a realm of politics that was not personal—that was, in fact, professional and philosophical—and from that realm she retreated. Howard Bay remembers Hammett giving her some Engels to read. She did her best, but Bay could see she had little interest in such material. For her, politics were a matter of temperament. She had strong feelings about war and peace and about fascism and communism, but she had almost no ideas about these subjects worth listening to.

After confessing her agnostic position to Vice-Premier Zdenek Fierlinger of Czechoslovakia and adding that the Cominform action against Yugoslavia was none of her business, Hellman was compelled to tell him that she liked Yugoslavs "as people." This wily old diplomat must have had to stifle a laugh. But he just smiled and said, "So do we." She also felt obligated to say she had heard that "large sections of the youth" did not like the Czech Communist government, and it would have been scandalous if she had not raised the question of Jan Masaryk's "suicide." Naturally, Fierlinger was most understanding of her qualms. The disaffection of the youth was blamed on the German occupation, and, according to Fierlinger, while Masaryk certainly did not welcome communism, he would have worked with it had he not committed suicide in anguish over a "painful disease in the bones of his hand."

With regard to a rehearsal of *The Little Foxes* in Belgrade, Hellman was blunt, for here she was sure of her ground. The scenery and costumes were fine; the acting was very uneven. As in Moscow, the actors were overdoing it, with Birdie "too drunk," Oscar "too sly," and Horace "too sick." After a long day of sight-seeing, her feet hurt and she could not suppress her yawns during the premiere of the play. Her hosts giggled and nudged her. The play was a huge success, with the playwright standing on stage taking bows and receiving a large ovation. At a drunken party afterwards she "loved everybody, including a man who was making the same speech for the second time."

At the climax of her trip, Hellman found Tito "easy and informal" and ready to talk. She wanted to know if he thought there would be war. No, he was sure there would not be; he did not think Americans would have the support to wage another war, and America could not fight alone. Hellman gamely spoke in

Wallace's favor when Tito asked her about domestic politics. She surely did not believe that Wallace "had grown and strengthened in the face of attacks which were often not based on rational disagreement, but on vulgar snideness," although that is what she told Tito. She was nearly as miffed at her candidate as she was at his opponents. After the interview, the Yugoslavs were amazed that she had not asked their leader about his rift with Stalin. "But I don't think you should ask a man if he has been unfaithful to his wife," was her reply. This provoked much amusement. It was similar to what she had said to the Czech official, reducing political affairs to family squabbles. It may be possible to make analogies between private and public life, but to leave the argument at that is to becloud it. She was taken with Tito's simplicity and lack of pomposity, and was sure that Yugoslavia's troubles with Russia were simply a "disagreement between two Socialist states [who did not] think alike, all the time, all their lives, as if they were robots and history were a stone monument waiting unchanged to allow all men to meet around her at the minute, in complete agreement." Here she was exhibiting a suppleness of response entirely lacking in the red-baiters at home. It is a pity she did not think through the implications of her parting reflections: "Communists have always seemed to me highly moral people, sometimes too moral for comfort." Whole classes of people have been wiped out by Communists who were certain they understood the objective laws of history. Hellman was lucky she never had the benefit of that stern morality that made her so uncomfortable.

The trip home via Paris revived memories of the Spanish Civil War—probably because she heard talk of De Gaulle's failure to come to power "because he has been too openly fascist, and too stupid in revealing it." Before she had left for Europe, Norman Mailer recommended she see an exciting new play, *Montserrat*, by Emmanuel Robles. The drama of Simon Bolivar's revolution in Venezuela in 1812 took hold of her, and she decided to adapt the French play for the American stage. Hellman's decision meant abandoning her efforts to turn *The Naked and the Dead* into a play.

Back home in late October, Hellman was almost immediately plunged into a crisis with Hammett. "He would now become so grossly drunk as to be unendurable," Diane Johnson writes. Hellman refused to see him, to have anything to do with him. Other people stayed away as well. Finally, Hammett could not move. Still, he refused to have Hellman called. Finally she was contacted, but she refused to help until her secretary offered to go instead. Realizing that that would be unfair, Hellman took Hammett in—dt's and all. Later, at a hospital, the doctor told Hammett he would be dead in a matter of months if he did not stop drinking. Hammett swore off liquor and kept his word.

Setting to work on *Montserrat*, Hellman wrote its author posing questions about historical details and about the main characters. She commissioned a literal translation, and by the end of the year was enlisting Malcolm Cowley's help. In those days he had a "reputation for finding versions of foreign speech that sounded right in English." But the play did not arouse his enthusiasm, and to this day he is "not proud" of the work he did on Hellman's text. "Her version of *Montserrat* seemed to me too simple-minded and lacking in emotional complexity. After a few weeks our collaboration faded away." He admired her as a "woman of courage" and regretted that he could not have been "of help in one of her projects." She evidently underestimated what it would take to adapt another writer's work for the stage, for she wrote Cowley, "I don't think I would ever have started Montserrat if I had known the amount of work." The problem with her play, as with her politics, was its simple-mindedness. Her view of the world was melodramatic, and reviews would suggest that only a tragic sensibility could have brought off Robles's rather turgid presentation of the conflict between individual and political choices.

The three-day Cultural and Scientific Conference for World Peace at the Waldorf-Astoria Hotel in New York in March of 1949 serves as a kind of epilogue to Hellman's Cold War politics. After this conference, and after *Montserrat*, she would write an entirely different kind of play, one that was removed from politics and from the fiery atmosphere of her best-known stage work. The State Department regarded the peace conference as a Communist front—"merely part of the Cominform's attempt, launched last year at Wroclaw (Breslau), Poland, to win the minds of the world's intellectuals," as *Newsweek* (April 4, 1949) put it. Visas had been granted to "seven Russians and fifteen other delegates from Iron Curtain countries," but nineteen other delegates from Western Europe and Latin America were refused entry into the country on the grounds that they were Communists or fellow travelers whose views were against the interests of the United States.

Much of the press and many prominent liberals attacked the conference, or at best implied that it was a highly compromised peace effort. The lead paragraph in *Newsweek*, which provided the fullest account of the conference, suggested that the aims of the conference were much closer to Stalin's than to Truman's, since there had been a call for "scrapping the Truman Doctrine, the Marshall Plan, and the Atlantic Pact." Appease the Soviet Union and there would be peace—this is how *Newsweek* saw it. The State Department issued a report recounting how the Soviet Union had thwarted cultural and scientific exchanges between the American and Russian peoples. Professor Sidney Hook of New York University organized anti-Communist liberals into a rival organization, Americans for Intellectual Freedom when he was refused permission to speak at the Waldorf.

The chairman of the Waldorf conference, Professor Harlow Shapley, a Harvard astronomer, pointed out that in fact a diversity of political views were represented, including that of the Communists, and that all "cultural questions have a political coloration." Skeptical reporters saw only red or the pinkish tinge they associated with Wallace Progressives. What bothered the press and anti-Communist liberals was that the invited Russians would not speak their minds—since to do so would jeopardize their security, perhaps their very lives, at home. For example, the Russians refused to address the issue of the split between Tito and Stalin. Shapley was either naive or disingenuous when he counseled reporters, "This is a peace conference. Let's keep politics out."

Norman Cousins, editor of the *Saturday Review of Literature*, made news when he decided to address head-on the auspices under which the conference was held. Shapley saw the speech beforehand and was shocked, then conferred several times with Hellman and others. To no avail, they tried to get him to modify his attack. Speaking to an audience of two thousand people, Cousins referred to the pickets outside of the Waldorf who were calling attention to the fact that the conference was being held by "a small political group, the Communist Party," which "owes its primary allegiance not to America but to an outside government." Cousins was reminding the audience—which had immediately turned hostile and was jeering and booing him—of what had disturbed liberals since the day of the pact: why was it that criticism of Soviet Russia was out of bounds? Why was it that the Soviet Union was always the first country that had to be appeased? *Newsweek* reported that "in the rear of the ballroom a girl smashed a plate in rage" when Cousins affirmed that "Americans want peace . . . but not peace at any price." According to *Newsweek*, after Cousins's speech, Hellman rose to remark, "I would recommend, Mr. Cousins, that when you are invited out to dinner you wait until you get home before you talk about your hosts." It was typical of this *grande dame*'s code of etiquette that she should chide the speaker for his incivility, as if that would immediately discredit what he had to say.

Newsweek was not entirely fair to Hellman or to the conference. The magazine was clearly biased and chose to heighten the drama and tension. In *The New York Times* (March 26, 1949), the reaction to Cousins's speech was reported to be "subdued hissing and booing." There was no plate-breaking, and the conclusion of his speech was greeted with "moderate applause." Hellman sounded conciliatory and critical. She thought that Cousins "might better have made the address at one of the conference's panel sessions than at the dinner." She most certainly did not approve of the booing and hissing. She criticized Sidney Hook, although *The New York Times* does not report what she said. Other accounts say that Hellman admitted that both the Soviet Union and the United States were responsible for the Cold War. She wanted the cycle of blame stopped so that both sides could work for world peace. She was arguing for cultural coexistence.

John Melby arrived in Washington on January 4, 1949, after three years in China. The FBI took note of a rally against HUAC that Hellman apparently attended. An FBI informant "advised that in the fund drive [to abolish HUAC] LILLIAN HELLMAN donated $250.00." Melby sent a letter to Hellman on January 16 thanking her for a Christmas cable. He was going home to El Paso for a month to see his boys and to make arrangements for a divorce. He spoke with Hellman by phone on March 12. They were cordial, but there were no immediate plans to meet. Neither of them knew that the State Department was already beginning a check of Melby's record to ascertain his loyalty. He was given a temporary assignment in the Philippines. From there he wrote her few letters, and she anguished over their lack of contact. Had their opposing political views destroyed his affection for her? In truth, Melby was uneasy, "more worried than she about their political differences," as Robert Newman puts it. As in politics, so in love, she wanted peace but was unable to resolve the conflicts in herself and in her times that would have made peace possible. And she was about to embark on a play production that was to be the stormiest in her stage career. After *Montserrat*, she would perforce reevaluate her life and career, and write another play, *The Autumn Garden*, which would try to make sense of why she had left so much undone.

15

MONTSERRAT

New York/Princeton/Philadelphia/ New York

(1949)

My relationship with Lillian—oh yes, we were on a first-
name basis—was an odd one. I directed two of her plays,
she was intimately connected with the production of a play
of mine, and she directed me in a play of hers. I am fairly
outgoing, yet I never got closer to her than one would to a
telephone operator who might phone a wake-up call every
morning for weeks on end. It was more of a non-relation-
ship, until it culminated (entirely my fault) in a permanent
antagonism on her part.

—Emlyn Williams, correspondence with author

She was a sweet, womanly person . . . soft and sentimental
under all that tough exterior. She wanted to know people
more intimately. After a wonderful dinner at her New York
apartment, Lillian urged me to tell the cook how much I
had enjoyed dinner. "She would be so pleased." I felt we
were able to break beyond all those facades and like
each other underneath. On the surface, however, I could
not imagine her getting close to any man. Had I lived closer
to her, I would have liked to know her more. I felt she was
living under a self-constructed suit of armor. She felt
more powerful that way.

—John Abbott, interview with author

E mlyn Williams first became aware of Lillian Hellman in 1939, when he read and was tremendously impressed by *The Little Foxes*. It was exactly his sort of play—wise, astringently witty, unsentimental, and perfectly crafted. Then, in New York in late 1940, Herman Shumlin directed Ethel Barrymore in Williams's play, *The Corn is Green*. The director pressed the playwright's wife, who knew her husband's work intimately, to attend rehearsals. (He himself was unable to do so, owing to the war in Europe.) Since Shumlin had the deepest respect for Hellman's judgment, she, too, came to many of them. This arrangement meant that Hellman met the wife of the author—traditionally an ominous event—to boot, she was the British wife of a British author, and nobody has ever accused Hellman of being an Anglophile. But Williams's wife was the soul of tact, and all was well. She did mention in a letter to Williams, however, that "Miss Hellman must be difficult to know."

1941: *Watch on the Rhine* was enjoying its big success in New York, and Williams's producer, Hugh Beaumont, asked him to direct the play in London. The playwright had never directed a work that was not his own, having always feared he might be tempted to tamper with the text, due to an unconscious urge to present the play as he would have written it. He was doubtful until he read the play. Like *The Little Foxes*, *Watch on the Rhine* seemed perfect to him, and the production was a triumph. He wrote Hellman to say how much he had enjoyed directing the play. She did not answer.

1942: Williams agreed to direct *The Little Foxes* in London. There was one snag—a big one: Bette Davis had just been a huge hit in the movie version. Beaumont and Williams realized then that the only star who could compete with that publicity was the one who had made the success of her career in the New York production. They cabled Tallulah Bankhead. And back came her ecstatic, "Darlings, Yes Yes YES!!" Her communication was smartly followed by a terse message from the author: "Cannot allow London production with Bankhead." That was that. The London production was a failure.

1945: Hellman in London. Her first meeting with Williams, supper at the Savoy. As Williams arrived, he thought, "I'm looking forward to this, she and I have so much in common." Besides being contemporaries (they were both forty) they had the theater and mutual respect, as well. He remembered reading that she prided herself on fearless honesty. This sounded fairly unnerving, but his hopes remained high. Williams was soon reminded of his wife's comment, "Miss Hellman must be difficult to know." He found that an understatement. That evening he realized that Hellman perfectly exemplified the difference between wit and humor: while in her plays she was gracefully witty, her private personality lacked humor to the point of grimness. The conversation dried up. He was cheered by only one agreeable moment, when she asked him if he would direct *Another Part of the Forest* in London. Unfortunately, he had a prior commitment.

Early 1949: Hellman and Kermit Bloomgarden, her producer, sent Williams, on holiday in New York, a script of the new Hellman play *Montserrat*. It was, ostensibly, an adaptation of a French original, but it was a Hellman play nevertheless—lean, sardonic, and chilling, the political message mercifully overshadowed by the dramatic eloquence. The part of the villain, Izquierdo, offered Williams was a fine one, and he quickly accepted. He assumed that Shumlin would direct but learned it would be Hellman, and he looked forward to rehearsals.

Late 1949: The evening before rehearsals started, Williams had coffee with Hellman and Bloomgarden, so that they could have a brief discussion of his part. Most actors who are faced with an important role in a new play, however good, find half a dozen unimportant phrases difficult to say, for all sorts of reasons, and are anxious for help from the author or director. Feeling that Hellman must have been sharply conscious of the fact that he was also a playwright, Williams had been extremely careful to keep his very tentative suggestions to a minimum.

Hellman's apartment was, of course, centrally heated, but the temperature, from the moment Williams arrived, seemed unaccountably to fall. His preliminary mention—conventional but sincere—of his enthusiasm about the play and the part fell flat. And when he got to those "tentative suggestions," ice began to form. They were mostly to do with Americanisms in the text, which he found uncomfortable because the play was set not in New York in 1949, but in Venezuela in 1812; for instance, he asked if he could say "He must be mad" instead of "He must be crazy," and "They think they're clever" instead of "They think they're smart." Hellman apparently thought him British-persnickety, and shook her head; her face, "not—at the best of times—suffused with human kindness, was of stone," he recalls. Kermit's reaction, from what Williams could see of it (so firmly was the producer under her thumb), was noncommittal. The actor did not get a thing—not a syllable, not a comma. "Ah well . . . " was his response.

John Abbott, who played the part of Juan Salcedo Alvarez in *Montserrat*, provides a persuasive explanation of why things went awry so quickly between Williams and Hellman:

> The affinity between Lillian and Emlyn was, of course, love of the Theatre with a big "T"—that is to say the capability of theatre to say things in a powerful, memorable way: but while Emlyn was satisfied to thrill audiences with the horror of seeing young men entering old ladies' homes with the head of his recent victim in a hatbox, Lillian despised what she would consider desecration of the theatre's use and in expressing her views on the matter she was often more than outspoken. This bone of contention was never dragged out in the open, that I am aware of, but one felt that Emlyn was aware that he was not being treated as an equal in the literary field.

"Lillian would have regarded any suggested changes in her language as an 'impertinence,' Abbott observes. When he ventured to change "Come quick," to "Come quickly" she would not allow it. When he suggested that his character would be too proud of his grammar to make a grammatical slip, she said only, "I hate adverbs!" How she proposed to get along without them was not explained to Abbott. But the actor did not think her rude. Instead, he realized it was her way of saying actors would not be permitted to "improve" her scripts. Abbott remembers her saying that during one of her productions a producer remarked, "We'll put that right during the rewrites." "Rewrites!" asked Lillian. "*What* rewrites!"

During the first day rehearsals, John Abbott remembers Hellman saying, "Now I haven't worked out any moves for anybody. But if you move around, it will probably come out all right." Abbott had never heard of such a thing. He was appalled: "That's all I want to know, where I am to stand. So I found myself a place in the middle of the stage and sat there and didn't move a foot. It seemed all right to me." Hellman was never one to say much in praise. At the dress rehearsal, she remarked, "I can only tell you you were good. I suppose other people would say 'you were *wonderful*,' but I never use that expression." She came into Abbott's dressing room on the first night and said "murd." He didn't know what she meant. Of course, he soon caught on that she meant *merde*.

Williams remembers that after the first two days of rehearsal, two flaws emerged. The first: it became clear that the first-class playwright whose stagecraft, when she was at her typewriter, was masterly, had become an entirely different person when faced with a bare stage and twenty eager actors. She was lost. "Why are you still standing *there*? . . . Try something different. . . . You're making the line sound unconvincing, somehow. . . . " One actor asked, "Miss Hellman, am I masking Julie?" and she looked at him as if she did not understand what he meant. Such a drawback, in a director who disarmed the cast by admitting she was "new to this, help me, kids!"could have been overcome by friendship with actors who, Williams could tell, would have collaborated with enthusiasm. But it was not to be, for there was a second flaw—a fatal one.

Good actors are sensitive as racehorses and crave a firm but loving hand. Hellman's was neither; when she was not wavering, she was hectoring. "No, no, how many times must I try to make you understand." Julie Harris (Felisa), who was just embarking on her distinguished acting career, remembers there was a division in the cast, with veterans like Williams, John Abbott, and Reinhold Schunzel mixed in with much younger, inexperienced actors. "Lillian would say to us young people, 'Look at those older actors; they know how to do it. Watch them.' Which the young people resented very much." Harris recalls that "she was absolutely the worst kind of director." Scenes and lines were dictated at a faster and faster pace. Harris remembers Hellman complaining to actors: "Why are you so slow? Why don't you speak up?" Constantly saying "don't" is probably the worst thing a director could do to an actor. Actors tend to tense up when not given the opportunity to test their wings, Harris suggests. Performances are shaped by cunning directors—like Jed Harris. Once, when an actor was doing too much gesturing with his hands, Harris stopped him abruptly: "I don't want any of your low comedy tricks in this play. It isn't that kind of play. If you do that once more I'm going to fire you and you are the best actor in America for the part." The actor remembered Harris's ploy; it seemed "the perfect way to deal with a misbehaving actor, threatening him but flattering him at the same time." Hellman lacked Harris's theater sense.

If Hellman was usually deaf to actors' suggestions, it may have been because she had experienced how recalcitrant they could be to her own direction. The old timers, in particular, thwarted her. Over the years Reinhold Schunzel (Salas Ina) had developed a way of dragging out pauses, and Hellman could not manage him. She wanted the actor to wear a wig. Schunzel hated wigs and never wore makeup. At a dress rehearsal he put the wig on backwards. "Mr. Schunzel, it's horrible. Take it off." He smiled and got his way.

Schunzel once amused his fellow actors when Lillian asked him to sit by the fire. He gazed at her for a moment, as though he could scarcely believe what he had heard, then he adjusted his glasses, looked at his script, then at Lillian and said:

"You vant I should move to the feuer?"
"Yes, Mr. Schunzel." After another pause he looked
at his script again.
"You vant I should sit in this chayer!"
"Yes, Mr. Schunzel." Again he examined his script, he
looked at the chair, he looked at the fireplace,
shrugged, and did as he was bid.

The actors laughed, but Lillian could not have missed his insolence. Schunzel was hinting that he should have been invited to make suggestions. After all, both he and Williams were eminent directors in their native lands. Lillian, as far as Abbott could see, did not take exception to Schunzel's insulting behavior. Indeed, she later wrote Abbott that she and Schunzel met often after the production and remained friends.

Abbott did not feel close to Lillian during rehearsals, yet sometimes when he sat next to her in the auditorium, she would ask his opinion about staging or the delivery of a line, here and there. Abbott remembers Nehemiah Persoff, who played Antonanzas, being puzzled about the meaning of a line. Hellman turned to Abbott and said, "how can you explain wit?" "She was not the first director who knew what she wanted but did not know how to teach the way to do it," Abbott concludes.

Howard Bay was sure that Hellman never understood actors. "As a director she operated on the premise that we're all intelligent people. We can explain what we want. And then you just go ahead and do it." Bay laughed, "It doesn't work that way. And *Montserrat* was the classic case." Bay felt it was a weak, didactic play, but

Hellman thought it said something important. She had assembled the wildest assortment of actors Bay had ever seen in one cast. No two actors matched. John Abbott remembers the director assembling the cast once to talk about the play. She tried to give them a feeling about the Spanish character, the time period, and so on. Abbott felt that her talk was performed as a "duty rather than something she had to say." This was fine with Abbott, who remembered a previous director, Harold Clurman, who wanted to spend a whole morning discussing a play. A fellow actor, Ralph Richardson, told Clurman, "No, we don't do that in England." Get on your feet and do it; it emerges as you go along—that summed up the English school of acting.

Williams remembers that a simple, daunting truth dawned on everybody: their director *did not like actors.* More and more she gave the impression that she thought that theirs was a demeaning occupation and that all performers were "sissies"—including the women. The result was that the cast was not only out of Hellman's reach, they were faced with a powerful phenomenon that was a contradiction in terms: a sort of anti-Fascist dictator. And they were frightened of her.

Hellman's problems became aggravated by what Williams calls "the director's nightmare." Steven Hill, playing Montserrat, turned out to be miscast. Bloomgarden and Bay begged Hellman to replace him. "He's a caricature of an Actor's Studio actor," Bay told her. "You don't know what he is going to do next or why. He throws everybody else off." Hellman could not make up her mind about him. She asked Williams if he agreed with Bay. Wary of getting involved, he said "Lillian, I'm too near him onstage to judge, you must decide." When pressed, he did confess that Hill, though talented, was a mumbling member of the method school of acting and did seem to give a cue as if he hated to part with it.

Method acting was a mystery to Hellman. She was much more comfortable with actors like John Abbott, who came from the English school in which "you aim at what you're going to do right from the beginning, and then you have it in mind, and you don't dig around in a rag bag hoping something will be pulled out eventually." Hellman gave the impression that all the actor needed to know was in his or her lines—so just study the lines. Actors who came to the early rehearsals with their lines memorized, as Julie Harris did, gained the playwright's approval. Abbott remembers Hellman once telling him Shumlin's remark to her that all her plays needed was a stage manager, meaning that they played themselves. To some extent, with a good cast, Abbott believed this was true. Virginia Bloomgarden thought this was so for *Another Part of the Forest*, where the brilliant ensemble acting obviously had nothing to do with Hellman's direction—or, more properly speaking, her nondirection.

Abbott did have one "little bit of a tiff" with his director. He was playing the role of Juan Salcedo Alvarez, an actor, who has a big scene in which Izquierdo (Williams) presses him to play his own death as he would do it on stage. Hellman had run out of ideas as to where to stage this. Abbott recalls, "and she said, 'I imagined it played up here,' and she pointed to upstage behind a table. I said, 'Oh, no.' I didn't think that spot—perhaps in the middle of the stage. 'Well, there's no need to ridicule everything I say.' " Hellman was defensive and probably felt, Abbott imagined, that she had made a bit of a faux pax. He regretted challenging her authority with his rude comment, "I didn't come to play this part behind the furniture!" After that Kermit Bloomgarden said, "I'm going to talk to Lillian about the actor's problem. She has to see the actor's point of view." In spite of feeling irate over Hellman's treatment of him in his most important scene, Abbott got on well with her and was invited out to Hardscrabble and to her house on Eighty-second Street.

Who would replace Steven Hill? Again, Hellman consulted Williams. "I said, 'Paul Scofield?' 'Oh, I auditioned him in London, Kermit and I found him kind of effeminate.' " Williams raised a silent eyebrow. Then he had an idea. "My film's playing in the next block, there's a boy in it *I* think is just right." The movie was one Williams had written and directed, *The Last Days of Dolwyn*, and Hellman rushed to see it. Her verdict: "No, he's not strong enough, no." She did not mention the movie, and Williams would have been surprised if she had. The "boy" was Richard Burton. Williams did not ask if she also found him "kind of effeminate."

Steven Hill, in Abbott's view, was a gifted actor who had intended to wait until he felt ready to give a filled-out performance. The producers were afraid to trust him. Rehearsal time on Broadway is horrendously inadequate, and Hill had been caught fishing around for his character when the rest of the cast was ready to open. Abbott remembers Hill was asked to show how he intended to play Montserrat:

but he just smiled and gave us an estimate of some weeks ahead; which meant that the first date would have to put up with a very embryonic rendering. . . . Redfield [Hill's replacement] put together a safe performance, but it lacked the sensitivity Steve's would have had. Kermit told me that when Steve was given his notice the boy simply said, "Okay." A rather touching reaction I thought, but Kermit said, "You know that's not natural—he's a sick boy!"

When the play opened in Princeton, Hill, the method actor, was death. After final dress rehearsal in Philadelphia, Hellman, Bloomgarden, and Bay repaired to a coffee shop. She was still trying to figure out the method. Hellman turned to her producer, "Kermit, you were with the Group Theater [the birthplace of the method]. Tell me about improvisation." Kermit explained the exercises assigned in class: "I remember once we were given the problem of constructing the life of an orange." Hellman said, "Let's go home." The next morning she was at the theater early and asked Howard, "How quick can we get Billy Redfield down here?" He was there by noon, and he went on that night. Fortunately, he sat at a desk for much of the play and could read Montserrat's lines from a script. Redfield did fine. He had gotten off a train, taken a cab to the theater, and asked "Where do I come on?"

Rehearsals grew more and more horrendous; Redfield, the plucky replacement, did his best. Consistent with Williams's determination to keep out of trouble, he avoided discussion to the point of seeming—he felt—enigmatic. There was, between him and his director, only one passage of arms. It happened at a rehearsal actors both look forward to and dread: the first uninterrupted run-through of a whole act, still without scenery, costumes, or props; lines are still not solidly implanted, and the producer, director, designers, understudies, and so on are all out in front. It is something of an ordeal for the actors, so it is imperative that the mental concentration of the cast should not be disturbed.

Five minutes into the run-through, from the middle of the dark auditorium, there was a loud click and a flash. Five minutes later, another click and flash. Then, in the middle of a dramatic confrontation on stage, another. Then another. With each flash, the actors were more and more thrown. Although a disciple of strict professional behavior, Williams found all of this beyond endurance.

Knowing that none of the others was in a position to protest, he reminded himself that he *was* the head of the company, stopped in mid-sentence and called out into the darkness, "Lillian, what *is* all this?" Of course, Williams knew what had happened. Hellman's voice rang out, even colder than his: "It's somebody taking pictures, surely you can tell?" "But you hadn't even warned us," he said, "all those explosions, reminded me of the London Blitz!" It was a cheap retort, which stung her into just as cheap a return. "The London Blitz," she announced, sharp as a knife, "was nothing to what happened to Stalingrad!" There was a pause. Williams had to respond somehow, and he heard himself saying, "Oh Lillian, were you there?" The rehearsal continued—flashless. The incident was never mentioned again, which (Williams feels) was just as well, since neither of them had come out of it with good marks.

Things went from bad to worse. After opening in Philadelphia, the confusion in the reviews made Hellman even more mixed up and uncooperative; the hectoring began to seem more like bullying. Between her and the actors there stood a barrage of non-communication. One after the other, members of the cast spoke to Williams of their unhappiness; at the last rehearsals a couple of the actresses were reduced to tears.

It seemed that Williams was the only one immune. He felt he was lucky enough to have an actor-proof part and the experience to tackle it without help from the director, who left him severely alone. It is hard to believe, however, that he did not have some anxiety about how he would be received in a production that seemed to be headed straight for disaster. His continued policy of uninvolvement caused him to feel somehow guilty and vaguely smug; this, and the sadly ironic spectacle of a fine author doing harm to her own play, led him to embark on the rashest move he has ever made. He has regretted it for thirty-seven years.

Williams decided to write to Hellman voicing the feelings of the cast, to the effect that while she was a fine playwright, she just did not understand actors and handled them the wrong way. He would read the letter to the company before mailing it, feeling that by putting their unhappiness into words, he would be restoring their confidence and helping them feel it was not they who were inadequate. He would exhort them to grit their teeth and fight through.

Williams did read the letter to them, and it did make some of the actors feel better—although John Abbott remembers being dismayed by the letter and refusing to sign it. He did not feel it was an actor's place to challenge a director. He had been engaged to play a part and had no control over who was chosen to direct it. Abbott told Reinhold Schunzel, the elder member of the company, that "it would be so hurtful for the morale of the company if this ever got out." Schunzel quite agreed and spoke to Emlyn: "If I were a guest in England, I wouldn't behave like this. What would you think of me?" Either Williams saw his reasoning or the lack of backing made him drop the idea. In any case, Williams remembers there was a more positive reaction which—obtusely—he had not foreseen. The cast begged him not to send the letter, as his telling the powerful Miss Hellman how unhappy they were would be certain to prevent their ever working for her again. Williams complied, of course, and everyone was sworn to secrecy. A few months later, at Sardi's with John Abbott, Hellman let out the fact that she knew all about the letter. Abbott was surprised and asked, "How ever did you find out?" And she said, "Well, you don't think I'm going to tell *you*."

After the play's New York opening, Williams learned that "somebody" had told Hellman of the letter. In fairness, he thought he should send it to her, although he carefully cut out the phrases that suggested the cast had criticized the director. There was no reaction. After the play closed, it gradually dawned on Williams how unwise he had been, especially for a playwright who had directed his own plays. Had he really expected that Hellman would listen to an actor? A saint would have taken offense, never mind Lillian Hellman. He knew retribution was on the way. Two letters arrived at the same time: one from Hellman, one from Bloomgarden. The letters were much the same, except that Hellman's was vituperation, pure and simple, with words like "gross disloyalty . . . monstrous . . . mischief-maker . . . sabotage. . . . " Williams felt he deserved what he got.

Clearly, he had to write back. He did his feeble best, calling their letters "the longest delayed delayed-action bomb in history." Williams seemed to remember that in his dressing room in New York, during the third week of the *Montserrat* schedule of performances and after Hellman knew about his letter, she visited him—more friendly than ever—and asked if he would help the play run longer by taking a salary cut. Did that comply with the famous Hellman moral code of the truth at all costs, down with hypocrisy? Where was the Hellman integrity? In her vituperative letter, Hellman mentioned that William Wyler had seen Williams's London production of *The Little Foxes* and had been so appalled by the way it was done that he had had Hellman in fits of laughter describing it. Williams was puzzled by this, and in his reply asked why she had urged him to direct a new play of hers three years later. Hellman did not answer him.

The postscript to the play, as far as Williams was concerned, was Hellman's paragraph about *Montserrat* in *Pentimento*: "I directed the play in a fumbling frightened way, intimidated by Emlyn Williams. . . . I do not blame Mr. Williams for his disapproval of me, though the way he showed his disapproval had a bad effect on the actors." Williams was at first incredulous, then fascinated. He respected her for admitting that she had "fumbled." But a frightened, intimidated Lillian Hellman? Was she referring to his letter? But that was not composed until after rehearsals were over. She had managed to turn the tables on him, neatly and completely. It was not she who had demoralized the cast, it was Williams, and he had frightened and intimidated her in the bargain! To him, it was a provocative glimpse of Hellman's psychology, if only a glimpse. When she wrote all that, had she believed it? Or had she, over the years, *made* herself believe it? Williams could not decide. Was he to conclude that she had sensed that here was one of the few actors who were not frightened of her—a novel realization which may have jolted her into being frightened of *him?* He could only see that his own experience of the woman was at odds with the image of a woman who was incorruptibly truthful. Asked for a final comment, Williams thought a moment: "A brilliantly gifted woman: it would have been fascinating to get to know her . . . I wish I had."

Montserrat received respectable reviews, but several critics identified flaws in the direction and in the writing:

> The play's lack of movement appears to be aggravated by Miss Hellman's rigid, unimaginative staging. (*Variety*, November 2, 1949)

> Miss Hellman's direction is uneven, frequently leaning to the static. (*Billboard*, November 5, 1949)

> Miss Hellman . . . took a pedestrian view of stage direction. (John Gassner, *Forum*, December, 1949)

In her comments at the time of the play's premiere, Hellman came perilously close to saying there was no need for directors. "Directing . . . is no great feat," she told Murry Schumach (*The New York Times*, October 23, 1949). Elia Kazan, Jed Harris, Herman Shumlin "and maybe one or two others" might make "creative contributions" to a production, but the play was the thing. It was enough that she had written short speeches and detailed stage directions. What more could actors want? And the idea that a director needed some special knack for "handling" actors was rejected out of hand. There was no such thing; it would be like playing God.

The play centers on Montserrat, the Spanish army officer who aids Simon Bolivar against the Spanish army of occupation in Venezuela in 1812. Although Montserrat is a traitor to Spain, he is on the side of revolutionary history—just as Kurt Muller in *Watch on the Rhine* is a traitor from the Nazi point of view but is on the side of democracy. Like Kurt, Montserrat is a vulnerable hero; he accepts human failure without capitulating to it:

> There is no man without a time of defeat and an hour
> of turning back. Bolivar had his defeat, he had his time
> of mourning, and passed through it. They may catch
> him tonight and kill him. But he will not turn back
> again. I know that as surely as I know that I am willing
> to die for it.

But unlike Kurt, Montserrat has no context (no family and no riveting personal history) in which to build his belief in the revolutionary future. Several reviewers complained that the play never dramatized the moral and political vitality of the revolution Montserrat defends. On the contrary, nearly every reviewer was taken with the evil Izquierdo, triumphantly and suavely played by Emlyn Williams. Montserrat agonizes over the deaths of six innocent people who Izquierdo has rounded up to kill, one by one, unless Montserrat divulges Bolivar's hiding place. Izquierdo is implacable and functions as the one truly active character on stage. As a result, he becomes—especially in the hands of a skillful actor like Williams—the fascinating cynosure of the action. As execution follows execution with all-too-predictable regularity, the tension of the play diminishes. As several reviewers noted, William Redfield, as Montserrat, had his head in his hands for most of the performance, immobolized by grief and by a script and staging that allowed him no means of countering Izquierdo's pyrotechnics.

Harold Clurman, in *The New Republic* (December 5, 1949), was the only reviewer to realize that in making *Montserrat* her own, Hellman had ruined it. It was an existentialist play, not a revolutionary one, Clurman explained. It was a drama about choice. Facing the certainty of death, a man does what he feels he must. "The play's protagonist, Montserrat, can be no more certain that life will bear him out in his nobility than the antagonist, Izquierdo, can vouch for the efficacy of his cynicism." In Robles's play, the nature of Bolivar's revolution does not need to be dramatized; the revolution does not have to compel the audience's belief. The existentialist hero cannot know if the future "will prove him right." All he can do is take "individual responsibility" for his actions. "What distinguishes his choice of action is that it is undertaken in behalf of millions of others. This is the existentialist ethic," Clurman pointed out. *Montserrat* was not a 1930s play about "the struggle for freedom." Instead the play centers on the passionate debate between Montserrat and Izquierdo. "Izquierdo should be as hot in his unbelief as Montserrat in his belief," Clurman insisted, whereas Williams, "a good actor, gives us a cold villain." In this most devastating critique of Hellman's writing and direction from a theater professional, one who obviously appreciated Robles's original and highly successful European play, it is apparent how completely misguided was the American production of *Montserrat*. "Her direction makes neither shape, sense nor good red excitement," Clurman concludes.

Robles held a similar opinion and wrote several years later to Ph.D. student Marie Kilker that Hellman had adapted his play in an "abusive manner." He tried to forbid the publication of her adaptation in her *Collected Plays* and took her to court. She relied on a contract she believed gave her the right to publish *Montserrat*, but she assured Robles her version of the play would not be offered for production by Dramatists Play Service.

Regina, Marc Blitzstein's operatic version of *The Little Foxes*, opened at nearly the same time as *Montserrat*. It was hailed by some critics, condemned by others. Clurman, feeling that *Regina*, like *Montserrat*, had completely misconceived the original from which it was adapted, remarked, "One might as well try to set double-entry bookkeeping to music as to make those 'little foxes' sing." The wonder is that less than two years later, Harold Clurman would be directing *The Autumn Garden*.

16

THE AUTUMN GARDEN
New York/Hardscrabble/Martha's
Vineyard/New York
(1950–1951)

An autumn garden is one which by winter time will fade
and not be a garden any more. It's a chrysanthemum
garden. The people in the play are coming into the winter
of life.

—Lillian Hellman, interview with Vernon Rice in *New York Post*,
March 6, 1951

F.B.I.
Gentlemen
  Why isn't Lillian Hellman picked up as a Red? She
speaks at all their meetings & gave a check for $2,600 for
the cause. During the last war, she was the guest of Mr.
Stalin & even sold her jewelry for the Russians. She has
entertained many notables from Poland & Russia & always
speaks how wonderful those countries are.
  What has she done for our soldiers?
  Very truly yours

—Author unknown. Letter to FBI, April 24, 1951

These were shocking times. In January 1950, Alger Hiss, president of the Carnegie Endowment for International Peace and previously a high State Department official, was convicted of two counts of perjury, stemming from his denial that he had passed on secret government documents to Whittaker Chambers when the latter was in the employ of the Communist underground. The lean, handsome Hiss, well-educated and well-connected, was the very epitome of the eastern establishment. If he could be guilty, then who could be exempt from suspicion?

There is no question that the cause celebres like the Hiss case badly frightened people and that the Communist menace was exaggerated. Judge Kauffman, in the Rosenberg espionage trial, would accuse the two defendants of having contributed to the outbreak of the Korean War. Lillian Hellman's view of the Cold War—that it was no more than a time of scoundrels who invented the Hiss case and others like it—is insupportable. The reactionary congressmen of HUAC were right on one fundamental point. As Allan Weinstein demonstrates in *The Hiss-Chambers Case*, sympathy for Soviet Russia had led some government officials like Hiss to turn over information to Communist agents. Had Hellman spoken frankly with her friend, the novelist Josephine Herbst, she would have discovered that Hiss and Chambers had indeed known each other and that Hiss's denials were outright lies. The HUAC-McCarthy witch-hunt was despicable in many respects, but it was not just the creation of the "cheap baddies" she dismisses in *Scoundrel Time*.

The irony of the intense FBI scrutiny that Hellman came under in this period, is that she and Hammett were leading very private, quiet, and introspective lives. Hellman was writing her least political play, *The Autumn Garden*, which she came to believe was her best work for the stage. Although not a political play, *The Autumn Garden* is about how people make and break their faith in each other. It is decidedly a play of middle age, in which a mature artist reviews the record of several characters' lives in order to measure the degree to which human beings can be loyal to one another and to their best visions of themselves. It is no accident, then, that *The Autumn Garden* was written during this Cold War hysteria, in which "friendly" HUAC witnesses repudiated their past, named their partners in Communist crime, and justified informing for the higher good—the democratic state to which they owed allegiance.

In making a case for herself before HUAC in 1952, Lillian Hellman talked about her family background; it was, she implied, the surest proof that she had not been disloyal. In preparation for writing *The Autumn Garden*, which was to have its roots in autobiography, Hellman felt compelled to go home for a month to New Orleans in January 1950. She needed to visit her aunts, "to press the memories of them and their boardinghouse freshly into her mind," as Richard Moody puts it. *The Autumn Garden* is a drama of memory. Along with her final original stage work, *Toys in the Attic*, it has more in common with her memoirs than with her previous plays. To Ward Morehouse of the *New York Sun* (December 16, 1949), she announced, "I'm going to write my memoirs some day." The many characters in *The Autumn Garden* almost crowd out the action and retard the dynamic of the play; a more supple form of narrative would be required for a writer who always wanted to write novels but who told Morehouse, "I simply haven't the guts to try it. Just too scared." She admitted to writing short stories, which she said were "not very good." This was John Melby's impression, too, when she sent him a few fictional pieces when he was still in China that he felt were poorly conceived. The short story form would also find its place in the memoirs.

In February 1950, Hellman was all set to get on with her new play, but then "was struck with a six-week siege of headaches and stomach sickness that kept her from the typewriter." Hammett was in Hollywood working on a script for William Wyler. Wyler's wife Talli remembers how the director waited and waited for the screenplay until Hammett finally had to return the money he had taken for writing it. He had dried up as a writer but would continue to make jokes about one opus or another he intended to finish—such as "The Valley Sheep are Fatter."

In mid-March, Hellman invited John Melby—recently returned from a foreign service post in Southeast Asia—to the farm. They had met briefly in Washington on her way to New Orleans. She had stayed at his apartment in Georgetown, and they enjoyed each other's company at lunch, where they discussed friends in Moscow and New York, music, the theater, and the various trips each had taken. Always frank with Hellman, Melby mentioned that there was another woman in his life, Hilda Hordern, Ambassador Stuart's secretary in Nanking. Hellman was not all distressed by this news. It was a happy and comfortable weekend at the farm, with Melby unwinding from the stress occasioned by his divorce. To their surprise, Hellman and Melby resumed their lovemaking, although neither of them gave voice anymore to the possibility of a permanent relationship. Their feelings ran very deep, however, and in testimony two years later at Melby's security hearing,

Hellman put it this way: "The relationship at this point was neither one thing nor the other: it was neither over nor was it not over." An FBI informant was watching Hellman, for her file records Melby's visit. He would see her once more in April, letters would be exchanged throughout the year, and Hellman would call him at Christmas.

In spite of looming political troubles, 1950 may have been the happiest year of Lillian Hellman's life. Certainly, her memoirs glow with the memory of it. Hammett had quit drinking. There was an openness about him, a loving quality that had nothing to do with sexuality. He cared a great deal about Hellman's writing and continued to help her with it. The touching side of Hellman came out in Hammett's company. She would say to him, "Now Dash, I want you to tell me after lunch I'm to go back inside and go to work." He'd say, "Okay, Lilly baby." After lunch: "Lilly." "Oh, you son of a bitch, leave me alone." And he'd say, "Lilly." Nobody else could move her. He had her number. While Lillian was digging up flowers one day, he said to Virginia Bloomgarden, "You know, she doesn't trust that the seeds know what to do when you put them in the ground. So she's got layers. If you dig down there, you would find that there's a whole world of flowers three feet under and maybe four feet under."

Catherine Kober remembers both the tender and the rough sides of these days at Hardscrabble. She loved their big poodles. One of the dogs had puppies and Catherine wanted to have a look. So that her feelings would not be hurt, Hammett and Hellman very carefully explained to her that if she approached the dog, she might get growled at and bitten. The poodle would protect her puppies, and Catherine must not think the dogs had changed their minds about her.

"Dash really knew what it was like to be a child, and I don't think Lillian quite got it," Catherine recalls. He would take her to the upstairs room and point out the birds' nests telling her to be very quiet so as not to frighten the birds. He knew—unlike most people who visited Hardscrabble—what to say to a child. This was very important to Catherine, for her mother was dying and no one seemed to realize the impact of this loss on the little girl. Catherine, a city child, wanted to go look at the chickens.

They were in different sections. There were the orange-footed blue-beaked ones and the blue-footed

> orange-beaked ones, and you weren't supposed to get
> them messed up. Well . . . I forgot to close the door to
> the coop. Lillian got very angry. She had cause to. She
> was the one with the peck marks on her hands. The
> chickens did not like being sorted. I think Dash tried
> to calm her down. He may have said, "This is what
> you can expect from a kid."

Hammett took more of an interest than ever in Hellman's new
play. Although he was not writing, he still had considerable
income from various literary properties. She divided her time
between Hardscrabble and Martha's Vineyard—with time out for
a brief summer trip to England and France—as she went through
the usual process of writing and revising. At the Vineyard, she
saw a good deal of her respected friend Van Wyck Brooks and read
two acts of *The Autumn Garden* for him. Later she would apologeti-
cally write him for an endorsement to be used in advertising for
the play. Hammett's criticism was not easy to take: "I don't know
what's happened, but tear this up and throw it away. It's worse
than bad—it's half good." But she seemed to thrive on his hard
words, which turned to praise of the final draft: "It's the best play
anybody's written in a long time. Maybe longer." It seemed the
farm would be "the right place to live" for the rest of her life,
especially since her time with Hammett settled into "a passionate
affection."

The Autumn Garden is set in a summer resort on the Gulf Coast,
about a hundred miles from New Orleans. The playwright's original plan was for a plot centered on the two Tuckerman sisters,
modeled after her aunts, and on their devotion to their brother, a
character based on her father. The lives of several middle-aged
vacationers would also be explored, as they had undoubtedly been
by Hellman as a child in her aunts' New Orleans boardinghouse.
The play quickly became too congested with characters and action,
and at some point Hellman decided to set aside her initial idea—
the triangle involving a brother and two sisters—which would
eventually be taken up again in *Toys in the Attic*. In revision, the
play became the story of Constance Tuckerman's summer resort,
and the relaxed atmosphere of the Gulf Coast replaced some of
the rather harsh confrontations between characters in the first
draft. It was not so much conflicts between people—which had
been the primary concern of earlier Hellman dramas—but the

confusion within people that dominated the composition of *The Autumn Garden*. As many critics have remarked, the playwright seemed to shift from an Ibsenian focus on social issues to Chekhovian probing of human character.

Perhaps the most interesting changes Hellman made in the writing of *The Autumn Garden* have to do with dialogue. Each subsequent draft became less talky. Often the playwright cut out qualifying words. For instance, when Rose Griggs asks her husband Ben, a retired general, whether he likes her dress, his reply is altered from "It's very nice" to "It's nice." An insignificant change, it might be argued, except that changes like this one occur with such consistency throughout the final script (dated October 17, 1952) that the cumulative effect is impressive. In this case, Ben's weariness with his silly wife is better expressed in two words rather than three. Some lines were shortened because of awkwardness and overstatement. For example, "But somewhere in the middle years, how wonderful to be alone" became "It's fine to be alone." The language was tightened; three-line speeches got reduced to two lines. The spare and economical prose is absolutely necessary in a play that has almost none of the melodrama of Hellman's earlier work. The language has to be pointed, since the confrontations in this play occur within characters. They must be able to articulate their self-awareness without the usual repetitiousness and amplification that would naturally occur off stage. The achievement of *The Autumn Garden* is that for all the pruning of wordage, the speech patterns are authentic—"real" in the sense that they are akin to what would be heard in actual conversation. Indeed, some opening-night reviews complained that the play was too "discursive." Yet Hellman was careful not to let the characters talk out all of their emotions; rather, the shaping of dialogue reveals personalities and frames of mind.

The example Hellman was fond of citing was the lengthiest speech in the play, Ben Griggs's reflection on what he has made, or failed to make, of his life. The speech went through several drafts, none of which ever satisfied Hellman, and which Hammett finally revised when she gave up in disgust. One of Hellman's attempts:

> There comes a time in most lives when you can still
> move around—when there is still room within your-
> self, and enough in you to use it and go some other

way. I don't know at what age other people understand that—but I have no excuse: I knew it ten, fifteen
years ago—but I let it run past me, thinking that when
I knew the way to go, of course I'd take it. (*With great
feeling*) Well I found out. There are no minutes of great
decision. Only a series of little ones coming out of the
past. You don't suddenly turn around—because it's
too damn late, and you've let it go too long.

Another Hellman draft:

And so there are no minutes of big decision. No time
when you can suddenly turn around. All those years
when you promised yourself the day would come
when you would wipe out the mistakes, or do the
work you'd never done, or think the way you'd never
thought, or have what you've never had—
    (*Shakes his head*)
No. That's not for people like me. I guess it has to be
the sum of it all, of a whole life, and none can be
thrown out as you tell yourself you can wait for the
great day. Can't do it that way. Well, I let it all run past
me, all the wasted time, sure that when I knew the
way to go, nothing could stop me. Then suddenly it
gets too late.

Hammett's rewrite:

So at any given moment you're only the sum of your
life up to then. There are no big moments you can
reach unless you've a pile of smaller moments to stand
on. That big hour of decision, the turning point in
your life, the someday you've counted on when you'd
suddenly wipe out your past mistakes, do the work
you'd never done, think the way you'd never thought,
have what you'd never had—it just doesn't come suddenly. You've trained yourself for it while you
waited—or you've let it all run past you and frittered
yourself away. I've frittered myself away, Crossman.

Hammett's version is the full realization of what Hellman intended
for the speech. Her two drafts read as they might be said off stage,

with the character coming to the point only at the end of the speech. Hammett, on the other hand, states the theme in the first sentence. And there is no need for the playwright to indicate emotion ("with great feeling," "shakes his head"). Readers or viewers of the play respond to the cadence of the words, to everything they know about the defeated Ben Griggs at this point in the play. Hammett knew actors would need no help in interpreting these devastating lines, and his removal of all directions to the actor and reader is in keeping with similar revisions Hellman made throughout her final script. Hammett's version is also more dramatic because the full cost to Ben is held in suspense until the last line, when he switches from the second person singular "you" to "I." Not until the very last line does Ben take full responsibility for his philosophical insight. That the final words should be addressed to Ned Crossman seals the dramatic effect and motivation of the speech, since Ned has also frittered away his life waiting for the "big hour of decision." Hammett obviously put an understanding of his own life into the play. He was never able to get his writing going again, and he knew all about the elaborate preparations he had made for his own "big moment," which, as a writer, never materialized. At one point, Hellman wanted him to direct the play, but he jokingly declined, saying that at fifty-seven it was too early to start a new career. He ought to wait until he was at least sixty.

The Autumn Garden is a retrospective play. "Let us be as we were," Nick Denery urges Constance Tuckerman, the woman he loved but left twenty years earlier. Each of her summer resort house guests is forced to evaluate his or her own present stance in the light of past experience. "Does anybody improve with age?" is the question Ned Crossman, the play's shrewdest intelligence, asks. Ned sees all too clearly the illusions these middle-aged characters have about changing their lives or reliving their youths, but he is so critical that any kind of improvement becomes impossible, and his insights result in another way of "frittering away" a life. By middle age, *The Autumn Garden* suggests, it is nearly impossible to make major changes in personality. It is possible, however, to live with fewer illusions, to see life more plainly without embroidering it. This is Sophie's position: "I do the best I can." If she seems excessively modest to the other characters, like Constance, who have romanticized reality, Sophie (another one of Hellman's mature Europeans) also seems to get nearer to the heart of things—to realizing that characters like Ned have never tried very hard to change or to do the best they can.

The plot of the play turns at the opening of the third act, when Nick Denery, home from Europe to see Constance and to play the role of visiting celebrity-artist, is discovered sleeping in Sophie's company. In fact, there has been no seduction, but small-town Southern morality condemns the young woman as much for appearances as for reality. Hellman's revision of the discovery scene again reveals judicious cutting of lines—authentic enough in their own right—that slowed the action of the play and made it less stage worthy. The material in brackets were deleted:

> MRS. ELLIS: Who is this.
> SOPHIE: It is Mr. Denery.
> MRS. ELLIS: (*Turns to stare at her*) [Yes, I recognize him.] What's he doing here?
> SOPHIE: He became drunk and went to sleep.
> [MRS. ELLIS: Sophie, what nonsense are you talking?]
> [SOPHIE: No, Mrs. Ellis, not nonsense. He became drunk and he went to sleep.]
> MRS. ELLIS: He has been here all night? (*Sophie nods*) What's the matter with you? Get him out of here immediately.

The somber quality of the play is often relieved by a humor that punctuates its characters' youthful illusions. Ben Griggs is bored with his wife Rose, who pretends to be a young flirt. When she tries to reawaken his interest by describing her love in Teheran, Ben replies, "He sounds like a good man. Go to him, Rose, the flying time is nothing now." Similarly, Mrs. Ellis, who has grown tired of Nick's childish interference in the lives of others, tells him: "My advice is to try something intellectual for a change. Sit down with your champagne—on which you've been chewing since early afternoon—and try to make a paper hat out of the newspaper or get yourself a nice long piece of string."

The maturity of *The Autumn Garden* is evident in the complex ways the characters regard themselves, even in the midst of their illusions. Rose, the least self-aware character in the play, nevertheless realizes, "I play the fool." She tells her husband she is scared, and much of her childish behavior reflects her uncertainty about herself and her fear that she has no one to help her. At the same time, her husband knows that she will continue to "play the fool" and that he will grow to like it even less. Her dependence on him is real, but it is also a "reality" that both of them have conspired to enforce. They have, in effect, fooled each other—a common occurrence in *The Autumn Garden*, where the very word "fool" is mentioned by several characters who feel they have betrayed the best in themselves and who ask Constance's question: "Well, what *have* I built my life on?" The emphasis given to this query lifts the play to another level of awareness, and it is characteristic of Hellman's maturity that she can manage this adult moment in one line.

By the end of 1950, *The Autumn Garden* was virtually finished and the playwright was looking forward to rehearsals. She felt it was too late in the season for her to undertake direction of the play, and Harold Clurman was hired—probably because of his reputation for deftly handling Chekhovian drama. An extraordinarily good cast was assembled. Fredric March would play Nick Denery, a philandering artist come home to toy with memories of his abandoned love Constance Tuckerman (played by Carol Goodner). Jane Wyatt was coaxed by Clurman into taking the role of Nina Denery, Nick's long-suffering wife. As many reviewers noted, Wyatt made the best of a thankless part, for there was not enough written for Nina to make her a completely realized character. Florence Eldridge March, everyone agreed, was perfect as Rose Griggs, and Clurman would devote many hours to making sure the scenes between Eldridge and Colin Keith-Johnson (playing Ben Griggs) were just right—to the chagrin of Wyatt, who felt the director welshed on his promise to help her with a difficult role she had been most reluctant to accept. Ethel Griffes turned in a stylish performance as the acerbic Mrs. Ellis, and Joan Lorring as Sophie more than held her own with the distinguished veterans in the cast.

Going into rehearsals, Hellman knew she had the elements of a first-rate production. But would the actors and the director realize her vision of the play? Florence Eldridge remembers Harold Clurman as a

> gentle, sensitive man—rather overawed by Lillian. She had a small desk in front of a center seat in the fourth or fifth row of the theater with a light behind it at which she made notes. Poor Harold would give a piece of direction and then almost jerk his head off looking

over his shoulder to see if it was approved. I once asked Lillian if she'd enjoy writing if a critic stood behind her with a red pencil making notes after each line. She just laughed and said, "It's not the same at all." However, when we rehearsed to play again for a fall tour, Harold was relaxed and inventive and it was really a better production because of his relaxation. Lillian was in Europe and he felt free to be creative in his own way.

According to Jane Wyatt:

> I think Harold made up his mind—"I am not going to have a fight with Lillian Hellman. *Everybody* has a fight with Lillian Hellman. I'm going to say, 'Yes, Lillian. No, Lillian. Yes, Lillian.' " He didn't put any punch into the play, although Chekhov was his forte.

Howard Bay recalls:

> It was not a happy thing. Lillian did interfere with the direction. She was rather literal-minded. She'd say, "Harold, so and so should. . . ." That wasn't the way Clurman directed. Rehearsals would stop for the arguments. And Harold went his own merry way. They tried to get me to be a referee once and a while. But I slithered away from that one.

In the introduction to Richard Moody's biography of Hellman, Clurman remembers that the playwright warned him that he "should not take offense if at times she appeared unjust in any critical complaints she might make in the course" of their work together. He had occasion to remember her admonition during a rehearsal at which he gave to the cast certain cuts in the text that the playwright had authorized. Hellman was uncharacteristically late, so he decided "to go ahead and effect the cuts, which I emphasized were the author's." When Hellman arrived, Clurman was quick to explain that he told the cast several times that the cuts were *hers*. Nevertheless, she "felt injured, almost insulted, by what she considered a breach of proper behavior. The play's words belonged to *her* and only she had the right to deal with them. I had preempted her auctorial prerogative." Although Clurman believed the theater is "nothing if it is not the art of collaboration," his conclusion was that Hellman had "no talent for collaboration." She was a writer first of all, and directors, scenic designers, actors, and others were, in Clurman's words, "intrusive strangers" to her.

Having worked with Hellman on the *Days to Come* disaster fifteen years earlier, Florence Eldridge was in a position to observe a somewhat more relaxed playwright, very entertaining and pleasant. But Hellman was not a person an actor could count on. Sometimes, backstage during a performance, Hellman looked very lonely. She would go and sit next to the actors. "One night she spoke of how lonely she was, and we said, 'well, we're just going to go out and have some supper. Do you want to come and have supper with us?' 'Oh,' she said, 'I'd love to do that.' In the next act somebody had turned up, and she was sorry but she couldn't come." Actors were not Hellman's cup of tea. In many ways, Eldridge liked her, but she was aware of characteristics she would not want to tangle with. "Lillian was quite a vain woman, really. She dressed beautifully. And either she felt actors weren't intellectual enough to entertain her or she may have not liked to cope with such attraction as they might have."

Lucille Watson, who had been stunning as Fanny Farrelly in *Watch on the Rhine*, was engaged to play the somewhat similar part of Mrs. Ellis. Watson was charming—"the enchanting Miss Watson," is how Jane Wyatt (Nina Denery) thought of her. At the first rehearsals, Watson would always bring a chair to put her feet up, because Harold Clurman liked to talk. "He would talk and talk and talk about the play," Wyatt recalls. One day, Watson leaned over to Wyatt and said, "If that little man goes on talking for five minutes more, I'm going to get up and leave." The director kept talking. Watson got up, rolled up her deck chair, and walked out the stage door. "We all watched her go out. And she never came back." During another of Clurman's talks, Kent Smith, who had the role of Ned Crossman, nodded off. Harold said, "Kent, are you asleep?" Kent said, "No, no, just . . ." In *Pentimento*, Hellman says Watson had rehearsed with the cast for three days. Watson supposedly told another actor that she could tolerate the playwright because she was "a toilet-trained Jew," but that the director put her out of patience because he was "just plain Jew."

The actress playing Sophie was not interpreting the role very well and had to be replaced just four or five days before the opening in Philadelphia. This was a very grave risk to take, Wyatt thought, since this Chekhovian play depended so much on the ensemble playing of the entire cast. Hammett, who was closely following rehearsals, wrote Maggie Kober on February 18 that the play looked "wonderful, but all of the acting still needs a lot of work and some of it needs a great deal." The actors seemed mechanical to him at this point and had not really got inside their roles. Eldridge was really working at it, and he was sure she would be "theatrically successful." Still, he thought "things don't look too hot for the Philadelphia opening." Clurman, in Hammett's view, was not pressing hard enough, although Hellman was more concerned about Clurman than Hammett was. On February 24, Hammett wrote Maggie that Joan Stanley, who had preceded Joan Lorring, was making Sophie "cute and not much else," and Keith-Johnson was "making a droop out of General Griggs." Perhaps this is why Clurman spent so much time with Eldridge and Keith-Johnson. Later in the rehearsal period Hammett changed his mind about Clurman: "Without going so far as to call him a great director, I think he's done well with the play, better, I dare say, than Lillian could have done if she'd directed it." At precisely this point, Hellman and Kermit Bloomgarden had a talk with the cast. Bloomgarden said he could book another week—maybe in Boston. All of the cast said yes; Clurman said no. Wyatt thought the director had another show coming up and that he could not stand working with Hellman any longer. The cast said, "Please, Harold." "No, you're all just fine. I think we'd all just get stale."

So the play was taken directly to New York City. "There should have been at least another week with the play, with the new cast member to sort the whole thing out," says Wyatt. Wyatt started fussing about Clurman's direction. He had directed her in the Clifford Odets play *Night Music*. She had never done any work for the Group Theatre and was a bit intimidated. "The first thing Harold said to me was, 'Now look, we know you can act; we know you can laugh, you can cry, so don't try to do anything.' Well, you've no idea how much courage that gave me." She loved working with Clurman and Elia Kazan in *Night Music* and felt she had been given a chance to shine in her role. When she was given the script for *The Autumn Garden*, she found it hard to read. The Nina Denery part was short, and the character's first entrance was just awful. When Wyatt walked out on the stage, there was Hellman, who the actress had never met before. Hellman was absolutely convinced that Wyatt was right for the role. The actress said, "Harold, if I do this play, it means leaving my husband and family. I don't really feel right for it, and it's such a hard part. You have to promise that you're really going to look after me and help." "Oh Jane, of course," was Clurman's soothing reply. In fact, Wyatt complains, he was of no help at all.

> He spent the entire time directing Florence Eldridge and Colin Keith-Johnson. We'd all sit around there, hour after hour, while he'd work on scenes between Eldridge and Keith-Johnson. Clurman never got to me. We finally got to Philadelphia, and I burst into tears on the stage and said, "Harold, I don't know what's the matter with you. You've let me down. I feel like a sore thumb. I hate myself. I'm embarrassed, and you've never said a goddam thing to me!"

It was a big deal, and everyone was all over Wyatt calming her down. She did not know what to do with the first scene, when Nick and Nina Denery enter. "Nina stands there for *hours and hours and hours*. And nothing to do. Nowhere to go, nowhere to sit down, nowhere to stand up. You don't know who the heck she is. It's a brute of a scene," explains Wyatt.

Then Hellman took over and started to direct some of the scenes. She gave Wyatt confidence, although Wyatt remembers that some of her direction was rather inept. She would say, "Well Jane, that first entrance isn't too bad. What you do is you go forward two steps, and you go over here maybe, and then maybe you. . . . " Wyatt did not think that helped much. Yet Hellman gave her courage, and gave her notes on the character and the situation in which Nina Denery found herself. Hellman was responsive to the frustrated actress, commenting, "Yes, Jane, that is bad. Let's change it." Later, Clurman came backstage to tell Wyatt how pleased he was with the development of her role. "That's because Lillian and I have been working on it," she told him. He was shocked, but Wyatt reminded him that he had been of no help at all. With Hellman's assistance and the time to settle down, Wyatt finally felt good about her role. She has fond memories of the playwright and of being invited out to Hardscrabble Farm.

Virginia Bloomgarden still remembers her own distress over Brooks Atkinson's opening-night review in *The New York Times*

(March 18, 1951), with the last line describing *The Autumn Garden* as "boneless and torpid." Telford Taylor, a good friend of Fredric and Florence March, remembers this opening night and others as being devoid of the emotionalism usually associated with Broadway productions. Hellman in particular, would take the reviews—good and bad—with the face of an old Roman. There were never any tears shed. She might indulge in jibes at the critics (well, you can't expect any better from that son of a bitch") and in a little horse play, but the predominant pose she adopted was one of the stiff upper lip. In general, the reviews were disappointing—not negative, but not as enthusiastic about what Hellman's friends thought might be one of her biggest hits. Even Harold Clurman, in *The New Republic* (March 26, 1951), faulted Hellman for a certain lack of humanity.

> The author is just with her characters; she sees them with a certain smiling asperity, an astringent, almost cruel, clarity. But she is unable to reveal in their weakness that which still makes them part of what is blessed and great in life. . . . Hellman is a fine artist; she will be a finer one when she melts.

Wyatt sensed a similar ungiving strain in the playwright's reading of human nature. Eldridge, on the other hand, thought her character, Rose Griggs, was a very silly woman who Hellman had humanized—so much so that people often told the actress how deeply sorry they felt for the character she played.

Several reviewers were impressed with what the *Time* (March 19, 1951) critic called the "vividly drawn and brilliantly differentiated" characters. Characters, rather than plot, dominated the play, and this was a welcome if startling development for critics who had spent years deriding Hellman's melodramas. In the *New Yorker* (March 17, 1951), Wolcott Gibbs suggested the playwright was mellowing, making her points "slowly and gently." There was some "pity in her attitude toward the species of man." Yet he complained of the "theatrical exaggeration in the drawing of all the people in the play. The old lady is too witty, the artist too objectionable, the drunk too wise, and the general too tired and spiritual to be completely convincing."

Virginia Bloomgarden took the lukewarm reception of *The Autumn Garden* very hard. The play ran for 102 performances—barely qualifying it as a "hit." Hellman would have none of Bloomgarden's tears, although she was impressed that Bloomgarden, at twenty-nine, should care so deeply about the middle-aged characters in the play. Bloomgarden was moved by the speech Hammett had written for General Griggs and by the tragedy of these characters who had waited for something "big" to happen in their lives. Of opening night, Hammett wrote Maggie Kober on March 11 that the cast seemed "very good" to him and Hellman, but that was because they had been so awful at the preview performances the previous two nights. In actuality, on opening night, they were giving "an adequate but mediocre performance." He was writing from Hardscrabble, where "Madame and I came up yesterday." Hellman was upstairs with a heating pad against her back. She had fallen on the cellar steps that afternoon. Hammett did not think much damage had been done.

In March and April, Hellman busied herself about the farm. There was a brief excursion to Boston for a talk at Wellesley, dinners, a concert, and a radio broadcast in New York. By mid-April, Hammett had been entrusted with his new granddaughter, Ann. He wrote Maggie Kober that Hellman was "quite nuts about her." He was invited to a conference in Paris, and Hellman was put out with him because he refused to go. "Madame has a firm belief that one should go almost anywhere for almost any purpose if it's free, and of course she's been trying to get me to France for years," he wrote Kober. Sun, "springness," and his granddaughter seemed to invigorate Hammett. Hellman was getting to be even more of a nuisance about Ann. She demanded to know whether people thought Ann was beautiful. They had better think so, Hammett commented, if they were going "to stay off her son-of-a-bitch list." When the proper words of praise for this most beautiful child were spoken, Hellman would look at Hammett in confirmation of her own opinion. He suspected that Hellman was "boring a great many people." Hellman also took to writing Ann's mother, Jo Marshall, about this "wonderful baby." Hellman liked Ann, she told Marshall, because she was so "calm and pleasant and at peace with the world. You give me great pleasure by allowing her to come." Hellman was looking forward to Marshall's visit. Hellman recalled that Jo was not much older than Ann when they first met at the Hollywood Knickerbocker Hotel. "You were three, and I'd like to think I was about fifteen. But I guess I wasn't." To Jo, Hellman confided that Hammett seemed younger now than when she first met him. He was "one of the few people in the world who has grown more interesting in time." Hellman wanted to know if there was anything Marshall particularly wanted to do on her visit. This was the gracious, loving Hellman at her best.

As Hellman suggests in her memoirs, she and Hammett took great delight in nature, and his letters to Maggie Kober during this period are filled with observations about robins and chickadees, flowers and insects. He was waiting for the summer birds. The "year-rounders are busy with new spring-stuff in the woods: business will pick up in a couple of weeks." On May 1, they were expecting the delivery of one of Zilboorg's black poodle puppies. He and Hellman seemed—albeit momentarily—at peace with the world.

As busy as she was with the play, and as domesticated as life seemed with Hammett, Hellman had not forgotten John Melby. In February, she had seen him for lunch in Washington and confided to him how much Hammett had changed from his drinking days. Melby had remarried, but this did not seem to upset Hellman. They had so much to talk about—her play, his travels, politics. They both detested HUAC, the stupid charges that the State Department people had "lost China," and the increasing search for scapegoats. The previous August, Melby had been promoted to Foreign Service Officer Class II, and a brilliant career seemed ahead of him. He was not aware that his security status was already in question, and that he and Hellman would soon become part of the scapegoating phenomenon they deplored. She sent Melby an inscribed copy of *The Autumn Garden*: "For John as always and as before. Lillian, May 1951."

That same month, Hellman took on a brief assignment for the University of Michigan. For the past few years, Professor Roy Cowden of the University of Michigan had invited the playwright to read student dramas for the prestigious Hopwood Awards. Arthur Miller, Norman Rosten, John Ciardi and other important writers had won Hopwood prizes as undergraduates and gone on to distinguished careers. It was common practice to invite notable authors to judge the annual competition.

Professor Cowden wrote identical letters to all judges of the contest, explaining that they would be expected "to read not more than half a dozen manuscripts" in each of the major and minor categories. It was a heavy load. He was careful to point out the very tight schedule to which judges would have to adhere. They had to read the plays, rank them, and return them within two weeks. In the previous year, Hellman had begged off with her admittedly strange excuse that reading other people's plays upset her so much she could not concentrate on her own. But for the 1950–1951 competition, Cowden received a letter from Edith Kean stating that Hellman had just finished her play and would be pleased to read for Cowden.

On May 3, 1951, Cowden sent manuscripts by express mail. All material was to be returned to him "express collect" no later than May 18. There were six plays in the major category but only two plays in the minor one. "If you think neither is worthy of a prize, I hope you will say so," advised Cowden. By May 11, he had sent a note to Clifford Odets, thanking him for his prompt report and return of the manuscripts. On May 18, Hellman's manuscripts had not arrived. In response to a telegram from Cowden Hellman wired on May 22 that she could not meet his deadline. She still had three manuscripts to read and wanted to know if she should proceed. By May 23 she had made progress but thought the plays were a bad lot, and she objected to the tight schedule that required her to read eight manuscripts and to his telegram urging her to complete her work. Cowden did not receive the manuscripts until May 30, at which time she reiterated her poor opinion of the plays. They revealed no talent, and she saw no potential in any of the manuscripts. She realized she sounded harsh, but it was her practice not to encourage writers who showed no aptitude. Her suggestion was to reserve the awards for another year. She was surprised at the pressure put on her by Cowden's telegrams. Having made a living as a professional reader, she took her job seriously, which meant reading slowly and carefully. She would never have taken on the task if she had known she would have only two weeks.

Of course, Cowden was obliged to thank her for reading the manuscripts and to point out that he had clearly indicated the time limits in his letter of invitation. He even enclosed a copy of the original for her. He made no other comment on the way she had told him his business. Clifford Odets had in fact written Cowden with a similar opinion of the plays. He had been up all night reading them, and although he was not enthusiastic, he conscientiously ranked the plays. He found a play in the minor category deserving of praise and an award.

At the beginning of July, four Communists convicted under the Smith Act jumped bail. Hammett was not surprised when three FBI agents showed up at Hardscrabble, since he was listed as an officer of the bail fund. Acting on information from a confidential source, "whose reliability was not determined," the agents set up a road block at the intersection of the road leading to the farm. Both Hellman and Hammett were interviewed and denied knowing the fugitives or where they might be found. Hellman invited the agents to have a look around the premises. The results, as reported in her file, were "negative," and the surveillance of her farm was discontinued.

Diane Johnson adds that "Lillian was coldly polite, drove them around in her car, insisting they look everywhere, that they talk with the farmer, Gus Benson, and his wife and go up in the attic." For Hellman it was "horrible to realize they had been denounced by neighbors, perhaps someone quite close by." This kind of "detective" work must have seemed to Hammett sillier than anything he had ever written for pulp magazines like *Black Mask*. The FBI seemed incapable of ratiocination—how could it do better when it spoke only the language of crime reports, where Lillian Hellman's married name was sometimes listed as an "alias"?

Are you now or have you ever been a member of the Communist Party? This question would be the Cold War's refrain. Under the Smith Act, which became law in 1940, aliens could be deported for activities considered un-American or subversive. The law became a handy tool for convicting alleged Communists, many of whom had come to the United States from Europe. By July 9, 1951 Hammett was in court refusing to testify about his role in putting up bail for the Communist fugitives. He would not reveal the names of hundreds of people who had contributed to a bail fund for the convicted. In fact, Hammett, a trustee of the Congress, did not know the names of the contributors, but he refused to say even that much to a grand jury, because he felt this would be cooperating with a system that used the Smith Act to persecute people not for their disloyalty, but for their unpopular opinions.

Hammett would soon be put in prison and serve a six-month jail term. After his arrest, bail was put at one hundred thousand dollars. Diane Johnson gives a detailed account of Hellman's frantic efforts to raise this large sum. She was successful because several good friends came through for her, but then the judge decided not to accept bail. The ordeal unnerved her. She cried not only for

Hammett but for the friends who had made sacrifices for his release.

Hammett's attorney delivered a note to Hellman. She was to get out of the country—to take one of those European trips she liked so much. Hammett did not need, at this late date, any proof of her love. On July 13, Hellman wrote what must have been one of the most galling letters of her life to Mrs. Shipley at the passport office, requesting a passport so that she could work on a film adaptation of *A Doll's House* for Hoche Productions of Paris. It was a most distinguished play, and she needed the work and the money. She might also be able to direct the London production of *The Autumn Garden*. "Most certainly I do not intend, and shall not, take part in any political activity of any kind," she assured Mrs. Shipley.

Hellman could no longer avoid knowing that she was considered a subversive. She had been blacklisted in Hollywood and visited at her farm by the FBI. She denied emphatically to Shipley that she was a Communist or a member of the Communist Party, although she admitted her association with many "left wing organizations." Some of her activities may have been "foolish," she said, but she had never been disloyal or unpatriotic. She was not actively engaged in politics, although her name might still appear "on the rolls of some organizations."

Hellman felt she had to demonstrate her loyalty. So she summarized for Shipley her role as cultural ambassador to the Soviet Union. She noted that Averell Harriman felt her trip had been "the most useful in the making of good relations of any foreigner who had been to Moscow." As an American delegate to the UNESCO meeting on a Theater Institute she had acted "with sense and discretion, and in the best interests of my country." J. B. Priestley, she believed, would testify in support of her claim and that her arrival had ensured the participation of several prominent European playwrights. She found it "sad" to have to boast about her accomplishments and to affirm her loyalty as a "rather old-fashioned patriot." In other times, such words would not have to be written, "because they are implicit in the person and are too good to be flaunted about." She also gave John Melby as a reference, and contacted Melby to warn him that Shipley might call. One of Shipley's staff did phone him, asking about the Moscow trip and if Melby had any reason to suppose that Hellman was a Communist. Melby said that he had seen no evidence of it, and three weeks later Hellman got her passport.

It was extraordinary that Hellman should write in this way about herself. But she was desperate to get away, and Hammett knew that traveling might be her salvation. In his diary for August 3, 1951, Arthur Kober gave some indication of just how grim things were for Hellman. He wished he could be of more help, but his wife was dying. He was anxious to be free of his own burdens. "I have enormous guilt about Lil who feels I've let her down. Guilt, because I have. I guess." She sailed on August 7 for England. She sent him a postcard from London indicating that nothing had come of her plans. Presumably, she was referring to the adaptation of *A Doll's House* or the directing of *The Autumn Garden*. She would write him again soon, she said, but she had had a difficult week and was very tired.

On September 8, she wrote to Jo Marshall from Claridge's, reiterating what she had told Kober and complaining that "nothing goes right." She was "tired and nervous and worried." Not doing the filmscript for *A Doll's House* was a big disappointment, for she was terribly worried about money. She had had "no direct word" from Hammett. The three weeks before she had left for Europe were the "worst" in her life. She was not even "grateful for the loss of six pounds. So many things happened so quickly and all of them went with such bad luck." Yet Hammett's messages to Jo were "fine and cheerful. He is most certainly a man of great inner dignity and courage, and I only hope he feels as cheerful as he sounds. If you have had any news, will you write to me? Write to me anyway and tell me how you are."

On September 19, 1951, during a HUAC hearing, screenwriter Martin Berkeley named Hellman as one of several persons present at an organizational meeting of the Hollywood Communist Party in June 1937 at Berkeley's house. Philip Dunne remembers Berkeley as an unstable character who did not have the respect of his colleagues. He passed himself off as a friend of Hammett's, although there is no evidence to support his claim. Ring Lardner, Jr., who had been at the meeting in question, is certain that Hellman had not attended. In *Scoundrel Time*, Hellman recalls that Hammett told her that she and Berkeley might have been at the same luncheon party once, but that that was the extent of their association. Berkeley's charge, however, was enough to bring her to the attention of HUAC. When she was questioned, it was established that she was in Hollywood at the time of Berkeley's meeting, but that was all.

By the end of September, John Melby had received an interrogatory from the State Department Security Office. This was a list of questions directed at officers whose loyalty or security was suspect. Melby was in shock, for he had gone from one success to another. The first three questions, moreover, had to do with Hellman. How well did he know her, and what were her political beliefs? Melby gave candid answers about their relationship—he knew of her left-wing activities, but he did not consider them subversive. Other questions probed Melby's politics and relationships with other people.

Melby wrote to Hellman telling her about the questions, and she replied, asking if she could be of help. He could think of nothing at the moment. Near the end of November, however, he was hit with a supplemental interrogatory informing him that the Security Board was aware of his visit to Pleasantville in the spring of 1950. He was to explain that trip. Now Melby was worried, for he had told no one about his Pleasantville excursion. Was Hellman's phone tapped? he wondered. He was impressed with government intelligence, and for the first time contemplated the notion that Hellman actually might have been a Communist. There would have to be a meeting between them in Washington. He had expected to be branded as one of those State Department officials who had "lost China." Now it seemed that his whole career was to hinge on his affair with Lillian Hellman. Neither of them could quite believe it. He thought it was none of the government's business to inquire about their intimacy, and decided not to embarrass Hellman. However, he would later have to amend his interrogatory to admit that the visit was more than "social."

Hellman remained active in public affairs. On December 1, she participated in a Harvard Law School symposium about the state of serious American drama. Along with Richard Rogers and Marc Connelly, she did not give too much weight to the current popularity of musicals; fashions changed quickly in the theater. According to *The New York Times* (December 2), Hellman suggested that there

was nothing wrong with the serious theatre that was not also awry with books, life or other facets of modern life. People under present tensions possibly lacked the "serious desire to think seriously," but this was nothing that had not happened before and would happen again in some later generation, she said.

On December 9, 1951, Dashiell Hammett, in poor health, was released from prison. Four nights later, Hellman had dinner with Arthur Kober and other friends and went to see Henry Fonda in *Point of No Return*. Kober does not mention in his diary if she enjoyed herself, but other entries for December suggest that she was in an awful state. On December 2, she had gotten angry at Kober, berating him for his "derelictions." He was at a loss as to what to do, and thought it might be the end of their friendship. What did she expect of him? he wondered. They were both in tears. It had been a tough year for Kober. His wife Maggie had died that summer. He had written to Sam Marx, saying, "I don't suppose I'll ever meet a sweeter, gentler or braver girl than Maggie in this, the graying portion of my life." It was "some small comfort" to know that she had, "at last, the peace for which she has for so long wanted." At Christmas, Hellman was lavishing gifts on Kober and his daughter Catherine. In summing up 1951, Kober was still troubled by "the fight with Lil, the jailing of Dash."

17

HUAC

Washington/New York/
Cambridge/Washington
(1952)

I cannot and will not cut my conscience to fit this year's fashions, even though I long ago came to the conclusion that I was not a political person and could have no comfortable place in any political group.

     —Lillian Hellman, letter to HUAC, May 19, 1952

In mid-February, John Melby and his new wife were Lillian Hellman's guests for the opening of *The Autumn Garden* in Washington. Melby and Hellman met twice to discuss his security investigation. They anticipated that she would be called before Congress and questioned about her past. Hellman was fearful that this witch-hunting period would last a long, long time. She was having trouble getting assignments; no new play was in the works. Always one to make a story better, in *Scoundrel Time* she puts her selling of Hardscrabble Farm in 1952, after her testimony before HUAC. Actually, the farm was gone by the end of 1951. She knew her idyll in Pleasantville was over.

On February 21, Hellman was served with a subpoena. She wanted to avoid testifying about her period in Moscow, for then she would have to talk about John Melby and also Averell Harriman, who had plans for a presidential campaign. She did not want to do anything that would jeopardize the men's reputations. The smear tactics of McCarthy could compromise Harriman's hopes. In the first draft of *Scoundrel Time*, Hellman tried to tell this part of her Cold War story, but she later wrote Melby that she could not figure out how to include him. As a rule, it had been her practice not to write about friends who were still alive, and perhaps this is why she carefully avoided explaining her relationships with Melby and Harriman. The result, however, makes the issue of "naming names" the centerpiece of *Scoundrel Time*, and the very personal story of her efforts to protect men she loved and respected is untold. What makes her stand even more compelling now is that she was shielding not only her associates in radical politics but also members of the very foreign policy establishment she was accused of subverting.

In other ways, *Scoundrel Time* misrepresents the significance and the human drama involved in testifying before Congress. Hellman was hardly the first witness to insist that she would talk freely about herself but would not identify other associates when questioned about her political activities and affiliations. Joseph Rauh, Hellman's attorney, did see unique aspects in her case. Having met Hellman at one or two social events in late 1951, he did not know her well when she first came to him with her subpoena. She came to Rauh with Abe Fortas's (later a Supreme Court justice) notion about taking a moral position, but in fact, Rauh suggests, the position they adopted turned out to be quite different.

> You see, she was different from Arthur Miller. He just was not going to tell them what the hell the names of other people were. If he went to jail, so be it. She walked in the door with a little different story: "I am not going to jail." Now apparently that resulted from a conversation she had had the night before with Dashiell Hammett. He told her she was not the kind of person who could survive prison. He knew. He'd been there. She made four conditions which, when put together, seemed impossible: first, she wasn't going to jail; second, she wasn't going to name names; third, she didn't want to plead the fifth amendment; fourth, she wanted to tell all about herself. That would have been a good law school exam. Had she gotten on the stand and told about herself, she would have

waived her privilege against self-incrimination. Then she would have had to answer about others or go to jail.

They decided she was going to say she was not now a member of the Communist party, and "we'd let her go a year or two back" in her testimony. Then she was going to plead the fifth amendment, which she would be willing to give up if HUAC agreed not to ask her about others. At first, Rauh's strategy was to have her write a letter to be distributed at a press conference after the hearing, explaining what she had done. Then he realized that that would be an "anticlimax. Let's do it right in the middle of the goddam hearing and blow the thing up." It was a dramatic scene worthy of a playwright. So they wrote a letter to Chairman Wood outlining their position. Most of the writing was Rauh's, but the ringing phrases were hers. Rauh remembers telling Hellman, "The test of whether we win or lose depends on the newspaper headlines. Will they print 'Lillian Hellman Stands on Conscience, Won't Name Other People,' or 'Lillian Hellman Pleads Fifth Amendment'?"

Although Hellman gave Rauh a very difficult legal problem to solve, he felt comfortable defending her because he was sure that she had never been under Communist party discipline, even though she had stated in an early draft of her HUAC letter that she was a Communist party member between 1938 and 1940. In *Scoundrel Time*, Hellman states that she was never a party member but that she attended several party meetings and that it would not have mattered to her whether she signed a party card. These are probably the same meetings she had in mind when she told Melby she had attended Marxist study groups in the late 1930s. From Kober's diaries, Ralph Ingersoll's recollections (as conveyed to his biographer Roy Hoopes and to Hilary Mills), and from her position on the Soviet invasion of Finland, it is clear that Hellman moved leftward toward the party between 1935 and 1940, without ever quite relinquishing her independence. Nowhere in *Scoundrel Time* is she forthcoming about this radical development in her thinking. Rauh himself had forgotten her admission of Communist party membership and was surprised by it when he recently examined his papers, now on deposit with the Library of Congress.

In Rauh's papers, there are two drafts of Hellman's HUAC letter—both of which are different from the one released to the press. The rough drafts make a fascinating study, for they reveal that at no point could Hellman bear to reveal why she had become a radical. The earliest draft (dated April 1952) contains many of the same phrases found in the final version—although she had not yet formulated her most memorable language. Her position was expressed negatively; that is, she explained what she felt government should not do: compel a citizen "to hand over his conscience." She refused to do that and would not make herself "today's cheap favorite by doing so." In her second paragraph, she admitted Communist party membership but hastened to say she was a "most inactive member" and witnessed no more than discussions of Marxism and current events. After approximately two years she left the party in 1940, and she was never encouraged or pressured to rejoin. The rest of this early draft was long winded and rambled on about her trip to the Soviet Union, her participation in Popular Front causes, and her efforts on behalf of the Progressive party. The last two paragraphs were a verbose version of her remarkably compressed language in the published letter.

The second draft was more conciliatory. Hellman admitted she joined the party in 1938 without thinking about the "serious step" she was taking. She supposed she was motivated by her "experience in Loyalist Spain the year before." She stated that she had acted without "any real information about the nature of the Party," and she thought "its ultimate aims were humanitarian and idealistic." She admitted she was "wrong." She did not balk at saying so, and she felt no "bitterness towards the misguided lady who asked me to join." She finessed the issue of the Hitler-Stalin pact. She believed the Soviet Union had become disillusioned after Munich in 1938, and she was sympathetic to its alliance with Nazi Germany. But she was in total disagreement with the Communist party's "glorification of Nazism" and noted that *Watch on the Rhine* was written at "the height of Nazi-Soviet collaboration." After World War II, she continued to support the Soviet Union because she had seen how devastated it had been by war and could not bring herself to believe "Russians would ever again want war." Now she was not certain how to judge Soviet actions.

If these letters were written to appease Joe Rauh, who insisted Hellman must give a straight account of her political past, they were not successful. In a letter to Hellman dated 30 April, 1952, Rauh noted the second draft would not serve as a "public vindication." Her statement seemed "too cavalier." The public considered "Communist membership and Communist activities extremely serious steps." There was no point in confessing party membership if she could not categorically admit she was wrong and give reasons why she was wrong. Her letter was "so little critical of the Communist movement in America that it will be generally considered an acceptance of it." He did not want to offend her, but he was obliged to point out that her statement of Communist affiliation was "likely to be compared by unfriendly sources to a lady retiring from the Republican party because she is tired of politics, although she still thinks Bob Taft [the leader of Conservative Republicans] is a dear sweet thing." In effect, Hellman was equating "membership in the Communist Party with membership in a ladies' literary society or 'good works' club," Rauh wrote Hellman. In his view, Hellman sounded naive:

> When you say that you drifted away from the Communist Party because you seemed to be in the wrong place, doesn't it have a certain air of getting into Schubert's when you wanted to be at the Majestic? When you refer to the Communists as people who were going your way, don't you just confirm what the House Committee is setting out to prove about you?

Rauh knew that the "implications" he was drawing were not true, yet that is surely how hostile readers of her statement would react. He suspected she was unwilling to take a stronger stand criticizing her involvement with Communists for fear that she would be regarded as buckling under to public pressure to recant her radical past. He shrewdly pointed out that she "should no more refrain from saying things for that reason than you should actually say them because you were in fact afraid of public opinion."

Whatever else Hellman may have done, her willingness to produce *Watch on the Rhine* during the pact period convinced Rauh of her independence, and his reading of her character suggested she had never been under "anyone's discipline." Her beautifully crafted final draft of the letter wisely left out specific mention of party membership and stood on her moral principles. Attorney and client continued to have deep disagreements, however. Rauh was the leader of the ADA, and he was strongly anti-Communist:

> We used to argue, and I'd say, "But Lillian, as a woman who believes in freedom, how can you feel that we

shouldn't criticize the Communists?" The difference between us was that I felt that since the Communists did not believe in freedom, it was the duty of those who did to be critical. She said, "When the Communists are being unfairly treated, and you admit they are [he agreed that their rights were not adequately protected], then I'm not going to add to the attack." This was sort of Thoreau type of argument. If honest men are in jail, the place of all honest men is in jail. Her point seemed to be that if the Communists were being unjustly criticized, she was not going to justly criticize them. We thought enough of each other to narrow our disagreement to that extent.

Rauh was ably assisted by Daniel Pollitt, now a professor of law at the University of North Carolina. Rauh and Pollitt had become specialists in representing labor unions and in dealing with HUAC—primarily because so many other law firms were reluctant to take loyalty and security cases. When Rauh hired him, he pointed out to Pollitt that in the competition for prestigious positions, there were always many well-qualified people. In such a field of impressive aspirants for jobs like attorney general, the fact that Pollitt worked for Joe Rauh would probably be held against him.

Pollitt spent 80 percent of his time dealing with various Congressional committees investigating people under suspicion. There were many ambiguities in the law, and Pollitt puzzled over exactly when a client could plead the fifth amendment. It was easy to waive the privilege of the fifth amendment once a witness began answering questions, but it was also difficult to claim it. Pollitt wrote a fairly lengthy memorandum on the subject. Whatever troubles Hellman had with money, she was a paying client, and it was a good idea to thoroughly research the fifth amendment issue while they had a client who could afford to pay them for it.

HUAC was a vicious committee. Many of the labor clients Rauh and Pollitt represented had been subpoenaed. Inevitably, HUAC would make a drama out of asking witnesses to name people they knew were members of the Communist party. Well, everybody in the labor movement knew Communists, and many labor officials had been active in Communist front organizations. Pollitt remembers a HUAC committee member pointed out to one labor official that it had come to HUAC's attention that there were six former card-carrying Communists involved in his union's strike against the Singer Sewing Machine Company. He said, "Well, it may be a surprise to your Committee, but I can think off hand of about sixty."

Pollitt spent about four days trying to decide whether Lillian Hellman had done something illegal, so that she could honorably plead the fifth amendment. She had provided Pollitt with a statement of all of her political activities that might have prompted the HUAC subpoena. Obviously, Pollitt was trying to forecast the questions the committee would ask her. He thinks he might have been anticipating later Supreme Court rulings by focusing on anything in her background that might make a link in a chain of evidence that could be used against her.

In *Scoundrel Time*, Hellman does a brilliant job of evoking the nerve-wracking weeks before her HUAC appearance. She had dinner with Clifford Odets, who blustered about showing HUAC his courage as a "radical man." Like Elia Kazan, he had lost his nerve and finked on his friends. Hellman knew herself well enough not to engage in any false heroics. It was all she could do just to keep calm. She was on the phone several times to Melby.

Before leaving for Washington, where she was to testify on May 21, Hellman called Harry and Elena Levin in Cambridge and asked if she could spend the evening with them. It was very short notice, but they were happy to have her. Levin remembers that she first came to Harvard University sometime in the late 1940s at the invitation of Louis Lyons, curator of the Niemann Foundation, who used to arrange "weekly colloquies between his group of visiting newspapermen and some distinguished person from the great world outside. One or two faculty members known to be interested in that person's field were also invited," and that is how Harry Levin met Hellman. Levin, Irving Babbitt Professor of Comparative Literature Emeritus, remembers that "it was still uncommon to hear women holding forth at Harvard in those bad old days; but she met that tough-minded audience of reporters on their own ground, and her straight talk made a sharp impression on us all." It was Levin's understanding that she later beat the reporters in a game of poker. Soon Hellman was friends with both Harry and Elena, and she took a warm interest in watching their daughter grow up. Harry would make trips to New York, where he and Hellman would have dinner and go to the theater. The couple spent a few summers living in a cottage at Vineyard Haven next door to Hellman that she found for them. Other summers they took a cottage in Chilmark or stayed at Cape Cod and visited her often at Martha's Vineyard.

Just days before her testimony before HUAC, the Levins spent a very animated evening with Hellman talking politics. Politics were very much on their minds because of the HUAC hearings. Elena had come to America from Russia at the age of twenty-two with her sisters and brother and old nurse. They had been brought over through an American friend of her late father's. A member of the liberal gentry, Elena's mother was executed as a Social Revolutionary by the Bolshevik regime. Elena's uncle had been Minister of Justice in Kerensky's government, and her grandfather had been Minister of Justice for the Czar and had introduced Alexander II's program of judicial reform. She remembers seeing "very much eye to eye" with Hellman. Hellman, in Elena's words, was "quite anti-Communist, but liberal-left. It was a very sympathetic, congenial conversation. But she did not tell us a word about her testimony in Washington." In fact, they did not know that she was scheduled to testify until they read about it in the newspapers. When Elena saw Hellman again, she said "It's amazing. You just didn't give us a hint of what you were about to do." There had been no indication of nervousness or concern from Hellman. Elena admired her behavior. "She probably needed somebody who was detached from the whole thing. . . . She just wanted to compose herself. It was the beginning of our real friendship."

In Washington on May 16, Hellman helped John Melby with his case before the Loyalty Board. This may have been when they exchanged the letters they had sent to each other. Hellman did not want to be in the position of surrendering Melby's letters to any investigating committee. She also engaged in some desultory shopping, went to the zoo, called Hammett, and finally bought herself an expensive dress. It was probably the best thing she could do, treating herself to a luxury she was convinced she would no longer be able to afford. On May 21, she faced her ordeal.

Hellman heightens the tension in *Scoundrel Time* by reporting a last-minute call to Joe Rauh from Thurman Arnold (at one time assistant attorney general and then Abe Fortas's law partner). Arnold had told Rauh that he was making a "martyr" of Hellman. In *Scoundrel Time*, Rauh is shown as having second thoughts while Hellman stubbornly sticks to their original approach, telling him she cannot make "quick turns." She instructs Rauh to call Arnold back, thank him for his advice, but to stay the course. To William Wright, Rauh denied consulting Arnold. He would not have asked for advice, and Arnold would not have volunteered it. Rauh has to be believed on this point; he was never one to back down or to change course suddenly. He certainly would not have changed his legal strategy at the last minute or upset a client by suggesting a new tack hours before a hearing. By then he had already shown enormous courage and resourcefulness in confronting Congressional committees. Although Hellman is approving of Rauh in *Scoundrel Time,* he does not escape the regrettable tendency in her memoirs to denigrate others to the benefit of herself. Hellman is clear, however, about how helpful her attorney was in preparing her psychologically for the hearing. Rauh knew how easy it was to make mistakes under the strain. If she sensed herself weakening, he could arrange for one break for her to go to the ladies' room. His other piece of advice was not to make jokes—it was a bad reaction, "a kind of embarrassment" witnesses experienced when they were insulted by the committee.

Lillian Hellman has often been praised for her fortitude in confronting the committee. She stood by her principles. This was an act of civil courage. It was also a supremely brave thing for any human being to do. You take a taxi cab to the House Office Building and walk up a flight of maybe thirty steps. Then you enter the rotunda. You wait for an elevator, but there's a crowd there. So it is simpler to walk up the marble circular stairway holding onto the solid brass handrail. Then you enter the Caucus room. Maybe you are five minutes early, and the committee is ten minutes late. The waiting period. People are buzzing behind you. Nobody comes up and shakes you by the hand. Ever since you entered the room, photographers' flash bulbs have been exploding in your face and continue to do so throughout your testimony. Your lawyer objects about the lights bearing down on you. Pollitt never knew anyone who was not nervous under such circumstances. Some of the tough union bosses might have looked composed, but they had been hardened by years of adversarial situations. Pollitt himself never got used to it. He was always nervous.

The press would be there—maybe twenty or thirty reporters sitting across from the witness table along one wall of the room. Then there would be row after row of seats behind the witness, occupied by an audience of perhaps five or six hundred that was

usually hostile. It was a huge room—the size of a football field—
with perhaps a hundred-foot ceiling and two massive chandeliers.
Hellman was lucky to have such a feisty, experienced pair of
attorneys representing her. Organizations having conventions in
Washington would organize excursions to the HUAC hearing; it
was their "un-American Activities Day," as Pollitt puts it. During
one of Rauh's appearances before the Senate Internal Security
Subcommittee, the bell rang for a roll call, and the subcommittee
members adjourned for a vote. The International Ladies Garment
Workers Union was visiting, and the woman in charge asked Rauh
to give a talk about what they were witnessing. He got up and
said, "This lousy committee is trying to undermine democracy
right here in the halls of Congress." A couple of senators drifted
back into the room as Rauh was taking questions.

Another time, Rauh worked out a deal with HUAC that there
would be no pictures of a witness who was called to testify on his
daughter's graduation day. The witness did not want his appearance on the six o'clock news spoiling his daughter's prom. When
Rauh's witness was called, the photographers' lights were on.
According to Pollitt, "Joe said, 'wait a minute, wait a minute. The
deal is no lights, no cameras.' The committee counsel said, 'Well,
that's while they're testifying, not while they're walking up here.'
Joe said, 'I'll be goddamned,' and walked over to the wall socket
and pulled out the plug." No lights.

Hellman was seated at a table approximately twenty feet from
the podium, what she called a "raised platform," like a stage. It
was a forbidding set-up, with the congressmen in position to look
down on her as she was sworn in. There were a few preliminary
questions. To one reporter, the forty-six-year-old witness looked
"trim figured" in her "close-fitting black hat and . . . tailored
brown-and-black checked silk dress." She "clenched a handker-
chief in clasped hands as she testified," but consulted Rauh only
once. As the committee zeroed in on Martin Berkeley's allegations,
Rauh instructed his client to mention her letter. Hellman expressed
her willingness to discuss Berkeley's testimony and her desire to
refer them to her letter. "To be fair to myself I think I have worked
very hard over this letter, and most seriously. I would like to ask
you once again to reconsider what I have said in the letter." This
was the playwright's master stroke. She was earnest; she was
appealing to a sense of fair play. Committee counsel Frank Tavener
replied: "In other words, you are asking the committee not to ask

you any questions regarding the participation of other persons in the Communist Party activities?" He had jumped to a conclusion, and Hellman shot back: "I don't think I said that, Mr. Tavener." She could not have made a cagier reply. The ground had completely shifted in her favor. The committee had to deal with her letter, to "clarify the record," as Chairman Wood put it. This, in turn, gave Rauh his opening. With the press eager to learn more about the letter, Rauh directed Pollitt to pass around copies. The chairman objected, but Rauh told Pollitt, "go ahead." Pollitt is sure he is embellishing his memory, but he seems to recall the sergeant-at-arms being directed to throw him out of the room. No such exchange is recorded in the official proceedings, but Hellman is surely right in *Scoundrel Time* that the transcript did not record all that was said.

As the committee grilled her about membership in the Communist party, she realized that her refusal to answer their questions made it seem as if she was hiding the truth. Neither Rauh nor Pollitt remembers what for Hellman was the most dramatic moment of all: when she heard someone from the press gallery say, "Thank God somebody finally had the guts to do it." Hellman presumed the statement was in reference to her letter. There is no question that this is what she wanted to hear, and Rauh and Pollitt provide no reason for disbelieving her, except that Rauh believes that Hellman's flair for the dramatic probably got the best of her. Rauh and Pollitt, who knew the letter was victory enough for them, had no need of an instantly gratifying reaction from the press. Hellman did. And she could not resist adding that when the press gallery voice was greeted by Chairman Wood's threat to remove the press from the room, the voice answered. "You do that, sir." The polite but steely rejoinder sounds just like the way Hellman would write the scene for a play.

The cunning of Hellman's position resided in her letter to HUAC, in which she made them appear as if they were preventing her from testifying about herself due to legal provisions in the fifth amendment—the provision being that once she testified about herself she would have to testify about others or be cited for contempt. Her letter made her seem entirely reasonable. She was a lay person bewildered by the law, a person of conviction and conscience who only wanted to do the right thing. Even better, there was the letter itself, smack in the middle of the official transcript of the hearing. She could have her uninterrupted say.

Unlike the Hollywood Ten, she did not tell the committee to go to hell—although in *Scoundrel Time* and in later interviews, she says that was exactly what she would have dearly loved to do. She was not smug or self-righteous—at least not in the letter or in her testimony. As in all of her communications with Mrs. Shipley at the passport office, Hellman presented herself as a dissenter who respected authority. It would have been very hard to send this principled woman to jail. If *Time* (June 2) is to be believed, her sex had something to do with her escape from HUAC's dragnet: "After she had been excused, Chairman Wood said gallantly: 'Why cite her for contempt? After all, she's a woman. . . .' "

In retrospect, of course, Hellman's victory over HUAC is not so surprising, but at the time, neither Rauh nor his client could be sure how the questioning would go, how Hellman would stand up under the pressure, or how her testimony would be reported in the press. HUAC was clumsy. Much time was spent determining her whereabouts in 1937—just so that Martin Berkeley's testimony that she attended a Communist party meeting could seem plausible if not provable. What if she had been asked point blank whether she had supported the pact? What if she had been asked about Hammett and their attendance at Marxist study groups? And what if—as Hellman had dreaded—her Moscow period was explored in detail? She was most fortunate that HUAC was obsessed with the Martin Berkeley "friendly-witness" approach to interrogation. Like the FBI, HUAC relied on informants, so-called experts because they were ex-Communists. Consequently, investigators developed no sense at all of Lillian Hellman's complex fellow-traveling politics. Senate committees, Pollitt points out, were much rougher on witnesses who took the fifth amendment: "You mean to tell me that an honest answer would tend to incriminate you? Have you ever engaged in espionage against the United States?" Each subsequent question would make the witness look even worse.

After the hearing, Rauh rushed Hellman out and entrusted her to Pollitt, who took her out for a drink. They had won, and Rauh did not want the committee to have time to reconsider. He was right. The next day, in *The New York Times*, the focus was not on her invocation of the fifth amendment but on her statement of conscience. In *Scoundrel Time*, Hellman recalls with pleasure that Murray Kempton wrote an article about her in the *New York Post* (May 22, 1951) entitled "Portrait of a Lady." Precisely so. She had set a standard of correct behavior that few would want to challenge.

Pollitt remembers being joined after the hearing by John Melby. It was a kind of rescue, since Pollitt was without the funds to pay for Hellman's drinks. In *Scoundrel Time*, Hellman says Pollitt is referring to a meeting a few weeks before the hearing, that Melby (she calls him a State Department official) did not join them after the HUAC testimony. But Melby confirms Pollitt's memory. According to Hellman, Rauh came along later, kissed her, patted Pollitt on the shoulder a few times, ordered sandwiches, and announced, "Well, we did it."

Pollitt thought Hellman had a "crush" on Rauh:

> Every time we would get in a taxi cab, she'd put her hand on his thigh. He would cross his legs. He probably was aware of it, embarrassed, and decided to put it out of his mind. After the hearing she said to Joe, "Let's go and have a drink," and he said, "Dan will go in with you, and I'll check the phones and be with you shortly." Well, I thought that he didn't come because the job was over and he didn't want to get involved in her celebrations.

Rauh says he never thought about Hellman in sexual terms. "Maybe [because] I'm happily married. I don't know. But the number of stories I have heard about her sex life are rather incredible to me." A few years later, Hellman would broach the idea of a more intimate relationship with another of her attorneys.

To this day, Rauh chuckles over how much has been made of Hellman's "moral victory" over HUAC. "The fact is, she did have to plead the fifth amendment. There was no way out of it, given the conditions she put up." He never thought she would go to jail, given his legal strategy. "She could have gone to jail if she had talked about herself, not pleaded the fifth amendment, then refused to answer about others." Arthur Miller's first-amendment argument was much more moral, as far as Rauh is concerned. He has fond memories of Hellman; she was a good client and became a good friend. Her letters to him later were lyrical and full of praise. But he cannot accept the image of her as a heroine, a leader of "the moral forces."

Since the appearance of William Luce's play, *Lillian*, based on

Hellman's memoirs, Rauh has been asked whether her version of the hearings is accurate.

> I would say it is Lillian's dramatization of it. I don't want to say anything that throws doubt on her veracity. . . . It was pretty exciting. Even if I had told the story in a pedestrian way, it would still be pretty exciting. But when she got done with it, it was better than a Babe Ruth home run.

LILLIAN HELLMAN

Howard Meyer remembers his young girlfriend: "She was never a beauty, but she had a beautiful figure. One of her tales, when she was working for Liveright, concerned an editor who wanted her to read a manuscript, and she was just an office girl who probably had made her brightness apparent. A second editor asked, 'Why in hell do you want Lillian to read it?' 'Because she has a beautiful figure,' the first editor replied."

State Historical Society of Wisconsin

Performing Arts Research Center, The New York Public Library at Lincoln Center

ARTHUR KOBER

Arthur was charming and good-looking and full of promise. This snappy and energetic man could carry Hellman along on his good spirits without overwhelming her, for he was also "shy and sensitive"—always "a sweet man," according to many of his friends. *Wisconsin Center for Film and Theater Research*

LILLIAN HELLMAN

Hellman even frightened her fellow writers because she was so aggressive, "so powerful in her speech—saying nuts" to the movie producers, as Albert Hackett remembers so well. "She was somebody wonderful to have on your side, but then you were afraid she'd go too far," he concludes.

HAMMETT'S PRINCETON HOUSE

The final draft of *Days to Come* was written at
90 Cleveland Lane in Princeton, New Jersey,
where Hammett had rented a Colonial-style, five
bay, three floor, seventeen-room house in the
fall of 1936. Isolated near the end of a street that
had few dwellings on it, it seemed the ideal
place to get away from New York and
Hollywood, to sober up, to work on a new
novel, and to be near Lillian as she readied *Days
to Come* for its Broadway opening in mid-
December.

This was a woman known for her
outspokenness and yet at the same time was
very feminine. "What she did for me really was
to make a man out of me, no quarrels about
it," said John Melby. (Melby's Chinese visa
photograph with his "Shanghai haircut.")
Courtesy of John Melby

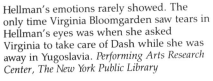

Hellman's emotions rarely showed. The
only time Virginia Bloomgarden saw tears in
Hellman's eyes was when she asked
Virginia to take care of Dash while she was
away in Yugoslavia. *Performing Arts Research
Center, The New York Public Library*

The famous photo of Dashiell Hammett arriving in Hollywood.
Springer/Bettmann Film Archive

Hellman was living in a beautiful large house up on a hill. Randall Smith began to "hang out with her." He was very impressed with the big Cadillac she allowed him to drive. She had plenty of money, so they could have dinner wherever they wanted. She dressed extremely well, though he noticed clothes did not hang well on a body with broad shoulders, large breasts, narrow hips, and no bottom "that amounted to anything." But she was always elegantly neat. *USC Special Collections, Hearst Newspaper Collection*

Courtesy of Randall Smith

ARTHUR AND MAGGIE KOBER

It had been a tough year for Kober. Maggie had died that summer. He had written to Sam Marx, saying "I don't suppose I'll ever meet a sweeter, gentler or braver girl than Maggie in this, the graying portion of my life." It was "some small comfort" to know that she had, "at last, the peace which she has for so long wanted." At Christmas, Hellman was lavishing gifts on Kober and his daughter Catherine. *Wisconsin Center for Film and Theater Research*

While in Rome in 1953, Hellman met Stephen Greene, a painter and recent winner of a prix d'Rome, in *Scoundrel Time,* she pictures herself as very lonely and isolated during her European trip. "She was not *alone,*" Stephen Greene emphasizes. *Courtesy of Stephen Greene*

Dashiell Hammett testifying before the Senate Committee, March 1953. *UPI/Bettmann Newsphotos*

LILLIAN HELLMAN

"She'd say whatever came into her head. Many things struck her funny, and she was very funny."
She was "girlish," recalls William Alfred. *Theatre Collection, Museum of the City of New York*

Virginia and Kermit Bloomgarden with Hellman. Bloomgarden's actress wife, Virginia, found Hellman to be a tough, formidable person unwilling to concede much to others. Hellman seemed to resent Virginia's presence, yet she respected the young actress's political work at the Stage Door Canteen and her acting talent. *Courtesy of Virginia Bloomgarden Chilewich*

Arthur Cowan and Tally Richards

Cowan had been a boxer during his Harvard Law School days and was proud of his still trim body, which he liked to show off at the beach. *Courtesy of Tally Richards*

ARTHUR COWAN IN HIS CHERISHED LIBRARY
Courtesy of Tally Richards

Stephen Greene took this photo of Hellman at Martha's Vineyard in
1955. *Courtesy of Stephen Greene*

LILLIAN HELLMAN, LEONARD BERNSTEIN, TYRONE GUTHRIE

Hellman thought up the idea of getting Tyrone Guthrie as director for *Candide*. She hoped he would be a good disciplinarian for all the collaborators. She thought he looked so much like Charles de Gaulle that he would come in and behave like a general "to us troops." *The Bettmann Archive, Inc.*

Fishing relaxed Hellman. "When she fished she wasn't so angry," said Jack Koontz, one of her fishing companions. *Courtesy of Louis Zetzel*

By 1940, Hellman had become worried about her drinking, but she was reluctant to think of herself as an alcoholic. "Do you ever have a drink before you go out to a party?" her psychiatrist, Gregory Zilboorg, asked. "Oh yes, I always do," she replied. "Then you are an alcoholic," he concluded.

Nora Ephron, Lillian Hellman, Carl Bernstein, and Bob Woodward arrive for the benefit premiere of *All the President's Men*. *UPI/Bettmann Archive*

LILLIAN HELLMAN: PUBLIC FIGURE
UPI/Bettman Archive

18

THE AFTERMATH
Philadelphia/New York/Washington
(1952–1953)

Here is the master flaw on which the whole loyalty-security
program broke down, the assumption contrary to the
whole spirit of English Common Law: because of the
overriding needs of state security, informants must be
protected, and the right of someone accused . . . to confront the purveyor of charges face to face, to cross-examine
that person, challenge his credibility, examine his accuracy
record—these Common Law rights no longer count.

—Robert Newman, *Cold War Romance:*
Lillian Hellman and John Melby

We are more keenly aware of the implications of the play
[*The Children's Hour*] today because slander is now a common factor in the life of the nation, accepted by many
reputable people as an evil necessary to a search for
genuine traitors.

—*The New York Times*, Review of the revival of *The Children's Hour*,
December 19, 1952

On April 4, 1952, six weeks before her HUAC appearance,
Hellman conferred with John Melby in Philadelphia, where
he was attending a meeting of the World Affairs Council. They
had dinner, took a stroll, and had a nightcap at her hotel—all duly
noted by the FBI agent assigned to follow them. The next day,

they again had dinner and went up to her room for a drink. They wondered how much HUAC knew about their relationship. Hellman was worried about being cited for contempt of Congress. The intensity of their times together resulted in a resumption of lovemaking. Melby did not leave until the next morning, when Hellman was to return to New York and he to Washington.

They did not see each other again until June, when Melby stopped by Hellman's apartment in New York for lunch. Neither of them had any new information, and Melby thought it was unlikely she would be asked to appear at his hearing. He still was not in a position to know how seriously his relationship with Hellman had jeopardized his career, but his continuing involvement with her testified to both his affection and his refusal to be intimidated. For her part, Hellman was prepared to testify if need be.

June 26, 1952. 10:00 A.M. Room 210, New State Building. State Department Loyalty Security Board meeting. Melby's record as a diplomat was unassailable; it was Lillian Hellman who had gotten him into trouble. Throughout his hearing and subsequent appeals, the board could never understand why Melby had continued to see Hellman after their affair in Moscow. Since she was a Communist, or at least a fellow traveler, it was their view that a foreign service officer should have refused all contact with her. The impressive evidence mustered by Melby's counsel proved beyond doubt that he was an extraordinarily effective diplomat of unquestioned integrity, but this did not count. Neither did Melby's pointing out that Hellman had never had the slightest interest in the details of his work. Of course, they had talked politics, but she had never asked him to betray a confidence and he had never volunteered any sort of information that might be considered a government secret.

The board could not believe that Melby was not aware of her Communist affiliations, even though he testified that no one to his knowledge had ever called her a Communist. He knew, certainly, that she was a leftist, perhaps even a fellow traveler in the 1930s, but he denied knowledge of the links the FBI had purportedly established between Hellman and figures like Gerhard Eisler, who had fled the country to avoid jail on a passport fraud charge. In fact, the FBI's information was flimsy—unsubstantiated gossip about Hellman's having hosted a dinner for Eisler.

To the board, Melby sounded too naive to be truthful. He was a sophisticated diplomat; surely he had sense enough to know Hellman's views were Marxist. In his testimony, Melby made clear that he did not think she was a political person or had much interest in political philosophy or the details of political life. She had so described herself in her HUAC letter. Her communism, if that is what it was, was sentimental and temperamental. He put it best when he said:

> She was very sympathetic to the Russian people and what was going on in the war. I think that that emotional reaction led her to condone things for the Russians that she would not condone for her own country. And I think that her horror at war led her to attribute better motives to the future of Russian foreign policy in terms of peace and war than I would have, and I think better motives than she would now.

But the board was exercised about Hellman's HUAC testimony. As far as they were concerned, she was a fifth-amendment Communist. Melby pointed out that Rauh had advised her not to go back more than three years in her answers to HUAC questions about Communist party membership. To go back any further would have compelled her to answer all questions, and her refusal to do so would have invited a contempt citation. So the erroneous impression was created that she had stopped answering questions because the committee was nearing the period in the past when she had been a party member. No one has ever said it better than did John Melby. Lillian Hellman had a double standard that she was loathe to acknowledge publicly, and that she would apologize for ever so slightly in *Scoundrel Time*. But the board was not convinced because they had ex-Communist Louis Budenz's statement from the FBI that Hellman had been a secret member of the party in 1950. Since Melby had no access to FBI files, he could not effectively combat the board's inference. He was disturbed by the insinuations that the board had evidence of which he was unaware, and he began to wonder whether Hellman had told him enough about her past. Yet, as Robert Newman observes, Melby showed absolutely no contrition over his relationship with Lillian Hellman.

Subsequent hearings covered much of the same ground, as if the board was waiting for Melby's breakdown. Over the next several months Melby worked diligently to clear his name. None of his appeals was successful, and he was never able to resume his foreign service career. When Hellman and Melby met with Joe Rauh on July 2 and July 12, Rauh was upset to hear that Melby's whole case centered on Hellman. She was angry. Hellman did not even know Gerhard Eisler, so she certainly had not hosted a dinner for him, and she was not a party organizer for front groups. There would be two more meetings with Rauh, on September 22 and December 27–28. Melby had a new attorney who was considering having Hellman testify. She was naturally concerned about how much she would have to say; she would rather not talk about the romance, and Rauh thought there were ways to minimize that kind of testimony. At the final meeting of the year, she seemed ready to appear before the board if deemed necessary by Melby's attorney. Then, as Robert Newman points out, Melby made a critical mistake: he accompanied Hellman to the plane she was taking back to New York. The transcript of a later State Department hearing is marked with an exclamation mark next to Melby's admission: "I drove her out to the airport."

With so much discussion of "secret informants," it is no wonder that Hellman decided to do a revival of *The Childrens' Hour*. The play seemed prophetic. It was about a whole world that had been infected by evil—a world that reacted childishly to allegations that the moral order had been subverted. The consequences of informing and character assassination became the central theme of *The Children's Hour* in an era that reacted in horror to the very idea of Communists, just as Mrs. Tilford responds in disgust to the very notion that Karen and Martha are lesbians. It was as if the order of things was contaminated. Associating with the unclean, as John Melby would find out, meant that one's own moral sense had been corrupted—or so it seemed to many of society's representatives.

Hellman knew the play had faults and considered rewriting parts of it. In the end, she did little more than change a few lines that seemed too "literary," improve the motivation of certain characters, and change some entrances and exits that seemed slightly awkward in the original. She hoped to effect the biggest improvement in the play by directing it herself. She was determined not to repeat the mistakes that had made *Montserrat* a disaster. She would get to know her actors better. Pat Neal would play Martha, and Hellman adored her. Kim Hunter was cast as Karen; the playwright took her out to lunch. Hunter remembers that it went very well. "We talked about how each of us worked. It was then that she said, 'I can count the directors I have faith in on one hand,' " The honored few were not available. A good choice would have been Elia Kazan, but since he had disgraced himself before HUAC, Hellman would not have him. Hellman was aware of her own limitations, and she confided to Hunter:

> On *Montserrat*, idiot that I was, I thought I could go in there and somehow talk actor's language. I don't know what actor's language is! All I managed to do was screw myself up and screw them up. I didn't understand what I was saying. None of that foolishness for this production. I am going to talk in my own language, and if you don't understand what I'm saying, if it makes no sense in terms of the actor's needs, then we'll sit down and talk it out.

Hunter thought Hellman was marvelous, a no-nonsense person with a surprising, cockeyed sense of humor. "It was unexpected and would sort of pop out at you. I also found her a very warm person. Even when she was still, you could tell there was something bubbling there below the surface. There was nothing cowlike about Lillian." First meeting Hellman was rather intimidating, but that went away. Hunter felt they had a built-in advantage because Hellman knew the play worked. The playwright was not in a vulnerable position as director. The rapport between Hellman and Neal also helped to break down any strangeness Hunter might have felt about working with "this lion in our theater community."

Hunter warned the playwright that she tended to work very slowly. "As long as we're talking about how we all work, I better get that off my chest right now, too. Things don't happen like that with me. Gradually I sort of mush into the play, the situation, the relationships, the character—everything." Hellman said, "Good to know, good to know."

Before rehearsals, Hellman had a gathering of the cast at her New York home. She explained why it was her intention to direct her own play. Naturally, she was pleased with the success Herman Shumlin had made of *The Children's Hour*. However, she did not think Herman had really understood her play. She talked about the original reviews. They said the first act was very exciting, the second act was marvelous, and in the third act the play just sort of disappeared. She said, "If I can accomplish what I am setting out to do in this production, the reviews will read quite differently. They will say the first act is very slow, the second act is lovely, and the third act is the play." Shumlin had been so intrigued with the child, Mary, that he had made the play be about the liar, Hellman told them. "It's not about the liar," she said, "it's about the lie. If I can get the reviews to say that, then it will be my play. Bless Herman, but he didn't do right by me."

In rehearsal, Hellman could not seem to help herself.

> ROLLYSON: After you told her about your working slowly, did it make a difference in the way she treated you?
> HUNTER: To a certain extent . . . No, no. We do what we do.

Hellman would get caught up in external things. Because Hunter was still struggling with how she would handle her part, she would fuss with her hair. Hellman would say, "A New England schoolteacher would never do that!" To calm Hellman down, Hunter would try not to do things with her hands. In the end, Hunter knew her gestures would fall into place when the part was mastered. She was still at an early stage in putting her performance together—talking, listening to what was going on, and not trying to give a complete characterization. But she was getting so bogged down with the detailed instructions the director was throwing at her—the Shumlin approach without Shumlin's tact—that one day Hunter said, "Lillian, this afternoon can you just not talk to me at all? I want to use the rehearsal all just for me. Just ignore what I'm doing, and then tomorrow, talk to me all you want. I have a task I have set for myself." That was fine with Hellman. At the end of the day, Hellman said to Hunter, "Well, I don't know what your task was that you set for yourself, but what you ended up doing was what I've been talking about all the time." Of course, Hunter knew her director was right, but Hellman's method of directing had distracted Hunter from the main point of the rehearsal.

For all of her problems with Hellman, Hunter is firm in calling her a "bloody good director." The actress remembers, in particular, Hellman's handling of the scene after Martha has shot herself. It was hard for Hunter not to cry. Hellman told her, "You must not cry. You must not. Even if it is only the first few rows that see the tears, they will not think about what is happening. They will watch the tears. *Please,* never cry." This was a tough request, says Hunter. "When you're trying not to cry is the time you cry. It was a fight for me the entire run. Of course, she was right. And I knew it; [she was] absolutely right." The crucial scene for the play, however, was the second-act confrontation between Mrs. Tilford (Katherine Emmet) and the two women, supported by Karen's fiancé Joe Cardin. (Robert Pastene). If that went well, the whole play went well. The emotional intensity had to be held at a peak throughout the scene; any letdown of feeling ruined what was to come.

Iris Mann, the bright adolescent actress who played Mary, impressed Hellman. Hellman would talk to her as though she were a full-fledged adult. Mann would then get up on stage and not be able to do what Hellman had just explained to her. Finally, the director realized that she was talking to Mann as if the girl had the experience of an adult, which of course she did not. According to Hunter, Hellman realized "She doesn't, *really,* understand emotionally what I'm talking about. Intellectually, she understands, but she cannot translate it into anything she can relate to. I've got to start talking to her as a child." It was very, very hard for Hellman, and the cast sympathized with her problem. Hellman found it a real trial to deal with the other children in the cast as well. Jose Vega, the assistant stage manager, remembers working with Hellman and her having him relay instructions to the kids.

Virginia Bloomgarden, an actress before she married Kermit Bloomgarden, very much wanted to play Karen's part. It was a role she was willing to fight for. It took a lot of complicated negotiations with Hellman to get to understudy Hunter and eventually to replace her in the role a few weeks before the play ended its run. Although Hunter's memories of Hellman are mostly sunny, Bloomgarden remembers a director who was not so kind to Hunter. "I spent an entire afternoon after a run-through performance when Lillian had torn her to pieces. I sat out there dying, and I thought, 'you want to put yourself in the lion's mouth?' " Hellman was trying to correct the balance between Neal and Hunter. Neal was dominating the play like a leading woman. Hellman said derisively to Hunter, "You're not playing Stella!" (Hunter was the original Stella in *Streetcar Named Desire*). "Karen is probably one of the strongest women that's ever been written, even though she's extremely feminine," and that was not coming through, suggests Bloomgarden, who had played Karen the season before in summer stock, with Hellman's permission. Hellman was devastating and Hunter was in tears. Bloomgarden went back stage to Hunter's dressing room and said, "I am really putting myself into the lion's mouth because my husband is the producer. This may not help you a lot, but I think it is important that you have a sense that no matter how demanding Lillian is of you, she's that much more demanding of herself." The other thing to keep in mind, said Bloomgarden, was to weed through the attack for the main line of Hellman's direction. Hellman was insulting, giving Hunter a blanket dismissal and suggesting she could play only one kind of role. From Bloomgarden's standpoint, Hellman was also trying to tell Hunter that she was playing a "character-ingenue," but the director did not know enough to put it that way. All Hellman had to say was that Karen was stronger than Martha. "Why doesn't she know this? She wrote the play," Bloomgarden remembers saying to herself. Jose Vega is under the impression that Hellman talked about replacing Hunter. In a fit of impatience, the director had exclaimed, "Oh she's never going to do it!"

If Virginia Bloomgarden was wary of interfering in the production, she had good reason. She rarely found it easy dealing with Hellman, who held certain grievances against her. Her husband Kermit was absent-minded and often forgot to tell her that they had been invited by Hellman to her country home. She once turned on Virginia and said, "You're very rude." Virginia replied, "What do you mean?" Hellman complained that she had never received notice when they decided not to come to the country. Virginia felt she always had to protect Kermit—"better me than him." The tone of Hellman's reproofs was always, "you really ought to learn better." Kermit's absent-mindedness was legendary. Jose Vega remembers the story of the producer getting into a cab and saying, "Corona, Corona," when he wanted to buy some cigars. And the time when the Bloomgardens were in a cab and Kermit stepped out to get a paper, then immediately hailed another cab, forgetting all about his wife.

Virginia remembers a day in July when she and Kermit were supposed to drive Hellman out to Long Beach to visit Arthur Kober. They were to pick her up at 9:00 A.M. The night before, they stayed up late listening to Adlai Stevenson's acceptance speech at the 1952 Democratic Convention. They overslept by about ten minutes. When they called Hellman, she was furious.

"Did Kermit call her? No, I called her," says Virginia. This was always the case for the wife of a producer who avoided confrontations with his playwright. They drove up to Hellman's building; she was outside tapping her foot. Virginia was driving, with Kermit beside her. He got out of the car and sat in the back. Hellman got in the front seat and immediately went after Virginia. Their lateness was inexcusable. This was a period when Virginia was in therapy. She had asked Hellman's advice about a psychiatrist, and Hellman had discussed with Gregory Zilboorg who Virginia should see. "I said, 'Lillian, I'm sorry. But we did get to bed very late.' " They were going across the Triborough Bridge when Hellman said, "Don't give me any of that. You ought to find out from your analyst why you were late." Then Hellman hit her on the arm. Virginia said, "I don't think this is a subject of discussion for you and me. I'd also appreciate it, since I'm driving, if you wouldn't hit me." Kermit, in the back seat, remained silent.

The Children's Hour premiered on December 18, and most of the reviews vindicated Hellman's direction. A few reviewers repeated the criticism of the third act that had been noted on the play's debut. The reviewer in *Time* (December 29, 1952) saw it exactly as Hellman wished:

> It is in the last act that something at once harsher and more humane begins to blow through the story, and with the very last scene—when the surviving schoolmistress faces an enlightened, remorseful old lady— that the play takes on, emotionally and morally, a sense of the tragic.

Similarly, Henry Hewes, in the *Saturday Review* (January 10, 1953), noted that, "Miss Hellman appears to be less concerned about malicious and irresponsible accusers than she is about the credence given them by 'good' and 'righteous' people." In general, Hellman received high marks as a director, and few critics compared her approach to Shumlin's. Hewes was the exception. He advised her to stop directing her plays: "One relentless and uncompromising Lillian Hellman is enough for any mortal to take in an evening at the theatre."

Although the entire cast was praised, Kim Hunter was often singled out. In the *New York Herald Tribune* (December 19, 1952),

Walter Kerr remarked that hers was "the truest and most moving playing . . . as the teacher who loses both her school and her love before justice is done." In the *New York Post* (December 19, 1952), Richard Watts, Jr., thought, "Miss Hunter gives the finest performance I have seen an actress offer all season." Although many reviewers praised Pat Neal as Martha, some were concerned that she had overplayed her part. "Her work is markedly mannish from the outset, a suggestion which tends to cloud the issue before it can be joined," Kerr suggested. "Miss Neal, as the girl who discovers that there is really abnormality in her, rather gave the secret away in an early scene, but she plays the final episode admirably," concluded Watts. Perhaps Hellman did Neal no favors by aiming all her rehearsal ammunition at Hunter. It is curious that critics noticed Neal telegraphing Martha's lesbian tendencies, for this approach was something Hellman had considered but abandoned in her notes for the play almost twenty years earlier. Kim Hunter does not remember Hellman consciously directing Neal in this manner, although they may have had private conversations to which Hunter was not privy.

The most provocative criticism of the revival came from Eric Bentley in *The New Republic* (January 5, 1953). Several reviews had noted the parallels between the play and McCarthyism that made the production an allegory of the Cold War period. Bentley spelled them out. To be a lesbian was tantamount to being a Communist. For two acts of the play, innocent schoolteachers are under suspicion and then attacked for being lesbians (or Communists). In the third act, the structure of the play and of the allegory break down. Just when the audience is aroused by this fine melodrama of good people assaulted by evil, it learns that Martha is, in fact, a lesbian (Communist). The moral issues are thus confused. Is it a social play about an unjust society, or a psychological play about flaws in human character? The abrupt change in focus creates this either/or dilemma for Bentley.

Apparently, Bentley was far more logical—or more shrewd?—in his reactions to the play in 1952 than his contemporaries. Surely, what the audience identified with was Martha's anguish over realizing she does not know herself as well as she thought. She is so hard on herself because she has been so defiant of the society that has condemned her. Her human tragedy moved people in 1952. They did not react, as Bentley did, by saying, "Aha! You see society had a point. There are perverts (Communists) in our midst." On the contrary, the audience saw the theme of self-knowledge and the theme of social conflict separately. Logically, the two themes are tied together, but one has to set aside one's feelings of identification with Martha to condemn the play as coldly as Bentley does. He was not wrong; indeed, he came to the play with a kind of objectivity that is remarkable. It would be another generation before Arthur Miller, in *After the Fall*, dramatized precisely the contradiction Bentley identified—that of a society that did not know itself and therefore was vulnerable to a campaign of hysteria against communism.

Surely, this question of what he should have known troubled John Melby. The Loyalty and Security Board pounded away at him with the implication that he ought to have realized how tainted a lover and companion Lillian Hellman was. How could he not know? He must be hiding something. How could he be trusted, when he associated with such a subversive person?

Like Martha in the crucial second-act scene of *The Children's Hour*, Hellman would have her chance to confront her accusers. In January 1953, as the reviews of the revival were coming in, Melby's new attorney, John Volpe, was arguing that Hellman should be allowed to testify before the board. In her own person, Volpe contended, she could demonstrate that there was no reason for Melby to suspect that she was "a dangerous person." Volpe wanted to summon other honorable and respectable people—Averell Harriman, Louis Kronenberger, and Mrs. Christian Herter—all of whom had known Hellman for years and had been "entertained in her home . . . spent weekends at her farm." They were not the kind of people who would befriend a secret party member—which is how the board now seemed to view Hellman after her HUAC testimony.

The board agreed to listen to Hellman, provided she limit herself to testimony bearing directly on Melby's case. They did not want to give her the opportunity to clear herself of all of the charges in her FBI file and in her HUAC hearing. With Rauh's counsel, she wrote a letter on February 2, similar to the one sent to HUAC, which again had the effect of getting her uninterrupted point of view into the record. She began the letter by noting she had wanted to speak on Melby's behalf all along and had been "puzzled" that she had not been previously called on to do so. Her involvement in politics was as a writer and dramatist trying to work for peace. She emphatically denied that she had done anything "disloyal or subversive," and she was at a loss as to how Melby's association with her "could possibly cast any doubts" on his career. In fact, she "most strongly resented any suggestion that such could be the case." As with HUAC, she was ready to answer all questions about herself, but it must be understood that her coming to the hearing was "in no sense and to no degree" an admission that she was guilty of "any wrongdoing."

Two days later, Hellman was in Mrs. Shipley's passport office. She wanted permission to go abroad to work on a screenplay for Alexander Korda. The playwright was desperately short of money. There had been tremendous legal costs involved in her HUAC case. (She had written to Van Wyck Brooks of "combing lawyers out of my hair.") There were also Hammett's attorneys to pay. And then the IRS had brought judgments against both of them of several hundred thousand dollars which they evidently owed in back taxes. Money from Hollywood had always been a significant source of income, but being blacklisted prevented her recouping her losses. Korda was getting her at a bargain price. At the moment, she seemed unable to write a new play. William Wright suggests that Hellman exaggerates her financial difficulties in *Scoundrel Time*. He cites the profits from the revival of *The Children's Hour*, and she was getting shares as both author and director. This is true, but the play had a run of only six months. "It got lovely reviews and then no business. It was very tight as to whether we could make it at all," Kim Hunter remembers. One night Hellman complained to Howard Bay that Jed Harris had seen the production and not liked one of the sets. Bay replied, "Neither did I. Didn't Kermit tell you that he slashed the budget?" Hunter remembers Bloomgarden addressing his backers and the cast: "I think there is a great audience out there for this production. But I think they can't afford it. Will you all stick together with me?" Everyone took cuts and agreed to two performances on Sundays. The older generation that had seen the play was not coming back; the younger generation did not have the price of tickets. The play did not make money for anyone, but Bloomgarden held things together, saying, "I can't stand the idea that this play won't last the season." In *Fanfare*, Richard Maney reports that the play did not recover its costs.

These were the circumstances in which Lillian Hellman had her meeting with Mrs. Shipley. The passport chief read through the list of Hellman's involvements in leftist organiziations and then surprised her by asking, "Tell me, Miss Hellman, do you think most of the friendly witnesses have been telling the House Un-American Activities Committee the truth?" No, the playwright did not think so. "The kiddies have been playing games on all of you, Mrs. Shipley, and you deserve the tricks they played because you pushed them into it." Shipley did not appear to take offense at this remark. Indeed, she agreed with Hellman that "many of them were lying. They will be punished for it." Hellman did not think so. They would get away with it, and people like Hellman, in the meantime, were having trouble getting work—which was the point of her appearance in Shipley's office. The playwright promised not to engage in any political activities while in Europe.

On February 5, after spending time with Melby's attorney, Hellman sent a follow-up letter to Shipley. She reiterated that she needed to go abroad for her employment. She categorically denied she was a member of the Communist party or that she had any "affiliation with the Communist party of any kind whatsoever." Her life, she insisted, was not political; her friendships were not based on politics. She had always thought of herself as "completely independent" and cited her production of *Watch on the Rhine* during the pact period. She mentioned that the party had often attacked her plays—the most recent instance (which she did not note) was *The Autumn Garden*. She had left the Progressive party when she found herself in "fundamental disagreement" with it. Before her last trip to Europe, she had written a letter to Shipley promising not to engage in political activities and she had kept her word. She did not relish relinquishing any of her rights to speak freely, but the promises to Shipley had been "made in honor, and I will continue to respect them." She closed her letter, "I am, more than I can say here, grateful to you for the courtesy and kindness you have always shown me."

Hellman would eventually get her traveling papers, even though Shipley had no compunction about denying passports to American citizens suspected of subversion. As Robert Newman demonstrates in a thorough analysis of Shipley's actions on Hellman's passport requests, Shipley could not have believed that Hellman was a Communist. The FBI files did not persuade her. The meetings between Shipley and Hellman must have been most impressive. Here were two women who thought very differently, but who could still speak the same language in so far as they both professed great regard for law and authority. It is unlikely that Hellman feigned this attitude. She was no anarchist, no matter how much she might inveigh against the established order. Indeed, she craved order and authority and worried most about the uses to which power was put.

The same day Hellman wrote Shipley, she followed John Melby to Room 1210–H of the State Department building, where he testified in the morning and she in the afternoon. She began by giving her recollection of their meeting and subsequent relationship. In all significant matters, she echoed Melby's own memory. She noted, in passing, that they had political disagreements. She put this in the context of her friendships with conservatives whom she was "very devoted to." There were many people she did not talk politics with, knowing they would not share her convictions. Although she and Melby had been lovers, and had allowed their passion for each other to revive sporadically, she thought of him now as a cherished friend. They were "very devoted to each other and very respectful of one another." Hellman could not have known that these very words would damn Melby in the board's judgment. They were underlined in the transcript of her testimony, and the board took every opportunity to probe the personal feelings of this couple and to indicate that it found their continuing association baffling and unacceptable. Robert Newman's analyses of the board transcripts concludes that in itself Melby's relationship with Hellman was enough to doom his efforts to reverse the board's decision.

On March 26, 1953, Hammett appeared before Joseph McCarthy's Senate subcommittee, which was investigating charges that pro-Communist books were stocked in libraries abroad run by the State Department. Hammett received much rougher treatment than did Hellman. His use of the fifth amendment was attacked, and he was asked whether he had engaged in espionage, whether he wanted to see a Communist government installed here, and so on. For Hellman, it was a very bleak time. In retrospect, John Melby believes it was a time in which he should have acted. The truth was that his hearings had thrown him together with Hellman in such a way that he realized how powerful their feelings still were for each other. At the time, Melby could not give up on his career; for several years he would nurture hopes that somehow the board's decision would be reversed. In the meantime, Hellman was leaving for Europe. After her return, they would see each other intermittently and write infrequently. Yet whenever they met, they could pick up right where they left off. There is in Melby's memories now a tone of lament, almost a cry for what he and Hellman might have made of their lives.

19

ABROAD
Rome/London/Biarritz
(1953)

I can't tell you, particularly since I've been here, how much
I have wanted you to be here, too. It was two years ago
now that we thought of it, and then everything began to
pop. And how many years before that did we think of
being together? The older I grow the more I am haunted by
the need of people doing things at the time they should be
done—and the less I seem to do them.

—Lillian Hellman, undated letter to John Melby

From Rome, Hellman wrote Henry Sigerist about her contract
negotiations with Alexander Korda, which "took much time
and energy. (Hollywood people are babies next to English lawyers)." Her political news was grim. Did he know that *The Children's Hour* had been banned in overseas libraries? Had Sigerist
heard from his good friend Gregory Zilboorg? "He's an absolute
stinker: he owes me a letter and I still don't know if he ever got my
cable from Milan. [Sigerist and Hellman had had a brief, pleasur-
able meeting there]. I think maybe after you have analyzed a
woman you must be good and sick of her."

In July, Hellman wrote to Melby about her sojourn in Europe.
She felt as though she were living in a vacuum, paralyzed. She
saw a few friends, but did not seem to enjoy the company of many
people. Her screenwriting was proceeding slowly. She inquired

about his wife Hilda and craved news of "home life." She asked him to forgive her "disconnected letter." This is the period she writes about in *Scoundrel Time,* when she suspected she was being watched by the CIA and it appeared that she might have to return to America to testify before McCarthy. Hammett gave her advice about how to check up on her spies. In 1960, the CIA would begin intercepting her correspondence to and from the Soviet Union.

While in Rome, Hellman met Stephen Greene, a painter and recent winner of a Prix de Rome. They had mutual friends, and in the spring of 1953 Hellman wrote him that she would be coming to Rome. He called her, and soon they were seeing each other all the time. He remembers that she was "terrified all that summer and extremely vulnerable." Her life had changed so drastically. Hammett's rapidly deteriorating health, the HUAC and State Department hearings, and the ruin of Melby's career were all very disturbing. Greene remembers her talking about Melby; it was obvious to him that she cared very deeply for Melby. She had no doubt that because of her friendship with Melby, he had lost his position.

One of the things Greene found "sort of bewildering" was how much Hellman talked about Hammett in the midst of enumerating her other affairs. It was always "Dash this and Dash that, and intermittently she would also mention how busy she'd been with other men, and how 'Margaret Sullavan got that man away from me,' and so on." Greene remembers once saying, "Lillian, you were married to Arthur Kober for a while. Why did you marry him? You never mention him." She did not know why. "It was the thing to do at the time," she told him. It made no sense to Greene, "particularly for a woman who really prided herself on an absolute clarity of recall." She would say, "Now I know exactly what I said four weeks ago." They would have disagreements on this issue. Greene thought that nothing was ever that clear, and that Hellman's life was no exception. It had its share of ambiguity. He was amused at some of Hellman's declarations: "I don't know anything about romantic love." This was an astonishing statement for a woman always in pursuit of passion, for someone Greene found "warm and compassionate and kind. But when it really came push to shove, she had demons at her all the time." One sign of this was the way she kept changing her mind.

In reading *Scoundrel Time,* Greene disputes the impression given that Hellman had no money. "I swear it's not true." He saw her at least twice a week and her lifestyle was not that of someone who worried about money. "You don't go to Biarritz and rent a place when you're that poor," as Hellman did later that summer. She had money, although "compared to what she had been used to," Greene was certain that it must have seemed to Hellman that she was impoverished.

Greene remembers being with Hellman during the encounter with Sam and Frances Goldwyn described in *Scoundrel Time*. In fact, years later, Greene kidded her about not remembering which part of the cafe they had sat in. It was an embarrassing meeting for Hellman because it was the first time she had met Goldwyn since being blacklisted. She had told Greene that at one time she was one of the highest-paid screenwriters in Hollywood. Sam Goldwyn lived up to all of the amusing stories told about him. Greene can still hear him:

> "Ah, Italy. Oh, Romeo and Juliet! I love it." There was
> a plaster mural on the wall—real junk, pseudoclassical
> Greek. "Just look at that. Look what this country has
> done. If I wasn't so busy, I'd have them take it off the
> wall, crate it, and have it sent back to Hollywood."

Greene talked politics with Hellman. He asked her point blank if she was a Communist. She said no. He asked her if she knew whether Hammett was, and she said she did not know. It was hard for him to believe. How could people be that close and not know? he wondered, yet he realized they had the kind of relationship that did not permit them to pry into each other's privacy. One evening, while talking with her about political commitments, Greene mentioned that someone in his family (now deceased) had been a party member. They were in an apartment that both of them suspected was bugged by the State Department. Lowering her voice, Hellman said that there were certain things that he must never tell anyone, anyone. For the most part, Greene feels that has been profoundly wise advice. "I trust it may be proper to think that Lillian herself used that advice," he concludes.

Greene still remembers Hellman's extraordinary comment about actors: "You know in the nineteenth century, no proper hostess, no proper woman, would let an actor into her sitting room." How a theater person could express such an active dislike of actors was more than Greene could understand. Other Hellman friends in

Rome, Joe and Bobbie Weinstein, who Hellman first met in the late 1930s during her activities on behalf of the Spanish Civil War refugees, were less puzzled by Hellman's attitudes. Bobbie knew from previous productions of Hellman's plays that she only had respect for world-class actors. Very few—Patricia Neal, Maureen Stapleton, Irene Worth—deserved her attention; the rest were just part of the theater crowd, hangers-on.

Bobbie could see how distressed Hellman was over her HUAC experience, yet as always the playwright came out "on top," in her friend's estimation. Hellman was remarkably resilient and carried on a vigorous social life, in spite of her plaintive correspondence. In *Scoundrel Time*, she pictures herself as very lonely and isolated. But she was not *alone*, Stephen Greene emphasizes.

Greene introduced Hellman to William and Rose Styron. The novelist wanted Hellman to have a copy of *Lie Down in Darkness*. She said to Greene, "Don't tell Bill, I don't like the book." Later, when Greene and his wife were back in New York, Hellman told him what a wonderful writer Styron was. She was a great friend, very loyal, and really believed that "everything is clear." And yet in terms of her own actions, life was not that way at all. Another time in Rome, Greene mentioned what a gifted singer Anita Ellis was. Hellman responded, "She can't be anybody if I haven't heard of her." When Hellman got back to New York, she found that Ellis was singing a Kurt Weil concert with Leonard Bernstein at Lincoln Center. Hellman said, "Oh, she's a great, great singer."

Hellman was "totally blank" on the subject of her own contradictions. Greene would discuss it with her. He saw nothing wrong with these inconsistencies—"that's the way most people are"—but she would not give an inch, seeing no discrepancy at all between what she sometimes said and what she actually did. They cared very deeply about each other, and Greene's observations never seemed to disturb her.

On top of all of her other troubles, Hellman was beginning to suspect that Alexander Korda might give her problems with her script, an adaptation of Jessica Mitford's novel, *The Blessing*. He seemed a little too disinterested. This was a shrewd assessment, because shortly it would become apparent that Korda was bankrupt and Hellman would not be getting her money. She wrote to Melby about these concerns, and added that she was "tired of Europe, sick of traveling, and forever sick of not living with somebody I want to be with." She suggested that given the Cold

War–McCarthy atmosphere, Melby probably would find it extremely difficult to get along even if reinstated as a foreign service
officer. In this feeling, she was also prescient, Melby now realizes.
She pointed out that he would have to work with "men less liberal
and less conscientious" than he was. The world was out of whack.
"Nothing fits, nothing at all," she wrote. She signed off very
affectionately, and even made fun of her complaints, saying, "I am
a crotchety old lady today."

By mid-August, Hellman was in Biarritz, trying to finish the
script for Korda. She had gotten sick on the car trip from Rome to
Biarritz. She had been looking forward to an apartment the Wylers
had rented for her, but she wrote to Melby that it had "turned out
to be a real little horror, sitting out over a main trucking road."
She could stand it only one night, and it had cost her plenty to
settle with the landlord. Now she was at the Miramar, "an elegant,
19th century version of Atlantic City." Ten more days ought to be
enough to get her commitment to London Films out of the way.
She sent a similar letter to Stephen Greene, but going into greater
detail about her illness. She thought her physical upset was the
culmination of what she had been feeling in London and Rome.
Much of her anguish stemmed from being just "plain sick." She
had over-analyzed her odd behavior in Rome, her "terrible physical depression and weakness."

From London, Hellman wrote Melby on the day she delivered
the script to Korda. She was pleased with it, although she realized
it needed more work. It was her impression that Max Ophuls, the
director, liked it; Korda hated it. He treated the screenwriter as
though she were an "office boy who should be paid off and
forgotten." According to Hellman, Korda then reversed himself,
telling Ophuls on the phone that he liked the script, without
informing her of his change of mind. She was shaken by this
turnabout, admitting that it did not take much to unnerve her. In
the past, she would have tossed the script at Korda and abandoned
the project. But she was desperate for income. Either she was
"growing old" and fearful of trouble or just resigned to the fact
that she was in no position to stir things up. She wanted to say "to
hell with it all" and was planning to come home soon. As concerned as she was about herself, Hellman did not forget that
Melby's whole career hung in the balance, and she commended
him for having taken his bitter experience "with such good grace

and good nature, so much better than I have taken less important things."

The one highlight of Hellman's trip to England was Stratford, where she saw a "magnificent" *King Lear* with Michael Redgrave. Otherwise, there had been several uncomfortable dinner parties with "very conservative ladies and gentlemen." She had had it with their criticism of cowardly American intellectuals. In response, she was "childishly patriotic" and sounded like the chamber of commerce. This was very like her behavior in the Soviet Union when her foreign friends attacked America. She knew they had a point—she would make it herself in *Scoundrel Time*—but she could not bear to hear it from the English. She admired them for their devotion to liberty and for their reasonableness. Now, "if they could only cook and stop the rain."

By the end of the summer, Hellman and Melby were reunited in New York and at Martha's Vineyard. But they had other concerns and obligations. Melby had to find a job. Hellman was giving Hammett money. She felt she owed it to him, although she resented him for needing it. He was reaching the stage where he could not take care of himself. Yet he had overseen arrangements for the road tour of *The Autumn Garden* while she was away in Europe. Theirs was not a bond she would break, even though he never asked her for help and never expected her to stay with him to the end. Had he felt more beholden to her, she might not have felt so bitter about his dependence.

Toward the end of the year, she wrote her revered friend Sigerist, who was concentrating on several volumes of his life's work, *History of Medicine*. She had come home in October "not wanting to sit around and listen to all that comes after"—especially "an enormous back income tax assessment. Europe began to seem like an old vacation." She was trying to work, but it had been so long since she had tried to write in New York City. Once the writing flowed, the place probably would make no difference. Yet she wanted to get her life "to where it had roots; final roots." Hammett was fine but too thin and, as usual, cheerful. She sent Sigerist her "deep, deep good wishes for the new year."

20

ADAPTATIONS

(1954–1958)

The girl was a lark in the skies of France, high over the heads of her soldiers, singing a wild, crazy song of courage.

—*The Lark*, Hellman's adaptation of *L'Alouette* by John Anouilh

I am not the optimist I once was.

—*Candide*, Hellman's adaptation of Voltaire's satire

Louis Kronenberger knew Hellman needed work, and he arranged for her to edit Chekhov's *Selected Letters* in his Great Letters series for the Farrar, Straus publishing company. Hellman admired Chekhov and his work and was intrigued by the society in which he had matured. Her introduction is lively, and her many turns of phrase suggest a writer having fun with a historical period (1860–1904), not a scholar soberly sizing up its significance:

> Great feudal landlords and princes and upper-class sons were learning the refinements of the West—they admired and envied them at the same time they patriotically rejected them—but they were mixing the good things and tossing them about. No sooner had the aristocracy learned to play a pretty waltz than the new merchant gentry bought the piano from under them. Fine linens were sent off to Holland to be cleaned, but the owner of the linen forgot to bathe.

In these contradictory times, Chekhov developed "a reasoned life" and a "definite outlook." Naturally, what she called his "toughness of mind and spirit" appealed to Hellman. Discussions of his politics must have reminded her of her own plight. She noted that some regarded Chekhov as a "political radical who desired the overthrow of a rotting society."

As with Chekhov, Hellman would have liked to have it said of her as she said of him in her introduction that she was a writer of "deep social ideals and an uncommon sense of social responsibility." She approved of Chekhov's wariness of how Constantin Stanislavsky sentimentalized his plays, for it must have struck a familiar note for Hellman, who was always worried about how her works were oversimplified in production. Chekhov also had his problems with actors, and Hellman doubtless appreciated what she terms his refusal "to deal in the large words of stage palaver." He was a much harder and sturdier moralist than productions of his plays suggested. In her view, he wrote "sharp comedy," satire. And he was an artist of economical means: "He learned, too, that writing for the stage is primarily the technique of paring down." The social Chekhov also attracted her: "He liked pretty women, he liked wine and a party, he kept open house for his friends, he enjoyed music and fishing and bathing and gardening and money and fame." He had taken a daring trip across Siberia—as had Hellman. In sum, he was a figure who she was able to bend to her liking. As usual, she had done a thorough job on his life and career, and her introductions to each phase of his biography make for compelling and informed reading.

To Henry Sigerist, Theodore Roethke, and others, Hellman gave money as her reason for writing adaptations, but it was work for which she had considerable respect—as her 1966 writing class at Yale would learn. Collaboration may not have been as fulfilling as original work, yet it sustained her and provoked her to work quickly and efficiently.

There were meetings with Leonard Bernstein in early 1954 about *Candide*, a project that she had suggested to him in September 1950. At that point, she wrote Theodore Roethke to say that her new project looked "nice." Still, it seemed a crazy thing to do, and she and Bernstein were arguing over who should be their lyricist. She also complained that she was working on "too many things," that people were confiding to her all their troubles, and that she had just gotten over a virus. "I look terrible and I am a dope," she wrote. Finally, the Bernstein-Hellman team settled on lyricist John La Touche. At Martha's Vineyard in the summer of 1954, all three began working on Hellman's book for *Candide*. Kober reported in his diary that on one occasion, La Touche, Bernstein, and Hellman were "testy with each other." Later, La Touche would drop out of the production of *Candide* and be replaced (on Harry Levin's recommendation) by Richard Wilbur.

While work continued intermittently on *Candide*, Hellman decided to devote most of her attention to Jean Anouilh's play, *L'Alouette*. Although the French playwright had concentrated on the religious and political implications of the Joan of Arc story, Hellman perfected a drama about conscience with a surprising amount of humor. *The Lark* is clearly her best adaptation in any form and would long ago have been recognized as one of her finest works had the play been originally hers.

Hellman commissioned several literal translations—first from students at Columbia and then from two students at Harvard, also recommended by Harry Levin. The Harvard team was to get one hundred dollars for fifty pages. When they delivered their translation, she declined to pay them because they had not single-spaced dialogue in play script form. It was a silly controversy, with "ugly words" from both sides. It was an embarrassment to Professor Levin. John Simon, one of the students, would become a drama critic who would blast Hellman's work in print at every opportunity. Hellman was touchy about money and about what she got for her money. She could be very generous but resented even the slightest possibility she had been taken advantage of. She went around telling friends about how one poet and his wife had not paid her back the fifty dollars they had borrowed. She was affronted by a party guest at Lionel and Diana Trilling's apartment who asked to share a limousine Hellman and Mike Nichols had ordered one late, stormy night in New York to take them to their East Side residences. Diana Trilling remembers that Hellman was on the phone the next day, complaining about a triviality that Trilling thought should have been beneath her notice. How much could it have cost Hellman to allow this self-invited traveling companion to use the car for the short distance between where they were dropped and where he was going?

It took Hellman about four months to craft a complete script of *The Lark* that still needed much work. The ending bothered her and there were several efforts to rewrite it. She was struggling to find the right balance between Joan of Arc's gruesome burning at the stake and the basic optimism of her heroine's vision of a renewed France, a renewed world. As usual, the playwright had done her homework. She had studied Joan in historical sources, taken notes on other historical figures, and constructed a chronology of Joan's life. In Hellman's characteristic fashion, many speeches were pared down, others were cut entirely, and a few new lines inserted.

Lillian Hellman's Joan (Julie Harris) is a down-to-earth woman very much like the playwright herself. This means that although Joan has had visions, she does not rhapsodize about them much. An angel appears to her with the injunction to save France from English domination. Joan contends that it is for man to fulfill God's plan through his own actions, not through a passive acquiescence in divine intervention and revelation. Joan does not proselytize; rather, she approaches the dauphin and his supporters in terms of what they should be doing for themselves and for their country. The English are not really her concern at all, except in so far as they prevent the French people from expressing their own identity. She is, in short, a patriot sharply critical of her own country but profoundly loyal. Reviewers did not see the parallel between the dramatist and her heroine. They were not thinking in biographical terms; indeed, they approached the play more as a translation than an adaptation—although Walter Kerr had a sneaking suspicion that Joan was Hellman's own.

Richard Moody has shown that while Hellman "retained the basic pattern of the original," her changes were "incisive" and constituted a considerable improvement over Christopher Fry's English version. Intellectual argument got reduced to the minimum, he notes, and the whole play took on a "biting briskness." He thought it clever of the playwright to suggest religious overtones through Leonard Bernstein's music rather than through words. Where Fry went for the lofty Joan, Hellman opted for the tough peasant:

> FRY: Get thee behind me, foul Satan, and don't tempt
> me again.
> HELLMAN: Go away, you filthy, stinking devil.

In a sharply satirical way, Hellman linked the fascination with the sexual, the subversive, and the religiously fanatical. Joan's basically healthy, straightforward views get perverted when reamed through the obsessions of the religious and political authorities, who are themselves corrupted by desires and concerns they have projected onto Joan:

> JOAN *(to The Promoter):* You've lied, Canon! I am not as educated as you are, but I know the Devil *is* ugly and everything that is beautiful is the work of God. I have no doubts. I know.
>
> THE PROMOTER: You know nothing. Evil has a lovely face when a lovely face is needed. In real life the Devil waits for a soft, sweet night of summer. Then he comes on a gentle wind in the form of a beautiful girl with bare breasts—
>
> CAUCHON *(sharply):* Canon, let us not get mixed up in our private devils.

The looniness of figures like the Promoter (Roger De Koven) must have seemed to Hellman akin to the crazed, almost prurient interests of the investigating committees in her own time. The English, for example, are much concerned with their "intelligence service," which, Warwick (Christopher Plummer) suggests, ought to be able to predict all forms of subversion. For Hellman, this must have been the precursor of the national security state put into business by Truman at the end of the war. As a politician, a kind of English overlord of France, Warwick states he "cannot afford the doctrine of man's individual magnificence." Joan's call to conscience, in other words, must be crushed.

Joan is like Lillian Hellman—and like her Kurt Muller, a vulnerable hero. When the dauphin (Paul Roebling) tells Joan he is afraid of opposing the English, Joan admits her own fears: "I've been in danger every minute of the way, and every minute of the way I was frightened. I don't want to be beaten, I don't want pain, I don't want to die. I am scared." Yet she acts as if she is not afraid; there is no other way but to "go on, go on. And you do go on." Ralph Penner, one of Hellman's students at Yale, remembers words like these that were almost a refrain from his teacher. She was frightened; she did not know what would come next. Yet Penner observes that Hellman seemed in control of herself. Similarly, in Rome in 1953—at perhaps the most single frightening moment of Hellman's life—Bobbie Weinstein observed a terribly scared woman who never let up, who was always there for her friends. Hellman's anxieties would wake her up, and she would smoke all night. She was a restless sleeper. It was Richard Wilbur's impression that she often needed someone like her maid Helen to be near her in the middle of the night to keep her from fears. Smoking soothed her. "Another person less uneasy than she could have got rid of that, but it was impossible to imagine her doing so," Wilbur concludes.

There is no play in which Hellman put more of herself. It was a cry of conscience: "But what I am, I will not denounce. What I have done, I will not deny," Joan maintains. As for her idealism, it is tempered with a recognition of political and psychological realities. Joan obeys her voices because they talk "good sense." She sought to put the silly dauphin on the throne because only through him could she accomplish her hopes for France. It might almost be Lillian Hellman justifying her support of Henry Wallace:

> JOAN (*comes forward, smiling, happy*): Oh, Warwick, I wasn't paying any attention to Charlie. I knew what Charlie was like. I wanted him crowned because I wanted my country back.

Reviews of *The Lark* show that Hellman and Bloomgarden were right in presuming that the perfect actress for Joan was Julie Harris. Harris was an electrifying performer who, in Walter Kerr's words, caught "the precise combination of country-girl naiveté and irresistible boisterousness. . . . There isn't a languid bone in her wired-together body, and she has a voice that would do credit to the noisiest kid on anybody's city-block" (*New York Herald Tribune*, November 18, 1955). In the *Journal American* (November 18, 1955), John McClain noted Harris's "fragile and beguiling sincerity." Harris was twenty-nine when *The Lark* premiered. *Time* featured her in a cover article, and many reviewers suggested that it was she who gave energy to the play. On opening night her fellow actors applauded her. She was supported by a brilliant cast, including Boris Karloff (Cauchon) and Theodore Bikel (Robert De Beauducourt).

The resounding success of *The Lark* came as somewhat of a surprise. In London, the Christopher Fry version had not been particularly successful, and it was doubtful that the Gallic intellectuality of the play would appeal to Broadway audiences. As was the custom for most Hellman plays, rehearsals were awful on the actors and on the director, Joseph Anthony, who had to put up with the playwright's continual interference. He felt she compromised him in front of the actors. She talked about replacing him. But Kermit Bloomgarden was firm, and his wife Virginia remembers *The Lark* as being one production in which he handled Hellman quite well. The playwright was there every day, nudging and badgering everybody. Anthony had the actors doing a kind of mime business at the beginning of the play. When Hellman saw it, she threw it all out. Julie Harris remembers sitting in the orchestra pit with Hellman after a break in the rehearsals. "Why are they so slow? Why don't they know it?" the playwright fretted. Harris had worked in *Montserrat* and knew Hellman well enough to ask, "How long did it take you to write this play?" "Well, six months—a year," Hellman said. "Well, give us three weeks. We only have three weeks," Harris told her. Harris liked and admired Hellman the writer, but she found Hellman "humanly so frail. She was like a child, a willful child. She should have known why actors needed loving and careful treatment. In all her books she talks about how she hated the theater, how she didn't go to see plays anymore, but the theater gave her her life. The theater is why she's famous. And that kind of bitterness—I thought, 'You're just like a little child.' " Harris was dismayed by Hellman's prejudices. "She didn't see things straight."

The irritable, short-tempered personality was associated in Harris's mind with Hellman's drinking. Drinking made Hellman more self-centered. There was no question in Bobbie Weinstein's mind that Hellman's impatience and quick mood changes were heavily influenced by her drinking. Years later, Harris saw Hellman in the hospital after a throat operation. She asked Hellman if she was finally going to quit smoking. Hellman whispered defiantly that she would never stop. She would hide her cigarettes under the pillow if need be. Harris could not see any sense in Hellman's attitude. "You see, there was that willful child. 'I will not stop smoking. It may be killing me. But I will not stop. And they can operate to doomsday, but I will go on smoking.' " Is that sensible? Harris wondered. To Harris, this was also an alcoholic symptom—the inability to control compulsive behavior. The power to reason seemed to be absent.

Although Harris brilliantly executed Hellman's Joan, the actress describes herself and the playwright as being on "opposite islands." Harris was "very much in love with Joan as a saint, not as a political creature." There was one scene in which Harris was on her knees praying to Saint Michael, and Hellman asked, "Do you have to get down on your knees?" Harris said, "Well, when people pray, they pray on their knees." Hellman said, "Oh, I guess so, but I do hate it." John Abbott suggests that perhaps Hellman viewed herself more on God's level. The Catholicism, the whole religious aspect of the play, was distasteful to her. Harris recalls that Hellman and Bloomgarden cut a good hour out of Anouilh's play—especially the arguments between the Inquisitor and the churchman, which Harris found so fascinating. Harris wanted to know why. Bloomgarden and Hellman said, "Oh, the American audience will never go for it." The actress thought it was a cop-out.

The reviewers, on the other hand, were thankful that the drama dispensed with the "towering phrases" usually found in ecclesiastical exercises for the stage. It was a "beautiful, beautiful play," exclaimed John Chapman in the *New York Daily News* (November 18, 1955). He was impressed at how the drama handled two points of view: the story of Joan as a "piece of history" and Joan's own account of her life. The staging admirably captured the double focus, since there was no scenery in the "usual sense. Merely a few levels of steps and platforms, and lights." This allowed the play to range widely in time and space rather than being restricted to a chronological structure. Joan the myth, and Joan the person, were caught in the fluidity of staging that blended past and present. In *The New York Times* (November 18, 1955), Brooks Atkinson noted that very few props were used—"a few benches, a portable throne, a rude stake for the ghastly burning." The addition of a cyclorama on which "shadow designs" were projected identified particular settings or places in Joan's life. It was a magical, dynamic evening in the theater. On November 19, 1955, the *Times* carried an item titled "All Critics Unite in Lauding 'Lark.' "

Hellman continued working on *Candide*, writing to Stephen Greene that it was a "most difficult job . . . a theatrically dangerous project [that] could easily fall on its face." But she enjoyed working with Leonard Bernstein, "a bright and pleasant man." Vittorio De Sica had offered her a film job in Italy but she was committed to finishing the play. An opera version of *Candide* was a rather daring project, and Hellman wrote Greene, "I don't know what the hell I am doing, but pray for me. It could be wonderful and it could be something awful." The "income tax mess cleaned me out," she said, and she was worried about her friends, all of whom seemed to be in some kind of trouble. New York was not a good place to write.

In an "Audition Precis," Hellman vouchsafed what had brought her to *Candide*:

> But few men have ever argued about the wonderful comedy of the book, the dash, the speed, the roaring-river quality that was the mark of the genius who wrote it. To many it is far the greatest satire ever written, hitting out in all directions, enclosing all human nonsense in a never halting rush to the end. It is the greatest piece of slap-dash every written, at the greatest speed.

Candide is Voltaire's naive hero, student of the philosopher Pangloss, who has counseled the young man that this is the best of all possible worlds, that all things are for the best—including war, rape, pillage, earthquakes, and so on. Voltaire's heightened prose mimics the action of his story; that is, adjectives assault a hero who has been flogged by an invading army of Bulgars and has witnessed his teacher being hanged, his good Samaritan Anabaptist drowned, and his beloved Cunegonde violated. Voltaire piles on Candide a series of misfortunes and misadventures, any one of which would be enough to undo a hero's faith in providence. Yet Candide blithely goes one, rarely giving way to pessimism about the absurdity of existence. When he does question the gruesome nature of his fate, he usually is befriended by some fellow sufferer—as is the case during his public humiliation in the auto-da-fé held after the Lisbon earthquake:

> Candide, stunned, stupefied, despairing, bleeding, trembling, said to himself: —If this is the best of all possible worlds, what are the others like? The flogging is not so bad, I was flogged by the Bulgars. But oh my dear Pangloss, greatest of philosophers, was it necessary for me to watch you being hanged, for no reason that I can see? Oh my dear Anabaptist, best of men, was it necessary that you should be drowned in the

port? Oh Miss Cunegonde, pearl of young ladies, was it necessary that you should have your belly slit open?

He was being led away, barely able to stand, lectured, lashed, absolved, and blessed, when an old woman approached and said, —My son, be of good cheer and follow me.

If life is a catalog of disasters in *Candide,* it is also a tribute to the senseless, comical, and somehow energizing human spirit that refuses to acquiesce to one misfortune after another. Voltaire also satirizes romanticism in Candide's ridiculous devotion to Cunegonde, yet the hero's worldwide search for his raped and aging beloved has an enviable doggedness to it. As a human being in search of love, Candide's fate had to interest Hellman almost as much as her own. It would not trouble her at all that Voltaire savages his sentimental characters; after all, this was precisely her attitude in *The Little Foxes* and other plays. Whether she realized it or not, *Candide* was the perfect foil to *The Lark.* Where the earlier adaptation emphasizes there is an order to human existence in spite of the folly of human beings; the latter ridicules the so-called order and dwells on the chaos of human events. Hellman is known for the rigidly controlled designs of her plays, but those designs are really the obverse expression of a personality that takes aim at all targets and that just barely manages to control itself. And this is true of Hellman from her first unpublished play, *The Dear Queen,* to her last work for the stage (another adaptation) *My Mother, My Father and Me.*

In Hellman's book for the musical *Candide,* the swing from optimism to pessimism is more pronounced than in the original. And there is a rather grave expression of wisdom that comes from an awareness of what experience has taught callow youth. "We will not live in beautiful harmony because there is no such thing in this world, nor should there be. We promise only to do our best and live out our lives," Candide contends. At the conclusion of the play, he will not think "noble" any more than will Kurt Muller, who objects to Fanny Farrelly's condescending use of the word in *Watch on the Rhine.* Candide has become, in Hellman's play, a realist, who counsels Cunegonde that they should love each other as they are, not as they would hope themselves to be.

In *The New York Times* (November 18, 1956), Leonard Bernstein pointed out the contemporaneity of *Candide:*

Puritanical snobbery, phony moralism, inquisitorial
attacks on the individual, brave-new-world optimism,
essential superiority—aren't these all charges leveled
against American society by our best thinkers? And
they are also charges made by Voltaire against his own
society.

In the *New York Herald Tribune* (November 25, 1956), Hellman
remarked that she had first read *Candide* when she was "very
young" and had continued to read it every five or six years after
that because of its humor and its "attack on all rigid thinking, on
all isms."

By the summer of 1955, Hellman was working hard on *Candide*
with Leonard Bernstein and Richard Wilbur. She had met the latter
at Harvard in the early 1950s. He had been one of Harry Levin's
students. Hellman and Wilbur hit it off immediately, and he
remembers their talking a great deal about Dashiell Hammett. She
liked Wilbur's translation of Molière's *The Misanthrope* and thought
the poet's style would be appropriate for the lyrics of *Candide*, on
which she had been working with a series of collaborators for
some time. After a few conferences in New York, where Wilbur
submitted a few sample lyrics to Bernstein and Hellman, he began
in 1956 working full time on the show. According to Wilbur's
agent, 83 percent of the lyrics were the poet's. Because of changes
in the story line, a lot of good work by other lyricists (James Agee,
Dorothy Parker, John La Touche) disappeared. Wilbur did extensive revisions and with Bernstein and Hellman thought up several
new numbers. The poet remembers seeing an early version of
Hellman's book for *Candide*. It was not very Voltairian—she did not
have his kind of wit—but it was very funny. Originally, her plan
was to have incidental music, as in *The Lark*. Then, as she talked it
over with Bernstein, the play began to have numbers. It would be
a play with music—not yet a musical comedy or opera. Because
she was working with other writers, Hellman tended to revise the
play scene by scene rather than fully drafting new versions, as was
her custom. Whole scenes were thrown out, and her "book" for
Candide became, in Wilbur's words, the "connective tissue" between the lyrics and music.

At the comic opera stage, collaboration proved difficult for
Hellman and Wilbur because areas of dominance were difficult to
demarcate. Yet Wilbur did not think of them as "clashing egos."

The Little Foxes: Tallulah Bankhead as Regina Giddens

The director Herman Shumlin told Hellman that the flamboyant Bankhead was "wild" about the play, and he thought she would "do fine" if her propensity for staging outrageous scenes could be kept in check. *Free Library of Philadelphia*

The Little Foxes: Regina (Tallulah Bankhead), Mr. Marshall (Lee Baker), Leo Hubbard (Dan Duryea), Ben Hubbard (Charles Dingle), Oscar Hubbard (Carl Benton Reid)

Ben is being ironic when he assures Marshall that the Hubbards are "very close," since they are hardly a loving family. But, in another sense, they *are* "very close" in the way in which they try to outfox each other while making sure that the family, as an economic enterprise, prospers.

The Children's Hour: Dr. Joe Cardin (Robert Keith), Martha Dobie (Ann Revere), *seated,* Mary Tilford (Florence McGee), Karen Wright (Katherine Emmet)

Dr. Joseph Cardin tries to reason with Mary Tilford: "Look, everybody lies all the time . . ." *Theatre Collection, Museum of the City of New York*

These Three: Martha Dobie (Miriam Hopkins), Karen Wright (Merle Oberon), Joe Cardin (Joel McCrea)

It has often been said that Hellman sanitized *The Children's Hour* for the movies and tacked on a happy ending; in fact, she sold Goldwyn and William Wyler on a script that preserved the principal theme of the play—the power of a big lie—and that resolved the story of the love triangle better than the play. *Wisconsin Center for Film and Theater Research*

The camera lingers a moment on Martha in *These Three;* she is disconcerted and a little disappointed—perhaps because she has tried too hard with Joe. *Wisconsin Center for Film and Theater Research*

Watch on the Rhine: Teck de Brancovis (George Coulouris), Kurt Muller (Paul Lukas), David Farrelly (John Lodge), Sara Muller (Mady Christians)

David Farrelly is a much weaker version of his deceased father, a distinguished diplomat; nevertheless, he shows some backbone in his support of Kurt when he is blackmailed by the Romanian nobleman, Teck. *Free Library of Philadelphia*

In *Watch on the Rhine*, Kurt must murder Teck. The lives of Kurt's fellow anti-Fascists cannot be risked by allowing Teck to leave the Farrelly home with information that could be used against them. *Free Library of Philadelphia*

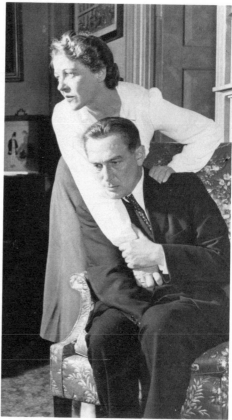

Watch on the Rhine: Sara Muller (Mady Christians), Kurt Muller (Paul Lukas)

In many ways Kurt is a ruined man, a vulnerable hero—as his wife Sara senses when she encourages him at the end of Act Two: "Don't be scared, darling. Don't worry, you'll get home. Yes, you will." *Free Library of Philadelphia*

The North Star: Koyla (Dana Andrews), Karp (Walter Brennan), Damian (Farley Granger), Claudia (Jane Withers), Marina (Anne Baxter)

On June 22, 1941, Germany invades the Soviet Union. Members of a Soviet collective farm, North Star, are hiking to Kiev. Much of the movie is taken up with their efforts to get back to the village once they encounter the invasion forces. *Wisconsin Center for Film and Theater Research*

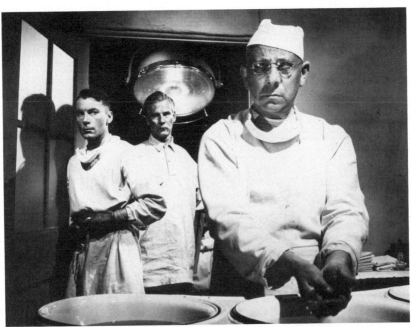

The North Star: Dr. Max Richter (Martin Kosleck), Dr. Kurin (Walter Huston), Dr. Otto von Harden (Eric von Stroheim)

Toward the end of the film, there is an exciting confrontation between a Nazi doctor (Erich von Stroheim) and the Russian Dr. Kurin (Walter Huston). Von Harden is not so much a dedicated Nazi as he is a collaborator, a believer in might makes right. He authorizes the blood transfusions that threaten the lives of the village children. Kurin, a humane, peaceful man, a scientist who has retired to village life, is forced to kill von Harden in a compelling encounter in the hospital. The conflict between von Harden and Kurin is reminiscent of the Teck de Brancovis-Kurt Muller confrontation in *Watch on the Rhine. Wisconsin Center for Film and Theater Research*

The Searching Wind: Alex Hazen (Dennis King), Sam Hazen (Montgomery Clift), Emily Hazen (Cornelia Otis Skinner)

Herman Shumlin remembered Clift's "amazing amount of intensity" in the closing speech of the play, but the actor would balk at the director's insistence that this intensity could be produced during every rehearsal. "I can do it, Herman, I can do it," he'd mutter, and then Herman would shout, "Then do it, goddamn it!"
Museum of the City of New York

The Searching Wind (movie version): Cassie Bowman (Sylvia Sidney), Alex Hazen (Robert Young), Emily Hazen (Ann Richards)
Courtesy of The Academy of Motion Picture Arts and Sciences

Another Part of the Forest: Patricia Neal as Regina Giddens with co-stars Scott McKay and Leo Genn

The only actor in the cast close to Hellman was Patricia Neal, then a very young, beautiful actress in her first major stage role. "With people Hellman liked she was extraordinarily nice. People she just worked with she didn't even see. She would walk in, and there would be people all around her saying hello, and she didn't even hear them," Jose Vega, the play's assistant stage manager, recalls. *Theatre Collection, Museum of the City of New York*

Another Part of the Forest (movie version): Regina Giddens (Ann Blyth), Ben Hubbard (Edmund O'Brien), Marcus Hubbard (Frederic March), Lavinia (Florence Eldridge).

Father and son confront each other in Hellman's post-Civil-War melodrama of family conflict and capitalistic competition.

The Lark: Joan of Arc (Julie Harris)

Harris was on her knees praying to Saint Michael, and Hellman said, "Do you have to get down on your knees?" Harris replied "Well, when people pray, they pray on their knees." Hellman said, "Oh, I guess so, but I do hate it." John Abbott (a member of the *Montserrat* cast) suggests that perhaps Hellman viewed herself more on God's level.

Toys in the Attic: Carrie Berniers (Maureen Stapleton), Julian Berniers (Jason Robards, Jr.), Albertine Prine (Irene Worth), Anna Berniers (Ann Revere)

When Julian arrives at his sisters' home with a wad of cash and his new wife, his sisters no longer have a purpose in life. Julian is no longer their toy.

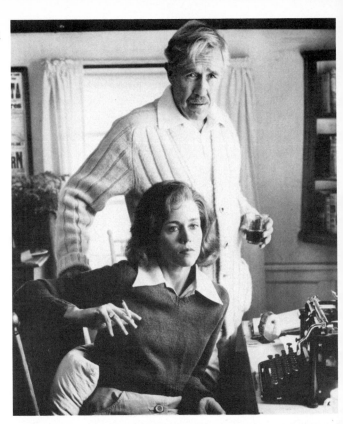

Julia: Jane Fonda as Hellman and Jason Robards as Dashiell Hammett

Julia: Vanessa Redgrave plays the "questionable" Julia and Jane Fonda plays Lillian as Hellman always wanted to look: a curly haired, blue-eyed blonde. *Phototeque*

They were at times "clashing talents," but they got along very well. In matters of the show they never quarreled, and they remained affectionate friends. Bernstein, who had superior experience in the musical theater, was inclined to push that advantage, which made something of a problem for the two writers. Although Wilbur enjoyed working with the composer, and though they had each other's respect, Wilbur does remember that they "chafed each other about a few lyrics," particularly about whether the words or the music should be written first for certain numbers. The poet would write a lyric he thought was best for the show, and the composer would say he had not been able to "set it," asking Wilbur to write something else. Hellman would often, though not always, take the poet's side, agreeing that Bernstein should try again.

It was Hellman's idea to get Tyrone Guthrie as director. She hoped he would be a good disciplinarian for all of the collaborators. She thought he looked so much like Charles De Gaulle that he might come in and behave like a general "to us troops." Actually, in Wilbur's memory, Guthrie did very little commanding.

> Every now and then he would lower the boom on somebody. He once gave me ten minutes in which to knock out some lines for the Lisbon scene, and I found to my surprise that I could do so. And I recall his saying on one occasion, "Now Lenny, you go and write that tune. I know that you weren't trying yesterday to write music. You were, in fact, water-skiing at Piggy Warburg's, weren't you?" Lenny went dutifully off and wrote some excellent music.

It was rather a lot to ask of Guthrie to keep these talents on their toes.

In his autobiography, Guthrie expresses enormous sympathy for Hellman. He felt she was working with "one hand tied behind her back." The collaborators agreed that first of all they had to have singers who would do "justice to the score." This meant that the acting often suffered when singers were asked to read lines and to develop scenes. They did not have the technical training that would show Hellman's writing to advantage. "This was no medium for hard-hitting argument, shrewd, humorous characterization, the slow revelation of true values and the exposure of false ones," Guthrie concludes. In her recent biography of Bernstein, Joan Peyser reports that during rehearsals the composer's score "was drowning Hellman's words." Even Bernstein's wife Felicia sided with the playwright's insistence that her lines be heard.

Candide proved to be a disappointment for nearly all concerned in the production. It received several respectable reviews and a few enthusiastic ones, but it managed to eke out a run of only seventy-three performances. Hellman would always be bothered by how much she had compromised her book for the play, but she remained on excellent terms with her collaborators and in print did not blame them for her own error in judgment. Only Ethel Reiner, referred to in *Pentimento* as the "lady producer," is censured for knowing nothing about music or the theater. According to William Alfred, Reiner was equally ignorant about poetry. When she interviewed Richard Wilbur, she said to him: "Who do you think you're kidding. I sent my secretary to a few big book stores. They had nothing by you and never heard of you." In the New York *Herald Tribune* (December 3, 1956), Walter Kerr called *Candide* a "spectacular disaster." Like several reviewers, he singled out Bernstein's music for praise, but he thought the direction and writing of the play heavy-handed. "Vague and meandering" was Tom Donnelly's verdict on Hellman's writing in the *New York World-Telegram* (December 3, 1956). Brooks Atkinson in *The New York Times* (December 3, 1956) noted that Hellman's Candide was not Voltaire's "blithering idiot" but a "disillusioned hero."

In *The New Republic* (December 17, 1956), Mary McCarthy provided the most incisive commentary on the play. The production, she wrote, was more like "a high school pageant than a social satire." Voltaire wrote about facing the facts; the play avoided them. This was especially true in the timid treatment of sex. In Voltaire's version, Candide had been banished from his home, and his romance with Cunegonde had been interrupted because he had been discovered making love to her behind a screen in her father's Westphalian castle. In the play, an outbreak of war is made to seem the cause of his troubles. Thus, Voltaire's point about the "old Adam," which is both Candide's salvation and his nemesis as it drives him into and out of his scrapes, is nullified. The play suffers, in the last analysis, from a failure of nerve.

McCarthy actually echoed some of Hellman's own doubts about what she had wrought. Her original version of *Candide*, on deposit at the University of Texas, clearly shows that she set out to be very faithful to Voltaire. Where concessions to middle-class Broadway taste in the production of *The Lark* proved, if anything, beneficial, similar considerations in *Candide* doomed the play. For example, Richard Wilbur's "Syphilis Song" was cut:

> Dear boy, you will not hear me speak
> With sorrow or with rancor
> Of what has paled my rosy cheek
> And blasted it with canker.
> 'Twas love, great love, that did the deed,
> Through Nature's gentle laws,
> And how should ill effects proceed
> From so divine a cause?

In spite of *Candide*'s poor reception and her problems with the script, Hellman had enjoyed herself. The play became the occasion for one of those happy accidents in life that *Candide* itself burlesqued. Ethel Reiner, producer of *Candide*, went to Dallas looking for financial backers. She called on her friend Howard Meyer—the same Howard Meyer who had dated Lillian Hellman in 1923. When Reiner told Hellman she had run into Meyer, the playwright brightened up and was most anxious to see him. In New York, there was reunion of boy and girlfriend. The meeting with Meyer was brief, but it brought back many fond memories. As he was leaving Meyer said, "Good night, Lillian." In recognition of their former intimacy, she responded, "Oh, that voice." He was charmed all over again. They would see each other one more time, when she would go to Dallas in 1979 to do a series of interviews with Marilyn Berger.

Hellman excelled in the creation of intimate scenes, little dramas she would put on with the help of her friends. Nothing endeared her more to intimates—even those who had mixed feelings about her—than her taking them into her confidence about the most personal matters. To Arthur Kober she wrote, "Last week I had a small growth on the skin of my vagina, do pardon the word and look it up, if necessary, but I was not allowed to treat it very seriously and Abe [her doctor] had the whole operation finished in ten minutes." Her hold over people was nothing less than seductive. And there is nothing her friends or even former friends enjoy more than to recount Hellman's choicest anecdotes and dramas.

Richard Wilbur:

> I remember our sitting down on the beach in front of her place one day, making up a play in which we would co-star. We pondered at length what the action would be, what form the courtship would take, and what names would be given the characters. She thought I should be "Boy" something-or-other; as for her name, we never decided that, though it was going to be very floral. Arthur Kober turned up during our story-conference, and gently declined to participate, not being in our foolish mood.

Although Hellman sounded like "pure New York," she was fond of playing the Southern lady. Her ability to be "relaxedly personal" seemed to Wilbur a Southern feature of her existence. She liked all of the things a man might do for a woman. She adored flowers. She liked being handed into cars or the chair being held for her. Any kind of courtliness delighted her.

Frances FitzGerald:

> Philip Rahv met Lillian at a party and then was invited to dinner by her. Because she had a rather large New York residence and a housekeeper, he assumed there was going to be a big dinner party. Two days before the dinner, she called him up and asked him what he wanted for dinner. She must have somehow known that he fancied himself as an enormous gourmet. In fact, he adored food, and he knew she had this wonderful cook. He suddenly realized that she was drawing him into a more intimate relationship. When he got there, it turned out there was dinner for two. This was one of his examples of her terrific gift for seduction.

Diana Trilling:

> When I used to go to her house for lunch—which I very often did—there would be a setting similar to the seduction of Philip Rahv. It would be a winter day, and there would be this lovely living room with a fire

and a little table, beautifully appointed, set up in front
of the fireplace—beautiful linen and silver. The maid
Helen would put the lunch on the table and then leave.
Lillian, who was usually wearing a velvet hostess
gown, would get up and close the doors behind Helen,
so that the room was very private, cut off from the rest
of the house. I'd always ask myself, "Now what?"

It was all very intimate, but Trilling set up her own signals, and
her feeling was that Hellman was not about to take a chance on
that.

"If you want to know what the secret of Lillian's power over
people was, it was an extraordinary gift for intimacy—even when
you didn't have it, she made it," Trilling recalls.

She would tell you the most personal things about
herself. And you would feel enormously flattered. I
remember a scene when I had come to visit her and
she wasn't feeling well. She was lying on a kind of
Madame Recamier couch. I was sitting on a chair
nearby. I don't remember why, but I spoke humor-
ously of having had to have a small operation on my
belly button. She said, very, very solemnly and most
dramatically, "Diana, do men have belly buttons?"
And then she went into gales of laughter, which of
course I joined. She said, "I haven't seen a man un-
dressed for so long I can't remember." This wasn't of
course true, but it suited the occasion.

Another time she said she had discovered a scar on
the underside of her breast. "The doctor said that I
had been bitten, but I explained that that was not
possible," Lillian went on gravely: "Diana, do you
think I could have bitten myself on the bottom of my
breast?"

The thing was, Trilling concluded, that Hellman in sharing these
intimacies with you, "made you feel unique."

William Alfred, who met Hellman in the summer of 1954 at
Harvard during a symposium on verse drama, remembers, "she
was such wonderful company." She regaled him with stories about
The Lark. Boris Karloff (who played Cauchon) told a method actor

who was giving everyone fits, "Will you for Christ's sake stop talking and start acting." Of a famous playwright, who kept referring to "Lillian and I" as if they were "the theater," Hellman remarked to Alfred, "If he says that one more time, I'm going to pop him!" She was absolutely honest about her feelings, Alfred recalls. "She'd say whatever came into her head. Many things struck her funny, and she was very funny." She was

> girlish. It might seem strange to say that about her nowadays, when people conceive of her as a "walking Medea," but she was open and would bubble over. Whatever you did for her, she enjoyed enormously. You'd take her out for a steak dinner, and you'd think she'd never had one before. She always gave a sense that you and she and some other friends belonged to a closed group that was really rather wonderful to belong to.

For company at the Vineyard or in New York, Hellman might entertain her physician, Samuel Standard, the Perelmans, the Hacketts, the Levins, the Styrons, the Greenes, and sometimes the Weinsteins, who were good friends of Herman Shumlin. Bobbie Weinstein cannot remember exactly how it happened, but during the mid-1950s Hellman and Shumlin had a romantic revival which lasted a few years. If these friends did not dine with Hellman in the city or come together at the Vineyard for beach parties and picnics, they might meet at Sardi's. Arthur Cowan, an attorney from Philadelphia and the subject of a profile in *Pentimento*, was Hellman's guest from time to time. Her broad array of friends was extraordinary. Ephraim London, another prominent attorney, began to see Hellman socially and was intrigued by how many lawyers she knew. She was fascinated by his family's involvement in politics—his uncle had been a socialist and a congressman. Later, he would do legal work for her gratis, and she would embarrass him by telling other lawyers that London was the only attorney who had never charged her a fee.

Hellman definitely thought of herself as having a circle, and to be a member of that circle certain requirements had to be met— although the rigor of her demands would not reach full expression until after the ailing Hammett died in 1961. Her life then became a literature of its own, with the appearance of *An Unfinished Woman* in 1969. But the fielding of a Hellman team, a cohort of followers, was definitely in the making before Hammett's death. Coming from John O'Hara, it might sound like sour grapes—he called them the "Hammett-Hellman-Perelman-Kober group," or the "Kronenberger-MacLeish-Mason Brown-Lillian Hellman pack, a mutual assistance group that are very influential but who bore me to death. They get together and all try to say the same thing first and regard it as intellectual conversation, and freeze if there is the slightest deviation from their line."

Hellman liked to cultivate promising young writers who might join her fold. She wrote an admiring letter to Herbert Gold about his novel *The Prospect Before Us* (1954) and was instrumental in getting him a grant from the National Institute of Arts and Letters and later a contract for a play that was to be an adaptation of one of his short stories. He first met her at a party in New York in 1956. Budd Schulberg was there, too, and he was trying to explain to Hellman why he had been a cooperative HUAC witness. She backed up and said, "Don't get near me, Budd, I don't want to talk to you. Don't touch me, Budd." He was following her, still trying to justify his testimony, and she was making a scene. The result was that both writers turned to Gold to explain their sides of the argument. Schulberg had come to feel that Communists were evil, and he regretted his contact with them, whereas Hellman felt proud—even arrogant—about her statement of conscience.

There would be other scenes. Maurice Zolotow had written an admiring portrait of Tallulah Bankhead; he had also recanted his early 1930s enthusiasm for communism and the Soviet Union and was known as a staunch anti-Communist. He had been invited to a party at which many of the theater's greatest names were in attendance. There was Lillian Hellman, sitting on a couch. She shot him a baleful glare, and suddenly said in a loud, raspy voice, "Well, you goddam Fascist, what are you doing here?" He blushed red all over, but she would not let go. "Who are you writing lies about now?" Zolotow walked away and sat next to Aldous Huxley, who wanted to know what the shouting was about. Zolotow tried to explain to him about the Bankhead-Hellman controversy. No one else spoke up, even though many of Zolotow's friends were there and knew that Hellman was suspect for her pro-Soviet opinions.

In nearly all things, Hellman was either pro or con. There was precious little room for the in-between in her world view. One was either an ally or an enemy. In her role as mother-patroness, she would introduce Gold to important people, praise him, invite him to dinner, and plan things that would be for his benefit. She had a rigid sense of propriety and expected Gold to play by her rules. She also wanted her young men to be *hers.* Rather innocently, he assumed that as a single man he had a right to bring a lady to one of Hellman's dinners. The hostess did not like it at all and was rude to Gold's companion.

Lillian did not take kindly to younger women, especially when they married male friends of her own generation. "She could be very arrogant and very jealous," Telford Taylor recalls. He was about to marry a woman who was a former student and considerably younger than him. She was twenty-seven at the time she met Hellman in Taylor's company at a dinner party:

> I told my wife I was going to be talking to somebody writing a biography of Lillian, and she said, "Well, I can remember only one thing about Lillian Hellman. I have never felt like such a 'nothing' in my life." I remember she was sitting next to Lillian and that Lillian never gave her a word. I was on to this and was amused rather than angry.

Bobbie Weinstein could have told Gold that it was a rule with Hellman that one did not bring guests who had not been explicitly invited. Impromptu visits were also discouraged. Diana Trilling remembers her acute embarrassment over Hellman's boorish treatment of her secretary, who on the spur of the moment called her on Martha's Vineyard asking if she could stop by with her teenage son. Hellman offered the boy something like coffee, which he politely refused, but he asked if he might have some sherry. With a liquor cabinet filled with just about anything a guest might request, Hellman said no, she had no sherry.

Hellman could also be an importunate hostess. Richard Wilbur remembers getting a call during the summer of 1956—"Lillian was asking us to yet another party." Social life at the Vineyard was incredibly busy. He was working and was tired. His wife was on the phone, and he remembers saying, "Dear God, let's not go to another party." Hellman was told that the Wilburs would have to "pass on this one."

Lillian began to press her and said, "It's going to be a nice party. I'm going to have shish kebab with fish instead of meat. It's going to be experimental food, and then Sam Barber will be there. She began naming guests. And I said to my wife, "If she really is so disappointed that we're not coming, then let's go." Mrs. Wilbur accepted the invitation. The next day in the grocery Lillian and my wife met, and in a very public way Lillian exploded at her over tables of vegetables, "You didn't want to come to my party. You only decided to come when I mentioned Sam Barber, and you became star-struck."

Things calmed down in a day or two, and Hellman and the Wilburs were warm friends as before. It was clear to Richard Wilbur, however, that in her fits of temper Hellman was capable of getting things very wrong. In spite of her devotion to truth, she would stubbornly hold to a misguided version of things. She wanted the Wilburs by her and felt very insecure about their loyalty when they hesitated about her party.

People put up with a lot from Hellman. There were many friends who could not accept her politics and who had to pass her own brand of loyalty tests. Yet their fascination with her overrode their reservations. Herbert Gold suggests it was because she was not only a prominent figure, "she had magnitude. She gave you the sense that this was a great person." One of Diana Trilling's friends once asked her, "How could you ever have been friends with that Commie?" Trilling's answer: "All my life I had wanted to know a large-sized woman, a woman with dimension, daring and imaginative, with boldness of vision, and I thought that I would find her in Lillian." "Well, did you?" Trilling's friend wanted to know. "No, what I found was a woman sitting around in a rocker in a hotel in the Catskills saying, 'He didn't remember my birthday; she didn't send me a card at Christmas; he didn't bring me a flower.' She was always checking up on people, chalking up. That's what she was always talking about." Yet Hellman was interesting; she was "big." And she courted the Trillings assiduously.

Lionel Trilling had known Hellman since the late 1920s before he and Diana were married. They had not been close friends, but he knew Louis Kronenberger and Howard Meyer and saw Hellman from time to time, usually at parties. During the late 1950s, Trilling would meet Hellman at meetings of the American Institute of Arts and Letters, and he would come home and report to his wife that Hellman wanted to be friends with them. He told Hellman, "our politics are so unalike, it's not going to work." But she seemed to have no understanding of what he was talking about. He was bewildered. How could she not realize that they took diametrically opposed positions on the Soviet Union? As they were walking out of a meeting one day, Hellman said, "I think we are fundamentally for the same things." Diana Trilling recalls that this was Hellman's "line on many things. If you were for democracy, if you were for justice, if you were for equality of the blacks and other minorities, it meant that your politics were the same as hers. It's so extraordinarily simple-minded." Lionel said, "But Lillian, our differences are a matter of public record." She blanched, as if he had said something absolutely shocking. "Because all of this was swimming in some wonderful atmosphere of political virtue," Diana concludes. Nevertheless, the Trillings were willing to give it a try. "We made a pact not to talk about politics."

It is Diana's impression that Hellman was looking for an affair with Lionel. Everyone knew that Hellman was pretty direct about wanting to go to bed with the men she liked. Evidently, she made no overt proposal to Lionel, as she had with many other men—including Stuart Rose, the editor of the *Saturday Evening Post*, a tall, slim, elegant man who had been a cavalry officer during World War I. Rose told Maurice Zolotow that Hellman had propositioned him one day at lunch. "How would you like to come up to my apartment and fuck?" she wanted to know. He looked at her and said, "No thanks." It is Diana's impression that Hellman would have liked Lionel to enter the list of those men who would regularly come by her New York residence and look in on her. "When Lillian found that she was failing to attract Lionel, she switched her attention to me," Diana observes.

Politics would always be a sore point between Hellman and the Trillings. When the Soviets prevented Boris Pasternak from receiving the Nobel Prize in 1958, Diana remembers saying something about the outrage of not allowing him to be published and read. Hellman got sharp and asked her what made her think that it was any better in the United States. "It's a hell of a lot better in this country," Trilling replied. Hellman countered by pointing to the persecution of Hammett. But it was Hammett's free choice to adopt the politics that had got him into trouble, Trilling suggested. The next day, Hellman phoned Diana: *"Never, never,* are you to speak that way about Dash to me. *Never."* The Trillings and Hellman continued to see each other, but there was a noticeable strain. Bobbie Weinstein, one of Hellman's three or four closest female friends, points out that Hellman was so used to intimidating people that only the firmest tones would get through to her.

Hellman often told Norman Podhoretz that she was not a "political person." He could never believe her; he found her "political to the core." Like many people, he discovered that her grasp of politics was not profound. In this, she was like many literary people Podhoretz knew who did not involve themselves in the details of electoral campaigns. "But those who are political will respond to public events in a more or less predictable pattern," he points out. She may no longer have been "an automatic apologist for the Soviet Union," but she would be there to support whatever seemed the radical position at the time. "Her own radicalism was real, but it lacked content: it was a disposition, a stance, an attitude, and yet not the less persistent for its substantive emptiness," Podhoretz concludes.

Many of Hellman's friends who were much closer to her than Podhoretz echo his view. When Khrushchev gave his famous speech in 1956 denouncing Stalin's crimes, Hellman condemned Khrushchev for turning on the very leader who had been responsible for Khrushchev's successful career. At first, this seems astonishing—that Hellman could only think of the ingratitude and not the enormous evil that had been exposed. Yet in Lillian Hellman's psychology Khrushchev was another informer! John Melby feels she was half joking and half serious. There was more than a grain of truth in what she said as far as he was concerned. Khrushchev was part of a world of gangsters, and he did have nerve decrying Stalin's sins. Hellman was taking the long view of history. She even predicted that Stalin would be vindicated one day. Melby believes she had in mind the changes in historical perspective that rehabilitate great figures like Napoleon and that turn former enemies like Germany and Japan into staunch allies.

Hellman once confessed to Catherine Kober that she and her generation had been naive about Stalin. Bobbie Weinstein recalls that she and Hellman expected the Soviet Union to eradicate evils like anti-Semitism. In their enthusiastic endorsement of the new world they thought he was creating in the Soviet Union, they had not considered seriously the implications of events like the Moscow trials. The whole discussion between Hellman and Kober took perhaps forty seconds, and Hellman was not the least bit defensive about her past. She was simply explaining where she had gone wrong. In private, especially in conversation with a younger person, she had no trouble specifying her political errors. In public, and with enemies, however, she was a different person. Admitting that her pro-Soviet politics had been wrong would have aided McCarthy and Cold War campaigns against radicals. And Hellman was loyal to Hammett. Her deepest feelings about radicalism were tied up in his person. She once told Ephraim London that Hammett had forbidden her to join the party. In her memoirs she suggests that Hammett did not confide in her about his party membership—perhaps for her own protection. If she was not the optimist she once was about the Soviet Union, she could not change her politics without seeming to betray him.

21

TOYS IN THE ATTIC

(1957–1960)

I think I wanted to say that not all kinds of love—so-called love—are noble and good, that there's much in love that's destructive, including the love that holds up false notions of success, of the acquisition of money.

—Lillian Hellman, interview with Seymour Peck, in *The New York Times*, February 21, 1960

"Liberal," she said, with something resembling battle fatigue. "It's so vague. In America at this point, it means no more than I'm-not-mean-to-my-mother."

—Lillian Hellman, interview with Fern Marja, in *The New York Post*, March 6, 1960

After *Candide*, Hellman seemed stuck. She suggests in *Pentimento* that she was already preparing for her departure from the theater, although she would write two more plays and attempt others. The late 1950s, in her view, were not congenial for the writer. On May 6, 1957, at a Drama Guild symposium in New York, she suggested that the writer "who has always been the rebel in the last ten years has become the conformist." On May 21, 1958, in an interview with Richard Stern at the University of Chicago, she spoke of the "mush-headedness" of the times and, in Stern's words, of a generation's "feeling of tranquility and . . . lack of exploration." She told Seymour Peck that people were trying too hard to get along and were using words like "love" much too loosely. At a party recently, a reasonably intelligent woman had told Hellman how she was "filled with love" for everyone there. Hellman told Peck that it was fine to say one was having a good time or that it was a nice party, but that there was "a lot of bunk going around about how we must all find love, we all need love." Hellman confided to Peck that she had fallen into the habit of saying "the big, soothing thing." It is hard to think of her acquiescing to the status quo, but the FBI was surprised to find her amenable to an interview on April 8, 1957. She was "quite friendly to the agents and was very courteous," according to her FBI file. Her case was then considered closed, since "her last CP activity was in the middle 1940s."

Hellman took to encouraging novelists and poets to write for the stage. She courted both Theodore Roethke and Saul Bellow, promising them help as a producer. From time to time there would be announcements of her various projects. *The New York Times* for February 16, 1958, carried an article about the "Hellman-Osterman Producing Firm" which was planning to bring Albert Camus's adaptation of Dostoyevsky's *The Possessed* to Broadway. Quarrels with Osterman were often the result of her sudden changes of mind. In the end, she had to admit that she did not make a good producer.

Hammett realized Hellman needed to write a new play. He also knew she needed some kind of spur, a story that would get under her skin and activate her deep-seated anger over injustice, so he suggested this scenario: "There's this man. Other people, people who say they love him, want him to make good, be rich. So he does it for them and finds they don't like him that way, so he fucks it up, and comes out worse than before. Think about it." She wrote about half of what was to become *Toys in the Attic*. She had trouble dramatizing the man as the center of the play. Her inclination was to reconceptualize the story so that it centered on his sisters, his wife, and her mother.

In several ways, *Toys in the Attic* took up where *The Autumn Garden* left off. In that play, Nick Denery was the center of the women's attention, flattering and cajoling and having his way with them. But he was a most unsympathetic character, and his illusions about his debonair self were subsumed in the many tales the playwright wanted to tell about the middle-aged characters who shared Nick's propensity to fool themselves. *Toys in the Attic* would tell the other part of the story—how two sisters had created a brother, Julian, all for themselves, a brother mated to their desire to exert total control over a world of their own making.

Early drafts of *Toys in the Attic* specify that it takes place in New Orleans in 1912. As Hellman scholar Theresa Rose Mooney points out, 1912 "was an important one in Hellman's childhood." In 1911, her father's business had failed and the family had moved to New York. For the first time, Hellman began to see her native South as an outsider who would return for six-month periods. Her unusual divided perspective, a result of seeing her New Orleans family in two very different locations, is reflected in all of her "Southern" plays. *Toys in the Attic* is unique in that it comes closest to autobiography. The play uses more facts from Hellman's life and relies more heavily on her bifurcated sensibility. She obviously had in mind her father and his two sisters.

In an early draft, one of the sisters is called Hannah. Jenny also appears in a list of names for characters in the play. The differences between the sisters who Hellman describes in *Pentimento* are magnified in the play. Carrie is a version of Jenny, the younger and prettier sister, who seems less down to earth than Hannah (based on Anna). In both the play and *Pentimento*, the older sister (Anna/Hannah) seems to be in charge, yet in subtle ways that only gradually become apparent, the younger sister (Jenny/Carrie) actually dominates the relationship. She is, as Hellman avers of Jenny in *An Unfinished Woman*, more "complex" than her older sister. In *Pentimento*, the author suggests that most women living together "take on what we think of as male and female roles." But the drama of her aunts' lives that fueled *Toys in the Attic* was the "mix-about" of the two women, the curious independent-dependent roles Hannah and Jenny played vis-à-vis each other.

Julian is an exaggerated Max, failing at every business he tries. References to the behavior of the rich, the obsession with how money influences human character, appear in almost every scene of the play and are reminiscent of those Newhouse conversations about finances described in *An Unfinished Woman*. There was tremendous power to be had in the possession of money. The only time in *Toys in the Attic* that Julian feels supremely confident is after he has big money and can talk with his wife's wealthy mother as an equal. The mother, Albertine Prine, has a black lover, Henry, and is obviously drawn from Hellman's memories of her Aunt Lily and Peters, Lily's black servant. Julian never quite realizes how his sisters have manipulated him through their seemingly generous outlay of loans every time he has gone bust. Max's sisters did not hold him with their money, but Hellman realized that they had a way of monopolizing his affection to the detriment of her mother and even of herself. When Max turned to other women, Lillian took it not so much as a rejection of her mother as a rejection of herself. In *Toys in the Attic*, Julian's wife is given the name Lily, and it is Lily who ultimately ruins his business deal as a result of her mistaken belief that he will run off with another woman, the wife of Cyrus Warkins, the town's ruthless businessman. Lily's love for Julian is all-consuming, and she cannot imagine that his relationship with Mrs. Charlotte Warkins (a former lover) is just business, that Julian has simply collaborated with the woman in selling a valuable piece of property to her wicked, unscrupulous husband. When Lily phones Cyrus to tell him about his wife and Julian, Warkins's confederates attack Julian and rob him of the cash he has been flaunting around town. Thus Lily unwittingly destroys not only Julian's fortune but his independence. He will again have to depend on her and his sisters. Lillian Hellman had to see herself in Lily's wilfulness, in her strident sense of absoluteness, in her panic when she cannot have Julian all to herself. In an early draft of the play, Lily recites the "Mama forgive me, Papa forgive me" prayer that *An Unfinished Woman* quotes Hellman as having said.

There were other family models for Julian and Lily. In an early draft, it is hinted that Lily is a drug addict—as was Hellman's Aunt Lily, and it is implied that much of Lily's erratic behavior in the play stems from her morphine habit. Aunt Lily's husband, the hearty, open-minded, and generous Uncle Willy, is another prototype of Julian. In the play, Lily suspects that Julian married her for her dowry; in *Pentimento*, it is implied that Willy married Lily for her money so that he could carry on the business deals that made him and broke him several times. As Theresa Mooney suggests, Willy's "love of the Louisiana bayou country, his ease with simple pleasures, his relish of Cajun foods, and his pleasure in duck hunting" are all a part of Julian when he says: "Anybody asked what I missed most in Chicago, I'd have said a bayou, a bowl of crayfish, a good gun for a flight of wild ducks coming over—Going to buy a little place up there, first thing."

To Emmy Kronenberger, it seemed that Hellman was exploring her dark side in *Toys in the Attic*. The whole plot of the play seemed to revolve around the way Hellman used people. Kronenberger recalls that

> Lillian was a great one for lending people money. But oh boy, there were ties, strings. Just to hold control. Nothing was ever done for anybody unless in some way it went back to Lillian. It couldn't be an open-handed thing.

This is why she once refused Hellman's offer of a loan for a new home. Hellman had lent some money to Louis Kronenberger after *The Children's Hour,* and then expected him to check in with her. She would make calls to his home, shrieking at him for one thing or another. Emmy thought Hellman acted as if she owned Louis. There were ugly incidents later with Kermit Bloomgarden and others, when Hellman would call in her loans, demanding immediate payment—no matter how inconvenient for the borrowers. She admired people like Arthur Cowan who could handle money well.

Hellman may have drawn on her own personality and family background as a way of authenticating for herself the compulsive, repetitive behavior she dramatizes in *Toys in the Attic.* The drama is Freudian and surely influenced by her own psychoanalysis, by her own probing of the unconscious—the attic of memories—for the toys, the seemingly little playthings that end up making the patterns of our lives. When Julian arrives at his sisters' home with a wad of cash and his new wife, his sisters no longer have a purpose in life. Julian is no longer their toy. He comes thinking he is their liberator. With his help they now can afford to take their long-planned trip to Europe, quit their jobs, and lead, in every way, independent lives.

Anna is more willing than Carrie to accept the new Julian. She knows "things have changed. That's as it should be." Carrie, on the other hand, tends to dwell on the family past and will not let go of her brother. In a shocking scene she is confronted with Anna's charge that she has always "lusted" after him. Julian's obtuseness and secretiveness complicate matters considerably. He understands much too late that he has overwhelmed his sisters with gifts and promises of an easy future. He never reckons with his wife's terrible feelings of being shut out. Lily is scared of her husband's temporary impotence—"Julian couldn't have me last night"—and does not appreciate the tremendous tension he experiences in dealing with Cyrus Warkins. As a result, Lily thinks she must vie with Carrie and Anna for Julian's love. Like Carrie, Lily feels rejected. To her rather aloof mother, Albertine Prine, Lily cries, "I was beloved, Mama, and I flourished. Now I'm frightened." Lily has never thought of herself as attractive and, like Carrie, is desperately trying to hold on to Julian. The scenes between Carrie and Lily are deeply affecting and ironic because the women are unable to realize how much they have in common.

It is curious that Julian, who describes himself as "kind of broken" before his financial windfall, should inspire so much passion. Lily deliberately injures herself in the hope that Julian will "cure" her. His gift, it seems, is his love, which is uncomplicated by selfishness. From the start of the play he is seen giving his money away, distributing large tips, and asking a taxi driver and a furniture mover to name their children after him—as if, indeed, Julian were a saint. More properly, he is akin to Hammett, a "sinner-saint," profligate and principled. Julian knows by the end of the play that he has been downright stupid in handling both his business and personal affairs, but he has done so with so much vitality, with so much good feeling for humanity, that he is able to shrug off his worst defeat: "Plenty of room in this world for everybody. Just got to fight for it. Got to start again, start again."

It took Hellman nearly three years to get *Toys in the Attic* right. She knew the play still had faults, but she never saw the virtue of tinkering. There was too much chance of spoiling what was good. She had had considerable trouble with plot and with motivation. During a period when she could not get beyond writing the first half of the play, Hellman told Richard Stern that Carrie had a "beau whom she's never married . . . because she's been in love with her brother all her life." As the playwright noted, it was highly unusual for her to discuss an uncompleted play in public, but she wanted to gauge how it might be received. At Martha's Vineyard, she read a version to Harry Levin and Richard Wilbur. Later she admitted to Don Ross in the *New York Herald Tribune* (February 21, 1960) that she "wanted to try out the sound of the man on men." In one draft, Lily wrecks Julian's plans by shooting and crippling him. There was also a confrontation scene between Dino Scarlotti (later changed to Cyrus Warkins) and Julian. It was ineffective because the playwright tried to express too many themes—including Carrie's shame that Julian has been involved

with a corrupt businessman. In this rejected scene, Scarlotti re-
neges on his business deal because his wife has betrayed him. He
refuses to make money on that. Hellman was trying too hard to
link money and love, to show how they compromise each other.

Until *Toys in the Attic*, Diana Trilling had never seen a play in
production. "Sometime when a play of yours is being produced,
invite me down. I want to watch it being directed," Trilling said to
Hellman. The playwright kindly remembered the request, and
Trilling found herself in an empty theater in the fourth row
watching director Arthur Penn work with actors: Maureen Stapleton (Carrie), Anne Revere (Anna), Irene Worth (Albertine Prine),
Jason Robards, Jr. (Julian). It was the scene in which Lily holds up
a knife, calling it her "knife of truth." To Trilling this was nonsense—what is a knife of truth?—but she was fascinated by the
director's behavior, his caution in preserving the ego of all the
performers. "If he wanted to tell an actor to speak a little louder or
softer, he did not give instruction in front of the other actors.
Instead, he took the player aside, and put an arm around his
shoulder, and quietly whispered to him, 'Perhaps if you could do
that a little differently,' " Trilling recalls. After an hour or two, she
had to leave. "I'll walk out with you," Hellman said. At the door
of the theater, Trilling told her, "I had such a good time. My
goodness, it's interesting to watch—the amount of time that is
spent over any one scene, it's extraordinary." That evening, Hellman telephoned: "Diana, you and I have both been psychoanalyzed, and we know enough about unconscious motives to understand what was going on this afternoon. You left the theater
without saying a word in praise of my play." Trilling gulped. She
could not bring herself to say that she did not like the scene.
Lamely, she talked about how absorbed she had been in the stage
work. She confesses that she is a terrible liar and did not do well
with a friend who left "no stone unturned. When I hadn't praised
her, she called me up and demanded it."

For *Toys in the Attic*, Howard Bay and Arthur Penn had a big
problem explaining to Hellman that they did not need an enclosed
set with ceilings. She was rather literal-minded about such things,
but she liked working with these two professionals very much and
respected their judgment. The play had a spectacular cast, but
there were problems. Both Jason Robards and Maureen Stapleton
were drinking heavily. One day after a rehearsal, Bay and Hellman

joined Stapleton in the bar. Stapleton said, "Lilly, you should not address the troops." Hellman's scorn for actors was by now legendary, but Stapleton—as many of Hellman's friends testify—knew how to handle the playwright. Stapleton was honest and direct and had such towering talent that Hellman acknowledged her authority.

After a preview in Boston, Bay, Penn, and Hellman went over to a second-floor room at the Ritz Hotel. The playwright was in a state because Robards had not given a very good performance. Hellman demanded to know what had happened. Penn started to explain that actors are very mercurial people. They are sensitive and cannot be expected to perform the same way every night. The playwright would have none of it and sent Penn to the telephone to reach Robards.

On February 25, 1960, the New York opening of *Toys in the Attic* was a tremendous success—second only to *The Children's Hour* in the length of its run (at 556 performances). Even reviewers who felt little enthusiasm over the characters or who identified faults in the plot greeted the play as a mature work that considerably enlivened an undistinguished theatrical season. Walter Kerr, in the *New York Herald Tribune* (February 26, 1960), acutely observed the nearly perfect blend of acting and writing. Robards had captured the "nervous tension" in Julian's "small-boy exuberance." When he came on stage showering his sisters with gifts, the audience almost immediately became uneasy, sensing that this was a man who had never had a success before. Stapleton, "in the dismayed edges" of her smile, foreshadowed, on Robards's first entrance, the divided feelings the sisters would have about Julian's success. Similarly, Kerr noticed Anne Revere's "reserved gratitude" and the stirring of fear as her character, Anna, tried on the clothes Julian had brought for her. "Miss Stapleton's eyes dart from object to object as though each were subtly contaminated. Miss Revere, walking sigh that she is, seems always to be holding a secret doom at bay, though not distantly at bay."

The actors' gestures were extremely important because of the playwright's sparce style. Characters had thoughts that were not "explicitly spoken." Hellman had written a "limpid, unfussed, intuitively-shaped language," Kerr concluded, in praise of her honesty and directness. Anne Revere's rehearsal script shows that the playwright had worked at precisely the effect Kerr lauds: the tensions in the characters had to be *acted* because they were never explained in so many words. Revere wrote a note to herself: "Anger at Carrie is a result of frustration in losing Julian. She sets out to go because there is now no family—She lived for her family and now there is no family so she'll live for herself." Anna never says anything like this when she prepares to leave home with the ticket Julian has provided for the European trip, yet Revere's note is part of the play's subtext, of what the audience grasps without having to be told.

Albertine Prine (played by Irene Worth) is the most fascinating character in the play. It seems somewhat odd that Kerr would say that Worth performs Albertine with "demoniac power," but perhaps he had in mind the fact that Albertine is the most focused character in *Toys in the Attic*. Her calm self-sufficiency and austere refusal to rationalize her behavior are very appealing in the context of characters who are so laden with illusions. But Albertine's very independence is what drives her daughter away from her. Albertine needs no one except her lover, Henry, and thus Lily feels rejected by her mother. In Albertine's scenes with Julian she is amusing because she is understated and droll. Again, Revere's script shows that the playwright knew what to leave out—as in this exchange in act two between Lily and her mother (the portions in brackets were cut):

> LILY: You haven't seen anybody in years, except Henry,
> of course. [Nobody ever came to our house.]
> ALBERTINE: [You could have had anybody you wanted,
> certainly I never interfered. And you had the fanci-
> est debutante party in years, and the dullest. Are
> young people in Chicago as conforming as they are
> here? I'm sure not. In a big city—]

It would not be inappropriate for Albertine to think these words, but to say them on stage would be to destroy the tautness of characterization Hellman was aiming for. Clearly, Albertine is a nonconformist; there is no need for her to criticize others. Indeed, she is much too aloof to argue with Lily about such things. Albertine's very strength—her detachment from societal rules—is what isolates her and alienates her daughter. To have Albertine justify herself to Lily, to inquire into Julian's and Lily's life in Chicago, vitiates her self-contained personality.

The tensions underneath civilized behavior that Kerr observes explode at the end of the play in Julian's savage beating. Several characters have done great psychological harm to one another and to themselves: Carrie and Anna have great hatred for each other; Lily has injured herself in the hope that Julian will be forced to attend only to her; and, in general, there is a high level of hostility in the way Lily treats Henry and in the way Carrie has had to work for years for a mean-minded employer. There is also anger and envy at the rich and at crude manipulators like Cyrus, whose wife has conspired with Julian to profit from a land deal with her husband that will allow her to leave him. A few years later, Hellman would agree to work on a screenplay of *The Chase* which explicitly dramatized the mood of violence that would initiate the sixties. When Jason Robards staggered on stage, looking as if several teeth had been knocked out, his face swelled up, nose broken, ears and cheeks gashed, and clothing torn and dirtied, the audience gasped. Many people could not look at him. Dr. Benjamin Gilbert, a Broadway house physician, noted in *The New York Times* (August 21, 1960) that there had been "three cases of heart attack, and nine cases of assorted shock, hysteria and fainting among members of the audience." Robards believed that people felt "something very personal about the beating. It must recall something in their own lives or in the lives of people they know." In the play, Carrie has set up Julian for this punishment by making sure Lily is able to tell Cyrus where her husband is to meet with Mrs. Warkins. The depth of her possessiveness and of her anger are very disturbing. Underneath the conforming customs of the 1950s lay a deep undercurrent of violent feeling. Soon Lillian Hellman would find herself involved in Norman Mailer's bizarre stabbing of his wife.

22

THE DEATH OF DASHIELL HAMMETT
(1960–1961)

Do you want to talk about it?
No. My only chance is *not* to talk about it.

—Lillian Hellman to Dashiell Hammett, late 1960—*An Unfinished
Woman*

Nearly every reviewer who praised *Toys in the Attic* suggested that it was an ugly play about the meanness of the human spirit. It was a tough, ruthless exposé, yet reviewers wanted people to see it—if only with half-averted eyes. As in *Another Part of the Forest*, Hellman had sensed the coming of a new age and she was brutally honest. The earlier play had forecast the anxiety of a postwar world, and it had come too soon. The audience would not accept it, even though *Another Part of the Forest* is in no way inferior to *Toys in the Attic*. The later play came at the end of the 1950s and in the midst of the failure of a postwar pax Americana. Marcus Hubbard's cynicism was too much to take in 1946; Albertine Prine's wry reflections on love in 1960 were apposite. She was a nonconformist in an age of conformity that was about to undergo a sea of change.

Nursing a dying Dashiell Hammett—lung cancer had been diagnosed—Hellman was not herself in any position to herald a new age of radicalism. In 1958, Hammett had given up his small place in Katonah, New York, and stayed with Hellman in New York City or at the Vineyard. He had accompanied her on a trip for the Boston tryout of *Toys of the Attic* and had attended the play's premiere in New York, but now he went almost nowhere. He was too weak, too tired. Many of Hellman's friends, like writer Norman Podhoretz, never saw Hammett and had the impression he was not interested in meeting them. He was a burden for Hellman, and she sometimes let other people know how put out she felt. In the main, however, she stuck by him and was fiercely protective of his privacy.

At the same time, Hellman was attracted to Norman Mailer, who was putting his enormous talent to the test of public life, even though she deplored many of his opinions and was dismayed at the show he made of himself. On the one hand, he was writing outrageous essays. "The White Negro" delved into the therapeutic uses of violence and suggested that the very marginality of blacks might have taught them to exist with an originality that had been dulled in a white-dominated society. A "White Negro" was a hipster who took from jazz, and from other aspects of what was still called "Negro" life, a style that was more than unconventional, it was a challenge to the whole status quo. On the other hand, Mailer was no beat poet, no societal drop out. He was mainstream New York, an avid literary party-goer, a nice Brooklyn boy (though he hated to admit it), and an aspirant to elective office. Mayor Mailer. Like Hellman, he enjoyed large social occasions and had mutual friends whose politics clashed. At this point, he was still friends with Hellman and Diana Trilling.

November 19, 1960, the night Mailer stabbed his wife, was preceded by a chaotic party meant to celebrate his decision to run for the office of mayor of New York. Neither Hellman nor Trilling was there that night—nor were the promised powerful political figures whose presence might have saved the party from capitulating to "an undercurrent of violence." Richard Gilman remembered "fights quickly broken up in corners, sexual stalkings and contretemps, envies and jealousies staging themselves as group therapy." The party seemed to be the culmination of scrapes Mailer had been getting into. Then, too, there seemed to be his frustration at not being taken seriously, at not being able to effect change. At the height of a "disastrous drunken evening" when, as Hilary Mills puts it, the writer's "ego had been severely battered," he went after his wife Adele, with whom he was want to quarrel violently, and stabbed her with a "two-and-a-half-inch-long penknife." She was wounded in the upper abdomen and back. He just missed her heart.

Hellman told writer Peter Manso that Mailer called her from Bellevue Hospital, where he had been committed by a judge for psychiatric observation. Mailer was broke and wanted to know if she could bring him five hundred dollars. Of course, she always wanted to help a friend. Hammett called her "a sucker and often a goddamned fool," and would not let her go. Even though he could barely walk, he got out of bed, locked the door, and put the key in his robe. In spite of her protests, he vowed that, as weak as he was, he would break her arm if she tried to get the key from him. An hour later, Hammett relented, but Hellman did not say if she went to Mailer. She also made a mystery of why Hammett was so opposed to her going:

> He used a sentence that I'll never repeat because it was
> anti-Norman. And Dash liked Norman. Many years
> later I told Norman this story, but he denied it ever
> happened. Which might show Norman's good nature
> and sweetness.

Hellman's feelings about Mailer were odd. That she liked him, there was no doubt. Norman Podhoretz remembers her flirting with Mailer. Yet she disapproved of him, and he often came in for criticism in her Yale writing course. Podhoretz and Diana Trilling first met Mailer at Hellman's house, and both of them became close friends with him.

After the stabbing, Trilling wrote to Mailer and sent him books while he was incarcerated. As soon as he could get to a phone, he called her, and the day after he got out, he went to see her. She must have talked to Hellman the day before Mailer visited her. Hellman was taken aback: "Oh, you're not going to see him alone." She tried to persuade Trilling that Mailer was dangerous. Trilling laughed. "Compared to me, Lillian was a pirate, a highwayman. She lived an infinitely more daring life than I ever did, and here she was warning me not to live so dangerously!" It seemed to Trilling absolutely absurd for her to be scared of Mailer. "I said to myself, 'She's not worried about my safety. She's jealous of the relationship. This is just bitchness.' "

Some time later, after the friendship with the Trillings had declined considerably, Hellman confided to Diana Trilling that

Mailer had been at her house one evening and had raced around the house after her, trying to rape her. Finally, Hellman had locked herself in her bedroom, while Mailer banged on the door in an effort to break it down. The only way she had been able to quiet him was by calling through the door that she had not had anything to do with a man for a long time and was frightened. Had all this really happened? Trilling wondered. "Well," says Trilling, "I took this story with a certain reservation. It didn't fit my picture of Norman." Yet the stabbing had been a shocking event, and Trilling did not quite know how to assess Hellman's story.

Soon Trilling began to notice that something had happened in Mailer's relationship with her. He was very guarded and no longer relaxed and friendly. "Suddenly an idea struck me. 'My God! Lillian has done a *Children's Hour* on me. She has told Mailer that *I* said that he had tried to rape *me*.' " Could Hellman's rape fantasy, if that is what it was, have suddenly been made to be Trilling's? That certainly would have made Mailer most uncomfortable with Trilling—"If Lillian had indeed told Mailer that I was saying that he had tried to rape me, it would make me out to be a very sick person." It bothered Trilling so much that she decided someone had to know, in case it ever came into any kind of public use, so she told William Phillips, an editor of *Partisan Review* and an old friend of hers. She never had any proof of her suspicions; it was an intuition, and perhaps had no basis at all in actual fact. There never seemed a way to broach the subject with Mailer, "so that to this day Trilling is not sure whether she was reading Hellman's conduct accurately or indulging a fantasy" of her own.

Hellman revised her life to suit herself. It was sometime in the late 1950s that she casually remarked to Trilling, "Of course, you're two years older than I am." Diana laughed and pointed out that she and Hellman were exactly the same age—both were born in 1905 and they had known this for years. She thought Hellman was joking. "But she wasn't; she was dead serious. She had just lopped two years off her age. And I was supposed to accept that and go along with it. . . . I didn't even try to say to her, 'Lillian, don't try to lie to me that way. That's stupid.' I just let it go by." There was no rupture, then, between the Trillings and Hellman, but their differences in politics and in feelings colored a friendship that slowly dissolved in the 1960s.

In late 1960, Hammett, still the subject of FBI and IRS scrutiny, was an acutely isolated figure guarded by Hellman "like a lioness," observes Catherine Kober. There were things Hellman could do to make him more comfortable, for this was the beginning of the years when she would receive many honors and invitations and when her position as a literary figure was secured. In May 1960, for example, she was elected a fellow of the American Academy of Arts and Sciences. About the same time, Harvard's Faculty Committee on Dramatics invited her to give the Theodore Spencer Memorial Lecture on Drama at Sanders Theatre (Harvard's largest auditorium). The invitation had come partly through Harry Levin's suggestion, but officially from Archibald MacLeish, an old friend who was also teaching at Harvard. At the informal reception at Levin's house, he introduced her to a new, bright, young dean, McGeorge Bundy. "Those two incisive minds hit it off together extremely well," Levin recalls. Not long afterward, Bundy, MacLeish, and Levin hatched the idea of bringing Hellman back to teach a regular course in playwriting.

Harvard was a congenial place for Hellman. She had come to Boston often for tryouts of her plays, and a fellow playwright, William Alfred, was also teaching at Harvard. He had even taken one of his classes to a performance of *Toys in the Attic*. But if she was to teach there, arrangements had to be made for Hammett as well. There was a nursing home at the corner of the street on which the Levins lived. At Hellman's request, Elena Levin visited the home to see if it would be appropriate for Hammett to stay there while Hellman taught at Harvard. Elena was shocked at the atmosphere. The manager of the home took her into a lovely room, beautifully furnished, with an elderly gentleman sitting in it. The manager indicated that the room would be available in two or three weeks. Perhaps the room's present occupant was deaf, but talking that way in his presence was to Elena an appalling act of insensitivity. When Hellman heard about it, she said it would not matter. Hammett would not pay any attention to people anyway, and certainly not to what they said.

In any event, Hammett did not live to see the nursing home, and Elena Levin's impression was that his death was a relief for Hellman. His long illness had been very wearying for her, and his physical and psychic agony had been great. In his last year, few people saw him. He was fond of Virginia Bloomgarden, who visited him regularly. Catherine Kober loved Hammett and came to see him during his last months. Like many of the children he had charmed at Hardscrabble, she could never forget his extraordinary sensitivity to the child's world. In her book, he was a saint, and it devastated her to see how isolated he felt. On one visit, she caught him looking at a photograph of his daughters. As he turned to her, he put the picture facedown—his visage was a tragic portrait of a man with a broken heart who felt completely alone. Hammett's relationship with his daughter Mary had been difficult for years. There had been violent quarrels. His other daughter, Jo, was more even-tempered and got along well with both her father and Hellman, but she lived far away and had her own family to take care of. Jo sensed that Hellman would have liked Jo to relieve her of the burden Hammett had become. Hellman became somewhat bitter and resentful when Jo made it clear she could not have her father with her. The sight of Hammett could be unnerving. He had aged so profoundly, he looked like death itself.

On January 10, 1961, Dashiell Hammett died. In his last days, Hellman tried to get him to say what their relationship had meant to him. As always, he was most reluctant to say they had done well. While his letters to her were often very tender and amusing, he could not seem to display his affection openly. His nurse remembers his running to the phone in his eagerness to speak with Hellman, yet in person he was usually reserved. It was like Hellman to want more from him, even if she had to write an amusing statement he laughingly signed as his tribute to her:

> Nov. 25, 1960
> 7:10 am
>
> On this thirtieth anniversary of the beginning of everything, I wish to state:
>
> The love that started on that day was greater than all love anywhere, anytime, and all poetry cannot include it.
>
> I did not then know what treasure I had, could not, and thus occasionally violated the grandeur of this bond.
>
> For which I regret.
>
> But I give deep thanks for the glorious day, and thus the name "Thanks-giving."
>
> What but an unknown force could have given me, a sinner, this woman?
>
> Praise God.
>
> Signed.

Dorothy Parker, the Bloomgardens, Patricia Neal, Leonard Bernstein, Arthur Kober, the Trillings, Louis Kronenberger, Norman Podhoretz, and Philip Rahv were among the three hundred people who attended Hammett's funeral. Hellman delivered a eulogy. She knew he would not want words spoken, but she had to honor him and to explain the significance of his life: "He didn't always think very well of the society we live in and yet when it punished him he made no complaint against it and had no anger about the punishment." If Hammett had been highly critical of his native land, he had also defended it in two wars. He had contempt for heroics, but "he was a patriotic man, very involved in America."

Hellman has been accused of exaggerating the place of Dashiell Hammett in her life. It is true that she did not tell the whole story of their time together, but in the end, who knows what the whole story is or how to tell it? If she had a reverent view of this man, so did many other men and women, and these others agree with her portrait of him as a "sinner-saint." Julie Harris, who did not know him at all, saw him in the back of a theater and immediately formed the impression of a saintly man. Virginia Bloomgarden, Catherine Kober, Patricia Neal, Lee Gershwin, Albert and Frances Hackett, and many others venerated him. It broke Lee Gershwin's heart the day Hammett sat in her living room and told her he would never write again. She said she found him such a loving, giving man. He had a way of taking an interest in friends that makes them mourn him to this day. "I wish you would write a book about *this* man, not the drunken sot that seems to beguile so many people," Catherine Kober says.

At Vineyard Haven in the late 1950s, Richard Wilbur and his family saw a great deal of Hammett. Wilbur liked him for many of the reasons Hellman did:

> His impatience with fraud, his integrity, his good stories. My son Christopher was sort of taken up by Dash. This eight-year-old boy, who had a command of baseball statistics, was very much respected for them by Dash, who also knew what Ty Cobb's lifetime batting average was. He would not come down when there were a lot of guests. I suppose Lillian wouldn't ask him down for fear that he would once again hear somebody say something pretentious and go upstairs in disgust.

With Wilbur, Hammett was willing to talk about the who-dun-it form and how it had developed in moral sophistication. They did not talk politics, although Wilbur remembers him as a man who was interested in everything. Trivial chat with him was informed chat. He was mortally sick, but he still seemed very much a man. He and Hellman would have a "joshing relationship" with each other. As Hellman said, to Wilbur Hammett was an old woman about his clothes. Even when he was hanging around in a bathrobe, it was a good bathrobe from Abercrombie's. Wilbur knew, because Hellman sent him some of these clothes after Hammett's death.

Hammett is everywhere in Hellman's memoirs. Even when she is not directly writing about him, he is still there as a kind of offstage presence. His death was the greatest misfortune of her life, even though she went on to build a whole new career for herself. In his recent memoir, Jerome Weidman has explained better than anyone what it meant for Hellman to have Hammett as a companion. Hammett brought out the best in Hellman, Weidman feels. His presence somehow diluted hers. Hellman once asked Weidman if he knew what made her tick. "No," he lied. "Piss and vinegar" was her answer. And it helped to know that, Weidman remarks, if you were to spend any time with her. Hammett once referred to Hemingway as a "smuck." "I think you mean 'schmuck,' " said Weidman's wife Peggy.

> "I mean he's a horse's ass," Hammett said.
> "In that case the proper word is putz," Lillian Hellman said.
> "Is it?" Peggy said to me.
> "I'm not sure," I said.
> I knew a schmuck from a putz, but I knew something more important. Contradicting Lillian was not a rewarding activity.
> "But in certain cases it is," I added diplomatically.
> "Hemingway is such a case," Lillian said.
> That ended that subject, as in her house many did.

According to Weidman, the feeling between Hammett and Hellman was never "overtly sentimental," but "it was almost palpable the moment you came in the door." Once Weidman overheard Hammett and Hellman discussing the screenplay for *The North*

Star. They sounded like businessmen negotiating methodically and systematically, or like workmen "calling off measurements to each other as they prepared to cover a basement floor with linoleum." Hellman disagreed over one of Hammett's suggestions. "He laid it out once more: a, b, c, d. Like a hammer tapping in the tack to hold down the linoleum. Pause. 'No,' Lillian said. Without impatience. Without irritation. But with unmistakable firmness. Exactly like his. Both voices hard, clear, and impersonal. Both starting again from the beginning." By lunchtime the problem was licked and they were telling funny Hollywood stories.

In *An Unfinished Woman*, Hellman mentions a moment when she is writing about Hammett and is compelled to get up and rail against him. The dialogue with him continued after his death. She would do everything in her power to save him for herself. She would wangle the copyrights to his work, fend off his would-be biographers, and threaten lawsuits against directors who wanted to film his life story. In the process, she made a myth of his life and of her life with Hammett. But the materials of the myth were on hand. Enough was there to set pen to paper, to elaborate an image of her better half. At least one of her friends believes that the way she posed for certain photographs, the way she held herself, was Hammett's way as well.

23

HARVARD
(1961)

"I really don't think you can teach writing," Miss Hellman
said to a visitor after the class. "But what you can do is to
show the kiddies what not to do and give them some
simple rules, which, if they are any good, they'll violate
later anyway. You can also give them themes and characters to work with. This is valuable."

—Don Ross, "Lillian Hellman Teaches What Can't Be Taught,"
New York Herald Tribune, April 23, 1961

January 26, 1961. Hellman sent Gladys and Van Wyck Brooks a
postcard from the Beverly Hills Bungalos, Beverly Hills, California. She was there for what "everybody" had assured her would
be a good "change of scene." She was not so sure. She was
preparing to leave in a week for Cambridge, where she would
begin teaching.

March 11, 1961. Hellman was living at Harvard's Leverett House.
She had been referred to Dr. Louis Zetzel by the wife of a Harvard
law professor. Dr. Zetzel took her medical history. Her father had
died at the age of seventy-four, a victim of senile dementia. Her
mother died at the age of fifty-five of cancer of the bowel. She told
Zetzel she had been divorced for thirty years. (Later he would
meet Kober and be touched by the warm, tender relationship
Hellman and Kober had.) She had had polyps of the vocal chords
removed in 1960. The duck bone incident in 1945 was also noted
for the record. She had had the usual childhood illnesses. This was

just a routine checkup and Hellman had no specific complaints—
except for some concern about her chest. She was particularly
conscious of her chest, she thought, because of Hammett's emphysema and respiratory problems. Her self-diagnosis was that there
was nothing organically wrong. She had some difficulty sleeping,
but this had always been a problem. She told Zetzel she did not do
much drinking, but she did smoke a little. As he later learned, she
was an inveterate smoker. He never saw her without a cigarette in
her mouth. He attributed some of her insomnia to the smoking.
He also found that she drank much more than she had admitted.
The results of the physical exam were negative: heart sounds
normal, blood pressure normal, no masses in the abdomen, and
the lungs were clear, skin was dry, reflexes were normal and so
on.

Hellman had coped very well with Hammett's death. Elena
Levin feels that Hammett's absence freed Hellman to throw herself
into her teaching, which she seemed to enjoy enormously. But the
physical exam and comments she made to friends suggest she had
periods of anxiety. She felt vulnerable and even undesirable.
Hellman always wanted a love affair with somebody. After Hammett died, Herbert Gold remembers her saying, in a very touching
way, "I'll probably never be in bed with another man." Of course,
this would not be true. In fact, at Harvard she would enter into an
affair with a dashing chemistry professor.

Teaching a regular college course was a new experience for
Hellman. She frequently demanded help with " 'how to teach'—
something with which she was naturally, and excusably, unfamiliar," according to Professor Walter Jackson Bate, who was chairman of the English department. He had met her socially several
times, liked her, and looked forward to her stay. But giving
Hellman advice was never easy. For Bate, it meant spending hours
with her in the midst of his own busy schedule as chairman,
teacher, and writer.

> I'd be summoned to go to her place for "lunch" to tell
> her what to do and how. It would have taken a tenth
> of the time if she'd have consented to come to the
> office and ask what she wanted. But, unfamiliar with
> busy academics, and being used—as she implied—to
> having people at other colleges wait on her, she
> thought the sophisticated approach was that of a New

York publisher's "cocktails-and-lunch." So I'd drop things and go over, and, after social chit-chat would face questions: "What am I supposed to do with the kiddies?" ("Well, have them submit plays or parts of plays. . . .") "Do I have to read amateur plays by the kiddies? And what am I supposed to say to them?" ("Say what you think. . . .") "Well, how do I say that? . . ." Et cetera. So it would continue for a couple of hours, to be renewed a week later. I confess that, having a lot to do, I began to feel frustrated.

Hellman exploded when Miss Helen Jones, the aged secretary for the English department, neglected to get the first of Hellman's three public lectures (April 17 and 24 and May 1, to be given at the Loeb Theater) announced in the *Harvard Gazette*, a kind of calendar published each week of upcoming events. The lecture had been advertised in large posters all over campus, and a sizeable audience had showed up, but Hellman was not mollified. As Bate recalls:

> My first inkling of this was an irate phone call from Lillian (she never appeared at the office in person) expressing outrage, and demanding that our poor, aged secretary be fired. When I tried to calm her, she kept asserting, "I am not used to having this at other universities, where they really get out the *red carpet* for me!"

The secretary was not fired, and Bate received no more invitations to lunch. He supposes Hellman was still upset over Hammett's death and more than a little "spoiled by the treatment she'd been given at various places." But Harvard had so many distinguished visitors and celebrities that it was impossible to provide red carpets. Another faculty member recounts having introduced one of Hellman's public lectures. He described her as a "thorough professional." After the event, she let him have it. Evidently, she thought the term "professional" was insulting and got herself into a vindictive fury. After that, the faculty member steered clear of her and felt she was the most spoiled woman he had ever met.

Helping Hellman prepare to teach seems to have been as scarifying as the production of a Hellman play, yet she was a rousing success in the classroom. Ken Stuart, one of her students, kept a journal account of her class, and from his notes it is obvious that she was a conscientious, demanding, and inspiring teacher. Like the other students in the course, he had been admitted on the basis of a piece of writing he had submitted to Hellman. In his case, it was a *Harvard Lampoon* parody of a screenplay of *Pride and Prejudice* as it would have been done by Eisenstein. He got to know her a little better than other students because he drove her Jaguar from New York to Cambridge. It was his impression that she had not taught before, and she wanted to be sure she was doing a good thing. She made it clear that she was not teaching playwriting. Two plays were assigned for reading—*Three Sisters*, by Anton Chekhov, and *Danton's Death*, by Georg Büchner—and students were required to write scenes with dialogue, but much of the class centered on short stories: "Felix Krull," by Thomas Mann, "The Prussian Officer," by D. H. Lawrence, and "Eveline," by James Joyce. Hellman knew she could not really teach writing; what she could show students were good examples of it. Now a publisher and teacher of writing classes, Stuart sees very clearly that Hellman had hit upon a procedure often used by teachers:

> You have to get the people together and first of all see what kind of animals we have here. Then you obviously tell them what you know about the business and at the same time you find out what they can do, and you tailor your comments accordingly. She was a very practical, smart, shrewd, tough, cagey lady.

Stuart vaguely recalls that Hellman was upset by the death of Hammett and may have mentioned the fact in class. His journal has one passage on Hammett that suggests his recollection is right. Teaching was an attempt to get herself together and to replace what had been lost with Hammett's death. Stuart observed her eating with faculty at Leverett House, and he remembers how important her maid Helen was in her life. But Hellman wanted a warmth and intimacy in her course. Sometimes she would bring food—especially sweets—for her students. They were her "kiddies," by which she meant no condescension. The term appeared in a newspaper article and she did not want the students to think she was disparaging them. She was maternal and tough, a coach and a guide. She gave the class her number at Leverett Towers, told them mornings were the best time to call, and arranged a few social occasions when she could speak with them outside of class. At the end of the course, each student received an inscribed copy of her collected plays. A few students kept in touch with her, including Stuart, after he had been suspended from Harvard because of a prank. She answered his letter inquiring about a writing job in Hollywood, saying she could not recommend it. It was a very tough life. She was sorry he was not in school and told him to cut out the pranks—it was "small potato stuff." She hoped he would come out to Martha's Vineyard to see her in the summer.

Hellman had shrewdly chosen works of literature that might be particularly appealing to young writers. "Felix Krull," for example, is narrated by a young man who is profoundly impressed by an actor's performance in the theater and who takes on various roles. "Eveline" is the story of a young woman poised to make an enormous decision to leave her native land with her lover. Much of the fiction deals with dramatic turning points in young people's lives. Hellman rarely spoke about writer's lives, but in the case of Georg Büchner, who died at twenty-three, she thought it important—perhaps because he had managed to accomplish so much in one play and at such a young age.

Stuart wrote five stories for Hellman's class—all of them takeoffs on the literature she had the students read. Her point was not that they were to copy from the models she provided them; rather, they could take—she actually used the word "steal"—from Joyce or Lawrence or Mann whatever intrigued them and then make their own stories. Hellman rarely used herself as an example, but she did remark that *Toys in the Attic* had its roots in *Three Sisters*. Hellman made sparing comments on student manuscripts. In Stuart's case, she always summed up her reactions in a sentence or two at the end of a story:

> act of kidnapping too large for short story
> story not about anything—ultilise character—make Betty fast & narrator not liking fast girls
> have fight at party & after fight find out winner doesn't want what he fought for
> tighten story up
> theme—people will fight for what they don't really want
> transition rough from realism & fantasy & then end realistic

These brief critiques show that she was concerned with the strategy of storytelling. Did the student have a subject he could handle within the confines of the form? Were plot and characterization sufficiently defined? Did the story's theme emerge crisply? In the one story of Stuart's that really engaged her attention, she made marginal comments throughout to the effect that he was being too explicit and needed to omit some of his narrator's commentary. She had questions about the meaning and consistency of the narrator's remarks. She circled and questioned bad phrases. In every way, she gave the impression that she was deeply concerned about the craft of writing. On this particular story, they had an argument. Stuart remembers Hellman pushing him to clarify what his narrator meant by the term "moral code." He did not think the story needed more elaboration and later came to feel it was his teacher's own interest in articulating moral issues that led her to ask for such changes in his story.

Sometimes Hellman would read students' stories in class without revealing the names of the authors. She always picked something she could praise, knowing full well that writers' egos were fragile. She wanted the students to talk about their work and was careful not to be too critical in class. Stuart and another student, Peter Benchley, remember a shocking piece by another student. Stuart sat in class wondering what Hellman would say about this castration story. It was discussed seriously, without undue emphasis on the subject matter. The author of the story, Bob Thurman, was, according to Benchley, "a wild, reckless kind of writer." It was his impression that Hellman thought Thurman had guts.

February 18: Hellman's first class began at the beginning. Her first comments focused on "fascinating the audience." It had to be done in the first few minutes. Shock tactics would not work; obscenity would just alienate people. Making a story or play realistic was not the writer's first consideration. Consider the audience first—the effect of speech on the audience—and let them know who was who as soon as possible. Every character should have a distinct way of speaking—the possibilities were endless. Shaw's characters, for example, were all properly differentiated, yet they all talked Shavian language.

For the next class, Hellman wanted to see a page or less, double-spaced, of dialogue, with one or two people on stage. The audience was given to understand that a long journey is taking place. Any tone—comic or serious—was acceptable. Some kind of tension had to be set up, some excitement generated for the audience, and some hint given as to how the play would be resolved. A problem had to be posed, and actors had to have something to do on stage. In the course of giving her instructions, Hellman referred to other dramatists like Shaw, Racine, and Shakespeare to illustrate her points. Although she would lay down rules, she also showed how great writers defied the conventions. The third act of *Man and Superman* had no action; *Troilus and Cressida* had characters on stage with nothing to do. In *Three Sisters*, Chekhov brushed aside the usual kinds of details playwrights feel obliged to supply about their characters. It is never clear, for example, whether the army doctor, Tchebutykin, lives in the same house with the sisters, rents a room, or has some other living arrangement. Hellman pointed out the similarities between *Toys in the Attic* and *Three Sisters*. Her story of two sisters always planning to go to Paris parallels the story of three sisters always wanting to go to Moscow. In both plays, the sisters focused on their recently married brother, and the theme of both works demonstrated that the aimless quality in the characters would be the same no matter what environment they chose to live in. Getting away to Paris or Moscow would have made no difference, according to Hellman. She cited her own play in this instance merely to suggest that other people's work could be used as a springboard for one's own writing.

Be careful about "recognition scenes," Hellman warned her students. She thought this was a trap female writers often fell into. Hellman mentioned she had done a parody of a Katherine Mansfield story for a French magazine to point up this fault. Harping on style was also dangerous. A writer's material should dictate style, as Joyce's did in *Ulysses*. Experiment for its own sake was of no value. A writer had to have something to say, and the subject matter had better be interesting. And always, put people ahead of the theme. Let people lead, she told her students. Here is the gist of what she had to say about good playwriting:

> You don't need so many words. "Yes" can sometimes be just as good as having someone explain why they're saying yes. Elaboration of emotion lots of times is unnecessary. The writing is more forceful and simple without elaboration. Cut out stage directions and description of characters. If you can't *do* the character, *don't*.

There were two good stage directions, as far as she was concerned: to get somebody somewhere or to indicate emotion. Elaborate descriptions of stage sets were usually a waste of time and bred sloppiness. Novelists and story writers had to describe characters; if the playwright followed their tack, the characters would not be able to speak for themselves.

To emphasize her point about characterization in plays, Hellman returned to *Three Sisters*. She noted that Olga was the only sister who really worked; while the other two talked about work, Olga did not—a sure sign that she was the only true worker. By asking perceptive questions about the characters, Hellman demonstrated how shrewdly Chekhov constructed his play. Why did everyone put up with Solyony, a particularly boorish personality? Because life was so aimless in this Russian province; there were no alternatives. In Moscow, Solyony would have been replaced by a fifth-rate pianist, Hellman remarked. The constant illusions to Moscow evoked the picture of a great city and helped to define the "grimy" confinement of provincial life. All of the characters were beautifully differentiated—including Vershinin's wife, who never appears on stage. Hellman might have added that she stole this technique from Chekhov, for the fate of Cyrus Warkins's wife is one of the most moving events in *Toys in the Attic*, although she is only described by Julian. Chekhov relied almost exclusively on dialogue to render characters. He was also extremely economical, selecting only crucial details to define each character.

Hellman felt the turning point in *Three Sisters* was Vershinin's speech in act one on the provinciality of the town. There was no way to conquer its darkness, it backwardness, in a generation, but he projects a future when, in two or three hundred years, the majority of mankind will be living a "beautiful, marvelous" life. Man must prepare for this glorious future—expect it, and it will happen. Irina, who longs for Moscow more intensely than her other sisters, sighs and says that future should all be written down. But, as Hellman shrewdly suggested to students, the speech only reveals the basic insincerity of the characters, since they are unwilling to change the way they live. As much as she treasured Chekhov, Hellman said he did not have the nerve of a great writer, of a Tolstoy. Chekhov's writings were life scale but not larger than life.

Hellman's first class had a kind of shape to it. She had begun by talking about realism and its limits and had ended by expertly taking apart a fine writer's strengths and weaknesses in the realistic vein.

Subsequent classes were of the same consistently high quality. Thomas Mann's "Felix Krull" was picked for its fast-paced story-telling. Hellman went through an elaborate analysis of how the story was constructed and of how the characters were played off against each other. Her explanations were studded with references to Dickens, Hemingway, Faulkner, Shaw, Thomas Wolfe, T. S. Eliot. Her discussions of fiction often brought her back to drama. Make every line in a play count. Take out those phrases you had fallen in love with. This was a favorite maxim Hellman enjoyed repeating to Richard Wilbur and which she had put into an article published just after the premiere of *The Little Foxes*. One student remembered Hellman's picture of writing as creating a Christmas tree: you get the tree, adorn it with ornaments, and finally take all of the ornaments off, so that the barest, sparest of trees is left. Cut exposition wherever possible; there just is no time to lead up to things. Be direct and simple: that was a much harder task than writing in a complicated, fancy fashion. Above all, hold yourself to what you were doing. The mark of a professional writer was to finish a piece. If you do not like it, throw it away. But do not abandon work in progress. She was an exigent writer and teacher, in her student Peter Benchley's estimation. As she read student stories, Hellman was pleased to tell the class their writing was improving. The bad news was that only four students had followed her first assignment properly. Evidently, some of the work had been sloppy, and she found that quite "rude." She told the students that Howard Bay (one of the few people she let read her manuscripts), S. J. Perelman, and William Styron would be coming to class to talk about writing and the theater.

On March 22, the teacher brought chocolates to class. Earlier classes had cookies and mints. She began by talking about adaptation. This had become one of the themes of her class, since she was in effect having students adapt their own stories from the models she was requiring them to study. She said she had considered adapting D. H. Lawrence's *The Fox* as a one-act play, but decided she was not able to because it was already a perfect story. The implication was that successful adaptations were motivated by a writer's belief that he or she could improve in some way on the original. Hellman would expatiate on this idea at great length in her Yale writing class in 1966.

"Felix Krull," "Eveline," and "The Prussian Officer" were all stories that lent themselves to Hellman's concern with psychology. She wanted to show students how a writer had to be true to the characters. Eveline and the Prussian officer's orderly were simple people, and the writer had to restrict himself or herself to delineating personalities who could not articulate reasons for their actions. These were stories about instinct, not understanding.

Howard Bay came to class to give a professional set designer's view of the contemporary theater. Besides commenting on the development of lighting and stage sets, he spoke of the contribution a designer could make to a play. With Hellman's realistic plays, a set helped the audience identify immediately with the action. Hellman admitted the set designer was often a convenient scapegoat: "everybody talks about lighting to avoid talking about other things." She thought an audience should absorb a set and then forget about it when the actors took over the play.

Class for March 29 opened with a discussion of "Eveline." She is a simple person—which does not mean "not bright." Rather, the central character is uncomplicated and decides not to change her life for reasons she will never understand. Why does Eveline turn back from going to America with her beloved? Joyce is good enough not to be explicit. Hellman would make the same point about the relationship between two soldiers in "The Prussian Officer." Lawrence does not say whether latent homosexuality is his subject, and it would be reductive to say it is. Hellman did believe "Eveline" suggests several explanations for the main character's behavior, and she enumerated them for the students:

a) duty
b) fear of unknown
c) love for what is known and worry about what is not known
d) never would have loved Frank unless she had problems—nice simple dutiful good girl

The richness of the story depended, however, on not boiling everything down to one reason. In writing such a story, moral explanations, in particular, would be out of place. This was—Hellman reiterated—a story of instinct. Very rarely do people like Eveline fall in love, and Joyce is not writing a great romance, she concluded.

The class for April 19 featured a dialogue between William Styron and Lillian Hellman. They agreed that most short stories could not have much expository prose. Flashbacks were also difficult to handle. The conversation led to a writer's experience. It was not necessary to be well-traveled; most writers had enough experience to work with by the time they were twenty-five. It was true of Faulkner, of Emily Dickinson, of many writers. Still, at least one student (Peter Benchley) thought this was odd advice coming from Hellman, a writer who had experienced such a varied life. There was much speculation on why writer's write. But it is not clear from Stuart's journal if Hellman or Styron suggested that "writing is a form of giving mother's milk back to the universe through the symbolic use of pen and ink." Most writers had fathers who they admired but who were not terribly successful. Writers were trying to justify their fathers' failures to the world. The artistic instinct involves a power drive, a desire to create something beautiful. What is clear is that both writers were throwing out ideas, not pronouncing axioms.

Toward the end of the term, Georg Büchner's play, *Danton's Death* was taken up. On January 6, 1961, Hellman had written to George Freedley at the New York Public Library requesting biographical material on Büchner. She wanted to know what material was available in English, including translations of Büchner's plays. Could Freedley have somebody do her this "great favor"? She had a very sick friend (Hammett) and was not able to "get out of the house." Büchner lived to be only twenty-three and had written several fragments and this flawed masterpiece. He was a science student and an activist in radical politics. He barely escaped with his life when his associates were apprehended in a failed revolutionary plot. Büchner died in Zurich of pneumonia. His play, Hellman believed, was the work of a brilliant, practical mind disgusted with the ways of revolution yet a revolutionary at heart. He set his play in 1794, a time when the fathers of the revolution were being guillotined. Danton, Hellman felt, was a failure as a character. Büchner provided him with no action, yet Danton embodied a significant insight: any man who asserts himself against historical process will probably be ruined; nevertheless, people always have and always will try to defy history. Hellman saw the play's theme as stating that the men who make revolutions are not always the men who carry them out; indeed the men who make revolutions are often devoured by them. The three-act play contains an extraordinary number of scenes; act two alone contains seventeen. As Hellman noted, Büchner's technique was cinematic and naturalistic. He was trying to capture both the panorama and the fragmented quality of revolutionary reality. Still, there were too many characters in the play. Although Hellman does not seem to have said so, she must have admired Büchner's effort to write a novel in dramatic form—as she had so often tried to do. And she certainly must have identified with his disillusionment with politics (her phrase), for it was her own—even as she was a revolutionary at heart. She loved the play's "cold, brilliant villain," St. Just. Why not? That is surely how she would have written him. There was an arbitrariness about Büchner's throwing in so much, and this was characteristic of most young playwrights, she told her class.

S. J. Perelman came to class in early May. He talked about the influences on his writing style, about how writers had to steal from one another until they developed a style of their own. He spoke of the comic writers he revered and regretted that this kind of prose was not taken more seriously. He had noticed that people would laugh to tears seeing a Marx brothers movie, come out into the lobby and say to each other, "wasn't that silly," and forget it. If they saw an Ibsen tragedy, they talked and cried about it all the way home. Yet humor, great satire, was often the product of serious anger—witness Voltaire's *Candide*. There was much discussion of technique and about how great writers did not let it show. Perelman then discussed agents. "Irving Lazar's opinion on anything was of about as much value as a dung beetle's. You might as well go out in a field and ask a crow." Hellman seemed to take over the discussion at this point. Villains, if there are such things, should not sound like villains or appear to be openly plotting, she explained. Villains, in fact, were often comic. In *The Little Foxes*, Ben Hubbard makes fun of himself—which is an easy way of making a villain come across. As she went on, Hellman became more specific about certain prohibitions in the theater: do not use weak, declining words ("even," "ever," "very"); do not announce actions ("Please be seated. I'm going to begin a long talk."); don't start a play if you do not have enough material to get you through the first act. Hellman was wary of large statements and grand endings. She still rued the conclusion of *The Children's Hour*, she told the students.

Although she had rules—even prejudices—Hellman made it

clear to students that she was laying down the law as she understood it. There was no question but that she might be wrong about some things, but this was her course and she could only teach it as she saw it. When a student suggested that the orderly in "The Prussian Officer" and the officer he kills were "morally equal," Hellman objected. "We don't have to argue whether your interpretation is right or mine is right. Maybe you're right. But you're going to have to take my interpretation for the purposes of this course. Is that clear?"

When it came time for the grades to be submitted, Hellman called her friend Bill Alfred. "Is there any way I can fail anybody who handed me in something every week?" she asked. Alfred said, "No, Lillian. You can't do that." She said, "Oh, okay." Then they went out to dinner, and Alfred asked her about the grade. She said, "I gave him a C, and I wrote, 'You're too damn slick for your own good!' " There is no doubt, however, that she was fond of her students and was sincere when she told journalist Don Ross that "in general, they are much better educated and poised than she was when she was a student at New York University and Columbia."

Dr. Zetzel saw Hellman again on May 20. She felt fine. The time at Harvard was a "good stretch" and she was returning to New York. She was already at work on Burt Blechman's novel, *How Much*, adapting it for the stage. Among other things, she would fasten on the book's satire of generational change. Being at Harvard had quickened her desire to become involved, to write about the young, and to stay young, creatively and exuberantly. The play would have tremendous energy. Hellman was still aiming for a power that was barely under control, a power capable of blowing a stage to bits.

24

MY MOTHER, MY FATHER AND ME
(1961–1963)

I thought, I think now, that it is a funny play, but we did not produce it well and it was not well directed. More important, I found that I had made some of the same mistakes I had made with *Candide*: I changed the tone midway from farce to drama and that, for reasons I still do not understand, cannot be done in the theatre.

—Lillian Hellman, *Pentimento*

Lillian Hellman, playwright, was beginning to have her place in American letters acknowledged. In 1961, she received the Brandeis University Creative Arts Medal and an achievement award from the women's division of the Albert Einstein College of Medicine of Yeshiva University. In 1962, she was elected to the vice-presidency of the National Institute of Arts and Letters. In *World Theatre* (Autumn 1962), Arthur Miller praised her for the "remorseless rising line of action in beautifully articulated plays." Many more honors and tributes were forthcoming.

All of this praise may have made Hellman feel fossilized. She was determined to do something different. She was looking for fresh material and thought she found it in Burt Blechman's novel, *How Much*. It is narrated by Berney Halpern, a nice mixed-up Jewish boy who feels he must participate in every fad in his quest to find himself. He lives in an unruly house with his mother, father, and grandmother.

Hellman was known for the well-made play. She would write a drama that seemed almost chaotic. But she had never written about her Jewish background. *My Mother, My Father and Me*—the title she gave her play—is Jewish with a vengeance. She was nagged by her reputation for melodrama; the new play would be a farce. With the exception of *The Searching Wind*, her work usually needed only one set. Now Howard Bay would be challenged to use the entire stage to suggest scenes taking place in many different locations—an apartment living room, bedroom, a restaurant, a factory, a nursing home, a department store, and so on. Although she would bring her new work to Broadway, it had the flavor of an experimental off-Broadway production. After the tremendous success of *Toys in the Attic*, Hellman was nothing if not daring. She had abandoned an original play to work on this adaptation.

For all of the seeming breaks with her past, *My Mother, My Father and Me* actually proved to be a return to origins. *The Dear Queen*, after all, had been a farce. Although it was never produced and Hellman sometimes appeared to disown it, for years she numbered the manuscript of each new play counting *The Dear Queen* as the first. Thus, a draft of *Watch on the Rhine*—her fourth produced play—was labeled "Play No. 5." Hellman had begun her career in collaboration with Louis Kronenberger by satirizing middle-class values. The royal characters in the play do not know what to do with their lives and look to the middle class for new models of behavior. As with *My Mother, My Father and Me*, *The Dear Queen* has fun with people who have not really grown up. Lord Warn, the advisor to the royal family, puts it to Sophia, the dear, dowager queen: "you and your whole family are charming—but you are children."

The title of Hellman's last completed play suggests autobiography. The play takes place, in a sense, in the mind of Berney Halpern, who ultimately "finds himself" by writing a novel about his family and himself. As in Blechman's novel, Berney still lives with his parents, even though he is well into his twenties. His father is a struggling businessman whose major concern is how much things will cost him. How much will it cost to put his wife's mother into a nursing home? How much will Berney's various occupations and hobbies set him back? Will his wife's shopping sprees bankrupt him? Berney is at odds with himself and his world and shifts comically from being a photographer, to a folk singer, to a medical student, to any number of "in" things that speak to his social conscience.

In *The Dear Queen*, the seventeen-year-old Elizabeth, a princess with nothing to do, prefigures Berney Halpern, who is a kind of privileged Jewish prince. Elizabeth masquerades as different people. She has pretended to be Voltaire's mistress—also "a Greek courtesan—without underwear." Both Berney and Elizabeth would prefer to let things hang out. They want to defy conventions and be their own people. Berney idealizes blacks and sees them as functioning more authentically than whites. He berates a white musician for even attempting to play jazz, since that is clearly (in his mind) the province of blacks. Elizabeth is also looking for something fulfilling. She drags a spinning wheel around with her and announces that she is spinning cloth for the poor. "If only we could live a free life—like the people out there [outside the palace]—I wouldn't have to invent things"—is her lament. In *The Dear Queen*, it is Jews who are exotic, not blacks. In explaining her choice of husbands, Sophia exclaims to her family, "It is no secret that I've been sick of you all for years. I really wanted a postman or a Jewish person."

In *An Unfinished Woman*, Hellman alludes to her childhood worship of blacks, her feeling that somehow they were more genuine. She turned to them because, like Elizabeth, she was sick of her own well-heeled family. The Newhouses were hardly aristocrats, yet they set themselves up in style and certainly treated their blacks as peasants. In her plays, it is often black women or lower-class servants who function as the voice or the chorus of truth. Hellman knew this was—in some degree—an affectation on her part and sometimes satirizes it as such in her plays. She was very much like her young, earnest characters. She could not resist pointing out to her Harvard class that reviewers seemed to miss the fact that she had named Lily in *Toys in the Attic* after herself. Alexandra in *The Little Foxes*—particularly the movie version—is a very accurate portrait of the self-righteous, obnoxiously innocent adolescent that Hellman portrays in *An Unfinished Woman*. Bodo, in *Watch on the Rhine*, has a similarly annoying habit of pontificating about his morality. In *The Searching Wind*, Sam Hazen may be a mouthpiece for Hellman's high principles; he is also her insufferably moralistic alter ego. Most of these young characters are opinionated and yet without a direction in life. The playwright had to be most sympathetic. She was twenty-nine years old before her first successful drama was produced, and she was still complaining about her mother's interference in her life. By her own account, she floundered for years before she found herself. Certainly, her family's preoccupation with money and business and her father's own commercial failure enter into her attraction to the material in *My Mother, My Father and Me.* The very title, of course, is Hellman's own, and it serves to focus attention not on materialism—as does the novel's title—but on family relationships. *An Unfinished Woman* begins with a family history that suggests the roots of many of Hellman's strongest emotions stemmed from "my mother, my father and me."

There is no plot to the play because there is no logic to the characters' lives. Mrs. Halpern, exhibiting much of the daffy behavior attributed to Hellman's own mother, cannot hold any conversation without changing the subject. Her attention span is that of the shopper. When a new item attracts her, she loses complete control of her train of thought. Similarly, Mr. Halpern's mind is market-oriented: will his shoes sell? His shoe company fails—just as Max Hellman's failed. No one seems interested in Berney, except insofar as he can be made into a product of the family. At the same time, he is incredibly spoiled and seems to have every expensive plaything he has requested from his father. This is not exactly the kind of treatment Hellman had from her parents, but it is close. Certainly, her mother and father never understood her career—any more than Berney's parents can understand his inchoate efforts to lead a committed life. Hellman's mother was rather fey; her father, charming, but ultimately not in tune with her desires. In the play, Berney's grandmother, Jenny, insists that he strike out for himself. In Blechman's novel, she is a much weaker character who lacks the independence Hellman gives her. The novel also includes a black cook and housekeeper, Hannah, who will not put up with any of Berney's nonsense or that of the other white characters. Hellman must have been struck by how much of Blechman's novel fit her own background—two of Blechman's characters were named Hannah and Jenny. Sophronia, Helen, and Hellman's two aunts provided a kind of sensible stability that was lacking in her parents. Similarly, Berney's only sources of healthy criticism are Hannah and Jenny.

A story Hellman liked to tell about her parents helps to explain why her treatment of family life in *My Mother, My Father and Me* is at once so devastatingly funny and sordid. On the way to the premiere of *The Children's Hour*, Max Hellman, a mischievous wag, told his nervous, gullible wife Julia to be prepared for a shocking event, a scandal: their daughter was going to have a character actually go to the toilet on stage. After the play, Julia turned to her husband and said with great relief, "I told you Lillian would not do a thing like that!" The story was outrageously amusing, but it was also demeaning to all concerned. The truth was that Hellman's parents did not know how to cope with her success; she never figured out why she was so fond of them and yet so angry. Surely, part of what vexed her was that neither parent knew what it meant to her to have a career. Similarly, Berney Halpern does not just want to live or to have a job; he seeks a meaning, a purpose, in existence, and his parents do not have an inkling of how painful thwarted ambition is for him.

As usual, the playwright took about eighteen months to work in methodical fashion on her adaptation. She began with notes for a first draft. Dialogue came rather quickly and whole scenes were rapidly fleshed out. The main problem for Hellman was to gauge how much of the original novel she should use. The length of scenes diminished or expanded as she sought to achieve the right balance. Her rehearsal script shows that she was still making line changes after the play went into production. She added many new characters—Mr. Kelly, Styron, Binkie-Pie—who would appear for only a scene or two. She quite deliberately created more characters than appeared in the novel—perhaps because the main figures, Mr. and Mrs. Halpern, were essentially one-joke characters and other kinds of comic relief were needed. The large cast was outstanding: Anthony Holland (Berney), Ruth Gordon (Rona Halpern), Walter Matthau (Herman Halpern), Helen Martin (Hannah), Lili Darvas (Jenny Stern, Berney's grandmother), Henry Gibson (Binkie-Pie), Heywood Hale Broun (Mr. Kelly). Since she did not have the novelist's option of satirizing society in a narrative, these characters dramatized the ridiculous insincerity and the stupidity of the times. Mr. Kelly is the no-nonsense, persistent IRS man who cannot accept Mr. Halpern's dishonest bookkeeping. Binkie-Pie is a half-beatnik, half-Hammettized writer of hardboiled, so-cially conscious fiction. Styron (named after the novelist) is there to satirize current fashions in social protest:

> BERNEY *(to Styron):* I wish I had been born a black man.
> I wish I had a chance to raise up a downtrodden
> people.
> STYRON: Ain't you a Jew, Mr. Berney?
> BERNEY: Yes, but nobody does anything to us anymore.
> STYRON: Well, pretend you a nigger. Lot of people do
> now.

William Alfred—not only a close friend but a fellow dramatist—
did not like the play:

> You see what happened was that Lillian sometimes
> would get infected with those strange New York rages
> for a particular book. And that book came at the end
> of a period of material about fighting with your par-
> ents and so on. I went to the Vineyard and read it. You
> always had to tell her the truth. I said, "I don't see
> why you're doing this." She gave me one of her
> Maggie and Jiggs looks, so I shut up like a clam.

When Hellman showed her manuscript to Howard Bay, he thought
it was a mistake. "Lillian had these periodic changes of life. She
thought she should get with it." *How Much?* was a "throwaway"
and should be dramatized as such. Bay thought Hellman had
spent too much time developing her characters. Hellman wanted a
realistic set, but to the designer that posed a problem because the
play breezed from one location to another with abandon.

Kermit Bloomgarden was also wary, and his wife Virginia
pleaded with him not to produce it. But he felt he owed it to
Hellman and went ahead—although he had trouble raising money
for the play and had to invest the funds he was saving for his
children's college education. Gower Champion was hired to direct,
and in retrospect, no one seems to remember why. He was highly
successful with musicals and seemed to have some gift for comedy,
but there was no reason to suppose that he understood how to
stage this offbeat drama. "I'm afraid she picked Champion because
he was 'hot' that season," says William Alfred. Walter Matthau,
who played Berney's father, thought Champion was Hellman's
choice because she could "bulldoze him into whatever she wanted
to do. I don't think Gower Champion ever understood that play."
The director "blew a whistle and rehearsals started on time, but it

wasn't much help," according to Howard Bay. Hellman was her usual self. Matthau remembers that "she wanted to hear the words and see the character *immediately.*" Since the actor had a loud voice and no patience with method acting, he suited the playwright. She was at rehearsal every day, and he found her to be an intimidating presence in the theater.

When Heywood Hale Broun, who got the part of Mr. Kelly, read the script, he thought that it was a strange play of ideas, but that it had a lot of brilliance. He did not know whether it would come off. In any event, he was dismayed to see it received like a "dirty version of the Goldbergs [an early television show]." Broun places much of the blame for the production's failure on Gower Champion. Hellman fussed about the director. Broun was puzzled. Why not go to Bloomgarden and say, "This is my play, and I don't want Champion to do it." He wondered if this was part of her Southern heritage—that no matter how tough you are, "the *ladies* do not generally go up against the gentlemen." By the time Champion was fired and Arthur Penn was brought in, it was too late. According to Broun, Hellman realized something had gone wrong in the course of rehearsals and said, more than once:

> "It is time we had black and Jewish villains." She thought we had gone too far the other way from the stereotype of the cringing Jew and the childlike Negro. But for the play to work, it would have to be directed with a cold, brittle French style, so that you realize this is not naturalism. Well, Gower Champion directed the beginning of it like a kind of warm, human comedy, so that when the black maid suddenly said to Tony Holland (Berney), as he's strumming his guitar and singing about "niggers," "Who are you calling a nigger, you kike," the audience went through the floor. That was the end of the play—they withdrew from it.

Matthau told Hellman he thought the play was anti-Semitic. To which she replied, "Just because I'm a Jew doesn't mean I can't pick on Jews." Matthau agreed, but for a dramatization he thought she had to "watch the continuous usage of bigotry heaped on one specific group for specific sociological and political purposes." Hellman remained vehement in rejecting Matthau's charge, although he thought she felt a little guilty that he had pointed out the problem. Martin Peretz, who first met Hellman when she was teaching at Harvard and later worked with her on the Committee for Public Justice, also told her the play was anti-Semitic:

> "Oh, Marty, you're always worried about the Jews. You always see anti-Semitism."
> I said, "I love *Portnoy's Complaint*. I didn't think that was an anti-Semitic novel."

Heywood Hale Broun believed that the play verged on anti-Semitism. But the playwright was willing to take that risk. He remembers Hellman saying, "always to make the Jew, the Negro, a hero is also a form of condescension." Everybody in the play was no damn good, as far as she was concerned. "It was a bitter Volpone play," suggests Broun, and actress Ruth Gordon caricatured Rona Halpern, Berney's mother, the Jewish woman shopper with gusto. Broun remembers her playing the role without any scruples about making her character a stereotype. The curious thing is that Matthau and Hellman remained friends after the production. In fact, his wife and Hellman often went on shopping sprees together.

Interviewer Christine Doudna asked Hellman whether she was "conscious of being Jewish." Certainly, Hellman replied, "but I don't clearly know what it means to me." To another interviewer, Sylvie Drake, she admitted, "I myself make very anti-Semitic remarks but I get very upset if anybody else does. I wasn't brought up as a Jew. I know almost nothing about being one—I'm sorry to say—though not sorry enough to go to the trouble of learning." Richard Wilbur remembers that he and Hellman "had a constant vein of chat going" about her Jewishness. Wilbur was attracted by the possibilities of becoming Jewish. He asked Hellman what his chances were. She had a strong liking for things Jewish, especially the cuisine. Albert Hackett remembers several weekend parties with Hellman at which the menu consisted of several Jewish delicatessen items. But anti-defamation was certainly not one of her great causes. If she was critical of Jews, Wilbur took it as a sign of her comfortable sense of being Jewish. Coming from someone else, her criticism might have seemed racist. Wilbur recalls that she hated "all those damn power craft out in the harbor in front of her house at Martha's Vineyard. She referred to them as 'stinkpots'—

which everyone else did—and also called them 'Jewish cocktail boats.' " "Rappaport" was for her a Jewish name for a certain category of obnoxious characters. If, for example, some unauthorized persons invaded a play rehearsal, she would not be content until she got "those Rappaports" out of the theater. William Alfred finds it hard to believe that Hellman even understood the charge of anti-Semitism—so much of her milieu was Jewish. Alfred also challenges the view that the playwright's targets in *My Mother, My Father and Me* were just Jewish. When Rona Halpern orders things from various department stores, she says "let's enjoy a little beauty." "Well," Alfred suggests, "that's Irish, too."

Alfred remembers parts of the original production vividly. He was there opening night. He sat next to a woman who seemed to have been marinated in about six martinis, and she was very, very Boston. Every time he would laugh, she would turn to him and say, "Really." The difficulty was not only the play, it was the casting. Although actress Lili Darvas, received excellent reviews, Alfred thought that to cast Darvas, one of the most famous beauties in the world, as a kind of annoying grandmother (Jenny) was a mistake. The other thing was that while Howard Bay's set was beautifully intricate, it was mounted on trolleys. Every time it switched, it reminded Alfred of the Seventh Avenue subway on a hot August afternoon. Scenery was mounted on squeaking runners, and they would "set your teeth on edge," Alfred remembers.

With few exceptions, reviews of *My Mother, My Father and Me* were respectful of Hellman's talent but damning of the play. Critics noticed she was trying something new—that there was a theater-of-the-absurd quality in the outrageous, manic behavior of the characters. She was a great admirer of Beckett and once told William Alfred that she did not see what was left to write for the theater after Beckett. It was his taking drama to extremes that must have appealed to her. The problem—as she herself recognized—was her inability to make the tone of the play consistent. The drama wobbled, as the *Time* magazine reviewer put it (April 5, 1963). As satire, it lacked the "moral suasion . . . that comes from being half in love with what one loathes, cherishing the sinner while hating the sin." Hellman never understood this kind of criticism. To accede to it would have meant being soft on people— a hard thing to do for a woman whose psychiatrist had told her to take a "cold view" of herself.

Several reviewers noted that the pacing of the Gower Champion production was off. While the Jewish nature of the play was acknowledged, the consensus was that Hellman's true target was the middle class—which meant just about everybody. The most insightful reviews came from Michael Smith in *The Village Voice* (March 28, 1963) and Emory Lewis in *Cue* (April 6, 1963). Smith observed that Hellman's play had improved on Blechman's novel by its "closer definition of the relationship between Berney and his grandmother." Jenny had "an old-world dignity and directness" that provided some perspective on the looniness of contemporary life. At the same time, Hellman avoided sentimentality or nostalgia, since Jenny's values could not be enforced in the present. Rather, Jenny, facing death, gives Berney the money that will liberate him from his family. It is money that should have been for her own last days and she gives it without the assurance that Berney will make proper use of it. But it is a gesture, Smith rightly points out, "a break forward into the unknown." It is also, as William Alfred notes, characteristic of a playwright who saw money as power, who had Sophie in *The Autumn Garden* and Regina in *Another Part of the Forest* recognize that their liberation depended on the power of money.

In his book, *Stages: The Fifty-Year Childhood of the American Theatre*, Emory Lewis regarded *My Mother, My Father and Me* as a "high point of theatre in the 1960s." He agreed that the production was a disaster—for many of the same reasons Heywood Hale Broun has given. "Everything needed to be done in an exaggerated, stylized fashion, in the Molière manner of the Comédie Française. The settings could have been suggested rather than detailed," Lewis wrote. The play was a parable of middle-class life, not a realistic documentary about it. In his trenchant summary of the characters, Lewis demonstrates that Hellman wrote a play that showed no mercy:

> This mama has nothing in common with the cloyingly sentimental, loving, impossibly wise woman of our folklore. The father is a sniveling, harried bore, too busy cheating the government and borrowing to pay his bills to notice his family. The son is a walking wreck, trying to find himself in folk music, beatnik literature, and other frenzied pursuits. His liberalism is as phony as a three-dollar bill. Grandmother is quite unwanted, and finally the hypocrites place her in a

home for the aged. The son finally loses his identity among the American Indians, though—along with other noble savages—he must don war-paint and sell cheap trinkets to the tourists.

Lewis notes that Edmund Wilson admired the play's harshness—the very ungiving quality that disturbed most reviewers. Robert Lowell also praised the play for its "weird inventions, its wit, and the gay variety of its anguish." The poet identified Hellman's originality: she can be grim and funny. Her unpleasant criticism redeems itself because it is entertaining and provocative, because there is so much energy and wit in her misanthropy. But these were literary opinions that did not count on Broadway, Lewis suggests. Gerald Weales has said almost the same thing about *Candide*, the only musical he can think of in which the "verbal wit is so demandingly intellectual. This fact, plus the tone of the show as a whole—a cynicism that is satirical, even moral, rather than conventionally sentimental—may explain its failure on Broadway."

To Lewis and to Weales, the poor reception of both *Candide* and *My Mother, My Father and Me* was largely the result of deficiencies in the audience, not in the playwright—notwithstanding Hellman's confessions of inadequacy with respect to both plays. Her utter lack of sentimentality—Tennessee Williams and Arthur Miller, for example, do seem soft-minded next to her—probably does explain why critics and audiences (part of the great middle class) have not warmed to some of her plays. She has never been a liberal or a middle-class playwright, and her contempt for liberalism is in part responsible for her losses.

However, this is not the whole story. In her quest to be as clear as possible, Hellman sharpens her characters to such a point that some of their humanity is sheared away. Take a look at Lewis's bald summary of the characters in *My Mother, My Father and Me* and you see both her great strength and weakness. Her characters stand out in bold relief, but there is no contrapuntal force within them, no inner tension against which they might react. They are all one thing. Now consider Willy Loman or Blanche Dubois. Their lives may be as out of control as Hellman's characters' lives are, but Willy and Blanche are human enough to sense, if not to rectify, their faults. Willy is a gripping character because he has suppressed many truths about himself. That is why he comes home after running his car off the road at the beginning of the play. The same can be said for Blanche, who is well aware of why she puts a shade over a naked light bulb, even if she glosses over her aging with a poetic flair. The truth is there waiting for these characters to grasp. And that truth remains vivid—so much so that Willy and Blanche have become a part of the American mythos. In the end, what debilitates *My Mother, My Father and Me* is not that Hellman attacks too many targets; it is not that she lacks a plot; it is not that her theme is hackneyed. In the end, it is her characters that do not quite live. They have their brilliant moments, but as soon as the play is ended, they deflate. It is in performance alone that they exist; in performance, a Hellman character may be more vivid than anything her contemporaries brought to the stage. Her dialogue is often better than Miller's, more precise than Williams's. But there is more to creating character than skewering personalities.

After *My Mother, My Father and Me*, Hellman would attempt other plays but never finish them. In interviews, she sometimes insisted that she might have another play in her. In her memoirs, she mentions it as a possibility but thinks it unlikely. Right after the failure of her last drama, she vowed to Walter Matthau that she would never write another one. She would write other kinds of books; she did not want to have to depend on producers, directors, and actors. She always seemed like a tough old lady to Heywood Hale Broun, but "that play hurt a lot," he recalls. It ran only a few weeks. Actors took pay cuts and a small cult following developed, but there was not enough interest in it to continue. Shortly after *My Mother, My Father and Me* closed, Hellman ran into S. J. Perelman and Broun, whose play, *The Beauty Part*, had also just closed. They were walking along Broadway and she pointed to a little Mom-and-Pop candy store and said, "Sid, why don't we open one of those? We can sell cigarettes and razor blades. We're just two old Jewish failures." It was the only time Broun ever heard her speak without self-confidence or arrogance.

THE MATTER OF MEMORY

(1962–1968)

I always had a trick memory. I can forget the name of
someone I had dinner with two nights ago and remember
in vivid detail the face of someone I never met but saw
sitting across the room 20 years ago.

—Joan Cook, "Furniture Collection That Charts Lillian Hellman's
Career," *The New York Times*, November 13, 1967

E ven though *My Mother, My Father and Me* was a failure, nearly
every review professed enormous respect for Lillian Hellman.
Critics wanted it said that she was one of the prominent playwrights of her age. It must have occurred to her that she had
enormous literary capital on which to draw. Even *Montserrat*,
revived in 1961, received some respectful reviews. In September
1962, Hellman wrote to Cheryl Crawford (one of the best producers
on Broadway) that she was pleased Crawford was interested in
reviving *The Autumn Garden*. Academics regularly included the
playwright in their surveys of twentieth-century drama, graduate
students began writing dissertations on her dramatic career, and
in 1963 the University of Texas acquired several of her manuscripts
and other papers. Her body of work in the theater was ranked very
highly. If she could not match the grandeur of Eugene O'Neill's
output, there was no one else to whom she could be compared
except the later generation of Arthur Miller and Tennessee Williams. Many of her contemporaries—Elmer Rice and Clifford
Odets, for example—still interested scholars and theater-goers,

but their careers did not compare favorably with hers. Plays like *Watch on the Rhine,* which might seem too much a part of their own time, remained vivid because of her wonderful ear for human speech and her deft characterization. As Allan Lewis suggested in *American Plays and Playwrights of the Contemporary Theatre* (1965), Hellman was the most "resilient" dramatist of her generation and worth discussing in the light of Ibsen and Chekhov.

Renewed interest in Hellman's work was not always helpful, of course. In March 1962, a new film version of *The Children's Hour* appeared, starring Shirley MacLaine, Audrey Hepburn, James Garner, and Miriam Hopkin, as the aunt (who played Martha in *These Three*). William Wyler, director of *These Three,* thought he could now bring to the screen an accurate version of the play, without the bowdlerization of 1930s' censorship. Hellman had produced an outline for a new film but did not write the screenplay. Few critics liked the movie. The play now seemed incredible. How could a whole community have believed a child's accusations of lesbianism? Hellman did not like this version either, and she knew why. Wyler was too faithful to the original. The times had changed, and in order for *The Children's Hour* to be successful it had to be completely rewritten. In *Hellman in Hollywood,* Bernard F. Dick shows that Wyler was not only bound by the 1930s play, he also failed to go much beyond what he had tried to do in *These Three.*

In December 1962, Simone Signoret brought an adaptation of *The Little Foxes* to the French stage. It was not well received, and Hellman hated it. Signoret's feelings were hurt, especially because she felt the production had been misrepresented in *Pentimento.* It was not true, Signoret insisted in *Nostalgia Isn't What It Used to Be,* that two weeks before the production Hellman had told her and the cast what was wrong with the production. On the contrary, the actress had implored the playwright to take a more active part in rehearsals, and it was only twenty-four hours before the actors were to perform that Hellman arrived to blast them with a "verbal shower" of criticism that was devastating. Signoret writes:

> Does one really forget? Or does one arrange? Or does one contrive? . . . Lillian, you know perfectly well that you only arrived the day before the opening. . . . Perhaps I should have written you a letter after I read *Pentimento.* I didn't do it. At the time it didn't seem

that important. Today, since all this is a matter of my memory, I don't see why I shouldn't confront mine with yours.

Autobiographical passages began to appear in some of Hellman's journalism in these years, but most of this writing is ephemeral, and there is not much indication that she had hit upon a form that might rival her success in the theater. In 1965, the producer Sam Spiegel invited her to write the screenplay for *The Chase*. It was her first big movie assignment since she had been blacklisted fifteen years earlier. Arthur Kober's diary records how she relished Spiegel's attention, showing off his gift to her of a diamond pin. By April, the Spiegel assignment had soured, and she was regaling Kober and the Hacketts with stories about Spiegel's perfidy. "He's the monster now," Kober noted.

The movie was based on several Horton Foote stories, a television play, and a novel. Bernard F. Dick has discovered that Spiegel hired someone to do a preliminary screenplay, then Hellman was called in to do a revised version. The final product was mostly her writing, as she admitted in a letter to Dick and in an interview with Fred Gardner. She complained that her work had been botched by rearranging scenes. She was also disturbed by the graphic violence—although this aspect of Foote's work and the Southern location (a small Texas town) must have attracted her, for she built into the screenplay the character of Val Rogers, who is reminiscent of Cyrus Warkins in *Toys in the Attic*. The power of money—an obsession with all of the characters in *The Chase*—invited Hellman's interest in the screenplay. Everyone accuses the sheriff (Marlon Brando) of having been bought off by Rogers (E. G. Marshall). The plot of the movie centers on Bubber (Robert Redford), the town's good-natured ruffian, who has escaped from prison. Bubber is a romanticized figure—like Julian in *Toys in the Attic*—in that he is both loved for his high spirits and condemned for his recklessness. But unlike Julian, he becomes a scapegoat for the community's rage against the rich. On the one hand, Bubber is his own man and that is admirable; on the other hand, as his own man he threatens a community that is afraid of confronting Rogers and the power of money. Everyone, in one way or another, owes his or her livelihood to this rich man. They hate him but they resent Bubber, who has chosen not to play by the rules set down by the wealthy. Hellman makes Tarl, Texas, a company town, so that some of the attitudes expressed in *Days to Come* are also reflected in *The Chase*.

In *The New York Times* (June 20, 1965), Peter Bart reported that "Lillian Hellman told friends she was intrigued by the prospect of dissecting a Texas town, in the light of the Kennedy assassination, to reveal the undercurrents of brutality." She seems to have had in mind a cruelty in society that permitted discrimination not only against blacks but against the poor. But Arthur Penn made the film into an orgy of violence, and Hellman was so distressed by it that she stopped speaking to him. *The Chase* is a crude work, and most characters are meanly caricatured. In itself, this should not have bothered Hellman—given her own penchant for character assassination in *My Mother, My Father and Me*. However much the shooting style and structure departed from her intentions, she must accept blame for the dialogue, in which characters speak their feelings in such an obtrusive way that one cannot escape the conclusion that she was writing a message picture. When the sheriff puts a black man in jail for his own protection, he announces, "Some of those people [the townspeople] are just nuts. I have to lock up a man here just to stop them from killing him."

In an interview with Irving Drutman (*The New York Times*, February 27, 1966), Hellman noted that "what was intended as a modest picture about some aimless people on an aimless Saturday night got hot and large, and all the younger ladies in it have three breasts—Well, it is far more painful to have your work mauled about and slicked up than to see it go in a waste-basket." She was through working on any project that would mean collaboration. She reminded Drutman that before the introduction of sound, the movies had been a director's medium. Writers like Fitzgerald and Faulkner never knew how to contend with movies made by committee. The Europeans had found a solution by often having the director write the film or work so closely with a few writers that the product looked like the accomplishment of one person. Of course, this is how Hellman had worked for Goldwyn. She then went on to make an interesting suggestion to Drutman which showed that she was still actively engaged with the film medium:

> Why not a new kind of script? A kind of outline of action, the sequences in order, the characters loosely defined, the end in view. Beyond that—and that, of course, is a great deal—you would write only the first

few lines of each scene, leaving the rest to be impro-
vised, going loose with what is there, or throwing it
out, if something better came along.

The idea was to give the director a firm plan but to allow for
flexibility within the structure so that he would not feel "as
cramped as he often does now." She thought she would like to try
such a script. It is a pity that Robert Altman (one of her favorites)
or John Cassavetes—directors who have approximated the approach she advocated—did not give her the opportunity to try it.

In early 1966, Hellman taught at Yale. She had come at the
invitation of her close friend John Hersey, master of the university's Pierson College. On the first day of class, she told her eight
students she was teaching an "exploratory course." She found
them a little too formal and pointed out that the class would only
work if they learned to talk to one another. She encouraged
interruption and argument. She wanted them to take seriously
what they were doing, not what they had done. They were there
to find out if they liked writing enough to keep doing it. She was
not a composition teacher and would not be instructing them in
the mechanics or the grammar of writing. She was there to give
them feedback, to tell them if she thought their writing worked.
She hoped she would have good suggestions on how to fix what
was wrong. Students were free to accept or to reject her advice.
The examples of writing she chose to discuss differed from her
Harvard syllabus. The first class was devoted to a discussion of
Gertrude Stein's lecture at Oxford in 1926, "How Writing is Written." Her students inquired about Stein's handling of repetition
and the use of time in writing. Hellman not only responded to
questions, she admitted that there were certain points she was not
sure of. The important thing was to understand the context of
Stein's lecture, which was designed, Hellman thought, to "give
you the impression that she is talking to you." In other words,
Stein was not speaking as a college professor but as a working
professional who was being as intimate as she could with her
audience. This was a provocative way to begin a class, to define for
students where Hellman herself was coming from.
Hellman was on the Yale campus three days a week and stayed
in a suite of rooms, which were right across from a tiny courtyard
next to where her class was held. Hersey often invited students to

social affairs, where they got to meet many writers in a casual, give-and-take atmosphere. Ralph Penner, one of Hellman's students, remembers that she broke her class into two sections, and on successive weeks would have the students to dinner—"or tried to. It didn't work in either case. She kept trying to cook steak and kept incinerating it." He had the impression that she was not a "home person." He remembers Hellman had a "strangely maternal" attitude toward her students. It was odd, he thought, because she had relatively little contact with them. She often talked to her students of being frightened. She did not know what was going to happen next. Her fears were not specific and to Penner it seemed she had learned to cope with them extremely well.

Penner heard a teacher speaking as a New Yorker with Southern overtones. Hellman's speech was clipped and straightforward. On social occasions, and after about six Scotches, her talk wandered and she became parenthetical. In the classroom, much of her time was taken up with her cigarette. Frequently she did not look right at a person. She spent a lot of time gazing out the window. She wore conservative, dark colors, except for one blinding red suit that she liked. Her hair was the most outlandish thing about her. It was very thick, very blond, and completely out-of-date—"a bouffant with wings," Penner recalls. "There was this incredible craggy face with an unbelievable nose and hair that should have been on a six-foot-tall model. From the back—if she was sitting down—you'd have absolutely no idea that this wrinkled, crazed face was going to look into your face when she turned around."

Nearly all of the Hellman reading assignments were short— things like Kafka's letter to his father. She emphasized that to write a good story, one really had to want to do that. And she was not counting on students to have inspiration. Consequently, they should think of themselves as writing adaptations of the works she assigned for reading. If they were to become professional writers, the chances were that a significant part of their time would be spent on adaptations. In addition, they would learn a great deal about different genres, about how a novelist had to look at certain material from the vantage point of his or her form. Adaptation was often a good way of seeing which works of literature really lived. She felt that if a work could withstand the transition from one form to another, there was a core that was valuable.

Students listened to the cast recording of *Candide* and were required to read John Gay's *Beggar's Opera* and Marc Blitzstein's translation of the *The Threepenny Opera*. Forbidding them to check the Kurt Weill music, she asked the students to create a sequence in a musical, including one up tempo song and one ballad. The temptation to find the actual music was very strong, Penner recalls. She seemed very pleased with her work on *Candide* and was "hellbent in demonstrating that a song could not just be dumped into a musical. It has to be part of the ongoing action. If possible, it should give you more insight into the characters or situation."

Hellman told the students to read *Robinson Crusoe* in a week. Penner did not know how the other students felt, but his reaction was, "Come on, this is a tome! And a boring one, at that." He tried to read it but quit in disgust. He was totally unprepared for the fact that the whole class had done pretty much the same thing.

> We all arrived for class, sat down—fakers, all of us, sitting there with our notebooks and our copies of *Robinson Crusoe*, bent to look as though we had read them. She came in and asked a couple of questions. In about two minutes it was clear that not one of us had so much as gone past the first three pages. That was when the shock took place. Lillian Hellman's look was one that could make you feel that you had failed or succeeded. "Do I take it that not one of you has read this?" We all put our heads down. There was a silence. We looked up and she was sitting there with tears streaming down her face. We got nervous. One of us said, "What's wrong?" She said, "No, I'm trying to figure out what I did wrong." She blamed herself for the fact that we had not read the book.

In the ensuing discussion, the students confessed that they found the novel a colossal bore. She said, "Yes, but only because of the way it is written." One student asked, "Isn't that the point about successful writing?" She said, "Not always." She explained that there were some things that they would have to go through even if they are not presented well or to one's liking, simply because what is there is important. *Robinson Crusoe* was significant because it was one of the basic plots in literature: a person marooned. The assignment was to do a treatment of that plot in their own terms.

Penner's story idea was to have somebody trapped in the Badlands. In a forty-five-minute consultation, one-to-one, Hellman "stomped all over the idea right at the very beginning." She thought it was ridiculous. "If he got in, he can get out. You have to make sure that your premise will be solid." Penner suggested that the character might be injured. "Ah, now we're hitting pay-dirt," she said. "Doesn't that change the idea of the story?" Penner wondered. She said, "No, the point is that the person is marooned. You have to make clear the person cannot get away." The student always found his teacher frank but never mean. Unlike other professors, she did not "pussyfoot." When writing was bad, she said so. There were "no big windbag explanations." There may have been occasions when she hurt people's feelings, but students also knew they were free to disagree with her. "You had to be able to state flatly what your case was. Wrangling sessions were a big waste of time." After one two-hour discussion, she told a student, "Look, we could choose any one of a series of points of view and argue them fairly cogently. That is not going to help you. What you have to do is find out where the absolutes are." Her most frequent criticism was, "this can't happen." She felt that the basic conception of a literary work had to be unassailable. From that point, a writer might make mistakes but the work as a whole would hold up.

Penner remembers her dealing very much in absolute ideas: if something was important, it was important and worth all matter of effort. In most things, she made clear choices. Her two favorite adjectives were "good" and "bad." Penner remembers her speaking at length about people who were "bad friends." The class asked her, "Isn't that a contradiction?" She said, "No, not at all. People do things well or they do them badly. And some people are bad friends." This was said in connection with her strong feelings about the McCarthy era. Penner saw that she was absolutely dumbfounded over friends who had informed on one another.

Hellman had a horror of adjectives. "Verbs, verbs, verbs," she would say. She taught students how to go through a manuscript and strike out verbiage. Often big words were discarded for simpler ones. It was as if, in Penner's words, adjectives were to be used like heavy spices: "You are very sparing with them and very careful about which ones you use. Whatever you place in as an adjective is going to be an incredible amount of color, and you better maintain that for the object or person throughout the piece." Penner thought Hellman had reservations about fiction. It clouded, muddled things. Her plays were so clear, and the ambiguity of the finest fiction seemed to trouble her. Dialogue was her forte; writing it was "bare bones time, kiddies," she would say.

Hammett was often a topic of conversation in class. It was not hard to figure out that her affair with him was on a par with that of Katharine Hepburn and Spencer Tracy. "This was a burning flame in her memory," as Penner puts it. One Hammett story (he was always referred to in class as "Hammett") had to do with their vacation on a Caribbean island with a very confusing bunch of people. She was trying to work out some story idea and could not seem to stop talking. Finally Hammett told her to just shut up. She asked him why. He said, "You've already solved the problem five times. If you find a solution, will you for Christ's sake just use it!" Hellman relayed this story to illustrate a point: she did not want her students to beat things to death. If it's good, leave it alone.

Penner had other writing teachers. What made Hellman distinctive was that she never talked to students about "wordsmithing."

> She never got involved in talking about the beauties of a particular sequence of phrasing or how to choose the right word. She dealt with it in a very abrupt and sometimes brutal, mechanical manner: "You have a story to tell, well tell the damn story." The question she asked us more than any other was, "Why did you write this?" And more often than not, we had absolutely no answer. That was when *that* paragraph would be scratched out. "Do you need this?" "Well, ah, I'm not sure." "You're not sure? Good, out!"

Sometimes Hellman talked about her contemporaries. Norman Mailer was committing unpardonable sins because he was ambiguous about what he really believed. "His problem is, he's just so damn in love with himself." About herself, she was unapologetic. She obviously liked her work, but she did not see any point in self-aggrandisement. She was angry at Mailer because he was misusing a great talent. Another target was William Styron, although she took him apart in a much quieter fashion. Politics was never a big issue in the classroom, although Penner recalls that she disliked *The Crucible* because it "smacked of politics." She felt Arthur Miller was pressing his point too far. Most critics, she believed, were not helpful because they did not explain how they had arrived at their judgments or how an author might improve on his or her work.

Open-ended criticism was useless. Late in the course, she reminded students that her own remarks on their papers were not necessarily true. If they disagreed with her, they had to be strong enough to ignore her criticism. She graded students on a pass, high pass, or pass with honors system. In the first few class sessions, she explained that students could not fail the course but they had better put forward a good effort. Penner could see she was amused by the whole concept of a writing course in college, by her very position—the honorary degrees and so on. Writing per se, everyone knew, could not be taught. And she disliked academic puffery.

Hellman was there because John Hersey had invited her. Penner found Hellman's friendship with Hersey intriguing because as personalities they were at opposite ends of the spectrum. "She was a very brusque, tough individual. He was a very contemplative, sensitive, and caring person. And he let you know that the moment you met him." Penner could tell that Hersey held Hellman in great esteem. For him, she was a kind of bellwether about life.

For Penner, Hellman's course was the most impressive experience of his college career. There was a purity and directness about her presentations in the classroom that he never forgot. She nurtured talent. She gave her home telephone number to students and expected them to call if they needed help with their writing. At the same time, she maintained a distance from her students because—Penner came to believe—while it was her tendency to want intimacy, she had been hurt by close relationships many times. In a private consultation with Penner, she would be very personal, but

> all of a sudden that would stop and she would say, "In any case, you have to fix this." When she was feeling comfortable with you, she would call you by your first name; when she was about to read your beads about something she would refer to you as "Mr. So-and-so."

Sometime after Hellman's course, Penner called her in New York. He was working on a story, had written himself into a corner, and could not find the way out. She was very kind and remembered instantly who he was. She was most willing to help and offered sensible advice. He had to sift through the story patiently, she told him, to weigh the elements and decide which one needed to be changed. The solution might be as simple as having a character leave rather than enter a room. The story had to be looked at as a problem that could be laid out on a table, and by moving two pieces you could change what it looked like. Penner's recollection is very like Jerome Weidman's observation of Hellman and Hammett's workmanlike approach to writing.

During the course, Hellman confided in her students that she was writing her memoirs. She was hard put to explain why, and said she was not at all sure she knew what she was doing. "I can guarantee you that this is not going to look like a book of memoirs by anybody else." In 1964, an interview with John Phillips and Anne Hollander in the *Paris Review* made Lillian Hellman matter in a new way. Suddenly it was not just her writing style but her style of life that was significant. The interview was prefaced by a long introduction. Hellman was described as living in a white house "at the bottom of a sandbank in the town of Vineyard Haven, Massachusetts, on the island of Martha's Vineyard." Her home was modern, with "lots of big windows and a wooden deck facing the harbor." Hellman liked to watch the ferries of the Woods-Hole-Martha's Vineyard-Nantucket Steamship Authority bringing visitors to this "teeming, heterogeneous resort." She was not a half-mile from the ferry dock, yet in this "exposed situation" she managed to work well. What Phillips and Hollander did not mention is how carefully Hellman had contrived this setting. The home had been designed by Howard Bay; it was an extension of her theater work, an expression of a writer who would come to make a theater of her life.

This was a new house and part of Hellman's bid for a new career. The shape of that new career had not yet been determined, and it would have to coexist with her old one—just as her new house was situated near (but not in sight of) her old one, which she had sold when Hammett died. Phillips and Hollander pointed out that the old house was more like Cape Cod, with its "painted shingles and climbing roses, plainer and more regional in its architecture, like a Yankee farmhouse of the last century." There was a "complex of boxlike rooms," in which Hellman's guests were accommodated. The "far east wing of the house" was made out of the shell of an old Cape Cod windmill. That is where Hammett had lived, an isolated figure who rarely socialized with Hellman's people.

Phillips and Hollander devote a long paragraph to evoking the

Hammett mystique, with the implication that Hellman provided this austere, cultivated man with a sanctuary. The interview itself reads like a preview of her memoirs, with Phillips and Hollander anxious to tell the reader that Hellman is a multidimensional figure not easily captured on the page, "being at once angry, funny, slyly feminine, sad, affectionate and harsh." At the time, she was working on her reminiscence of Hammett for a collection of his stories. She admitted to her interviewers that Hammett would not have wanted her to reprint his early work; such a private man would not have welcomed her exposure of his life. She was asked about everything—her dramas, screenplays, politics, friendships, opinions of various writers, and so on. Many of the attitudes familiar to readers of her memoirs appear in the interview.

Her decision to write about "Lillian Hellman" could not have been easy. On January 21, 1966, in response to a request for her cooperation in a biography of Theodore Roethke, she seemed willing, but added, "I do have a barrier against writing down memories, and have never been able to do it. Maybe everything becomes set and forever for me when it is written down." Was she disingenuous? Perhaps. It was always her guise in her memoirs, however, to present herself as a most reluctant witness to her own life. Hellman disliked writers like Mailer who made themselves into their own heroes and heroines. In May 1964, *Show* magazine published her savagely funny attack on *After the Fall*. She was outraged at what she conceived to be Arthur Miller's barely disguised exploitation of his life with Marilyn Monroe. In December 1963, *Ladies Home Journal* featured her report on the civil rights movement's march on Washington in 1963; her heritage as a Southerner and memories of Sophronia naturally came into play. There were desultory articles on a theater festival in Edinburgh and on Pope Paul VI's trip to the holy land.

Could these pieces be forged into a book? Hellman reviewed her occasional writing from years past and concluded that it was not very good. Maybe she could "do better with the same memories." In any event, she decided it was not enough merely to collect and edit old material; she would have to build her career anew—past and present. She decided to return to the Soviet Union to refresh her recollections. To novelist Edwin O'Connor she wrote, "I think I'll be off to Moscow about October 10 [1966], complaining every inch of the way about a sore back and maybe other things." There was a moving reunion with her friend and translator, Raya Orlova, which Hellman writes about in *An Unfinished Woman*. Hellman cried because she knew she was no longer the young woman who had braved that risky trip across Siberia in 1944. The "new shabbiness" of postwar Moscow saddened her, and she felt ill at ease in a different era. As she later wrote a Russian friend, Helena Golisheva, returning to Russia "was a strange experience for me; I found myself often feeling lost, and yet feeling homesick for Moscow and all of you when I left." The Russians were silent when she referred to their wartime leader: "Stalin is not a good man to quote these days," she notes in *An Unfinished Woman*. She never got over this change in sentiment; *her* Stalin would always remain an ally—even when she most reluctantly had to admit that the evidence of his atrocities was overwhelming. Rather than really trying to understand what had happened, she reverts in *An Unfinished Women* to moral relativism: "They condemn Vietnam, we condemn Hungary. But the moral tone of giants with swollen heads, fat fingers pressed over the atom bomb, staring at each other across the forests of the world, is monstrously comic." If there is truth in her conclusion, by equating the actions of one side with the other, there is also evasion. Was the moral scale balanced? There is an allusion to labor camps and to the fact that Stalin sent some of his own soldiers to the camps. She quotes a Russian as saying, "The old crazy man Stalin believe that if Germans had you prisoner, perhaps you wished to be prisoner, or perhaps you talk secrets to them." Rather than confront a malign system, Hellman attributes this evil to "the old crazy man"—as if all that is at stake is Stalin's deterioration.

Hellman may have gleaned much more from her Russian friends than she ever put in print, especially from Lev Kopelev, Raya Orlova's husband and Aleksandr Solzhenitsyn's companion in a labor camp. She did know that in 1945 Orlova had been interrogated for receiving gifts in 1945 from Hellman, a foreigner. Orlova had been in trouble over Hellman's gift of an expensive hearing aid for her father. In a preface to Lev Kopelev's memoir, *To Be Preserved Forever*, Hellman remarks that "the bureaucracy, as silly as most, decided that there was something mighty odd about my sending so costly a gift, and they had hounded Raya with questions. Asses all and everywhere." Again, there is almost no interest in discovering *why* Orlova was "hounded." *Is* it the same everywhere? In *An Unfinished Woman*, Hellman notes that after 1945 there were no letters from Orlova and she "put some of it down to Slavic putting-off-until-tomorrow . . . some other wall had gone up for both of us." When they met, Orlova told her she had not known how to "write about herself or her country in the postwar Stalin years." Perhaps Orlova was being close-lipped about the Stalinist terror, but could Hellman have been naive enough to accept such a simple explanation? In *Memoirs*, Orlova speaks of her gradual disaffection from the Soviet system. Hellman was aware of Orlova's growing doubts, but she did not really want to know about them. They discussed the twentieth Communist Party Congress (1956), where Khrushchev had denounced Stalin. Orlova asked her how Hammett had reacted to this exposure of evil. Hellman said, "Raya, you always think that the world is revolving around your country. Nobody gives a damn about your Congress." Orlova replied, "But Lillian, the twentieth Party Congress wasn't just an event in our country, it was a world event."

It was at Raya and Lev's apartment that Hellman met Solzhenitsyn, who at that time was a hero for many:

> I was impressed, of course, with Solzhenitsyn, but I cannot say I was attracted to the silent, strange figure. There was something out of order, too odd for my taste. Certainly I admired him, as a writer and a man, but Raya sensed that I felt something else, and she forced it out of me as we stood in front of Pushkin's Leningrad house a week later. She started to cry, saying how painful it was to her that I, whom she loved, had not immediately loved Solzhenitsyn. Friend should love friend. . . . I think in America this scene would have made me laugh; in Russia it made me feel sad and foreign.

Hellman does not vouchsafe what it was that made her draw away from Solzhenitsyn, and Orlova will not say. But it is not difficult to guess what happened. In this period, Orlova and Kopelev were still dissenters within the system. Hellman intuited that Solzhenitsyn, on the other hand, was his own man. For him, it was not a matter of a revolution gone wrong; the revolution itself was a mistake. It was very astute of her to see what Orlova had not yet divined—that Solzhenitsyn was against the system *per se* and not just against the abuses of socialism.

By November 10, 1966, Hellman was back from Europe and

writing to Jay Martin, who wanted to speak with her about his biography of Nathanael West. She was on a tight writing schedule and was "only free on certain days and certain hours," but if he could give her a "week's notice," an appointment could be arranged. Before taking off for a vacation in the Virgin Islands at the end of December, she wrote to John Melby mentioning her "two weeks in Moscow. That long pole of memory got deeply stirred." Although their contact had been sporadic, Hellman never lost interest in Melby or in his career.

Hellman planned a second trip to the Soviet Union for May of 1967. She had not been able to locate many of the people she had wanted to see on her previous visit, and was coming at the invitation of the writers' union. On March 13, she mailed a letter to Orlova explaining that she had written a lengthy account of her visit in 1966 and was bringing it along with her articles written in 1945. Her memoir was moving slowly, and she disliked writing about herself. She could not "somehow, reach the right tone." She said she was uncertain about the length of her stay. It depended, in part, on how plans went for a revival of *The Little Foxes* in New York.

For the 1967 visit, Maya Koreneva was selected as Hellman's translator. Koreneva, a member of the Gorky Institute of World Literature of the USSR Academy of Sciences, was working on a thesis on American drama since World War II. She had written five or six pages on Hellman's postwar plays and had read the rest of her work, except for the adaptations. She had seen *Another Part of the Forest* and *The Autumn Garden* produced by the Moscow Art Theatre, and she had met Hellman briefly during the 1966 visit, while attending the playwright's lecture on contemporary American literature at the Library of Foreign Literature, Moscow University. She felt she was well prepared to assist this prominent and respected American writer.

Although Koreneva had an official position as translator, it was clear from the start that she and Hellman would meet on a personal level. Hellman was very friendly and asked her about her studies. In reply to Koreneva's questions, Hellman frankly admitted she disliked the theater and did not see much of it. She joked with Koreneva and suggested her translator knew more about American theater than she did. She had trouble sitting through plays—in part, because of the bad back she had complained of to Edwin O'Connor. In Leningrad, they attended a Maxim Gorky play, which accentuated atmosphere rather than action. Its slow movement, the many pauses when the only sounds heard were the creaking or slamming of a door, a scraping of a chair over the floor, or somebody's sobbing, powerfully conveyed the idea of a pitiful waste of life, but the torpid rhythm was unbearable for Hellman. She blamed her early exit on her back, "as if she felt she had to apologize so as not to hurt other people's feelings." After the performance, she praised the director for his work.

Hellman wanted very much to see a ballet in Leningrad but was told it was difficult to get tickets. She was kept in uncertainty an entire day and then notified by the administrator of the theater that it was impossible for him to get a single ticket. Hellman was outraged, yet very reserved and dignified in talking about her disappointment. She could not understand why they could not just put her in the director's box. It would have been such an easy solution, she told Koreneva. It was not the absence of tickets that bothered Hellman but rather what she seemed to think was "a breach of courtesy," to use Koreneva's words. Hellman also felt that if persons like Sergei Eisenstein had been still around, such an incident would not have occurred.

Koreneva was not sure how she should address Hellman: Miss Hellman? or simply Lillian? Finally, after much agonizing, she settled on "Miss Lillian"—to the delight of the playwright, who told her translator that that was what Faulkner called her. He was "always very courteous, the perfect gentleman," Hellman told Koreneva. Clearly, Hellman cherished the memory of her days with Faulkner and Hammett. Koreneva did not know Hammett's work at all, but she could see that Hellman revered his honesty and courage. She spoke of him as a man, not as a writer. He was an "indisputable authority" for Hellman—a judgment Koreneva reached by measuring the tone of Hellman's words, not the substance of them. Hellman spoke of Hammett quite naturally. "It came through as something unconscious, as having nothing to do with a deliberate pose or position, taken with an eye to look 'better,' " Koreneva concludes. Hellman spoke proudly of Hammett's burial in Arlington National Cemetery, which surprised Koreneva, who "felt it remarkable that an avowed liberal should appreciate the signs of national esteem so much."

Naturally, Hellman reminisced about her trip to Russia in wartime. Koreneva remembers Hellman telling her many of the same memories recounted in *An Unfinished Woman*. Foremost for her was always Eisenstein. The bond she had with him and a few others was deeply emotional, Koreneva thought.

Hellman was always elegantly dressed. Koreneva remembers a dark blue dress made of some expensive woolen fabric, cut very simply but with immaculate lines. Another was silk with a dark-blue background. Both dresses had vertical slit pockets in their skirts, which Hellman thought very convenient and advocated them as if they were her own invention. She also wore a reversible overcoat that was grey on one side and dark red on the other. At Pushkin's memorial museum she took off her coat and handed it to the man in the cloakroom. When she came to collect the coat, the old man handed it to her with a smile showing that while Hellman and Koreneva were in the museum he had sewn on a tab so that now it could be hung on a peg. Hellman was very amused and touched by his friendly gesture. He did not know who she was; he was just trying to help one of those "crazy Americans." They left, with Hellman saying *spassibo* (thank you). Later, she removed the tab.

Hellman had trouble wearing a pair of crocodile-skin shoes she had brought with her. Her "loose ankle" made her stumble, she told Koreneva. They were brand new, and she offered them to Koreneva. Another time she observed that Koreneva would look nice in a short dress with a full skirt—which was in fashion then. Yet another time, she mentioned that Koreneva's hair needed cutting. Koreneva was not in the least bit offended by these personal remarks. They seemed to be offered in a very friendly way. Hellman was not reproachful. Koreneva took her comments as "an amiable piece of advice given to one who obviously does not pay enough attention to one's appearance." Hellman became very dear to Koreneva, and both of them tried—as best they could—to correspond and carry on their friendship.

Politics was another natural topic of conversation. Hellman was very frank and outspoken in public and in private about her opposition to the Vietnam War. On one occasion, during a meal at the Metropol, a large old restaurant from the prerevolution days, Hellman spotted McGeorge Bundy, who she identified to Koreneva as a very powerful proponent of the war. Bundy recognized her, came over to the table, and began talking. "With all the smiling and joking and laughing that went on one could easily conclude that what he (or she) was watching was a happy reunion of long separated friends. I'm sure Lillian Hellman felt that with her wit and flirting she served her cause better than with frowns and abuse," Koreneva concludes.

A man from Moscow radio asked Hellman for an interview. At first everything went well. In due time, the interviewer asked her about Vietnam and she expressed her dissent. But then she said something critical about the Soviet Union. The interviewer would not have it. She told him she would not allow the interview to be broadcast without the critical remarks, and the interview was canceled.

Koreneva and Hellman discussed Khrushchev. Koreneva had mixed feelings about him. She supported his policy of liberalization, particularly his efforts to rehabilitate the victims of the atrocities during the personality cult period. But she felt he made a ridiculous figure of himself in his escapade at the United Nations, and she was appalled by Khrushchev's rather vulgar views on art. Hellman advised Koreneva to "pay attention to primary things." From that point of view, nothing could match the importance of Khrushchev's efforts to do away with former repressive practices. She also argued that his appearance at the United Nations made him look not like a clown but rather like a human being—not some effigy.

Hellman wanted to know if Koreneva felt a repressive anti-Semitic atmosphere. Koreneva is not Jewish and was not speaking for Jews when she answered that her generation—the people she knew—did not have such prejudices. It was her honest opinion that anti-Semitism was not an official policy then. Hellman seemed glad to hear these words and said this marked an improvement since her wartime visit. Koreneva felt this was a subject Hellman had probably taken up with her old Russian friends.

Hellman saw a good deal of Raya Orlova and Helena Golisheva (another Hellman translator) at Golisheva's house in the country. Golisheva wanted to translate *Watch on the Rhine* if she could omit the children from the play. Hellman would have liked to have her play produced in the Soviet Union, but not at the expense of altering the text.

Hellman's plays have had an interesting reception in the Soviet Union. Reviews of *The Little Foxes* and *Another Part of the Forest* were very favorable. By the late 1940s and the onset of the Cold War, the same plays were heavily criticized and the author was rebuked for misunderstanding and misinterpreting social forces and the class struggle. By the end of the 1950s, the tone of the reviews changed again and Hellman was back in favor.

One day Koreneva took Hellman to visit Olga Bergholz, a poet who Hellman met during the war. Bergholz had suffered terribly during the siege of Leningrad and during the Stalinist years. Bergholz had survived all those hardships in a way that only increased the respect and admiration Koreneva had for her. Now she was dying and could not really communicate with others. There was very little for Koreneva to translate. Hellman's questions and remarks came haltingly. Bergholz's answers followed in the same manner—clusters of words or even single words separated by long pauses, words that seemed suspended in the air. It was as though they communicated more through their eyes than through the words they spoke. Their eyes searched each other, but for what truth Koreneva could not say. Koreneva recalls:

> We were both impressed when we left Bergholz, so much that we could not speak. I'm afraid we never spoke about it again. When it was impossible to avoid the subject with other people, Hellman just stated the fact that she visited Bergholz. But she did not say anything about how the visit went. As if she did not wish to make that great suffering trivial by talking about it.

Koreneva had met many American writers in the Soviet Union— John Steinbeck, John Cheever, Edward Albee, Arthur Miller, Denise Levertov, Robert Lowell, and others. They all impressed her as feeling they had a moral duty to their country and to their people.

> Their consciousness of it as a group is far greater and stronger than that of any other group I've ever met, though I realized I happened to get acquainted with "the cream of the cream" of American culture. What struck me most about Lillian Hellman as a person— and it distinguishes her for me from any other man or woman I knew or know—was that from the very first moment I felt the presence of a great mind, a great intellect. I had this feeling until the end of her stay here. And I did not feel anything like it with anybody else.

Hellman was somewhat uncomfortable at the fourth national congress of the Union of Writers. She had known nothing about it when she arrived in Moscow, and she wanted to leave before it opened. Only after several requests from writer's union officials did she agree to stay for the opening. Hellman showed Koreneva a short, one-page speech—"nice and friendly" is the way Koreneva characterizes it. Hellman concluded by proposing a toast to the freedom that writers and the country at large had then. She wished the congress success. As Hellman later told Martin Arnold, (*The New York Times*, May 31, 1967) "too many Soviet writers had been punished for their views, but that since she was in the country, she felt she could not refuse" the invitation to speak. Hellman was never one to show bad manners in Moscow. On May 22, Georgi M. Markov, a novelist, began the meeting by advising writers to "free mankind from the dirt and filth" of western society. Hellman was joined by C. P. Snow and his wife, Pamela Hansford Johnson, but left Moscow for New York after the opening session. Martin Arnold reported Hellman's view that Soviet intellectuals were "determined to make the fight for their own freedom to write as they wish to write." She thought this feeling of independence cut across generations, and it was in marked contrast to the Soviet Union of twenty years before. She wanted to stress, however, that "none of the intellectuals were against the Government, but that they merely were fighting for the freedom to criticize it." She was impressed with their erudition and facility with languages, and with the fact that, in some cases, they knew more about American writers than she did. On June 3, in the *New York Post*, she told Helen Dudar that there seemed to be "infinitely less interference" now with writers, although she described herself "as a writer concerned that Russian writers are 'in jail for what they wrote.' "

The fall 1967 revival of *The Little Foxes* was a triumph, with an all-star cast including George C. Scott, Anne Bancroft, E. G. Marshall, Richard Dysart, and Margaret Leighton. Hellman worked very closely with director Mike Nichols. At the first full-cast rehearsal, she explained that she had grounded her play in "an amazing time in America . . . when new money-making activities were burgeoning and a new element was assuming domination of local economies." The play was about a "stratification of society," she suggested, in tune with Nichols's idea that *The Little Foxes* was not merely a period piece. "It has a lot to do with now," Nichols said—perhaps having in mind the protests of the sixties against vast concentrations of economic and political power.

Hellman did everything she could to help the production—including filing an unsuccessful suit against CBS, claiming they had no right to show the William Wyler film of *The Little Foxes* on television. A few critics were outraged by the acclaim accorded this new production of the play. In the December 21, 1967, issue of the *New York Review of Books*, Elizabeth Hardwick called the play "a catalogue of sentiment about the Old South." Attacking the historical accuracy of *The Little Foxes*, she said it purveyed a view of the South that many "serious historians believe to be a legend, not to say a cliche." This was hardly a worthy argument. Would anyone think to attack the value of Shakespeare's *Richard III* because it does not measure up to historical scholarship? Hardwick seriously misread the play. Hellman was not soft on the Old South, or on characters like Birdie—although her audiences sometimes were. Hardwick wanted to see a "tragic conflict" in Horace instead of an "unbelievably idealistic" attitude. This might have been an interesting development, but it was not within the range of dramatic possibilities Hellman chose to consider—a point Richard Poirier made quite tellingly in his rebuttal to Hardwick (*New York Review of Books*, January 18, 1968).

Hardwick's was the opening shot in a campaign against Hellman by those who disliked her person, her politics, and her plays. In the years to come, Hellman would be denigrated as a commercial, middle-brow playwright. Hardwick even went so far as to say that the plays were awkwardly constructed and that Hellman was writing "an American version of Socialist realism." John Simon (*Commonweal*, December 1, 1967) dragged in the charge of melodrama once more and condescended to praise a few of her plays as effective broadsides or inferior Chekhov.

Edmund Wilson, in "An Open Letter to Mike Nichols" (*New York Review of Books*, January 4, 1968), rose above this critical acrimony to suggest that Hellman's plays did not fit neat categories, and that the playwright herself wrote plays that were far superior to such terms as "tragedy" and "comedy." Her plays were neither one nor the other; even better, she wrote without needing to consider categories. Indeed, he pointed out that her last play, *My Mother, My Father and Me*, was quite a novel piece of work, hampered by staging that was entirely too realistic.

In a fine analysis of her career, an academic critic, Jacob Adler, called Hellman "the single most important American Ibsenian outside of Arthur Miller." He carefully reviewed the charges of melodrama and found Hellman using the form for viable dramatic purposes. The Hubbards, for example, were so specifically drawn that they probably could not be considered "typical of a class of exploiters, whether Southern, American, or universal." The playwright drew on her family and on history to create these characters, but they have a life of their own that makes Hardwick's attack irrelevant. Hellman was more than a superior craftsman. Adler argued that her presentation of evil could be "matched in almost no other playwright." Her wit and humor—even when it was the "gallows humor" she pointed out to the cast of *The Little Foxes* in 1967—was often ignored by critics. "There is hope in Miss Hellman's world—hope, indeed, in the very act of presenting it," Adler concluded.

With the revival of *The Little Foxes*, with the critical adulation and condemnation, the most natural thing for Hellman to have done would be to write about the theater, but Hellman hated the theater. When Moss Hart sent her a letter complaining that she had written a "dismissive sentence" about his autobiography, *Act One*, she noted that her words were "dismissive" only in a "world where people use very large words, sometimes knowing what they mean, more often not caring, throwing the opposite ones about when the time suits." The values of the theater world, she pointed out to Hart, were not her values, and this was perhaps why she had reservations about his book.

To Joan Cook in *The New York Times* (November 13, 1967), Hellman stated she was "working on a collection of memory pieces." There was plenty to work with. In Hellman's New York townhouse, Cook observed mementos of childhood "tucked in among her warm woods, and the soft greens and yellows that predominate in the easy amalgamation of furniture" from the productions of her plays. There was a Victorian chair from *The Little Foxes*, an early American highboy from *The Children's Hour*, a Sheraton bird cage from *The Autumn Garden*, an Empire love seat from *Watch on the Rhine*, a Victorian love seat and two Sheraton chairs from *The Searching Wind*. Pictures of a "ruffled, beribboned and suitably sullen" Hellman hung in the upstairs hall. There was a faded photograph of her mother with "dark hair piled high" in a fashion the playwright wanted Anne Bancroft to emulate in the 1967 revival of *The Little Foxes*.

The reminiscence of Hammett for an anthology of his work published in 1966 provided a way out of Hellman's dilemma over how to write about herself without writing about the theater. He was intrinsically interesting. There was much to say about him even after he had stopped writing. She found it bearable to talk about herself in relation to the other; indeed, it was the best way to get an angle on herself. She could be selective. Let memory lead the way; make no effort to write a chronological autobiography. Disdain the idea of becoming a bookkeeper of one's own life, as she put it in *An Unfinished Woman*. Talk about work only when it was amusing or dramatic. The title she eventually arrived at, *An Unfinished Woman*, was perfect, for it gave promise of incompleteness, fragmentation, and made a virtue of it. It seemed more honest to have gaps—to leap, for example, from Russia in 1944 to Russia in 1966. That is how memory works. The grain, the feel of experience recalled, would be her aim.

On July 15, 1968, Hellman wrote to Helena Golisheva. Hellman expected to complete her memoir by the end of September or October. Little, Brown was very pleased with the book, but she had reservations. It always seemed to be the case that she did not get the pleasure she ought to out of "decent work." *An Unfinished Woman* was a "strange book, full of holes." It was an "odd experience" writing about the past, discovering the things she remembered and the things that had "gone past" her and that might have been of "greater importance."

26

AN UNFINISHED WOMAN
(1969)

———

I do regret that I have spent too much of my life trying to
find what I called "truth," trying to find what I called
"sense." I never knew what I meant by truth, never made
the sense I hoped for. All I mean is that I left too much of
me unfinished because I wasted too much time. However.

—Lillian Hellman, *An Unfinished Woman*

What matter if I live it all once more?
Endure that toil of growing up . . .
The unfinished man and his own pain,
The finished man among his enemies.

—W. B. Yeats, "A Dialogue of Self and Soul"

With *An Unfinished Woman*, Lillian Hellman received the best reviews of her career as well as a National Book Award. The book was an enormous popular and critical success. She had managed, in nearly every reviewer's estimation, to be honest, courageous, and direct, and pointed in her remarks yet understated, in what Stanley Young (*The New York Times Book Review*, June 29, 1969) called her "short and modest memoir." "That's Lillian Hellman for you, speaking frankly and telling all, diamond-hard in her judgments, yet leaving the deepest things unsaid," praised John Barkham (*New York Post*). John Beaufort (*Christian Science Monitor*, June 24, 1969) was taken by the portraits of Hellman on the front and back covers of the first edition, revealing "the uncompromising look-you-in-the-eye candor of the Hellman gaze." The tone of these reviews is interesting, for the woman and her writing are taken as the same thing, as though she *is* her style. Barkham is so seduced by her manner that he concludes, "Of the surface stuff—the hit plays, the public admiration—there's virtually nothing at all. She always was a woman of character and her book mirrors it precisely." Are her plays and the attention they have received really "surface stuff"? Would a thoughtful account of her place in the American theater really be of minor importance compared to the literary and political gossip that fills *An Unfinished Woman*? Is it so fine of Hellman to reduce her Hollywood screenwriting, for example, to anecdotes about rolling condoms and fights with Sam Goldwyn? It is not that these amusing and instructive episodes do not belong in her book, but why are they made to stand for a career? Reviewers did not take up Hellman's own confession that she never made the "sense" she hoped for. Worse than that, almost no one seemed to notice that many of her stories are calculated to evade the very "truth" she hoped to capture.

Joseph Epstein (*The New Republic*, July 26, 1969) thought he was praising *An Unfinished Woman* when he said it had the "quality of a very superior American movie of the thirties. . . . It is the work of a woman at once knowing yet without cynicism, tough yet generous, honest yet reticent—a female and super-literate Humphrey Bogart." It never seemed to occur to him that his very words revealed that the Lillian Hellman of *An Unfinished Woman* was a literary invention and should be discussed as such. Hellman was so skillful at eliding over her political life that Epstein termed her "an unexceptional blend of thirties radicalism." Young was more accurate when he suggested, "Miss Hellman keeps intact the hidden channels of her own beliefs."

Edward Sothern Hipp (*Newark Evening News*, September 14, 1969) was one of the few critics of the book: "There are too many gaps, too much substitution of hazy philosophy for graphic autobiography." Robert Lasson (*Washington Post Book World*, June 22, 1969) was virtually alone in not being charmed by Hellman's memoir. "The book has no structure," he complained. It begins as an autobiography, veers into diary entries, and ends with portraits of people important to the author. There are marvelous glimpses of the thirties and forties, but evidently Lasson was not impressed by Hellman's conclusion that these experiences were not meant to add up. Christopher Lehmann-Haupt (*The New York Times*, June 30, 1969) was less censorious but clearly disappointed: it is a "slight and sparse, pieced together" book. He got to see nothing of the writer at work, although he enjoyed her "peppery anecdotes." He wanted more "news from the interior" and seemed dismayed by Hellman's disappearance into "diary entries written years earlier." He pointed to her conclusion in disbelief. Surely Hellman could find a better way to sum up her life than shrugging it off with the word "However." Yet he wanted to honor her intention: "She has given a detailed portrait of a person who doesn't want to be protrayed. And she makes us understand."

Hellman surely had a right to produce a memoir as opposed to an autobiography, but there were consequences to that approach that left her less than the honest person reviews raved about. Had she chosen to write a chronological autobiography, she would have had to show how her politics developed. She could not have permitted herself to jump over the pact period or to omit the fact that she had supported the Moscow purge trials. She would also have had the hard job of figuring out her writing career. What had it meant to write both screenplays and dramas? What were the influences on her writing? As a teacher, she proved that she had reflected on these matters, yet they did not interest her as a memoir writer. She left herself open to Robert Lasson's speculation that "her best plays were written a long time ago and by now they may have less meaning to their creator than to their admirers." In fact, Hellman was often distressed when critics did not rate her as one of the very best American playwrights. John Beaufort (*Christian Science Monitor*, July 24, 1969) wondered if Hellman meant to give "the snub supreme to the players and other collaborators who animated her dramas by not mentioning them at all."

A few reviewers believed that the memoir's style was influenced by the playwright's experience. V. S. Pritchett (*Life*, June 27, 1969) thought it was the theater that had taught Hellman to break up her memoir "into short, strong scenes and to present herself with remarkable directness." Robert Kotlowitz (*Harper's*, June, 1969) suggested that ending *An Unfinished Woman* with "However" derived from the plays, "the plots neatly tied up and easily comprehended, while an uneasy sense of the future and its ironic dependence upon the past lurks just beyond the final curtain." Many reviewers assumed that the "crackling dialogue" of the memoir was attributable to the playwright's hand.

Kotlowitz was acute when he spotted the fact that Hellman "still indulges an old, tired snobbishness about Hollywood, a kind of offended superiority in the face of social gaucheries committed by arriviste producers and their dull wives, some of whom were even known to go so far as to eat grapefruit at dinner." This also struck Hammett's daughter, Jo Marshall, when she read *An Unfinished Woman*. She recalls that both her father and Hellman were incredible snobs about California architecture and customs and favored European styles. It pained her to see such bright people be so small-minded.

Kotlowitz also had reservations about the "overfastidiousness" of the book. Surely there was more to say about growing up as a Jew in the South. And why mention Gregory Zilboorg and then give almost no idea as to what her psychoanalysis was about? There was also a lack of generosity in her failure to mention her contemporaries in the fifties and sixties. "It is close to stubborn affectation to pass so much by," said Kotlowitz.

Kotlowitz was getting at a tone in *An Unfinished Woman* that most reviewers did not have the time or the space to explore. In the most insightful review of the memoir, Dorothy Rabinowitz (*Commentary*, December, 1969) identified "a tone so composed around the self and its two units of feeling (irritability and love) that it makes no distinctions among experiences or among objects." Rabinowitz analyzed, for example, Hellman's account of the march on Washington:

> She can grow irritated with Martin Luther King, impatient with his dream, as she says, because he reminds her of too many Southern preachers of her childhood. If she cannot love him, she must be irritated with him: he has that place assigned by childhood memory and there is nothing to be said beyond that—that, and the fact that he is a kind man, as she says—and she wanders off to look for something to eat. It is that kind of sensibility: one is either here or there, right or not, irritating or loved.

This is Hellman's world of absolutes, and her readers have admired her for just this quality: her candid willingness to admit prejudice. But if she is true to herself, the result is often the snobbery Kotlowitz picked up on. Hellman had almost no ability to see value in the things that interested other people. She was intolerant in the extreme.

Rabinowitz suggested that Hellman was schooled in this intolerance by Dashiell Hammett. Hellman admired his "refined hauteur, his willingness to snub people who were wrong or who bored him." Many of Hellman's friends also admired Hammett's refusal to suffer fools, but such "irritability of mind"—as Rabinowitz called it—"has its dangers." When Hellman emulates Hammett—as in the numerous times she drops a subject in her memoirs by saying or implying "to hell with that!"—she excludes "all the other emotions one may have about things one does not happen to love. There are many things Miss Hellman does not love, and she is merely, and monotonously, irritable about all of them," Rabinowitz concluded. What Hellman does not like, she cannot understand. It is no wonder, then, that her literary and political likes and dislikes were the stuff of melodrama, and never the material for a probing, intellectual, emotional self-examination.

An Unfinished Woman ends very strongly because it deals with Dorothy Parker, Helen, and Dashiell Hammett—the people she loved. As Hellman often said, she was neither an autobiographer nor a historian. The form of the reminiscence—short and tightly controlled—is her forte. The only plot she needs is the one supplied by memory. Her aim is to give her feeling for a person and the feel of that person, so chronology is not important—indeed, it would defeat her wish to convey a compact version of her companions.

Several reviewers noted that Hellman had produced the finest portrait of Parker they had ever read. Hellman emphasizes that she and Parker were of a different generation, had different kinds of wit, did not like each other on first meeting, and struck up an improbable friendship that lasted to the day of Parker's death. They tended to avoid certain subjects—like their writing—and did not like each other's male companions. Yet they never had a fight, and Hellman treasured Parker as much for her faults as for her virtues. They wanted to amuse each other and evidently did not feel they were in competition. As they grew older, the friendship became tenuous. Parker continued to drink heavily, and Hellman found her friend "dull and repetitive" at such times. Without apology or excessive explanation, Hellman lays out her feelings:

I was tired of trouble and wanted to be around people who walked faster than I and might pull me along with them.

And so, for the next five years of her life, I was not the good friend I had been. True, I was there in emergencies, but I was out the door immediately they were over. I found that Dottie's middle age, old age, made rock of much that had been fluid, and eccentricities once charming became too strange for safety or comfort.

This is a good example of the plain and simple Hellman who has been justly praised.

In some ways, Parker's fate was Hellman's own, for they had a kinship unacknowledged in *An Unfinished Woman*. In Hellman's old age, "much that had been fluid" would turn to rock, and her endearing eccentricities would become a trial for her closest friends. As Epstein points out, they were also alike in their refusal to "con themselves" and in their savage exposure of sham. Politically, they were very close—although Hellman does not make anything of this in *An Unfinished Woman*. Surely Hellman's phrase about Parker, "a tangled fishnet of contradictions" ought to be applied to herself as well. Both women loved to socialize with the rich, even as their radical politics called for a leveling of society, although Hellman did not follow Parker in sentimentalizing radicals or in treating the rich "with an open and baiting contempt." Nevertheless, both women were Socialists On High who rarely formed friendships with working-class radicals.

There were aspects of her friendship with Parker that Hellman chose not to write about but which continued to fascinate her. For instance, why had she so often checked her anger in Parker's presence? To Jo Ann Levine (*Christian Science Monitor*, December 21, 1973), Hellman confessed, "I would be very angry that she had no money and lived so extravagantly and left most people to pay the bills. (Mostly me.)" For a woman prone to rage, Hellman exercised, in her own view, "great restraint" where Parker was concerned. Perhaps she did so because she knew Parker was incorrigible and could not "live anywhere but in a semi-first-class place." To have made scenes with Parker would only have embarrassed them both. Hellman remembers one visit from Parker at her old Martha's Vineyard house. Hellman had to leave for three days and fixed three casseroles for her friend, labeling them Monday, Tuesday, Wednesday, as well as some hard-boiled eggs and sandwiches, taking care to show Parker where everything was. She even kept the oven on, so that all Parker had to do was follow Hellman's written instructions. When Hellman returned,

> nothing had been touched, except a large piece of cheese, and there wasn't even any asking her why, there wasn't any sense. I don't think she would have been able to tell me. I was upset with all the trouble I had gone to, but I do think I know why she did that— she didn't like to do what she didn't know how to do. It embarrassed her.

Hellman does not add that for such pains she did expect an ultimate reward. According to a friend, the playwright Howard Teichmann, who met Hellman sometime after Parker had died, Hellman was furious with Parker:

> That goddamn bitch Dorothy Parker. . . . You won't believe what she's done. I paid her hotel bill at the Volney for years, kept her in booze, paid for her suicide attempts—all on the promise that when she died, she would leave me the rights to her writing. At my death, they would pass to the NAACP. But what did she do? She left them *directly* to the NAACP. Damn her!

In an interview with Nora Ephron, Hellman gave a much calmer version of her upset: "It's one thing to have real feeling for black people, but to have the kind of blind sentimentality about the N.A.A.C.P., a group so conservative that even many blacks now don't have any respect for, is something else. She must have been drunk when she did it." The truth is that Hellman felt she had a right to the money. Yet who was she to decide on the proper causes for Parker to fund? And why assume the bequest was no more than the act of a dipsomaniac? Hellman eventually got around to the real point, telling Ephron that she had expected to have the rights to Parker's literary property at least until her own death.

Jo Marshall is troubled about one aspect of the Dorothy Parker section in *An Unfinished Woman*. Hellman makes clear that Hammett never had any use for Parker. When Marshall's father would visit her in California, he would make a point of taking her to see Parker. Knowing that he did have intense likes and dislikes, Marshall could not imagine him seeking out the company of someone he despised. On another occasion, her father asked her what she thought of Parker. Marshall said she liked her, but Parker seemed to her a little "soppy"—like someone who walked around with a damp hankie. Hammett became very angry and appeared offended by the remark.

Marshall agrees with Hellman that Hammett did not share Hellman's fondness for Helen Hellman's maid. Hammett thought Helen was a bit of a clod and that Hellman sentimentalized her. Helen was like a "stone wall," Marshall remembers him saying. Of course, he did not see in Helen the Sophronia who Hellman cherished, and he could not ignore Helen's rudeness to Hellman. To Levine, Hellman admitted that she had cut out the very worst scenes with Helen: "It's too painful for me to remember—but we often got along very, very badly. We had furious fights, she and I. I don't think I wanted to lie about it. It's just that I didn't want to remember it." Like Sophronia, however, Helen could take her employer's measure—much as black servants in Hellman's plays offer the shrewdest commentary on their white superiors.

One of the most intriguing aspects of the Helen presented in *An Unfinished Woman* is her ability to handle certain situations better than her employer. An incident in Hellman's home with a peculiarly excited young black man proves to Hellman that she does not even glimpse what is immediately apparent to Helen—that the boy is on drugs. Rather than enlisting Hellman's help, Helen banishes her from the room and deals swiftly and authoritatively with what otherwise might have been an ugly incident. It is one of those moments when Hellman, without saying as much, realizes she is out of her element. In relationships with people she loved, she was able to see her limitations clearly.

Hellman acknowledged that, like many white liberals, she labored under certain illusions about blacks. Yet her southern upbringing and proximity to blacks gave her the confidence to suggest that Helen really hated white people. Hammett was an ex-Catholic and, in Hellman's view, as proud and self-loving as Helen. He thought Helen was confused because her Catholicism taught her to forgive; she loved Hellman but had a pent-up anger against whites that she found difficult to admit. Hellman's arguments with Helen often centered on her opinion that her servant was a "house nigger" with a "real-pretend love for white people." Helen's feelings were hyphenated in the sense that her treatment of Hellman was, in equal parts, rude and affectionate—as when she would hit Hellman on the arm as a sign of approval for something that had been said.

Perhaps Hellman was too close to Helen to see what a comical pair they made when they were together. Sometimes Helen was a kind of sidekick. William Alfred is still amused with memories of how competitive Hellman was about everything, and how coming back from a fishing trip with Alfred she said to Helen: "He got five. I got seven." Alfred remembers that "wonderful Helen" would give him fish all the time. Lillian would say, "He doesn't like fish." And Helen would say, "He do like fish. He's a Catholic."

Hellman once told Alfred the story of how Helen had been sent to her by an agency. At the time, Hellman was very ill with the flu, and Helen was there for the day. Hellman fell asleep. At her Eighty-second Street townhouse, there was a landing, across from which was a bedroom Hammett slept in when he was very ill. On the other side was Hellman's bedroom-study. Hellman had been having hallucinatory dreams. When she woke up, she looked down the stairway and there was a lump on the landing. It was Helen, who had slept on the landing rather than going home. Hellman said, "Come here. What are you doing? If you're going to sleep here, sleep in the bed in that other room." Helen said, "Well, Miss Hellman, because you're from the South I didn't think you would want me to do that." Alfred regarded Helen as a very special woman, a great woman.

Alfred remembers that when Hellman was at Harvard, she had Helen, a very good housekeeper, with her. It was Helen's habit to use lemon oil to polish the furniture. There were two very special chairs that belonged to Archibald MacLeish's wife, "a very fussy lady." Unthinkingly, Helen placed the bottle of lemon oil on one of these 1950s Louis XV chairs.

> She was a large lady, and as she was polishing the arms and legs of the other chair, she kicked the bottle, which spilled all over the lemon silk covered seat of the chair. That night I had been invited for dinner.

Lillian and Helen weren't talking. Lillian said, "Madame's on her high horse." They probably had had enormous words that day. That night Lillian made crepe suzettes for dessert. She put on so much brandy that when she threw the match in, it exploded and burnt her eyelashes and widow's peak. Helen came in, and then they made up. Helen threw her arms around Lillian and said, "Oh, Miss Hellman." It was very touching.

Jeanne Noble, vice-president of the National Council of Negro Women, wrote a letter to *The Atlantic* (July 1969) praising Hellman's rare ability to portray "the inner world of black domestics." She was struck by the authenticity of Hellman's relationship with Helen. "We blacks usually 'turn off' the very second whites speak of 'loving their domestics,' " but Hellman's words about Helen's and Sophronia's strength and vulnerability thoroughly convinced Noble.

Most reviewers noted that Dashiell Hammett's presence was felt everywhere in *An Unfinished Woman*, not just in the section devoted to him. Stephen Greene was struck by the uncanny quality of Hellman's memory. Visiting Martha's Vineyard in the mid-1950s he found Hammett every bit as impressive as she made him seem when she told Greene about him in Rome. There were phrases Hammett used that were reproduced vividly and with absolute accuracy in her memoir. Carlos Baker, Hemingway's distinguished biographer, was moved to write to the *New York Review of Books* (March 6, 1966), where an excerpt of her remarks on Hammett had appeared: "It's by far the best writing in print about him, and makes a fine portrait-in-depth of a kind too rare in this or any other time."

Just as Hellman thought she was "nobody's girl," Hammett was his own man. They shared many similarities, but their differences were very telling:

It does not matter much to me that I don't know if Hammett was a Communist party member: most certainly he was a Marxist. But he was a very critical Marxist, often contemptuous of the Soviet Union in the same hick sense that many Americans are contemptuous of foreigners. He was often witty and biting

sharp about the American Communist party, but he
was, in the end, loyal to them.

This passage sums up Lillian Hellman's complex, often confused,
political and personal attitudes. It did matter whether Hammett
was a party member, and it was not enough to know what he
believed. Party members were under discipline; this meant taking
positions that might violate individual conscience; this meant
putting Russia first, even if a party member was contemptuous of
the Soviet model; this meant, in the end, abrogating freedom of
choice. The tragedy of Dashiell Hammett's life is that a man of so
much character, so much conviction, remained committed to the
party. He knew the party had let him down, had broken his heart,
yet he refused to say so. This is precisely what Hellman praises
him for. In her own case, she was less disciplined but more fervent
in embracing the Soviet model. It was the *vision* of a new world, a
more just society, that appealed to her imagination. Understanding
the details of dialectical materialism, on the other hand, was rough
going. She did not have Hammett's mind for Marxism. For Hellman, principles were like friendships: you stuck with them; you
were loyal. This kind of loyalty, this kind of love, blinded her. It is
no wonder that in her memoir she never made the sense she had
hoped for.

27

HEROINE OF CULTURE

(1968–1973)

I think that for my generation, whether one was politically
conscious or not, personal life and political life were
separate. Recently with Vietnam and Cambodia, and then
very suddenly with Kent State University, the two have
become one. Our lives are political now.

> —Mike Nichols, interview with Lillian Hellman,
> *The New York Times,*
> August, 9, 1970

Bad review in book section Lillian Hellman plays—call her
to commiserate. Testy but relaxed.

> —Arthur Kober's diary, June, 18, 1972

O n December 3, 1968, Lillian Hellman attended a conference at Princeton sponsored by the Institute for Advanced Study. More than one hundred prominent intellectuals had been invited to discuss contemporary affairs. John Kenneth Galbraith, professor of economics at Harvard, suggested, "the lesson of the past year is that organization can be opposed." He was thinking of protests against the Vietnam War and of dissident movements in iron-curtain countries. President Johnson had been forced from office. Galbraith's rhetoric reflected the buoyancy of the sixties. If the world was in crisis, a whole generation of students was willing to work for change. The next day, George Kennan gave a speech that harshly condemned the raucous protests of the young. He argued for the restoration of "decorum" in public life. He was roundly condemned by many of the conference's participants—notably Lillian Hellman. According to *The New York Times* (December 4), she wondered how a man of her generation could hold convictions so opposed to her own. She thought her generation were "messers" and defended the very students Kennan attacked:

> "God knows many of them are fools, and most of them will be sellouts, but they're a better generation than we were. Since when is youth not allowed to be asses? Many of us spoke today as if Freud never lived. There's nothing to be despairing about except the American liberal."
>
> At that point, a divinity student in the audience, Sam Brown, rose to deliver an impassioned defense of his generation—crediting it with such roles as turning America around from its pursuit of an impossible military victory in Vietnam.
>
> He said that he understood what it felt like to be in love with an older woman, for he had just fallen in love with Miss Hellman.

Kennan was not alone in his beliefs, but he certainly could not count on much support. Hellman had to acknowledge that "he did a very brave thing; he refused to be a swinger."

Lillian Hellman was very much in swing with the sixties. On July 1, 1969, she was quoted about her students at Harvard and MIT in the *The New York Times*: "It's the pleasantest generation I've ever seen." She found them to be well-mannered and capable of being embarrassed when she complimented them on their "manly good nature."

> During the Harvard bust I got so sick of hearing the endless arguments about the ethics of breaking into buildings. Why was it necessary for everyone to have a flag pinned on him that says, "Moral dinner party attitude"? Who likes to see anything destroyed? But who likes what we did? My parents didn't like it when I got drunk or left home.
>
> I've been asking myself how many parents will stand behind their children, and I'm not sure many of

them will. You're not sure that when parents denounce students they're not denouncing their own
sons. But I don't think these kids are going to be
frightened as we were—they're not old enough to fear
betrayal.

Hellman seemed to be rejuvenated by the very public nature of the
protests in the sixties. They were reminiscent of her own political
involvements in the thirties and forties. But very little politics
entered her classroom in a direct way, although in *An Unfinished
Woman* she mentions being baited about Vietnam by Harvard
students. She told them to go to hell. This was a very different
generation from her 1961 Harvard class. Yet, if anything, she was
more enthused about her teaching. When she was not able to
reach them, she "usually got help from one or the other of them,"
she told Lewis Funke in an interview. To Gloria Emerson (*The New
York Times*, September 7, 1973), Hellman recalled that the student
movement had taken her by surprise. There was no precedent for
it in America, and "it was a great pleasure to see it. It took me
quite a while to realize they meant what they said. . . . I don't
think I recognized its importance. I know I didn't. I'm sorry to say
I learned a kind of caginess during the McCarthy period."

By now Hellman was very much a part of college life, socially
and academically. She was very comfortable in the classroom,
especially at Harvard, and at ease with faculty and administrators.
Her opinions were avidly solicited, and she was urged to write
more about her colorful life. Martin Peretz invited her to his
Harvard classroom. Students wanted to know about the Wallace
campaign. She claimed she had not known it was run by Communists. Somebody asked, "How could you all be so naive as not to
realize what was going on?" Peretz himself had just been intensely
involved in Eugene McCarthy's presidential campaign. Her timing
was perfect. "Well, you know, it's a very heady thing running a
man for President. Sometimes you sort of lose your senses—oh
sorry, Marty."

In her sixties, Hellman was every bit as competitive sexually and
intellectually as she had been in the thirties. There had been a
faculty member at Harvard in the early sixties with whom Hellman
had had an affair. He had subsequently married. At the end of the
decade, she saw him again in the company of mutual friends.
Hellman spent a weekend ignoring her former lover's wife and

monopolizing his time. These dear friends of hers were dismayed to see Hellman act this way. She was not the person they had become so fond of. She was doing everything she could to make her former lover's wife miserable and uncomfortable.

In 1969, Lionel Trilling was a visiting professor at Harvard and Hellman was teaching at MIT. Diana Trilling felt she should invite Hellman for lunch, even though their friendship then was nearly extinct. There was a strain between them, and it was difficult to relax. The conversation turned to Yugoslavia, for Hellman was having an affair with Vladimir Dedijer, who had turned against his fellow Yugoslav dissident Djilas. They were a curious pair, Dedijer and Hellman. Did Hellman find his politics acceptable?

If Hellman was not slowing down, there were signs that her health was beginning to deteriorate. It was not until 1969, during her third exam with Dr. Zetzel, that she admitted to smoking three packs of cigarettes a day. She had trouble with pulsations in her lower extremities, which suggested circulatory problems. Zetzel sent her to an orthopedist, who discovered that she had a tear of the anterior branch of the fibula ligament in the ankle. The bone was not broken; she was given an elastic stocking.

In April 1970, Hellman joined John Melby, John King Fairbank of Harvard, and others in a program sponsored by the Committee of Concerned Asian Scholars. This group vehemently opposed the Vietnam War and, according to Robert Newman, "saw in our involvement in that unhappy land the lingering influence of McCarthyism and the 'loss' of China." The meeting in San Francisco was well attended and Hellman was the star. One of the participants, Jim Peck, recalls that she was "forceful, intense, eloquent, and had the audience in the palm of her hand." It was the last time John Melby and Lillian Hellman saw each other. The FBI noted the San Francisco meeting and what it termed "Hellman's support of New Left and antiwar groups."

Hellman took heart from these public meetings and had it in mind to challenge the Nixon administration's attack on civil liberties. She evidently recognized that the protests and the repression of the sixties were quite different from both the social activism of the thirties and the passivity of the fifties. Whatever the New Left stood for, it did not concern itself with the Marxist, pro-Soviet movement of earlier decades. Certain government officials actually admitted there were abuses of power and did not revert to McCarthy's tactic of blaming domestic problems on subversives. Ramsey Clark, a former attorney general, had published a book on crime in which he openly criticized J. Edgar Hoover.

These changes in the political zeitgeist emboldened Hellman. She conceived of a broad-based organization that would confront institutions like the FBI head-on. Called the Committee for Public Justice, this organization would inform citizens of threats to their freedom. While Hellman relied on many people in her inner circle—John Hersey, Mike Nichols, William Styron, Jerome Wiesner (president of MIT), Ephraim London, Hannah Weinstein—for a core of support, she purposely sought out influential people and celebrities who were no more than acquaintances and who might even disagree with many of her literary and political judgments. She made the issue of liberty, not herself, important and—especially at the beginning—did not thrust herself into a visible leadership role.

Robert Silvers, co-editor of the *New York Review of Books*, was a most interesting choice for the committee. He had first met Hellman in the company of his friends, Robert and Elizabeth Lowell, in the late sixties. When Silvers visited Philip Rahv at Martha's Vineyard, he would see Hellman socially. She was a friend of Jason Epstein, who was very close to Silvers. In spite of these mutual friends, Silvers and Hellman were not intimate. Indeed, the *New York Review of Books* had published Elizabeth Hardwick Lowell's attack on *The Little Foxes* in December 1967, and he remembers he did not see much of Hellman afterward. Then, in the summer of 1970, he received a call from her asking him if he would join with a group of people at her New York apartment. She felt there was a threatening atmosphere in the country.

There was no doubt that Hellman was the central figure in the committee. She raised a considerable amount of money from friends and through benefit dinners, although such contributors as Thomas Brandon, head of Janus films, gave large sums to the organization. Hellman was not highly informed about many of the legal issues addressed by the committee, but she was very actively involved in the practical matters of running an organization and consulted often with Silvers and others. She was concerned to have a range of people with different political views working with the committee—indeed, she did not want it identified as a leftist group. Scholars working with the FBI and former prosecutors were invited to attend the committee's conference on the FBI at Princeton in 1971. Hellman did not just want big names for the committee. They had to be people with ideas, and she was careful not to make the organization the creation of celebrities. When the names of famous actors were proposed as members, she often rejected them, according to Silvers.

The conference on the FBI was highly successful and resulted in a publication edited by Stephen Gillers, executive director of the committee. Much later, the committee sponsored a conference on Watergate, chaired by Kingman Brewster, then president of Yale. From its early days, however, the committee included nationally known lawyers and former government officials. In December 1970, the Committee took out an impressive full-page ad in *The New York Times*, asking what had happened to the Bill of Rights. To have Telford Taylor, a prosecutor at the Nuremberg trials, Ramsey Clark, and Burke Marshall, a former assistant attorney general, all of whom were listed as on the executive committee, in Hellman's camp was extraordinary. The ad was timely, for on November 18, 1970, *The New York Times* had carried an article on Clark's criticism of the FBI. Hoover, Clark contended, had become obsessed with his own reputation. FBI agents lacked objectivity, the FBI stifled internal criticism, and only those facts that fit the director's ideology were collected. Hellman must have been particularly pleased by Clark's assertion that the FBI's probe of the Communist party was a "terribly wasteful use of very valuable resources." Why was it "so difficult to begin civil rights investigations" and inquiries into "unlawful police conduct"? Clark wanted to know. Clark and the committee were particularly exercised about preventive detention, "no knock" police authority, the failure of the federal government to guarantee the constitutional right of black children to desegregated education in the South, wiretapping, a Federal "blacklist" of scientists, anti-riot laws that abrogated the right of free speech, the "unleashing" of National Guard troops and police officers on campuses, and efforts to intimidate protest groups and the media. Listed as standing behind Clark's statement were Robert Coles (psychiatrist), Norman Dorsen (general counsel of the American Civil Liberties Union), Burke Marshall, Robert B. Silvers, Telford Taylor, and Jerome Wiesner.

Stephen Gillers, now Professor of Law at New York University, left private practice at Dorsen's urging to head the committee—at first on a part-time basis. Very quickly, however, the committee became his major responsibility. He first met Lillian in early 1971 at a Greenwich Village restaurant, The Cookery, then owned by,

Barney Josephson, a well-known thirties radical. Gillers remembers that Lillian tried a little bit of everyone's plate, which endeared her to him. He was attentive to her and to her view of how the committee should operate. They got along extremely well and would spend hours on the phone exploring in great detail the committee's work, but he witnessed several instances of her harshness with others. No one lectured Lillian about her hostility, but "we tried to deflect any kind of harangue she might have set off on," Gillers comments. Although Robert Silvers found Hellman polite and friendly in his own dealings with her, he remembers that she was rough on the young women who worked for the committee and not above humiliating them in front of others. This was often the case with Hellman—whether it was the staff of the Committee for Public Justice, Helen, secretaries, or actors. It was a cruel tendency even her fondest friends do not deny. Silvers witnessed aspects of her behavior that he thought were quite appalling. She was often manipulative and bullying.

Hannah Weinstein, a movie producer associated with Hellman since the days of the Waldorf peace conference, joined Hellman in believing the aims of the committee would be best furthered by large public events. Many committee members were lawyers and scholars who preferred study projects, carefully organized analytical conferences, and a newsletter on the activities of the Justice Department written in a convincing, objective tone. That, they thought, would be the most effective way of dealing with civil liberties problems. The conferences on the FBI and Watergate pleased Hellman, but she was disappointed that the committee did not have more of a mass appeal. It is Silvers's impression that she wanted rallies organized in places like Madison Square Garden, that "she looked back to the days when there were such rallies in the thirties." She looked for the drama in which she herself would have a role at least some of the time. "Therefore, she was often quite critical of the more lawyerly and scholarly work of the committee." As Stephen Gillers puts it, "we lawyers saw issues, legalisms, Lillian saw movements and morality plays." But she continued to raise money before withdrawing from the committee in the late seventies.

Telford Taylor feels she became disappointed in her rich friends who did not contribute more money to the committee, and in lawyers like Taylor himself who eventually committed themselves to other projects. Her view that the committee should also inspire people to become better citizens and not just issue lawyer-like reports was probably right, Gillers concedes, but the lawyers could not see themselves as social activists.

Hellman's views were often simplistic and subject to abrupt changes. Gillers could see that she did not have a well-thought-out political philosophy. Rather she was motivated by questions of fairness and of character. Robert Silvers recalls that Hellman "was in many ways not very sympathetic. But I did believe that the work of this committee had its use—particularly during the Nixon period—so I thought it was worth collaborating with her." Martin Peretz, publisher of *The New Republic*, is chagrined by his association with Hellman and the committee:

> Here was a lady with a certifiably stupid political intelligence and there would sit Burke Marshall, Telford Taylor, myself. Even if we were sort of on the left with her, some of the things she conceived of doing were just so stupid. And we would chirp along like castrati. There was a way in which she had a moral authority over people despite the patent corruption of her own position. She was vindictive and people were afraid of her. They still are—from the grave!

Hellman made judgments about people as one might about a character in a play. Once she decided that someone was bad, you could not say, "But hey look Carter did x or y, and that's good." If she didn't like someone, she didn't like him, and that was it. She had antennae that alerted her to the characterological acceptability of a prominent person, to the bad guys in her play, Gillers concludes.

By the end of the decade, Hellman was involved in her libel suit against Mary McCarthy and had lost interest in the committee; its activities ceased.

Throughout the early seventies, Hellman kept busy teaching and writing her next memoir. In February 1971, she was at Berkeley teaching, among other things, Melville's classic story, "Bartleby, the Scrivener." In an interview with Beverly Koch in the *San Francisco Chronicle* (February 14), she said the theater was no longer dying; it was dead. Perhaps that is why at Harvard in 1968, now at Berkeley, and the next year at Hunter College she took more time in class to speak about screenplays. Students knew all about movies; they rarely read or saw plays. At Hunter she also taught Nathaniel Hawthorne's short story, "My Kinsman, Major Molineux." She had long ago perfected her method of working from short literary pieces as models for students who could not possibly, in her view, have enough experience to write about their own lives. She told her Hunter students that she had declined director Joseph Losey's offer to do a movie of Joseph Conrad's *The Secret Agent*, but she wanted them to read it and tell her in two pages how they saw the story "in terms of motion pictures. It's an almost perfect movie script" she assured them. Hellman had a few "personality battles" with Hunter students who did not live up to her high expectations. Although she had interviewed all of the students, she was not satisfied with some of them. They did not read enough. Hellman taught Edith Wharton, Henry James, and Thomas Mann. There was much excitement about Hellman's teaching on campus, and her colleague at Hunter, Alex Szogyi, who was head of the Distinguished Professorships Committee at the time, remembers the feedback from students as having been very positive.

Szogyi, a professor of French, and Comparative Literature, had arranged for Hellman's appointment, helped pick the books for her class, found the students, and did everything necessary to make her feel comfortable and successful. As he puts it, "I came into Lillian's life at a time when I was useful to her." Szogyi had been one of Robert Penn Warren's students, and he had met Hellman at the annual Christmas dinner given by Penn Warren and his wife, Eleanor Clark. Between Penn Warren and Hellman there was the utmost respect and fondness, and Szogyi got to know her through these annual dinners at a time when her playwriting career was mostly over and her memoirs had not yet made her famous. It was to him she turned when she wanted research done on the word "pentimento." She also confided in him her agonies in writing about Julia. It saddened him a little that she never gave him a copy of the book in acknowledgment of his help, but she had a way of forgetting.

At the Penn Warrens, Szogyi found Hellman "restless and prone to be the unexemplary guest. She did best with the tête à tête, where one was subject to her merciless scrutiny." Szogyi, also an accomplished playwright and food critic, has provided one of the most evocative portrayals of Hellman's seductiveness. To be alone with Hellman meant her wonderfully sensual and gravelly voice could then be the focus of attention. . . . The truth is, she was modish, she dressed awfully well to show those good legs and had a natural chic that few could emulate. . . . She had a marvelous palate. She cooked like a dream. . . . Her borscht was as good as her gumbo. Seeing her work, cooking, absorbed by the problems of timing and flavoring, one understood her uncanny knack for salting an anecdote and spicing a memory.

Szogyi once cooked a dinner with the Penn Warrens in Hellman's honor. He served caviar and his mother came and cooked part of the meal. Hellman walked in as the last of the guests and said, "Oh, I just went to the most boring party, and they served so much caviar! It's so boring!" Szogyi suggested she might do well to leave since he was serving caviar. She said, "Good, let me eat some." And she ate it, graciously.

Szogyi cannot remember Hellman ever having mentioned a word about her looks. There was an aura and uniqueness about her that was entrancing. Her theatrical personality was very appealing:

She was phenomenally unusual looking, but if you spent one minute with her, you could only think she was beautiful. I was mesmerized by her. I thought she was so wonderful looking. She didn't look like anybody else. You could talk forever with her. She was a great conversationalist, constantly making you laugh, and saying the most outlandish things and enjoying it—doing imitations. She hated Simone Signoret and did a terribly unfair imitation of her. . . . We talked about people, food, life, literature, and the pursuit of happiness.

Hellman liked to screen her own calls. If she did not want to speak with you, she would do an imitation of her maid or housekeeper announcing that "Miss Hellman's not in."

Szogyi does not describe himself as a close friend, but feels that for that very reason Hellman was able to "give a lot" to him. She knew she risked nothing with him; he was not part of her regular entourage. He was a "safe commodity." They had much in common—a love of food, cooking, literature, and certain animals, like bears and poodles. He felt close to her because, like him, she had raised a "dynasty of poodles." Szogyi liked to think she had the personality of a poodle: "intelligent, charming, affectionate, and caring—but also vengeful if things didn't go her way. She could be merciless if she didn't approve."

Hellman was also open to new experiences and thoroughly enjoyed the horoscope Szogyi did for her, which came about because she told him she was in doubt about the date of her birth. It occurred to Szogyi that Hellman might be coquettish about her birthdate, yet she seemed genuinely curious as to whether he could determine it. She said her father had never wanted her to know her age and that the hospital records had been destroyed in a fire. As a professional astrologer, Szogyi ascertained (based on her feelings at the time of Hammett's death) that she was born in 1906. In fact, Hellman's 1905 birth certificate can be obtained from the Bureau of Vital Statistics in New Orleans.

When Szogyi first met Hellman, Peter Feibleman, a young novelist, was "number one" in her life. Indeed, Szogyi came to believe Feibleman was the "love of her life." Her closest friend seemed to be Mike Nichols, and Hellman went out of her way to ask Nichols to direct one of Szogyi's plays, but the director had already chosen someone else's work. Szogyi was the only one in the United States to have translated all of Chekhov, and Hellman often spoke with him in a tongue-and-cheek way about how much she had "stolen" from the Russian writer. This was the one influence on her work she readily admitted. She seemed to have her own private ax to grind against the theater and would constantly tell Szogyi she never went to see plays. Then she would invite him to the theater. "I thought you never went," he said. "This is an exception," she replied sternly. "You'll remember it." She did not want to go to the theater but she would go. And she was very eloquent about it. Although she did not like the *Hot L Baltimore*, for example, Szogyi recalls she

> gave a critique of what we were seeing that was more canny than anything we subsequently read in the papers. She knew instantly it would succeed, and she predicted the importance of the playwright. She didn't need more than a moment of a work to decide what she thought about its ultimate value, just as she didn't

need more than a spoonful of a dish to decide about the value of a restaurant.

Hellman's health was beginning to go. Szogyi knew she had glaucoma. Some years earlier, she had tried to give up smoking; hypnosis had not helped her to stop. "Some good soul had suggested marijuana. Can you imagine me smoking seventy-five pot cigarettes a day?" she snorted. In 1966, Ralph Penner had noticed that she was often out of breath during class. In September 1973, she told journalist Gloria Emerson that her energy was flagging. It was harder for her to express anger as vehemently as she would like: "The other day I tried to hit a boy with an umbrella but I couldn't reach him." At about the same time, however, she had better luck with a truck driver—perhaps because he was nearer and her weapon was a package she was carrying. In spite of her physical fragility, she swam every day when she was at Martha's Vineyard.

Szogyi could see that Hellman was bitter about her physical decline. He also found her terribly disappointed over her declining reputation as a playwright. When he wrote an appreciative article on her theatrical career, she was enormously grateful. This was surprising to him, though she insisted he had changed her life. Why should such a major talent be beholden to him? he wondered. But he had caught her at a particularly vulnerable time. Of course, she had a hard exterior, but in Szogyi's view that toughness was necessary to protect herself. She was extraordinarily sensitive and could be hurt very easily, he found. When Arthur Kober died in 1975, Szogyi wrote her a note, and she was so delicate about it, so touched that he should think of her. When his mother died, she could not have been nicer to him.

Szogyi also knew of the dark side of intimacy with Hellman. "She had a way of torturing people who were close to her." One person Szogyi had introduced to Hellman came up to him in the street and said, "I'll never forgive you for ruining my life." It was because she would fight for what she thought of as her rights. There was this child in Hellman that kept coming out.

She related to her childhood so much. She would talk to you about what it was like to be a little girl with your party dress. . . . You could sense that her childhood was precious and how hurt she was by so many things.

In *Pentimento,* Hellman observes, "It is the lifelong problem of only children that they doubt all affection that is offered, even that which has been proved." When interviewer Jerry Tallmer (*New York Post,* October 13, 1973) asked her why she felt this way, she replied, "Because as an only child you never have enough of anything. Because you're so spoiled all the time, and a lot has led to wishing for more." There was this insatiable quality about her—it inevitably meant that she would go to extremes, alienate people, and demand more than most people were willing to give.

It was this tendency in Hellman's character that led to Szogyi's parting company with her. There came a point when she became obsessed with one of his friends, and she would interrogate Szogyi about him. There was no quarrel; it was just harder to maintain their warm relationship. Except for this one unfortunate aspect of their friendship, he felt she had treated him with the utmost respect and tenderness. Some time later, he invited her to return to Hunter to talk about food. "Sweetheart, I can't come because I'm too weak, but I'll send you a recipe," she replied.

When Hellman's *Collected Plays* was published in 1972, Szogyi wrote the most positive review of the volume for *Saturday Review* (August 12, 1972). With the finesse of a practicing playwright and theater critic he identified her best work in fresh terms.

> [*The Little Foxes*] scintillates with an electric performance by Regina and struggles without it, actually more dependent on a touching Birdie and an obsequious Leo. The play is one of the best examples we have ever had on the American stage of the effective use of melodrama. *Another Part of the Forest,* fascinating because it came after, in 1947, and not before, is a much better play, brilliantly constructed, more subtly orchestrated, and, in this writer's guess, her finest work. *Toys in the Attic* is the best written, the only one in which poetry pre-empts prose at every turn, with the most provocative characters, best illustrating Lillian Hellman's foremost theme: the desire for flight and the inevitability of inertia.

Rather than worrying the issue of melodrama to death, he takes the work on its own terms. He is careful to show that in theater the relationships between characters *in performance* can make a major difference in how a play is received. And like Hellman's student Ralph Penner, Szogyi appreciates how the playwright orchestrates her work and voices her characters. In *Another Part of the Forest*, in particular, every character has a distinctive vocabulary and rhythm. *Toys in the Attic* is indeed her poetic play because it is so much about states of feeling—about Lily's deep emotional investment in her vision of Julian which comes into conflict with Carrie's romance with her brother. In turn, this naive sentimentality is counterpointed by Albertine Prine's dry wit and Anna's abrupt figures of speech. Unlike most of Hellman's critics, Szogyi is able to step back from the individual plays and articulate their overall thrust. What Regina wants most is to soar, to move beyond the domestic tyranny of her life. She is much more than just a conniving little fox. What Anna and Carrie have always feared is the same thing: what if their tidy, domestic existence is overturned—as seems probable when Julian returns home? He turns over the very ground on which they have built their lives. What matters most to Julie Rodman in *Days to Come* is that she escape the awful staleness of her marriage. This is why she is drawn to Leo Whalen, the labor organizer who promises to upset the status quo. Even the malevolent Mary in *The Children's Hour* is striking out and running away from the discipline of school. Look how much more fascinating she is than her docile classmates. Sara Muller in *Watch on the Rhine* has gone to Europe to get out from under a domineering mother. Without Sara's return home with her husband and family, Fanny Farrelly and her son would never have been "shaken out of the magnolias." Like Hellman herself, her characters must fall out of trees to discover their true natures. Alex Hazen in *The Searching Wind* has betrayed his own brilliance by never making the hard choices. He is surely a victim of his own inertia. *The Autumn Garden* is about nothing if it is not Hellman's definitive treatment of middle-age malaise. In *Montserrat*, the characters are trapped by the staid lives they have made for themselves and are frightened to death by the revolutionary impulse. *Candide* contains no greater attack on self-complacency, on the view that this is "the best of all possible worlds." It is a work of art—in its original form and in Hellman's adaptation—that is an all-out assault on foolish optimism. Nothing drove Lillian Hellman, the playwright and the person, like dissatisfaction with the way things are. This is why she was attracted to her comic characters—like Berney Halpern in *My Mother, My Father and Me. The Lark,* of course, is the quintessential work of an artist for whom flight was foremost.

The other reviews of *Collected Plays* deeply disappointed Hellman. A particularly nasty piece of criticism appeared in *The New York Times Book Review* June 18, 1972. It rehashed the old charges of melodrama and was written as though the playwright needed to be taken down a peg or two. Only a few reviewers had any notion of what she had accomplished in her plays. It seemed to escape notice that this was a body of work worth a discerning appraisal. In this respect, Hellman has always been right. The level of dramatic criticism in this country has been very low.

Hellman has been best served by doctoral students who have patiently studied her manuscripts and shown what a meticulous, deliberate craft she made of writing. Richard Moody's book, appearing at the same time as *Collected Plays,* is a pioneering effort to evaluate her manuscripts. Yet it never occurred to reviewers of *Collected Plays* that Hellman might have used the volume as a way of finally coming to terms with her stage work. Recently, Cynthia Bailey Denham produced a dissertation comparing *Collected Plays* with the first editions of Hellman's dramas. In the case of every play, subtle changes were made in dialogue, overly explicit stage directions were excised, and structural faults were corrected. The most extensive revisions appeared in *Days to Come,* where nearly 25 percent of the text was cut. The lines Florence Eldridge complained about in 1936 were omitted, for Hellman realized the actress was right: there was no proper motivation for Julie's statement that she loved Whalen. The 1936 version:

> WHALEN *(gets up, looks at her)*: What are you talking about, Mrs. Rodman?
> JULIE *(angrily)*: I've told you. I've told you. *(Then softly, quietly.)* I'm in love with you. It was the first evening you talked to me—*(Smiles, bitterly.)* When you didn't know who I was. Well, you know who I am now.

Hellman's 1972 version:

> WHALEN. What are you talking about, Mrs. Rodman?
> JULIE. *(angrily)*: I've told you. I've told you. *(Then softly,*

quietly) I want to stay, I want to stay here. I mean,
I—

In the later version, Julie is more true to the confused, vacillating character of the rest of the play. In the original stage version, her forwardness spoiled the playwright's point about a woman who was one of several characters who did not know their own minds. The 1972 version of *The Little Foxes* tones down Addie's maternal lines and strengthens Alexandra's. In this instance, the change seems influenced by the screenplay. In *Watch on the Rhine*, Kurt's highly idealistic speeches about good men fighting for a better world are muted by the inclusion of qualifying words such as "perhaps" and "might." Hellman was probably influenced by her own bitter experience in the postwar years, but she was also making Kurt more realistic and giving him a more believable rhetoric. One of his big speeches is cut in half, for the play does have a tendency toward proselytizing. Sentence by sentence, speech by speech, Hellman re-imagined her plays. In 1941:

> KURT: In every town and every village and every mud
> hut in the world, there is always a man who loves
> his children and who will fight to make a good
> world for them.

In 1972:

> KURT: In every town and every village and every mud
> hut in the world, there is a man who might fight to
> make a good world. . . .

Every play benefits from similar kinds of revisions.

It is not surprising that Lillian Hellman would take such care with her plays. They mattered deeply to her. Had she written a preface to *Collected Plays*, as Arthur Miller had done for his volume in 1956, more attention would have been paid to her oeuvre. But she disliked writing theater essays and criticized Miller for producing too much journalism. Yet, in deciding not to write a brief for her own work, she did herself a disservice. Without her help, no one seemed to notice that her *Collected Plays* was the outcome of a kind of "seeing and then seeing again"—a phrase she would use to define her next, highly successful memoir, *Pentimento*.

28

PENTIMENTO
(1973)

Old paint on canvas, as it ages, sometimes becomes transparent. When that happens it is possible, in some pictures, to see the original lines: a tree will show through a woman's dress, a child makes way for a dog, a large boat is no longer on an open sea. That is called pentimento because the painter "repented," changed his mind. Perhaps it would be as well to say that the old conception, replaced by a later choice, is a way of seeing and then seeing again.

That is all I mean about the people in this book. The paint has aged now and I wanted to see what was there for me once, what is there for me now.

—Lillian Hellman, *Pentimento*

M any reviewers noticed that the method of *Pentimento* had evolved out of the three character portraits concluding *An Unfinished Woman*. Reviews for this second book were concerned more with style and structure and somewhat less with the writer herself. In some ways, *Pentimento* has been regarded as a novel by critics looking for central themes. Hellman begins with "Bethe."

The miserable lesson that love is no refuge from the world's great violence was one that Lillian Hellman learned early, and the lesson is repeated in almost every chapter. (Penelope Mesic, *Chicago Tribune*, September 23, 1973)

> *Pentimento* is about different forms of love and commitments, many of them conflicting and very difficult, and how one chose and continues choosing among and between them, being *responsible* for the choices and accepting that necessity, too. (Eliot Fremont-Smith, *New York Magazine*, September 17, 1973)

While *Pentimento* was very well received, critics began questioning the form of reminiscence:

> [*Pentimento*] somehow draws the threads of the various narratives together in a way that is clearly satisfactory to the author and more mysteriously so to the reader. This is a strange, fascinating book, which attempts to impose the clear structures of fiction upon the real world, yet gains in artistry whenever the untidiness of reality breaks in to confuse the pattern. (*Times Literary Supplement*, April 26, 1974)

Such language suggests that Hellman is inventing as well as remembering her life. She says as much in her definition of "pentimento." Of course, this is true also of *An Unfinished Woman*—of any autobiography or memoir—because memory is selective. All writing is, in one sense, fiction, a construct. But in *Pentimento*, Hellman is calling it to mind.

Most reviewers were captivated by "Julia." It is the most riveting piece in the book and it reads like a screenplay. It jumps around in time and place, and it is nicely balanced between the intrepid Julia and the fearful, yet ultimately stalwart Hellman. Naturally, "Julia" would make a good movie. The film rights for "Willy" were also purchased. Hellman told many friends and several interviewers that she was surprised to learn that she would be a character in the film *Julia*. It is very hard to believe that Hellman was that oblivious to the fact that she had now made of herself what Diana Trilling would later call "a heroine of culture."

What made *Pentimento* so "strange" and "fascinating" was that its author, who had been lavishly praised for her candor, was writing more and more of what had to be fiction. To the reviewer in the *Times Literary Supplement*, the dialogue of *Pentimento* sounded like fiction. This suspicion had not occurred to readers of *An Unfinished Woman*, who found Hellman's truth-telling inseparable from her style.

There is a sense in which all writers are liars and thieves. Like many writers, Hellman would joke about stealing from authors she admired. What writer of fiction would not want to make a good story better by reshaping or omitting some inconvenient fact? Many of Hellman's friends can speak of her inventiveness, of her tendency to embroider her life. Richard Wilbur, for example, feels that Hellman's memory may have exaggerated the importance, to her, of certain European experiences; that she may have made far too much of her friendships with the French writers Phillipe Soupault, Louis Aragon, and others. Wilbur believes she did revere the truth. He finds her memories of people he knew—Helen Jackson, Dashiell Hammett, and Arthur Cowan—very accurate. Yet like all human beings, her memory could be faulty, her perceptions distorted by her emotions. She could even have clear visual memories of things that may not have happened. This phenomenon is not unusual. Wilbur has found some of his own childhood memories, for example, not to be true—even though he has vivid recollections of them. To challenge Hellman, however, even in a joking way, was to invoke her wrath—as Wilbur learned to his chagrin at an awards dinner. He turned to her and said, "Isn't it strange you've turned into a memoir writer because you have such a rotten memory. How do you develop any notion of what you ought to put down on paper?" To his surprise, she lit into him. "What are you talking about? I've kept diaries all my life. I can prove anything I put on paper!" He took pains to mollify her, but later received a scorching letter. It began: "Dear Dick: I don't know whether I should say 'dear' or not." He wrote back, expressing his regard for her work and pointing out that wherever he was familiar with the background of her memoirs he could say she was accurate. He was distressed at having offended her, but explained that his remarks were occasioned by the fact that all during their friendship she had made jokes about her rotten memory. He did not mean to say that she was a liar. (This letter preceded the public attacks on Hellman's veracity.) Yet what is the appropriate response to a writer who categorically states, "I trust absolutely what I remember about Julia"? The statement itself is a fiction, a bid for authority that only a novelist can justify. In a memoir, such a statement says more about the writer than about the events he or she is about to narrate.

Hellman's veracity would never have become such a big issue—it had become *the* issue of her life by the time she died—if she had not made truth her province. Hellman's peculiarity as a writer is that she does not seem to have realized how much of an imaginative construct she made of her life, even though the very term she employs, pentimento, is a polite way of talking about her prevarication. To repent is not just to change one's mind; it is an act of contrition.

What makes *Pentimento* an authentic book is that it is true to the pull of memory in human lives. Not everyone can write, but everyone does have a collection of portraits—a Bethe, an Uncle Willy, a Julia, an Arthur Cowan, and so on. How to judge Hellman's portraits in a biography is a difficult matter. Hellman never divulged Julia's true identity—if indeed there ever was a single person answering Hellman's memory of Julia. Bethe, Uncle Willy, and nearly all the others described in *Pentimento*, are dead. It is somewhat different, however, in regard to Arthur Cowan, whose story received scant attention in reviews of *Pentimento*.

Several of Cowan's friends, acquaintances, and relatives can vouch for much of the portrait Hellman limns of him. He was an eccentric Philadelphia lawyer, who Hellman met shortly after a poetry reading in the early fifties. Many people have found his life and death a great mystery and are no more certain of him than Hellman is in her book. He traveled widely and was constantly buying new, expensive automobiles, courting young women, and complaining about the steaks he would compulsively order in expensive restaurants. His politics were erratic, and there were many quarrels between him and Hellman because of his reactionary tendencies. Yet he was a very generous man and was helpful even to people whose politics he despised. But he could also be obnoxious. John Melby remembers going to Cowan's Philadelphia office at Hellman's suggestion to inquire whether Cowan might be interested in contributing to the National Council on Asian Affairs. Cowan was pleasant enough, but Melby has never forgotten the image of the attorney sitting down at his desk and rudely putting up his feet, right in Melby's face.

Cowan had been a boxer during his Harvard Law School days and was proud of his still-trim body, which he liked to show off at the beach. He was usually engaged in some sort of "rigorous" diet. He always had to have the newest camera, but never knew how to use it. He had specialists for his teeth, for his eyes—even for his gall bladder. He never was satisfied with his face and went through several operations to improve his looks. He could dress very elegantly, spoke impeccable French, and admired the world of writers. Cowan was an enormously successful attorney and stock market investor. As his friend Molly Howe is quoted as saying in *Pentimento,* Cowan could talk about money "the way some people talk about poetry." For all his eccentricity, however, Cowan was a dear friend to many, many people and left an extraordinary impression on them. It is Hellman's view in *Pentimento* that Cowan wanted it that way.

Hellman describes Cowan's residence as a "handsome old house in Rittenhouse Square" furnished "with ugly draperies, the furniture heavy expensive copies of what the movies think is an English greathouse library." Hellman hated the dark room and the "ugly draperies" that hid the light. When she drew them aside to see the view, Cowan reacted vehemently. In *Pentimento,* this exchange between them deftly encapsulates his manic, finnicky side:

> "My books! My books! Don't do that."
> "Don't do what?"
> "Don't let in any light. It will harm the bindings. Why don't you know such things? I'll tell you why— because you don't have a fine binding in the world."
> "I don't like them," I said. "If I had the courage, I'd throw out all my books, buy nothing but paperbacks, replace them—"
> "I can't stand what you're saying, I can't stand it. You're not fit to touch a book in this house. I forbid you to *touch my books.*"

The craziness, as Hellman tells it, is all on Cowan's part.

Cowan was a litigious man, involved in one lawsuit after another, talking money constantly, courting Hellman yet shying away from her because, she believed, he did not really want her. According to Hellman, he accused her of wanting to marry him, but she could not imagine doing so. She turned over her records to him. He made money for her. She treats this aspect of their relationship as if it was of complete indifference to her. He was a man of extreme prejudices. Germans he could not abide. He drove fast cars recklessly and could fly off the handle at any moment. In the chaotic splendor of his life, he seemed to Hellman "a man of unnecessary things,"—a phrase she repeats twice, as though it were the refrain of her story. She sensed that whatever internal coherence had kept Cowan together was gradually breaking down. He died in as mysterious and contradictory a fashion as he lived: in a car wreck in Spain, purportedly on some secret mission for the U.S. government. Surviving him in the accident was his companion, a nineteen-year-old German girl. This German girl, according to Cowan's family, was not in the automobile, and her presence at the accident seems to be Hellman's dramatic touch.

Why did Lillian Hellman write about Arthur Cowan? To be sure, he was a fascinating figure in her life, and she must have admired his loyalty to friends with whom he disagreed. Richard Wilbur remembers she loved to "bat the breeze" about people like Cowan:

> We could sit and talk for half an hour about whether Arthur Cowan had been crass in pulling out a fifty-dollar bill and handing it to the waitress in the Old Oyster House in Boston and thus keeping the restaurant open fifteen minutes beyond its closing time. We would talk about what fifty-dollars meant to him, whether the smile on his face as he did it had been the gloating smile of a rich and powerful man, or whether he was trying to be amiable. We could brood over a gesture of that sort and enjoy ourselves enormously.

But there were many such people who did not make it into Hellman's memoirs, let alone receive their own chapter.

Hellman and Cowan were far more alike than one would imagine from her account. Hellman loved the power of money. She liked to be courted and to be lavished with gifts. She was always talking about taking people to court and had a temper every bit as volatile as Cowan's. She does not say that she and Cowan had a romance. William Wright assumes they did. With John Melby, she was always frank about her affairs, and he is positive that Hellman and Cowan were not lovers. She raises the issue of jealousy only once in her portrait of Cowan, but given her sense of competitiveness with other women, it is hard to believe that his predilection for young, beautiful girls did not greatly disturb her. It is probably the case that he was Hellman's suitor without sex. He confided to one young female companion who asked whether he had been physically intimate with Hellman, "No. It would be like going to bed with Chief Justice Frankfurter!"

After reading about Hellman's Arthur Cowan it is surprising to learn that in some respects he probably was afraid of her. Virginia Bloomgarden Chilewich found Cowan a "lovely man" with whom she once enjoyed a delightful dinner at the Polo Lounge in the Beverly Hills Hotel. Afterward he said, "Don't tell Lillian." She wondered what was the matter. She was married to Kermit Bloomgarden and she saw nothing improper in a meal between friends. But Cowan was insistent. "Don't tell Lillian. She'll kill me. Or maybe she'll kill you." Chilewich was intrigued. Later, as he drove her to the airport when she was leaving for New York, he again implored, "Listen, *really don't tell Lillian.*" Chilewich understood that Hellman could be difficult, but she wanted to know what Cowan was afraid of. "Lillian's going to decide you and I have had an affair?" she asked Cowan. "Let her decide it." In spite of her own troubles with Hellman, this was one area that did not bother her at all. Still later, in New York, he wanted to be sure Chilewich had not spoken with Hellman about the dinner. "You know I really like you," he said. "I like you too," she replied, "but you're reading something into this." But all he could think was that Hellman would be furious.

Thomas McBride, the son of the attorney Hellman mentions in *Pentimento*, recognizes a great deal of the Arthur Cowan his father knew quite well since their college years together. The McBride family went with Cowan to see *Toys in the Attic* and visited Hellman at Martha's Vineyard. Everyone had their share of arguments with Cowan. Cowan's face would turn purple, and Mrs. McBride would say, "Arthur, Arthur, calm down. You're going to have a stroke." It was embarrassing going to restaurants with Cowan because he would make a ruckus about the food or have fun with a waiter: "How could you serve slop like this! Get this out of here! . . . The last time I was here, the chef cooked a wonderful dish of fried mockingbird's tongues. Would you check to see if that is on the menu this time?" He loved to tell jokes, McBride recalls. "Even when they weren't funny, you had to laugh watching Arthur convulse with laughter." He was also a great story teller. At Cowan's funeral, McBride remembers his father referring to Cowan's involvement with a secret government agency in the last, mysterious months of his life. Cowan had said something like,

"They want me to go back. I don't want to go back." He was speaking of returning to Europe on some kind of mission and seemed morbid about it.

The dialogue attributed to McBride's father in *Pentimento* strikes his son and daughter, Mary Robinson, as true—albeit it is put into Hellman's finished style. For example, his father would not have used a phrase like "kick through" to describe how Cowan would support his friends. McBride doubts the emphasis Hellman put on Cowan's fuzzy sense of time. He remembers that "Arthur always seemed to know exactly what was going on, where he had to be, when he had to be there." Unless Cowan had some purpose in misleading Hellman, it is hard to believe he was so vague about things.

Although Hellman mentions Cowan's love of books and his facility with French, McBride and other friends remember him as a more studious, literate man than the one in her memoir. Besides his impressive command of French literature, he was well versed in Dickens. Robinson remembers Cowan as an accomplished conversationalist who had a real knack for involving others in discussion. His wonderful stories energized people. He had an enchanting way of weaving his reading into his conversations. Although he could be infuriating, Robinson takes exception to Hellman's picture of the man as a perpetual adolescent. Certainly he had an immature side, but the details Hellman emphasizes distort the person Robinson knew.

Both Mary Robinson and Marilyn Raab, the daughter of Cowan's sister Sadie Raab, believe that Hellman wrote her piece on Cowan in anger. They feel writing about Cowan was "cathartic" for a woman who felt rejected. She was after Arthur, never got him, and it rankled her, they suggest. She has Thomas McBride, Sr., saying that she was the only woman Cowan really respected and confided in. This simply was not so. McBride's own wife was a very bright woman whom Cowan was fond of and respected highly. They shared a love of French and often spoke it to each other. Sadie Raab is barely mentioned in the Hellman portrait, even though she and Hellman knew each other and met often. Cowan was very attached to his sister. She managed his properties and looked after his business interests. Sadie's daughter Marilyn remembers how the whole family looked up to Cowan, a glamorous, elusive, legendary figure with contacts in the brilliant world outside of Philadelphia. Such omissions only matter because they suggest Hellman was going on her own feelings alone and made little attempt to understand other aspects of Cowan that made him quite another person for other people.

After Cowan's death, Hellman pestered Sadie Raab mercilessly about his estate. Raab got so angry that she sent back Hellman's letters and manuscripts (given to Cowan as gifts) and said she wanted nothing more to do with her. Cowan had told his sister of the location of a will in a certain bank's safety deposit box, but when Raab checked the box with her accountants, no such document was found. Indeed, no will ever turned up, in spite of an extensive search, but Hellman was sure Cowan had left money for her, and she was suspicious of Cowan's family. She was especially upset when a few women did receive money when they produced notes of Cowan's promising them large sums of money. It was the opinion of Thomas McBride, Sr., that the "holographic wills" were legal. Hellman suggests in her portrait that Cowan had given Helen such a note but she had torn it up. The implication is that the other women did something disreputable.

In *Three*, Hellman acknowledges getting letters from people who "denounced" her and her "picture of Arthur." One woman wrote to defend him; another expressed her deep hatred for him. Hellman thought some of the other letters may have come from members of Cowan's family, who she suggests were not very interested in learning about the true circumstances of his death. One of Sadie Raab's friends wrote to Raab declaring "how sad, vindictive and greedy (after a fashion) is the chapter on your brother."

In her usual proud-humble fashion, Hellman appoints herself as the flawed but loyal elegist of this "remarkable, generous, valuable, eccentric man. . . . He deserved something better than the sentiments of his family, most of whom he disliked, and something better from me if I could only have found it or said it." Hellman knew something was missing from her own perception of the man. Her lack of "self-penetration"—to use literary critic Patricia Meyer Spacks's term—is remarkable. Cowan clearly called forth from her very strong feelings about romance and money, yet she comes nowhere near examining the deep sources of Cowan's hold on her. As one of her severest critics, John Simon, says about her one-sentence dismissal of her marriage to Arthur Kober, "From our forthright, outspoken author, we have the right to expect something more." Similarly, literary critic Clive James complained of

Hellman's "pronounced tendencies toward that brand of aggressive humility, or claimed innocence, which finds itself helpless to explain the world at the very moment when the reader is well justified in requiring that a writer should give an apprehensible outline of what he deems to be going on."

Tally Richards was one of those young, beautiful models Cowan courted. She met him in 1948 at a cocktail party in New York City for André Maurois's nephew Gerald. After the party, she had dinner with Cowan at a Greenwich Village restaurant. Several months later, she was doing a fashion show at a hotel in Philadelphia, saw him in the dining room, and renewed their acquaintance. They began to see each other frequently. The first few years were turbulent, but their relationship gradually changed to a deep-seated, tender, caring one that lasted until his death in 1964.

Both Cowan and Richards had contradictory personalities—a rock-like center and swirling, exaggerated feelings on the surface. When they met she was an impressionable young woman. Cowan was twenty-three years her senior, cultured, articulate, and successful. She was impressed and fascinated by him. She did not know what she was to him at the beginning of their relationship—a beautiful child, a table decoration?

Along with Lillian Hellman, Molly Howe, and others, Richards received gifts from Cowan—including a Matisse print and several small watercolors of Paris street scenes by unknown artists. They were the first prints she owned. She was also presented with autographed books. Cowan once remarked that Lillian Hellman did not understand why he gave books to people like Richards. Her answer was that people like her appreciated them more. Cowan liked that answer.

Richards may have been the girl across the room at the party (mentioned in *Pentimento*) in Hellman's honor who stared at her all evening. Richards remembers going to a large party Cowan gave in Philadelphia, and feeling out of her element. She sat in a corner all evening. The most vivid memory of the party was her enormous pain in consorting with the literati:

> I wanted to be like Lillian Hellman, and, according to
> a book of self-portraits of writers, collected by a New
> York bookseller and now a published book, Lillian
> Hellman wanted to *look* like me.

Now a successful art dealer in the Southwest and a writer comfortable among the literati, Richards can thank Cowan for introducing her to a larger world.

> The chapter about Arthur in *Pentimento* angered me at first. Although factually correct in small things such as the books, the will, the talk of an early death, the diets, the shaved chest, Hellman's writing lacked the warm humor and affection of Molly Howe's letter which was included in the chapter and brought Arthur to life again. Arthur's theatricals were intended to amuse, entertain, and shake those around him from a lethargic existence. Now, after several years, after reaching an age psychologically unattractive to men, I can empathize with Hellman's taste of bitters. Empathize with the courage it takes to live with desire, coupled, as Katharine Hepburn recently put it, with the "inability to attract the finest beast in the jungle." I feel that for Hellman great success and the warmest most generous friendship did not make up for that one inability.

29

SCOUNDREL TIME
(1972–1977)

But I don't want to write my historical conclusions—it isn't my game. I tell myself that this third time out, if I stick to what I know, what happened to me, and a few others, I have a chance to write my own history of the time.

—Lillian Hellman, *Scoundrel Time*

. . . the title may refer not only to the "period of scoundrels" that it chronicles, but also to the mean elements of time itself, and to the corrosive nature of bitter memory.

—Sam A. Portaro, Jr., *Christian Century*, May 15,1985

Lil has begun to confuse herself with George Sand. I see all the preliminary symptoms of *folie de grandeur*; she regards herself as a historical character, and as someone who has known her since 1928 or thereabouts, I am becoming alarmed lest those men in the white jackets armed with butterfly nets suddenly appear and entice her into their wagon.

—S. J. Perelman, quoted in Dorothy Herrman, *S. J. Perelman:*
A Life

With Richard Nixon in the White House during the years Hellman was writing *An Unfinished Woman* and *Pentimento*, it is not surprising that she would compare her ordeal in the fifties with Vietnam and Watergate in the late sixties and early seventies.

She spent the whole summer of 1973 watching the Watergate hearings on television. Vice President Agnew's resignation astonished her: "If you or I did what Agnew did, we'd be in jail. All that talk about permissiveness—remember *that*?" In her book, Agnew and his lot were pious villains who were all the more dangerous because of their "patriotic talk." The seventies were potentially worse than the fifties because the scoundrels were not clowns like McCarthy. Halderman, Erlichman, and Mitchell had more concentrated power than did the politicians of an earlier generation.

Hellman's own political past was only alluded to in *An Unfinished Woman* and *Pentimento*—which is perhaps why she enjoyed such good press. The pressure of the times and of her own participation in the Committee for Public Justice pushed her into writing a memoir about the McCarthy era. She had tried to write such an account twice before and had never been able to achieve the right tone. It would have to be written as a morality play—that was the only standard she could bring to political life—and she would have to be the protagonist, a role she could not cast herself in until after the great success of her previous two memoirs. By 1976, there was a reading public primed for anything that had Lillian Hellman as its heroine.

This was, after all, the Lillian Hellman who participated in panel discussions of women's liberation and whose appearance at Bryn Mawr College in 1974 was reported in a *Philadelphia Bulletin* headline calling her a "literary giant." This was the same Lillian Hellman whose cooking recipes appeared in *Vogue*, who wrote in autobiographical fashion for *Travel and Leisure* magazine about her trip to Martinique. She was a writer who could command five thousand dollars from *The New Republic* for a fragment of an unfinished play. This woman of fashion had her new Park Avenue cooperative put on the spring house-tour of apartments. An amusing trip to Florida she took with the Hacketts and S. J. Perelman was the subject of a humorous article in *The New York Times*. Then there were all of those honorary degrees and literary awards that kept Hellman squarely in the public eye. She was on the *au courrant* list—named as one of the most influential women of 1975 by the National Newspaper Enterprise Association. College graduates at Barnard heard her enjoin them to participate in the political process, and her words went into the newspapers. A theater night in New York honoring Hellman was attended by Mike Nichols, Jane

Alexander, Warren Beatty, Ellen Burstyn, Jane Fonda, Christopher Plummer, Jason Robards, Maureen Stapleton, Leonard Bernstein, and many others, and excerpts from her plays were performed. As noted in the press release, the whole evening was "held for the benefit of The Committee for Public Justice, founded by Miss Hellman five years ago to work for the protection of citizens against threats to their constitutional rights and liberties." Hellman had recently attached her name to a legal suit aimed at preventing Nixon from claiming the Watergate tapes and papers as his personal property.

Interviewers began to discomfit Hellman by calling her a person of great integrity and candor, even though she had never really explained her past involvement in politics and how it related to her new prominence. That she had been unable to write about it earlier could not serve as an excuse now. She was vulnerable on the issue of Stalinism. Sooner or later, she would be called on it. In fact, in 1974, at the height of her popularity, Meyer Levin published *The Obsession*, a memoir about his alleged blacklisting in the New York literary and theatrical world, in which she figured as one of the principal villains.

In *The Obsession*, Levin tells the story of how in 1950 he discovered *The Diary of Anne Frank* in a French translation. For him it was "the voice from the mass graves" he had been searching for after years of reporting on the Holocaust as a war correspondent. He assisted Otto Frank, Anne's father and the sole surviving member of the family, in finding an American publisher. Levin's review in *The New York Times* helped bring the book to the immediate attention of a large audience. In return, the writer asked Frank to give him the first opportunity to adapt the diary for the stage. Frank agreed, and Levin submitted a draft of his script to Cheryl Crawford, a major Broadway producer.

In *The Obsession*, Levin is extremely vague about dates and on how many drafts he worked on before finishing the play. According to Levin, Crawford at first praised his draft and then abruptly rejected it. When pressed for reasons, she admitted that Lillian Hellman had found the script unstageworthy. Eventually, Crawford dropped her option on the play and Kermit Bloomgarden took it up. By this time (1955), bringing *The Diary of Anne Frank* to the stage had become Levin's obsession. He quickly lost control of it as a literary property because of his unacceptable draft and suspected a conspiracy had deprived him of his literary right to dramatize the diary.

If there was anyone with a more melodramatic imagination than Lillian Hellman's, it had to be Meyer Levin. He eventually concluded that his play had been suppressed because it was too Jewish, and that Hellman had instigated the hiring of Frances and Albert Hackett—her non-Jewish friends—to write an adaptation emphasizing the universal elements in Anne Frank's story. Why would Lillian Hellman do such a thing? Levin thought it was because she was an anti-Zionist Stalinist hostile to the uniqueness of Jews and the Jewish historical experience.

Levin's paranoia is so thoroughgoing in *The Obsession* that it is difficult to separate the credible and incredible elements in his story. He took Bloomgarden to court, claiming that the producer and his writers had plagiarized his play. He won a jury verdict supporting his charge. Subsequently, the judge threw out the jury verdict. Ephraim London, who somehow managed the feat of being friends with both Hellman and Levin, dismisses Levin's suspicions out of hand. He points out that Levin eventually produced a good play, but the version Levin proudly proclaimed as better than the Hacketts' Pulitzer Prize–winning adaptation (in 1956) was not the one Cheryl Crawford or Kermit Bloomgarden first saw. At some point, Bloomgarden did receive a version from Levin that he liked, but by then the Hacketts were well into their adaptation. Furthermore, several other producers had also rejected Levin's earlier versions.

Albert Hackett does not recall ever having seen Levin's version. He and his wife Frances did consult with Hellman and she provided advice about the structure of the play—in particular, where to place the Chanukah scene—but none of the writing was hers. Albert remembers that Hellman's main objection to the Levin version she saw was that there was too much "moral breast-beating." Since the Hacketts' play contains dialogue not in the original diary but in Levin's play, a case can be made for plagiarism; the Hacketts need not have actually seen a script to have picked up cues from Bloomgarden and Hellman. But the really disturbing issue is political: *Did* Hellman maneuver her friends into writing a drama that skirted the Jewish content of the play?

In reviewing the whole Meyer Levin controversy, Sander L. Gilman has recently argued in *Jewish Self-Hatred: Anti-Semitism and the Hidden Language of the Jews* that Anne Frank was in many ways an assimilated Jew:

> One of the central proofs that Levin brought in his court suit against the Hacketts was the use of a specific scene placed at the conclusion of the second act: "Here, now, was the Chanukah scene, just as I had placed it, as the climax at the close of the second act. Anne, extremely excited, hurrying about distributing her gifts, the excitement mounting and mounting—something seemed wrong to me. The way they had done it was more like Christmas." Indeed, the Chanukah celebration is so presented in the Hacketts' play. But what is the parallel in the diary itself? On December 7, 1942, Anne Frank records that Chanukah and St. Nicholas's Day fell almost together. Chanukah was celebrated, but "the evening of St. Nicholas's Day was much more fun." In December 1943 there are five separate entries recording her joy at the coming of St. Nicholas's Day and Christmas. It is on St. Nicholas's Day that good little boys and girls are rewarded with gifts, while bad children receive coals in their shoes. Anne Frank was typical of assimilated Jews, who adopted Christian religious observations without any religious overtones in lieu of a Jewish religious celebration. Both versions of the play thus create a speaking Jew, and being Jewish, at least in the world of the theater, is tied to the image of religion, if not to religion itself. The language that Anne Frank is made to speak is stage English, just as her diary was written in literary Dutch, so there is no specific linguistic marker for her identity. She does not speak with a Jewish accent, does not mix bits of Hebrew in her discourse. The authors, no matter what their political persuasion, must give her some type of identification as a Jew.

Regardless of how "Jewish" Meyer Levin's adaptation of the diary might have been and of the question of his play's quality, there can be no doubt that the Hacketts had the dramatic license to make Anne Frank both a Jew and an example of suffering humanity. As

Victor Navasky points out in his review of *The Obsession*, the decision to understate the play's Jewishness may have been a wise esthetic decision. This seems to have been Hellman's reaction when she called Levin's version "moral breast-beating."

Yet there is no question that Hellman was anti-Zionist. She was a part of the thirties' Stalinist old guard that looked to the Soviet Union to abolish anti-Semitism. In effect, this meant abolishing what she seems to have regarded as the ethnocentrism of Jewish-ness so disagreeable in Israel and in people who made being Jewish an issue. She quarreled with Herbert Gold about his support for Israel. Martin Peretz has no doubt at all that she found Israel something akin to an anachronism in the modern world. Her attitude actually was in line with Soviet foreign policy, which criticized the Israelis for the occupation of Arab land. Although she never denied she was Jewish, she had little interest in defining herself as a Jew. Peretz and Levin put it more strongly: to Peretz, she was antagonistic toward the very idea of a Jewish state, to any form of Jewishness that set itself apart from the mainstream; to Gold, she was "almost a self-hating Jew, a Jew-hating Jew."

Hellman expressed what Jewishness she had in curious ways. According to John Hersey, "When anything seems unspeakable to her, she will shout 'Oy!' and cross herself." Ring Lardner, Jr., observed that Hellman had known very little about the seder she attended at her friend Hannah Weinstein's house, although she was curious and kept asking questions about it. Hellman probably would not have seen an issue in "universalizing" the Anne Frank story, since her sense of Jewishness had become inseparable from her participation in American culture as a whole. Joseph Cohen, an English professor at Tulane University, points out that Hellman's family was not part of the massive Jewish emigration from Eastern Europe to America between 1880 and 1920. As German Jews, a group quite separate from the people of Levin's generation, Hellman's family would have been "well-assimilated" in New Orleans by 1850 and already tied to big investment firms and banks "because of the cotton trade." She would have come from a background that would have made Levin and other Eastern European Jews seem paranoid and inferior. Stephen Birmingham remembers having lunch with Hellman at the Ritz-Carlton in Boston, where she told him she'd read and enjoyed his book *Our Crowd*, which stimulated her to regale him with "funny anecdotes about similarities in her upper-crust, German-Jewish upbringing in New

Orleans" and imagines she had included these stories in her memoirs. But the contrary is true. Except for a few scattered comments, Hellman has nothing to say in her memoirs about being Jewish. Both she and Arthur Kober found the religious aspects of Jewish life distasteful, although Kober often made the lives of Jews the subject matter of his stories. In a study of what she regards as Hellman's anti-Semitism, Bonnie Lyons points out that Hellman's plays and memoirs exhibit, if anything, a conversion to Christian concepts of honor. At the very least, Hellman is unwilling to see *anything* in specifically Jewish terms. Kurt Muller is careful to note that the anti-Fascists he is trying to ransom are "not only Jews." Julia says much the same thing. For Lillian Hellman, there are no specifically Jewish issues—not even the Holocaust. That stance in itself surely constitutes the denial of a heritage, Lyons argues. In researching an article for the *Tulanian* (Fall 1983), David Fyten was unable to get Hellman to comment on Lyons's essay "The First Jewish Nun on Prytania Street."

When Ephraim London first discussed Levin's charges against her, Hellman laughed; when the allegations appeared in *The Obsession*, she was furious. She told London that he could not continue as her friend if he also saw Levin. He told her in no uncertain words that he did not pick his friends on the basis of whether or not they pleased her. If she really wanted to know, he was also friends with red-baiters, with a murderer, and with many other people he was sure Hellman would not approve of. She calmed down, and London learned that she actually liked to be talked to that way. He remained one of her dearest and most loyal friends. Herbert Gold, on the other hand, was banished from her coterie when she saw a blurb he had written for *The Obsession*. In an exchange of letters, he explained that he recognized Levin's faults, but that Levin also had many good points, and Gold was not about to give him up. This is similar to what London had said. The difference was that Gold had been a kind of protégé of Hellman's. Hellman asked how dare he betray her by befriending Levin? Gold answered that he would tell anyone how grateful he was for Hellman's help, but he did not take back his support for Levin. Gold had always maintained some distance from Hellman, not wanting to be caught in her orbit. Now there seemed no way to mend their break.

The implication of *The Obsession* is that Lillian Hellman could put the word out on someone. She could see to it that Levin never got produced in New York, that his books never got prominently reviewed, that he never got invitations for television and radio interviews. He did not say that Lillian Hellman alone was responsible for his blacklisting—if that is what it was. But her influence had been something to reckon with.

Even if Meyer Levin was phobic on the subject of Lillian Hellman, there is no question that her attitudes and her behavior made her a proper target of his paranoia. As Martin Peretz explains:

> In the intellectual world there was this very deep fissure between the identifying Jews and the universalizing Jews—who of course were not truly universalizing. Their homeland was Russia, whether they were born there or not. That's certainly true of Lillian. Those of us who were a different kind of Jew were an offense to her. She said I was provincial and parochial. . . . Once my wife and I were having dinner with Lillian and Hannah Weinstein. Lillian was going on about the Nazi-like Israelis, and Hannah said, "Stop this Lillian, this is crazy! This is completely out of whack!" She was fanatically anti-Israel. And with the Israelis she had the most scrupulous moral norms. . . . It wasn't so much that their behavior offended her. The existence of the Jewish state tells them [the universalizers] that there are a lot of people in the world who say we Jews are really—no matter how idiosyncratic we are— we're a people just like everybody else. We have criminals, we have murderers, we have armies, we have governments that are corrupt and inefficient. And for those people who have emancipated themselves from the confines of religiosity to find that for a lot of Jews that emancipation means being just like the gentiles politically—what's so special about that?

Hellman, Philip Rahv, and the novelist Alan Lelchuk fought over precisely this issue. Rahv, who moved from Stalinism to anticommunism, took as his last name the Hebrew word for rabbi. As Peretz puts it:

> That is the nom de guerre he chose in the Communist movement. So there is a statement of ambivalence

from the moment he enlists in the Communist International. His will left his entire estate to the state of Israel—not to a Jewish charity or to Hebrew University, which some childless Jews might do. This was raw! This meant buying planes! . . . Once at a dinner party at Billy Abrahams' apartment in Boston . . . Lillian and Philip got into the nastiest, most rancorous dispute. She said that his Zionism was an atavism.

Hellman felt uncomfortable talking about Zionism. It represented everything that was antithetical to her vision of history. Hellman's politics—her devotion to the Soviet Union, the notion of creating a new world—meant that any emphasis on Zionism or ethnicity was repugnant. Zionism was, in Peretz's words, a standing reproach to everything Hellman believed:

> Historically the Zionists turned out to be right. What were they saying? That Europe is doomed for the Jews. Liberal democracy won't save us. The Socialists won't save us. And the Communist revolutionaries won't save us. Whatever else may be wrong with Zionists, on that fundamental insight they were absolutely right.

With characters like Levin dredging up her past, it was imperative that Hellman provide her own *Scoundrel Time* script. She said as much in a letter to Joseph Rauh (January 22, 1974) asking for his help in checking facts for her new memoir: "Mr. Meyer Levin has begun the red baiting all over again." Hellman had only to look to a passage in *Pentimento* to see how *Scoundrel Time* would take shape. In remembering Arthur Cowan, she alludes to her rage over his seeming stupidity about McCarthyism. Apparently, he did not understand her HUAC testimony, why she had had to sell her farm, or why she had been blacklisted. Her strong feelings provoked a "storm" she could hardly contain, and she realized her disturbance had to do with "a kind of tribal turn against friends, half-friends, or people I didn't know but had previously respected." She was not mad at Nixon, McCarron, and the other cold warriors. She was upset with American intellectuals who found "fancy reasons" for not coming to the aid of those hounded by HUAC. She was disgusted with HUAC witnesses who confessed to sins of subversion they had never committed. She dramatized herself as an injured innocent who had been deprived of "a child's belief in tribal safety."

No reviewer, so far as I know, took issue with this remarkable passage—probably because it was not presented as political analysis but as deep personal feeling, a digression in a character portrait. Yet the passage contains the essence of *Scoundrel Time*: the naive, confused, but principled Lillian Hellman angrily wondering why her intellectual friends and acquaintances had no guts. As history, her comments are bunk; as autobiography, they reveal her extraordinary talent for projecting her personality on the times.

To what tribe does Lillian Hellman refer? She writes as though intellectuals were all part of one club. The only period in her lifetime when anything approximating a "tribe" existed was during the Popular Front of the thirties, when liberals and radicals and leftists of all persuasions were united by their antifascism. Even then, the notion of a "tribe" would have been dubious, since John Dewey and others were raising questions about the horrors of the Moscow trials and forced collectivization. Certainly, by 1939, any semblance of coherence in the intellectual community was destroyed by the Hitler-Stalin pact.

As far as HUAC was concerned, Hellman steadfastly refused to see that some witnesses—whatever their fears about losing their jobs, whatever their craven desire to make up stories of subversion—also were genuinely ashamed of their collaboration with Communists. They were dupes and admitted as much. Could Lillian Hellman ever have confessed that she was wrong, let alone that she was duped about such fundamental matters? Hardly. All she could see was that the "tribe"—which never existed in the first place—had let her down. This is about as immature a political position as one can possibly take. To maintain such willed innocence is also to remain pure, to have absolutely no compassion for others and no insight into her own sentimental politics.

In *Pentimento*, Hellman was already setting up her reference to the tribal Trillings as "old respected friends" who finked out on her by refusing to see history her way. In a new preface to his novel *The Middle of the Journey*, Lionel Trilling called Whittaker Chambers a "man of honor." Trilling had known Chambers at Columbia University, where they were students together in the twenties. Both Lionel and his wife Diana detested Chambers's actions as a Communist agent. In fact, Diana felt Chambers had

"blood on his hands" and refused to shake hands with him. But
Lionel felt he knew Chambers well enough to say that Chambers
was not a man to bear false witness against Alger Hiss. Chambers,
in other words, had a code of honor. This is all Lionel had meant
to say.

The Trillings were associated with Philip Rahv and William
Phillips, editors of the *Partisan Review*, which had begun under the
aegis of Stalinism but had reversed itself even before the Hitler-
Stalin pact. The journal was staunchly anti-Stalinist, yet the journal's editors at one time or another, had also been a part of
Hellman's social circle—if not her tribe. At first, there was great
uneasiness among writers who had contributed to *Partisan Review*
and other liberal publications as to how to respond to Hellman's
gross distortions of the McCarthy period. *Scoundrel Time* was not a
book that could be easily avoided. Any intellectual who lived
through Hellman's time had to come to grips with her blanket
condemnation of a whole generation of political thinkers and
activists. It was also irritating to have to read the initial reviews in
influential periodicals and newspapers like *The New York Times Book
Review*, *Newsweek*, the *Chicago Tribune*, *The Nation*, *Commonweal*, *The
Washington Post Book Review*, and many other journals that treated
Lillian Hellman as the paragon of political virtue and concentrated
on her brave stand before HUAC without noticing how much of
her own political history she had omitted. Virulent anti-Communists like Sidney Hook and William Buckley wanted to review
Scoundrel Time for *The New Republic*. Martin Peretz, still a friend of
Hellman's, was in a quandary. He felt she was vulnerable—that
she had "made herself vulnerable. She told people she was vulnerable with the iciest deliberation." Finally, Alfred Kazin was Peretz's
choice. Although Kazin had some hard feelings about the politics
of the thirties, he tried to be balanced about the past. As late as
February 1974, Hellman had sent Kazin a card from Sarasota,
Florida, evidently responding to a question he had asked about
her "friendship" with Solzhenitsyn. She was not that close to the
Russian writer, she wrote Kazin, but she had met him "a number
of times with Lev Kopelev, his old comrade & my friend." At
another time she wrote Kazin from Montego Bay, Jamaica, thanking him for a "nice letter" and complaining about "too much food,
too much jabber with Dukes and rich Jews." Kazin was Peretz's
old friend and a most valued contributor, but his review was "so
devastating and devastatingly personal" that Roger Rosenblatt, the

literary editor, and Peretz decided not to print the piece. According to Peretz, it discussed Hellman and Helen:

> Here was this woman who loved black people, and Kazin recounted episodes—equivalences of which I had seen between Lillian and Helen. It wasn't implausible—this bitchiness and cruelty and peremptoriness. But was it relevant to the book? There were some good reasons for rejecting the review: this is an *ad hominum* attack on Lillian Hellman. But of course it's hard to write about Lillian Hellman without being *ad hominum* because it's not a book. It's about me! Falsifications of me.

Although Peretz did not tell her, he is sure she knew he had refused the review. In fact, Kazin had sent a letter to *The New York Times Book Review* mentioning that his piece had been rejected and did some vociferous complaining in New York literary circles. In retrospect, Peretz feels he was intimidated out of printing the review. Hellman was already grousing about a conspiracy against her book. Still worried about whether he could let Hellman's book pass, Peretz decided to do "something really cowardly about it." He published John Hersey's affectionate speech about Hellman. That became his "excuse for a review of *Scoundrel Time*."

> She calls me one day several weeks after I had turned down the Kazin review but before the Hersey piece appeared. She says, "Will you call your friend Pat Moynihan and tell him to call off the dogs." That is a quote. I said, "Lillian, I have not the slightest idea what you're talking about." She described an anti-Communist conspiracy presided over by Moynihan, agented by Nathan Glazer, Alfred Kazin, Norman Podhoretz. It's comic that anybody would think that Norman Podhoretz and Alfred Kazin could possibly be in the same conspiracy. They're not even in the same conspiracy of the Elders of Zion. From her experience in the Communist orbit she had a view about how people behaved intellectually and politically—that everybody was under some kind of explicit or at best implicit or tacit discipline.

Reviews of *Scoundrel Time* were changing from positive in the spring to mixed and negative in the summer and fall of 1976. Murray Kempton's appraisal in the *New York Review of Books* (June 10, 1976) was indicative of the trend. He had much admiration for her bravery before HUAC; in fact, he was one of the very few journalists who had said so in print at the time of her testimony. Nevertheless, he was offended by her "candid snobbery." Kempton thought that Hellman had a smug and lofty view of anyone who cooperated with the committee and that she distorted the role of people like Kempton's friend, James Weschler. Kempton believed Hellman's book was honest but not "quite true"; it lacked "self-understanding." It distressed him to see her mean-spirited descriptions of Henry Wallace's parsimony and frugal eating habits. While professing great respect for Hammett, Kempton pointed out that Hellman had much simplified what it meant to be a Communist loyalist:

> We wonder what he [Hammett] might have said to Miss Hellman on the night he came home from the meeting of the board of the Civil Rights Congress which voted to refuse its support to the cause of James Kutcher, a paraplegic veteran who had been discharged as a government clerical worker because he belonged to the Trotskyite Socialist Workers Party.

In *Scoundrel Time*, Hellman, at her moralizing best, asks, "Since when do you have to agree with people to defend them from injustice?" Did she ask her beloved Hammett this question when he and his fellow Communists refused to defend James Kutcher? Kempton mentioned Kutcher not to discredit Hellman but to show that Hammett and Hellman's political decisions were not as simple and as absolutely principled as she suggests in her memoir.

In the fall issue of *Dissent*, Irving Howe expressed his outrage at Hellman's tepid admission that she had taken "too long to see what was going on in the Soviet Union." This was an amazingly mild way of characterizing her Stalinism after years of the Soviet Union's tyranny over its own people and its satellites in Central and Eastern Europe. Then, for her to say that "whatever our mistakes, I do not believe we did our country harm" was too much for Howe:

Dear Lillian Hellman, you could not be more mistaken! Those who supported Stalinism and its political enterprises, either here or abroad, helped befoul the cultural atmosphere, helped bring totalitarian methods into trade unions, helped perpetuate one of the great lies of our century [that Stalin's Russia stood for the making of a new, better world], helped destroy whatever possibilities there might have been for a resurgence of serious radicalism in America. Isn't that harm enough?

Nathan Glazer (*Commentary*, June 1976), Sidney Hook (*Encounter*, February 1977), Alfred Kazin (*Esquire*, August 1977), and many other intellectuals involved in fighting both communism and Joseph McCarthy wrote reviews taking strong exception to *Scoundrel Time*. The dispute became front-page news in *The New York Times* on September 28, 1976, with the headline "Diana Trilling Book is Canceled; Reply to Lillian Hellman is Cited." Four passages in a book of essays under contract to Little, Brown (Hellman's publisher) constituted Trilling's disagreement with Hellman. The publisher asked her to delete the passages; she agreed to amend one but insisted that the others remain intact.

Although the friendship between Trilling and Hellman had lapsed by the late sixties, they were still on speaking terms, and Hellman had given Trilling advance warning about the passage on her husband Lionel in *Scoundrel Time* and assuring her that she did not include the Trillings in her "scoundrel" category. Lionel had been ailing and died while Hellman was writing *Scoundrel Time*, and it was therefore Diana's responsibility to explain her husband's remark about Chambers that had so dismayed Hellman. Diana and Hellman had never agreed on the subject of the Cold War, and it could not have been surprising to Hellman that Trilling would want to have her say. Yet Diana says Hellman spent the entire summer of 1975 trying to seduce her into not attacking *Scoundrel Time*:

It was most extraordinary to watch all of Martha's Vineyard fall into line. Who has such power? I had five summer dress-up dresses, and I did not know how I was going to get through the summer. Because of Lillian I was being invited to these grand homes, night after night after night. It was a massive movement. The next summer [after the public falling-out with Hellman] I couldn't even get back the house I had the previous year. An ice-cold Martha's Vineyard. None of these people ever invited me again.

Trilling does not allege that Hellman phoned her friends requesting that they snub her. "No, that isn't the way it is done at all. I doubt the people would obey such an overt command. It was just that she talked against me, and they knew how they must behave. Of course, she could also say quite openly, 'You take her side, and you can never come to my house again.' "

There is no question but that Lillian Hellman operated in this way, even though in a *New York Times* interview (November 17, 1976) she ridiculed Trilling's comments on her ostracism. No one close to her could for a moment doubt that she expected complete loyalty. Even Norman Mailer nullified his endorsement of Trilling's book of essays, *We Must March My Darlings* as soon as Hellman objected to it. Hellman had pointed out to Mailer that it would be the second time he wrote a blurb for a book that attacked her—the first offense had been his support of *The Obsession*. According to Hellman, Mailer apologized to her. According to Trilling, Mailer phoned the publisher and weakened his comment in such a way that the blurb was worthless.

Very few people had the presence of mind and confidence to tell Hellman off the way Ephraim London could. It is not unusual for public figures to have a protective core of friends. Biographers often find this to be the case with Marilyn Monroe, John F. Kennedy, and others. Hellman, however, took this phenomenon a step further, so that Martha's Vineyard became her kingdom. Those who managed to remain friends to the end—John Hersey, Richard Poirier, Robert Brustein, William and Rose Styron, Jerome Wiesner, Mike Nichols, and a few others—were sworn to secrecy. Lillian Hellman established her own discipline—much to the dismay of biographer Hilary Mills, who thought she could interview Hellman's friends the Styrons and other Vineyard people she had grown up with. It was Mills's idea to explain how Hellman had such a hold on these people, but none of them would speak to her.

Before the controversy with Hellman, it had occured to Diana Trilling that Little, Brown might very well take exception to criticism she might have of a popular and highly respected author. She alerted her publisher in advance to the fact that she might include an unfavorable review of *Scoundrel Time* in her book of essays. Roger Donald, the Little, Brown editor with whom she was working, assured her that was no problem, but when Little, Brown received Trilling's manuscript, it cancelled her contract. Trilling pointed out that she was critical of several public figures in her book. Their only concern was Hellman. Roger Donald made a public statement that they considered Trilling's remarks to be a personal attack on Hellman. Hellman denied seeing or hearing about the passages in question. She said she did not know about the discussions between Little, Brown and Trilling "until two weeks after they took place." Hellman made it seem as though she had encouraged Trilling to "print anything, anywhere and at any time, that is the truth." Even though there had always been tensions between the two women, Hellman acted befuddled about Trilling's book:

> I was told it contained a hysterical personal attack on me. . . . This is deeply puzzling to me. Diana and I are old friends, and we spent the summer on the same island—Martha's Vineyard. Our houses were within a mile of each other, and she came a number of times for dinner and lunches. I thought everything had been straightened out.

This was disingenuous, to say the least—although Hellman had to admit "there had been some bad feelings between her and Mrs. Trilling after 'Scoundrel Time' came out."

Some publishers supported Little, Brown's decision to drop Trilling, suggesting they had to be loyal to their authors. Among well-known writers, Kurt Vonnegut was almost alone in castigating Little, Brown for having refused to support Trilling's right to say what she pleased. Trilling herself thought the cancellation was a form of censorship. One of the offending passages was read to Hellman over the telephone:

> Since the publication of this symposium [on liberal anti-communism] in 1967, the issues which come within its orbit have continued to divide the intellectual community with ever-increasing acuteness, albeit

with always-diminishing intellectual force. The most recent document of this division is Lillian Hellman's "Scoundrel Time."

Little, Brown objected to her reference to Hellman as an example of "diminishing intellectual force." Hellman burst out laughing when she listened to this proposed deletion and said, "I don't give a damn. . . . My goodness, what difference would that make?"

Hellman steadfastly maintained that she had refused to see or hear the passages about her. Trilling thinks otherwise. She concedes that Hellman probably did not actually call people and say, "Don't print Diana Trilling." It would have been more subtle—a matter of Hellman making her displeasure known to her minions, who would have had no trouble guessing what had to be done. Like her friends, her publisher must have known what a premium Lillian Hellman put on loyalty.

In a long footnote to *We Must March My Darlings*, published by Harcourt Brace Jovanovich in 1977, Trilling summing up her reactions to *Scoundrel Time*. Her words accurately reflect the views of many anti-Communist liberals:

> The fact that McCarthy used the Communist issue wholly for opportunistic purposes does not mean that communism didn't exist as a danger in the world or that the murderous Soviet regime lacked active powerful support in America, particularly in the entertainment industry.

Not only was Hellman all wrong in her interpretation of Lionel Trilling's "man of honor" statement, she did not even have straight the most elementary facts about Whittaker Chambers. Allan Weinstein, author of the definitive book on the *Hiss-Chambers* case, succinctly exposes Hellman's ignorance:

> Sections of *Scoundrel Time* took up the argument for Hiss's innocence and his frame-up, with Hellman observing that "Facts are facts . . . and there never had been a chance that, as Trilling continues to claim . . . Chambers was a man of honor." Hellman offered three major sets of "facts" to support her belief in Alger Hiss's innocence: that Chambers hid his microfilms in

a pumpkin for a long period of time (every news account in 1948 and all subsequent books on the Case pointed out that Chambers placed the films in the pumpkin on the morning of the day he turned them over to HUAC); that "most of the frames [of the five roll of microfilm] were unreadable" (also well publicized was the fact that only one roll was illegible, while the two strips of State Department documents were perfectly "readable"); and that the "pumpkin papers"—finally released to Hiss and other researchers in 1973—were found "to contain nothing secret, nothing confidential" (which applied only to the non–State Department rolls). Hellman's insistence that she "wasn't a historian" was thus amply vindicated.

Perhaps the most measured response to *Scoundrel Time* came from William Phillips in *Partisan Review*. Phillips began by calling Hellman "an honorable and gifted woman, and a friend," some of whose "facts and political conclusions" needed correcting. First, *Partisan Review* had a much clearer record of opposition to McCarthy than Hellman suggested. Richard Rovere, Arthur Schlesinger, Dwight Macdonald, and Philip Rahv had all written anti-McCarthy statements. Second, many ex-Communists, including Rahv and Phillips himself, had lost opportunities to write for certain journals and to teach at universities. They were not Hollywood celebrities and did not receive the publicity accorded to Hellman. His point was that these anti-Communists had not been silent and had not escaped blacklisting, yet Hellman wrote as if liberals had thrived while only radicals were punished during the McCarthy terror.

Phillips was candid in suggesting that if liberal anti-Communists did not come to the defense of those attacked by McCarthy, it was because some of those attacked "were Communists and what one was asked to defend was their right to lie about it." His own feeling, which he imagines was shared by others, was that "Communists did not have a divine right to a job in the government or in Hollywood—any more than I felt I had a right to a high-salaried job in an institution." Did Lenin or Trotsky or Rosa Luxembourg demand employment from the capitalist enemy? Phillips asked. Hellman, unfortunately, made almost no distinctions whatsoever—between the anti-communism of the left and of the right, for example. It was wrong of her to say that liberal anti-communism had led to—even if it was perverted by—Richard Nixon, who took advantage of the communism phobia to get himself and his kind into office. The link she forged between McCarthyism, liberal anti-communism, Vietnam, and Watergate was fallacious, said Phillips:

> I, myself, do not believe that even the conservative intellectuals were responsible for Watergate. That is too simple a reading of the forces behind these macabre phenomena. But, clearly, those anti-Communists who were socialists or liberals and who have been at least as critical of our own society as they have been of Russia have no more to do with Nixon than with McCarthy.

Phillips closed his piece on *Scoundrel Time* by expressing his dismay over Garry Wills's introduction to the book, which he felt was "far below the level of his earlier writing." Evidently, Wills's piece was intended as a historical overview of the kind Hellman herself felt inadequate to supply. Unfortunately, the whole volume becomes even more skewed by his tendentious rhetoric: "A newly aggressive Truman had launched the Cold War in the spring of 1947 with his plan to "rescue" Greece and Turkey. Simultaneously he introduced a new loyalty program. . . ." Wills writes as if the Soviet Union had not yet taken over Poland and exhibited its own aggressive foreign policy. Wills's answer to hysterical anti-communism is to stand it on its head: "We are not merely a country. We are an Ism. And truth must spread without limit; it cannot countenance error." This is precisely what anti-Communists had always said about Soviet intentions: the U.S.S.R. believed in the infallibility of its ideology and would try to conquer the world with it. All along the line, Wills tries to make history fit Hellman's biases.

Only at one point does Wills take issue with Hellman. He rhapsodizes about her extremely individualistic code of honor, which meant she could not have believed that HUAC and

> men like McCarthy and Chambers were sincere. The ideologue's mentality is so foreign to her that she must explain fanaticism to herself as mere opportunism. In fact, the Red-hunters were so dangerous precisely

because they considered themselves saviors of the country from a diabolical plot.

Because Hellman had "spent her life creating vivid and individual people on the stage . . . the thought of a McCarthy intent on destroying whole classes and types of people is almost too horrible to contemplate," Wills concludes.

The implications of Wills's insight are fascinating. Substitute the name Stalin for McCarthy throughout Wills's argument. Whether it was Stalin or McCarthy, she could not imagine a *policy* of mass extermination, or a personality activated by a policy. Stalin is the "old crazy man" of *An Unfinished Woman*; McCarthy and his followers are shady confidence men in *Scoundrel Time*. The fact is, Hellman's politics were always *personal*. She was honest when she told John Melby and HUAC that she was not a political person, that she did not really understand politics even though she was heavily involved in it. Her loyalty was to people she felt deeply about—above all to Hammett. Her politics were, at best, secondhand, borrowed clothing. When attacked, she could only put her head down and bully her way through. Her phrase for McCarthy and his ilk is "cheap baddies." This is a comic-book version of politics, with Hammett as Superman. All right, she implies, Stalin was a bad man. But she cannot see beyond that—that his ideology mandated the murder of whole classes and types of people. What ultimately vitiates *Scoundrel Time* is not just Lillian Hellman's effort to cover up her political past, to rationalize her radicalism, and to expose the cowardice of others. The problem with *Scoundrel Time* is Lillian Hellman. She did not have the mind for it. Her effort to separate herself from politics was doomed from the beginning. It was impossible to write about herself without making political judgments, but political judgments were exactly what she was not qualified to make. She was a moralist, and moralism, by itself, does not yield a political vision. Taken as a metaphor, as another one of the dramatist's morality plays, *Scoundrel Time* is emotionally fulfilling. As a political memoir, it is, in Hilton Kramer's words, "one of the most poisonous and dishonest testaments ever written by an American author."

When Diana Trilling's book appeared in the spring of 1977, reviewers were still mulling over Hellman's charge that liberals had let her down. Thomas Edwards, in *The New York Times Book Review* (May 29, 1977), thought Trilling's words were harsh enough to have provoked a duel between gentlemen in another age. Edwards was inclined to sympathize with Hellman and resist Trilling's too comfortable view of American government. Bruce Cook tried to be evenhanded in the *Saturday Review* (May 28, 1977), and remarked that Trilling had not written fighting words. In *The New Republic* (August 20 and 27, 1977), Irving Howe surveyed the considerable damage done by American Stalinists—as he had in his review of *Scoundrel Time*—but took the occasion to suggest that

> where some or many of the anti-Stalinist intellectuals
> went astray was in allowing their warranted concern
> with Stalinism to tempt them into an increasingly rigid
> conservatism, or to distract them from the fact that in
> the United States, during the 1950s and then in the
> Nixon years, the major danger came from the right.

In Howe's view, Diana Trilling was not prepared to admit that "a politics complex and supple enough to cope with this multitude of enemies" from the left and the right had not been developed. There was "some justice" in Hellman's belief that liberals had not done enough to combat McCarthy and other rightists and reactionaries. Indeed, liberals took some comfort in watching Stalinists brought to judgment. Howe made clear, however, that Trilling did not minimize the dangers of the right in her writing; rather, her "liberal position" was "strong, in principle, but not nearly so strong, in application." If this was not a vindication of Hellman, it was a helpful clarification of her views; for she objected to liberalism "as a mode of social activism"—to use Howe's phrase. Liberals had the right words, Hellman noticed, but how did they translate in practice?

Yet Hellman was constitutionally incapable of even thinking through a position as sophisticated as Trilling's. During this period Martin Peretz and his wife stayed at Hellman's Vineyard house for a weekend. At dinner with the Herseys and John Phillips (son of J. P. Marquand) the discussion turned to communism. Peretz said:

> Lillian, I understand that the McCarthy period was an
> evil episode in American history. But let's put that
> aside for the moment. In some way, some of the
> people for whom you cared the most died because of

their commitment to communism, which has turned out to be a very ambiguous business.

Peretz was trying not to offend Hellman, but he had to observe that Hammett and several other loyal Communist friends of Hellman's had been imprisoned, that a Czech Communist friend had been executed by the Communists, and that Julia had died for that better world communism had not delivered. Was the sacrifice of these people worth it? Without saying a word, Hellman got up and went upstairs, leaving her guests. Either Hersey or Phillips said, "I think she's not coming back." Peretz and his wife came down for breakfast the next morning, when Hellman acted as if nothing had happened.

Sometime after the appearance of *Scoundrel Time*, Peretz was helping the Jerusalem Foundation raise money. Someone suggested to him that it would be easy to get a donation from Roy Cohn, an attorney infamous for his work as Senator McCarthy's counsel. "He's always looking for some way to make himself seem respectable," Peretz's friend said. So Peretz called Cohn, who happily agreed to put together a group of big contributors. Cohn hosted a cocktail party attended by George Steinbrenner, the probate judge of New York, the mayor of Jerusalem, and other prominent figures. On the gossip page of the *New York Post* the next day, an item appeared about Cohn and Peretz hosting a Jerusalem party. When Peretz arrived home from work, his wife Ann said, "Lillian has been ringing the phone off the hook all day. She is fit to be tied. You better call her." As Peretz tells it:

Lillian begins: "Roy Cohn—how could you do this to me! McCarthy, fascism, the Rosenbergs, Dashiell Hammett, tuberculosis, prison!" I felt put upon, but she was a friend. I said, "Lillian, you're right, it was a bad mistake, a bad error in judgment." "Error in judgment! This is the most disgusting, immoral. . . ." And it was clear there was no way she was going to let me off the hook or let me apologize. There were various things in our relationship that rankled her, and this was the consummation of it all. She continued to belabor me. How could I do it to her? Well, I didn't do it to her. Finally, I said, "Lillian, it's true. I did not host this party with Roy Cohn, but it is true I attended a party in his house, and that I initiated it. But at least I never socialized with Stalin." She hung up the phone and that was the last time we ever spoke to each other.

30

JULIA

(1976–1986)

Julia is very much like the title of the book, she is an
obscured character whom you can just catch through the
"varnish and the smoke," but you only perceive outlines
and contours.

—Vanessa Redgrave, interview with Judith Weinraub, *The New
York Times*, October 31, 1976

I wish I could answer your question about "Pentimento,"
but the plain fact is that I can't. Don't you find that you
never know quite what you have written, nor the reasons
for it? Or maybe I just don't ever want to know.

—Lillian Hellman, letter to Solita Solano, October 24, 1973

By the fall of 1976, Lillian Hellman was no longer just a
"heroine of culture." She was a legend in her own time. As
Liz Smith put it in the *New York Daily News* (October 15, 1976), it
had been "a hot month for Hellman." The Diana Trilling fracas
was just the beginning. There was also the "scandale" of Hellman's
interview with Rosalynn Carter which was "commissioned and
turned down by *The Times*," then picked up by *Rolling Stone*.
"Obviously, in spite of criticisms that the Hellman view of Mrs.
Jimmy Carter is 'poorly written' and/or 'doesn't say anything,'
someone agrees with me that even Ms. Hellman's laundry list
would be of lively interest to the literati," Smith suggested. The
"capper to Big Lil's saga" was her pose for a fur advertisement,

with the caption, "What Becomes a Legend Most?" Smith could not resist adding:

> P.S. Hellman, who suffered during the McCarthy blacklist days, when she was accused of leftist leanings, took the Maximilian mink for her pains.
> I ask you, doesn't that sound like a dyed-in-the-mink capitalist to you?

The movie *Julia* (distributed by 20th Century-Fox) was going into production. Seventies radicals Jane Fonda and Vanessa Redgrave would play Lillian and Julia. "Julia" was now Hellman's signature story. On October 29, 1974, she read it at Bryn Mawr and was so moved that "she had to stop and hold her breath for a moment before she could go on." The same year, she read it for a Bill Moyers Television interview and broke down crying. Filming had to be suspended for an hour. There was yet another public reading of "Julia" in 1977, during her visit home to New Orleans.

"Julia" is the quintessential Lillian Hellman story for many reasons. As Kathleen Bell puts it in her master's thesis, "Julia is the pure character," parts of whom appear throughout Hellman's plays. Out of Julia comes, so to speak, the motherlode; it is no accident that she is given the name of Hellman's own mother. In *The Nation* (November 5, 1977), Robert Hatch noticed now Vanessa Redgrave plays Julia's "selfless, smiling dedication to her cause, and motherly indulgence of Lillian." It is not hard to see that Julia represents everything Hellman wanted to be: beautiful, dedicated, and self-sacrificing, a nurturer of talent and of principle, compassionate and demanding, democratic and radical. Julia rebels against her family with none of Regina's nasty self-interest. She is upset with the status quo but is without Julie Rodman's aimless sexual politics. Julia is as generous as Julian but knows what to do with her money. If she is as lovely and tolerant as Hellman's own mother, Julia is also much more decisive and worldly wise. Julia's articulate criticism of the status quo is not spoiled by Cassie Bowman's bitterness. Julia is a much better doctor than Joseph Cardin because she has a sounder understanding of the body politic. Kurt Muller comes the closest to her. With his broken hands and tender concern for his family, he is a precursor of the Julia who loses a leg in her fight against fascism and produces a baby. What makes Julia such a satisfying wish-fulfilling character is that she represents everything Hellman was looking for: a person who would take personal responsibility for healing the world. In *The Searching Wind*, Sam Hazen's strident last speech makes his mother and father personally responsible for the policy of appeasement that led to war. His anger over the leg that must be amputated and his attack on his parents does not seem quite appropriate because he puts too heavy a load on individuals. He has fought for his country, but has he earned the privilege of condemning his parents? *Julia*, on the other hand, is Hellman's purest and most integrated character, because from childhood she takes on the troubles of the world and establishes her absolute right to make moral and political judgments—to see politics and personal relations as the same thing. Indeed, her politics are so much a part of her character that they seem not the expression of ideas but the embodiment of her whole personality. This is surely what Lillian Hellman wanted for herself.

Julia the movie accomplishes what neither Hellman's plays nor her memoirs can quite manage. Right from the beginning, it fuses the images of Hellman, Julia, and Hammett—the masculine and feminine, mother and father, and political and personal principles of the Lillian Hellman legend. Even the bald synopsis of the movie's beginning contains the essential myth of the writer's life:

> In 1934, the writer, Lillian Hellman (JANE FONDA) is working on her first play at the Beach House on the East Coast of the United States where she is living with Dashiell Hammett (JASON ROBARDS). The writing is not going well and while Hammett gives constant, invaluable support, Lillian's memory returns again and again to her childhood friend, Julia (VANESSA REDGRAVE).

The Child's Hour is about two women committed to each other and to their cause. They have put everything they have into the school. While the play is not overtly political, it is about what happens to people who invest their whole lives in what they believe, only to find their investment viciously attacked. The world they worked for is destroyed—one of the women is destroyed, and the other must somehow carry on. In *The Children's Hour*, Karen is left with those last trying minutes of the play that Hellman never could correct. In *Julia*, the problem of an ending is finally solved with the opening and closing images of Lillian Hellman in a boat, a still figure recalling her past, stirring the waters of memory, carrying on Julia's message. Viewers of the film could not know that to Hellman fishing alone always seemed to mean self-sufficiency. She once told William Alfred she always went out fishing alone in a boat on her birthday to avoid phone calls, but mostly to prove to herself she could still cope. Although the movie *Julia* makes no direct reference to Hellman's work other than *Pentimento*, it surely constitutes a kind of coda to her whole career.

Hellman did not write the script for *Julia*, but she kept in close contact with its producer, Richard Roth, who relayed her detailed suggestions to the director, Fred Zinneman. She was consulted on casting, and it was she who got the director and producer to accompany her to see Vanessa Redgrave in a Broadway production of *Lady from the Sea*. Soon afterward, Zinneman felt that Redgrave was the only actress who could possibly play Julia. Hellman was very worried that her own place in the film would seem too prominent. Keep the focus on Julia, she kept telling Roth. She wanted more scenes from Julia's childhood showing her protesting conditions of poverty. Hellman disliked all the "fake butch" scenes that showed her constantly smoking. She wanted a little more tenderness shown between herself and Hammett and wanted to be portrayed calling him Dash, not Hammett, which she thought made her sound "fake-tough." But above all, she did not want Lillian to be the leading character. She wrote to Roth saying she was pleased he admired her, but "send sables instead and cut me way down." She sent in other corrections, some of which were followed and others of which were not. Hellman was never entirely pleased with *Julia*. She felt there was not enough historical background. To Martin Peretz's surprise, she complained that Zinneman was playing down the Jewish aspects of the story, yet this was something he found her doing all the time herself. Given her high standards and her understandable touchiness about the portrayal of herself, Hellman's complaints were mild. She must have sensed how good the filmmakers were at getting her myth on screen.

It almost did not matter what the reviews said about *Julia*. With the unusual instance of a best-selling author portrayed on the screen while still alive, with two female stars known for their radical politics, and with Jason Robards, one of the age's finest actors, playing the handsome Hammett—about whom there had been a mystique many years in the making—the picture could not lose. The outcome of the film was set from the start:

> What other movie has had its trailer built into an Academy Awards presentation, the way "Julia" did last March [1977], when Jane Fonda made a speech introducing Lillian Hellman, who, head erect, acknowledged a standing ovation? (Pauline Kael, "A Woman For All Seasons?" *New Yorker*, October 19, 1977)

Hellman now had an aura about her. Not only was she up there on the screen, she was also the legend around whom various associations tended to gather:

> There is a moment in the film, when Lilly and Dash are talking about the difference between sable coats and what really matters, when we're reminded of something else. Some months ago Hellman appeared in a full-page ad in *The New Yorker* draped in a fur coat, with the caption "What Becomes a Legend Most?" On one level, that ad was appalling. Yet, on another level, there was something magnificently defiant about that face, as deeply grooved as W. H. Auden's, staring out at the world from an ostentatious shell. You could almost hear her cackling, after too many drinks, "Well, why the hell not."—(Martin Knelman, "Starring . . . The Writer," *The Atlantic*, November 19, 1977)

When reviewers began to make up dialogue for Lillian Hellman, when she reminded them of other august literary figures, when— in other words—she was *seen* to be operating on different levels at once as writer-celebrity, negatives and positives were almost beside the point. Whatever was said could not possibly hurt a career that had become larger than life.

Jane Fonda had been signed for the part of Lillian Hellman after reading scenes from the playwright's work at a benefit dinner in 1975. There were aspects of Hellman that troubled the actress— principally her "bad temper and irritability." Fonda never really identified with Hellman, but she did come to "care about her very much." In the *New Yorker* (October 10, 1977), film critic Pauline

Kael noticed now Fonda used the endless smoking of cigarettes and body language to create "a driven, embattled woman—a woman overprepared to fight back. This woman doesn't have much flexibility. You can see that in the stiff-necked carriage, the unyielding waist, even in the tense, muscular wrists, and in her nervous starts when anything unexpected happens." Yet as a personality and as a writer, Fonda's Hellman never quite comes alive, although Kael identified the more authentic moments:

> When—as Lillian—she walks into Sardi's on the opening night of her hit, twitching slightly from drunken nervousness, reveling in the attention she's getting while stiffly living up to her own image of herself as the distinguished playwright, you want more of her.

Balling up sheets of paper and throwing a typewriter out the window is hardly an adequate way of dramatizing a writer's life, although biographer Fred Guiles is surely right when he says this is not Fonda's fault. While the image-making qualities of *Julia* are superb—there are countless film frame portraits that recall *Pentimento*—the trouble lies in the writing. Dorothy Parker is discarded as a character, and we do not get to see how these two tough women, in Guiles's words, "could neutralize each other and become warm, affectionate friends."

The absence of a shrewd and sardonic Dorothy Parker throws all attention, of course, on the Julia-Lillian relationship. Of those who cared to question the film, Kael was the most perceptive in probing Julia's unreal purity. "Who can believe in the Julia Hellman describes," Kael asked,

> the ideal friend of her early youth, the beautiful, unimaginably rich Julia who never fails to represent the highest moonstruck ideals? If ever there was a character preserved in the amber of a girlhood crush, she's it.

Of course, Julia is described as a "girlhood crush," in *Pentimento*. But Kael's point was that Hellman (not just the screenwriter, Alvin Sargeant) is imagining Julia from an adolescent point of view. Julia is what the young Hellman–old Hellman *wanted* her to be. As Redgrave realized, Julia is the "obscured" character; she is the friend Hellman never quite had. Julia is, in Kael's irreverent words, a "saintly Freudian Marxist queen, on easy terms with Darwin, Engels, Hegel, and Einstein." She would have been a joke but for Redgrave's presence, which gives the character "an ethereal, storybook wonder," Kael concluded.

Julia put Hellman into the celebrity category. She became a news item and revered public figure:

> Dustin Hoffman/Lillian Hellman, 'If I spent the rest of my life in a room with this writer,' says the actor, 'she'd never bore me. She's the toughest, softest person I ever met. She transcends sex. I'd vote for her for President.' "—"My Favorite Woman," *Good Housekeeping*, November, 1976.

> In the fall of 1976, *The Autumn Garden* was revived and received a very respectful review from Walter Kerr— "This 'Garden' is Nearly Perfect," *The New York Times*, November 28, 1976

> The October 1976 issue of *Ms.* carried Hellman's drawing of herself titled, "What I wanted to look like and don't." Around the picture Hellman had placed comments, "Blonde curls, natural . . . Deep blue eyes, natural."

> In the winter of 1977, the Baltimore Center Stage was performing *Toys in the Attic* while Washington's Arena Stage was doing *The Autumn Garden*. A nonprofessional theater in Silver Spring, Maryland, produced *The Little Foxes*—Richard L. Coe, "The Importance of Being Lillian: A Hellman Mini-Festival," the *Washington Post*, February 20, 1977.

> "On the subject of education, Hellman was somber: 'American education has taken an enormous slide in the last seven or eight years.' She did not exempt Ivy League colleges."—Henry S. Miller, Jr. interview with Hellman, *Harvard Magazine*, January-February 1978.

> In April 1978 Hellman attended a conference on the twenties at Rutgers University—Leslie Bennetts, "Who Paved the Way," the *New York Times*, 10 April 1978.

It was even news when Hellman tried to stop the production of an off-off-Broadway version of *Toys in the Attic*—"Lillian Hellman Fails to Bar her 'Toys' From Opening," *The New York Times*, May 12, 1978.

In August 1978 Hellman flew into Wolf Trap Virginia for Leonard Bernstein's sixtieth birthday concert:

Hellman was scheduled to give the final speech of the evening during the concert. Nobody had seen a copy, but they knew it would be typically spectacular. Hellman had suggested that she might read it to Bernstein on the telephone and he disappeared for 10 minutes to talk to her. On his return he told Mrs. Shouse [Bernstein's Hostess]: "I told her to go ahead and read it. It will be prickly and there will be some raised eyebrows and hurt feelings, but I don't see any other way."

In her speech, the last of the evening, Hellman interrupted the generally congratulatory tone of other remarks with a brief, moving tribute to Bernstein's wife Felicia, who died recently. "There are people in this disorderly universe who should not die . . ." she said. "When they are gone, reduction takes place."

She referred to her collaboration with Bernstein on "Candide" and said their friendship had survived that test but it was not easy. "When the hurricanes were over—and it took a long time—our true affection for each other was delicately stitched together by his wife.

She said that only sick people like pain but that only artists can transform it into beauty, and she predicted "a new period of creativity" for Bernstein arising from the pain of his loss. She wished him "40 more years of work—and 40 isn't enough, Lenny, maybe it will take 50."—Joseph McLellan and Lon Tuck, "Night of Nights for One of America's Arts Heroes," the *Washington Post*, August 26, 1978.

In October, 1978, the new WPA Theatre launched its second season with "the first revival ever allowed of Lillian Hellman's 1936 play, 'Days to Come.' This is

Julia 511

the first production of the play that Ms. Hellman has allowed in 42 years and she will personally attend the rehearsals."—Press release, Alan Eichler Associates.

In an article called "Hellman: Recovering," the *New York Post* (17 December 1978) reported:

> Bed rest for author Lillian Hellman, who is home recuperating from an operation for glaucoma in her left eye. Hellman underwent surgery several days ago at Columbia Presbyterian Hospital. A spokesman says she feels fine but that it's still too early to determine how successful the operation was.

In the *Washington Post* (January 25, 1979) Richard Cohen suggested that

> About the only woman who comes close to Bacall . . . is Lillian Hellman. There are some similarities—the long affair with Dashiell Hammett, for instance, and Hammett's superficial kinship to Bogart. He is the writer, after all, who created what may be Bogart's greatest role—Sam Spade in "The Maltese Falcon." But the thing cannot be carried too far. Hellman has a body of work, an artistic, political and a personal commitment that has made her the darling of feminists. She has truly become a legend in her own time and one reason is that she has lived long enough to help write it herself.—Richard Cohen, "Bogie's Widow Famous for Being Famous."

The Julia story enhanced Hellman's mystique. She claimed she could not reveal Julia's identity because members of her family were still alive and might sue. Ephraim London, her attorney, insists this was a genuine concern. But Hellman knew a good story and how tantalized people were by her intimations. Stephen Gillers was full of questions about Julia, and Hellman was responsive—adding details to the story by way of satisfying his curiosity. To Martin Peretz she would suggest Julia came from a family like . . . and she would throw out a few names. With Talli Wyler, she was even more vague, and like Hellman's other friends, Talli got nowhere near solving the mystery. So far, no friend of Hellman's has admitted to knowing Julia or her actual name.

As early as May 1974, shortly after *Pentimento* was published in England, Clive James suggested in the *New Review* that the "Julia chapter, like all the others, happens in a dream. Despite the meticulously recollected minutiae, the story reads like a spy-sketch by Nichols and May." Why, for example, were the instructions to Lillian so complicated? "To have been there, to have seen it, and yet still be able to write it down so that it rings false—it takes a special kind of talent." James had no grounds for supposing the Julia chapter was not true, other than Hellman's own writing. Nearly everyone she wrote about was dead, and it did not occur to most reviewers—until Hellman raised the issue herself with a term like *Pentimento*—to diligently question the extent to which the author was working from fact.

Through the second half of the seventies, Hellman's growing legend rankled people like Mary McCarthy—an anti-Stalinist since the 1930s who had for years detested Hellman's politics and writing. On January 25, 1980, McCarthy appeared on the "Dick Cavett Show," and in response to his question on overrated writers, she jumped on Hellman, calling her a bad and dishonest writer. When asked by Cavett to clarify her opinion, McCarthy declared that everything Hellman wrote was a lie, including every "and" and "the." Perhaps a week later, Cavett got a call from Hellman, who was very upset. She felt the host should have defended her. Cavett was sorry she was taking it so hard, and asked her if she would like to respond to McCarthy's remarks on television. Hellman thought there would be little point in appearing on television stating that she was not a liar. Instead, less than a month later, Hellman brought a libel suit against McCarthy, Cavett, and the Public Broadcasting Corporation, asking $2.25 million in damages.

The suit sent shock waves through the literary and publishing community. Much more was at stake than just a fight between bitter literary rivals. Although many writers thought McCarthy had gone too far in attacking Hellman, was it right or fair of Hellman to bring a libel suit? Norman Mailer wrote a public appeal asking both women to drop the confrontation which was poisoning the atmosphere of literary life. Ending the controversy was unlikely, since Hellman was pressing McCarthy for a public apology on television. Mailer himself has often been severely critical of fellow writers, and he must have realized how the freedom to criticize would be harmed by the suit. Many of Hellman's friends—like William Alfred—expressed their disapproval of Hellman's resort to the courts, but she angrily and stubbornly went ahead. Her attorney Ephraim London is quite blunt about the libel suit's purpose. Hellman was certain that McCarthy's brutal attack would be followed up by others, and she wanted to punish anyone who went so far as to call her a liar. Yet London had an impressive reputation as a civil liberties lawyer, as a staunch defender of first-amendment rights. What was he doing initiating a libel suit? Martin Peretz wondered. "The first amendment guarantees the right of speech; it doesn't guarantee the right to lie about someone," London replied to his critics.

Hellman, herself a caustic critic of others, was blatantly trying to intimidate those who would exercise the same privilege. Never was it clearer that she had put herself in another category altogether—freedom of speech for everyone, except those who attacked Lillian Hellman. For some years now she had been a wealthy woman. Besides substantial royalties from her memoirs, there were sales of movie rights, revivals of her plays, an inheritance from a relative. "Let's go to the best restaurant in Boston," Hellman would say to Harry and Elena Levin. "I'm rich." There is no question that she could afford to be litigious—even better, Ephraim London took no legal fees from her. McCarthy, not very well off to begin with, was heavily burdened by the legal expense of defending herself. Hellman knew this.

If Hellman really thought McCarthy and others would be daunted, she was greatly mistaken. McCarthy took off for Princeton to consult with Carlos Baker, Hemingway's biographer, for she was sure Hellman had lied about her relationship with Hemingway. Baker told her about the correspondence between Hemingway and Max Perkins in Firestone Library. After lunch she examined the letters and came out, Baker understood, with just the material she needed to prove that Hellman had indeed lied. In the meantime, Hemingway's third wife, Martha Gellhorn wrote what many people have taken to be a devastating exposure of Hellman's lies. Although "Julia" was not yet the central issue, Gellhorn made it clear that she had grave doubts about that story too. Gellhorn titled her piece "Close Encounters of the Apocryphal

514   *LILLIAN HELLMAN*

Kind," which George Plimpton, editor of *Paris Review*, changed to "Guerre de Plume." What neither McCarthy nor Gellhorn knew was that ever since the appearance of *Pentimento*, Dr. Muriel Gardiner, whose life story paralleled Julia's in many important respects, was wrestling with what to do about what seemed to be on appropriation of her life story. Historian J. C Furnas, a friend of Gardiner's for fifty-odd years, recognized the resemblance between Gardiner and Julia immediately and wrote to his friend Philip Dunne that Hellman would eventually find herself in trouble for this outrageous theft.

The tone of Gellhorn's essay set the standard for subsequent assaults on Hellman's veracity. Gellhorn put Hellman in the category of "apocryphiars," writers with self-serving, spiteful fantasies that were retailed by scholars and biographers—no matter how absurd and implausible were the printed words. The trend toward *"apocryphism,* a meld of apocryphal story and apocryphiar" was growing at an alarming rate—in other words, the telling of stories about the famous by the famous who in the same breath make themselves more famous.

In her best literary policewoman fashion, Gellhorn documents that Hellman is a lousy, lying historian who has inflated her own importance. Gellhorn knows the Spanish Civil War period best because she was there with Hemingway during most of it. At every turn, Gellhorn proves that Hellman's chronology is out of whack. This is true within *An Unfinished Woman* and *Pentimento* and between the two memoirs, where dates conflict. Just the chronology for the year 1937, for example, would have Hellman in several places at once—in Moscow, with Julia in Vienna, and in Spain. And where to fit in Hellman's trip to Helsinki—also in 1937? Furnas notes that in one of the early stories in *Pentimento*, Hellman says that after her experience in Germany in the very early 1930s, she never returned again. What happened, then, to the 1937 trip in which Hellman carried money for the anti-Fascist cause? Where Gellhorn was present at meetings between Hellman and Hemingway, Gellhorn's memories contradict Hellman's at every point. On facts about the bombing of cities, on the food available to Hemingway and others, and on the whole period, Hellman was wrong. "Her incomprehension of that war is near idiocy," Gellhorn concludes.

When Muriel Gardiner's autobiography appeared in 1983, many of its readers could no longer doubt that she was Julia in all important respects, save for the fact that she had survived the war, had not lost a leg, and had been psychoanalyzed not by Freud himself but by one of his most trusted disciples. Gardiner was amazingly tolerant of what her friends took to be Hellman's plagiarism. Furnas suggests that as a psychoanalyst, Dr. Gardiner was "accustomed to dealing with human eccentricities" and was therefore exceedingly open-minded about this "extraordinary imposition." Gardiner was curious, however, and wrote to Hellman. She never received a reply. Hellman denied receiving the letter and rejected the suggestion that she had modeled Julia on Gardiner, although Gardiner and Hellman had a mutual friend, the attorney Wolf Schwabacher, who could have told Hellman all about Gardiner's exploits. Gardiner remembered Schwabacher telling her about Hellman. Through it all, Hellman treated the growing controversy as so much nonsense.

Stephen Spender, who had had an affair with Gardiner during the war and who had lived for a time in Vienna, was certain that Hellman's Julia was Gardiner. How could there be two such American woman active in the anti-Fascist resistance, both medical students and psychoanalysts? Gardiner herself checked with her contacts in Europe. There was absolutely no one who came forward with evidence that another American woman had been working in the underground during those years. Hellman's only response was that no underground movement kept good records or archives.

In June 1984, *Commentary* published Samuel McCracken's " 'Julia' and Other Fictions by Lillian Hellman." He went far beyond Gellhorn's demolition of Hellman's chronology and characterization of events. He checked the London telephone book for 1938 to show there was no listing for the funeral home to which Julia's body supposedly was taken. He checked the passenger list of the ship Hellman sailed on after going to England to claim Julia's body. Hellman was not on the list. At every point where evidence of Julia's existence or death might be checked, McCracken found nothing. On the face of it, he found the Julia story ridiculous. Why would Julia assign more than half a dozen people to help Hellman carry money for the anti-Fascists? The dangers of such an operation would only increase as more people were included. Why would Julia herself take part, since her wooden leg would make her conspicuous? Why smuggle money at all? "Miss Hellman herself says that the Morgan Bank had been sending Julia large sums of money all over Europe," McCracken points out. Once McCracken gets started on the discrepancies and contradictions, he cannot help but observe that Hellman's handling of details would "disgrace a third-rate thriller." Muriel Gardiner, a veteran at underground work, had also wondered about the improbabilities. Her own autobiography is written in such a sober, self-effacing way, and she is described as such a figure of integrity by all of her friends and associates, that her own reservations about Hellman's story must be given the greatest weight.

During this public excoriation of Lillian Hellman's memoirs, depositions were being taken in the libel suit. McCarthy denied that her statements about Hellman during the Cavett interview were "statements of fact." Her opinion of Hellman as a dishonest writer was based principally on the three volumes of memoirs.

> In my opinion, these works distort events which are part of the history of the plaintiff's time, distort and aggrandize her relationship to those events, and are harshly unfair to many individuals, a few of whom are still living or were at the time of publication, but most of whom are dead and unable to defend themselves. I did not address myself to the question of prevarication per se, which would require a conscious intention to state an untruth. With respect to many of her statements, which I find dishonest, it may well be that plaintiff has persuaded herself of her version of the truth and is deaf to any other. The result is, in my opinion, pervasive falsity.

McCarthy was asked to give examples of the "plaintiff's intellectual dishonesty." Foremost in McCarthy's mind was Hellman's slighting of people who had taken positions before HUAC braver than hers, who had freely discussed with the committee their own activities but who refused to divulge the names of others: "One reading plaintiff's memoirs comes away with the clear impression that plaintiff was the first and only witness to offer to take such a position." McCarthy attacked the device of the voice from the press gallery—"Thank God somebody finally had the guts to do it"—and the notion that Abe Fortas would have said it was time to take a moral position before HUAC and not depend on the legalities of the fifth amendment. McCarthy referred to the HUAC testimony of Sidney Buchman, "a prominent Hollywood writer and producer, given on September 25, 1951, a full eight months prior to plaintiff's appearance. Buchman's case had to be known to both Rauh and Hellman, McCarthy pointed out. He did exactly what Hellman wanted to do but did not. He explained his own activities but refused to name names. He did not invoke the fifth amendment. "It was by no means certain the plaintiff would have been cited for contempt if she refused to name names" and relied on the fifth amendment, McCarthy wrote. "In fact the committee had, prior to plaintiff's appearance, failed to prosecute witnesses who had admitted their memberhsip in the Communist Party but who had refused to name others." Arthur Miller had also taken a more courageous stand, talking about himself and not taking the fifth amendment. He was cited for contempt of Congress, but this was reversed on appeal. "By plaintiff's own proclaimed standards the conduct of Buchman and Miller before the Committee was more courageous than hers. Hence it is my opinion that the lack of reference throughout plaintiff's memoirs to either Buchman's or Miller's conduct before the Committee in plaintiff's memoirs is self-aggrandizing and dishonest," McCarthy concluded. Like Murray Kempton, she deplored Hellman's slighting references to James Weschler. McCarthy than went on to expose the fact that Hellman was no innocent who misunderstood the import of the Moscow purge trials.

On the question of Buchman matters were more complicated than McCarthy allowed. He did receive a citation for contempt in February of 1952, and that may have frightened Hellman. Ultimately he was fined $150 and given a one-year suspended sentence. His behavior after his testimony was certainly more conciliatory than Hellman's. After his HUAC appearance in 1951, he issued a statement thanking the committee for its courteous treatment of him. On March 9, 1953, the *Hollywood Citizen-News* carried a statement by Buchman's attorney, Edward Bennett Williams, that his client "would report to authorities any subversive activities on the part of persons who had been in the party with him."

To an interviewer, Hellman explained that she knew there were others who had taken positions before HUAC anticipating her own, but she was wary of going beyond the scope of her own experience:

> I did start out by writing about many of the people I admired—Paul Sweezey (the Marxist economist) and

Leo Huberman among others. But then I thought that
if I just mentioned a few, then it would seem as if they
were the only people I admired. So I took them out. In
any case the book is about myself. It isn't a history.

Did she not see that she had miscalculated—that in concentrating
on herself, she still made historical judgments on people like
Kazan and Odets? Had she included the story of John Melby's
ordeal during the McCarthy period and of her efforts on his behalf,
she would surely have seemed a more sympathetic character. But
her feelings for Melby were apparently too personal and unresolved for *Scoundrel Time*. In September 1975, she wrote him that
her second raft of the memoir was finished. Although she had
asked him for information, their history "touched" and "pained"
her, and she was unable to do it justice. This was no reflection on
what they had shared. She took their affair "seriously," yet its
inconclusiveness upset her. She was not sure they comprehended
what had happened to them. In any event, she believed her failure
to write successfully about them was surely an indication of how
deeply she still cared for him. Another reason, concious or unconscious, may have been her esthetic need to keep the Hammett
myth intact. How to make room for Melby when Hammett had
already been cast as her leading man? One day at the Vineyard,
she had Howard Bay write about a 1947 strike of the craft unions
and about backstage politics. She did not use a word of it, but
more to the point he was disturbed by how she made everything
turn on herself. "I said, 'Lillian, you should have subtitled it *How I
Lost Hardscrabble Farm.*' "

Mary McCarthy's big guns were saved for "Julia." Her deposition states:

According to the story, plaintiff who was in Paris in
the late summer of 1937 on the point of leaving for
Moscow to attend a theater festival undertook a mission at Julia's request made by telephone from Vienna
to act as a courier for the anti-Nazi underground by
carrying money from Paris to Berlin on the way to
Moscow. Plaintiff was briefed for her mission by Johann (agent #1), a man who visited her at her Paris
hotel. At the appointed time, agent #1 met plaintiff at
the railroad station in Paris and put her on the train

where she met W. Franz (agent #2) previously described by agent #1 as his nephew. Agent #2 gave her
a large hat box and a box of candy. Attached to the hat
box was a note from Julia which contained certain
instructions. In the plaintiff's compartment were a
large young woman (agent #3) and a thin young
woman with a cane (agent #4) who shepherded her
through the sticky moments of the train trip—one of
them being the German customs inspection. When the
train finally reached Berlin, plaintiff wearing a large
fur hat stuffed with currency was accompanied on the
platform by agents #3 and #4 and was greeted effu-
sively in English by a middle-aged woman (agent #5).
The man accompanying agent #5, agent #6 directed
plaintiff to Albert's restaurant near the station where
Julia was waiting for her. Among other things, Julia
told plaintiff that they would be eating caviar but that
Albert (apparently agent #7) had to send for it. The
caviar arrived in due course and was consumed with
wine. Julia, who had described herself as too noticeable because of her crutches (we learn that she lost a
leg during the Fascist instigated riots in 1934 in Vienna) took the fur hat with the money and went to the
bathroom, emptied the hat and returned it to the
plaintiff. When the time came for plaintiff to return to
the railroad station, Julia told plaintiff that the man
(agent #7 or #8) who will take care of you has just
come into the street. Julia also told plaintiff that on
arriving at the station she would be met by another
man (agent #8 or #9) who would board the train and
travel to Warsaw in order to see her safely out of
Germany. Plaintiff is not sure if she ever saw agent #8
and #9. He does say goodbye to her through her
compartment door when the train arrives in Warsaw.
While the procedures described by the plaintiff can
give a certain Hitchcockian lift to a movie script, I
cannot believe they would ever be used in an underground operation. That an experienced underground
operative such as Julia and her associates would involve eight or nine agents in addition to Julia herself
in a mission in which a neophyte (plaintiff) is the

actual courier seems completely incredible. The high
visibility aspect of the operation, the expensive fur hat,
the effusive greeting on the railroad platform, the use
of a restaurant as a place of delivery, bringing in caviar,
receipt of money by the too noticeable Julia is also in
my opinion completely beyond belief.

McCarthy also pointed out that in *An Unfinished Woman*, Hellman
stated she was greeted in Berlin by a young Russian consular
officer. Would such an exchange of money have taken place in
public, in Berlin, especially since the courier was a well-known
Jewish radical? McCarthy asked. Then there was the problem of
the other Julia figure in *An Unfinished Woman*:

I find it difficult to believe that plaintiff knew two
women, both with medical careers, both Marxists,
both Americans killed in Vienna in the 1930s by or as
a result of the Nazis. One, Julia, and the other the
Alice of *An Unfinished Woman*. Her father was a rich
Jew from Detroit, and "she was already started on the
road to Marxism that would leave her as a student
doctor to be killed in the Vienna riots of 1934"—the
same riots that resulted in the loss of Julia's leg. . . .
Were Julia a true story, one would have expected
friends of this brave woman to step forward with
information establishing her identity. . . . The only
hero or heroine the plaintiff allows posterity to honor
is plaintiff herself. In my opinion, if Julia is a true
story, plaintiff's writing of this woman in such a
mysterious and melodramatic manner constitutes a
kind of grave robbery.

Many of the discrepancies Gellhorn and McCracken identified
were also enumerated by McCarthy—as well as a catalog of the
great number of people Hellman had demeaned in her memoirs:
Hemingway, Henry Wallace, Erroll Flynn, Clifford Odets, Morris
Ernst, Lucille Watson, Tallulah Bankhead, and Alan Campbell. "I
might also mention John Dos Passos who died a year after publication of *An Unfinished Woman*," McCarthy added. The novelist
had been profoundly disturbed that Communists had gained control of the Loyalist cause, and Hellman had trivialized his concerns.

McCarthy did not claim to have discovered all of Hellman's dishonesty; to do so would be "unduly burdensome," and she did not think it was "required." As she put it in a later deposition, it was the general tone of Hellman's writing that McCarthy found unconvincing and false.

Throughout her testimony, McCarthy emphasized that she was giving her opinion. Expressions of opinion, she knew, were not libelous. Ephraim London sought to demonstrate that McCarthy was not merely expressing a literary opinion:

> The defamatory statements were not made in a review of a book or books. They were made on a televised program in which Miss McCarthy appeared to tout her most recent unsuccessful novel. McCarthy has, in fact, not written any literary criticism for ten years. . . . McCarthy's statement was a statement of alleged fact spoken about one who earns her living as a professional writer—in recent years a writer of memoirs. Such statement, when false—and no one pretends it is true—is libelous per se. It may be noted that at the time McCarthy made the statement she had not read all of the plaintiff's memoirs. [McCarthy had admitted this in her deposition.] McCarthy's statement was made with malice, with knowledge of its falsity. McCarthy conceded [in her deposition] that when she was interviewed on the Cavett program she meant not that plaintiff's "writing is made up of literal lies" and she continued "I don't mean literally nothing when I say 'Nothing in her writing rings true.' I don't mean, of course—say perhaps seventy per cent of factual statements are probably true—I don't mean that."

In her deposition, Hellman noted that McCarthy had been attempting to discredit her for years. Hellman quoted an interview that McCarthy had done with her brother, actor Kevin McCarthy. When he asked her what she had against Hellman, she replied:

> Well, I never like what she writes. There was a little episode back in 1948 when I was teaching at Sarah Lawrence. She was in the sun parlor telling the students that the novelist John Dos Passos had betrayed

the Spanish Loyalists. She was defaming Dos. I couldn't stand this woman brain feeding these utterly empty innocent minds and thinking she could get away with it.

Hellman branded this incident as being "in every respect, untrue." Hellman obviously relished reading another question Kevin McCarthy had put to his sister: "In print you have the reputation of being cold and ruthless, a bitter quill dipped in venom. Critics say you are taking revenge on someone or something. What is your response?" McCarthy's answer, "Balls," was quoted by Hellman, who said McCarthy had answered her brother's question with "her usual wit." Hellman also quoted a *Paris Metro* interview with McCarthy in which she said Hellman's every word was false, including "and and but." Hellman noted that the interviewer described how "McCarthy's steady smile has grown into a full grin." Neither this last statement, nor the almost identical one on Cavett's show, were literary criticism, as far as Hellman was concerned.

> My opinion of Miss McCarthy has not been expressed publicly, and I've not responded to any of her increasingly virulent attacks before the latest. I was reasonably sure after the telecast of libel ensued that if I did not take action, I would suffer more vicious slanders.

Hellman was at pains to prove that in legal terms she was not a public figure, in which case malice on McCarthy's part would have to be proved. McCarthy would have to be shown to have made "false remarks in reckless disregard of the truth."

> My attorney informs me that the term public figure has special meanings in libel law. One definition he read to me was of a public figure for all purposes; that is, he said, a person who assumes roles of special prominence in the affairs of society or who occupies a position of persuasive power and influence. I am certainly not such a person. I may have had some prominence as a playwright and a writer, but I have not had or assumed a role of prominence in the affairs of society. And certainly I do not and never did occupy a

position of power and influence. My life is a private one. I do not try to influence anyone other than my friends. I appear in public only when I dine out or see a play or travel or, on rare occasions, lecture. . . . The term public figure, Mr. London informed me, also applies to one who thrusts himself or herself to the forefront of particular public controversies to influence the resolution of the issues involved. (A particular public controversy being one that gave rise to the defamation). I did not, of course, thrust myself to the forefront of controversy with McCarthy. On the contrary, I suffered her insults in silence even after the broadcast of her defamation and after this action was instituted. I do not believe I can possibly be considered a public figure under either of the definitions for the purposes of this action.

Hellman's and her attorney's arguments persuaded the judge in so far as he refused to dismiss the suit when Benjamin O'Sullivan, McCarthy's attorney, made a motion for a summary judgment. The action against Cavett was dismissed because the judge found he played no part in the preparation or editing of the program. McCarthy's language, in Judge Baer's words, "does not clearly pass the test of an opinion." Although the judge conceded there were those who "believe that constitutional protection should be broadly applied where one author/critic sets out after another author/critic," and Hellman had a "verbal arsenal" powerful enough to answer McCarthy "in kind," he felt the "average listener" might well recognize McCarthy's "verbal hyperbole" and still conclude that a substantial portion of Hellman's memoirs were false. He took note of the fact that McCarthy had "only limited exposure to the works of the prolific" Miss Hellman at the time she labeled her a liar.

Many people were astonished to hear that Hellman was not a "public figure." Floyd Abrams, a New York first-amendment expert who represented the media in libel cases, took issue with Judge Baer and believed his decision would not be upheld. "I believe that Judge Baer is wrong in his analysis and that his ruling is inconsistent with a wide range of decisions concluding that football coaches, low-level actors and minor city officials are all public figures."

Stephen Gillers agrees and does not see how Hellman could have ultimately won her case because McCarthy's views of Hellman were clearly hyperbole. In 1984, she asked him whether she was right in suing McCarthy. Gillers does not remember exactly what he answered, although he is sure he communicated his belief that the suit should be dropped. He came away with the impression that she had mixed feelings about the wisdom of her case.

Had Hellman not died, London is sure he would have won the suit against McCarthy. Certainly Hellman thought she would win. After winning the first round in the suit, she sent him a card with two words on it: "My hero." It reminded London of the title cards in silent films. In *Suing the Press*, a recent book-length study of libel cases, Rodney A. Smolla suggests that "had the case gone to trial and then to a jury, there is an excellent chance in today's legal climate that Lillian Hellman would have won a substantial jury award." Smolla bases his conclusion on the fact that many judges have treated "statements that are ostensibly opinion as factual, thus subjecting those who express such statements to possible liability."

The matter of Julia was never tried. London was absolutely convinced of the basic truth of Hellman's story. At the same time, knowing Hellman, he had no doubt that she had embroidered the story considerably. Several people, London insists, knew about Hellman's trip to Berlin with the money in her hat. This was the truth he believed was undeniable. Before the trip to Berlin, Hellman had told several people about it—so many in fact, that London thought if it had been him, he would have canceled the trip. Said London, "Even Louis Fraad, my brother-in-law, who was a medical student in Vienna at the time, knew that the events of Julia took place. I was shocked that he did. And my brother-in-law knew Lillian only very slightly." But Fraad was quite sure that the woman in question is Muriel Gardiner. He was not aware of any other American woman and doubts that Julia could have been anyone other than Gardiner. Julia was the one aspect of the case that deeply troubled London. He knew it would have been painful for Hellman to divulge Julia's true identity. He kept telling her that sooner or later she would have to surrender the true name of her friend.

Although Hellman affected an aloofness from the accusations that she had borrowed Gardiner's life for "Julia," on two occasions she phoned Gardiner and tried to arrange a meeting. There is every reason to suppose from William Wright's account that the two women were wary of each other. Gardiner certainly must have wondered about Hellman's motivations. Robert Silvers recalls that a writer who distrusted Hellman was trying to get in touch with Gardiner to advise her not to agree to a meeting. Silvers believes

> The thought was that Lillian might see her and say, "Well, are you sure that you are Julia?" And Mrs. Gardiner, in her very precise way, might have said, "I can't be entirely sure." At which point Lillian might immediately have announced to the press, "I have seen this woman and she refuses to identify herself as Julia."

In commenting on the veracity of "Julia," London—ever loyal to Hellman—observes that she "was a good dramatist, and she would certainly not have hesitated to add some dramatic touches."

> Rollyson: I suppose what you're telling me is that in *Pentimento* in a section called "Julia" Lillian Hellman writes a story. It's a kind of drama. And the drama in some way is based on some real feelings and a real person, but a great many of the details might not be true.
> London: Might not be true, that's right.
> Rollyson: And that's what you would have had to say in court?
> London: That's what I would have had to say in court unless Lillian gave me more details.
> Rollyson: Do you think she would have if pressed?
> London: I think she might have if I told her these things would be assumed to be untrue.

London concedes the possibility that almost all of the plot of "Julia" is invented. If one takes his point, then much of the argument with her chronology and her plot is beside the point. She would use dates, seasons, and times of the year to give verisimilitude to the narrative and not to document where she was and when. She states quite clearly in *An Unfinished Woman* that she has no intention of being the "bookkeeper" of her own life. Surely,

she created chronology for her convenience and probably manipulated dates consciously and unconsciously. In spite of what
Samuel McCracken thinks, even first-rate thrillers are often full of
inconsistencies. That Hellman hopelessly mixed up dates does not
make her a liar. Even the precise Mr. McCracken (or his editors)
can get a date in the recent past wrong—he gave 1973 as the release
date for the movie *Julia*. Much of the "Julia" plot that seems so full
of holes to Hellman's hostile critics did not bother *Pentimento*'s
reviewers, for their sympathies were with her.

It does not seem fair to attack Hellman on the question of
probability, since the issue is not whether the story she tells is
plausible but whether it is true. Is it probable that Julia would have
seen Hellman in Berlin? Hellman makes clear how deeply the two
women wanted to see each other, how often they had not been
able to meet, and how desperately Julia needed Hellman as her
messenger to and from the outside world. The point of the story is
that both Julia and Hellman are taking risks that involve personal
feelings, not just political convictions. Granted, an underground
operative most likely would not have behaved this way and Muriel
Gardiner would not have engineered such a plan. But the fact is
that Hellman's Julia does, and that the Julia *imagined* by Hellman is
a person quite separate from Gardiner, even though the scaffolding
of Julia's character seems to be built upon Gardiner's.

Fellow writers wonder whether Hellman crossed the line between fiction and fact in believing in her characters. Did these
characters *become* her life story? Herbert Gold talks about moments
in the creative process when the writer almost believes that his or
her characters actually exist. Writers are sometimes compelled to
believe in the reality of their fictional creations in ways that would
be deemed pathological lying in others. There is no question that
Julia is at the heart of Hellman's life and deeply expressive of her
feelings. How much of Julia existed apart from Muriel Gardiner is
not certain. Nor is it certain to what extent the term *Pentimento* is
meant to be Hellman's confession that she is not only re-seeing
her life, she is re-inventing it. In his biography of Jane Fonda, Fred
Guiles surely speaks for many Hellman readers who are aware of
the "Julia" controversy:

> Making herself a heroine of the Resistance movement
> against the Nazis was doubtless an old fantasy of Miss
> Hellman's. Tough, "scrappy," a companion and lover

Dash Hammett once described her, and antifascist, she must have resented the fact that throughout this period she had American ties, contracts in Hollywood, and a decent man who needed her with him in New York and Hollywood. But while we can believe in the character of Julia, in the fact that she once existed and did these things—we can even believe in her death at the hands of the Nazis—it is more difficult to accept Lillian Hellman herself as a character under those circumstances. With the death of her old friend Dorothy Parker in 1967 following on that of Dotty's husband, Alan Campbell, Hellman must have repented the more prosaic facts of her trip to Europe with the Campbells, and placed herself square in the middle of this dangerous mission. . . . Alternatively we can take this very contrived espionage plot another way. Perhaps Julia or someone in the Resistance movement did ask Miss Hellman to be a courier of some currency into Berlin. She told Dorothy Parker about it soon afterward but kept it from Alan Campbell, who was known to be a gossip. It was risky and it was successful—done and filed away in the mind as of no great moment.

Guiles could be right, for Hellman did tell the Julia story sometime in the fifties to John Melby, so that he was not surprised at all to read it in *Pentimento*. At the very least, the "fantasy" of Julia, if that is what it was, was a long time in the making. Howard Bay and Ralph Ingersoll believed Hellman had a very powerful ability to fantasize. Like many of her friends, Bay did not believe the Julia story. He speculated that it had grown in her mind over many, many years.

In *Hellman in Hollywood*, Bernard F. Dick suggests that sometimes Hellman's memory was confused, while other times her contradictory dates may have been intentional in order to prevent the very tracing of events to which the zealous McCracken and the determined Gellhorn have devoted themselves. That Julia is given the name of Alice and dies in 1934 in *An Unfinished Woman* does not perturb Dick at all; the author simply decided to tell more of the story in *Pentimento*. This is a common enough feature in the fiction of Faulkner and many others, but it disconcerts readers of memoirs. Until readers begin to look for such things, discrepancies in dates, minor characters who are killed off and get renamed as major characters, are not usually noticed. Hellman herself may not have noticed, since she—like many of her readers—passionately identifies with the story she has to tell. For readers like Dick who see Julia as central to all of Hellman's work—as I do—the fictionalizing that assuredly took place seems less important than the artistic and biographical truth that for Lillian Hellman, Julia was real.

31

RASPBERRIES

(1980–1984)

But memory for all of us is so nuts. . . . It's no news that
each of us has our own reasons for pretending, denying,
affirming what was there and never there.

—Lillian Hellman, *Maybe*

I s *Maybe* (1980) a "story," as Hellman subtitles it, or is it part
four of her memoirs? Sarah Cameron, the object of fascination
in *Maybe*, is an obscure figure who Hellman never knew really
well. In the course of a lifetime, Sarah goes through many guises,
and Hellman is never sure of the truth of Sarah's tales or how
much Hellman herself may have misremembered, misperceived,
or invented. There are conflicting reports and assessments of
Sarah's romantic and melodramatic life, which has touched Hellman in peculiar ways from the twenties to the present. Memory
itself is a maybe in Hellman's book. All memories are stories,
Maybe implies, however much we hope our recollections are true.
Sarah is just an extreme case, and this is why she interests
Hellman—although the author says she does not understand Sarah's hold on her.

In her review of *Maybe* in *The New Republic* (August 2 and 9,
1980), Maggie Scarf suggests:

Sarah seems to be almost an object of fantasy, or of a
schoolgirlish crush. She is (as is standard for the ob-

jects of such crushes) many things that Hellman herself is not: an arch-WASP, a beautiful patrician girl.

Maybe takes "Julia" a step further by implying Hellman has a need for the story of a Sarah/Julia. The need—though not necessarily the woman—actually exists. At one point, Hellman concludes that Sarah has made up the story that she and Hellman have had the same lover, Alex, and that he has told both of them they smelled. With no real evidence, Hellman takes the story as Sarah's kindness toward her—perhaps because there are unstated similarities between the two women. Sarah consorts with gangsters and claims to have been witness to the aftermath of a murder. More prosaically, Hellman dines with Frank Costello and studiously avoids crime talk. Like Julia, Sarah leads the mysterious, adventurous life that intrigues her comparatively staid counterpart, Hellman.

Maybe is an extraordinary departure for Hellman. Although she had previously admitted the faultiness of her memory, her admissions were in the manner of asides—self-protecting confessions of fallibility that were quickly disposed of in her crisp, judgmental portraits of people in her life. *Maybe*, on the other hand, has italicized passages that are about nothing but the vaguenesses and prejudices of memory. Because she refers to herself, to her growing blindness, to Dashiell Hammett and other figures familiar from her other memoirs, *Maybe* seems to be nonfiction. In *The New York Times Book Review* (June 1, 1980), Robert Towers was "tantalized" by the book but ultimately disappointed. It was all so unresolved. Hellman digressed about her own life and never seemed to come to the point about Sarah. Towers noted problems with chronology—a sure sign that he considered the book a memoir.

William Abrahams, Hellman's editor at Little, Brown, wrote to *The New York Times* (July 20, 1980) in reply, noting that *Maybe* was not a "historical document." Take it as "the author described it," he suggested. Implicit in Hellman's idea of "story" is a blend of fact and fiction, and *Maybe* is about finding meaning through making up stories. Hellman meets several people with stories about Sarah. Sarah's son and ex-husband have very different accounts of her—each of which are possibly true. Both praised and blamed in the past for her precise plotting, reviewers took Hellman to task for *Maybe* because it was too ambiguous.

The tone of *Maybe* is also new for Hellman. Perhaps because of her growing physical infirmity—her letters from this last period are full of news about various operations and ailments—there is an uncharacteristic admission of her defenselessness. She is bothered for years by Alex's remark that there was a "high odor" in her private parts. Her behavior becomes obsessive; she takes baths three times a day, sniffs herself relentlessly, and bothers the men in her life about her smell. As Maggie Scarf puts it, Hellman seems closer to the comical, vulnerable Birdie of *The Little Foxes* than to the "competent, scrappy, smart Regina." In *Maybe*, Hellman allows herself to talk about "feminine hurts and feminine humiliations."

In *Newsweek* (June 2, 1980), Walter Clemons reported he was surprised by Hellman's "book about the erosion of certainty and the unknowability of truth." Taking note of recent attacks by Diana Trilling, William Buckley, and Mary McCarthy, he accurately predicted, "It is now open season on Hellman, and she will get lambasted for this book." In the *Village Voice* (May 19, 1980), Vivian Gornick's review of *Maybe* succinctly described the change in fashion:

> It is rare that a gifted writer who lives a long and full life does not write one memoir too many. Almost inevitably, a wise or witty sense of event capitulates to the overwhelming I. Style begins to override content, experience becomes rhetoric, and the work falls into self-parody. When that happens, the last not-so-good volume sometimes makes the reader rethink the early first-rate ones. Looking back with a reluctantly educated eye, one sees that much that is here at the end— the posturing, the self-importance, the self-dramatization—was there at the beginning.

The "tone of emotional ellipsis" that once seemed such a fine thing in the memoirs actually hid the truths Hellman was not honest enough to confront. Gornick cited a passage from *An Unfinished Woman* about a Russian acquaintance who asked Hellman why she seemed depressed: "Maybe just too much of myself. Of knowledge that has come too late, or wisdom I can't make use of now or don't want to. All kinds of things." Such sentences now invited the critic's skepticism. Too many of them made Gornick "distrust the content, to feel it served the rhythm, that experience was being pushed around inside a stylishness of expression that should be taking orders, not giving them." In sum, said Gornick,

"Hellman is hiding inside her own creation." Hellman was not really being intimate with the reader; on the contrary, the prose was carefully constructed to obviate "real pain" and "real vulnerability." It was as if Hellman were implying, "I should give *you* that? Fat chance."

Certainly, the story of smelly private parts is the kind of fake come-on Diana Trilling came to suspect. With the really intimate issues, Martin Peretz felt, Hellman withdrew, went up to her room. To Gornick, *Maybe* seemed "an impoverished piece of writing that verges severely on self-parody." The prose still has grace, and the "associativeness" that allowed the author to link her life to Sarah's is impressive, but there is no hidden depth, no richness to be had out of sentences that are "nothing more than their own skimpy selves. There is no unspoken thought or feeling tied to weighted allusion somewhere beyond the page. What you see is what you get." Two important things went wrong with Hellman, Gornick concluded: her "inner time stopped for her, and then she made a literary enterprise out of honesty."

Gornick was a little too hard on Hellman and a little too caught up in the very negative trend she identified in the first paragraph of her view. What makes *Maybe* a remarkable work of art, a "story," is that for once the author is only as good as her words. The empty rhetoric Gornick complains about is meant to stand for no more than the intangible nothingness of memory. Hellman's *donnée* is that she is purblind—physically and metaphorically. She cannot know how she smells to others and therefore cannot know whether her perceptions of herself are true. One's own smell is as intimate a possession as one has, and yet one does not have it. So it is with Hellman's own life. After three memoirs, all she could say was maybe. For Alex to suggest she had an odor that she had never noticed shook her whole sense of herself. A corollary of Alex's rejection of her is Sarah's deliberate snubbing of her on two occasions, when Hellman is forced to announce, quite formally, that she is "Lillian Hellman." As famous, as feisty, as intimidating as Hellman was, a part of her always felt unacknowledged—even rejected. There were never enough gifts for her, parties in her honor, literary awards, revivals of her plays, lovers, students, or friends to satisfy her.

It was gratifying, however, to see several good productions of her plays in the eighties. A revival of *Watch on the Rhine* at the Long Wharf Theater in New Haven came to New York. Hellman responded enthusiastically. While some reviewers thought the cast was inadequate and that the war drama was dated, the questions the play posed—to what extent are human beings responsible for one another? Is there an obligation to come to the defense of people whose freedom is threatened?—were still clearly relevant to most reviewers. If Kurt's heroic commitment seems simple-minded and antique, his cry of conscience is not. It is an open question whether *Watch on the Rhine* is dated or out of fashion. Certainly, an Eastern European actor coming from a culture dominated by an evil Soviet presence might play Kurt with a conviction American actors find difficult to summon in the years since Vietnam and Watergate.

Hellman was also particularly pleased with a 1982 production of *Another Part of the Forest* in Los Angeles. Robert Fryer, the producer, remembers that she was in very feeble health and came to the first rehearsals with a walker. She was always very well dressed, "very chic." As to be expected, she was firm about every aspect of the production and about how the actors should approach their parts. She often came backstage to confer with Ralph Beaumont, the stage manager. She was enormously pleased with the way the play was handled, and went every day to rehearsals. They seemed to rejuvenate her. Eventually, she was doing without the walker. The cast and crew grew very fond of her.

The Little Foxes, with Elizabeth Taylor in the title role of Regina, earned a million dollars in its tour of several cities. Most reviews were respectful, a few were harsh. But as with *Julia*, it hardly mattered: audiences were enthralled by the beautiful movie star in her first stage role, taking on a classic of the American theater. As a play, *The Little Foxes* did not receive much discussion, except for the usual charge of melodrama. A refreshing exception was the reviewer in the *New Yorker* (May 18, 1981), who welcomed "the old-fashioned complexity of its plot, as well as the variety of family relationships that it risks examining. How reassuring, in these parched days of plotless, tongue-tied two- and three-character plays, to observe six or eight people onstage at the same time, all going at one another hammer and tongs!" Paying attention to the acting and the characterization, the reviewer noted, "The most complicated personage onstage is Ben Hubbard, who is shrewd, resilient, and without a shred of self-deception; Anthony Zerbe embodies him admirably, letting us see, for example, that when Ben talks in tiresome clichés it is because there are times when that is the cleverest thing to do." Hellman had turned down many offers for a Broadway revival of *The Little Foxes* with other stars, but she thought the forty-nine-year-old Taylor was the "right person at the right age at the right time" to play Regina. She had been prompted by Mike Nichols to consider Taylor and accepted the actress after hearing her read for the part. Only once did the Nasty Old Lillian get out of hand. During dinner with Taylor and others involved in the production, she mentioned wanting to come to one of the run-throughs of the play. Taylor groaned and asked Hellman to wait until opening night—meaning only that she wanted the playwright to see the production at its best. Naturally, this is not the way Lillian Hellman took it, and she screamed her diapproval at Taylor. According to William Wright, the actress quickly saw that the playwright had misunderstood and was quite willing to forget the unpleasantness.

A revival of a different sort also occupied a small part of Hellman's time during these years. Her memoirs were to be brought to the stage. William Luce, author of *The Belle of Amherst*, a highly acclaimed play starring Julie Harris as Emily Dickinson, was approached by producers Ann and Bob Shanks about an adaptation of Hellman's memoirs. An admirer of Hellman's "literary achievements and moral ideals," Luce joined her and Ann Shanks for lunch at a Beverly Hills restaurant. He remembers a virtually blind Hellman ordering a chocolate soufflé for dessert.

> As I was talking to her, she picked up her fork for the first bite. She was squinting at the area before her, and I watched her hand wandering around uncertainly. Finally she scooped up the cigarette resting in the ashtray. It was a perfect balancing act, as she brought the fork and cigarette toward her mouth, with ashes an inch long still attached to the butt. I paused in my conversation and gazed, fascinated by what I was seeing. I should have stopped her, but I didn't. I don't know what possessed me. I was transfixed. Fortunately, Ann reached out and grabbed her hand just in time.

Hellman gruffly told Luce he had her approval. She had seen *The Belle of Amherst* and had checked him out with Harris. Hellman then shrugged, and something in her tone made him hesitate. He asked if she was sure he was "the one for the job." "Yes," she said, "and I seldom say yes."

Other than the memoirs, Luce worked from Marilyn Berger's television interviews with Hellman and from transcripts of her HUAC testimony. Luce admits that his motive with *Lillian* was to bring her "to the stage in as winning a way as possible, while maintaining the integrity of that effort." Since she had script approval, he was not free to stray from the persona of the memoirs. He considered it was an honor working with "America's great woman of letters" and told her so. He could "tell that she was pleased."

One of Luce's first decisions was the setting for the play: Lillian outside of Dash's hospital room in the last hours of his life, recalling their years together and all that brought her to him. Evidently, she liked this setting very much but felt Luce had waited too long in his first draft to let the audience know Hammett was offstage dying. In a later draft, Luce made Hammett's offstage presence clear near the beginning of the play. Before submitting the first draft to Hellman, Luce went over it with his producers. The revised first draft was then submitted to her. She could no longer read copy, so the actress Dorothy McGuire (one of the stars of the Los Angeles revival of *Another Part of the Forest*) tape-recorded the play. Luce met with Hellman four times and spoke with her on the phone. The last two meetings were in early 1984 at Talli Wyler's house, where Hellman was a guest. These were work sessions in her upstairs suite, to which she would be carried by a male nurse or by Luce and Bob Shanks. She was all business about the writing of the play and never "imperious or self-important," Luce recalls:

> She had dictated notes after hearing the play. The notes were excellent suggestions. She asked for deletions of certain anecdotes in favor of others which are not in her books. I remember when I stepped into her bedroom for that meeting, she peered at me and said, "You and I are natural enemies." And then, she laughed.
>
> I knew what she meant. She was allowing me to touch her writings and fashion them into something else.
>
> Lillian's state of mind was unclouded when I worked with her, which was not so many months

before she died. Her health was gone. She was frail, almost blind, but she did manage to walk, with some- one at her side. She smoked constantly. She once asked me to sit close to her, without the window behind me, so that she could see more clearly.

Luce did not make any reference to the Julia story in the play because it had been the subject of a movie and of so much controversy. He and Hellman never spoke of it. The last time he saw her at Talli Wyler's, he kissed her goodbye, then stepped into the hall while Ann and Bob Shanks spoke with her. He heard her say to them, "Please tell Bill how much I like him. I find it difficult to say so." It almost broke his heart to hear her say that, and to realize that this articulate woman was unable to speak a simple endearment to him. About two months before she died, he called her about some revisions she had requested. Her last words to him were, "It's my voice. Thank you." It was one final turn at the theater, although Hellman did not live to see it.

Hellman's last winters were spent in places where the weather was easiest on her lungs, which is why in January 1984 she came to Talli Wyler's home in Beverly Hills. William and Talli Wyler had taken vacations and visited with Hellman many times in the past forty years—for ten days in the south of France in 1947; in Rome on Alex Korda's yacht in 1953; in Rome and Florence in the fifties; in New York City and Los Angeles in the sixties. By 1984, traveling to California was a big production for Hellman. It meant renting a car and a house, hiring a staff, and so on. It was more than she wanted to cope with. In the summer of 1983 she had written to Wyler asking if she could come out and rent two bedrooms and a third room for her cook. The house was neatly divided into guest and master bedrooms, and with her children grown up and moved away, it was easy for Wyler to accommodate her friend and for both of them to preserve their privacy. Hellman stayed for two months.

In addition to her lung and eye problems, Hellman had had a pacemaker since 1981. When she was facing the ordeal of heart surgery, Peter Feibleman asked his friend Rupert Allan to call Hellman and explain his own experience with open-heart surgery. Allan did not know Hellman at all, but she seemed reassured by his steady, even explanation of how the pacemaker had eased his difficulties. He warned her that after the operation she would probably go through a terrible depression. She seemed very grateful for his call. At Wyler's, Hellman was very ill and attended by nurses day and night. She had to be carried to her car. But with all of that, her determination to go on was really amazing and admirable. "I made a note," Wyler says, "[to] remember it. Because every day she did *something*. You would think that she would want to just relax, but no, every day she had them get her dressed, fix her hair, put a little makeup on her face, and she would go out." Hellman loved to be wheeled around the big Irvine Ranch Market with its wonderful produce, meats, and fish. She also enjoyed going out with friends to a restaurant, although this was always a production in itself:

> Wyler: Just to get her there, out of the car, carried through the place—which meant that everybody there was gawking.
> Rollyson: Did you have any idea of what Hellman thought of all this? Would she have wanted that attention?
> Wyler: She loved it. She couldn't see it, but she had to be aware of it. A slight hush would fall over the place [laughter] and everybody would be whispering "Who is that?" Of course she loved it.

For the most part, Wyler and Hellman led separate lives and sometimes called each other up on their separate telephone lines. But Wyler made a point of seeing Hellman every day. If Hellman had people for dinner, she did not feel obligated to invite Wyler. It worked out very well.

Hellman was very moody and as combative as ever. She was always threatening to sue people. There was something about the feistiness of Hellman's persona that had become legendary. Wyler could feel it. It was more pronounced than ever: "I think she played Lillian Hellman for a very long time, a very long time." She was often in a bad temper with her nurses; occasionally, Wyler would hear her shrieking at them. Hellman had a dictating machine, and she was working with Peter Feibleman on their book, *Eating Together: Recollections and Recipes*. He remembers her trying to sit up in bed at Wyler's, saying, "I'm no fun anymore," and then adding, "But I *was* fun, wasn't I?"

The cookbook was a reprise of the fun Hellman had had over

the years preparing meals and traveling. Several recipes were associated with New Orleans, with friends who had taught her about certain dishes, and with Feibleman, who had accompanied her on several of her trips in recent years. In their book, he recounts meals in "San Francisco; New Orleans; New York; Boston; Connecticut; Sarasota; Palm Beach; three islands in the Caribbean; two yachts in different waters; Maine; Mexico; Paris; London; Rome; Cairo; and (for two weeks) floating down the Nile." They quarreled frequently, and the subject was often food. According to Feibleman's own account, their spats were often very public and very loud. They could be an embarrassment to others, but they seemed to take great joy in culinary conflict. Style—the way one prepared oneself for dinner and for life—was of enormous importance to this couple.

None of Hellman's reminiscences in the cookbook lasted much more than three pages. While devastatingly ill, she seems to have hit on a method of presenting vignettes of the past, snapshots of the self on which she could dwell for her minute of history. She did not have breath for much more. Thus, there were glimpses of her third birthday party, at which she sat in a corner, cross, soiled her dress, and was scratched by her cat, and of her elegant sixteenth birthday party, at which she appeared in a Parisian "gold-shot satin" dress with "gold fringe at the hem" and danced in the rather odd fashion of the day: "The boy, whirling the girl around the floor, had to hold her by the waist while she leaned the upper part of her body backwards as far as it would go." This was a kind of "gym-dance trick, and it looked very ugly, but it felt very nice." At eighteen, Hellman scandalized her father and her two aunts by doing a piece of historical research that proved her grandfather was not the Civil War hero they had celebrated. She fondly remembered Paris in the twenties, when she was not yet a real writer but was taken up by some of the best. She had to get in a last dig at Simone Signoret, claiming the actress had instructed the cast of *The Little Foxes* to have nothing to do with her, so that she had had to eat alone in a lower-class restaurant in the neighborhood of the theater. Feibleman had amusing things to tell about her nude bathing. She would come to the beach fully clothed, cover herself with a towel, and squirm for several minutes until she emerged naked in the midst of curious onlookers. In the morning Hellman was usually in a happy mood. By noon "she began to think about subjects ranging from death to Hitler." She would spend hours worrying Feibleman and others about the menu for one of her parties, berating her guest of honor, Mike Nichols, for having put her to so much trouble. Ten years had been taken off her life, she would tell him, even though he had insisted that no party was necessary, that he wanted to rest. When Nichols's wife Annabel tried to mollify Hellman by saying her guests would be honored by their invitations, Hellman replied, "Fuck all of them . . . except the Herseys. Let's have a drink." Even in the hospital, she was irrepressible and cantankerous, cursing the hospital dietician and three night nurses who "had never heard language like that in their lives." When Feibleman took her home from the hospital and insisted on stopping on the road for a cheeseburger, this became the occasion for her "running commentary on the sad state of Jews in America as exemplified by my desire to put a slice of cheese together with chopped meat between a bun and eat it." Fast food gave them "something to argue about for the rest of the ride."

Amazingly, Hellman was keeping her life going, although it was apparent to Wyler that in a few months Hellman would die. Hellman could not see her plate to eat; only far-off shapes were visible to her now. To Wyler she seemed practically anorexic. She talked about food, had vast amounts of it cooked, but ate almost nothing.

One of the friends Hellman liked to visit in Los Angeles was Walter Matthau. He remembers her being carried around by a UCLA football player. She was coughing up a lot of phlegm, but her mind was sharp. One evening, while talking politics around the table, she heard somebody say something "right of center" that she did not like and she jumped on it. One of the last things she said to Matthau was, "Walter, I know you don't like me, but I'm in love with you." He said, "You know that I don't like you. Once again, you're wrong Lillian. Because I'm just as crazy about you as you are about me." She was nettled because he lectured her about smoking. He said, "Lillian, you're only smoking one cigarette at a time." And she replied, "Oh, shut up, Walter." She reminded him that he had never given anybody a hard time when he was smoking. (A heart attack had convinced him to quit). Hellman was determined to smoke constantly, and was defiant about it. Matthau saw her as a very nervous person; smoking gave her the illusion of a certain calm. (Smoking also closed the vascular network, undoubtedly giving her comatose and rather pleasant sensations in her extremities). Matthau knew this was the end for her, and by the close of the evening he was exhausted from just hoping she would stay together.

Frances FitzGerald remembers a visit in 1984 to Hellman in Los Angeles. As a child, FitzGerald first knew Hellman through her stepfather's cousin, Marshall Field, and his wife Ruth, who were dear friends of Hellman's. FitzGerald was in a position to observe the strong bond between the Fields and Hellman, a companionship that Hellman briefly alludes to in *Scoundrel Time*. To FitzGerald, Hellman seemed a wonderful and powerful figure who enjoyed consorting with rich and liberal friends. FitzGerald always felt she did not have "enough edges" for the prickly Hellman. It was not in FitzGerald's nature to revel in the intense personal dramas Hellman liked to stage. In 1984, the change in Hellman's physical presence was shocking—she looked "like a stick." Yet she still had it in her to flirt with movie stars. FitzGerald remembers that Hellman and Warren Beatty "used to have this thing going. She would bang him with her cane, and he would tell her something outrageous." The will was still there: "it was like this enormous voice coming out of a pipe."

The way Hellman saw purpose in everything impressed FitzGerald. It seemed that there was always someone doing something to her—hence the lawsuits. Where FitzGerald tended to see confusion in things, Hellman saw intention. An example is their last meal together, in which they spoke about a mutual friend who was having considerable trouble with her children. "They were killing her," FitzGerald remembers telling Hellman. Perhaps because Hellman had become increasingly insecure about her friendships and had taken to holding things against former confidants, she found it easy to twist information and believe in conspiracies—in this case, that a close friend's children were planning to do away with their mother. When FitzGerald arrived home from her California trip, Hellman called to say she had received a letter alerting her to the murder plot. Although she was barely able to recognize FitzGerald on her visit—Hellman nevertheless proceeded to "read" the letter over the phone, insisting that FitzGerald "do something about this." FitzGerald made some inquiries and was told by a neighbor that this friend had been having conflicts with her children that were "really killing her." Then FitzGerald realized what had happened.

Lillian had taken my words . . . words that were being lightly tossed around at the time, and she had transformed them into an actual plot, a mystery story. And she had put herself at the center of it by being the one who was the recipient of the news from [the friend's] Japanese housekeeper. Lillian was going to save her friend by this intervention. It suddenly occurred to me that this was where "Julia" had come from.

What particularly impressed FitzGerald was Hellman's fidelity to detail—to the imaginary letter, to the elaboration of particulars that seemed so realistic to her. FitzGerald was half-amused and half-horrified by the murder plot scenario (especially by the warning from a Japanese housekeeper FitzGerald knew did not exist).

Jo Marshall, who had also known Hellman since childhood, visited Hellman at Talli Wyler's house. Marshall found Hellman very weak but very brave. "Don't you ever get to New York?" Hellman asked. "Not very often," Marshall replied. "Well, you ought to come, and we'll go to the theater." Hellman would not concede that her infirmities would keep her from going anywhere. For some reason, Marshall observed that people were not as interesting as they used to be. "God, isn't that true," Hellman agreed. Hellman had always made life more interesting, Marshall remembers. What great stories Marshall had heard from her over the years. When Hellman told a story, she knew everything, down to the last detail. If she remembered something involving Marshall, it might not be the way Marshall remembered it, but Hellman was always sure of her version. For example, in 1950, Marshall had visited Hardscrabble, and it was only upon her return to California that she realized she was pregnant. Years later, in reminiscences about that period, Marshall happened to mention not knowing about her pregnancy during the visit, and Hellman said, "Don't you remember? You sat and you told Dash and me that you were expecting a baby." Hellman always had to be in the know.

Through the years, Marshall came to wonder about many of the things Hellman told her, things that always seemed to dramatize Hellman's feelings but did not square with the facts. Hellman had often claimed to Marshall that Marshall's mother had sued Hammett in Los Angeles for alienation of affection and that the story had been picked up by the New Orleans press. Hellman was identified as the cause of the action and was terribly embarrassed about it. She said she had the newspaper clipping of the notice, although she never showed it to Marshall. Marshall felt it would have been most unlike her mother to have published such a notice, and every account of Mrs. Hammett supports her daughter's feelings. On one of her last meetings with Hellman, Marshall said her mother could not have done such a thing. Perhaps Ashley A. Ash, an unscrupulous relative, had acted in her stead. Hellman exploded with laughter and said, "Wait a minute. Let me write that name down." What was behind the story, as far as Marshall was concerned, was Hellman's hatred of Mrs. Hammett.

The most dramatic story Hellman had for Marshall was saved for a letter dated November 25, 1980. It concerned Marshall's sister Mary, with whom Hellman had had increasingly bitter fights over several years. Ostensibly, Hellman was writing to console Marshall about the death of her mother. Hellman knew what it meant to be "cut off from the childhood one had lost anyway." Then she abruptly announced that she had "several large questions to ask." Many years ago, Hellman had decided that after Mrs. Hammett's death she would tell Mary that she was not Hammett's daughter, thinking that perhaps it would "straighten out" Mary to know this. Now that so much time had gone by, however, it might make things "even messier" to tell Mary that she was the offspring of a love affair between her mother and another man. Hellman was asking Marshall for advice. No one knew this secret except Hellman and an analyst Hammett had told. Marshall could not believe Hellman's letter; it only expressed another of Hellman's delusions about Marshall's mother. The first she had heard of the story was from Hellman, years earlier. Her mother supposedly had gotten pregnant by a soldier (she had worked in an army hospital), and out of the kindness of his heart, Hammett had married her and claimed the child as his own. Hellman had said she knew the name of the soldier but had long forgotten it. To Marshall, it seemed entirely out of character for her mother to have taken up with a soldier while seeing Hammett, but the "clever thing about Lillian was that she knew this was something my father could have done. He had it in him to act the cavalier," Marshall concludes.

By late March 1984, Hellman had returned to the East Coast. William Alfred found her angry with weakness and the fear of death, although the subject itself was never mentioned. She was irascible with everyone. He remembers her saying a few years earlier, "I dread the time when I won't be able to go out by myself in a boat and fish." The time had arrived. To Albert Hackett she would deny her diseases: "I don't have emphysema. Never had it." During previous summers at the Vineyard, they would go fishing together. With a cigarette in her mouth that had been lit by Hackett because her eyesight was so poor, and the rod in her hand, she made her play for the fish. It was wonderful to watch her waiting for the tug on her line. Hackett thought her cigarettes were doctored; there seemed to be almost no tobacco in them. "What in God's name have you given me?" she would say to him after he handed her a lit cigarette. Toward the end, he and his wife kept getting notes from her putting off dinner dates. She was just not "quite right."

Another of Hellman's fishing companions, Jack Koontz, sadly observed her physical deterioration over the six years he knew her. At first, she was

> still strong enough to conquer a bluefish, or even several bluefish at once, when we used heavy umbrella rigs to try and fill the fish box. She would fight the crank on the reel as the fish struggled on the end of the line, and then said she was getting just too old and too weak to do this sort of thing. When she got the fish into the boat, she made it clear whose turn it was to catch the next fish, because after that it was her turn again.

In the last two years of her life, all she could manage were scup and flounder. Sometimes speedboats would come too close and Koontz would warn her about the wake he feared would knock her down.

> She always did the same thing. She sat until the boat began to churn in the wake, then she got angry, grabbed the rail, stood up, and gave the guy the finger, hollering out that he had the whole ocean, so why did he have to bother us. Then we'd go back to fishing.

The summer of 1983 was Hellman's worst. She could no longer hold her rod steady. When she caught a fish, Koontz would have to hold it up in front of her "so she could feel its size and shape." Yet she was still able to catch the biggest fish, and her courage was impressive. Most people in her condition, Koontz notes, would have given up. But he believes fishing relaxed her. "When she fished she wasn't so angry."

Louis Zetzel and his wife were visiting a relative of hers for the weekend on Martha's Vineyard when they heard that Hellman was seriously ill. She was extremely pleased to get his phone call. They arranged a meeting and he was very moved by her condition. They talked at great length about the help she was getting. She knew nothing about the various things that could be done for blind people to increase their independence. She made use of several of his suggestions aimed at restoring her confidence. He had never had any success in stopping her smoking. It had become the topic of almost every conversation with her once he realized the extent of her addiction. It was a little dangerous now to be around Hellman and her cigarettes. She would put them down anywhere. Ring Lardner, Jr., found himself more than once in charge of watching her at parties to prevent fires. On her visit to New Orleans in 1977, she actually succeeded in setting her tissues on fire in front of an audience listening to her give a public reading.

The Christmas before she died, Hellman called Julie Harris in Cape Cod. Hellman was having a Christmas party and wanted Harris to be there. The actress had not heard from Hellman in years, but she thought it was wonderful of Hellman to remember her. From time to time, Kim Hunter would run into Hellman. In May 1984, she saw a blind Hellman with a nurse at a party hosted by Pat Neal for her youngest daughter Lucy. Hellman was there for perhaps half an hour. "I hugged her but had to tell her who I was," Hunter remembers. They had five minutes together. Hellman was not happy, but she was not going to let Neal down by not showing up for the party. Hellman was very sad and said to Hunter she was not worth anything anymore. She felt she had nothing more to say. To Hunter, it was as if Hellman just wanted to get it over with. Neal remembers Hellman coming to the party wearing a "magnificent Russian amethyst necklace. She looked divine. She wanted to know all about my Lucy's future plans; she was very eager to help the next generation."

John Melby spoke with Hellman in the spring of 1984 after John Hersey suggested he call her. She was so sick, it was difficult to have a conversation, but they did reminisce about their wonderful times together in Moscow and East Hampton. He was one of several friends she remembered in her new will, signed on May

25, 1984. Blair Clark (a friend and former lover), Mike Nichols and his wife Annabel, Rita Wade (Hellman's secretary), Barbara and John Hersey, Richard Poirier, William Abrahams, Howard Bay, Ephraim London, Raya Orlova, and many other friends received gifts of money or some of Hellman's prized furniture collection, art work, and other valuable items. Peter Feibleman was the recipient of substantial property and money as well as a 50 percent share of all royalties from her literary work. Other friends, including Melby, Ruth Field, William Abrahams (her editor at Little, Brown), Fred Gardner (a former student), and others received smaller shares of her estate. A "Lillian Hellman Recreational Trust" was established for children between the ages of eight and sixteen "who are year-round residents of Gay Head" on Martha's Vineyard. Jo Marshall and Mary Miller finally received the literary rights to their father's work which he had meant them to have and which Hellman had controlled since Hammett's death.

In a settlement with the IRS after Hammett's death in 1961, Hellman and Arthur Cowan had acquired control of all of his literary properties for the incredibly low figure of five thousand dollars. When Cowan died, his family did not contest Hellman's exclusive possession of Hammett's literary estate. Although it is clear from Hammett's will that he intended his daughters to hold the copyrights to all of his work, Hellman reserved them for herself. Hellman's letters to Jo Marshall suggest that she believed she was the only person to safeguard Hammett's life and work. Time and again, she gave Marshall peremptory instructions on how to foil plots by movie makers to dramatize her beloved Hammett's life. Marshall's husband called Hellman's schemes to thwart this or that intruder as the "mania of the month." Marshall suggests, "I think I must have always been a reminder that there had been a wife and children which weren't hers." In a letter to Marshall dated 18 December 1974, Hellman referred to "your father's debt to me." Hellman had taken care of Hammett for years and no doubt felt she was owed some of the income from his literary properties. A new collection of Hammett stories received front-page attention in *The New York Times Book Review*. Hellman said she thought the book would sell well and hoped to send Hammett's daughters money from the profits. Although Hellman spoke of accountants, attorneys, and complicated income tax problems, Marshall never really received an accounting of how the royalties earned by her father's work were distributed. At Christmas, she might get a gift of three thousand dollars but how such gifts figured into Hellman's mysterious calculations was never clear to Marshall. Over the years, Hellman's letters would contain this Dickensian refrain: "The terms of your father's will if you remember are: one part of everything to Mary, one part of everything to me, and two parts of everything to you." One letter from the late seventies included a five hundred dollar check for Mary and a one thousand dollar check for Jo, and Hellman said, "I would, of course, be glad to send you my $500, but it would cause some extra difficulty particularly in the light of what I hope to do in the future." As usual, Hellman was hinting that she would sort out the matter of what the daughters were entitled to from Hammett's estate. In fact, she never got to it—not even at a time when five hundred dollars would surely have caused her no difficulty. As Marshall puts it, "In this never never land of abundance we would be getting all of my father's fortune. . . . Reading this letter now, it sounds so patently insincere." This was the way Hellman tried to retain complete control. The notion that anyone should profit from Hammett's life, except herself, enraged Hellman. On 5 December 1975, she wrote to Francis Ford Coppola trying to dissuade him from doing a movie that would turn Hammett into a "character." She was referring to a novel Coppola had bought in which Hammett was portrayed as a detective solving a crime. Coppola was not deterred, and in a subsequent letter Hellman expressed her shock that in his reply to her the director stated that he "did not care" what happened to him after his death. She put this to him hypothetically: "Would you be willing . . . to see your Godfather movies after your death cut up and changed so that they turn into arguments for the reign of gangsters—what would amount to a justification for Fascism that most certainly you would have been the first to hate." She admired his work but threatened an invasion of privacy lawsuit if he went ahead with the movie. The movie was made; no lawsuit was filed. Coppola must have been mystified by Hellman's references to his work. After all, the issue was not the mutilation of Hammett's fiction but the use of Hammett himself for fictional purposes, a use (some would contend) Hellman had availed herself of. Marshall was enlisted as an ally only when Hellman got wind of someone wanting to interview the Hammett family. When Hellman picked first Stephen Marcus, then Diane Johnson to do Hammett's biography, she wrote to assure Marshall that they had the Hellman stamp of approval. For some reason, Marcus did not complete the book and delayed returning materials given to him by Marshall and others. Hellman explained in a letter dated 8 November 1978 that "Marcus was not a man of ill will. I think he has gone slightly nuts." Hellman instructed Marshall to be present at any interviews with her sister Mary and to make sure that "Miss Johnson does not see your mother at all." Hellman reminded Marshall that her mother was now senile. This was not quite the case, Marshall recalls, although she concedes that her mother at that point would have been able to make only a "little sense." In any case, Hellman always knew best and never for a moment considered that her own writing contributed to the very exploitation of Hammett's memory she decried in others.

On June 30, 1984 Lillian Hellman died of heart failure. "The Lillian Hellman Fund," another provision of Hellman's will, was set up for "gifts or grants" to anyone engaged in any field of writing or of scientific research who "is deserving of help," the recipients to be selected "without regard to race, creed, national origin, age, sex or political beliefs." "The Dashiell Hammett Fund," on the other hand, was established specifically for gifts or grants to persons advocating "political, social and economic equality, civil rights and civil liberties" anywhere in the world but "preferably here in the United States." Even in death, Hellman wanted to make a distinction between herself and Hammett and to demonstrate that it was not she who was the political person:

> I further request that the fiduciaries in making such selections shall be guided by the political, social and economic beliefs which, of course, were radical, of the late Dashiell Hammett who was a believer in the doctrines of Karl Marx.

Hellman also left a small fund for the care of her parents' cemetery plots in the Temple Israel Cemetery in Westchester County, New York. Hellman herself would be buried in a plot in Chilmark, Massachusetts, acquired by her friend Jerome Wiesner.

The University of Texas received Hellman's literary papers, except for certain manuscripts that went to Mike Nichols. Decherd Turner, director of the university's Humanities Research Center in Austin got a call from Hellman asking him to restrict her papers to her "one and only authorized biographer," William Abrahams, as designated in her will. This was a most unusual request, but it was acceded to in view of the fact that Hellman was making a gift of her papers to the university. Abrahams, the editor of all of her memoirs and a close friend, has exclusive use of her papers and is also one of her literary executors. A public announcement of his selection was made in March 1984. As with Hammett and Dorothy Parker, so with herself, Hellman did everything in her power to hand pick who would write her life. For twenty years, students of Hellman's career had had access to her papers at the University of Texas; now Hellman was destroying some of her papers, calling friends and sending telegrams to them asking that they not speak to William Wright or that they speak only with Abrahams. Not every friend obeyed what one of them has called "Lillian's cranky last wishes."

At Hellman's funeral, Peter Feibleman evoked how impossible it was for her to go on living. As one of her nurses said:

> This lady is half paralyzed; she's legally blind; she's having rage attacks that are a result of strokes; she has no way of stopping. She says things to people she doesn't necessarily mean and then she regrets them. She cries at night; she can't help that. She can't eat. She can't sleep. She can't walk. She can't find a comfortable position in the hospital bed that has been provided for her, or on the sofa, or anyplace in her life.

Many friends, especially John Hersey, believed it was Hellman's spleen that kept her alive. He told Martin Peretz that when she seemed to fail, a friend might shout Mary McCarthy! or Diana Trilling! and the blood would rush to all parts of Hellman's body as her anger was aroused. If such extreme measures were not called for, even the name of Martin Peretz might have been enough to get Hellman going. The last eighteen months of her life were a horror. Yet Annabel Nichols remembers reading Francis Parkman to Hellman and taking "excursions into unsolved mysteries in the newspapers." They went "overtime to finish Norman Mailer's new novel." Always, Nichols came away feeling she had learned something new from Hellman.

Christopher Lehmann-Haupt saw Hellman during the last two

days of her life. She was complaining bitterly that he should write something about the plight of the blind. It bothered her that there were so few recordings of great books. She was in obvious pain but did not dwell on it. Instead, she was concerned because she had accepted a "substantial advance" for a new book and she was not sure she would ever be able to deliver it. She had about fifty thousand words but thought it was "pathetically bad." Lehmann-Haupt tried to encourage her, suggesting she concentrate on the better parts—"your first drafts have always seemed bad to you," he reminded her. But she was in a state over not knowing which parts were "really bad and what just seems bad." If she could not sleep, why not spend her time dictating the book? Lehmann-Haupt asked. "Most of the time I spend trying to figure out ways to kill myself," she replied. A moment later she muttered, "I shouldn't have said that." Lehmann-Haupt promised to come back later in the summer to read to her from a new edition of *Ulysses*. She died the following night.

William Styron took Hellman out to dinner a few days before she died. Theirs had always been a stormy friendship. But Styron believed that he and others who remained her friends realized that her prickliness and titanic anger were not really directed at individuals. Her rage was cosmic; it came from a deep reservoir of hate over everything that makes this an unjust world. They had a good dinner carving up "a few mutually detested writers and one or two mediocre politicians," Styron recalled. Hellman was in enormous pain. Styron kept putting more padding under her to try to make her more comfortable. She said "she was cursed by God with having from birth a skinny ass," which "bolstered her skepticism of the existence of God." This was his cue to tell her that her "skinny ass" was made up for "with an ample and seductive bosom." She smiled. She was no more than a "fragment of a human being" at that point, but Styron "had a glimpse of . . . a young girl again in New Orleans with a beau and having a wonderful time."

As ill as Hellman was in her last two years, Stephen Greene remembers how involved she was in talking about handsome young men. To the very end, it was important to her that she be escorted and catered to by them. The last time Green saw her it was "absolutely frightening. Her eyes were red to the rims." He kept jumping up and lighting cigarettes for her. He was so embarrassed that he told her she looked well. It was a big mistake. He looked at her very plain, blue and white quilted bathrobe, and wondered why she had not gotten dressed. Instead of saying that, he reminded her of the beautiful silk dressing gown she had bought him at Gucci's. She said, "I never got you one." She seemed a little shy, and he was not sure whether she had forgotten the gift.

Over the forty-five years Howard Bay knew Hellman, she had become "a little more rigid, a little more positive, a little more arbitrary, a little more prejudiced—like everybody. That's what happens to everybody." The last time he saw her, he told her a story that intrigued her. Bay's father was a self-made man and very proud of his "Palmer penmanship." At eleven years old, Bay had asthma. His family lived in Seattle, but his mother took him to her family's home in Lincoln, Nebraska, to get away from the damp climate. At the end of the school year, mother and son took the train home to Seattle. Bay's father was not there to greet them at the station. They took a bus home to an empty house. On the kitchen table was a note in his father's wonderful penmanship:

> I'm leaving you folks. Don't forget to pick the raspber-
> ries. Signed, W. D. Bay.

"That was a wonderful story about the strawberries," Hellman responded. Howard said, "raspberries." And Hellman said, "No, it was strawberries."

NOTES

The Acknowledgments give complete information on my interviews. Unless otherwise noted, all interviews cited in the Notes were conducted by the author. Sources for each chapter are cited by author and title. The Bibliography gives full publication information for every written source, except for ephemeral or minor items which are cited fully in the Notes. Arthur Kober's unpublished autobiography, diaries, and letters from Hellman to Kober are housed in the Archives Reading Room of the State Historical Society of Wisconsin.

1. A LEGEND IN HER OWN TIME

P. 1   BRING BAD TROUBLE TO PEOPLE WHO . . . : Hellman's testimony before HUAC is included in Eric Bentley, *Thirty Years of Treason*.

P. 2   THE LETTER WENT THROUGH SEVERAL DRAFTS: interviews with Joseph Rauh and Daniel Pollitt.

P. 2   SHE ADMITTED HER MEMBERSHIP IN THE COMMUNIST PARTY: Joseph Rauh Papers, Library of Congress.

P. 2   TO HELL WITH ALL OF YOU: Hellman interview with Marilyn Berger in Jackson Bryer, *Conversations with Lillian Hellman*.

P. 3   I THOUGHT YOU WERE AN ENVIRONMENTALIST . . . : interview with Philip Dunne.

P. 3   LIKE A LOT OF PEOPLE: John Melby, letter to author.

P. 3   LOVED ATTENTION: interview with Richard de Combray.

P. 3   A NOTORIETY KICK: interview with Howard Bay.

P. 3   OVERSTEPPING HERSELF: interview with Talli Wyler.

P. 4   SHE WAS INTRIGUED BY THE WAY HELLMAN JUMPED AROUND . . . : interview with Jo Marshall.

P. 4   SAM MARX AND I: interview with Lee Gershwin.

P. 5   PHOTOGRAPHIC MEMORY: interviews with Talli Wyler and Philip Dunne.

P. 5   THE LEGEND IN HER OWN TIME CRAP: interview with Howard Bay.

P. 5   HER FUNERAL WAS REPORTED IN *VANITY FAIR*: Bob Colacello, "A Vineyard Vignette," *Vanity Fair*, September 1984.

P. 5   *MONSTRE SACRE*: interview with Talli Wyler.

P. 5   JOKED ABOUT HER GEORGE WASHINGTON NOSE: interview with Emmy Kronenberger.

P. 6   BLOW AGAINST FASCISM: Margaret Harriman, *Take Them Up Tenderly*.

P. 6   I HAVE A T. L. FOR YOU: interview with Talli Wyler.

P. 6   A STRIKE BY THE SCENIC ARTISTS: Sam Marx interview with Hilary Mills.

P. 7 SHE TRIED TO BLOCK A BIOGRAPHY OF DOROTHY PARKER: interview with Maurice Zolotow and correspondence from Hellman to Arthur Kober in Arthur Kober Papers.

P. 7 WHEN IT BECAME KNOWN THAT WILLIAM WRIGHT: interviews with Richard Wilbur and William Alfred.

P. 7 A MERCILESS SATIRE ON ARTHUR MILLER'S PLAY: "Lillian Hellman Asks a Little Respect for her Agony, An Eminent Playwright Hallucinates after a Fall Brought on by a Current Dramatic Hit," *Show*, May 1964.

P. 8 DEAR LILLIAN: Robert Brustein, "Epilogue in Anger," *The New Republic*.

P. 8 DIANE JOHNSON REPORTS IN *VANITY FAIR*: Diane Johnson, "Obsessed."

P. 8 SHE WAS A *VIPER*: confidential interview.

P. 8 DEEP HATRED OF LILLIAN . . . : interview with Zoe Caldwell.

P. 8 AT HELLMAN'S FUNERAL: quoted in Bob Colacello, "A Vineyard Vignette."

P. 9 SHE MUST HAVE KNOWN SHE WAS DYING: interview with Richard de Combray.

P. 9 LILLIAN TRIED A BIT OF EVERYONE'S PLATE: interview with Stephen Gillers.

P. 10 IF SHE LIKED YOU: quoted in Bob Colacello, "A Vineyard Vignette."

P. 10 CATHERINE KOBER HONORS HELLMAN: interview with Catherine Kober.

P. 11 SHE QUARRELED WITH EVERYONE: Robert Brustein, "Epilogue in Anger."

P. 12 I NEVER MUCH LIKED HIS HOUSE UN-AMERICAN COMMITTEE TESTIMONY: Hellman interview with John Phillips and Anne Hollander in Bryer, *Conversations with Lillian Hellman*.

P. 13 SHE WOULD LIKE TO BE A LIBERAL: Harriman, *Take Them Up Tenderly*.

P. 13 I CAN SEE THAT HELLMAN . . . : Alfred Kazin, letter to author.

P. 14 SHE NEVER FORGAVE HAMMETT FOR REFUSING HER HIS BED: Diane Johnson, *Dashiell Hammett: A Life*.

2. AN ONLY CHILD

P. 15 BORN ON JUNE 20, 1905: various sources report 1905. In a few cases, 1906 or 1907 are reported. She used the 1905 date in her testimony before the House Committee on UnAmerican Activities. An August 28, 1946 memorandum in her FBI file states that "the records of the New Orleans Board of Health, Bureau of Vital Statistics, reflect in Volume 130, Page 632, that the subject was born LILLIAN FLORENCE HELLMAN on June 20, 1905, at New Orleans, Louisiana. A copy of Hellman's birth certificate (sent to me by Hellman researcher Theresa Mooney) is available from the Bureau of Vital Statistics in New Orleans.

P. 15 MAX'S FAMILY HAD COME TO THE CITY FROM GERMANY: the exact date of the Hellman family's emigration to New Orleans has not been verified, although my researcher, Joseph R. Spilmann, Jr., checked several sources. Much of the genealogical information in this chapter is derived from Spilmann's research in the U.S. Census, New Orleans City Directories, other local sources in New Orleans, and from *three*.

P. 16 DEMOPOLIS IN THE NINETEENTH CENTURY: William Wright, *Lillian Hellman*.

P. 16 *THE PINK LADY*: Helen Dudar, "A Long Look Backward at the Comedy," *New York Post* Magazine Section, January 3, 1967.

P. 16   TRANSPLANTED SOUTHERNER: Glenn Whitesides, "Lillian Hellman: A Biographical and Critical Study."

P. 17   FIRST AND MOST CERTAIN LOVE . . . : *An Unfinished Woman.*

P. 18   A MAN OF GREAT FORCE: *An Unfinished Woman.*

P. 18   TO CLEAN THE CRAYFISH: *An Unfinished Woman.*

P. 18   I WAS CRAZY ABOUT OTHER PEOPLE'S LIVES: "A Successful Playwright Recalls Her Childhood in New Orleans," *New Orleans Times Picayune,* April 19, 1959.

P. 19   WONDERFULLY GOOFY: interview with Richard Wilbur.

P. 19   A GENTLE, VERY PLEASANT WOMAN: Fern Marja, "A Clearing in the Forest," *New York Post* Magazine Section, March 6, 1960.

P. 20   A HARD TIME ABOUT LIVING WITH HAMMETT: Hellman correspondence with Arthur Kober in Arthur Kober Papers.

P. 20   KILL THEM FOR IT: *An Unfinished Woman.*

P. 21   IN NEW YORK: Marja, "A Clearing in the Forest."

P. 21   FOLLOW SUSPICIOUS-LOOKING PERSONS: Harriman, *Take Them Up Tenderly.*

P. 22   ADULTS WERE MY ENEMIES: quoted in Whitesides, "Lillian Hellman: A Biographical and Critical Study."

P. 22   A PRIZE NUISANCE CHILD: Hellman interview with Hellman in Bryer, *Conversations with Lillian Hellman.*

P. 22   I DON'T LIKE THE PICTURE OF MYSELF: Hellman interview with Bill Moyers in Bryer, *Conversations with Lillian Hellman.*

P. 22   HER FIRST STORY: quoted in Whitesides, "Lillian Hellman: A Biographical and Critical Study."

P. 22   AN AIMLESS CHILD: Marja, "A Clearing in the Forest."

P. 23   NURSIE AND MADAM: Hellman interview with Marilyn Berger in Bryer, *Conversations with Lillian Hellman.*

P. 24   HE WAS SITTING ALONE: *Pentimento.*

P. 24   SEXUAL STIRRINGS: *An Unfinished Woman.*

P. 24   DANCING CLASS: *An Unfinished Woman.*

P. 25   A BIRTHDAY GIFT: *An Unfinished Woman.*

P. 25   MANY RELIGIOUS PERIODS: *Pentimento.*

P. 26   WAS NOT EVER TO FALL IN LOVE VERY OFTEN: *Pentimento.*

P. 26   WILLY'S MURDER: *Pentimento.*

P. 27   MOTHER, I HAVE HEART TROUBLE: quoted in Harriman, *Take Them Up Tenderly.*

P. 27   LOOKING UP THE NAUGHTY WORDS: unidentified newspaper clipping.

P. 27   HER REPORT CARDS: courtesy of Hilary Mills.

P. 27   HER PARTICIPATION IN DRAMATICS: Harriman, *Take Them Up Tenderly;* Whitesides, "Lillian Hellman: A Biographical and Critical Study."

P. 27   A COLUMN HELLMAN WROTE: Harriman, *Take Them Up Tenderly;* Whitesides, "Lillian Hellman: A Biographical and Critical Study."

P. 27   THE TWO GIRLS WOULD CUT CLASSES: Wright, *Lillian Hellman.*

P. 28   THEY WERE ENGAGED: interview with Emmy Kronenberger.

P. 28   A WILD AND HEADSTRONG GIRL: *An Unfinished Woman.*

P. 28   ALL I GOT OUT OF IT WAS A NOTEBOOK: 1935 newspaper clipping quoted in Whitesides, "Lillian Hellman: A Biographical and Critical Study.

P. 28   THE SUMMERS SESSIONS OF 1922 AND 1923: Hellman's registration at Columbia verified by Ruby Hemphill, Supervisor Transcripts & Inquiries, Office of Student Information Services, Columbia University.

P. 28   ALEXANDER WOOLLCOTT'S NYU CLASS: *An Unfinished Woman.*

P. 28   HELLMAN COPIED HABER'S PAPER: Wright, *Lillian Hellman.*

P. 28   ONLY ONE PROFESSOR EXCITED HER INTEREST: *An Unfinished Woman.*

P. 28   HER FAVORITE MEMORIES: *An Unfinished Woman.*

P. 28–29   HOWARD MEYER FIRST MET EIGHTEEN-YEAR-OLD LILLIAN HELLMAN: interview with Howard Meyer

P. 29   AN AFFAIR: *An Unfinished Woman.*

P. 29   THE MAN IN QUESTION: interview with Emmy Kronenberger.

P. 30   ROMANTIC SCENES IN HER WRITING: Richard Moody, *Lillian Hellman.*

P. 30   A SHY GIRL: *An Unfinished Woman.*

P. 30   NEVER A BEAUTY: interview with Howard Meyer.

P. 30   AFTER VERSAILLES: Daniel Aaron, *Writers on the Left.*

P. 31   HELLMAN EXPECTED TO BE FIRED: *An Unfinished Woman.*

P. 31   MADE A DATE THAT EVENING WITH HOWARD MEYER: interview with Howard Meyer.

P. 32   HOT AND HEAVY: interview with Howard Meyer.

P. 33   LADY WRITER STUFF: Hellman interview with John Phillips and Anne Hollander in Bryer, *Conversations with Lillian Hellman.*

P. 33   HELLMAN MET LEE GERSHWIN: interview with Lee Gershwin.

P. 33   THE ENORMOUS DISPLAY OF MAKEUP BOTTLES AND PERFUMES: interview with Diana Trilling.

P. 33   BUNK OF 1926: Moody, *Lillian Hellman.*

P. 34   SUMMER BACHELORS: *New York Herald Tribune,* September 26, 1926.

P. 34   MOSQUITOES: *New York Herald Tribune,* June 19, 1927.

P. 34   GRAND HOTEL: Moody, *Lillian Hellman.*

P. 34   KOBER BEMOANED HIS LOSING NIGHT: Louis Sobel, *The Longest Street: A Memoir.*

P. 34   THE LITTLE WOMAN WON'T LIKE IT: Louis Sobel, *The Longest Street: A Memoir.*

P. 35   SHE ALWAYS FANCIED HERSELF AS A GREAT POKER PLAYER: Howard Benedict interview with Hilary Mills.

P. 35   A SLY SENSE OF HUMOR: Sam Marx interview with Hilary Mills.

P. 35   MELLOWER AND IN AN INFERIOR POSITION: Howard Benedict interview with Hilary Mills.

P. 35   ONE OF THOSE ASTUTE AND SMART JEWISH GIRLS: Leo Friedman interview with Hilary Mills.

P. 35   TO ROCHESTER, NEW YORK: *An Unfinished Woman.*

P. 35   RAT-FUCK: Lillian Hellman and Peter Feibleman: *Eating Together: Recollections and Recipes.*

P. 36   A YEAR IN BONN: *An Unfinished Woman.*

P. 36   HASTY FLIRTATIONS: Moody, *Lillian Hellman.*

P. 36   RUMORS OF ROMANCE: Sam Marx interview with Hilary Mills.

P. 36   SID AND LAURA PERELMAN MARRIAGE: Dorothy Herrman, *S. J. Perelman.*

P. 36   HELLMAN HAD HER OWN COTERIE: Sam Marx interview with Hilary Mills.

P. 36–37   SHE WAS A RATHER NICE HOMELY GIRL: Sam Marx interview with Hilary Mills.

P. 37   HOW GOOD HELLMAN WAS TO KOBER'S MOTHER: Mildred Kober Mendelson interview with Hilary Mills.

P. 37   CRUSHED ALL MY PLANS: Arthur Kober, "Having Terrible Time," unpublished autobiography in the Arthur Kober Papers.

P. 37   DISTINGUISHED NONENTITY: Kober, "Having Terrible Time."

P. 37–38   A PASSIONATE AFFAIR WITH DAVID CORT: Wright, *Lillian Hellman.*

P. 38   GARDEN OF ALLAH: Bernard F. Dick, *Hellman in Hollywood.*

P. 39   SHE FOUND IT DEMEANING: *An Unfinished Woman.*

P. 39   MARX HAD NO CHOICE: Sam Marx interview with Hilary Mills.
P. 39   SAM GOLDWYN: Garson Kanin, *Hollywood*.
P. 40   A TEACHER: *An Unfinished Woman*.

3. SHE-HAMMETT

P. 42   I WAS THERE THE NIGHT SHE MET HIM: interview with Lee Gershwin.
P. 43   HER SECOND PLAY: introduction to Lillian Hellman, *Six Plays*.
P. 43   HE ALWAYS STOPPED HIMSELF SHORT: Johnson, *Dashiell Hammett: A Life*.
P. 43   PERENNIAL WORKBLOCKS: Kober letter to Fred Gardner in Arthur Kober Papers.
P. 44   ALL LAUGHS: interview with Albert Hackett.
P. 45   FOR TWO PINS: Kober letter to Fred Gardner in Arthur Kober Papers.
P. 45   THE WOMEN WENT UPSTAIRS: interview with Ruth Conte.
P. 45   HIS SUICIDAL FEELINGS: interview with Lee Gershwin.
P. 45   CATHERINE KOBER REMEMBERS THAT HER FATHER: interview with Catherine Kober.
P. 45   HELLMAN AND HAMMETT WERE HAVING A FLING: interview with Jo Marshall.
P. 45   LETTERS FROM THE ST. MORITZ: Arthur Kober Papers.
P. 46   HAMMETT'S LETTERS TO HELLMAN: Moody, *Lillian Hellman*; Johnson, *Dashiell Hammett: A Life*.
P. 47   DEEP UNEASINESS ABOUT SEX: Jay Martin, letter to author.
P. 47   HELLMAN FELT HER AUNTS WOULD DISAPPROVE: *Pentimento*.
P. 47   THE BEAUTIFUL SIDE OF MY FATHER'S FAMILY: *Pentimento*.
P. 48   I'M A CLOWN: Johnson, *Dashiell Hammett: A Life*.
P. 49   DOSTOYEVSKY SINNER-SAINT: *An Unfinished Woman*.
P. 50   WILLIAM FAULKNER: Joseph Blotner, *William Faulkner: A Biography*.
P. 50   DEEP RESPECT FOR HER TALENT: Meta Carpenter Wilder, letter to author.
P. 50   ARTHUR KOBER ENJOYED HAMMETT'S COMPANY: interview with Albert Hackett.
P. 51   WORKING ON A PLAY: "The Dear Queen" manuscript, Library of Congress.
P. 52   ACCORDING TO EMMY KRONENBERGER: interview with Emmy Kronenberger.
P. 52   WROTE TO JOHN GOLDEN: correspondence file of John Golden, Billy Rose Theatre Collection, New York Public Library.
P. 52   AT THE BILTMORE: Johnson, *Dashiell Hammett: A Life*.
P. 53   SHE MAY EVEN HAVE BEEN IN LOVE WITH HIM: Herrman, *S. J. Perelman*.
P. 53   HIS ANCESTORS WERE OF GENTLE BIRTH: Jay Martin, *Nathanael West*.
P. 53   HELLMAN DESCRIBED WEST: Martin, *Nathanael West*.
P. 53   NOVELESQUE ELEGANCE: interview with Heywood Hale Broun.
P. 53   EMBARRASSED HAMMETT: *An Unfinished Woman*.
P. 54   AN IMPERSONAL SIXTEEN-STORY BARRACKS: S. J. Perelman, *The Last Laugh*.
P. 54   PARIS OF THE IMAGINATION: Martin, *Nathanael West*.
P. 54   STEAMING OPEN HIS GUESTS' LETTERS: Martin, *Nathanael West*.
P. 54   SOMEWHAT REMOTE EMOTIONALLY: Jay Martin, letter to author.
P. 54   WEST WAS ENGAGED TO ALICE SHEPARD: Martin, *Nathanael West*.
P. 54   WHY, SHE ASKED PEP?: Jay Martin, letter to author.

P. 55   HELLMAN'S LACK OF GOOD LOOKS: interview with Emmy Kronenberger; Herrman, *S. J. Perelman*.

P. 55   BEING A BEAUTY: Hellman interview with Peter Adam in Bryer, *Conversations with Lillian Hellman*.

P. 55   HELLMAN WANTED HAMMETT TO WRITE POEMS TO HER: Hellman interview with Bill Moyers in Bryer, *Conversations with Lillian Hellman*.

P. 55   EMMY KRONENBERGER REMEMBERS: interview with Emmy Kronenberger.

P. 55   JEALOUS OF GREAT BEAUTIES: Hellman interview with Christine Doudna in Bryer, *Conversations with Lillian Hellman*; interview with Howard Bay.

P. 55   LILLY NEVER MADE A POINT OF BEING KIND WITH OTHER WOMEN: interview with Albert Hackett.

P. 57   A PERSON WITH RESERVES SO DEEP: *An Unfinished Woman*.

P. 60   A PLAY READER FOR FIFTEEN DOLLARS A WEEK: Moody, *Lillian Hellman*.

P. 60   NOTES FOR *THE CHILDREN'S HOUR*: Manfred Triesch, *The Lillian Hellman Collection at the University of Texas*.

P. 61   HELLMAN'S COMPLICATED, HALF-UNDERSTOOD FEELINGS: Doris Falk, *Lillian Hellman*.

P. 62   ON A RAINY DAY: interview with Lee Gershwin.

P. 63   A LETTER TO KOBER: Arthur Kober Papers.

P. 63   SHE WROTE TO KEEP HIM ABREAST OF HER LIFE: Arthur Kober Papers.

P. 64   HELLMAN RETYPED EACH NEW DRAFT: Robert Walker Hungerford, "Minutes in Lillian Hellman's 'The Children's Hour': Composition of the Play from Inception to Publication."

P. 65   THE FIRST FULL DRAFT: Edmund Fuller, "First Draft Analysis of Early Versions of 'The Children's Hour,' " Edmund Fuller Collection, Mugar Memorial Library, Boston University.

P. 66   HER PRELIMINARY NOTES: Triesch, *The Lillian Hellman Collection at the University of Texas*.

P. 68   EARLY DRAFT OF THE PLAY: Special Collections department of Mugar Memorial Library, Boston University.

P. 70   TELEGRAPHING ARTHUR KOBER: Arthur Kober Papers.

P. 71   AN ALTERCATION IN THE THEATER WITH SHUBERT: *Pentimento*.

P. 71   POWER AND PUNCH: Richard Maney, *Fanfare*.

P. 71   SET ASIDE OPENING NIGHT TICKETS: Moody, *Lillian Hellman*.

4. THREESOMES

P. 75   OVERBURDENED HER PLAY: Hellman, Introduction to *Six Plays*.

P. 75   ONE OF HELLMAN'S MOST PERCEPTIVE CRITICS: Joseph Wood Krutch, *Nation*, May 22, 1934.

P. 75   HER OWN NAUGHTY CHILDHOOD: Michael Mok, " 'The Children's Hour' Had to Be Written; 18th Century Gave Idea of Modern Play," *New York Post*, November 23, 1934.

P. 76   A TEST CASE: "American Play Banned," *The New York Times*, March 12, 1935; "Fight Boston Play Ban," *The New York Times*, December 16, 1935.

P. 76   *THE MELODY LINGERS ON*: The Dunne and Block screenplay, located in the Special Collections Department of Doheny Library, University of

Southern California, is a thorough reworking of what is called a "continuity by Lillian Hellman."

P. 77   GOLDWYNISMS: interview with Albert Hackett.

P. 78   HE WANTED TO TREAT WRITERS WELL: Bernard F. Dick, *Hellman in Hollywood*.

P. 78   FUCK HIMSELF: Arthur Marx, *Goldwyn: A Biography of the Man Behind the Legend*.

P. 78   PHILIP DUNNE TELLS THE STORY: interview with Philip Dunne.

P. 78   HELLMAN DOMINATED GOLDWYN: Sam Marx interview with Hilary Mills.

P. 79   IT WAS A COMPANY UNION: Nancy Lynn Schwartz, *The Hollywood Writers' Wars*.

P. 79   ROOSEVELT GAVE YOU A FEELING: Lillian Hellman interview with John Phillips and Anne Hollander in Bryer, *Conversations with Lillian Hellman*.

P. 79   SO POWERFUL IN HER SPEECH: interview with Albert Hackett.

P. 79   FAMOUS LADY WRITER: Schwartz, *The Hollywood Writers' Wars*.

P. 80   FELLOW SCREENWRITERS: interview with Philip Dunne.

P. 81   WE SHALL ALL BE TOGETHER: The screenplay of *The Dark Angel*, dated May 13, 1935, is on deposit in the Merle Oberon Collection of The Academy of Motion Picture Arts and Sciences.

P. 82   INGERSOLL STEPPED OUT ONTO THE TARMAC: Roy Hoopes, *Ralph Ingersoll*.

P. 82   HELLMAN WAS VERY PUT OUT WITH HAMMETT: Ralph Ingersoll interview with Hilary Mills.

P. 83   SO ANGRY AT SID: Herrman, *S. J. Perelman*.

P. 84   HELLMAN WROTE TO KOBER: Arthur Kober Papers.

P. 84   SHE KNEW THAT GOLDWYN: Marx, *Goldwyn: A Biography of the Man Behind the Legend*; Axel Madsen, *William Wyler*.

P. 84   RESTRICTIONS SET DOWN BY JOSEPH BREEN: Correspondence from the Breen office and Hellman's treatment for *These Three*: in the Motion Picture Association of America, Production Code Administration Files, on deposit at the Academy of Motion Picture Arts and Sciences.

P. 85   HELLMAN AFFIRMED THE ARTISTIC QUALITY OF FILM SCRIPTS: Hellman interview with Phillips and Hollander in Bryer, *Conversations with Lillian Hellman*.

P. 85   THIRTEEN-PAGE TREATMENT: On deposit at the Academy of Motion Picture Arts and Sciences.

P. 88   I HAVE SELDOM BEEN SO MOVED: Graham Green, *Spectator*, May 1, 1936.

P. 89   SENT HIM A TELEGRAM FROM CHICAGO: Arthur Kober Papers.

P. 89   ATMOSPHERE TOUR: Hellman interview with Lucius Beebe in Bryer, *Conversations with Lillian Hellman*.

P. 90   AS RALPH INGERSOLL PUT IT: Ralph Ingersoll interview with Hilary Mills.

P. 90   HAMMETT WAS SO DETACHED: Ralph Ingersoll interview with Hilary Mills.

P. 90   EMOTIONAL CRISIS: Hoopes, *Ralph Ingersoll*.

P. 91   EXTENSIVE NOTES FOR THE PLAY: Triesch, *The Lillian Hellman Collection at the University of Texas*.

P. 92   MARCH 8, 1933: Schwartz, *The Hollywood Writers' Wars*.

P. 93   STRIKES IN OHIO: Raymond Boryczka and Lorin Lee Cary, *No Strength Without Union: An Illustrated History of Ohio Workers 1803–1980*.

P. 94   I WAS IN THAT RACKET: *Pentimento*.

P. 95   A SPECIALIST IN HATE AND FRUSTRATION: *Nation*, December 26, 1936.

P. 95   IN HER DIARY: Herrman, *S. J. Perelman*.

P. 95   ISOLATED NEAR THE END OF THE STREET: L. Scott Bailey, interview with author.

P. 96   HELLMAN REMEMBERED THAT THE HOUSE: *Pentimento*.

P. 96   THE SLOANE FAMILY: William M. Sloane, correspondence and interview with author.

P. 96   SHE WAS QUITE VAGUE: interview with L. Scott Bailey.

P. 96   SHORTLY AFTER THE SCHOOL YEAR STARTED: Thomas H. Wolf, letter to author.

P. 97   TOWN AND GOWN: interview with William M. Sloane.

P. 97   NOT THE NORMAL KIND OF NEIGHBOR: interview with L. Scott Bailey.

P. 97   CONSIDERABLE DAMAGE: interview with William M. Sloane.

P. 98   NOT THINKING HARD ENOUGH: Introduction to *Six Plays*.

P. 98   THERE WAS AN ENORMOUS RESPECT AND ADMIRATION: interview and correspondence with Florence Eldridge.

P. 99   PEOPLE WERE RESTLESS: Richard Maney, *Fanfare*.

P. 100   IT WAS LIKE A DIRGE: interview with Florence Eldridge.

P. 100   I'VE CHANGED MY MIND: Maney: *Fanfare*; Hoopes, *Ralph Ingersoll*.

P. 100   ALAS, MY POOR ALENÇON: Florence Eldridge, letter to author.

P. 100   ONE OPENING NIGHT REVIEWER: Daniel W. Gilbert, *New York American*, December 16, 1926.

P. 102   THE DIRECTOR CALLED IT A PHONY: Michael Anderegg, *William Wyler*.

P. 102   MARTIN IS AN ENEMY OF SOCIETY: Dick, *Hellman in Hollywood*.

P. 102   BETTER THAN AN ORDINARY SLUM: Marx, *Goldwyn: A Biography of the Man Behind the Legend*.

P. 102   THE CENSORSHIP OF THE TIME: Breen's letter is in the Motion Picture Association of America, Production Code Administration Files, on deposit at the Academy of Motion Picture Arts and Sciences.

P. 103   DRINA'S ROLE AT THE EXPENSE OF KAY'S: Dick, *Hellman in Hollywood*.

P. 103   THE YEAR 1937: Dick, *Hellman in Hollywood*.

P. 104   THE ROMANTIC LEAD IS NOT AN INFORMER: Dick, *Hellman in Hollywood*.

P. 106   SIMPLIFIED CHARACTERS: John T. McManus, "The Screen," *The New York Times*, August 25, 1937; Richard Lockridge, "The Stage in Review," *New York Sun*, September 11, 1937; E. V. Lucas, "At the Pictures," *Punch*, December 1, 1937; Gilbert Seldes, *Scribner's Magazine*, November 1937.

5. DAY IN SPAIN

P. 107   SPANISH WAR STRICKEN: Burton Bernstein, *Thurber: A Biography*.

P. 108   DAY IN SPAIN: *The New Republic*, April 13, 1938.

P. 108   ANY CAUSE WOULD DO: Sam Marx interview with Hilary Mills.

P. 108   A WRITER'S DESTINY: Elinor Langer, *Josephine Herbst*.

P. 109   IN HOLLYWOOD IN THE THIRTIES: Schwartz, *The Hollywood Writers' Wars*.

P. 109   VARIOUS ACCOUNTS OF THE PARTY: interviews with Florence Eldridge and Philip Dunne; Carlos Baker, *Ernest Hemingway: A Life Story*: Peter Wyden, *The Passionate War*.

P. 110   SUPERANNUATED MURPHYS: *An Unfinished Woman*.

P. 111   ADVERTISEMENT IN *THE NEW MASSES*: "A Statement by American Progressives," *The New Masses, May 3, 1938*.

P. 112   AN IDEOLOGICAL BATTLEGROUND: Jeffrey Hart, "For Whom the Bell Tolled," *Commentary*, December 1986.

P. 112   UNMITIGATED REPRESSION AND TERROR: Ronald Radosh, " 'But today the struggles': Spain and the intellectuals," *The New Criterion*, October 1986.

P. 112   SOME LIBERALS: interview with Philip Dunne.

P. 113   DECEIVED BY HERBST AND OTHERS: See Langer, *Josephine Herbst*, for Herbst's and Hemingway's roles in trying to pacify and to deceive Dos Passos, and Hoopes, *Ralph Ingersoll*, for Archibald MacLeish's shock over the execution of his friend by the Loyalists. When Ralph Ingersoll sided with MacLeish, Hemingway branded Ingersoll a "coward."

P. 113   SPAIN WAS THE PLACE: Wyden, *The Passionate War*.

P. 113   MORE SCHOOLS IN A YEAR: "The Siege of Madrid" in *The Portable Dorothy Parker*, edited by Brendan Gill.

P. 115   IN AN EXCHANGE WITH DAN RATHER: Hellman interview with Dan Rather in Bryer, *Conversations with Lillian Hellman*.

P. 115   GRANDE DAME: Beatrice Ames quoted in Keats, *You Might as Well Live: The Life and Times of Dorothy Parker*.

P. 115   DUBBING HELLMAN MADAME: Dashiell Hammett Collection, the Humanities Research Center, University of Texas.

P. 116   THEY BELIEVED TOGETHER WITH MARX: Keats, *You Might as Well Live: The Life and Times of Dorothy Parker*.

P. 116   OUTRAGED AT WILLIAM CARNEY: "Richard Harding Davis, 1938," an unpublished manuscript in the Rutgers University Library, Special Collections and Archives.

P. 117   SPANISH DIARY: "The Little War" in *This is My Best*, edited by Whitney Burnett.

6. THE LITTLE FOXES

P. 121   DEALING WITH GOLDWYN: Ralph Ingersoll interview with Hilary Mills.

P. 121   A NEW FABLE: Hammett quoted in Moody, *Lillian Hellman*.

P. 121   IT IS RAINING HERE: Hammett quoted in Moody, *Lillian Hellman*.

P. 121   SHE LIKED SAM GOLDWYN: Ward Morehouse, "Broadway After Dark," *New York Sun*, March 11, 1939.

P. 121   HELLMAN'S APRIL 4 INTER-OFFICE COMMUNICATION: in The Bancroft Library, University of California, Berkeley.

P. 122   ESPY RETALIATED: in The Bancroft Library, University of California, Berkeley.

P. 123   WITT REMEMBERED: Schwartz, *The Hollywood Writers' Wars*.

P. 123   THAT DAMN COMMUNIST BRACKETT: interview with Philip Dunne.

P. 123   NIGHT AFTER NIGHT: quoted in Whitesides, "Lillian Hellman: A Biographical and Critical Study." For other important accounts of Hellman's research see Theresa Rose Mooney, " 'Southern' Influences in Four Plays by Lillian Hellman"; Triesch, *The Lillian Hellman Collection at the University of Texas*; Moody, *Lillian Hellman*.

P. 124   IT HAD LITTLE GROUND PLANS: interview with Howard Bay.

P. 124   SHE FAVORED STATISTICAL AND EMPIRICAL STUDIES: Mooney, " 'Southern' Influences in Four Plays by Lillian Hellman."

P. 125   CHARACTER SKETCHES AND PLOT OUTLINES: The playwright's notes on the main characters were published in a newspaper article that was not identified in the clipping file of the Billy Rose Theatre Collection, New York Public Library; Whitesides, "Lillian Hellman: A Biographical and Critical Study," and Mooney, " 'Southern' Influences in Four Plays by Lillian Hellman," also quote material from the character sketches.

P. 125   THE TITANESS IN BEER'S *THE MAUVE DECADE*: Mooney, " 'Southern' Influences in Four Plays by Lillian Hellman."

P. 128   THE FIRST FOUR DRAFTS OF THE PLAY: see Mooney, " 'Southern' Influences in Four Plays by Lillian Hellman."

P. 131   HAMMETT WAS HAVING A BREAKDOWN: interviews with Albert Hackett and with Philip Dunne; see also Dunne, *Take Two*.

P. 132   AIRMAIL HIM TO A TERRIFIED LILLIAN: Johnson, *Dashiell Hammett: A Life*.

P. 132   I'VE GAINED TWENTY POUNDS: Hammett's letter is in the files of Turner Entertainment, Los Angeles, California.

P. 132   THE TOUGHNESS OF HIS CRITICISM: Introduction to *Six Plays*.

P. 132   THE CASTING OF REGINA: *Pentimento*.

P. 133   SHE IS REPORTED TO HAVE HAD HER DOUBTS: Tallulah Bankhead, *Tallulah*.

P. 133   SHUMLIN TOLD GARY BLAKE: Gary Blake, "Herman Shumlin: The Development of a Director."

P. 133   THE LEGENDARY THEATRICAL GENIUS: Martin Gottfried, *Jed Harris: The Curse of Genius*.

P. 134   SORT OF A STAR: interview with Howard Bay.

P. 134   THINGS WERE ROUGH SOMETIMES: interview with Howard Bay.

P. 134   WE HAD THE PERFECT CAST: interview with Howard Bay.

P. 134   SHUMLIN EXTOLLED BANKHEAD'S POWER: Michael Mok, "The Man Who Found a Hit for Tallulah Just Made Her Forget She Was a Star," *New York Post*, February 28, 1939; Maurice Zolotow, *No People Like Show People*.

P. 134   BANKHEAD ENDED UP FITTING INTO THE ENSEMBLE: interview with Howard Bay.

P. 135   ONE ANECDOTE THAT SURVIVED THE REHEARSAL PERIOD: interview with Heywood Hale Broun.

P. 135   HE HATED TECHNICAL MATTERS: interview with Howard Bay.

P. 136   AFTER SHUMLIN: interview with Howard Bay.

P. 136   WILLIAM WYLER'S WIFE TALLI: interview with Talli Wyler.

P. 136   TERRIBLE TO ARTHUR: Ralph Ingersoll interview with Hilary Mills.

P. 137   SCREAMING AT LOUIS: interview with Emmy Kronenberger.

P. 137   THE WOMEN HELLMAN LIKED: interviews with Howard Bay, Albert Hackett, Randall Smith, Talli Wyler, Virginia Bloomgarden Chilewich, and Emmy Kronenberger.

P. 137   SMALL MARXIST STUDY GROUP: see *Cold War Romance: Lillian Hellman and John Melby*, forthcoming from University of North Carolina Press.

P. 138   HELLMAN CONFESSED THAT IN 1939: "The Times of The 'Foxes,' " *The New York Times*, October 22, 1967.

P. 138   BANKHEAD IMMEDIATELY CHALLENGED THE PLAYWRIGHT'S MEMORIES: "Miss Bankhead Objects," *The New York Times*, October 29, 1967.

P. 138   EN ROUTE TO BALTIMORE: Lee Israel, *Miss Tallulah Bankhead*.

P. 138–139   CONFUSING REGINA AND SHAKESPEARE'S LADY MACBETH: Israel, *Miss Tallulah Bankhead*.

P. 139   THE CHARACTER DOES NOT HOLD UP GENERALLY: Israel, *Miss Tallulah Bankhead*.

P. 140   THE CHARACTER BEN: interview with Richard Wilbur.

P. 141   TALLULAH BANKHEAD INTERPRETED REGINA: Helen Ormsbee, "A First Night is the Last Mile Until She Hears Her own Voice," *New York Herald Tribune*, February 12, 1939.

P. 141   FREDRIC MARCH REMARKED TO HIS WIFE: interview with Florence Eldridge.

7. THE PACT

P. 144   THE ELEGANT GERALD AND SARA MURPHY: *Pentimento*.

P. 144   HE WAS A COMMITTED MARXIST: interview with Jo Marshall.

P. 146   HER FBI FILE: A summary (dated June 16, 1941) details her involvement in what the FBI considered Communist front organizations and meetings: In February 1937, she was listed on the letterhead of the Citizens Committee for Support of the W.P.A. and was a member of the National Committee for the Defense of Political Prisoners. As of July 20, 1938, she was identified in the *Daily Worker* as Vice-President of the League of Women Shoppers, Inc. On October 19, 1938, she had spoken at a dinner at the Hotel Commodore in New York City for a drive to raise $150,000 to bring back 1200 American volunteers of the Abraham Lincoln Brigade in Spain. On November 17, 1938, she was one of several writers who petitioned President Roosevelt to stop trading with Nazi Germany. "In December, 1938, Lillian Hellman allegedly associated herself with the Progressive Committee to Rebuild the American Labor Party, which is reported to be the Communist wing of the American Labor Party." Hellman sponsored a New Year's Eve ball in 1938 under the auspices of the Non-Sectarian Committee for Political Refugees. Along with seventy-eight other writers, she signed an appeal for the lifting of the Embargo which prevented the Spanish Republic from buying arms for its defense. In February 1939 she was listed as a sponsor of the Veterans of the Abraham Lincoln Brigade. "On February 20, 1939 a reliable confidential informant forwarded literature of Films for Democracy, New York City, which indicated that Miss Hellman was a member of the Advisory Board of this organization. The informant stated that from what he had learned to date there seemed to be no doubt whatsoever that the organization was intended as a propaganda vehicle for radicalism. He further advised that the Committee and Advisory Board of the organization were made up of a mixture of genuine Liberals and radical fellow travelers of the Communist Party." The March 20 issue of the *Daily Worker* described Hellman as one of the directors of History Today, Inc., a group which sponsored a film "showing China's heroic fight against Japan's aggression. This was part of an effort to 'bring progressive films to the screens of America.' " In April she was one of the sponsors of The Spanish Refugee Committee. That month she also signed a letter in support of the Federal Arts Project. In May, she became a member of the Editorial Council of "Equality," a "Communist Front publication," in the FBI's view, dedicated to "a fight against anti-Catholic, anti-Negro, and anti-Semitic groups in the United States." In November she was sponsor of the Foster-Parent Plan for War Children, Inc., New York City.

P. 147   THEY PARTED COMPANY ON THE SUBJECT OF THE PACT: interview with
          Philip Dunne.

P. 147   COLLECTIVE SECURITY FOR ALL ANTI-FASCIST NATIONS: Dunne, *Take Two*;
          interview with Philip Dunne.

P. 147   HELLMAN HAD NO DOUBTS ABOUT THE PACT: interview with Ring Lard-
          ner, Jr.

P. 148   THE WAR IN EUROPE WAS PHONY: interview with Ring Lardner, Jr.

P. 148   HELLMAN'S ATTITUDES WERE SIMILAR TO RALPH INGERSOLL'S: Ralph Inger-
          soll interview with Hilary Mills.

P. 148   THEY QUARRELED OVER HIS SYMPATHETIC VIEW OF STALIN: Laura Hobson,
          Laura Z.

P. 148   I NEVER TALKED POLITICS WITH HER: Ralph Ingersoll interview with
          Hilary Mills.

P. 148   CODE WORDS: Langer, *Josephine Herbst*; Schwartz, *The Hollywood Writers'
          Wars.*

P. 148   HELLMAN WAS UNUSUALLY CIRCUMSPECT: from Hellman's FBI file:

          [Name blacked out] informed that Miss Hellman was a member of the
          Advisory Board of the HOLLYWOOD THEATRE ALLIANCE (1939).
          This organization was a Communist effort the purpose of which was
          to produce plays carrying out the propaganda line of the Communist
          Party. It was affiliated with the AMERICAN PEACE MOBILIZATION
          and those of this Alliance were extremely active in their opposition to
          the "imperialist" war, the position of the Communist Party at that
          time. The HOLLYWOOD THEATRE ALLIANCE went out of existence
          with the change in the Communist Party line brought about by the
          attack on Soviet Russia by Hitler. DAILY NEWS, April 5, 1939 [Name
          blacked out] stated that Miss HELLMAN, by her sponsorship of
          numerous organizations to prevent aid to England and France during
          the period of the pact between Stalin and Hitler and by her support
          of the AMERICAN PEACE MOBILIZATION in its efforts to defeat our
          national defense, and then by her later change to one of patriotism
          and all out aid to the allies, showed that she is in close sympathy with
          the line of the Communist Party in the United States.

P. 149   HER ATTITUDE TOWARD THE SOVIET INVASION OF FINLAND: Wright, *Lillian
          Hellman*, suggests "it is doubtful that Hellman went to Finland in
          1937. There was not sufficient time during her August visit to Paris,
          Moscow, Prague and Spain." He concedes she might have visited
          Finland on an earlier trip in 1937, when she was working on *The
          Spanish Earth*. But Finland had nothing to do with her involvement in
          the Loyalist cause, and it is hard to believe she would have spent two
          weeks there because she herself notes that the earlier trip to Europe
          in 1937 was cut short by a case of pneumonia.

P. 150   AN OUTSPOKEN ANTI-COMMUNIST: Zolotow, *No People Like Show People.*

P. 150   GIVING HELLMAN A SHOT OF BRANDY: Bankhead, *Tallulah.*

P. 150   FINLAND WEEK: Israel, *Miss Tallulah Bankhead.*

P. 150   SHUMLIN TOLD GARY BLAKE: Blake, "Herman Shumlin: The Develop-
          ment of a Director."

P. 151   SOCIALIST REFORMS HERE AT HOME: Johnson, *Dashiell Hammett: A Life.*

P. 151   COLLECTIVE SECURITY FOR PEACE: interview with Philip Dunne.

P. 151   ATTACKS ON PRESIDENT ROOSEVELT: interviews with Philip Dunne and
          Maurice Zolotow; see also Dunne, *Take Two.*

P. 151   HE WOULD VOTE FOR THE REPUBLICAN PARTY: interview with Jo Marshall.

P. 152   AUTHORITARIANISM OF THE PARTY: Hoopes, *Ralph Ingersoll.*

P. 152   AN ULTRAMONTANIST: Dunne, *Take Two.*

P. 152   WHEEL-HORSE COMMUNIST: Dunne, *Take Two.*

P. 153   EVEN THE SOVIET INVASION OF POLAND WAS RATIONALIZED: interview with Maurice Zolotow; see also Johnson, *Dashiell Hammett: A Life.*

P. 153   SHE WAS NOT COMMUNIST: interview with Lee Gershwin.

P. 154   THE STAR WAS NOT TO BE CROSSED: Eugenia Rawls, "Tallulah—The Story of a Friendship," unpublished manuscript in the Eugenia Rawls and Donald Seawell Theater Collection, Southern Historical Collection, University of North Carolina at Chapel Hill.

P. 155   COMMUNICATED ONLY THROUGH SEMAPHORES: Maney, *Fanfare.*

8. THE SPLENDOR OF PLEASANTVILLE

P. 157   SHE WENT TO INGERSOLL'S ANALYST: Ralph Ingersoll interview with Hilary Mills.

P. 157   THE AFFECTIONATE DRAWING GERSHWIN MADE: I wish to thank Lee Gershwin for showing me the Zilboorg drawing and for discussing the psychiatrist with me.

P. 157   WALRUS-LOOKING PERSONAGE: interview with Virginia Bloomgarden Chilewich.

P. 157   INGERSOLL DESCRIBED ZILBOORG: Hoopes, *Ralph Ingersoll.*

P. 157   A DISCUSSION OF *WATCH ON THE RHINE*: Zilboorg, *Man, Mind, and Medicine.*

P. 158   DO YOU EVER HAVE A DRINK?: interview with Richard Wilbur.

P. 158   LIKE ANY GOOD ANALYST: interview with Virginia Bloomgarden Chilewich.

P. 158   ONE ANALYST REMEMBERS: confidential source.

P. 158   HE HELPED HER: Hellman interview with Marilyn Berger in Bryer, *Conversations with Lillian Hellman.*

P. 158   ZILBOORG'S TREATMENT OF HELLMAN: Hellman interview with Christine Doudna in Bryer, *Conversations with Lillian Hellman.*

P. 159   UNERRING BELIEF IN THE RIGHTNESS OF ANY CAUSE: Hoopes, *Ralph Ingersoll.*

P. 159   ALL OF US HAVE GREAT HOPES: Hellman letter to Richard Wright, April 4, 1940, in the Beinecke Rare Book and Manuscript Library, Yale University Library.

P. 159   THIS NEWSPAPER OF TOMORROW: Hodding Carter, *Where Main Street Meets the River.*

P. 160   FIELD WAS MUCH IMPRESSED: Stephen Becker, *Marshall Field III: A Biography*

P. 160   REFORMED PRINCELING PLAYBOY: Louis Kronenberger, *No Whippings, No Gold Watches: The Saga of a Writer and His Jobs.*

P. 161   SNIDE ASIDES ON EMMY KRONENBERGER: Arthur Kober Papers.

P. 161   HELLMAN WAS DRESSED ALL IN WHITE: Sigerist, *Autobiographical Writings.*

P. 163   SHE RAN INTO THOMAS E. DEWEY: Harriman, *Take Them Up Tenderly.*

P. 163   THE CHARGES OF MILITANT ANTI-COMMUNISTS: Johnson, *Dashiell Hammett: A Life*; Hoopes, *Ralph Ingersoll.*

P. 164   HE WAS GIVEN TO EMOTIONAL DECISIONS: Carter, *Where Main Street Meets the River.*

P. 164   RESEARCH AND WRITING OF *WATCH ON THE RHINE*: Triesch, *The Lillian Hellman Collection at the University of Texas*.

P. 165   INTERVIEWS WITH PEOPLE: Charlotte Hughes, "Women Playmakers, *The New York Times Magazine*, May 4, 1941.

P. 165   ASK HERSELF POINTED QUESTIONS: Harriman, *Take Them Up Tenderly*.

P. 165   HELLMAN TOLD ROBERT VAN GELDER: Hellman interview with Robert Van Gelder in Bryer, *Conversations with Lillian Hellman*.

P. 165   HELLMAN WROTE ELEVEN ROUGH VERSIONS: Triesch, *The Lillian Hellman Collection at the University of Texas*.

P. 165   HOW SHE REMEMBERED HER SCHEDULE: Hellman interview with Robert Van Gelder in Bryer, *Conversations with Lillian Hellman*.

P. 166   A NOTICE ON THE DOOR OF HER WORKROOM: Harriman, *Take Them Up Tenderly*.

P. 166   CHRISTMAS IN 1940: Harriman, *Take Them Up Tenderly*.

P. 167   THE GREAT FORGOTTEN FIGURE: Sam Marx interview with Hilary Mills.

P. 167   ONLY ONE SENTENCE IN HER MEMOIRS: interview with Stephen Greene.

P. 167   SHE KIDDED HIM ABOUT AN OLD LETTER: Arthur Kober Papers.

P. 167   HAD HIM FOR BREAKFAST: interview with Talli Wyler.

P. 169   ARTHUR SOMEWHERE HAD LOST THE MAINSPRING: interview with Max Lerner.

9. WATCH ON THE RHINE

P. 171   AN EFFORT TO REWRITE *DAYS TO COME*: In The *New York Daily News*, April 28, 1941, Robert Sylvester quoted Hellman saying about *Watch on the Rhine*: "I'm not satisfied with it . . . I feel that there's one character too many, but I can't for the life of me figure out which one it is. It was the same way with 'Days to Come.' I'm sure that all that failure needed was the elimination of one character, maybe the villain, and it would have been all right." Sylvester reported that "there's a bare possibility . . . that Herman Shumlin might produce a special matinee or series of them of 'Days to Come' in rewritten form." Hellman mentioned that the cast of *Watch on the Rhine* had urged her to do it, but she was doubtful. In the end, she did not try to revive her second play.

P. 171   THEN IT OCCURRED TO HER: Hellman interview with Robert Van Gelder in Bryer, *Conversations with Lillian Hellman*.

P. 172   DAVID HAS FALLEN IN LOVE WITH MARTHE: In an early draft, Hellman made Marthe Teck's accomplice in the scheme against Kurt. This was unnecessary. By having Marthe and David resume a friendship begun in childhood, by having them fall in love, Hellman strengthened the plot and the connections between her characters.

P. 173   TAKEN IN A POKER GAME: In the *New York Daily News*, April 28, 1941, p. 35, Hellman spoke about the real life source for Teck: "That character is built on one of the most glamorous aristocrats in London . . . I was invited to his house for supper, although we had never met, and no sooner was dinner ended than I found myself $700 out of pocket in one of the weirdest, crookedest poker games in history. There was another wealthy, wacky, titled clown in the game, and he must have been clipped for $3,000. I always have to smile a little when I read weighty, important statements on England's future course by my one-time host and poker partner." Hellman refers to Romanian Prince Bibesco, his country's ambassador to Great Britain.

P. 173   EARLY DRAFTS OF THE PLAY: Triesch, *The Lillian Hellman Collection at the University of Texas.*

P. 174   A VULNERABLE HERO: In an earlier draft Sara states that Kurt has been "badly wounded in the spine." Hellman's concentration on Kurt's hands in later drafts makes his physical weakness more expressive and more intimate and more visible.

P. 177   THE WORKING MASS OF THE GERMAN PEOPLE: Triesch, *The Lillian Hellman Collection at the University of Texas.*

P. 177   ARRANGEMENTS WITH GOLDWYN: Moody, *Lillian Hellman*; Arthur Kober Papers.

P. 178   HELLMAN THOUGHT GOLDWYN HAD LIED: Arthur Kober Papers.

P. 178   PARKER AND CAMPBELL HAVE BEEN CREDITED: Whitney Stine and Bette Davis, *Mother Goddam.*

P. 178   WYLER'S LETTER OF FEBRUARY 10, 1941: Arthur Kober Papers.

P. 178   COULDN'T WE, IN THE PICTURE: Arthur Kober Papers.

P. 179   FIND A WAY OF DRAMATIZING: Arthur Kober Papers.

P. 179   BETTE DAVIS'S REVISED SHOOTING SCRIPT: in the Bette Davis Collection, Mugar Memorial Library, Special Collections, Boston University.

P. 180   SHE WROTE TO THE KOBERS: Arthur Kober Papers.

P. 180   THE ONLY WAY TO PLAY REGINA: Stine and Davis, *Mother Goddam*; Madsen, *William Wyler*; Anderegg, *William Wyler.*

P. 180   HUMANIZE THE BLACKS: Dick, *Hellman in Hollywood.*

P. 181   SHE WROTE THE ACTRESS: Tallulah Bankhead Collection, Alabama State Archives.

P. 182   A LETTER TO KOBER: Arthur Kober Papers.

P. 182   NEGOTIATED WITH BROADWAY PLAYWRIGHT MOSS HART: Arthur Kober Papers.

P. 182   HER LETTERS ALSO REVEAL: Arthur Kober Papers.

P. 184   ABOUT THIS EPISODE: Arthur Kober Papers.

P. 184   DINNER FORUM ON EUROPE TODAY: Hellman's letters to Horace Kallen, September 10, October 5, and October 27, 1941: in the Horace Kallen Papers, YIVO Institute for Jewish Research; "Governor to Shun 'Communist' Forum," *The New York Times*, October 4, 1941; "Lillian Hellman Speaks at Dinner to Aid Anti-Nazis in France," *The New York Times*, October 10, 1941.

10. HOLLYWOOD GOES TO WAR

P. 189   COMMAND PERFORMANCE OF *WATCH ON THE RHINE*: The New York Times, January 6, 1942.

P. 190   HAMMETT WAS SLOWLY WRITING THE SCRIPT: the Warner Brothers Archive in the Special Collections department of Doheny Library, University of Southern California, contains extensive material, including correspondence from Wallis to Hammett, on the making of *Watch on the Rhine.*

P. 190   SHUMLIN WROTE TO WALLIS: Warner Brothers Archive.

P. 191   HAMMETT'S DISQUISITIONS: A draft of Hammett's screenplay is on deposit at the Humanities Research Center, University of Texas at Austin; other copies of the screenplay can be found at the Lilly

Library, Indiana University, and at Doheny Library, University of Southern California. The Special Collections department of Doheny also has Hammett's screen treatment of *Watch on the Rhine*.

P. 191   THE MEXICAN OPENING: Dick, *Hellman in Hollywood*.

P. 191   HE'S PUT IN ONE SCENE: unidentified newspaper clipping in the files of the Billy Rose Theatre Collection, New York Public Library.

P. 192   *THE NEGRO SOLDIER*: The Bancroft Library, University of California, Los Angeles, holds a copy of the Hellman script.

P. 193   GOLDWYN WAS GOING TO MAKE THE NEGRO PICTURE: Arthur Kober Papers.

P. 193   SHE WROTE TO HAL WALLIS: Warner Brother's Archive.

P. 193   VINCENT SHERMAN WAS ENTHUSIASTIC: The Special Collections department of Doheny Library, University of Southern California, holds a copy of Sherman's script and the memos to and from Jack Warner.

P. 194   HAMMETT'S DAUGHTERS: Johnson, *Dashiell Hammett: A Life*; interview with Jo Marshall.

P. 195   HE BEGAN TO PAW HER: Johnson, *Dashiell Hammett: A Life*.

P. 195   AS SHUMLIN FEARED: Warner Brothers memos to Shumlin can be found in the Special Collections department of Doheny Library, University of Southern California.

P. 195   SHE WROTE WALLIS: Hellman's letter to Breen and Wallis are in the Special Collections department of Doheny Library, University of Southern California.

P. 196   SHE WROTE TO KOBER: Arthur Kober Papers.

P. 196   THICK RESEARCH BOOK: Hellman interview with Irving Drutman, unidentified clipping in the files of the Billy Rose Theatre Collection, New York Public Library.

P. 197   LETTER TO KOBER: Arthur Kober Papers.

P. 197   DASH WAS WRITING HER CHEERY LETTERS: quoted in Moody, *Lillian Hellman*.

P. 197   THE AFRICAN LANDING FORCE: Arthur Kober Papers.

P. 198   THEY HAD COME TO AN END: Arthur Kober Papers.

P. 198   HE WAS NEVER JEALOUS: interview with Howard Bay.

P. 198   TO SEE IF ANY OLD FRIENDS HAVE DAUGHTERS: Moody, *Lillian Hellman*.

P. 198   LILLIAN REALLY LIKED THE PICTURE VERY MUCH: Warner Brothers Archive.

P. 198   SHE WROTE TO KOBER: Arthur Kober Papers.

P. 199   LOVE-BIRDS: Arthur Kober Papers.

P. 199   ANOTHER LETTER FROM HAMMETT: quoted in Johnson, *Dashiell Hammett: A Life*.

P. 199   SHE WROTE JACK WARNER: Warner Brothers Archive.

P. 199   *MISSION TO MOSCOW*: Along with *The North Star* and *Song of Russia*, Mission to Moscow portrayed Stalin's Russia in highly favorable terms. During the McCarthy period, these movies were cited over and over again as the work of Communists. *Mission to Moscow* was particularly offensive to red-baiters because it justified Stalin's purge trials, the Hitler-Stalin Pact, and the invasion of Finland. That *Mission to Moscow* was made during the period of the United States wartime alliance with the Soviet Union did not matter to the red-baiters.

P. 199   LEWIS MILESTONE: "Mr. Milestone Beats a Plowshare into a Sword," *The New York Times*, March 14, 1943.

P. 200   AN ELABORATE RUSSIAN VILLAGE: Carol Easton, *The Search for Sam Goldwyn*.

P. 203   THE HARSHEST CRITICISM: Mary McCarthy: *Town and Country*, 1944; reprinted in *Film Comment*, January–February 1976.

P. 203   TIRED AND NERVOUS: Arthur Kober Papers.

P. 204   HE WAS SHOCKED: Johnson, *Dashiell Hammett: A Life*.

11. THE SEARCHING WIND

P. 205   SHUMLIN SAW A DRAFT: Moody, *Lillian Hellman*.

P. 205   RICHARD MANEY: "From Hellman to Shumlin to Broadway," *The New York Times*, April 9, 1944; see also Ward Morehouse, "Broadway After Dark," *New York Sun*, April 8, 1944.

P. 205   THE EARLIEST VERSION OF THE PLAY: Triesch, *The Lillian Hellman Collection at the University of Texas*.

P. 207   INDIVIDUALS MESSY IN THEIR PRIVATE LIVES: Earl E. Fleischman (Eugene Earl), "The Searching Wind in the Making," *Quarterly Journal of Speech*, February 1944.

P. 209   RAISE YOUR HAND A LITTLE HIGHER: interview with Julie Harris.

P. 210   SHE QUESTIONED HIM MORE THAN USUAL: Moody, *Lillian Hellman*.

P. 210   CASTING OF . . . THE FEMALE ROLES: interview with Howard Bay.

P. 211   THE SCRIPT HAD WEAKNESSES: Moody, *Lillian Hellman*.

P. 211   NOT TO CUT HER MATERIAL SO DRASTICALLY: interview with Virginia Bloomgarden Chilewich.

P. 211   LIKE DUMB ANIMALS: interview with Virginia Bloomgarden Chilewich.

P. 211   BLOOMGARDEN'S INTERCESSION: interview with Virginia Bloomgarden Chilewich.

P. 211   THE DIRECTOR WOULD GET GRIM AND TAUT: Maney, "From Hellman to Shumlin to Broadway, *The New York Times*, undated newspaper clipping.

P. 212   A SILENT DINNER WITH SHUMLIN: interview with Virginia Bloomgarden Chilewich.

P. 212   SHUMLIN REMEMBERED CLIFT'S AMAZING AMOUNT OF INTENSITY: Patricia Bosworth, *Montgomery Clift: A Biography*.

P. 214   HAMMETT'S AFFAIRS: interview with Bobbie Weinstein.

12. RUSSIA

P. 215   SLIPPED RATHER SHARPLY: Arthur Kober Papers.

P. 215   BAD, BAD HUMOR: Arthur Kober Papers.

P. 216   SHUMLIN WOULD WRITE TO KOBER: Arthur Kober Papers.

P. 216   SHIPLEY HAD REJECTED HELLMAN'S APPLICATIONS: I am indebted to Robert Newman for supplying me with a copy of the Passport file of correspondence and memoranda concerning Hellman.

P. 217   SHOPPING FOR LONG UNDERWEAR: interview with Ring Lardner, Jr.

P. 218   SHE WROTE HIM IN EARLY SEPTEMBER: The undated letter and the reply of MacLeish's secretary (dated September 4) are located in the Archibald MacLeish Papers, Manuscript Division, Library of Congress.

P. 218   A WIRE TO HAL WALLIS: Hal Wallis Collection, Academy of Motion Picture Arts and Sciences.

P. 219   HELLMAN WROTE THE KOBERS FROM THE SEATTLE: Arthur Kober Papers.

P. 220   AS ROBERT NEWMAN OBSERVES: *Cold War Romance: Lillian Hellman and John Melby*.

P. 220   SHE WOULD LEARN FROM ROBERT LOVETT: *An Unfinished Woman*.

P. 220   IN GOOD SHAPE: the Arthur Kober Papers.

P. 221   IT WAS GREAT FUN: Wright, *Lillian Hellman*.

P. 222   HER RUSSIAN TRANSLATOR: Raya Orlova, *Memoirs*.

P. 223   SHE RELUCTANTLY ASKED HERBERT GOLD: interview with Herbert Gold; Raya Orlova, letter to author.

P. 224   HARDLY LOVE AT FIRST SIGHT: My account of the Hellman-Melby romance relies heavily on Robert Newman's forthcoming book *Cold War Romance: Lillian Hellman and John Melby*, and on interviews with John Melby.

P. 225   A STEADY STREAM OF LETTERS: quoted in *Dashiell Hammett: A Life* by Diane Johnson.

P. 225   GOING OFF ON AN IMPORTANT TRIP: Hal Wallis Collection, Academy of Motion Picture Arts and Sciences.

P. 226   SPECIAL TENNIS COURTS: Orlova, *Memoirs*.

P. 226   FOR HEAVEN'S SAKE: interview with William Alfred.

P. 226   ROBERT MEIKLEJOHN: quoted in Newman, *Cold War Romance: Lilliam Hellman and John Melby*.

P. 227   SEEING THE FRONT: Raya Orlova interview with Hilary Mills; Raya Orlova, letter to author.

P. 230   THE IDIOT MAJOR: Raya Orlova, letter to author.

P. 230   NO LENIN: Orlova, *Memoirs*.

P. 230   BUT ORLOVA POINTS OUT: Raya Orlova, letter to author.

P. 231   KATHLEEN HARRIMAN SUSPECTS THAT: Wright, *Lillian Hellman*.

13. ANOTHER PART OF THE FOREST

P. 232   A CABLE AND A LETTER TO MELBY: Correspondence between Hellman and Melby is cited in Robert Newman's forthcoming book, *Cold War Romance: Lillian Hellman and John Melby*. As in the previous chapter, I am deeply indebted to Newman and to Melby for my reconstruction of this period in Hellman's life.

P. 235   A PRESS CONFERENCE IN NEW YORK: "Russia Acclaimed by Miss Hellman: Home, She Says Soviet Will Deal with Fascism—Hopes we Do the Same in U.S.," *The New York Times*, March 2, 1945.

P. 235   FUND-RAISING CAMPAIGN: "Fete Lillian Hellman, Raise $60,000 for Spain," *Daily Worker*, March 24, 1945.

P. 239   HELLMAN'S SECRETARY: Dashiell Hammett Collection, Humanities Research Center, University of Texas at Austin.

P. 240   SCREEN VERSION OF *THE SEARCHING WIND*: Academy of Motion Picture Arts and Sciences, Beverly Hills, California.

P. 241   CASSIE IS GIVEN MUCH STRONGER LANGUAGE: Dick, *Hellman in Hollywood*.

P. 242   AN INTERVIEW WITH LEWIS FUNKE: in Bryer, *Conversations with Lillian Hellman*.

P. 242   WARD MOREHOUSE: "Broadway After Dark," *New York Sun*, November 15, 1946.

P. 244   AS . . . DORIS FALK OBSERVES: *Lillian Hellman*.

P. 246 THE ENDING OF THE PLAY: For the most complete discussion of Hellman's composition of the play, see Mooney, " 'Southern' Influences in Four Plays by Lillian Hellman."

P. 247 SHE TOOK HIM TO COURT AND LOST: Wright, *Lillian Hellman*.

P. 248 WE USED TO SIT AT BREAKFAST: interview with Virginia Bloomgarden Chilewich.

P. 248 YOU COULDN'T STAND UP TO HER: interview with Jose Vega.

P. 248 HELLMAN'S DIRECTION: interview with Jose Vega.

P. 250 LILLIAN BEHAVED EXTREMELY WELL: interview with Virginia Bloomgarden Chilewich.

P. 251 RICHARD MOODY NOTES: *Lillian Hellman*.

P. 251 AS THERESA MOONEY SHOWS: " 'Southern' Influences in Four Plays by Lillian Hellman."

P. 252 EVEN HENRY SIGERIST: *Autobiographical Writings*.

14. COLD WAR

P. 254 THE EXTREMISM OF THE TIMES: Richard Walton, *Henry Wallace, Harry Truman and the Cold War*; Garry Wills introduction to *Scoundrel Time* (first edition).

P. 254 DUNNE'S WORDS: interview with Philip Dunne.

P. 255 OUR OWN PURGE OF COMMUNISTS: Dunne, *Take Two*.

P. 255 SINISTER AND REACTIONARY FORCES: Quoted in Walton, *Henry Wallace, Harry Truman and the Cold War*.

P. 256 I THOUGHT STALIN'S SPEECH: Walton, *Henry Wallace, Harry Truman and the Cold War*.

P. 257 MELBY WAS OUTRAGED: As in the previous chapter, I am deeply indebted to Newman, *Cold War Romance: Lillian Hellman and John Melby*, and to Melby for my reconstruction of this period in Hellman's life.

P. 258 THE INVITATION OF JULIAN HUXLEY: UNESCO correspondence is in the Manuscripts Department, Lilly Library, Indiana University, Bloomington, Indiana.

P. 259 TRULY A NOBLE LADY: Arthur Kober Papers.

P. 259 TELEGRAM TO KOBER: Arthur Kober Papers.

P. 259 UNDATED LETTER TO KOBER: Arthur Kober Papers.

P. 259 MISS HELLMAN, WHOSE PROBLEMS . . .: Manuscripts department, Lilly Library, Indiana University, Bloomington, Indiana.

P. 260 DOUBTS ABOUT THE VALUE OF THE UNESCO MISSION: Hellman's letter to Brooks is in the Special Collections department, Van Pelt Library, University of Pennsylvania.

P. 260 HELLMAN'S SECRETARY: Arthur Kober Papers.

P. 260 HELLMAN WROTE MAGGIE: Arthur Kober Papers.

P. 262 MELBY IS CONFIDENT IN HIS MEMORY: interview with John Melby.

P. 263 SHE COULD HAVE BEEN A DIPLOMAT'S WIFE: interview with John Melby.

P. 263 NOTHING ELSE REALLY MATTERS: interview with John Melby.

P. 263 AS PHILIP DUNNE POINTS OUT: *Take Two*.

P. 264 DUNNE POINTS OUT: *Take Two*.

P. 267 SHE WROTE MAGGIE KOBER: Arthur Kober Papers.

P. 267 RANDALL "PETE" SMITH: interview with Randall Smith.

P. 268 HARDLY A ROUGHNECK: Isabel Stein, letter to author.

P. 270   OTHER FACETS OF LILLIAN: interview with Virginia Bloomgarden Chilewich.

P. 271   WALLACE WAS A JERK: interview with Randall Smith.

P. 271   JOHN MELBY REMEMBERS: interview with John Melby.

P. 271   DEAR MR. WALLACE: Kimball.

P. 272   HELLMAN'S EMOTION: interview with Virginia Bloomgarden Chilewich.

P. 274   SOME ENGELS TO READ: interview with Howard Bay.

P. 275   A CRISIS WITH HAMMETT: Johnson, *Dashiell Hammett: A Life*.

P. 276   HELLMAN WROTE ITS AUTHOR: Marie Kilker, "The Theatre of Emmanuel Robles: An American Introduction with a Checklist on Criticism and Production."

P. 276   ENLISTING MALCOLM COWLEY'S HELP: Malcolm Cowley, letter to author.

P. 276   SHE WROTE COWLEY: Cowley Collection, Newberry Library, Chicago, Illinois.

P. 277   PROFESSOR SIDNEY HOOK: See his recent autobiography, *Out of Step*.

P. 278   ARGUING FOR CULTURAL COEXISTENCE: quoted in Cedric Belfrage, *The American Inquisition, 1945–1960*.

P. 278   AS ROBERT NEWMAN PUTS IT: *Cold War Romance: Lillian Hellman and John Melby*.

15. MONTSERRAT

P. 280   MY RELATIONSHIP WITH LILLIAN: This chapter relies heavily on a long written statement by Emlyn Williams and on interviews with John Abbott, Julie Harris, and Howard Bay.

P. 284   HARRIS'S THEATER SENSE: Gottfried, *Jed Harris: The Curse of Genius*.

P. 285   DRAGGING OUT PAUSES: interview with Howard Bay.

P. 285   MR. SCHUNZEL, IT'S HORRIBLE: interview with John Abbott.

P. 285   SCHUNZEL ONCE AMUSED HIS FELLOW ACTORS: John Abbott, letter to author.

P. 286   THE ENGLISH SCHOOL: interview with John Abbott.

P. 287   NONDIRECTION: interview with Virginia Bloomgarden Chilewich.

P. 293   ROBLES HELD A SIMILAR OPINION: Kilker, "The Theatre of Emmanuel Robles: An American Introduction with a Checklist on Criticism and Production."

P. 293   *REGINA*: Moody, *Lillian Hellman*, reports that Blitzstein "solicited" Hellman's opinion of *Regina*. She pointed out there were "un-Southern" words in the text—like "pinch" and "cram." "For your sweet tooth to crave" was a "bad line, very unlike Regina." Then Hellman offered this extended analysis of her creation and Blitzstein's version: "I don't think Regina is a flirt. She would flirt with Marshall for a reason; she would flirt with anybody for a reason, but I don't for a second believe she would flirt with the men in this town . . . no talk about another woman getting fat. I think she is long past such small feminine pleasantries . . . Regina must never, never, never answer the question, 'Are you afraid, Mama?' . . . and I think the whole approach to the Negro in the play is too sentimental. I think the original play had too much of such sentimentality and it was an artistic mistake. But I don't think we should increase the mistake."

16. THE AUTUMN GARDEN

P. 295   ALGER HISS: Allan Weinstein, *Perjury: The Hiss-Chambers Case.*

P. 296   JOHN MELBY'S IMPRESSION: interview with John Melby.

P. 296   SIEGE OF HEADACHES: Arthur Kober Papers.

P. 296   A SCRIPT FOR WILLIAM WYLER: interview with Talli Wyler.

P. 296   THE VALLEY SHEEP ARE FATTER: Hammett letter in the Dashiell Hammett Collection, Humanities Research Center, University of Texas at Austin.

P. 296   IN MID-MARCH: I am deeply indebted to Robert Newman and John Melby for my reconstruction of this period in Hellman's life.

P. 297   AN OPENNESS ABOUT HIM: interview with Virginia Bloomgarden Chilewich.

P. 297   THE TOUCHING SIDE OF HELLMAN: interview with Virginia Bloomgarden Chilewich.

P. 297   SHE LOVED THEIR BIG POODLES: interview with Catherine Kober.

P. 298   VAN WYCK BROOKS: correspondence between Brooks and Hellman in the Van Pelt Library, Special Collections, University of Pennsylvania.

P. 298   I DON'T KNOW WHAT'S HAPPENED: *An Unfinished Woman.*

P. 298   A PASSIONATE AFFECTION: *Pentimento.*

P. 298   IN REVISION: See Mooney, " 'Southern' Influences in Four Plays by Lillian Hellman," for a discussion of revisions; the final script of *The Autumn Garden* is located in the Manuscript Reading Room, Library of Congress.

P. 301   TOO EARLY TO START A NEW CAREER: Johnson, *Dashiell Hammett: A Life.*

P. 303   GENTLE, SENSITIVE MAN: interview and correspondence with Florence Eldridge.

P. 304   I'M NOT GOING TO HAVE A FIGHT: interview with Jane Wyatt.

P. 304   IT WAS NOT A HAPPY THING: interview with Howard Bay; see also Clurman, *On Directing* and *All People Are Famous* for insights into *The Autumn Garden* and explanations of the director's difficulties with the playwright.

P. 305   KENT, ARE YOU ASLEEP?: interview with Jane Wyatt.

P. 306   HAMMETT WROTE MAGGIE: Dashiel Hammett Collection, Humanities Research Center, University of Texas at Austin.

P. 306   WYATT STARTED FUSSING: interview with Jane Wyatt.

P. 307   BROOKS ATKINSON'S OPENING-NIGHT REVIEW: interview with Virginia Bloomgarden Chilewich.

P. 308   THE FACE OF AN OLD ROMAN: interview with Telford Taylor.

P. 309   MADAME HAS A FIRM BELIEF: Dashiell Hammett Collection, Humanities Research Center, University of Texas

P. 309   HELLMAN LIKED ANN: letter to Jo Marshall, courtesy of Jo Marshall.

P. 310   LETTERS TO MAGGIE KOBER: Dashiell Hammett Collection.

P. 310   HELLMAN HAD NOT FORGOTTEN JOHN MELBY: Newman, *Cold War Romance: Lillian Hellman and John Melby.*

P. 310   A BRIEF ASSIGNMENT FOR THE UNIVERSITY OF MICHIGAN: Hellman's correspondence with Roy Cowden is in the University of Michigan Graduate Library, Special Collections.

P. 312   ACTING ON INFORMATION FROM A CONFIDENTIAL SOURCE: Hellman's FBI file.

P. 312   LILLIAN WAS COLDLY POLITE: Johnson, *Dashiell Hammett: A Life.*

P. 312   HELLMAN'S FRANTIC EFFORTS: Johnson, *Dashiell Hammett: A Life.*

P. 313   THE MOST GALLING LETTERS OF HER LIFE: in Hellman's Passport file, Department of State.
P. 314   A POSTCARD FROM LONDON: Arthur Kober Papers.
P. 314   SHE WROTE TO JO MARSHALL: Hellman letter to Marshall, courtesy of Jo Marshall.
P. 314   SCREENWRITER MARTIN BERKELEY: interviews with Philip Dunne and Ring Lardner, Jr.

17. HUAC

P. 317   IN MID-FEBRUARY: Newman, *Cold War Romance: Lillian Hellman and John Melby*; intervew with John Melby.
P. 318   HELLMAN'S ATTORNEY: interview with Joseph Rauh.
P. 318   SHE WAS DIFFERENT FROM ARTHUR MILLER: interview with Joseph Rauh.
P. 319   WE'D LET HER GO A YEAR OR TWO BACK: interview with Joseph Rauh.
P. 321   WE USED TO ARGUE: interview with Joseph Rauh.
P. 322   WHEN RAUH HIRED HIM: interview with Daniel Pollitt.
P. 322   WHEN A CLIENT COULD PLEAD THE FIFTH AMENDMENT: For the intricacies of pleading the fifth amendment, see Pollitt's two articles, "Pleading the Fifth Amendment Before a Congressional Committee: A Study and Explanation," *Notre Dame Lawyer*, December 1956, and "The Fifth Amendment Plea Before Congressional Committees Investigating Subversion: Motives and Justifiable Presumptions—A Survey of 120 Witnesses," *University of Pennsylvania Law Review*, June 1958.
P. 322   HUAC WAS A VICIOUS COMMITTEE: interview with Daniel Pollitt.
P. 323   HELLMAN CALLED HARRY AND ELENA LEVIN: interview and correspondence with Harry and Elena Levin.
P. 324   ELENA HAD COME TO AMERICA: interview with Elena Levin.
P. 324   HELLMAN HELPED JOHN MELBY: Newman, *Cold War Romance: Lillian Hellman and John Melby*.
P. 325   RAUH DENIED CONSULTING ARNOLD: Wright, *Lillian Hellman*.
P. 325   POLLITT NEVER KNEW ANYONE WHO WAS NOT NERVOUS: interview with Daniel Pollitt.
P. 326   A HUGE ROOM: interview with Daniel Pollitt, who kindly took me through the Caucus room and explained the physical layout.
P. 326   UN-AMERICAN ACTIVITIES DAY: interview with Daniel Pollitt.
P. 326   ANOTHER TIME: interview with Daniel Pollitt.
P. 326   TO ONE REPORTER: Don Irwin, "Lillian Hellman Refuses to Say If She was Red," *New York Herald Tribune*, May 22, 1952.
P. 326–327 THE TEXTS OF HELLMAN'S LETTER AND THE COMMITTEE'S REPLY:

DEAR MR. WOOD: As you know, I am under subpoena to appear before your committee on May 21, 1952.

I am most willing to answer all questions about myself. I have nothing to hide from your committee and there is nothing in my life of which I am ashamed. I have been advised by counsel that under the fifth amendment I have a constitutional privilege to decline to answer any questions about my political opinions, activities, and associations, on the grounds of self-incrimination. I do not wish to claim this privilege. I am ready and willing to testify before the representatives of our Government as to my own opinions and my own actions, regardless of any risks or consequences to myself.

But I am advised by counsel that if I answer the committee's questions about myself, I must also answer questions about other people and that if I refuse to do so, I can be cited for contempt. My counsel tells me that if I answer questions about myself, I will have waived my rights under the fifth amendment and could be forced legally to answer questions about others. This is very difficult for a layman to understand. But there is one principle I do understand: I am not willing, now or in the future, to bring bad trouble to people who, in my past association with them, were completely innocent of any talk or any action that was disloyal or subversive. I do not like subversion or disloyalty in any form and if I had ever seen any I would have considered it my duty to have reported it to the proper authorities. But to hurt innocent people whom I knew many years ago in order to save myself is to me inhuman and indecent and dishonorable. I cannot and will not cut my conscience to fit this year's fashions, even though I long ago came to the conclusion that I was not a political person and could have no comfortable place in any political group.

I was raised in an old-fashioned American tradition and there were certain homely things that were taught to me. To try to tell the truth, not to bear false witness, not to harm my neighbor, to be loyal to my country, and so on. In general, I respected these ideals of Christian honor and did as well with them as I knew how. It is my belief that you will agree with these simple rules of human decency and will not expect me to violate the good American tradition from which they spring. I would, therefore, like to come before you and speak of myself.

I am prepared to waive the privilege against self-incrimination and to tell you everything yo wish to know about my views or actions if your committee will agree to refrain from asking me to name other people. If the committee is unwilling to give me this assurance, I will be forced to plead the privilege of the fifth amendment at the hearing.

A reply to this letter would be appreciated.
Sincerely yours

LILLIAN HELLMAN

DEAR MISS HELLMAN: Reference is made to your letter dated May 19, 1952, wherein you indicate that in the event the committee asks you questions regarding your association with other individuals you will be compelled to rely upon the fifth amendment in giving your answers to committee questions.

In this connection, please be advised that the committee cannot permit witnesses to set forth the terms under which they will testify.

We have in the past secured a great deal of information from persons in the entertainment profession who cooperated whole-heartedly with the committee. The committee appreciates any information furnished it by persons who have been members of the Communist Party. The committee, of course, realizes that a great number of persons who were members of the Communist Party at one time honestly felt that it was not a subversive organization. However, on the other hand, it should be pointed out that the contributions made to the Communist Party as a whole by persons who were not themselves subversive made it possible for those members of the Communist Party who were and still are subversive to carry on their work.

The committee has endeavored to furnish a hearing to each person identified as a Communist engaged in work in the entertainment field in order that the record could be made clear as to whether they were still members of the Communist Party. Any persons identified by you during the course of committee hearings will be afforded the opportunity of appearing before the committee in accordance with the policy of the committee.

Sincerely yours
JOHN S. WOOD, Chairman

P. 327   POLLITT IS SURE HE IS EMBELLISHING: interview with Daniel Pollitt.

P. 327   NEITHER RAUH NOR POLLITT REMEMBERS: interviews with Joseph Rauh and Daniel Pollitt.

P. 328   TO GO TO HELL: Hellman interview with Marilyn Berger in Bryer, *Conversations with Lillian Hellman.*

P. 329   IT WAS A KIND OF RESCUE: interview with Daniel Pollitt.

P. 329   A CRUSH ON JOE: interview with Daniel Pollitt.

P. 329   RAUH SAYS: interview with Joseph Rauh.

P. 329   A MORE INTIMATE RELATIONSHIP: confidential source.

P. 330   A BABE RUTH HOME RUN: interview with Joseph Rauh.

18. THE AFTERMATH

P. 331   HELLMAN CONFERRED WITH JOHN MELBY: My reconstruction of this period of Hellman's life is indebted to Newman, *Cold War Romance: Lillian Hellman and John Melby,* and interviews with John Melby.

P. 334   REWRITING PARTS OF IT: Hellman interview with Harry Gilroy in Bryer, *Conversations with Lillian Hellman,* and Moody, *Lillian Hellman.*

P. 335   WE TALKED ABOUT HOW EACH OF US WORKED: interview with Kim Hunter.

P. 336   IF I CAN ACCOMPLISH: interview with Kim Hunter.

P. 337   A TRIAL TO DEAL WITH THE OTHER CHILDREN: interview with Jose Vega.

P. 337   A LOT OF COMPLICATED NEGOTIATIONS WITH HELLMAN: interview with Virginia Bloomgarden Chilewich.

P. 341   HELLMAN SHOULD BE ALLOWED TO TESTIFY: Newman, *Cold War Romance: Lillian Hellman and John Melby.*

P. 342   HELLMAN WAS IN MRS. SHIPLEY'S OFFICE: Newman, *Cold War Romance: Lillian Hellman and John Melby.*

P. 342   SHE HAD WRITTEN TO VAN WYCK BROOKS: letter dated June 5, 1952 in the Van Pelt Library, Special Collections, University of Pennsylvania.

P. 342   MEETING WITH MRS. SHIPLEY: *Scoundrel Time.*

P. 343   A FOLLOW-UP LETTER TO SHIPLEY: in the Passport File, Department of State.

P. 344 THE SAME DAY HELLMAN WROTE SHIPLEY: Newman, *Cold War Romance: Lillian Hellman and John Melby.*

P. 344 A TIME IN WHICH HE SHOULD HAVE ACTED: interview with John Melby.

19. ABROAD

P. 346 I CAN'T TELL YOU: quoted in Newman, *Cold War Romance: Lillian Hellman and John Melby.*

P. 346 HELLMAN WROTE HENRY SIGERIST: in Manuscripts and Archives, Yale University Library.

P. 347 HELLMAN MET STEPHEN GREENE: interview and correspondence with Stephen Greene.

P. 349 JOE AND BOBBIE WEINSTEIN: interview with Bobbie Weinstein.

P. 349 SHE WROTE TO MELBY: Newman, *Cold War Romance: Lillian Hellman and John Melby.*

P. 350 A SIMILAR LETTER TO STEPHEN GREENE: courtesy of Stephen Greene.

P. 350 HELLMAN WROTE MELBY: Newman, *Cold War Romance: Lillian Hellman and John Melby.*

P. 351 SHE RESENTED HIM: Newman, *Cold War Romance: Lillian Hellman and John Melby.*

P. 351 NOT WANTING TO SIT AROUND: Hellman's letter to Sigerest is in Manuscripts and Archives, Yale University Library.

20. ADAPTATIONS

P. 353 MEETINGS WITH BERNSTEIN: Joan Peyser, *Bernstein: A Biography*

P. 353 SHE WROTE THEODORE ROETHKE: Theodore Roethke Papers, University of Washington Libraries Manuscript Section.

P. 354 AN EMBARRASSMENT TO PROFESSOR LEVIN: interview with Harry Levin.

P. 354 HELLMAN WAS TOUCHY ABOUT MONEY: interviews with Diana Trilling, Ephraim London, Bobbie Weinstein, Virginia Bloomgarden Chilewich; Catherine Kober; David Bloomgarden interview with Hilary Mills. In the late sixties and early seventies, Kermit Bloomgarden had several financial reverses and illnesses. Hellman had loaned him money before he went into the hospital. In 1971, Kermit's son David got a call from her demanding $5,000 immediately. He was twenty-five at the time and in night school studying for a major exam. She wanted the money *tomorrow.* As David recalls, "the day before the exam I made my way downtown to pick up a check that was sent to me from a brokerage house. I met her at her apartment on Park Avenue. I remember having this vitriolic exchange. I was surprised at myself and I was surprised at her. I told her that she had caught me at a time when it was particularly important to me and I didn't understand why she had to have the money that day. She said something about some loans being called in on her or something." In his diary for July 6, 1972, Arthur Kober recorded "Lil tells me of Kermit borrowing 5,000 & her loss. She won't talk with him & hasn't forgiven David." When Kermit developed a brain tumor in 1976 (the year he died, Hellman went to see him and they had several long talks. He still had enormous respect for her, but now there was a reserve between them. This coolness did not prevent Hellman from scolding Virginia (after her divorce from Kermit) for supposedly contributing to Kermit's financial problems.

After Arthur Kober's death in 1975, his daughter Catherine received $10,000 Hellman had set aside for him. Catherine had had a very hard time—years watching her mother slowly die, and then the recent death of her father. Her therapist advised her to assert herself and to confront Hellman, who wanted Catherine to give the money to the Committee for Public Justice. Catherine wrote to say she would be giving the $10,000 as seed money to a foundling hospital. Kober recalls that Lillian responded not with fury but with questions, and with the observation that so much money had already gone to the foundling home—which Kober had to concede was true. As Kober remembers it, Hellman asked, "Why are you giving the money here when your own background should direct you to support the Committee?" She made a very good case. But Kober's therapist egged her on to stand up to Hellman. In retrospect, Kober feels she should have acknowledged Hellman's argument, explained that she had already committed the money elsewhere, but shown her good faith by promising a contribution to the Committee, whose work she did respect. Had Kober explained that the $10,000 was going to help a friend's work at the foundling hospital, she is sure Hellman would have understood. Instead, coached by her therapist, she decided to fight the dragon. Hellman countered by writing a letter pointing out her father would have wanted her to give the money to the Committee. Kober thinks Hellman was probably right, but at the time a very troubled Kober considered Hellman's letter a form of "emotional blackmail." By the third or fourth exchange of letters, their stands were polarized. Kober said Hellman was an awful person and she could no longer consider her a friend. In retrospect, Kober puts the blame on herself and believes Hellman, from her point of view, acted justly. There was no further contact between them.

P. 354   AFFRONTED BY A PARTY GUEST: interview with Diana Trilling.

P. 355   THE RIGHT BALANCE: See the description of her revisions in Triesch, *The Lillian Hellman Collection at the University of Texas.*

P. 356   SHE WAS FRIGHTENED: interviews with Ralph Penner, Bobbie Weinstein, and Richard Wilbur.

P. 358   THE PLAYWRIGHT'S CONTINUAL INTERFERENCE: Wright, *Lillian Hellman.*

P. 358   KERMIT BLOOMGARDEN WAS FIRM: interview with Virginia Bloomgarden Chilewich.

P. 358   WHY ARE THEY SO SLOW?: interview with Julie Harris.

P. 358   HUMANLY SO FRAIL: interview with Julie Harris.

P. 358   HELLMAN'S DRINKING: interview with Bobbie Weinstein.

P. 358   I WILL NOT STOP SMOKING: interview with Julie Harris.

P. 358–359   OPPOSITE ISLANDS: interview with Julie Harris.

P. 359   A MOST DIFFICULT JOB: Hellman letter to Stephen Greene, courtesy of Stephen Greene.

P. 360   AUDITION PRECIS: Triesch, *The Lillian Hellman Collection at the University of Texas.*

P. 360   CANDIDE, STUNNED, STUPIFIED, DESPAIRING: *Candide,* Translated and Edited by Robert M. Adams (New York: W.W. Norton, 1966).

P. 362   HELLMAN AND WILBUR: interview with Richard Wilbur.

P. 362   REVISE THE PLAY SCENE BY SCENE: Hellman's revisions of *Candide* are discussed in Triesch, *The Lillian Hellman Collection at the University of Texas* and Moody, *Lillian Hellman.*

P. 363   GOT ALONG VERY WELL: interview with Richard Wilbur.

P. 363   TYRONE GUTHRIE AS DIRECTOR: interview with Richard Wilbur.

P. 363–364   GUTHRIE CONCLUDES: Tyrone Guthrie, *A Life in the Theatre.*

P. 364   ERROR IN JUDGMENT: Joan Peyser, *Bernstein: A Biography,* reports that there were tensions between Bernstein and Hellman during the collaboration on *Candide* and afterwards. Hellman once phoned a Bernstein collaborator on another project warning him that the composer was a monster and had been responsible for *Candide*'s failure. There were times when Bernstein obviously found her hard to take and would refer to her among friends as "Uncle Lillian."

P. 364   REINER WAS EQUALLY IGNORANT ABOUT POETRY: interview with William Alfred.

P. 365   SYPHILLIS SONG: Moody, *Lillian Hellman.*

P. 365   CANDIDE'S POOR RECEPTION: See Gerald Weales, *American Drama Since World War II,* for a much more positive view of *Candide.* Weales singles out Hellman for praise and contrary to most critical opinion cites Bernstein for weakening the play. On Hellman's work as an adaptor, see two articles by Henry W. Knepler, "*The Lark*: Translation vs. Adaptation: A Case History," *Modern Drama,* May 1958, and "Translation and Adaptation in the Contemporary Drama," *Modern Drama,* May 1961.

P. 365   OH, THAT VOICE: interview with Howard Meyer.

P. 365   HELLMAN EXCELLED IN THE CREATION OF INTIMATE SCENES: interviews with Richard Wilbur, Frances FitzGerald, and Diana Trilling.

P. 365   TO ARTHUR KOBER: Arthur Kober Papers.

P. 366   I REMEMBER OUR SITTING DOWN ON THE BEACH: interview with Richard Wilbur.

P. 366   PHILIP RAHV MET LILLIAN: interview with Frances FitzGerald. According to FitzGerald, shortly before Rahv died in 1973, Hellman wrote to him. "It was the sweetest thing. He was in a bad way, living in Cambridge and thinking of coming to New York, and she wrote this lovely letter (engaging and sympathetic) saying how wonderful it would be if he came. Her words were just great—a fine expression of friendship. Meanwhile he was telling dreadful stories about Lillian. He always told dreadful stories about everybody."

P. 366   WHEN I USED TO GO TO HER HOUSE: interview with Diana Trilling.

P. 367   WONDERFUL COMPANY: interview with William Alfred.

P. 368   A ROMANTIC REVIVAL: interview with Bobbie Weinstein.

P. 368   HOW MANY LAWYERS SHE KNEW: interview with Ephraim London.

P. 369   A HELLMAN TEAM: Matthew J. Bruccoli, ed. *Selected Letters of John O'Hara.*

P. 369   PROMISING YOUNG WRITERS: interview with Herbert Gold.

P. 369   YOU GODDAM FASCIST: interview with Maurice Zolotow.

P. 370   RUDE TO GOLD'S COMPANION: interview with Herbert Gold.

P. 370   SHE COULD BE VERY ARROGANT: interview with Telford Taylor.

P. 370   BOBBIE WEINSTEIN COULD HAVE TOLD GOLD: interview with Bobbie Weinstein.

P. 370   HELLMAN'S BOORISH TREATMENT OF HER SECRETARY: interview with Diana Trilling.

P. 370   SOCIAL LIFE AT THE VINEYARD: interview with Richard Wilbur.

P. 371 SHE HAD MAGNITUDE: interview with Herbert Gold.
P. 371 FRIENDS WITH THAT COMMIE: interview with Diana Trilling.
P. 371 LIONEL TRILLING HAD KNOWN HELLMAN: interview with Diana Trilling.
P. 372 STUART ROSE: interview with Maurice Zolotow.
P. 372 POLITICS WOULD ALWAYS BE A SORE POINT: interview with Diana Trilling.
P. 373 HELLMAN WAS SO USED TO INTIMIDATING PEOPLE: interview with Bobbie Weinstein.
P. 373 POLITICAL TO THE CORE: Norman Podhoretz, *Breaking Ranks.*
P. 373 KHRUSHCHEV WAS ANOTHER INFORMER: interview with John Melby.
P. 373 HELLMAN ONCE CONFESSED TO CATHERINE KOBER: interview with Catherine Kober.
P. 374 SHE ONCE TOLD EPHRAIM LONDON: interview with Ephraim London.

21. TOYS IN THE ATTIC

P. 375 THE CONFORMIST: "400 Writers Hold First U.S. Meeting," *The New York Times*, May 7, 1957.
P. 375 AN INTERVIEW WITH RICHARD STERN: Bryer, *Conversations with Lillian Hellman.*
P. 376 QUARRELS WITH OSTERMAN: Wright, *Lillian Hellman.*
P. 377 EARLY DRAFTS OF TOYS IN THE ATTIC: Mooney, " 'Southern' Influences in Four Plays by Lillian Hellman."
P. 378 TO EMMY KRONENBERGER: interview with Emmy Kronenberger.
P. 380 HELLMAN TOLD RICHARD STERN: Bryer, *Conversations with Lillian Hellman.*
P. 381 REJECTED SCENE: Triesch, *The Lillian Hellman Collection at the University of Texas.*
P. 381 INVITE ME DOWN: interview with Diana Trilling.
P. 381 AN ENCLOSED SET WITH CEILINGS: interview with Howard Bay.
P. 382 YOU SHOULD NOT ADDRESS THE TROOPS: interview with Howard Bay.
P. 382 ANNE REVERE'S REHEARSAL SCRIPT: the Anne Revere Collection, Mugar Memorial Library, Boston University.
P. 384 MANIPULATORS LIKE CYRUS: see Triesch, *The Lillian Hellman Collection at the University of Texas,* for a scene that makes explicit the play's attack on unscrupulous capitalism. Eventually Hellman decided to omit this scene and handle the story of Warkins and his wife indirectly. They never appear on stage, yet Julian's lament, in the last act, over Mrs. Warkins' grim life with her brutal husband is more effective than the actual scene as the playwright first wrote.
P. 384 ROBARDS BELIEVED: *The New York Times*, August 21, 1960.

22. THE DEATH OF DASHIELL HAMMETT

P. 386 NOVEMBER 19, 1960: Hilary Mills, *Mailer: A Biography.*
P. 387 HELLMAN TOLD WRITER PETER MANSO: Peter Manso, *Mailer: His Life and Times;* for another version of this story, see Hellman interview with Wayne Warga in Bryer, *Conversations with Lillian Hellman.*
P. 387 FLIRTING WITH MAILER: Norman Podhoretz interviewed in Manso, *Mailer: His Life and Times.*

P. 387 TRILLING WROTE TO MAILER: interview with Diana Trilling.

P. 387 COMPARED TO ME: interview with Diana Trilling.

P. 387 HELLMAN CONFIDED TO DIANA TRILLING: interview with Diana Trilling.

P. 388 A *CHILDREN'S HOUR* ON ME: interview with Diana Trilling.

P. 388 LIKE A LIONESS: interview with Catherine Kober.

P. 389 THEODORE SPENCER MEMORIAL LECTURE: correspondence and interview with Harry Levin.

P. 389 A NURSING HOME: interview with Elena Levin.

P. 389 FOND OF VIRGINIA BLOOMGARDEN: interview with Virginia Bloomgarden Chilewich.

P. 389 CATHERINE KOBER LOVED HAMMETT: interview with Catherine Kober.

P. 390 JO SENSED THAT HELLMAN: interview with Jo Marshall.

P. 390 HE WAS USUALLY RESERVED: Johnson, *Dashiell Hammett: A Life*.

P. 390 AN AMUSING STATEMENT: Johnson, *Dashiell Hammett: A Life*.

P. 391 HELLMAN DELIVERED A EULOGY: "Lillian Hellman Gives Eulogy at Hammett Funeral," *New York Herald Tribune*, January 13, 1961; "Hammett Eulogized by Lillian Hellman," *The New York Times*, January 13, 1961.

P. 391 A SAINTLY MAN: interview with Julie Harris.

P. 391 MANY OTHERS VENERATED HIM: interviews with Virginia Bloomgarden Chilewich, Lee Gershwin, Albert Hackett, and Catherine Kober.

P. 391 HIS IMPATIENCE WITH FRAUD: interview with Richard Wilbur.

P. 392 HAMMETT BROUGHT OUT THE BEST IN HELLMAN: Jerome Weidman, *Praying for Rain*.

23. HARVARD

P. 394 A CHANGE OF SCENE: Hellman's letter to Brooks is in the Special Collections department, Van Pelt Library, University of Pennsylvania.

P. 394 REFERRED TO DR. LOUIS ZETZEL: interview with Dr. Zetzel.

P. 395 HAMMETT'S ABSENCE: interview with Elena Levin.

P. 395 IN BED WITH ANOTHER MAN: interview with Herbert Gold.

P. 395 DASHING CHEMISTRY PROFESSOR: confidential source.

P. 395 HOW TO TEACH: Walter Jackson Bate, letter to author.

P. 396 THOROUGH PROFESSIONAL: confidential source.

P. 396–397 KEN STUART: I am indebted throughout this chapter to Ken Stuart's journal, to his recollections of the class, and to the papers Hellman assigned him to write.

P. 399 SHE WANTED STUDENTS TO TALK ABOUT THEIR WORK: interviews with Ken Stuart and Peter Benchley.

P. 400 SIMILARITIES BETWEEN *TOYS IN THE ATTIC* AND *TWO SISTERS*: see Jacob H. Adler, "Miss Hellman's Two Sisters."

P. 402 WRITING AS CREATING A CHRISTMAS TREE: interview with Peter Benchley.

P. 404 HELLMAN HAD WRITTEN TO GEORGE FREEDLEY: Billy Rose Theatre Collection, New York Public Library.

P. 406 MORALLY EQUAL: Don Ross, "Lillian Hellman Teaches What Can't Be Taught," *New York Herald Tribune*, April 23, 1961.

P. 406 TIME FOR THE GRADES: interview with William Alfred.

P. 406 SHE FELT FINE: interview with Dr. Zetzel.

24. MY MOTHER, MY FATHER, AND ME

P. 407 HER PLACE IN AMERICAN LETTERS: On June 4, 1961, Hellman was awarded an honorary Litt.D. by Wheaton College in Norton, Massachusetts: "Because you are a penetrating observer of human behavior as well as a superb architect of dramatic structure, your plays for over twenty-five years have continued to delight us with their skillful teaching. Deeply concerned with the problems of justice and injustice, with good and evil—the problems which are the source of all enduring literature—you have always had something valuable to say and have said it well, speaking freely through the exacting demands of realistic drama. Not only have you dramatized great issues but you have also found material in the quiet dilemmas from which no man is free. Your concern for truth, your gifts for characterization and for craftsmanship, place you among the most distinguished playwrights of our time."

On December 5, 1961, Hellman was elected to the American Academy of Arts and Letters. On June 5, 1963, she was awarded an honorary Litt.D by Douglass College, the women's division of Rutgers University: "As the watchman, as the searching wind, as the guardian or our most precious fruits of humanity and liberty, you have spoken dramatically and commanded us to be your attentive and applauding audience."

P. 408   THE DEAR QUEEN: a copy of this copyrighted play is available in the Manuscript Division, Library of Congress.

P. 408   NUMBERED IN THE MANUSCRIPT OF EACH NEW PLAY: Triesch, *The Lillian Hellman Collection at the University of Texas.*

P. 411   A SCANDAL: interview with William Alfred.

P. 411   HER REHEARSAL SCRIPT: Triesch, *The Lillian Hellman Collection at the University of Texas.*

P. 411   STYRON: Was Hellman having a little joke on her writer-friend? She must have known that he was working on *The Confessions of Nat Turner,* a novel narrated by a black insurrectionist slave.

P. 412   MAGGIE AND JIGGS LOOKS: interview with William Alfred.

P. 412   IT WAS A MISTAKE: interview with Howard Bay.

P. 412   BLOOMGARDEN WAS ALSO WARY: interview with Virginia Bloomgarden Chilewich.

P. 412   GOWER CHAMPION: interviews with Howard Bay, Walter Matthau, William Alfred, Martin Peretz, and Heywood Hale Broun.

P. 413   A STRANGE PLAY OF IDEAS: interview with Heywood Hale Broun.

P. 413   THE PLAY WAS ANTI-SEMITIC: interview with Walter Matthau.

P. 414   OH, MARTY: interview with Martin Peretz.

P. 414   BEING JEWISH: Hellman interviews with Christine Doudna and Sylvie Drake in Bryer, *Conversations with Lillian Hellman.* To Drake, Hellman said:

"I've asked myself many times what I would have liked to have been born and decided a long time ago that I was very glad I was born a Jew. Whether brought up as one or not, somewhere in the background there was a gift of being born a Jew. I don't want it to alter my point of view about things any more than I would want being a Catholic or anything else to alter my point of view, but I am glad of what I am.

"I felt absolutely violent during the Nazi period, certainly. I still do. I was in school in Germany when it first started. Later I saw Majdanek (a concentration camp in Lublin, Poland). I'll never recover as long as I live."

P. 414   THE POSSIBILITIES OF BECOMING JEWISH: interview with Richard Wilbur.
P. 415   THE CHARGE OF ANTI-SEMITISM: interview with William Alfred.
P. 415   A GREAT ADMIRER OF BECKETT: interview with William Alfred.
P. 416   MONEY AS POWER: William Alfred, letter to author.
P. 418   HELLMAN RAN INTO S. J. PERELMAN: interview with Heywood Hale Broun.

25. THE MATTER OF MEMORY

P. 419   HELLMAN WROTE TO CHERYL CRAWFORD: a letter dated September 7, 1962, is in the Billy Rose Theatre Collection, New York Public Library.
P. 420   WYLER WAS TOO FAITHFUL TO THE ORIGINAL: Madsen, *William Wyler.*
P. 420   BERNARD F. DICK SHOWS: *Hellman in Hollywood*
P. 421   BERNARD F. DICK HAS DISCOVERED: *Hellman in Hollywood.*
P. 421   THE FINAL PRODUCT: Hellman interview with Fred Gardner in Bryer, *Conversations with Lillian Hellman.*
P. 423   ROBERT ALTMAN: Hellman interview with Christine Doudna in Bryer, *Conversations with Lillian Hellman.*
P. 423   AN EXPLORATORY COURSE: interview with Ralph Penner. Unless otherwise noted, this account of Hellman's Yale class is based on Penner's remarks.
P. 423   STEIN'S LECTURE: Richard Shepard, "Lillian Hellman Teaching at Yale." *The New York Times,* February 1, 1966.
P. 429   THE *PARIS REVIEW*: in Bryer, *Conversations with Lillian Hellman.*
P. 430   A BIOGRAPHY OF THEODORE ROETHKE: Hellman's letter to Allan Seager is in the Bancroft Library, University of California, Berkeley.
P. 430   LADIES HOME JOURNAL: on February 27, 1964, *The New York Times* reported that the Curtis Publishing Company was "named today [February 26] in a $3 million libel suit filed in Circuit Court by Sheriff Dewey Colvard of Etowah County [Alabama]." The sheriff brought suit because of Hellman's *Ladies Home Journal* article that accused the sheriff's deputies of police brutality. In the March 1964 issue of *Ladies Home Journal* the publishers printed a retraction. Hellman's statement is printed right after the retraction:

"I was evidently misinformed about minor matters of fact. For example, I quote the young Negroes from Gadsden [Alabama] as saying that a boy who was lying in a hospital bed had cow prodders put to him by a sheriff and two cops. The Curtis Publishing Company has been informed by the Sheriff of Etowah County that neither he nor his deputies used the cow prodders on the boy. I therefore wish to apologize to Mr. Colvard because, as a white woman born in the South, and whose roots are most affectionately there, I do not blame any white Southerner for not wishing to be unjustly involved. But the fact remains that the cow prodders were used on the boy I wrote about by men I cannot identify at this minute of going to press. My article, in all important matters, tells the truth and I wish to disassociate myself from the above retraction. What is true should not be obscured by the fear of lawsuits."

P. 430   DESULTORY ARTICLES: "Scotch on the Rocks," *New York Review of Books,* October 17, 1963; "Sophronia's Grandson Comes to Washington," *Ladies Home Journal,* December 11, 1963; "The Land That Holds the

Legend of Our Lives," *Ladies Home Journal*, April 1964; "Lillian Hell-man Asks a Little Respect for Her Agony," *Show*, 1964. "Do better with the same memories, Hellman interview with Nora Ephron in Bryer.

P. 430 TO NOVELIST EDWIN O'CONNOR: Hellman correspondence with O'Con-nor is in the Boston Public Library.

P. 431 HELENA GOLISHEVA: Hellman's letter to Golisheva was intercepted by the CIA and obtained by the author under the Freedom of Informa-tion Act. According to Lee S. Strickland, Information and Privacy Coordinator of the Central Intelligence Agency, Hellman's letters to Soviet friends were acquired "under an intercept program called HTLINGUAL. This activity dealt with mail flowing between New York City and the USSR from 1956 until 1973, when the program was terminated."

P. 432 THE TWENTIETH PARTY CONGRESS: Raya Orlova interview with Hilary Mills; Raya Orlova, letter to author.

P. 433 WRITING TO JAY MARTIN: the letters to Martin are in the Huntington Library, San Marino, California

P. 433 SHE WROTE JOHN MELBY: Newman, *Cold War Romance: Lillian Hellman and John Melby*.

P. 433 NEVER LOST INTEREST IN MELBY: In 1955, she sent him $500 to be kept in a bank account. He would mail her cash for Hammett's expenses. This peculiar arrangement had to do with Hellman's fears that Inter-nal Revenue would check on how she was spending money on Hammett, and she did not want certain sums to be traced. When Melby sought an academic position, she wrote on his behalf. She wrote him in June 1959 after his disappointment in not finding government employment. She missed him and regretted the ties she had made that prevented them from being together. When he was working as an advisor for foreign students at the University of Pennsylvania in August, 1959, she dropped him a note: "Dear Prof. Melby, I have called you twice. Can a non-PhD ask how you are, and where? A non-PhD." When Kennedy was elected in 1960, she wrote him from London, where she was en route to Rome to consult with William Wyler about his film of *The Children's Hour*. She was delighted that "your candidate won for you. I hope to God, it will be good for the rest of us, too." She signed her letter with "much, much love." In July, 1966, she wrote him from Martha's Vineyard to express her delight over his appointment as head of the Political Studies depart-ment at the University of Guelph. In December of 1968, she sent congratulations for his highly regarded book, *Mandate of Heaven*. She could see that it was "excellent & important stuff." She often wanted to know when he would come to see her. When *An Unfinished Woman* was ready for print, she sent a letter promising him a copy and noting "You appear in the Russian stuff, and I think you will like your appearance." Her inscription in his copy reads "For John with much love & because he is in, importantly, this book. Lillian."

P. 433 A LETTER TO ORLOVA: intercepted by the CIA.

P. 433 THE 1967 VISIT: My account is based directly on a sixteen-page hand-written letter from Maya Koreneva, Hellman's Russian translator.

P. 433 BAD BACK: Hellman's letter to O'Connor is in the Boston Public Library.

P. 436 HELLMAN'S PLAYS: Maya Koreneva, letter to author.

P. 438 NONE OF THE INTELLECTUALS WERE AGAINST THE GOVERNMENT: Hellman had no use at all for exiles like Anatoly V. Kuznetzov. In an opinion piece for *The New York Times* (August 23, 1969), she attacked him for protesting the Soviet system only after "he was in the soft, welcoming arms of Britain." While in Russia he had saved his own skin by acting as an informer. She compared him with Whittaker Chambers—one of the most hated figures in her demonology of the Cold War. It was all right to be a Solzhenitsyn and go to prison for one's protest; anything less than that was "craven," as A. Ezergailis put it in his rebuttal letter to the *Times* on August 30. Never mind that in 1952 Hellman herself had been terrified by the prospect of prison. She did not deny Kuznetzov's statements about the suppression of free speech in the Soviet Union, but she could not let his remarks pass without her typical apology for the Soviet police state:

"Russia has made enormous advances in the way men eat, live and learn, but it is still in the days of the Revolution when it was perhaps understandable that men who were making a new world feared those who disagreed with them. Now they cannot tell a patriot from a bootlicker, a true artist from a panderer."

She noted that she had spent six months (it was more like three) on a cultural mission in the Soviet Union and returned briefly in 1966 and 1967. "Those are not the best qualifications for judging what Mr. Kuznetsov had to say, but they are better than the Academics who know the language and the history but who do not know the country, and as good as journalists and diplomats, who know the country but who often do not know the people because Russians are afraid of them." Hellman, who had virtually no Russian and was herself afraid of learning too much from people who did not like to hear her quote Stalin, presumed to judge Kuznetsov.

P. 438 FREE MANKIND: Peter Grose, "Soviet's Writers Given Party Line," *The New York Times*, May 23, 1967.

P. 438 AN AMAZING TIME IN AMERICA: Richard F. Shepard, " 'Little Foxes' Gets a Start in Low Key," *The New York Times*, September 29, 1967.

P. 440 A FINE ANALYSIS OF HER CAREER: Jacob Adler, *Lillian Hellman*.

P. 440 DISMISSIVE SENTENCE: Hellman letter (dated August 11, no year) to Moss Hart, in the Hart Papers at Wisconsin Center for Film and Theater Research, University of Wisconsin.

P. 441 HELLMAN WROTE TO HELENA GOLISHEVA: intercepted by the CIA.

26. AN UNFINISHED WOMAN

P. 442 A DIALOGUE OF SELF AND SOUL: Hellman was pleased when William Alfred recognized her allusion to this great poem in the title of her memoir.

P. 445 INCREDIBLE SNOBS: interview with Jo Marshall.

P. 448 THAT GODDAM BITCH: quoted in Wright, *Lillian Hellman*.

P. 448 AN INTERVIEW WITH NORA EPHRON: in Bryer, *Conversations with Lillian Hellman*.

P. 449 THE DOROTHY PARKER SECTION: interview with Jo Marshall.

P. 449 A BIT OF A CLOD: interview with Jo Marshall.

P. 450 A KIND OF SIDEKICK: interview with William Alfred.

P. 451   THE UNCANNY QUALITY OF HELLMAN'S MEMORY: interview with Stephen Greene.

P. 451   IT DOES NOT MATTER MUCH TO ME: *Scoundrel Time.*

27. HEROINE OF CULTURE

P. 455   SHE TOLD LEWIS FUNKE: in Bryer, *Conversations with Lillian Hellman.*

P. 455   MARTIN PERETZ INVITED HER TO HIS HARVARD CLASSROOM: interview with Michael Kinsley.

P. 455   IGNORING HER FORMER LOVER'S WIFE: confidential source.

P. 456   HELLMAN FOR LUNCH: interview with Diana Trilling.

P. 456   HER THIRD EXAM WITH DR. ZETZEL: interview with Louis Zetzel.

P. 456   ACCORDING TO ROBERT NEWMAN: *Cold War Romance: Lillian Hellman and John Melby.*

P. 457   ROBERT SILVERS: interview with Robert Silvers.

P. 458   STEPHEN GILLERS: interview with Stephen Gillers.

P. 459   ALTHOUGH ROBERT SILVERS: interview with Robert Silvers.

P. 459   TELFORD TAYLOR FEELS: interview with Telford Taylor.

P. 460   GILLERS CONCEDES: interview with Stephen Gillers.

P. 460   NOT VERY SYMPATHETIC: interview with Robert Silvers.

P. 460   HERE WAS A LADY: interview with Martin Peretz.

P. 460   SHE MADE JUDGMENTS: interview with Stephen Gillers.

P. 460   AT HUNTER: Fern Marja Eckman, "Lillian Hellman—Plenty of Class," *New York Post*, October 14, 1973.

P. 461   HER COLLEAGUE AT HUNTER: interview with Alex Szogyi; Alex Szogyi, "Lillian," *The Hunter Magazine*, July 1985.

P. 462   HER WONDERFULLY SENSUAL AND GRAVELLY VOICE: Szogyi, "Lillian."

P. 462   THE MOST BORING PARTY: interview with Alex Szogyi.

P. 462   SHE WAS PHENOMENALLY UNUSUAL LOOKING: interview with Alex Szogyi.

P. 462   HELLMAN LIKED TO SCREEN HER OWN CALLS: Szogyi, "Lillian."

P. 463   THE LOVE OF HER LIFE: interview with Alex Szogyi.

P. 463   THIS IS AN EXCEPTION: interview with Alex Szogyi.

P. 463   *HOT L BALTIMORE*: interview with Alex Szogyi.

P. 464   SOME GOOD SOUL: Szogyi, "Lillian."

P. 464   RALPH PENNER HAD NOTICED: interview with Ralph Penner.

P. 464   THE OTHER DAY: Jo Ann Levine, "Author Lillian Hellman—A Portrait in Words," *The Christian Science Monitor*, December 21, 1973; see also Gloria Emerson, "Lillian Hellman: At 66, She's Still Restless," *The New York Times*, September 7, 1973.

P. 464   SZOGYI WROTE HER A NOTE: interview with Alex Szogyi.

P. 464   I'LL NEVER FORGIVE YOU: interview with Alex Szogyi.

P. 464   SHE RELATED TO HER CHILDHOOD SO MUCH: interview with Alex Szogyi.

P. 465   COMPARING *COLLECTED PLAYS* WITH FIRST EDITIONS: Cynthia Denham Bailey, "Lillian Hellman's Revisions in 'The Collected Plays.' "

28. PENTIMENTO

P. 469   MANY REVIEWERS: Patricia Meyer Spacks, *The Female Imagination*; John

Simon, "Pentimental Journey," *Hudson Review,* Winter 1973–74; Clive James, *At the Pillars of Hercules.*

P. 470   FILM RIGHTS: "Hellman memoir Yields 'Willie' For a Film and Separate from 'Julie,' " *Variety,* July 31, 1974.

P. 471   HELLMAN'S MEMORY MAY HAVE EXAGGERATED: interview with Richard Wilbur.

P. 472   AN UNCLE WILLY: Carol Gelderman, *Mary McCarthy: A Life,* suggests Hellman's Uncle Willy and Aunt Lily are largely an imaginative projection of the real life originals.

P. 472   SEVERAL OF COWAN'S FRIENDS, ACQUAINTANCES, AND RELATIVES: interviews with John Melby, Martin Peretz, Marilyn Raab, Thomas McBride, Mary Robinson, Richard Wilbur, Harry Levin, Virginia Bloomgarden Chilewich, and correspondence with Tally Richards.

P. 472   JOHN MELBY REMEMBERS: interview with John Melby.

P. 474   PEOPLE LIKE COWAN: interview with Richard Wilbur.

P. 474   WILLIAM WRIGHT ASSUMES THEY DID: *Lillian Hellman.*

P. 475   LOVELY MAN: interview with Virginia Bloomgarden Chilewich.

P. 475   THE MCBRIDE FAMILY: interview with Thomas McBride.

P. 476   THE DIALOGUE ATTRIBUTED TO MCBRIDE'S FATHER: interviews with Thomas McBride and Mary Robinson.

P. 476   ROBINSON REMEMBERS: interview with Mary Robinson.

P. 476   SHE WAS AFTER ARTHUR: interviews with Mary Robinson and Marilyn Raab.

P. 477   ONE OF SADIE RAAB'S FRIENDS: letter supplied to author by Tally Richards.

P. 478   SHE MET HIM IN 1948: Tally Richards, letter to author.

P. 478   I WANTED TO BE LIKE LILLIAN HELLMAN: Tally Richards, letter to author.

P. 479   THE CHAPTER ABOUT ARTHUR: Tally Richards, letter to author.

29. SCOUNDREL TIME

P. 481   WHAT AGNEW DID: Jerry Tallmer, "Woman in the News: Lillian Hellman," *New York Post* Weekend Magazine, October 13, 1973.

P. 481   PANEL DISCUSSIONS OF WOMEN'S LIBERATION: Gloria Emerson, "Lillian Hellman: At 66, She's Still Restless," *The New York Times,* September 7, 1973.

P. 481   FIVE THOUSANDS DOLLARS FROM *THE NEW REPUBLIC:* interview with Martin Peretz.

P. 481   WOMAN OF FASHION: Leslie Bennetts, "Literary Giant Takes Post at Bryn Mawr, Lillian Hellman Gives Vivid Reading Here," *Philadelphia Bulletin,* October 30, 1974; Arthur Gold and Robert Fizdale, "Lillian Hellman's Creole Cooking," *Vogue,* June 1974: Lillian Hellman "Martinique," *Travel and Leisure,* January 1974; Lillian Hellman, "A Scene from an Unfinished Play, *The New Republic,* November 30, 1974.

P. 481   PARK AVENUE COOPERATIVE: Susan R. Giddin, "The Set That Lillian Built," *New York Post,* May 13, 1974.

P. 481   AMUSING TRIP TO FLORIDA: Israel Shenker, "Perelman Shaken Up by Florida's Charms," *The New York Times,* April 27, 1974.

P. 481   MOST INFLUENTIAL WOMAN: *Los Angeles Times,* August 19, 1975.

P. 481   COLLEGE GRADUATES: "For Truth, Justice, and the American Way," *The New York Times,* June 4, 1975.

P. 481   A THEATER NIGHT: John Springer Associates Press Release, "Theatre Honors Lillian Hellman," October 27, 1975.

P. 482   PREVENTING NIXON: Anthony Ripley, "U.S. Judge Rules Nixon Documents Belong to Nation," *The New York Times*, February 1, 1975; "Appeals Court Will Move Quickly on Nixon Records," *The New York Times*, February 2, 1975.

P. 482   THE HEIGHT OF HER POPULARITY: On October 29, 1973, it was announced in *The New York Times* that Hellman was one of four people honored by the American Civil Liberties Union for "outstanding contributions to civil liberties." On December 3, 1973, Hellman was inducted into the Theater Hall of Fame, "Notes on People," *The New York Times*, December 4, 1973. On December 7, 1973, "Notes on People," *The New York Times* reported that she received "the first Woman of the Year Award of the New York University Alumnae Club." On June 30, 1974, it was announced in "Notes on People," *The New York Times*, that Hellman had been "chosen to receive the prestigious Edward Mac-Dowell Medal for outstanding contributions to literature." *The New York Times* for April 20, 1975 noted she was one of "8 'Women of the Year' " honored by the *Ladies Home Journal*. October 6, 1976, *The New York Times:* "Actors Equity Association has named Lillian Hellman the recipient of the performers union's third annual Paul Robeson Award. . . . The Robeson award recognizes individuals who have shown 'concern for and service to fellow humans, respect for the dignity of the individual, freedom of expressions, universal brotherhood, and the artist's responsibility to the profession and the greater society.' " "Lillian Hellman Gets Lord & Taylor Award," *The New York Times*, November 10, 1977: "The award is given annually by the department to 'an outstanding individual whose creative mind has brought new beauty and deeper understanding to our lives.' " Joseph Brooks, the company's chairman and chief executive, extolled Hellman not only for her writing but for her "unshakable faith in the rights of the human being and for her unwavering crusade for personal dignity." Other recipients of the award included Albert Einstein, Ralph Bunche, and Margaret Chase Smith. Hellman received several honorary doctorates: New York University (reported in *The New York Times*, June 7, 1974); Smith College and Yale University (1974); Columbia University (reported in *The New York Times*, April 13, 1976).

P. 482   ONE OF THE PRINCIPAL VILLAINS: My account of the Levin controversy is based on interviews with Ephraim London, Martin Peretz, Herbert Gold, Virginia Bloomgarden Chilewich, Albert Hackett, and on *The Obsession*; see also "Meyer Levin's Suit Over 'Diary' Opens," *The New York Times*, December 14, 1957; "Levin Suit Dismissed," *The New York Times*, January 7, 1958; "Meyer Levin Wins $50,000 Over Play," *The New York Times*, January 9, 1958; Victor S. Navasky, "The Ordeal of Meyer Levin," *The New York Times Book Review*, February 3, 1974; Meyer Levin's letter of reply to Navasky and Kermit Bloomgarden's and Navasky's letters: *The New York Times Book Review*, March 3, 1974; Pearl K. Bell, "Meyer Levin's Obsessions," *Commentary*, June 1978; the replies by Levin and others with Bell's rejoinder: *Commentary*, September 1978; Stephen Fife, "Meyer Levin's Obsession," *The New Republic*, August 2, 1982; Joseph Shottan, "Who's the Scoundrel?" *Midstream*, October 1976. For an assessment of anti-Jewish attitudes in Hellman's work, see Bonnie Lyons, "Lillian Hellman: 'The First

Jewish Nun on Prytania Street,' " in *From Hester Street to Hollywood: The Jewish-American Stage and Screen,* edited by Sarah Blacher Cohen.

P. 485   SAY OY AND CROSS HERSELF: John Hersey, "Lillian Hellman," *The New Republic,* September 18, 1976.

P. 485   RING LARDNER, JR., OBSERVED: interview with Ring Lardner, Jr.

P. 485   HELLMAN'S FAMILY: Joseph Cohen, *The Tulanian* (Fall, 1983).

P. 485   FUNNY ANECDOTES: Stephen Birmingham, letter to author. In *The Dear Queen,* a Jewish veterinary surgeon, Dr. Bahnhof, keeps embarrassing his gentile friends by making direct references to his Jewishness.

P. 486   RELIGIOUS ASPECTS OF JEWISH LIFE: interview with Catherine Kober.

P. 486   HELLMAN LAUGHED: interview with Ephraim London.

P. 486   AN EXCHANGE OF LETTERS: interview with Herbert Gold.

P. 487   IN THE INTELLECTUAL WORLD: interview with Martin Peretz.

P. 488   MR. MEYER LEVIN: Joseph Rauh Papers, Library of Congress.

P. 490   BLOOD ON HIS HANDS: interview with Diana Trilling.

P. 490   A CODE OF HONOR: interview with Diana Trilling.

P. 490   ALFRED KAZIN WAS PERETZ'S CHOICE: interview with Martin Peretz.

P. 490   SHE WROTE KAZIN: Hellman's letters and cards to Kazin are in the Berg Collection of The New York Public Library.

P. 491   HERE WAS THIS WOMAN: interview with Martin Peretz.

P. 491   SHE CALLS ME ONE DAY: interview with Martin Peretz.

P. 493   STILL ON SPEAKING TERMS: interview with Diana Trilling.

P. 494   EVEN NORMAN MAILER: interview with Lillian Hellman in Manso, *Mailer: His Life and Times*; interview with Diana Trilling.

P. 494   MUCH TO THE DISMAY OF BIOGRAPHER HILARY MILLS: interview with Hilary Mills.

P. 494   THE CONTROVERSY WITH HELLMAN: interview with Diana Trilling; see also Robert D. McFadden, "Diana Trilling Book is Canceled; Reply to Lillian Hellman is cited," *The New York Times,* September 28, 1976; Michael Kernan, "Friends and 'Scoundrels': Publishing Fray Centered on the '50s," *The Washington Post,* September 29, 1976; Judy Klemesrud, "Lillian Hellman Denies Having Played a Role in Little Brown's Rejection of Trilling Book," *The New York Times,* September 29, 1976; Deidre Carmody, "Trilling Case Sparks Publisher-Loyalty Debate," *The New York Times,* September 30, 1976; Judy Bachrach, "Lillian Hellman on the Trilling Controversy," *The Washington Post,* September 30, 1976; *Newsweek,* October 11, 1976; Diana Trilling, *We Must March My Darlings*; Weinstein, *Perjury: The Hiss-Chambers Case.*

P. 499   IN HILTON KRAMER'S WORDS: "The Life and Death of Lillian Hellman," *The New Criterion,* October, 1984.

P. 500   THE MCCARTHY PERIOD: interview with Martin Peretz.

P. 501   SO PERETZ CALLED COHN: interview with Martin Peretz.

P. 501–502   HELLMAN AND COHN: interview with Martin Peretz.

30. JULIA

P. 503   I WISH I COULD ANSWER: letter to Solita Solano in the Janet Flanner-Solita Solano Papers, Manuscript Division, Library of Congress.

P. 504   SHE READ IT AT BRYN MAWR: reported in *Philadelphia Bulletin,* October 30, 1974.

P. 504   A BILL MOYERS TELEVISION INTERVIEW: Bryer, *Conversations with Lillian Hellman.*

P. 504   VISIT HOME TO NEW ORLEANS: Hellman and Feibleman, *Eating Together: Recollections and Recipes.*

P. 504   THE PURE CHARACTER: Kathleen T. Bell, " 'Julia' Characterization in the Plays of Lillian Hellman."

P. 505   THE BALD SYNOPSIS: Fred Zinneman Collection, Academy of Motion Picture Arts and Sciences.

P. 506   FISHING ALONE: interview with William Alfred.

P. 506   SHE KEPT IN CLOSE CONTACT: Hellman's communications with Roth are part of the record of the Fred Zinneman Collection, Academy of Motion Picture Arts and Sciences.

P. 506   THE ONLY ACTRESS: Susan Ferris, "Turning Lillian Hellman's autobiographical reminiscence into a movie called for intelligence, directorial skill, and two talented stars," *Horizon*, October 1977; Judy Klemesrud, "Vanessa Redgrave—'The Only Person Who Could Play Julia,' " *The New York Times*, October 2, 1977.

P. 506   JEWISH ASPECTS OF THE STORY: interview with Martin Peretz.

P. 507   NEVER REALLY IDENTIFIED WITH HELLMAN: Fred Guiles, *Jane Fonda.*

P. 508   NOT FONDA'S FAULT: Guiles, *Jane Fonda.*

P. 508   ABSENCE OF A SHREWD AND SARDONIC DOROTHY PARKER: Guiles, *Jane Fonda.*

P. 508   WHO CAN BELIEVE IN THE JULIA?: Philip French's review of *Julia* in *Sight and Sound*, Winter 1977–78.

P. 511   JULIA'S IDENTITY: interview with Ephraim London.

P. 511   FULL OF QUESTIONS ABOUT JULIA: interview with Stephen Gillers.

P. 511   WITH TALLI WYLER: interview with Talli Wyler.

P. 512   MCCARTHY APPEARED ON THE DICK CAVETT SHOW: I am grateful to Mary McCarthy and her attorney, Benjamin O'Sullivan, for supplying me with the depositions in the Hellman-McCarthy case, from which I draw my quotations from Hellman, McCarthy, Cavett, and London unless otherwise noted. Additional commentary is drawn from interviews with London, Peretz, Alfred, and from the following articles: Margot Slade and Tom Ferrel, "Literary Quarrel Turns Litigious," *The New York Times*, February 17, 1980; Norman Mailer, "An Appeal to Lillian Hellman and Mary McCarthy," *The New York Times Book Review*, May 11, 1980; John Simon, "Literary Lionesses," *National Review*, May 16, 1980; Michiko Kakutani, "Hellman-McCarthy Libel Suit Stirs Old Antagonisms," *The New York Times*, March 19, 1980; Robert M. Kaus, "The Plaintiff's Hour," *Harper's*, March 1983; Walter Goodman, "Literary Invective," *The New York Times Book Review*, June 19, 1983; Marcia Chambers, "Lillian Hellman Wins Round in Suit," *The New York Times*, May 11, 1984; William McPherson, "Hellman vs. McCarthy—in the Matter of 'Truth,' " *The Washington Post*, May 15, 1984.

P. 513   I'M RICH: interview with Harry and Elena Levin.

P. 513   MCCARTHY TOOK OFF FOR PRINCETON: Carlos Baker, letter to author.

P. 513–514 CLOSE ENCOUNTERS OF THE APOCRYPHAL KIND: Martha Gellhorn, letter to author.

P. 514   HISTORIAN J. C. FURNAS: interview with Philip Dunne.

P. 514   FURNAS NOTES THAT: J. C. Furnas, letter to author.

P. 517   THE QUESTION OF BUCHMAN: Bernard F. Dick, letter to author.

P. 517   TO AN INTERVIEWER: Caroline Moorehead, "A Witch-Hunt Survivor with Unfashionable Conscience Still Intact," *The Times* (London), December 3, 1976.

P. 518   HER SECOND DRAFT OF THE MEMOIR: Newman, *Cold War Romance: Lillian Hellman and John Melby.*

P. 518   *HOW I LOST HARDSCRABBLE FARM:* interview with Howard Bay.

P. 523   NOT A PUBLIC FIGURE: Lois Romano, "Ruling Backs Hellman," *The Washington Post,* May 12, 1984.

P. 524   STEPHEN GILLERS AGREES: interview with Stephen Gillers.

P. 524   MY HERO: interview with Ephraim London.

P. 524   THE BASIC TRUTH OF HELLMAN'S STORY: interview with Ephraim London.

P. 524   EVEN LOUIS FRAAD: interviews with Ephraim London and Louis Fraad.

P. 525   TO GET IN TOUCH WITH GARDINER: interview with Robert Silvers.

P. 526   THE REALITY OF THEIR FICTIONAL CREATIONS: interview with Herbert Gold.

P. 527   A VERY POWERFUL ABILITY TO FANTASIZE: interview with Howard Bay; Ralph Ingersoll interview with Hilary Mills.

P. 527   THE JULIA STORY: interview with John Melby.

31. RASPBERRIES

P. 531   THE REALLY INTIMATE ISSUES: interview with Martin Peretz.

P. 531–532   *WATCH ON THE RHINE: The New York Times,* October 16, 1979; *The New York Times,* December 27, 1979; *The New York Times,* January 4, 1980; *The New York Times,* January 7, 1980; *The Philadelphia Inquirer,* January 5, 1980; *The Nation,* January 26, 1980; *The New Yorker,* January 14, 1980; *New York,* January 14, 1980; *Newsweek,* February 4, 1980; *New Statesman,* September 26, 1980.

P. 532   *ANOTHER PART OF THE FOREST:* interview with Robert Fryer; see also Rick Talcove, "Another Part of the Theater for Lillian Hellman," *Los Angeles Daily News,* February 4, 1982.

P. 532–533   *THE LITTLE FOXES: Saturday Review,* July 1981; *The New Leader,* June 1, 1981; *People,* April 6, and May 25, 1981; *America,* July 18–25, 1981; *The Nation,* June 20, 1981; *Time,* March 30 and May 18, 1981; *New York,* May 18, 1981; *Variety,* April 7, 1982; *New Statesman,* March 29, 1982. Paul Harris, "Mad Scramble for Tickets," *Variety,* March 25, 1981; " 'Foxes' Profit Hits $1,075,000 to Date; Going to London," *Variety,* October 21, 1981: "The revival has been a financial bonanza not only for Taylor, Bufman [the producer], director Austin Pendleton and the cast, but also for Hellman, who's estimated to have earned upwards of $1,000,000 as her author's royalties.

P. 533   AN ADMIRER OF HELLMAN'S LITERARY ACHIEVEMENTS: William Luce, letter to author; press release for *Lillian;* William Luce, preface to Dramatist's Play Service edition of *Lillian.*

P. 533   AS I WAS TALKING TO HER: William Luce, letter to author.

P. 534   LUCE ADMITS: William Luce, letter to author.

P. 534   LUCE MET HELLMAN FOUR TIMES: William Luce, letter to author.

P. 534   SHE HAD DICTATED NOTES: William Luce, letter to author.

P. 535   WILLIAM AND TALLI WYLER: interview with Talli Wyler.

P. 535   PETER FEIBLEMAN ASKED HIS FRIEND: interview with Rupert Allan.

P. 536   ALWAYS THREATENING TO SUE PEOPLE: interview with Talli Wyler.

P. 538   WALTER MATTHAU: interview with Walter Matthau.

P. 539   FRANCES FITZGERALD REMEMBERS: interview with Frances FitzGerald.

P. 540   JO MARSHALL: interview with Jo Marshall.

P. 540   WHAT GREAT STORIES: At Hellman's funeral, Jules Feiffer captured the way Hellman's story telling evolved naturally out of her lifestyle: "She could take a marketing trip to Cronig's [on Vineyard Haven] and string it out into three well-made acts, quietly dramatic, surprisingly suspenseful. Who did she run into that she wanted to avoid? What slight would occur, what mishap at the check-out counter, the crisis of the meat counter, the incident of the vegetables, the adventure of the shopping cart, and all of this told in a growing, cigarette-gutted, booze-burnished croak, interrupted only by her own editorial asides, Isn't that extraordinary? Have you ever heard of such a thing? Have I gone mad? Maybe it's me. I'm sure it's me." *Vineyard Gazette,* July 6, 1984.

P. 541   ANGRY WITH WEAKNESS: interview with William Alfred.

P. 542   DENY HER DISEASES: interview with Albert Hackett.

P. 542–543   HELLMAN'S FISHING: statement by Jack Koontz in *Vineyard Gazette,* July 6, 1984.

P. 543   LOUIS ZETZEL: interview with Louis Zetzel.

P. 543   WATCHING HER AT PARTIES: interview with Ring Lardner, Jr.

P. 543   SETTING HER TISSUES ON FIRE: Theresa Mooney, letter to author; Hellman and Feibleman, *Eating Together.*

P. 543   JULIE HARRIS: interview with Julie Harris.

P. 543   KIM HUNTER: interview with Kim Hunter.

P. 543   PAT NEAL: statement in *Vineyard Gazette,* July 6, 1984.

P. 543   JOHN MELBY: Newman, *Cold War Romance: Lillian Hellman and John Melby.*

P. 543   HER NEW WILL: a copy can be obtained from Surrogate's Court in New York City.

P. 544   HELLMAN'S LETTERS TO JO MARSHALL: courtesy of Jo Marshall.

P. 545   SHE WROTE TO FRANCIS FORD COPPOLA: letters courtesy of Jo Marshall.

P. 546   THE UNIVERSITY OF TEXAS: interview with Decherd Turner.

P. 547   AUTHORIZED BIOGRAPHER: Edwin McDowell, "Lillian Hellman Names Abrahams Her Biographer," *The New York Times,* March 9, 1984.

P. 547   LILLIAN'S CRANKY LAST WISHES: confidential source.

P. 547   AS ONE OF HER NURSES: Hellman and Feibleman, *Eating Together.*

P. 547   THIS LADY IS HALF PARALYZED: Hellman and Feibleman, *Eating Together.*

P. 547   A FRIEND MIGHT SHOUT: interview with Martin Peretz.

P. 547   READING FRANCIS PARKMAN: statement in the *Vineyard Gazette,* July 6, 1987.

P. 547–548   THE LAST TWO DAYS OF HER LIFE: Lehmann-Haupt: "Plight of the Blind Who Love Books," *The New York Times,* September 6, 1984.

P. 548   A NEW BOOK: to interviewer Phyllis Meras (Bryer, *Conversations with Lillian Hellman*) Hellman mentioned she was at work on a new book. "It's about children I've known, and my editor is encouraging about it—perhaps much too encouraging."

P. 548   WILLIAM STYRON: statement in *Vineyard Gazette,* July 6, 1984.

P. 548   STEPHEN GREENE REMEMBERS: interview with Stephen Greene.

P. 549   RASPBERRIES: interview with Howard Bay.

BIBLIOGRAPHY

There are three useful bibliographies of Hellman's life and career: Mary Marguerite Riordan, *Lillian Hellman: A Bibliography: 1926–1978* (Metuchen, N.J.: Scarecrow Press, 1980); Steven H. Bills, *Lillian Hellman: An Annotated Bibliography* (New York: Garland, 1979); Mark W. Estrin, *Lillian Hellman: Plays, Films, Memoirs: A Reference Guide* (Boston: G. K. Hall, 1980). This bibliography is primarily a list of works by and about Hellman and her period that proved particularly useful in the composition of this biography. The Notes contain additional citations of material on Hellman's life and work.

WORKS OF LILLIAN HELLMAN
(in chronological order)

A. Drama

The Children's Hour. New York: Knopf, 1934.
Days to Come. New York: Knopf, 1936.
The Little Foxes. New York: Random House, 1939.
Watch on the Rhine. New York: Random House, 1941.
Four Plays. (*The Children's Hour, Days to Come, The Little Foxes, Watch on the Rhine*) With an introduction by Lillian Hellman. New York: Random House, 1942.
The Searching Wind. New York: The Viking Press, 1944.
Another Part of the Forest. New York: The Viking Press, 1947.
Montserrat. New York: Dramatists Play Service, 1949.
The Autumn Garden. Boston: Little, Brown, 1951.
The Lark. New York: Random House, 1956.
Candide, A Comic Operetta Based on Voltaire's Satire. Score by Leonard Bernstein. Lyrics by Richard Wilbur. Other lyrics by John Latouche and Dorothy Parker. New York: Random House, 1957.
Toys in the Attic. New York: Random House, 1960.
Six Plays: (The Children's Hour, Days to Come, The Little Foxes, Watch on the Rhine, Another Part of the Forest, The Autumn Garden) With an introduction by Lillian Hellman. New York: The Modern Library, 1960.
My Mother, My Father and Me. Based on Burt Blechman's novel *How Much?* New York: Random House, 1963.
The Collected Plays. Boston: Little, Brown, 1972.

B. Memoirs

An Unfinished Woman. Boston: Little, Brown, 1969.
Pentimento. Boston: Little, Brown, 1972.

Scoundrel Time. Boston: Little, Brown, 1976.
Three. (An Unfinished Woman, Pentimento, Scoundrel Time) With new commentaries
　　by Lillian Hellman. Introduction by Richard Poirier. Boston: Little, Brown,
　　1979.
Maybe. Boston: Little, Brown, 1980.
Eating Together: Recollections & Recipes, with Peter Feibleman, Boston: Little, Brown,
　　1984.

C. Editions

The Selected Letters of Anton Chekhov. With an introduction by Lillian Hellman.
　　New York: Farrar, Straus, 1955.
The Big Knockover: Selected Short Stories and Short Novels of Dashiell Hammett. With
　　an introduction by Lillian Hellman. New York: Random House, 1966.

D. Selected Contributions to Newspapers and Periodicals (Arranged Chronologically)

"Light Reading Good of Its Kind." *New York Herald Tribune Books,* November 28,
　　1926.
"Futile Souls Adrift on a Yacht." *New York Herald Tribune Books,* June 19, 1927.
"I Call Her Mama Now." *American Spectator.* September, 1933.
"Perberty in Los Angeles." *American Spectator.* January, 1934.
"The Theatre." (Review of *Barchester Towers) Time.* December 13, 1937.
"Day in Spain." *The New Republic,* April 13, 1938.
"A Statement by American Progressives, *The New Masses,* May 3, 1938.
"Back of Those Foxes." *The New York Times.* February 26, 1939.
"The Little Men of Philadelphia." *PM.* June 25, 1940.
"The Little War." *This is My Best,* edited by Whitney Burnett. Cleveland: World
　　Publishing Company, 1945.
"I Meet the Front Line Russians." *Collier's.* March 31, 1945.
"Author Jabs the Critic." *The New York Times.* December 15, 1946.
"The Judas Goats." *The Screen Writer.* December, 1947.
Reports on Yugoslavia. *New York Star.* November 4–10, 1948.
"Scotch on the Rocks." *New York Review of Books.* October 17, 1963.
"Sophronia's Grandson Goes to Washington." *Ladies Home Journal.* December,
　　1963.
"Land that Holds the Legend of Our Lives." *Ladies Home Journal.* April, 1964.
"Lillian Hellman Asks a Little Respect for her Agony: An Eminent Playwright
　　Hallucinates after a Fall Brought on by a Current Dramatic Hit," *Show.* May,
　　1964.
"The Times of The 'Foxes.' " *The New York Times,* October 22, 1967.
"Interlude in Budapest." *Holiday.* November, 1967.
"And Now—An Evening with Nichols and Hellman." *The New York Times.* August
　　9, 1970.
"The Baggage of a Political Exile." *The New York Times.* August 23, 1970.
"Martinique." *Travel and Leisure,* January, 1974.
"A Scene from an Unfinished Play." *The New Republic,* November 30, 1974.
"For Truth, Justice, and the American Way," *The New York Times,* June 4, 1975.
Foreword to *To be Preserved Forever* by Lev Kopelev. Philadelphia: J. B. Lippincott
　　Company, 1977.

E. Screenplays by Lillian Hellman, or by Lillian Hellman with Another Author, and Screenplays Based on Her Works

The Melody Lingers On, 1934.
The Dark Angel, written with Mordaunt Shairp, 1935.
These Three, 1936.
Dead End, 1937.
The Little Foxes, 1941.
Watch on the Rhine, written by Dashiell Hammett, edited with additional scenes by Lillian Hellman.
The North Star. New York: The Viking Press, 1943.
The Negro Soldier, 1944.
The Searching Wind, 1946.
Another Part of the Forest, written by Vladimir Posner, 1948.
The Blessing, 1953.
The Children's Hour, written by John Michael Hayes from Hellman's outline, 1962.
Toys in the Attic, writtten by James Poe, 1963.
The Chase, 1966.
Julia, written by Alvin Sargent, 1976.

WORKS ABOUT LILLIAN HELLMAN

Aaron, Daniel. *Writers on the Left, Episodes in American Literary Communism*. New York: Harcourt, Brace, World, 1961.

Adler, Jacob H. *Lillian Hellman*. Austin, Texas: Steck-Vaughn Company, 1969.

———. "The Rose and the Fox: Notes on the Southern Drama." *South: Modern Southern Literature in its Cultural Setting*. edited by Louis D. Rubin and Robert D. Jacobs. Garden City, New York: Doubleday, 1961.

———. "Miss Hellman's Two Sisters." *Educational Theatre Journal*. May, 1963.

Anderegg, Michael. *William Wyler*. Boston: Twayne, 1979.

Bailey, Cynthia Denham. "Lillian Hellman's Revisions in 'The Collected Plays.' " Ph.D. dissertation, Auburn University, 1986.

Baker, Carlos. *Ernest Hemingway: A Life Story*. New York: Scribner's, 1969.

Bankhead, Tallulah. *Tallulah*. New York: Harper and Brothers, 1952.

———. "Miss Bankhead Objects." *The New York Times*. October 29, 1967.

Becker, Stephen. *Marshall Field III: A Biography*. New York: Simon and Schuster, 1964.

Belfrage, Cedric. *The American Inquisition, 1945–1950*. Indianapolis: Bobbs-Merrill, 1973.

Bell, Kathleen T. " 'Julia' Characterization in the Plays of Lillian Hellman." Master's thesis, Florida Atlantic University, December, 1980.

Bennetts, Leslie. "Literary Giant Takes Post at Bryn Mawr." *Philadelphia Bulletin*. October 30, 1974.

———. "Who Paved the Way." *The New York Times*. April 10, 1978.

Bentley, Eric., ed. *Thirty Years of Treason: Excerpts from the Hearings before the House Committee on Un-American Activities. 1938–1968*. New York: The Viking Press, 1971.

Blake, Gary. "Herman Shumlin: The Development of a Director." Ph.D. dissertation, The City University of New York.

Blotner, Joseph. *Faulkner: A Biography*. New York: Random House, 1974.

Bernstein, Burton. *Thurber: A Biography*. New York: Dodd, Mead, 1975.

Boryczka, Raymond and Cary, Lorin Lee. *No Strength Without Union: An Illustrated History of Ohio Workers 1803–1980*. Columbus: Ohio Historical Society, 1982.

Bosworth, Patricia. *Montgomery Clift: A Biography*. New York: Harcourt Brace Jovanovich, 1978.

Briggs, John. *Leonard Bernstein: The Man, His Work, and His World*. Cleveland: World Publishing Company, 1961.

Bruccoli, Matthew J., ed. *Selected Letters of John O'Hara*. New York: Random House, 1978.

Brustein, Robert. "Epilogue in Anger." *The New Republic*. August 13 and 20, 1984.

Bryer, Jackson R., ed. *Conversations with Lillian Hellman*. Jackson: University Press of Mississippi, 1986.

Carter, Hodding. *Where Main Street Meets the River*. New York: Rinehart, 1953.

Clark, Barrett. "Lillian Hellman." *College English*. October, 1944.

Clurman, Harold. *On Directing*. New York: Macmillan, 1972.

———. *All People Are Famous*. New York: Harcourt, Brace & Company, 1974.

Colacello, Bob. "A Vineyard Vignette." *Vanity Fair*. September, 1984.

Davie, Michael. "Lillian Hellman: Life as Fiction." *The Observer*. November 9, 1986.

Dick, Bernard F. *Hellman in Hollywood*. Teaneck, N.J.: Fairleigh Dickinson University Press, 1982.

Downer, Alan S. *Fifty Years of American Drama, 1900–1950*. Chicago: Henry Regnery Company, 1951.

Dudar, Helen. "A Long Look Backward at Comedy." *New York Post* magazine section. January 3, 1967.

Dunne, Philip. *Take Two: A Life in Movies and Politics*. New York: McGraw-Hill, 1980.

Easton, Carol. *The Search for Sam Goldwyn*. New York: Morrow, 1976.

Emerson, Gloria. "Lillian Hellman: At 66, She's Still Restless." *The New York Times*. September 7, 1973.

Falk, Doris. *Lillian Hellman*. New York: Frederick Ungar, 1978.

Felheim, Marvin. "*The Autumn Garden*: Mechanics and Dialectics." *Modern Drama*. September, 1960.

Ferris, Susan. "Turning Lillian Hellman's autobiographical reminiscence into a movie called for intelligence, directorial skill, and two talented stars." *Horizon*. October, 1977.

Gelderman, Carol. *May McCarthy: A Life*. New York: St. Martin's Press, 1988.

Gellhorn, Martha. "On Apocryphism." *Paris Review*. Spring, 1981.

Gidden, Susan R. "The Set That Lillian Built." *New York Post*. May 13, 1974.

Gilman, Sander L. *Jewish Self-Hatred: Anti-semitism and the Hidden Language of the Jews*. Baltimore: The John's Hopkins University Press, 1986.

Gold, Arthur and Fizdale, Robert. "Lillian Hellman's Creole Cooking." *Vogue*. June, 1974.

Gottfried, Martin. *Jed Harris: The Curse of Genius*. Boston: Little, Brown, 1984.

Gould, Jean. *Modern American Playwrights*. New York: Dodd, Mead, and Company, 1966.

Grose, Peter. "Soviet's Writers Given Party Line." *The New York Times*. May 23, 1967.

Guiles, Fred. *Jane Fonda: The Actress in Her Time*. New York: Pinnacle Books, 1983.

Guthrie, Tyrone. *A Life in the Theatre*. New York: McGraw-Hill, 1959.

Hammett, Dashiell. *The Thin Man*. New York: Knopf, 1934.

Harriman, Margaret Case. *Take Them Up Tenderly: A Collection of Profiles*. New York: Knopf, 1944.

Hart, Jeffrey. "For Whom the Bell Tolled." *Commentary*. December, 1986.

Herrman, Dorothy. *S. J. Perelman: A Life*. New York: Putnam, 1986.

Hersey, John. "Lillian Hellman." *The New Republic*. September 18, 1976.

Hobson, Laura Z. *Laura Z: A Life*. New York: Arbor House, 1983.

Holmin, Lorena Ross. *The Dramatic Works of Lillian Hellman*. Stockholm: Almquist and Wiksell (distributor), 1973.

Hook, Sidney. *Out of Step*. New York: Harper & Row, 1987.

Hoopes, Roy. *Ralph Ingersoll: A Biography*. New York: Atheneum, 1985.

Hungerford, Robert Walker. "Minutes in Lillian Hellman's 'The Children's Hour': Composition of the Play from Inception to Publication." Ph.D. dissertation, University of South Carolina, 1980.

Irwin, Don. "Lillian Hellman Refuses to Say If She Was Red." *New York Herald Tribune*. May 22, 1952.

Israel, Lee. *Miss Tallulah Bankhead*. New York: Putnam, 1972.

James, Clive. *At the Pillars of Hercules*. Boston: Faber & Faber, 1979.

Johnson, Diane. "Obsessed." *Vanity Fair*. May, 1985.

———. *Dashiell Hammett: A Life*. New York: Random House, 1983.

Kanin, Garson, *Hollywood*. New York: Viking, 1974.

Keats, John. *You Might as Well Live: The Life and Times of Dorothy Parker*. New York: Simon and Schuster, 1970.

Kerr, Walter. "This 'Garden' is Nearly Perfect." *The New York Times*. November 28, 1976.

Kilker, Marie. "The Theatre of Emmanuel Robles: An American Introduction with a Checklist on Criticism and Production." Ph.D. dissertation, Southern Illinois University 1972.

Kimball, Penn. *The File*. New York: Harcourt, Brace, Jovanovich, 1983.

Klemesrud, Judy. "Vanessa Redgrave—'The Only Person Who Could Play Julia.' " *The New York Times*. October 2, 1977.

Knepler, Henry W. *"The Lark:* Translation vs. Adaptation: A Case History," *Modern Drama*. May, 1958.

———. "Translation and Adaptation in the Contemporary Drama," *Modern Drama*. May, 1961.

Kramer, Hilton. "The Life and Death of Lillian Hellman." *The New Criterion*. October, 1984.

Kronenberger, Louis. *No Whippings, No Gold Watches: The Saga of a Writer and His Jobs*. Boston: Little, Brown, 1970.

Krutch, Joseph Wood. *The American Drama Since 1918*. New York: George Braziller, 1957.

Langer, Elinor. *Josephine Herbst*. Boston: Little, Brown, 1984.

Layman, Richard. *Shadow Man: The Life of Dashiell Hammett*. New York: Harcourt Brace Jovanovich, 1981.

Lederer, Katherine. *Lillian Hellman*. Boston: Twayne, 1979.

Lehmann-Haupt, Christopher. "Plight of the Blind Who Love Books." *The New York Times*. September 6, 1984.

Levin, Meyer. *The Obsession*. New York: Simon and Schuster, 1973.

Levine, Jo Ann. "Author Lillian Hellman—A Portrait in Words." *The Christian Science Monitor*. December 21, 1973.

Luce, William. *Lillian*. New York: Dramatists Play Service, 1987.

Lyons, Bonnie. "Lillian Hellman: 'The First Jewish Nun on Prytania Street,' " in *From Hester Street to Hollywood: The Jewish-American Stage and Screen*. Edited by Sarah Blacher Cohen. Bloomington: Indiana University Press, 1983.

McDowell, Edwin. "Lillian Hellman Names Abrahams Her Biographer." *The New York Times*. March 9, 1984.

Madsen, Axel. *William Wyler*. New York: Thomas Y. Crowell, 1973.

Maney, Richard. *Fanfare: The Confessions of a Press Agent.* New York: Harper and Brothers, 1957.

———. "From Hellman to Shumlin to Broadway." *The New York Times*, April 9, 1944.

Manso, Peter. *Mailer: His Life and Times.* New York: Simon and Schuster, 1985.

Marja, Fern. "A Clearing in the Forest." *New York Post* magazine section. March 6, 1960.

———. "Lillian Hellman—Plenty of Class." *New York Post.* October 14, 1973.

Martin, Jay. *Nathanael West: The Art of His Life.* New York: Farrar, Straus & Giroux, 1970.

Marx, Arthur. *Goldwyn: A Biography of the Man Behind the Legend.* New York: Norton, 1976.

Milestone, Lewis. "Mr. Milestone Beats a Plowshare into a Sword." *The New York Times.* March 14, 1943.

Millichap, Joseph R. *Lewis Milestone.* Boston: Twayne, 1981.

Moody, Richard. *Lillian Hellman.* New York: Pegasus, 1972.

Mooney, Theresa Rose. " 'Southern' Influences in Four Plays by Lillian Hellman." Ph.D. Dissertation, Tulane University.

Moorehead, Catherine. "A Witch-Hunt Survivor with Unfashionable Conscience Still Intact." *The Times* (London). December 3, 1976.

Newman, Robert. *Cold War Romance: John Melby and Lillian Hellman.* (Forthcoming from University of North Carolina Press.)

Orlova, Raisa. *Memoirs.* New York: Random House, 1983.

Perelman, S. J. *The Last Laugh.* New York: Simon and Schuster, 1981.

Peyser, Joan. *Bernstein: A Biography.* New York: William Morrow, 1987.

Podhoretz, Norman. *Breaking Ranks.* New York: Harper & Row, 1979.

Pollitt, Daniel. "Pleading the Fifth Amendment Before a Congressional Committee: A Study and Explanation." *Notre Dame Lawyer.* December, 1956.

———. "The Fifth Amendment Plea Before Congressional Committees Investigating Subversion: Motives and Justifiable Presumptions—A Survey of 120 Witnesses." *University of Pennsylvania Law Review.* June, 1958.

Radosh, Ronald. " 'But today the struggles': Spain and the intellectuals." *The New Criterion.* October, 1986.

Ripley, Anthony. "U.S. Judge Rules Nixon Documents Belong to Nation." *The New York Times.* February 1, 1975.

———. "Appeals Court Will Move Quickly on Nixon Records." *The New York Times.* February 2, 1975.

Ross, Don. "Lillian Hellman Teaches What Can't Be Taught." *New York Herald Tribune.* April 23, 1961.

Schwartz, Nancy Lynn. *The Hollywood Writers' Wars.* New York: Knopf, 1982.

Shenker, Israel. "Perelman Shaken Up by Florida's Charms." *The New York Times.* April 27, 1974.

Shepard, Richard. "Lillian Hellman Teaching at Yale." *The New York Times.* February 1, 1966.

———. " 'Little Foxes' Gets a Start in Low Key." *The New York Times.* September 29, 1967.

Sievers, W. David. *Freud on Broadway: A History of Psychoanalysis and the American Drama.* New York: Hermitage House, 1955.

Sigerist, Henry. *Henry F. Sigerist: Autobiographical Writings.* Selected and translated by Nora Sigerist Beeson. Montreal: McGill University Press, 1976.

Sobol, Louis. *The Longest Street: A Memoir.* New York: Crown, 1968.

Spacks, Patricia Meyer. *The Female Imagination.* New York: Knopf, 1975.

Stine, Whitney, with Bette Davis. *Mother Goddam*. New York: Hawthorn Books, 1974.

Szogyi, Alex. "Lillian." *The Hunter Magazine*. July, 1985.

Tallmer, Jerry. "Woman in the News: Lillian Hellman." *New York Post* Weekend Magazine. October 13, 1973.

Triesch, Manfred. *The Lillian Hellman Collection at the University of Texas*. Austin: University of Texas Press, 1967.

Trilling, Diana. *We Must March My Darlings*. New York: Harcourt Brace Jovanovich, 1977.

Voltaire. *Candide*. Translated and edited by Robert M. Adams. New York: W. W. Norton, 1966.

Walton, Richard. *Henry Wallace, Harry Truman and the Cold War*. New York: The Viking Press, 1976.

Weales, Gerald. *American Drama Since World War II*. New York: Harcourt, Brace & World, 1962.

Weidman, Jerome. *Praying for Rain*. New York: Harper & Row, 1986.

Weinstein, Allen. *Perjury: The Hiss-Chambers Case*. New York: Knopf, 1978.

Whitesides, Glen. "Lillian Hellman: A Biographical and Critical Study." Ph.D. dissertation, Florida State University.

Wright, William. *Lillian Hellman, The Image, The Woman*. New York: Simon and Schuster, 1986.

Wyden, Peter. *The Passionate War: The Narrative History of the Spanish Civil War*. New York: Simon and Schuster, 1983.

Zilboorg, Gregory. *Man, Mind, and Medicine*. New York: Harcourt, Brace & Company, 1943.

Zolotow, Maurice. *No People Like Show People*. New York: Random House, 1951.

INDEX

adaptation, 420–21; London production, 281, 291; E. H. Lowell's attack on, 457; operatic version, 293; revisions in, 468; revivals, 137, 433, 438–39, 440, 509, 533–34; road tour, 154, 181; in Soviet Union, 236, 436–37; Yugoslavian production, 271–72, 274
"Little War, The" (LH), 117, 118
Litvinov, Maxim, 189
Liveright, Horace, 30
Lloyd, Harold, 72
Lodge, John, 175
Loebel, Herbert, 230
London, Ephraim, 368, 374, 457, 483, 486, 494, 511, 513, 521, 523, 524, 525; in LH will, 545
London Films, 350
Lorring, Joan, 303, 306
Losey, Joseph, 461
Louis, Joe, 192–93
Love (theme), 469–70
Love triangle (theme), 80, 84, 85–86, 87, 104, 205–6
Lovett, Adele, 220
Lovett, Robert, 220
Lowell, Elizabeth Hardwick, 457
Lowell, Robert, 417, 437, 457
Loyalists (Spain), 2, 109, 112, 113, 116, 137, 141, 150, 151, 218, 520, 521
Luce, Henry, 82, 159
Luce, William, 7, 329–30, 534–36
Lukas, Paul, 175–76, 191, 199
Lying, power of, 64–65, 67, 70, 84, 88, 336
Lyons, Bonnie, 486
Lyons, Leonard, 136
Lyons, Louis, 323

McBride, Thomas, 475–76
McBride, Thomas, Sr., 476, 477
McCarthy, Eugene, 455
McCarthy, Joseph, 115, 318, 344, 347, 350, 374, 456, 481, 493, 496, 498–499, 501; liberals' opposition to, 497, 500
McCarthy, Kevin, 521–22
McCarthy, Mary, 203, 364, 531, 548; LH libel suit against, 460, 512–14, 516–17, 518–24
McCarthy period, 11, 12–13, 225, 426, 455, 500–1, 504; LH distortions about, 490; LH memoir about, 481
McCarthyism, 261, 295, 340, 456, 488, 498
McClain, John, 357
McCracken, Samuel, 515–16, 520, 526, 527
McCrea, Joel, 86, 102, 104
McCutcheon, George Barr, 121
Macdonald, Dwight, 497
McGuire, Dorothy, 535
McKay, Scott, 247
McKelway, St. Clair, 182, 189–90
McKinley, William, 127
MacLaine, Shirley, 420
MacLeish, Archibald, 106, 217–18, 238, 261, 389, 450
McLellan, Joseph, 510
McManus, John, 106
Magic Mountain, The (Mann), 50
Mailer, Adele, 386–87

Mailer, Norman, 5, 268–69, 275, 427, 430, 494, 513, 548; stabbed wife, 384, 386–87, 388
Male Animal, The (film), 150, 153
Malkiel, Henrietta, 33
Malraux, André, 137
Maltese Falcon, The (Hammett), 44
Maltz, Albert, 120, 253–54
Man and Superman (play), 400
Maney, Richard, 99, 155, 205, 211, 342
Mann, Iris, 337
Mann, Thomas, 397, 402, 461
Mannerheim (head of Finnish government), 150
Mansfield (mayor of Boston), 76
Mansfield, Katherine, 400
Manso, Peter, 387
Mao Tse-Tung, 238
March, Florence Eldridge, 109, 141, 303–4, 305, 308, 311
March, Fredric, 80, 98n, 109, 141, 303, 308, 311
Marcus, Stephen, 546–47
Markov, Georgi M., 438
Marshall, Burke, 458, 460
Marshall, E. G., 421, 438
Marshall, Herbert, 80, 180
Marshall, Jo, 4, 144, 151–52, 194, 309–10, 314, 445; on LH memoirs, 449; and LH veracity, 541–42; and literary rights to Hammett's work, 545–47; relationship with Hammett, 390
Marshall, Margaret, 208
Martha's Vineyard, 494
Martin, Helen, 411
Martin, Jay, 47, 53, 54, 55, 433
Marx, Jake, 16, 18
Marx, Karl, 23, 28, 116
Marx, Sam, 4, 6, 35, 78, 108, 167, 316; on LH, 36–37, 38
Marx family, 16
Marxism, 231; in works of LH, 94
Marxist study groups, 137, 152, 159, 319, 328
Marxists, 255
Masaryk, Jan, 266, 274
Mason, Sophronia, 9, 17, 20, 25, 65, 70, 128, 430, 449, 451
Matthau, Walter, 411, 412, 413–14, 418, 539–40
Maurois, André, 478
Mauve Decade, The (Bear), 125
Maybe (LH), 11, 29, 36, 529–32
Mayer, Louis B., 38, 93
Me (Play: Kober), 35
Meiklejohn, Robert, 226
Melby, Hilda, 317, 347
Melby, John, 3, 137, 230, 231, 236–37, 256, 257, 260, 261–63, 266–67, 271, 273, 296, 313, 317–18, 323, 329, 331–32, 373, 433, 456, 472, 474, 499, 527; affair with LH, 222, 224–25, 226–27, 231, 232–35, 237–40, 242, 245–46, 257, 263, 266, 270, 296–97, 332, 344–45, 518; divorce, 278; foreign service career, 224, 238, 310, 332, 334, 347, 350–51; LH correspondence with,